RANDOM HOUSE WEBSTER'S

COMPUTER
& INTERNET
DICTIONARY

Third Edition

Random House Webster's
Computer & Internet Dictionary

Third Edition

Philip E. Margolis

Random House
New York

Random House Webster's Computer & Internet Dictionary, Third Edition

Copyright © 1999 by Philip E. Margolis

The Random House Living Dictionary Database™, is a trademark of Random House, Inc.

Trademarks
A number of entered words which we have reason to believe constitute trademarks have been designated as such. However, no attempt has been made to designate as trademarks or service marks all terms or words in which proprietary rights might exist. The inclusion, exclusion, or definition of a words or term is not intended to affect, or to express a judgment on, the validity or legal status of the word or term as a trademark, service mark, or other proprietary term.

This book is available for special purchases in bulk by organizations and institutions, not for resale, at special discounts. Please direct your inquiries to the Random House Special Sales Department, toll-free 888-591-1200 or fax 212-572-4961.

Please address inquiries about electronic licensing of reference products, for use on a network or in software or on CD-ROM, to the Subsidiary Rights Department, Random House Reference & Information Publishing, fax 212-940-7370.

Library of Congress Cataloging-in-Publication Data
Margolis, Philip E.

   Random House Webster's computer & internet dictionary / Philip E.
Margolis. -- 3rd ed.
     p.   cm.
   Rev. ed. of: Random House personal computer dictionary. 2nd ed.
c1996.
   Includes biographical references and index.
   ISBN 0-375-70351-9
   1. Microcomputers--Dictionaries. 2. Computers--Dictionaries.
  I. Margolis, Philip E. Random House personal computer dictionary.
  II. Title.
  QA76.15.M37 1998
  004.16'03--dc21   98-45280
                                    CIP

www.randomwords.com

Typeset and printed in the United States of America.

1999 Third Random House Edition

0 9 8 7 6 5 4 3
January 2000

ISBN: 0-375-70351-9

New York   Toronto   London   Sydney   Auckland

PREFACE

Back in 1995, when I prepared the second edition of this book, then called the *Random House Personal Computer Dictionary,* the World Wide Web was just beginning to create a small buzz in the computing world. But few realized then that the Web represented a paradigm shift in the way computers are used. Prior to the Web, personal computers were mainly machines for creating documents, analyzing data, and playing games. Today, PCs are portals into rich virtual environments—environments that offer a wealth of information as well as communities. Not surprisingly, *computerese* is evolving to describe things and situations that never even existed a couple of years ago. Words like *Web, Net, surf, chat, e-mail,* and *URL* have become commonplace. This new edition—retitled to reflect its changes—includes nearly 1,000 new terms, mostly in the Internet category.

Just as the Web is profoundly changing *computerese,* it's also changing the way computerese is documented. In 1996, I created an on-line version of the dictionary called the *PC Webopædia* (www.pcwebopedia.com). The Web site has undergone many changes and now serves as both an on-line glossary and a search engine for technology information. And just as the first two editions of the book contained the core information for the Web site, the expanded site now forms the basis for this new book.

While the electronic version of the dictionary has some obvious advantages—more frequent updates, full-text search engine, and hot-linked cross-references—printed books continue to be the preferred medium of choice for most people most of the time. This preference is probably due to the still rather primitive and clumsy computer interfaces, but may also be tied to a deeper human need for tactile feedback. It will be interesting to see whether the new generation of children who are growing up with the Internet will still choose printed matter over its electronic equivalents.

Once again, I owe thanks to my intrepid editor, Enid Pearsons, who has now masterfully guided the dictionary through three editions. And special thanks go to Charles Kozierok for reviewing the manuscript and pointing out many errors. I highly recommend his Web site, the *PC Guide* (www.pcguide.com) for more detailed information about computers. Of course, I accept full responsibility for any errors or omissions that remain. Lastly, thanks to the thousands of visitors to the PC Webopædia who e-mailed encouragement and questions and who asked repeatedly for access to this information in book form. It was the first time in my 20 years of being an author and technical writer that I received so much direct response from readers. This is one advantage of electronic publishing that I had not expected, and one that I find nearly irresistible—immediate feedback from readers :-).

Philip Margolis
Rockport, Massachusetts
October, 1998
pmarg@sandybay.com

LIST OF ILLUSTRATIONS

LIST OF TABLES

Guide to Computer Terms
by Category

Few things are more frustrating than looking up a word and finding that the definition contains ten new mysterious terms. I have tried to avoid these circular definitions as much as possible, although sometimes they're unavoidable. I have at least refrained from using terms that are not included in this dictionary. In addition, most of the definitions include cross references to lead you to more information about a particular topic.

The following list organizes terms into broad categories. If you are interested in learning about a particular area of computer science, you might start by looking up the terms in the appropriate category. You can start with any term and the cross references will lead you to related terms.

Adapters/Cards
accelerator board
adapter
add-in
add-on
board
card
daughtercard
DIP
driver
edge connector
expansion board
expansion slot
hot plugging
interrupt
on-board
PC card
printed circuit board
slot
sound card
television board

Addressing
absolute address
address
address space
base address
high memory
low memory
machine address
offset
relative address
thunk

Animation
3DO
ActiveX control
alpha channel
animated GIF
animation
fps
frame
mask
morphing
plug-in
SGI
Shockwave
sprite
tweening

Application Failures
abort
bug
crash
deadlock
down
fatal error
frozen
GPF
hang
invalid page fault
overflow error
runtime error
underflow

Application Programming Interfaces (APIs)
API
ASPI
CGI
DirectX
DMI
HLLAPI
ISAPI
JDBC
MAPI
MCI
MDI
NSAPI
ODBC
ODI
SDK
TAPI
TSAPI

Applications
accounting software
applet
application
autosave
bells and whistles
bloatware
CAD
CAD/CAM
CAE
calculator
calendar
CAM
close
compound document
contact manager
courseware
data processing
document management
e-mail client
end user
ERP
export
feature
handwriting recognition
import
legacy application
open
PIM

PKZIP
quit
run
runtime version
save
scheduler
shareware
spell checker
vanilla

Artificial Intelligence
agent
artificial intelligence
bot
cybernetics
expert system
fuzzy logic
genetic programming
handwriting recognition
language
natural language
neural network
optical character recognition
pattern recognition
robot
robotics
voice recognition

Audio
3-D audio
AC-3
AIFF
AU
digital audio
digitize
Dolby Digital
fps
MIDI
MP3
MPEG
RealAudio
sampling
sound card
streaming
WAV
wave table synthesis

Browsers
ActiveX control
bookmark
browse
browser
Internet Explorer
Java
JavaScript
Microsoft
Mosaic

Mozilla
Navigator
Netscape
plug-in
Shockwave
VBScript

Buses
32-bit
Access.bus
ADB
address bus
AGP
AT bus
burst mode
bus
bus mastering
CardBus
EIDE
EISA
expansion bus
external bus
Fibre Channel
HIPPI
hot plugging
I2O
IEEE 1394
Industry Standard
    Architecture (ISA) bus
interface
local bus
Micro Channel Architecture
    (MCA)
NuBus
PCI
PCMCIA
SCSI
USB
VL-Bus
VME bus

Business Presentation
area chart
bar chart
column graph
exploded view
legend
line graph
pie chart
presentation graphics
scatter diagram

Cables
coaxial cable
fiber optics
null-modem cable
twisted-pair cable
UTP

Caches
buffer
cache
disk cache
L1 cache
L2 cache
pipeline burst cache
RAM cache
RAM disk
VCACHE
write-back cache

CD-ROMs
CAV
CD-I (Compact
    Disc-Interactive)
CD-R drive
CD-ROM
CD-ROM player
CD-ROM/XA
CD-RW disk
CDFS
CLV
compact disc
disc
erasable optical disk
floptical
Green Book
magneto-optical (MO) drive
MSCDEX
MultiRead
optical disk
Orange Book
quad-speed CD-ROM drive
Red Book
seek time
White Book
WORM
Yellow Book

Chat
acronym
avatar
chat
chat room
emoticon
instant messaging
IRC
lurk

Client/Server Computing
client
client-side
client/server architecture
middleware
peer-to-peer architecture
thin client
three-tier

TP monitor
transaction processing
two-tier
WinFrame

Color
CIE color model
CMYK
color depth
color management
    system (CMS)
color matching
color separation
offset printing
Pantone Matching System
    (PMS)
process colors
RGB monitor
S-Video
spot color
true color
WYSIWYP

Color Printers
banding
bilevel printer
CMYK
color printer
color separation
contone printer
ink-jet printer
laser printer
snapshot printer
solid ink-jet printer

Communications
access
ADPCM
asynchronous
AT command set
bandwidth
baseband transmission
baud
bisync
bps
carrier
channel
circuit switching
codec
COM
communications
DCC
DTE
emulation
flow control
frame
full duplex
half duplex

handshaking
host
I/O
isochronous
modulate
noise
null-modem cable
parallel
polling
protocol
remote
serial
simplex
start bit
stop bit
synchronous
telematics
terminal emulation
UART
Winsock

Communications Software
communications software
emulation
remote control software
software modem
AT command set
Bell 103
Bell 212A
Binary File Transfer (BFT)
CCITT
communications
    protocol
DSVD
Group 3 protocol
Group 4 protocol
Hayes compatible
Kermit
RS-232C
RS-422 and RS-423
RS-485
SLIP
V.22
V.22bis
V.32
V.34
V.35
V.42
V.90
Xmodem
Ymodem
Zmodem

Compiling, Binding and Linking
bind
coff

compile
link
map
object code
source code

Computer Entertainment
3DO
MOO
MUCK
MUD
MUSH

Computer Industry Companies
ISV
OEM
Silicon Valley
VAR

Computer Science
architecture
computer literacy
computer science
computer system
digital
dynamic
ergonomics
IT
logical
meta
paperless office
physical
proprietary
sampling
stateless
system
transparent
virtual

Configuring Adapters
ASPI
configuration
configure
DIP
DIP switch
hot plugging
IRQ
jumper
plug-and-play
PnP
SCAM
setup
toggle

Connectors, Plugs and Sockets
BNC connector

connector
DIN connector
pinout
plug
RJ-11
RJ-45
slot
Slot 1
socket
Socket 7
Socket 8
Zero Insertion Force (ZIF)
    socket

Convergence
cable modem
CDMA
convergence
DSS
PC/TV
WebTV

Data
analog
attribute
BLOB
browse
comma-delimited
control character
convert
corrupted
data
data dictionary
data entry
data integrity
data mining
data processing
digital
digitize
escape sequence
export
fixed length
import
integer
ISAM
key
line feed
machine readable
metadata
petabyte
precision
punctuation
purge
random access
raw data
read
read-only
read/write

record
replication
sequential access
sign
variable length
variable-length record
write

Data Compression
ARC
codec
data compression
DCT
disk compression
file compression
lossless compression
lossy compression
LZW
MNP
MP3
MPEG
pack
packed file
PKZIP
sampling
tar
unpack
ZIP

Data Formats
AIFF
alphanumeric
ANSI Character Set
ASCII
ASCII file
BAK file
BCD
binary
binary file
binary format
BinHex
character
character set
convert
decimal
DOM
double precision
EBCDIC
export
extended ASCII
file format
floating-point number
format
hexadecimal
import
ISO Latin 1
leading zero
MIME

octal
padding
special character
text
text file
TNEF
Unicode
Uuencode

Data Sizes
bit
byte
escape character
exabyte
G
giga (G)
gigabit
gigabyte
K
KB
kilobyte
M
MB
mega
megabyte
nibble
petabyte
terabyte
word
yottabyte
zettabyte

Data Storage
ARC
archival backup
archive
backup
data recovery
gigabyte
HSM
incremental backup
mass storage
media
primary storage
RAID
restore
slack space
storage
storage device
store
terabyte

Data Structures
array
binary tree
character string
data structure
heap

hierarchical
leaf
list
matrix
pop
queue
stack
tree structure
vector

Data Transfer Rates
data transfer rate
Gbps
gigabit
Kbps
kilobit
MBps
Mbps
megabit
PIO

Databases
ADO
aggregate function
audit trail
BLOB
built-in function
DAO
data dictionary
data entry
data mart
data mining
data warehouse
database
database management
    system
DB2
dBASE
distributed database
field
fixed length
flat-file database
fourth-generation
    language
HyperCard
index
Informix
ISAM
JDBC
Jet
join
key
keyword
mail merge
merge
multidimensional DBMS
normalization
ODBC

OLAP
RDBMS
record
referential integrity
replication
report
report writer
RPG
SQL
SQL Server
stored procedure
table
two-phase commit
VSAM

Desktop Publishing
Acrobat
anchor
boilerplate
camera-ready
crop marks
desktop publishing
electronic publishing
greeking
hard return
imagesetter
Lino
Linotronic
offset printing
page layout program
preview
rule
ruler
screen
service bureau
style sheet
template
WYSIWYG
WYSIWYP

Directory Services
Active Directory
directory service
LDAP
NDS

Disk Drives
access time
areal density
ATA
bad sector
bay
cluster
crash
DASD
Defrag
defragment
density

disk
disk cache
disk compression
disk controller
disk drive
disk mirroring
disk optimizer
disk pack
drive bay
ESDI
FAT32
fault tolerance
FDHD
fdisk
format
fragmentation
half height
head
head crash
IDE interface
initialize
interleave
LBA
low-level format
MFM
mount
partition
phase change disk
PIO
RAM disk
RLL
ScanDisk
sector
seek time
server mirroring
SMART
Smartdrive
TPI
track
Ultra DMA
volume
volume label

Display Standards
8514/A
CGA
EGA
Hercules graphics
MCGA
MDA
NTSC
PGA
SVGA
VGA
video standards

Distributed Computing
Component Object Model

CORBA
DCE
DCOM
distributed computing
IIOP
OMG
OSF
RMI
SOM

Documentation
customer support
documentation
hard copy
help desk
man page
readme file
undocumented

DOS
ANSI.SYS
autoexec.bat
AUX
BAK file
BAT file
bootable diskette
COM
COM file
COMMAND.COM
CONFIG.SYS
DOS
EEMS
EXE file
expanded memory
extended memory
external command
fdisk
file allocation table
high memory
high memory area
himem.sys
internal command
LIM memory
low memory
MBR
MSCDEX
PC-DOS
PIF file
protected mode
TSR
UNC
VCPI
XMS

DVD
Divx
DVD
DVD + RW

DVD-RAM
DVD-ROM
DVD-Video

Electronic Commerce
BinHex
biometrics
Certificate Authority
digital cash
EDI
electronic commerce
ESD
SET
smart card

Electronic Mail
attachment
e-mail
e-mail address
e-mail client
emoticon
Eudora
flame
IMAP
instant messaging
LISTSERV
mail merge
mailbox
mailing list
mailing list server
Majordomo
MAPI
MIME
multicast
POP
S/MIME
SMTP
snailmail
spam
TNEF
Uuencode
voice mail

Encryption
cipher text
Clipper chip
cryptography
decryption
DES
digital certificate
encryption
key
plain text
Pretty Good Privacy
public-key encryption
RSA
symmetric encryption
symmetric-key cryptography

Error Correction
checksum
CRC
crc detection
even parity
Kermit
MNP
odd parity
parity
parity checking
Zmodem

Ethernet
100Base-T
10Base-2
10Base5
10BaseT
Ethernet
Gigabit Ethernet
IEEE 802 standards
shared Ethernet
switched Ethernet
switching hub

Expressions
arithmetic expression
Boolean expression
Boolean logic
conditional
expression
identifier
literal
mathematical
expression
scientific notation
static variable
subscript
variable

Faxing
digitize
fax
fax machine
fax modem
Group 3 protocol
Group 4 protocol
MFP
optical scanner
telecopy

File Management
alias
directory
document
dot
extension
FAT32
file

file allocation table
file management system
filename
folder
hidden file
ISAM
lock
NFS
NTFS
parent directory
path
pathname
redirection
root directory
slack space
subdirectory
text file
UNC
VSAM
wildcard character
working directory

File Transfer
anonymous FTP
Binary File Transfer (BFT)
BinHex
download
FTP
MIME
TFTP
upload
Uuencode
Xmodem
Ymodem

Flat-Panel displays
active matrix display
backlighting
CSTN
DSTN
dual-scan display
electroluminescent
    display (ELD)
flat technology monitor
flat-panel display
gas-plasma display
LCD
LCD monitor
passive-matrix display
plasma display
supertwist
TFT

Formatting
alignment
bleed
feathering
flow

flush
footer
forced page break
gutter
hanging indent
hard
header
hyphenation
justification
justify
landscape
layout
leader
left justify
margins
MuTeX
odd header
orientation
orphan
overstrike
page break
page layout program
pagination
pica
point
portrait
preview
proportional spacing
ragged
redlining
repaginate
soft
strikeout
style
style sheet
tag
text wrap
thumbnail
vertical justification
widow
word wrap

Formatting Standards
CSS
HTML
LaTeX
MuTeX
PDF
PostScript
rich text format
SGML
TeX
TrueType
XML

Foundation Classes
AFC
JDK

MFC

Graphical User Interfaces (GUIs)
alert box
AWT
branch
button
cascading windows
check box
choose
click
collapse
desktop
dialog box
double click
drag
drag-and-drop
graphical user interface
GUI
hot spot
I-beam pointer
icon
IFC
maximize
MDI
menu
menu bar
menu driven
minimize
moving-bar menu
overlaid windows
point
pointer
pop-up window
pull-down menu
push-button
radio buttons
scroll
scroll bar
shift clicking
size
split screen
tiled windows
title bar
window
X-Window
zoom

Graphics
aliasing
anchor
animated GIF
antialiasing
autotracing
Bézier curve
bit block transfer
bit map

anchor
animated GIF
CDF
CSS
DOM
dynamic HTML
frames
HTML
HTTP
hypertext
JavaScript
marquee
meta tag
PNG
SGML
tag
VRML
W3C
XML

Hypermedia
authoring tool
HyperCard
hyperlink
hypermedia
hypertext
image map

Input Devices
CCD
digital camera
digitizing tablet
grabber
HMD
input device
IrDA
joystick
light pen
pointing device
pointing stick
puck
source
standard input
stylus
tablet
touchpad
trackball

Integrated Circuits (ICs)
ASIC
CCD
chip
controller
DAC
DSP
integrated circuit
large-scale integration (LSI)
Moore's Law

nanotechnology
PLD
semiconductor
Texas Instruments
transistor
VLSI

Internet
ARPANET
BITNET
domain name
Electronic Frontier
    Foundation
extranet
finger
hop
IAC
IAHC
IANA
IETF
IIS
Internet
Internet Architecture Board
Internet Society
InterNIC
intranet
IP address
IP Multicast
IP spoofing
IP switching
IPng
LDAP
Net
NSFnet
NSP
on-line
PING
POP
RealAudio
smurf
Telnet
TLD
traceroute
TTL
whois
WINS

Internet Access
ADSL
channel bonding
connect time
dial-up access
Dial-Up Networking
DirecPC
fractional T-1
ISP
K56flex
L2TP

leased line
POP
PPP
RADIUS
SDSL
SLIP
T-1 carrier
T-3 carrier
WebTV
Winsock

Internet and Online Services
ActiveMovie
bulletin board system
CBT
cyber
cyberspace
distance learning
FAQ
information highway
netiquette
newbie
PointCast
pull
push
user group

Internet Backbone
I2
MAE
Mbone
NAP
NGI Initiative
OC
vBNS

Internet Protocols
ARP
BGP
BIND
BOOTP
CDF
CGI
CIDR
DHCP
DNS
DOM
FTP
HTTP
ICMP
IP
IP Multicast
IPng
IPsec
L2TP
Layer Two Forwarding
LDAP

mouse
mousepad
serial mouse
trackball
Xerox

Microprocessors
680x0
Alpha Processor
ALU
ASIC
chip
chipset
CISC
clock speed
coprocessor
CPU
CPU time
DAC
DSP
FLOPS
FPU
instruction
integrated circuit
Merced
MHz
microcode
microcontroller
microprocessor
MMU
Moore's Law
motherboard
Motorola microprocessors
nanotechnology
overclock
PGA
pipelining
primary cache
processor
RAMDAC
register
RISC
secondary cache
semiconductor
SIP
SPARC
SPEC
superscalar
tag RAM
transistor
ULSI
voltage regulator
VRM
wait state
Zero Insertion Force (ZIF)
    socket
zero wait state

Miscellaneous Standards
Centronics interface
CIE color model
Device Bay
DIN connector
ECP
EIDE
EISA
EPP
ESDI
Industry Standard
    Architecture (ISA) bus
IrDA
ISO 9000
PCMCIA
PnP
QIC
SAA
SCSI
ST-506 interface
TWAIN

Mobile Computing
ACPI
APM
battery pack
CardBus
EPOC
hand-held computer
HPC
memory effect
palmtop
PDA
pen computer
portable
power management
sleep mode
telecommuting
virtual desktop
Windows CE
ZV Port

Modems
acoustic coupler
answer-only modem
auto-answer
cable modem
channel bonding
direct-connect modem
external modem
fax modem
Hayes compatible
host-based modem
internal modem
K56flex
modem
on-board modem
RJ-11

software modem
terminal adapter
V.90
wireless modem
X2

Monitors
alignment
analog monitor
aspect ratio
autosizing
color monitor
composite video
console
convergence
CRT
DDC
degauss
digital monitor
display
display screen
DLP
dot pitch
dumb terminal
ELF emission
Energy Star
fixed-frequency monitor
graphics display system
graphics monitor
gray scaling
intelligent terminal
interlacing
mask pitch
monitor
monochrome
multifrequency monitor
multiscanning monitor
page-white display
PAL
paper-white display
pincushion distortion
pixel
raster
refresh
resolution
RGB monitor
S-Video
screen
screen flicker
smart terminal
terminal
touch screen
true color
TTL monitor
VDT radiation
VDU
Windows terminal

Motherboards
ATX
backplane
BIOS
daughtercard
form factor
heat sink
LPX
motherboard
NLX
POST
printed circuit board
voltage regulator
VRM

Multimedia
BLOB
digital watermark
HDTV
MCI
MPC
multimedia
multimedia kit
SMIL
streaming
television board
tweening
WebTV

Multiplexing
FDM
multiplex
multiplexor
PCM
TDM
TDMA
WDM

Network Interface Cards (NICs)
3COM
AUI
BNC connector
DLC
IRMA board
MAC address
NDIS
network interface card
ODI
protocol stack
transceiver

Network Management
audit trail
CMIP
DMI
IS
MIB

MIS
network management
remote control
RMON
SMS
sniffer
SNMP
spoof
system management
systems administrator
TCO
TP monitor
ZAW

Network Protocols
CMIP
DLC
hub
IPX
Layer Two Forwarding
NDIS
protocol stack
SAP
SDH
SMB
SNMP
SPX
xDSL

Network Topologies
bus network
ring network
star network
token bus network
token-ring network
topology

Networking Companies
3COM
Big Blue
Cisco Systems
DEC
IBM
Novell

Networking Hardware
3COM
backbone
bridge
brouter
concentrator
FRAD
hub
MAU
MTU
repeater
router
routing switch

switch
switching hub
transceiver
UTP

Networking Software
application sharing
distributed database
DSOM
mailing list server
monitor
name server
NetBIOS
NetWare
NetWare Loadable Module
network operating system
ODI
PPTP
RAS
remote control software
VTAM

Networking Standards
AppleTalk
ARCnet
ATM
CDDI
DCE
FDDI
HDLC
LocalTalk
OSI
SDLC
SDSL
SMDS
SNA
SONET
TOPS
X.25
X.400
X.500

Networks
AUI
broadband transmission
broadcast
carrier
cell
cell relay
CIR
circuit switching
client/server architecture
clustering
connectionless
connectivity
contention
daisy chain
dial-up access

diskless workstation
domain
domain name
DSS
enterprise
extranet
Frame Relay
gateway
heterogeneous network
hop
internetworking
intranet
IP switching
latency
leased line
load balancing
local
local-area network
log on
log out
MAN
MSCS
Named Pipes
Net PC
Netbeui
network
network computer
NFS
node
packet
packet switching
peer-to-peer architecture
proxy server
public carrier
pull
push
PVC
QoS
remote access
routing
socket
subnet
subnet mask
SVC
telematics
Telenet
Telnet
throughput
traffic
tunneling
Tymnet
vBNS
virtual circuit
VLAN
VPN
wide-area network
Wolfpack

Newsgroups
conference
emoticon
forum
LISTSERV
lurk
mailing list
mailing list server
Majordomo
moderated newsgroup
news reader
newsgroup
NNTP
PINE
post
SIG
sysop
thread
USENET

Notebook Computers
battery pack
docking station
laptop computer
Lithium-Ion battery
NiCad battery pack
NiMH battery pack
notebook computer
PC card
PCMCIA
port replicator
slate PC
subnotebook computer
transportable

**Object-Oriented
Programming**
BLOB
class
component
Component Object Model
CORBA
DCOM
encapsulation
IFC
JavaBeans
JavaSoft
object
object oriented
object-oriented program-
    ming
ORB
overloading
polymorphism
RMI
SOM
UML

Online Services
America Online
CompuServe Information
    Service
MSN
online service
Prodigy

Operating Systems
background
batch file
batch processing
BeOS
BIOS
boot
bootable diskette
clean boot
cold boot
command
command buffer
command language
command line
command processor
configuration file
control panel
control program
cooperative multitasking
CP/M
cross-platform
distributed processing
driver
embedded object
environment
EPOC
event
executable file
execute
fault tolerance
foreground
GPF
I/O
interrupt
interrupt vector table
job
kernel
launch
load
loader
MBR
memory resident
multi-user
multiprocessing
multitasking
multithreading
MVS
native
NetWare
network operating system

page printer
paper feed
PCL
pin
plotter
PostScript
ppm
print server
printer
printer driver
printer engine
printout
raster image processor
resident font
resolution enhancement
sheet feeder
smoothing
snapshot printer
soft font
spooler
thermal printer
toner
tractor feed
WYSIWYP

Procedures, Functions and Routines
aggregate function
argument
call
function
invoke
module
parameter
procedure
recursion
routine
RPC
stub
system call

Programming
ActiveX
algorithm
alpha version
benchmark
beta test
big-endian
bloatware
bomb
bubble sort
bug
bytecode
CICS
code
constant
contiguous
control

data type
debug
declare
delimiter
DLL
dummy
dump
dynamic variable
easter egg
encapsulation
filter
flag
flow control
front end
functional specification
garbage in, garbage out
geek
genetic programming
glitch
hack
hacker
hard coded
hardwired
heap sort
heuristic programming
High Performance
    Computing
interprocess
    communication (IPC)
ISO 9000
iteration
JDBC
kludge
library
line
listing
loop
macro
mask
memory leak
MPP
name
nesting
OCX
optimize
overhead
parse
patch
program
programmer
property
reverse engineering
runtime
runtime error
scalable
script
semantics
semaphore

simulation
socket
software engineer
software engineering
stateless
systems analyst
systems integrator
three-tier
time-out
tweak
two-tier
VBX
virtual machine
Year 2000 problem

Programming Languages
Ada
AppleScript
assembly language
awk
BASIC
C
C++
COBOL
CODASYL
compiler
Delphi
Eiffel
FORTRAN
fourth-generation language
GW-BASIC
high-level language
interpreter
Java
JavaScript
JScript
keyword
LISP
low-level language
machine language
microcode
Modula-2
MUMPS
Pascal
Perl
programming language
Prolog
pseudocode
QBASIC
query language
reserved word
RPG
Smalltalk
SQL
syntax
Tcl
UML
VBScript

personal finance manager
public-domain software
shareware
software
software licensing
software piracy
speech synthesis
upgrade
upward compatible
vaporware
viewer
warez

Software Companies
Apple Computer
Big Blue
Borland International
BSDI
DEC
IBM
Informix
JavaSoft
Microsoft
Netscape
Novell
Oracle
PointCast
Progress Software
Sun Microsystems
Sybase
Wintel
Xerox

Special Characters
asterisk
backslash
backspace
blank character
caret
EOF mark
EOL mark
ESC
graphics character
null character
pad character
tab character
tab stop
whitespace

Spreadsheets
absolute cell reference
aggregate function
automatic recalculation
cell
column
field
formula
label

Lotus 1-2-3
manual recalculation
range
recalculate
relative cell reference
spreadsheet
three-dimensional
    spreadsheet
VisiCalc

Standards
de facto standard
open
open architecture
proprietary
protocol
RFC
standard

Standards Organizations
ACM
ANSI
CCITT
Electronic Industries
    Association (EIA)
FCC
IAHC
IEEE
IETF
Internet Architecture Board
Internet Society
ISO
ITU
OMG
OSF
OSI
The Open Group
VESA
W3C

Supercomputers
High Performance
    Computing
HPC
supercomputer

Supercomputing
High Performance
    Computing
HIPPI
HPCC
parallel processing
supercomputer

Tape Drives
3480, 3490
DAT
DDS

density
DLT
helical-scan cartridge
QIC
tape
tape drive
Travan

Telecommunications
ADSL
auto-redial
B-channel
cell
cellular
centrex
CSU/DSU
CTI
DSVD
DTMF
Internet telephony
PBX
POTS
PSTN
RJ-11
T-1 carrier
T-3 carrier
telecommunications
telematics
telephony
TSAPI

3-D Graphics
3-D graphics
3-D software
AGP
CAD
CAD/CAM
Direct3D
DirectX
modeling
NURBS
OpenGL
ray tracing
render
texture
Z-buffer
Z-buffering

Transaction Processing
CICS
OLTP
TP monitor
transaction processing
two-phase commit

Types of Computers
Amiga
Apple Computer

clone
computer
desktop model computer
embedded system
kiosk
Macintosh computer
mainframe
minicomputer
NC
network computer
NUMA
personal computer
SOHO
TCO
turnkey system

Typography
ascender
baseline
boldface
bullet
caps
Courier font
cpi
descender
dingbat
drop cap
fixed pitch
font
font family
hyphenation
Intellifont
italic
kerning
leading
lowercase
micro-justification
microspacing
monospacing
outline font
pica
pitch
proportional font
proportional spacing
roman
sans serif
scalable font
serif
superscript
TrueType
TWIP
typeface
uppercase
x-height

UNIX
A/UX
AIX

awk
BSDI
daemon
FreeBSD
GNU
Linux
man page
POSIX
Solaris
UNIX
X-Window
Xenix

User Interfaces
active
Apple key
associate
autosave
box
case sensitive
character based
CICS
clipboard
command driven
context sensitive
control
Control key combination
copy
CUA
current
cursor
cursor control keys
cursor position
default
delete
documentation
ergonomics
floating
form
Help
highlight
hot key
insertion point
interactive
keystroke
learn mode
light bar
look-and-feel
modifier key
option
overwrite mode
prompt
recycle bin
reverse video
screen font
screen saver
select
shortcut

shortcut key
tear-off menu
undo
user
user interface
user-friendly
wizard

Video
digital video
digitize
fps
genlock
S-Video
sampling
streaming
television board
video
video capture
video editing
video overlay
VoD

Video Adapters
color depth
DDC
genlock
graphics accelerator
graphics coprocessor
graphics mode
PAL
RAMDAC
SGRAM
Texas Instruments Graphics
  Architecture (TIGA)
TI 34010
video adapter
video standards
WRAM

Video Formats
3DO
ActiveMovie
AVI
CD-I (Compact
  Disc-Interactive)
Cinepak
Common Intermediate
  Format
DirectX
DVD-Video
DVI
Indeo
motion-JPEG
MPEG
non-interlaced
QCIF
QuickTime

RealVideo
Texas Instruments Graphics
 Architecture (TIGA)
TI 34010
VESA
Video for Windows
XGA

Video Memory
AGP
color depth
RAMDAC
RDRAM
resolution
SGRAM
texture
video memory
VRAM
WRAM

Videoconferencing
application sharing
Common Intermediate
 Format
CU-SeeMe
distance learning
H.323
H.324
Mbone
multicast
NetMeeting
NetShow
QCIF
RealVideo
RTP
RTSP
videoconferencing
VoD

Virtual Memory
address space
demand paging
MMU
page
page fault
paging
swap
swap file
thrash
virtual memory

Virtual Reality
avatar
HMD
MOO
MUD
MUSH
QuickTime VR

virtual reality
VRML

Viruses
antivirus program
macro virus
Trojan horse
virus

Vocations
programmer
software engineer
system administrator
systems administrator
systems analyst
systems integrator

Web Development
Active Server Pages
ActiveX
Apache Web server
CGI
cookie
CSS
DOM
dynamic HTML
HotJava
JScript
log
log file
NSAPI
Perl
servlet
SSI
virtual server
Web server
Webmaster
Windows DNA

Windows
.INI File
ACPI
bootable diskette
CDFS
COM
DCC
DDE
Dial-Up Networking
DirectX
DLL
ESCD
fdisk
FTS file
GID file
himem.sys
MBR
Microsoft Windows
MIF

MSCDEX
MSCS
Network Neighborhood
NTFS
OCX
OLE
OSR 2
PIF file
Registry
Smartdrive
UNC
VFAT
Win32
Win32s
Windows
Windows 95
Windows 98
Windows CE
Windows DNA
Windows NT
Windows terminal
WINS
Winsock
Wintel
Wolfpack
ZAW

Wireless Computing
CDMA
CDPD
GSM
local-area wireless
 network (LAWN)
PCS
TDMA
wireless modem

Word Processing
annotation
append
block
boilerplate
clear
compound document
cut
editor
embedded command
even header
footer
header
insert
insert mode
line editor
mail merge
Microsoft Word
paste
replace
search and replace

A BCDEFGHIJKLMNOPQRSTUVWXYZ

abort To stop a program or function before it has finished naturally. The term *abort* refers to both requested and unexpected terminations. For example, many applications let you abort a search or a print job by pressing a specified abort key. On the other hand, programs can abort unexpectedly for any of the following reasons:

- bugs in the software
- unexpected input that the program cannot handle
- hardware malfunction

When a program aborts, you are usually returned to the operating system shell level. Contrast abort with *crash*, which makes the entire system, including the operating system, unusable.

⇒ See also BOMB; CRASH; HANG; QUIT; SHELL.

absolute address A fixed address in memory. The term *absolute* distinguishes it from a *relative address*, which indicates a location by specifying a distance from another location. Absolute addresses are also called *real addresses* and *machine addresses*.

⇒ See also ADDRESS; RELATIVE ADDRESS.

absolute cell reference In spreadsheet applications, a reference to a particular cell or group of cells that does not change, even if you change the shape or size of the spreadsheet or copy the reference to another cell. For example, in Lotus 1-2-3 and other spreadsheet programs, the cell reference "A3" is an absolute cell reference that always points to the cell in the first column and third row. In contrast, the reference "A3" is a *relative cell reference* that initially points to the cell in the first column and third row but may change if you copy the reference to another cell or change the shape and size of the spreadsheet in some other way. Absolute cell references are particularly useful for referencing constant values (i.e., values that never change).

⇒ See also CONSTANT; RELATIVE CELL REFERENCE; SPREADSHEET.

AC-3 The coding system used by Dolby Digital. The two terms *AC-3* and *Dolby Digital* are often used interchangeably.

⇒ See also DOLBY DIGITAL.

Accelerated Graphics Port See AGP.

accelerator board 1. Short for GRAPHICS ACCELERATOR. **2.** A type of *expansion board* that makes a computer faster by adding a faster CPU or FPU. Most modern computers are designed to accept simpler upgrades. Built into the motherboard is a socket in which the CPU sits. It is usually possible simply to remove the CPU and replace it with a faster model. This is particularly easy if the socket is a Zero Insertion Force (ZIF) socket.

⇒ See also BUS; COPROCESSOR; CPU; EXPANSION BOARD; FLOATING-POINT NUMBER; FPU; GRAPHICS ACCELERATOR; INTEL MICROPROCESSORS; MAIN MEMORY; MICROPROCESSOR; MOTHERBOARD; PC; RAM; ZERO INSERTION FORCE (ZIF) SOCKET.

access *v* **1.** To use. For example, programs can *access memory*, which means they read data from or write data to main memory. A user can access files, directories (or folders), computers, or peripheral devices. **2.** More specifically, *access* often means to read data from or write data to a mass storage device. The time it takes to locate a single byte of information on a mass storage device is called the access time. —*n* **3.** The act of reading data from or writing data to a storage device. **4.** A privilege to use computer information in some manner. For example, a user might be granted *read access* to a file, meaning that the user can read the file but cannot modify or delete it. Most operating systems have several types of access privileges that can be granted or denied to specific users or groups of users.

⇒ See also ACCESS TIME; BYTE; MASS STORAGE; MEMORY; RANDOM ACCESS; READ; WRITE.

Access.bus A serial communications protocol developed by Philips Semiconductors and Digital Equipment (DEC) in 1985 for connecting peripheral devices to a computer. *Access.bus* is designed for hassle-free installation and configuration of relatively low-speed devices, such as keyboards, monitors, and printers. Access.bus uses a bus topology, which enables it to support up to 125 devices.

A competing standard, *Universal Serial Bus (USB)*, is quickly becoming the serial standard.

⇒ See also BUS; SERIAL PORT; USB.

access code Same as *password,* a series of characters and numbers that enables a user to access a computer.

⇒ See also ACCESS; LOG ON; PASSWORD.

access control Refers to mechanisms and policies that restrict access to computer resources. An *access control list (ACL)*, for example, specifies what operations different users can perform on specific files and directories.

⇒ See also AUTHORIZATION; SECURITY.

accessory slot Same as EXPANSION SLOT.

Table 1
Typical Access Times for Different Computer Devices

Device	Typical Access Times
static RAM (SRAM)	5–15 nanoseconds
dynamic RAM (DRAM)	50–70 nanoseconds
EPROM	55–250 nanoseconds
read-only memory (ROM)	55–250 nanoseconds
Hard Disk Drive	6–12 milliseconds
Erasable Optical	19–100 milliseconds
CD-ROM	80–800 milliseconds
DAT tape drive	about 20 seconds
QIC tape drive	about 40 seconds
8 mm tape drive	40-500 seconds

---

access time The time a program or device takes to locate a single piece of information and make it available to the computer for processing. *DRAM (dynamic random access memory)* chips for personal computers have access times of 50 to 150 nanoseconds (billionths of a second). *Static RAM (SRAM)* has access times as low as 10 nanoseconds. Ideally, the access time of memory should be fast enough to keep up with the CPU. If not, the CPU will waste a certain number of clock cycles, which makes it slower.

Note, however, that reported access times can be misleading because most memory chips, especially DRAM chips, require a pause between back-to-back accesses. This is one reason why SRAM is so much faster than DRAM, even when the reported access times are equivalent; SRAM does not need to be refreshed like DRAM, so there is no pause between back-to-back accesses. A more important measurement of a chip's speed, therefore, is its cycle time, which measures how quickly two back-to-back accesses can be made.

Access time is also frequently used to describe the speed of disk drives. Disk access times are measured in milliseconds (thousandths of a second), often abbreviated as *ms*. Fast hard disk drives for personal computers boast access times of about 9 to 15 milliseconds. Note that this is about 200 times slower than average DRAM.

The access time for disk drives includes the time it actually takes for the *read/write head* to locate a sector on the disk (called the *seek time*). This is an average time because it depends on how far away the head is from the desired data.

⇒ See also ACCESS; CLOCK SPEED; CPU; CYCLE TIME; DATA TRANSFER RATE; DISK CACHE; INTERLEAVE; WAIT STATE.

accounting software A class of computer programs that perform accounting operations. The simplest accounting programs, sometimes called *personal finance managers*, are single-entry systems that automate check writing and record keeping.

Double-entry systems include functions for general ledger, accounts receivable, and accounts payable. More sophisticated systems also support functions for payroll, inventory, invoicing, and fixed assets. Some high-end systems even support sales analysis and time billing.

⇒ See also YEAR 2000 PROBLEM.

ACM Abbreviation of the *A(ssociation) for C(omputing) M(achinery)*, an organization composed of U.S. computer professionals. Founded in 1947, the ACM publishes information relating to computer science, holds seminars, and creates and promotes computer standards.

⇒ See also STANDARD.

acoustic coupler A device onto which a telephone handset is placed to connect a computer with a network. The acoustic coupler might also contain a modem, or the modem could be a separate device.

Popular in the 1970s, acoustic couplers are no longer widely used. Nowadays, telephones connect directly to a modem via modular telephone connectors. This produces better connections than acoustic couplers and avoids the problems produced by irregularly shaped telephones. Still, acoustic coupler modems are useful in some situations, such as in hotel rooms where the telephone cable is anchored to the wall. Modems that do not use an acoustic coupler are sometimes called *direct-connect modems*.

⇒ See also MODEM; NETWORK.

ACPI Short for *A(dvanced) C(onfiguration) and P(ower) I(nterface)*, a power management specification developed by Intel, Microsoft, and Toshiba. ACPI, which is included in Windows 98, enables the operating system to control the amount of power given to each device attached to the computer. With ACPI, the operating system can turn off peripheral devices, such as CD-ROM players, when they're not in use. As another example, ACPI enables manufacturers to produce computers that automatically power up as soon as you touch the keyboard.

⇒ See also APM; POWER MANAGEMENT; SLEEP MODE.

Acrobat A suite of programs developed by Adobe Systems, Inc., for creating and distributing electronic documents. Programs in the suite allow you to create a Portable Document Format (PDF) file for a document. You can then distribute the PDF file electronically to people who view the document with the Acrobat Reader. The reader is the best-known component of the Acrobat suite and is freely distributed by Adobe.

People viewing a PDF file (or document) with the Acrobat Reader see the document with the exact layout and typography intended by the author. This is its main advantage over other electronic formats such as HTML, where the layout can vary depending on the software being used. PDF has become one of the most popular formats for distributing documents between different types of computer systems.

⇒ See also PDF.

acronym Technically, a word that is formed by combining some parts (usually the first letters) of some other terms. For example, *modem* is the acronym derived from *mod(ulator)/dem(odulator)*. In everyday speech, the term is also used to refer to *abbreviations,* which are combinations of letters representing a longer phrase. For example, *CRT* is an abbreviation for *c(athode) r(ay) t(ube)*. The difference is that an acronym is pronounced as if it were a word rather than just a series of individual letters.

Newsgroups, chat rooms, and e-mail have spawned a rich set of acronyms and abbreviations for common phrases. A few of the more common ones are listed below.

⇒ See also CHAT ROOM; E-MAIL; NEWSGROUP.

Acronym	Meaning
ASAP:	As Soon As Possible
BTW:	By the Way
FWIW:	For What It's Worth
FYI:	For Your Information
IMHO:	In My Humble Opinion
IMO:	In My Opinion
LOL:	Laughing Out Loud
ROTFL:	Rolling On the Floor Laughing
RTFM:	Read the F***ing Manual
TIA:	Thanks in Advance

active Refers to objects currently being displayed or used on a computer. For example, in graphical user interfaces, the *active window* is the window currently receiving mouse and keyboard input. In spreadsheet applications, the *active cell* is the cell, usually highlighted, in which data can be entered or modified. The *active program* is the program currently running. When you enter a command, it usually applies only to the active elements.

⇒ See also CELL; GRAPHICAL USER INTERFACE; SPREADSHEET; WINDOW.

active backplane See under BACKPLANE.

Active Directory A new directory service from Microsoft; part of Windows NT 5.0.

⇒ See also DIRECTORY SERVICE; LDAP; NDS; WINDOWS NT; X.500.

active matrix See under ACTIVE MATRIX DISPLAY.

active matrix display A type of flat-panel display in which the screen is refreshed more frequently than in conventional passive-matrix displays and is therefore sharper and brighter. The most common type of active-matrix display is based on a technology known as *TFT (thin film transistor)*. The two terms *active matrix* and *TFT* are often used interchangeably.

⇒ See also FLAT-PANEL DISPLAY; LCD; TFT.

ActiveMovie A new multimedia streaming technology developed by Microsoft. ActiveMovie is already built into the Internet Explorer browser and will be part of future versions of the Windows operating system. Supporting most multimedia formats, including MPEG, ActiveMovie enables users to view multimedia content distributed over the Internet or an intranet, or on CD-ROM.

ActiveMovie's main competition is the QuickTime standard developed by Apple Computer.

⇒ See also MULTIMEDIA; QUICKTIME; STREAMING.

Active Server Pages A specification for a dynamically created Web page with a *.ASP* extension that contains either Visual Basic or Jscript code. When a browser requests an ASP page, the Web server generates a page with HTML code and sends it back to the browser. So ASP pages are similar to CGI scripts, but they enable Visual Basic programmers to work with familiar tools.

⇒ See also CGI; VISUAL BASIC.

ActiveX A loosely defined set of technologies developed by Microsoft for sharing information among different applications. ActiveX is an outgrowth of two other Microsoft technologies called *OLE (Object Linking and Embedding)* and *COM (Component Object Model)*. As a name, *ActiveX* can be very confusing because it applies to a whole set of COM-based technologies. Most people, however, think only of ActiveX controls, which represent a specific way of implementing ActiveX technologies.

⇒ See also ACTIVEX CONTROL; ADO; COMPONENT OBJECT MODEL; DIRECTX; JAVA; MICROSOFT; OLE; WINDOWS DNA.

ActiveX control A control using ActiveX technologies. An ActiveX control can be automatically downloaded and executed by a Web browser. ActiveX is not a programming language but rather a set of rules for how applications should share information. Programmers can develop ActiveX controls in a variety of languages, including C, C++, Visual Basic, and Java.

An ActiveX control is similar to a Java applet. Unlike Java applets, however, ActiveX controls have full access to the Windows operating system. This gives them much more power than Java applets, but with this power comes a certain risk that the applet may damage software or data on your machine. To control this risk, Microsoft developed a registration system so that browsers can identify and authenticate an ActiveX control before downloading it. Another difference between Java applets and ActiveX controls is that Java applets can be written to run on all platforms, whereas ActiveX controls are currently limited to Windows environments.

Related to ActiveX is a scripting language called *VBScript* that enables Web authors to embed interactive elements in HTML documents. VBScript is similar to Visual Basic, just as JavaScript is similar to Java. Microsoft's Web browser, Internet Explorer, supports Java, JavaScript, and ActiveX. Netscape's Navigator browsers support only Java and JavaScript, but there are plug-ins you can install that enable Navigator to support VBScript and ActiveX.

⇒ See also ACTIVEX; BROWSER; DYNAMIC HTML; INTERNET EXPLORER; JAVA-BEANS; OCX; SHOCKWAVE.

ActiveX Data Objects See ADO.

Ada A high-level programming language developed in the late 1970s and early 1980s for the U.S. Defense Department. Ada was designed to be a general-purpose language for everything from business applications to rocket guidance systems. One of its principal features is that it supports *real-time* applications. It also incorporates modular techniques that make it easy to build and maintain large systems. Since 1986, Ada has been the mandatory development language for most U.S. military applications. In addition, Ada is often the language of choice for large systems that require real-time processing, such as banking and air-traffic-control systems.

Ada is named after Augusta Ada Byron (1815–52), Countess of Lovelace and daughter of Lord Byron. She helped Charles Babbage develop programs for the *analytic engine,* the first mechanical computer. She is considered by many to be the world's first programmer.

⇒ See also HIGH-LEVEL LANGUAGE; MODULAR ARCHITECTURE; REAL TIME.

adapter 1. Short for EXPANSION BOARD. **2.** The circuitry required to support a particular device. For example, *video adapters* enable the computer to support graphics monitors, and *network adapters* enable a computer to attach to a network. Adapters can be built into the main circuitry of a computer or they can be separate add-ons that come in the form of expansion boards.

⇒ See also CONTROLLER; EXPANSION BOARD; VIDEO ADAPTER.

adaptive differential pulse-code modulation See ADPCM.

ADB Abbreviation of *A(pple) D(esktop) B(us)*, a type of communications pathway built into all versions of the Apple Macintosh computer since the SE. It is used to connect low-speed input devices such as the keyboard and mouse. ADB ports are designated with a special icon. A single ADB port can support as many as 16 simultaneous input devices.

⇒ See also BUS; CONSTANT; MACINTOSH COMPUTER; PORT.

add-in 1. A component you can add to a computer or other device to increase its capabilities. Add-ins can increase memory or add graphics or communications capabilities to a computer. They can come in the form of expansion boards, cartridges, or chips. The term *add-in* is often used instead of *add-on* for chips you add to a board that is already installed in a computer. In contrast, *add-on* almost always refers to an entire circuit board. **2.** A software program that extends the capabilities of larger programs. For example, there are many Excel add-ins designed to complement the basic functionality offered by Excel. In the Windows environment, add-ins are becoming increasingly common thanks to OLE 2.0.

⇒ See also ADD-ON; CARTRIDGE; EXPANSION BOARD; OLE.

add-on Refers to a product designed to complement another product. For example, there are numerous *add-on boards* available that you can plug into a personal computer to give it additional capabilities. Another term for *add-on board* is *expansion board*.

Add-on products are also available for software applications. For example, there are add-on report-generation programs that attach to popular database products such as MS-Access, giving them additional report-generation and graphics capabilities.

The terms *add-on* and *add-in* are often, but not always, used synonymously. The term *add-in* can refer to individual chips you can insert into boards that are already installed in your computer. *Add-on,* on the other hand, almost always refers to an entire circuit board, cartridge, or program.

⇒ See also ADD-IN; CARTRIDGE; EXPANSION BOARD; EXPANSION SLOT; PRINTED CIRCUIT BOARD.

add-on board Same as EXPANSION BOARD.

address 1. A location of data, usually in main memory or on a disk. You can think of computer memory as an array of storage boxes, each of which is one byte in length. Each box has an address (a unique number) assigned to it. By specifying a memory address, programmers can access a particular byte of data. Disks are divided into *tracks* and *sectors*, each of which has a unique address. Usually, you do not need to worry about addresses unless you are a programmer. **2.** A name or token that identifies a network component. In local area networks (LANs), for example, every node has a unique address. On the Internet, every file has a unique address called a URL.

⇒ See also ABSOLUTE ADDRESS; ADDRESS BUS; ADDRESS SPACE; BASE ADDRESS; DISK; E-MAIL ADDRESS; MAC ADDRESS; MACHINE ADDRESS; MAIN MEMORY; MEMORY; OFFSET; RELATIVE ADDRESS; SECTOR; TRACK; URL.

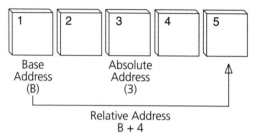

Figure 1: **memory addresses**

address bus A collection of wires connecting the CPU with main memory that is used to identify particular locations (addresses) in main memory. The width of the address bus (that is, the number of wires) determines how many unique memory locations can be addressed. Modern PCs and Macintoshes have as many as 36 address lines, which enables them theoretically to access 64 GB (gigabytes) of main memory. However, the actual amount of memory that can be accessed is usually much less than this theoretical limit because of chipset and motherboard limitations.

⇒ See also ADDRESS; BUS; CPU; MAIN MEMORY.

Address Resolution Protocol See ARP.

address space The set of all legal addresses in memory for a given application. The address space represents the amount of memory available to a program. Interestingly, the address space can be larger than physical memory through a technique called *virtual memory*.

⇒ See also ADDRESS; MAIN MEMORY; MEMORY; THUNK; VIRTUAL MEMORY.

ADO Short for *A(ctiveX) D(ata) O(bjects)*, Microsoft's newest high-level interface for data objects. ADO is designed eventually to replace *Data Access Objects (DAO)* and *Remote Data Objects (RDO)*. Unlike RDO and DAO, which are designed only for accessing relational databases, ADO is more general and can be used to access all sorts of different types of data, including Web pages, spreadsheets, and other types of documents.
Together with OLE DB and ODBC, ADO is one of the main components of Microsoft's *Universal Data Access (UDA)* specification, which is designed to provide a consistent way of accessing data regardless of how the data is structured.

⇒ See also ACTIVEX; DAO; ODBC.

Adobe Acrobat See under ACROBAT.

Adobe Photoshop A leading paint program from Adobe Systems, Inc. For many years, Photoshop has been the model against which other paint programs are compared. Initially, it ran only on Macintosh systems, which was a strong selling point for Macs, especially among graphic artists. Today, Photoshop runs on both Macs and Windows PCs.

⇒ See also DESKTOP PUBLISHING; IMAGE ENHANCEMENT; PAINT PROGRAM.

Adobe PostScript See POSTSCRIPT.

ADPCM Short for *A(daptive) D(ifferential) P(ulse) C(ode) M(odulation)*, a form of *pulse-code modulation (PCM)* that produces a digital signal with a lower bit rate than standard PCM. ADPCM produces a lower bit rate by recording only the difference between samples and adjusting the coding scale dynamically to accommodate large and small differences. Some applications use ADPCM to digitize a voice signal so that voice and data can be transmitted simultaneously over a digital facility normally used only for one or the other.

⇒ See also MODULATE; PCM; SAMPLING.

ADSL Short for *a(symmetric) d(igital) s(ubscriber) l(ine)*, a new technology that allows more data to be sent over existing copper telephone lines, known as POTS. ADSL supports data rates of from 1.5 to 9 Mbps when receiving data (known as the *downstream* rate) and from 16 to 640 Kbps when sending data (known as the *upstream* rate).

ADSL requires a special ADSL modem. It is not currently available to the general public except in trial areas, but many believe that it will be one of the more popular choices for Internet access over the next few years.

The ITU is currently defining an xDSL standard based on ADSL, called *G.dmt*.

⇒ See also ISDN; POTS; SDSL.

Advanced Differential Pulse-Code Modulation See ADPCM.

Advanced Graphics Port (AGP) See AGP.

Advanced Micro Devices See AMD.

Advanced Power Management See APM,

Advanced SCSI Programming Interface See ASPI.

AFC Short for *A(pplication) F(oundation) C(lasses)*, a set of Microsoft foundation classes written entirely in Java. The AFC sits on top of the Java Development Kit (JDK) and extends Sun's Abstract Window Toolkit

(AWT). A similar group of foundation classes is Netscape's Internet Foundation Classes (IFC).

⇒ See also AWT; CLASS; IFC; JAVA; JDK; MFC.

agent A program that performs some information-gathering or -processing task in the background. Typically, an agent is a given a very small and well-defined task.

Although the theory behind agents has been around for some time, agents have become more prominent only with the recent growth of the Internet. Many companies now sell software that enables you to configure an agent to search the Internet for certain types of information.

In computer science, there is a school of thought that believes that the human mind essentially consists of thousands or millions of agents all working in parallel. To produce real artificial intelligence, this school holds, we should build computer systems that also contain many agents and systems for arbitrating among the agents' competing results.

⇒ See also ARTIFICIAL INTELLIGENCE; DAEMON.

aggregate function A function that performs a computation on a set of values rather than on a single value. For example, finding the average or mean of a list of numbers is an aggregate function.

All database-management and spreadsheet systems support a set of aggregate functions that can operate on a set of selected records or cells.

⇒ See also DATABASE MANAGEMENT SYSTEM; FUNCTION; SPREADSHEET.

AGP Short for *A(ccelerated) G(raphics) P(ort)*, a new interface specification developed by Intel Corporation. AGP is based on PCI but is designed especially for the throughput demands of 3-D graphics. Rather than using the PCI bus for graphics data, AGP introduces a dedicated point-to-point channel so that the graphics controller can directly access main memory. The AGP channel is 32 bits wide and runs at 66 MHz. This translates into a total bandwidth of 266 MBps, as opposed to the PCI bandwidth of 133 MBps. AGP also supports two optional faster modes, with throughputs of 533 MBps and 1.07 GBps. In addition, AGP allows 3-D textures to be stored in main memory rather than video memory.

AGP has a couple of important system requirements:

- The chipset must support AGP.
- The motherboard must be equipped with an AGP bus slot or must have an integrated AGP graphics system.
- The operating system must be the OSR 2.1 version of Windows 95, Windows 98, or Windows NT 5.0.

AGP-enabled computers and graphics accelerators hit the market in August 1997. However, there are several different levels of AGP compliance. The following features are considered optional:

Texturing: Also called Direct Memory Execute mode; allows textures to be stored in main memory.

Throughput: Various levels of throughput are offered: **1X** is 266 MBps, **2X** is 533 MBps, and **4X** provides 1.07 GBps.

Sideband Addressing: Speeds up data transfers by sending command instructions in a separate, parallel channel.

Pipelining: Enables the graphics card to send several instructions together instead of sending one at a time.

⇒ See also 3-D GRAPHICS; 3-D SOFTWARE; GRAPHICS ACCELERATOR; NLX; PCI; TEXTURE.

AI Abbreviation of *artificial intelligence*.

AIFF Short for *A(udio) I(nterchange) F(ile) F(ormat)*, a common format for storing and transmitting sampled sound. The format was developed by Apple Computer and is the standard audio format for Macintosh computers. It is also used by Silicon Graphics Incorporated (SGI).

The format encodes audio data in 8-bit mono or stereo waveforms. AIFF files generally end with a **.AIF** or **.IEF** extension.

The AIFF format does not support data compression, so AIFF files tend to be large. However, there is another format called *AIIF-Compressed* (*AIFF-C* or *AIFC*) that supports compression rations as high as 6:1.

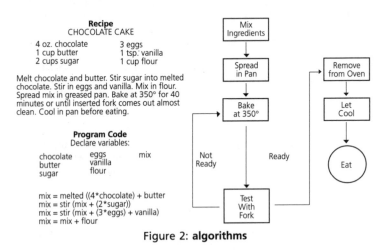

Figure 2: **algorithms**

AIX Abbreviation for *A(dvanced) I(nteractive) eX(ecutive)*, a version of UNIX produced by IBM. AIX runs on a variety of computers, including PCs and workstations.

⇒ See also UNIX.

alert box A small box that appears on the display screen to give you information or to warn you about a potentially damaging operation. For example, it might warn you that the system is deleting one or more files. Unlike dialog boxes, alert boxes do not require any user input. However, you need to acknowledge the alert box by pressing the Enter key or clicking a mouse button to make it go away.

Alert boxes are also called *message boxes*.

⇒ See also BOX; DIALOG BOX; GRAPHICAL USER INTERFACE; WINDOW.

algorithm A formula or set of steps for solving a particular problem. To be an algorithm, a set of rules must be unambiguous and have a clear stopping point. Algorithms can be expressed in any language, from natural languages like English or French to programming languages like FORTRAN.

We use algorithms every day. For example, a recipe for baking a cake is an algorithm. Most programs, with the exception of some artificial intelligence applications, consist of algorithms. Inventing elegant algorithms —algorithms that are simple and require the fewest steps possible—is one of the principal challenges in programming.

⇒ See also ARTIFICIAL INTELLIGENCE; BUBBLE SORT; HEAP SORT; HEURISTIC PROGRAMMING; PROGRAM; PROGRAMMING LANGUAGE; PSEUDOCODE.

alias An alternative name for an object, such as a variable, file, or device. On Macintoshes, you can assign aliases for files, which allows you to have icons for the same file in different folders. Windows provides the same functionality but uses the term *shortcut*. UNIX also supports aliases but calls them *links* or *symbolic links*.

⇒ See also DEVICE; FILE; NAME; VARIABLE.

aliasing 1. In computer graphics, the process by which smooth curves and other lines become jagged because the resolution of the graphics device or file is not high enough to represent a smooth curve. Smoothing and anti-aliasing techniques can reduce the effect of aliasing. **2.** In digital sound, aliasing is a static distortion resulting from a low sampling rate—below 40 kilohertz (Khz).

⇒ See also ANTI-ALIASING; JAGGIES; RESOLUTION; SMOOTHING.

alignment 1. When used to describe text, *alignment* is the arrangement of text or graphics relative to a margin. **2.** In reference to graphical objects,

flush left alignment means that text is lined up along the left margin.	*flush right alignment* lines up text along the right margin.
centered alignment means that text is aligned around a midpoint.	*justified alignment* means that text lines up along both margins.

alignment describes their relative positions. Most draw programs support an align command that allows you to align two or more objects so that their tops, bottoms, sides, or middles are aligned.

⇒ See also DRAW PROGRAM; JUSTIFICATION; MARGINS.

alpha blending See under ALPHA CHANNEL.

Table 2
Alphanumeric, Punctuation, and Special Characters

Alphanumeric Characters	Special Characters	Punctuation Characters	
a–z	Esc	;	semicolon
A–Z	Tab	:	colon
0–9		,	comma
		"	double quote
		'	single quote
		#	number sign or pound sign
		/	slash
		\	backslash
		*	asterisk or star
		^	caret
		.	period, point, or dot
		@	at sign
		&	ampersand
		~	tilde
		!	bang or exclamation mark
		-	dash
		=	equal sign
		—	em dash
		–	en dash
		…	ellipsis

alpha channel In graphics, a portion of each pixel's data that is reserved for transparency information. A 32-bit graphics system contains four channels—three 8-bit channels for red, green, and blue (RGB) and one 8-bit alpha channel. The alpha channel is really a *mask*—it specifies how the pixel's colors should be merged with another pixel when the two are overlaid, one on top of the other.

Typically, you wouldn't define the alpha channel on a pixel-by-pixel basis, but rather per object. Different parts of the object would have different levels of transparency depending on how much you wanted the background to show through. This allows you to create rectangular objects that appear as if they are irregular in shape—you define the rectangular edges as transparent so that the background shows through. This is especially important for animation, where the background changes from one frame to the next.

Rendering overlapping objects that include an alpha value is called *alpha blending.*

⇒ See also ANIMATION; GRAPHICS; MASK; PIXEL; RGB MONITOR.

alphanumeric Describes the combined set of all letters in the alphabet and the numbers 0 through 9. It is useful to group letters and numbers together because many programs treat them identically, and differently from punctuation characters. For example, most operating systems allow you to use any letters or numbers in filenames but prohibit the use of many punctuation characters. Your computer manual might express this rule by stating: "Filenames may be composed of alphanumeric characters."

Sometimes additional characters are considered alphanumeric: for example, on IBM mainframes, the characters @, #, and $.

⇒ See also CHARACTER; SPECIAL CHARACTER.

Alpha Processor A powerful RISC processor developed by Digital Equipment Corporation used in its line of workstations and servers. It is the only microprocessor, other than x86 microprocessors, that runs Windows NT. As of 1998, versions of the Alpha chip contain nearly 10 million transistors and run at clock speeds of from 300 to 600 MHz.

⇒ See also INTEL MICROPROCESSORS; MICROPROCESSOR; RISC; WINDOWS NT; WORKSTATION.

alpha testing See under ALPHA VERSION.

alpha version A very early version of a software product. Typically, software goes through two stages of testing before it is considered finished. The first stage, called *alpha testing,* is often performed only by users within the organization developing the software. The second stage, called *beta testing,* generally involves a limited number of external users.

⇒ See also BETA TEST; DEBUG.

Alta Vista The name of a software firm associated with Digital Equipment Corporation (DEC). Alta Vista offers software products you can use to locate and manage information on the Internet or a private computer network that uses Internet tools (an *intranet*). The best-known product from this company is the Alta Vista search system that anyone can use to find information on the World Wide Web. People often use the term *Alta Vista* to refer to this free search service.

The Alta Vista search service contains one of the largest Web indices. The index is maintained and generated by programs, called *robots* or *spiders*, that follow links on Web pages, download the pages, and then index them according to the words and phrases that the pages contain.

⇒ See also DEC; EXCITE; HOTBOT; INFOSEEK; LYCOS; MAGELLAN; OPEN TEXT; SEARCH ENGINE; SPIDER; WEBCRAWLER; WORLD WIDE WEB; YAHOO!.

Alt key Short for *Alternate key*, the Alt key is like a second Control key. Not all computer keyboards have an Alt key, but it is standard on all PCs. You use it in the same fashion as the Control key—holding it down while you press another key. For example, an instruction to use the Alt + P combination means that you should hold the Alt key down while pressing and then releasing the P key. The meaning of any Alt key combination depends on which application is running.

On Macintoshes, the equivalent key is called the *Option key*.

⇒ See also ASCII; CONTROL CHARACTER; KEYBOARD; OPTION KEY.

ALU Abbreviation of *a(rithmetic) l(ogic) u(nit)*, the part of a computer that performs all arithmetic computations, such as addition and multiplication, and all comparison operations. The ALU is one component of the CPU (central processing unit).

⇒ See also CPU.

AMD Short for *A(dvanced) M(icro) D(evices)*, a manufacturer of chips for personal computers. Along with Cyrix, AMD is challenging Intel with a set of Intel-compatible microprocessors. AMD's latest chip, the *K6*, supports MMX instructions.

⇒ See also CYRIX; INTEL; INTEL MICROPROCESSORS; K6; MICROPROCESSOR; MMX; PENTIUM MICROPROCESSOR.

American National Standards Institute See ANSI.

American Standard Code for Information Interchange See ASCII.

America Online A popular online service. It is often abbreviated as *AOL*.

⇒ See also COMPUSERVE INFORMATION SERVICE; MSN; ONLINE SERVICE.

Amiga A family of personal computers originally produced by Commodore Business Machines. Amigas are powerful personal computers that have extra microprocessors to handle graphics and sound generation. The Amiga operating system has had preemptive multitasking since its inception in 1985, 10 years before this feature found its way into Microsoft Windows.

Like older Apple Macintosh computers, the Amiga line of computers is built around the Motorola 680x0 line of microprocessors. Although the Amiga operating system is not compatible with other PC operating systems, such as DOS and Windows, there are emulation programs that enable an Amiga to run PC, Macintosh, and even UNIX programs.

Faced with financial hardships, Commodore sold the Amiga to a German company called Escom AG. Escom, in turn, also went bankrupt. In March, 1997, Gateway 2000 purchased the Amiga design.

⇒ See also GRAPHICS; MICROPROCESSOR; MIDI; PERSONAL COMPUTER.

analog Almost everything in the world can be described or represented in one of two forms: *analog* or *digital*. The principal feature of analog representations is that they are continuous. In contrast, digital representations consist of values measured at discrete intervals.

Digital watches are called digital because they go from one value to the next without displaying all intermediate values. Consequently, they can display only a finite number of times of the day. In contrast, watches with hands are analog, because the hands move continuously around the clock face. As the minute hand goes around, it touches not only the numbers 1 through 12 but also the infinite number of points in between.

Early attempts at building computers used analog techniques, but accuracy and reliability were not good enough. Today, almost all computers are digital.

⇒ See also DAC; DIGITAL.

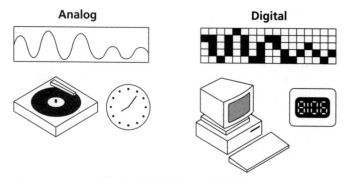

| Analog | Digital |

Figure 3: **analog vs. digital**

analog monitor The traditional type of color display screen that has been used for years in televisions. In reality, all monitors based on CRT technology (that is, all monitors except *flat-panel displays*) are analog. Some monitors, however, are called *digital monitors* because they accept digital signals from the video adapter. EGA monitors, for example, must be digital because the EGA standard specifies digital signals. Digital monitors must nevertheless translate the signals into an analog form before displaying images. Some monitors can accept both digital and analog signals. Some analog monitors are also called digital because they support digital controls for adjusting the display.

Most analog monitors are *multifrequency monitors*, which means that they are designed to accept signals at two or more preset frequency levels.

⇒ See also ANALOG; CRT; DIGITAL; DIGITAL MONITOR; FLAT-PANEL DISPLAY; MONITOR; MULTISCANNING MONITOR; VIDEO ADAPTER.

anchor In desktop publishing, to fix a graphical object so that its position relative to some other object remains the same during repagination. Frequently, for example, you may want to *anchor* a picture next to a piece of text so that they always appear together.

⇒ See also DESKTOP PUBLISHING.

AND operator A Boolean operator that returns a value of TRUE if both its operands are TRUE, and FALSE otherwise.

⇒ See also BOOLEAN OPERATOR; OPERAND; OPERATOR.

animated GIF A type of GIF image that can be animated by combining several images into a single GIF file. Applications that support the animated GIF standard, *GIF89A,* cycle through each image. GIF animation doesn't give the same level of control and flexibility as other animation formats, but it has become extremely popular because it is supported by nearly all Web browsers. In addition, animated GIF files tend to be quite a bit smaller than other animation files, such as Java applets.

⇒ See also ANIMATION; GIF.

animation A simulation of movement created by displaying a series of pictures, or frames. Cartoons on television provide one example of animation. Animation on computers is one of the chief ingredients of multimedia presentations. Many software applications enable you to create animations that you can display on a computer monitor.

Note the difference between animation and video. Whereas video takes continuous motion and breaks it up into discrete frames, animation starts with independent pictures and puts them together to form the illusion of continuous motion.

⇒ See also 3-D GRAPHICS; 3-D SOFTWARE; ALPHA CHANNEL; ANIMATED GIF; MODELING; MORPHING; MULTIMEDIA; SGI; SPRITE; TWEENING.

annotation A comment attached to a particular section of a document. Many computer applications enable you to enter annotations on text documents, spreadsheets, presentations, and other objects. This is a particularly effective way to use computers to edit and review work in a workgroup environment. The creator of a document sends it to reviewers, who then mark it up electronically with annotations and return it. The document's creator then reads the annotations and adjusts the document appropriately.

Many modern applications support voice annotations. If the computer is equipped with a microphone, the reviewer can voice comments orally instead of writing them. These voice annotations are digitized and stored with the document. When a reader of the document selects the annotation icon, the spoken message is played back through the computer's speakers.

⇒ See also WORKGROUP COMPUTING.

anonymous FTP A method for downloading public files using the *File Transfer Protocol (FTP)*. Anonymous FTP is called *anonymous* because you don't need to identify yourself before accessing files. In general, you enter the word *anonymous* or the abbreviation *ftp* when the host prompts you for a username; you can enter anything for the password, such as your e-mail address or simply the word *guest*. In many cases, when you access an anonymous FTP site, you won't even be prompted for your name and password.

You can use the Archie system to obtain a list of anonymous FTP sites and files available on each site.

Many FTP sites are protected. Unlike anonymous FTP sites, these restricted FTP sites can be accessed only by individuals who enter a valid username and password.

⇒ See also DOWNLOAD; FTP.

ANSI Acronym for the *A(merican) N(ational) S(tandards) I(nstitute)*. Founded in 1918, ANSI is a voluntary organization composed of more than 1,300 members (including all the large computer companies) that creates standards for the computer industry. For example, ANSI C is a version of the C language that has been approved by the ANSI committee. To a large degree, all ANSI C compilers, regardless of which company produces them, should behave similarly.

In addition to programming languages, ANSI sets standards for a wide range of technical areas, from electrical specifications to communications protocols. For example, FDDI, the main set of protocols for sending data over fiber optic cables, is an ANSI standard.

⇒ See also FDDI; PORTABLE; STANDARD.

ANSI Character Set A collection of special characters and associated codes adopted by the ANSI standards organization. The ANSI character set includes many foreign characters, special punctuation, and business symbols.

In Windows environments, you can enter ANSI characters by holding down the Alt key and typing the ANSI code with the numeric keypad. On Macintoshes, you can enter ANSI characters by holding down the Option key and typing a character.

⇒ See also ASCII; ISO LATIN 1.

Table 3 ANSI Characters			

Character	Name	ANSI Code	Macintosh Keystrokes
...	ellipsis	0133	Option;
'	opening single quote	0145	Option]
'	closing single quote	0146	Option Shift]
"	opening double quote	0147	Option [
"	closing double quote	0148	Option Shift [
•	bullet	0149	Option 8
–	en dash	0150	Option Hyphen
—	em dash	0151	Option Shift Hyphen
™	trademark symbol	0153	Option 2
©	copyright symbol	0169	Option g
®	registered trademark	0174	Option r
¼	one quarter	0188	font-dependent
½	one half	0189	font-dependent
¾	three quarters	0190	font-dependent

ANSI.SYS Pronounced *ann-see-dot-siss,* the name of a DOS device driver that makes a monitor conform to the ANSI standard. The ANSI standard specifies a series of *escape sequences* that cause the monitor to behave in various ways. For example, one escape sequence clears the screen while another causes all subsequent characters to be inverted.

In general, DOS programs do not use the ANSI codes because these codes are slower than the built-in BIOS codes. DOS programs that do use ANSI codes for compatibility with other devices require that you load the ANSI.SYS device driver in the configuration file, CONFIG.SYS.

Windows does not use ANSI.SYS at all.

⇒ See also ANSI; BIOS; CONFIG.SYS; DRIVER; ESCAPE SEQUENCE.

answer-only modem A modem that can receive messages but cannot send them. Only the most inexpensive modems are answer-only.

⇒ See also MODEM.

antialiasing In computer graphics, *antialiasing* is a software technique for diminishing *jaggies*—stairsteplike lines that should be smooth. Jaggies occur because the output device—the monitor or printer—doesn't have a high enough resolution to represent a smooth line. Antialiasing reduces the prominence of jaggies by surrounding the stairsteps with intermediate shades of gray (for gray-scaling devices) or color (for color devices). Although this reduces the jagged appearance of the lines, it also makes them fuzzier.

Another method for reducing jaggies is called *smoothing*, in which the printer changes the size and horizontal alignment of dots to make curves smoother.

Antialiasing is sometimes called *oversampling*.

⇒ See also JAGGIES; RESOLUTION; SMOOTHING.

antistatic mat A mat on which you can stand while repairing a computer or adding expansion cards. The mat absorbs static electricity, which might otherwise damage electronic components. Another way to eliminate damage caused by static electricity is to wear an antistatic wristband.

antivirus program A utility that searches a hard disk for viruses and removes any that are found. Most antivirus programs include an autoupdate feature that enables the program to download profiles of new viruses so that it can check for the new viruses as soon as they are discovered.

⇒ See also MACRO VIRUS; VIRUS.

AOL See AMERICA ONLINE.

Apache Web server A public-domain Web server developed by a loosely knit group of programmers. The first version of Apache, based on the NCSA httpd Web server, was developed in 1995. Because it was developed from existing NCSA code plus various patches, it was called *a patchy server* — hence the name *Apache Server.*

As a result of its sophisticated features, excellent performance, and low price (it's free), Apache has became the world's most popular Web server. By some estimates, it is used to host more than 50 percent of all Web sites in the world.

Core development of the Apache Web server is performed by a group of about 20 volunteer programmers, called the *Apache Group.* However, because the source code is freely available, anyone can adapt the server for specific needs, and there is a large public library of Apache add-ons. In many respects, development of Apache is similar to development of the Linux operating system.

The original version of Apache was written for UNIX, but there are now versions that run under OS/2, Windows, and other platforms.

⇒ See also LINUX; WEB SERVER.

API Abbreviation of *a(pplication) p(rogram) i(nterface)*, a set of routines, protocols, and tools for building software applications. A good API makes it easier to develop a program by providing all the building blocks. A programmer puts the blocks together.

Most operating environments, such as Windows, provide an API so that programmers can write applications consistent with the operating environment. Although APIs are designed for programmers, they are ultimately good for users because they guarantee that all programs using a common API will have similar interfaces. This makes it easier for users to learn new programs.

⇒ See also APPLICATION; HLLAPI; INTERFACE; OPERATING ENVIRONMENT; ROUTINE; RPC; SDK; TAPI; TSAPI; WIN32.

APM Short for *A(dvanced) P(ower) M(anagement)*, an API developed by Intel and Microsoft that allows developers to include power management in BIOSes. APM defines a layer between the hardware and the operating system that effectively shields the programmer from hardware details.
  APM is expected to be gradually replaced by ACPI.

⇒ See also ACPI; POWER MANAGEMENT.

app Short for *app(lication)*. A *killer app*, for example, is an application that surpasses (i.e., kills) its competitors.

⇒ See also APPLICATION.

append To add something at the end. For example, you can append one file to another or you can append a field to a record. Do not confuse *append* with *insert*. *Append* always means to add at the end. *Insert* means to add in between.

⇒ See also CONCATENATE; INSERT.

Apple Computer A personal-computer company founded in 1976 by Steven Jobs and Steve Wozniak. Throughout the history of personal computing, Apple has been one of the most innovative influences. In fact, some analysts say that the entire evolution of the PC can be viewed as an effort to catch up with the Apple Macintosh.
  In addition to inventing new technologies, Apple also has often been the first to bring sophisticated technologies to the personal computer. Apple's innovations include:

Graphical user interface (GUI). First introduced in 1983 on its Lisa computer. Many components of the Macintosh GUI have become *de facto* standards and can be found in other operating systems, such as Microsoft Windows.
Color. The Apple II, introduced in 1977, was the first personal computer to offer color monitors.
Built-in networking. In 1985, Apple released a new version of the Macintosh with built-in support for networking (LocalTalk).
Plug & play expansion. In 1987, the Mac II introduced a new expansion bus called NuBus that made it possible to add devices and configure them entirely with software.
QuickTime. In 1991, Apple introduced QuickTime, a multiplatform standard for video, sound, and other multimedia applications.
Integrated television. In 1993, Apple released the Macintosh TV, the

first personal computer with built-in television and stereo CD. **RISC**. In 1994, Apple introduced the Power Mac, based on the PowerPC RISC microprocessor.

⇒ See also GRAPHICAL USER INTERFACE; LocalTalk; MACINTOSH COMPUTER; NEXTSTEP; PLUG-AND-PLAY; PowerPC; QuickTime; RISC.

Apple Desktop bus See ADB.

Apple key A special key on Macintosh computers labeled with the Apple logo (see figure). On all but the oldest Apple computers, the Apple key serves as the Command key.

⇒ See also COMMAND KEY.

Apple Symbol

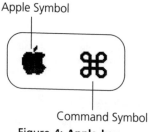

Command Symbol

Figure 4: **Apple key**

Apple Macintosh computer See MACINTOSH COMPUTER.

AppleScript A scripting language developed by Apple Computer that is integrated into the Mac OS starting with System 7.5. AppleScript provides an easy way to automate common tasks. AppleScript is also powerful enough to automate complex tasks and to customize the way applications behave.

AppleScript can be extended through *scripting additions* called *OSAX*. These add-on modules provide special resources and commands not available in the basic language.

⇒ See also MAC OS; MACRO; SCRIPT.

applet A program designed to be executed from within another application. Unlike an application, applets cannot be executed directly from the operating system. With the growing popularity of OLE (object linking and embedding), applets are becoming more prevalent. One example of an applet is a Java stock ticker that runs within the user's Web browser. A well-designed applet can be invoked from many different applications.

⇒ See also APPLICATION; COMPONENT; JAVA; OLE; SERVLET.

AppleTalk An inexpensive local-area network (LAN) architecture built into all Apple Macintosh computers and laser printers. AppleTalk supports Apple's *LocalTalk* cabling scheme, as well as Ethernet and IBM Token Ring. It can connect Macintosh computers and printers, and even PCs if they are equipped with special AppleTalk hardware and software.

⇒ See also LOCAL-AREA NETWORK; LOCALTALK; MACINTOSH COMPUTER; TOPOL-OGY.

application A program or group of programs designed for end users. Software can be divided into two general classes: *systems software* and *applications software*. Systems software consists of low-level programs that interact with the computer at a very basic level. This includes operating systems, compilers, and utilities for managing computer resources.

In contrast, applications software (also called *end-user programs*) includes database programs, word processors, and spreadsheets. Figuratively speaking, applications software sits on top of systems software because it is unable to run without the operating system and system utilities.

⇒ See also APPLET; APPLICATION SHARING; DATABASE MANAGEMENT SYSTEM; END USER; IDE; LEGACY APPLICATION; OPERATING SYSTEM; SOFTWARE; SOFTWARE LICENSING; SPREADSHEET; SYSTEMS SOFTWARE; UTILITY; WORD PROCESSOR.

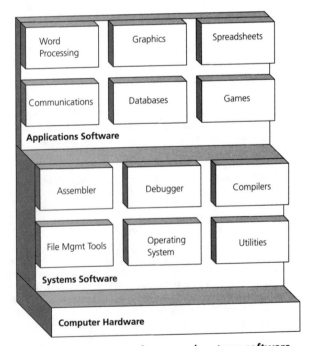

Figure 5: **applications software and systems software**

Application Foundation Classes See AFC.

Application Program Interface See API.

application sharing A feature of many videoconferencing applications that enables the conference participants to run the same application simultaneously. The application itself resides on only one of the machines connected to the conference.

⇒ See also APPLICATION; VIDEOCONFERENCING; WHITEBOARD.

application software See under APPLICATION.

Application Specific Integrated Circuit See ASIC.

applications software See under APPLICATION.

ARC To compress a file using the ARC format. The ARC data compression format, created by Systems Enhancement Associates, is particularly popular among bulletin board systems (BBSs). Another common format is *ZIP*.
Files that have been compressed with an ARC utility end with a .ARC extension. To decompress them, you need a utility called *ARC-E* (stands for *arc-extract*).

⇒ See also DATA COMPRESSION; ZIP.

Archie A program that enables you to search for files anywhere on the Internet by filename.

⇒ See also FILENAME; GOPHER; INTERNET.

architecture A design. The term *architecture* can refer to either hardware or software, or to a combination of hardware and software. The architecture of a system always defines its broad outlines, and may define precise mechanisms as well.
An open architecture allows the system to be connected easily to devices and programs made by other manufacturers. Open architectures use off-the-shelf components and conform to approved standards. A system with a *closed architecture,* on the other hand, is one whose design is *proprietary,* making it difficult to connect the system to other systems.

⇒ See also CLIENT/SERVER ARCHITECTURE; FUNCTIONAL SPECIFICATION; MODULAR ARCHITECTURE; OPEN ARCHITECTURE; PROPRIETARY; SCALABLE; STANDARD.

archival backup A type of backup in which all files are copied to a backup storage device. Archival backups are also called *full backup.* Contrast with *incremental backups,* in which only modified files are copied.

⇒ See also ARCHIVE; BACKUP; INCREMENTAL BACKUP.

archive *v* **1.** To copy files to a long-term storage medium for backup. Large computer systems often have two layers of backup, the first of which is a disk drive. Periodically, the computer operator will archive files on the disk to a second storage device, usually a tape drive.

On smaller systems, archiving is synonymous with *backing up*. **2.** To compress a file. —*n* **3.** A disk, tape, or directory that contains files that have been backed up. **4.** A file that contains one or more files in a compressed format. —*adj* **5.** In DOS systems, the *archive attribute* marks files that have been modified since the last backup.

⇒ See also ARC; ARCHIVAL BACKUP; ATTRIBUTE; BACKUP.

ARCnet Short for *A(ttached) R(esource) C(omputer) net(work)*, ARCnet is one of the oldest, simplest, and least expensive types of local-area network. ARCnet was introduced by Datapoint Corporation in 1968. It uses a token-ring architecture, supports data rates of 2.5 Mbps, and connects up to 255 computers. A special advantage of ARCnet is that it permits various types of transmission media—twisted-pair wire, coaxial cable, and fiber optic cable—to be mixed on the same network.

A new specification, called *ARCnet Plus,* will support data rates of 20 Mbps.

⇒ See also ETHERNET; LOCAL-AREA NETWORK; TOKEN-RING NETWORK.

area chart A type of presentation graphic that emphasizes a change in values by filling in the portion of the graph beneath the line connecting various data points.

⇒ See also PRESENTATION GRAPHICS.

areal density The amount of data that can be packed onto a storage medium. Areal densities are generally measured in gigabits per square inch. The term is useful for comparing different types of media, such as magnetic disks and optical disks. Current magnetic and optical disks have areal densities of several gigabits per square inch.

⇒ See also DENSITY; DISK; OPTICAL DISK.

argument In programming, a value that you pass to a *routine*. For example, if SQRT is a routine that returns the square root of a value, then SQRT(25) returns the value 5. The value 25 is the argument.

Argument is often used synonymously with *parameter*, although *parameter* can also mean any value that can be changed. In addition, some programming languages make a distinction between arguments, which are passed in only one direction, and parameters, which can be passed back and forth, but this distinction is by no means universal.

An argument can also be an option to a command, in which case it is often called a *command-line argument*.

⇒ See also OPTION; PARAMETER; ROUTINE.

arithmetic expression An expression that represents a numeric value. Other types of expressions can represent character or *Boolean* values.

⇒ See also EXPRESSION.

arithmetic logic unit See ALU.

arithmetic operator See under OPERATOR.

ARP Short for *A(ddress) R(esolution) P(rotocol)*, a TCP/IP protocol used to convert an IP address into a physical address (called a *DLC address*), such as an Ethernet address. A host wishing to obtain a physical address broadcasts an ARP request onto the TCP/IP network. The host on the network that has the IP address in the request then replies with its physical hardware address.

There is also *Reverse ARP (RARP)*, which can be used by a host to discover its IP address. In this case, the host broadcasts its physical address and a RARP server replies with the host's IP address.

⇒ See also DLC; IP ADDRESS; TCP/IP.

ARPANET The precursor to the Internet, ARPANET was a large wide-area network created by the U.S. Defense Advanced Research Project Agency (ARPA). Established in 1969, ARPANET served as a testbed for new networking technologies, linking many universities and research centers. The first two nodes that formed the ARPANET were UCLA and the Stanford Research Institute, followed shortly thereafter by the University of Utah.

⇒ See also INTERNET; NSFNET.

array In programming, a series of objects all of which are the same size and type. Each object in an array is called an *array element*. For example, you could have an array of integers or an array of characters or an array of anything that has a defined data type. The important characteristics of an array are:

Each element has the same data type (although they may have different values).

The entire array is stored contiguously in memory (that is, there are no gaps between elements).

Arrays can have more than one dimension. A one-dimensional array is called a *vector;* a two-dimensional array is called a *matrix.*

⇒ See also DATA STRUCTURE; DATA TYPE; MATRIX; SUBSCRIPT; VECTOR.

arrow keys Most computer keyboards contain four arrow keys for moving the cursor or insertion point right, left, up, or down. When combined with the Shift, Function, Control, or Alt keys (on PCs), the arrow keys can have different meanings. For example, pressing Shift + Up-arrow might move the cursor or pointer up an entire page. On Macintoshes, the arrow keys can be combined with the Shift, Option, and Command keys.

The exact manner in which the arrow keys function depends on which

program is running. Some programs ignore them.
The arrow keys are also called *cursor control keys*.

⇒ See also KEYBOARD.

artificial intelligence The branch of computer science concerned with making computers behave like humans. The term was coined in 1956 by John McCarthy at the Massachusetts Institute of Technology. Artificial intelligence includes

games playing: programming computers to play games such as chess and checkers.

expert systems: programming computers to make decisions in real-life situations (for example, some expert systems help doctors diagnose diseases based on symptoms).

natural language: programming computers to understand natural human languages.

neural networks: Systems that simulate intelligence by attempting to reproduce the types of physical connections that occur in animal brains.

robotics: programming computers to *see* and *hear* and react to other sensory stimuli.

Currently, no computers exhibit full artificial intelligence (that is, are able to simulate human behavior). The greatest advances have occurred in the field of games playing. The best computer chess programs are now capable of beating humans. In May, 1997, an IBM supercomputer called *Deep Blue* defeated world chess champion Gary Kasparov in a chess match.

In the area of robotics, computers are now widely used in assembly plants, but they are capable only of very limited tasks. Robots have great difficulty identifying objects based on appearance or feel, and they still move and handle objects clumsily.

Natural-language processing offers the greatest potential rewards because it would allow people to interact with computers without needing any specialized knowledge. You could simply walk up to a computer and talk to it. Unfortunately, programming computers to understand natural languages has proved to be more difficult than originally thought. Some rudimentary translation systems that translate from one human language to another are in existence, but they are not nearly as good as human translators. There are also voice recognition systems that can convert spoken sounds into written words, but they do not *understand* what they are writing; they simply take dictation. Even these systems are quite limited—you must speak slowly and distinctly.

In the early 1980s, expert systems were believed to represent the future of artificial intelligence and of computers in general. To date, however, they have not lived up to expectations. Many expert systems help human experts in such fields as medicine and engineering, but they are very expensive to produce and are helpful only in special situations.

Today, the hottest area of artificial intelligence is neural networks, which are proving successful in a number of disciplines such as voice recognition and natural-language processing.

There are several programming languages that are known as AI languages because they are used almost exclusively for AI applications. The two most common are *LISP* and *Prolog*.

⇒ See also COMPUTER SCIENCE; CYBERNETICS; EXPERT SYSTEM; FUZZY LOGIC; GENETIC PROGRAMMING; HEURISTIC PROGRAMMING; LISP; NATURAL LANGUAGE; NEURAL NETWORK; PROLOG; ROBOTICS; VOICE RECOGNITION.

AS/400 Short for *A(pplication) S(ystem)/400,* a line of IBM minicomputers introduced in 1988 and still popular today. Whereas most other minicomputer vendors have seen their market eroded by PCs and client/server systems, IBM has had reasonable success with its AS/400 series.

⇒ See also IBM; MINICOMPUTER.

ascender In typography, the portion of a lowercase letter that rises above the main body of the letter (that is, above the height of a lowercase *x*). For example, the letter *t*'s ascender is the part of the vertical line above the horizontal line.

⇒ See also BASELINE; DESCENDER; X-HEIGHT.

ASCII Acronym for the *A(merican) S(tandard) C(ode) for I(nformation) I(nterchange).* Pronounced *ask-ee,* ASCII is a code for representing English characters as numbers, with each letter assigned a number from 0 to 127. For example, the ASCII code for uppercase *M* is 77. Most computers use ASCII codes to represent text, which makes it possible to transfer data from one computer to another.

Text files stored in ASCII format are sometimes called ASCII files. Text editors and word processors are usually capable of storing data in ASCII format, although ASCII format is not always the default storage format. Most data files, particularly if they contain numeric data, are not stored in ASCII format. Executable programs are never stored in ASCII format.

The standard ASCII character set uses just 7 bits for each character. There are several larger character sets that use 8 bits, which gives them 128 additional characters. The extra characters are used to represent non-English characters, graphics symbols, and mathematical symbols. Several companies and organizations have proposed extensions for these 128 characters. The DOS operating system uses a superset of ASCII called *extended ASCII* or *high ASCII*. A more universal standard is the ISO Latin 1 set of characters, which is used by many operating systems, as well as by Web browsers.

Another set of codes that is used on large IBM computers is EBCDIC.

⇒ See also ASCII FILE; CHARACTER SET; EBCDIC; EXTENDED ASCII; ISO LATIN 1; TEXT FILE; UNICODE.

ASCII file A text file in which each byte represents one character according to the ASCII code. Contrast with a binary file, in which there is no one-to-one mapping between bytes and characters. Files that have been for-

Table 4
Standard ASCII (Control Codes and Space Characters)

Decimal Value	Abbreviation	Description
0	NUL	Null
1	SOH	Start of Heading
2	STX	Start of Text
3	ETX	End of Text
4	EOT	End of Transmit
5	ENQ	Enquiry
6	ACK	Acknowledge
7	BEL	Audible bell
8	BS	Backspace
9	HT	Horizontal tab
10	LF	Line feed
11	VT	Vertical tab
12	FF	Form feed
13	CR	Carriage return
14	SO	Shift out
15	SI	Shift in
16	DLE	Data link escape
17	DC1	Device control 1
18	DC2	Device control 2
19	DC3	Device control 3
20	DC4	Device control 4
21	NAK	Negative acknowledge
22	SYN	Synchronous idle
23	ETB	End transmit block
24	CAN	Cancel
25	EM	End of Medium
26	SUB	Substitution
27	ESC	Escape
28	FS	Figures shift
29	GS	Group separator
30	RS	Record separator
31	US	Unit separator
32	SP	Blank space character (Space Bar)

matted with a word processor must be stored and transmitted as binary files to preserve the formatting. ASCII files are sometimes called *plain text files.*

⇒ See also ASCII; BINARY FILE.

ASIC Pronounced *ay-sik,* and short for *A(pplication) S(pecific) I(ntegrated) C(ircuit),* a chip designed for a particular application. ASICs are built by connecting existing circuit building blocks in new ways. Because the building blocks already exist in a library, it is much easier to produce a new ASIC than to design a new chip from scratch.

⇒ See also CHIP; INTEGRATED CIRCUIT.

Table 5
Standard ASCII (Alphanumeric Characters)

33	!	49	1	65	A	81	Q	97	a	113	q
34	"	50	2	66	B	82	R	98	b	114	r
35	#	51	3	67	C	83	S	99	c	115	s
36	$	52	4	68	D	84	T	100	d	116	t
37	%	53	5	69	E	85	U	101	e	117	u
38	&	54	6	70	F	86	V	102	f	118	v
39	'	55	7	71	G	87	W	103	g	119	w
40	(	56	8	72	H	88	X	104	h	120	x
41	)	57	9	73	I	89	Y	105	i	121	y
42	*	58	:	74	J	90	Z	106	j	122	z
43	+	59	;	75	K	91	[	107	k	123	{
44	,	60	<	76	L	92	\	108	l	124	|
45	-	61	=	77	M	93	]	109	m	125	}
46	.	62	>	78	N	94	^	110	n	126	~
47	/	63	?	79	O	95	_	111	o	127	_
48	0	64	@	80	P	96	`	112	p		

ASP See ACTIVE SERVER PAGES.

aspect ratio In computer graphics, the relative horizontal and vertical sizes. For example, if a graphic has an aspect ratio of 2:1, it means that the width is twice as large as the height. When resizing graphics, it is important to maintain the aspect ratio to avoid stretching the graphic out of proportion.

The term is also used to describe the dimensions of a display resolution. For example, a resolution of 800 by 600 has an aspect ratio of 4:3.

Table 6
Extended ASCII (De Facto Standard for PCs)

Decimal Value	Character	Decimal Value	Character	Decimal Value	Character	Decimal Value	Character
128	Ç	160	á	192	L	224	α
129	ü	161	í	193	⊥	225	β
130	é	162	ó	194	┬	226	Γ
131	â	163	ú	195	├	227	π
132	ä	164	ñ	196	─	228	Σ
133	à	165	Ñ	197	┼	229	σ
134	å	166	ª	198	╞	230	μ
135	ç	167	º	199	╟	231	τ
136	ê	168	¿	200	╚	232	Φ
137	ë	169	⌐	201	╔	233	Θ
138	è	170	¬	202	╩	234	Ω
139	ï	171	½	203	╦	235	δ
140	î	172	¼	204	╠	236	∞
141	ì	173	¡	205	═	237	φ
142	Ä	174	«	206	╬	238	ε
143	Å	175	»	207	╧	239	∩
144	É	176	░	208	╨	240	≡
145	æ	177	▒	209	╤	241	±
146	Æ	178	█	210	╥	242	≥
147	ô	179	│	211	╙	243	≤
148	ö	180	┤	212	╘	244	⌠
149	ò	181	╡	213	╒	245	⌡
150	û	182	╢	214	╓	246	÷
151	ù	183	╖	215	╫	247	≈
152	ÿ	184	╕	216	╪	248	°
153	Ö	185	╣	217	┘	249	·
154	Ü	186	║	218	┌	250	·
155	¢	187	╗	219	█	251	√
156	£	188	╝	220	▄	252	ⁿ
157	¥	189	╜	221	▌	253	²
158	₧	190	╛	222	▐	254	■
159	ƒ	191	┐	223	▀	255	

⇒ See also AUTOSIZING; GRAPHICS.

ASPI Short for *A(dvanced) S(CSI) P(rogramming) I(nterface)*, an interface specification developed by Adaptec, Inc., for sending commands to a SCSI host adapter. ASPI has become a *de facto* standard that enables programmers to develop applications and drivers that work with all ASPI-compatible SCSI adapters.

⇒ See also SCSI.

assembler A program that translates programs from assembly language to machine language.

⇒ See also ASSEMBLY LANGUAGE; MACHINE LANGUAGE.

assembly language A programming language that is once removed from a computer's machine language. Machine languages consist entirely of numbers and are almost impossible for humans to read and write. Assembly languages have the same structure and set of commands as machine languages, but they enable a programmer to use names instead of numbers.

Each type of CPU has its own machine language and assembly language, so an assembly language program written for one type of CPU won't run on another. In the early days of programming, all programs were written in assembly language. Now, most programs are written in a high-level language such as FORTRAN or C. Programmers still use assembly language when speed is essential or when they need to perform an operation that isn't possible in a high-level language.

⇒ See also ASSEMBLER; COMPILE; LOW-LEVEL LANGUAGE; MACHINE LANGUAGE; PROGRAMMING LANGUAGE.

assign To give a value to a variable. In programming, you assign a value to a variable with a special symbol called an *assignment operator*. In many languages, the assignment operator is the equal sign (=). For example, the following C language statement assigns the value 5 to the variable x:

x = 5

Such a statement is called an *assignment statement*.

⇒ See also OPERATOR; STATEMENT; VARIABLE.

associate To *link* a certain type of file to a specific application. In MS-DOS and Microsoft Windows environments, the file's type is specified by its three-character extension. For example, the .DOC extension identifies Microsoft Word documents. Once a file type has been associated with an application, selecting any file of that type automatically starts its associated application and loads the selected file.

⇒ See also EXTENSION; FILENAME.

Association for Computing Machinery See under ACM.

asterisk Also called a *star*, a punctuation mark denoted by a 5- or 6-pointed snowflake shape (*). In many operating systems and applications, the asterisk is used as a *wildcard* symbol to represent any string of characters.

⇒ See also WILDCARD CHARACTER.

asymmetric digital subscriber line See ADSL.

asymmetric encryption See under PUBLIC-KEY ENCRYPTION.

async Short for ASYNCHRONOUS.

asynchronous Not synchronized; that is, not occurring at predetermined or regular intervals. The term *asynchronous* is usually used to describe communications in which data can be transmitted intermittently rather than in a steady stream. For example, a telephone conversation is asynchronous because both parties can talk whenever they like. If the communication were synchronous, each party would be required to wait a specified interval before speaking.

The difficulty with asynchronous communications is that the receiver must have a way to distinguish between valid data and noise. In computer communications, this is usually accomplished through a special *start bit* and *stop bit* at the beginning and end of each piece of data. For this reason, asynchronous communication is sometimes called *start-stop transmission*.

Most communications between computers and devices are asynchronous.

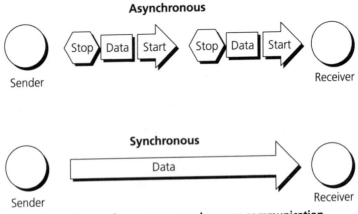

Asynchronous

Sender   Stop Data Start   Stop Data Start   Receiver

Synchronous

Sender   Data   Receiver

Figure 6: **asynchronous vs. synchronous communication**

⇒ See also COMMUNICATIONS; FLOW CONTROL; ISOCHRONOUS; START BIT; STOP BIT.

Asynchronous Transfer Mode See ATM.

AT Short for *advanced technology*, the AT is an IBM PC model introduced in 1984. It includes an Intel 80286 microprocessor, a 1.2 MB floppy drive, and an 84-key AT keyboard.

Today, the term is used more generally to refer to any PC with an 80286 processor.

⇒ See also INTEL MICROPROCESSORS; PC.

ATA Short for *AT Attachment*, a disk drive implementation that integrates the controller on the disk drive itself. There are several versions of ATA, all developed by the *Small Form Factor (SFF) Committee:*

ATA: Known also as *IDE*, supports one or two hard drives, a 16-bit interface, and PIO modes 0, 1, and 2.

ATA-2: Supports faster PIO modes (3 and 4) and multiword DMA modes (1 and 2). Also supports logical block addressing (LBA) and block transfers. ATA-2 is marketed as *Fast ATA* and *Enhanced IDE (EIDE)*.

ATA-3: Minor revision to ATA-2.

Ultra-ATA: Also called *Ultra-DMA, ATA-33,* and *DMA-33;* supports multiword DMA mode 3 running at 33 MBps.

ATA/66: A new version of ATA proposed by Quantum Corporation, and supported by Intel, that will double ATA's throughput to 66 MBps. The first ATA/66 computers are expected to be available in the first half of 1999.

⇒ See also CONTROLLER; DISK DRIVE; EIDE; IDE INTERFACE; PIO; ULTRA ATA.

ATAPI See under ATA.

AT Attachment Packet Interface See under ATA.

AT bus The expansion bus on the IBM PC/AT and compatible computers. The bus is the collection of wires and electronic components that connect all device controllers and add-in cards. The controllers are the components that attach to peripheral devices. The bus, therefore, is the main highway for all data moving in and out of the computer.

The AT bus, which runs at 8 megahertz and has a 16-bit data path, is the de facto standard for PCs. Because all IBM PCs (until the high-end PS/2 models) had an AT bus, it has been possible for manufacturers to produce expansion boards that will work with any PC.

The AT bus is sometimes referred to as the ISA (*Industry Standard Architecture*) bus. However, ISA also includes the XT bus, which is an 8-bit version of the AT bus.

As processors have become more powerful, and applications more demanding, the AT bus has turned out to be the chief bottleneck in PCs. In response, IBM introduced the Micro Channel Architecture (MCA) in 1987. However, MCA was not accepted by the computer industry because it was not backward compatible with the AT bus, so IBM has been forced to drop it.

A more successful alternative to the AT bus is the *Extended Industry Standard Architecture (EISA)*, a high-speed 32-bit bus architecture developed by a group of IBM's competitors. Unlike MCA, EISA is backward compatible with the AT bus, so a computer equipped with an EISA bus can accept AT or EISA expansion boards.

While EISA has had limited success, its speeds are still insufficient for modern graphical applications. The most common solution to bypassing the AT bus bottleneck is to include a local bus on the motherboard. A local bus communicates directly with the processor rather than using the standard computer bus. Currently, there are two competing standards for local buses: VESA local bus (VL-bus), promoted by the VESA standards group, and Peripheral Component Interconnect (PCI), designed and promoted by Intel.

⇒ See also BACKWARD COMPATIBLE; BUS; EISA; EXPANSION BOARD; IBM PC; INDUSTRY STANDARD ARCHITECTURE (ISA) BUS; LOCAL BUS; MICRO CHANNEL ARCHITECTURE (MCA); PCI; VL-BUS.

AT command set Pronounced *ay-tee command set*, the de facto standard language for controlling modems. The AT command set was developed by Hayes and is recognized by virtually all personal computer modems.

⇒ See also HAYES COMPATIBLE; MODEM.

AT keyboard An 84-key keyboard introduced with the PC/AT. It was later replaced with the 101-key *Enhanced Keyboard*.

⇒ See also KEYBOARD.

ATM Short for *A(synchronous) T(ransfer) M(ode)*, a network technology based on transferring data in *cells* or *packets* of a fixed size. The cell used with ATM is relatively small compared with units used with older technologies. The small, constant cell size allows ATM equipment to transmit video, audio, and computer data over the same network and to assure that no single type of data hogs the line.

Current implementations of ATM support data transfer rates of from 25 to 622 Mbps (megabits per second). This compares to a maximum of 100 Mbps for Ethernet, the current technology used for most LANs.

Some people think that ATM holds the answer to the Internet bandwidth problem, but others are skeptical. ATM creates a fixed channel, or route, between two points whenever data transfer begins. This differs from TCP/IP, in which messages are divided into packets and each packet can take a different route from source to destination. This difference makes it easier to track and bill data usage across an ATM network, but it makes it less adaptable to sudden surges in network traffic.

When purchasing ATM service, you generally have a choice of four different types of service:

Constant Bit Rate (CBR) specifies a fixed bit rate so that data is sent in a steady stream. This is analogous to a leased line.

Variable Bit Rate (VBR) provides a specified throughput capacity, but data is not sent evenly. This is a popular choice for voice and video-conferencing data.

Unspecified Bit Rate (UBR) does not guarantee any throughput levels. This is used for applications, such as file transfer, that can tolerate delays.

Available Bit Rate (ABR) provides a guaranteed minimum capacity but allows data to be *bursted* at higher capacities when the network is free.

⇒ See also CELL RELAY; ETHERNET; FDDI; FRAME RELAY; INTERNET; IP SWITCHING; QoS; TCP/IP.

Attached Resource Computer Network See ARCNET.

attachment A file attached to an e-mail message. Many e-mail systems support sending only text files as e-mail. If the attachment is a binary file or formatted text file (such as a Microsoft Word document), it must be encoded before it is sent and decoded once it is received. There are a number of encoding schemes, the two most prevalent being Uuencode and MIME.

⇒ See also E-MAIL.

Attachment Unit Interface See AUI.

attribute 1. A characteristic. In a word processing application, an underlined word would be said to have the *underline attribute.* In database systems, a field can have various attributes. For example, if it contains numeric data, it has the *numeric attribute.* **2.** In database-management systems, the term *attribute* is sometimes used as a synonym for *field.* **3.** In DOS systems, every file has *file attributes* that indicate several properties of the file. For example, they indicate whether the file is read-only, whether it needs to be backed up, and whether it is visible or hidden.

⇒ See also DOS; FIELD; FILE; HIDDEN FILE.

ATX The modern-day shape and layout of PC motherboards. It improves on the previous standard, the *Baby AT form factor,* by rotating the orientation of the board 90 degrees. This allows for a more efficient design, with disk drive cable connectors nearer to the drive bays and the CPU closer to the power supply and cooling fan.

⇒ See also ATX; BABY AT; FORM FACTOR; MOTHERBOARD.

.au See under AU.

AU Short for *au(dio)*, a common format for sound files on UNIX machines. It is also the standard audio file format for the Java programming language. AU files generally end with a *.au extension*. On PCs, two other popular sound formats are WAV and MIDI.

⇒ See also DIGITAL AUDIO; MIDI; WAV.

audio card Same as SOUND CARD.

Audio Interchange File Format See AIFF.

audit trail A record showing who has accessed a computer system and what operations he or she has performed during a given period of time. Audit trails are useful both for maintaining security and for recovering lost transactions. Most accounting systems and database management systems include an audit trail component. In addition, there are separate audit trail software products that enable network administrators to monitor use of network resources.

⇒ See also LOG FILE; SECURITY.

AUI Short for *A(ttachment) U(nit) I(nterface)*, the portion of the Ethernet standard that specifies how a cable is to be connected to an Ethernet card. AUI specifies a coaxial cable connected to a transceiver that plugs into a 15-pin socket on the network interface card (NIC).

⇒ See also COAXIAL CABLE; ETHERNET; NETWORK INTERFACE CARD.

authentication The process of identifying an individual, usually based on a username and password. In security systems, authentication is distinct from *authorization*, which is the process of giving individuals access to system objects based on their identity. Authentication merely ensures that the individual is who he or she claims to be but says nothing about the access rights of the individual.

⇒ See also AUTHORIZATION; BIOMETRICS; CHALLENGE-RESPONSE; CHAP; DIGITAL SIGNATURE; KERBEROS; PAP; PASSWORD; RADIUS; USERNAME.

authoring tool Also known as *authorware*, a program that helps you write *hypertext* or *multimedia* applications. Authoring tools usually enable you to create a final application merely by linking together objects, such as a paragraph of text, an illustration, or a song. By defining the objects' relationships to one another, and by sequencing them in an appropriate order, authors (those who use authoring tools) can produce attractive and useful graphics applications. Most authoring systems also support a scripting language for more sophisticated applications.

The distinction between authoring tools and programming tools is not clear-cut. Typically, though, authoring tools require less technical knowledge to master and are used exclusively for applications that present a mixture of textual, graphical, and audio data.

⇒ See also HYPERTEXT; MULTIMEDIA; PROGRAMMING LANGUAGE; SCRIPT.

authorization The process of granting or denying access to a network resource. Most computer security systems are based on a two-step process. The first stage is *authentication*, which ensures that a user is who he or she claims to be. The second stage is authorization, which allows the user access to various resources based on the user's identity.

⇒ See also ACCESS CONTROL; AUTHENTICATION; EXTRANET; SECURITY.

authorware Same as AUTHORING TOOL.

auto-answer A feature supported by many modems that enables your computer to accept incoming calls even if you are not present. In *auto-answer mode*, a modem attempts to establish a connection whenever the telephone rings. This is an important feature if you are offering a service to which others can subscribe.
  Auto-answer is also a critical feature for fax modems because it enables you to receive fax documents while you are away. All fax machines are auto-answer.

⇒ See also FAX MACHINE; FAX MODEM; MODEM.

autoexec.bat Stands for *auto(matically) exec(uted) bat(ch)* file, the file that DOS automatically executes when a computer boots up. This is a convenient place to put commands you always want to execute at the beginning of a computing session. For example, you can set system parameters such as the date and time, and install *memory-resident* programs.

⇒ See also BATCH FILE; BOOT.

automatic acceleration See under DYNAMIC ACCELERATION.

automatic recalculation In spreadsheets, a mode in which all cells are recalculated whenever a value changes. Automatic recalculation ensures that the spreadsheet data are always up-to-date, but it may make working on the spreadsheet slower. Alternatively, you can specify *manual recalculation*, where you must explicitly instruct the application to recalculate.

⇒ See also RECALCULATE; SPREADSHEET.

auto-redial A feature supported by many modems that allows the modem to continue redialing a number until it makes a connection. This is a useful feature if you subscribe to an online service that is frequently busy.

⇒ See also MODEM.

auto-repeat A feature of some keys on computer keyboards that causes them to repeat as long as they are held down. Most keys are auto-repeat.

⇒ See also KEYBOARD.

autosave A feature supported by many applications in which the program automatically saves data files at predetermined intervals. This is an important feature because it reduces the amount of work you would lose if your system crashed. Usually, you can specify how often you want the application to save data.

⇒ See also CRASH; SAVE; WORD PROCESSING.

autosizing Refers to a monitor's ability to automatically adjust the raster (the rectangular area being displayed) depending on the resolution of signals being received. For each different resolution (e.g., VGA, SVGA, etc.) the monitor needs to readjust the raster so that it fits within the physical dimensions of the display screen and maintains the aspect ratio of the image.
⇒ See also ASPECT RATIO; MONITOR; RASTER; RESOLUTION; SVGA; VGA; VIDEO ADAPTER.

autosync monitor Same as MULTISCANNING MONITOR.

autotracing The process of converting a bit-mapped image (or *raster* image) into a *vector* image. In a bit-mapped image, each object is represented by a pattern of dots, while in a vector image every object is defined geometrically.

Most autotracing packages read files in a variety of bit-mapped formats (PCX and TIFF are the most common) and produce a file in a vector format such as *Encapsulated PostScript (EPS)*. The conversion techniques used, and the accuracy of the conversion process, differ from one package to another.

Autotracing is particularly useful for manipulating images produced by an optical scanner. Scanners produce bit-mapped images that cannot be manipulated by sophisticated tools until they have been converted into a vector format through autotracing.

⇒ See also BIT MAP; BIT-MAPPED GRAPHICS; EPS; OPTICAL SCANNER; PCX; POST-SCRIPT; TIFF; VECTOR GRAPHICS.

AUX Stands for *Aux(iliary) port*, the logical name in DOS systems for the standard communications port. This is usually the same as COM1.

⇒ See also COM; PORT.

A/UX Pronounced *ox*, Apple's version of UNIX, which runs on some versions of the Macintosh.

⇒ See also UNIX.

auxiliary storage Same as MASS STORAGE.

avatar 1. A graphical icon that represents a real person in a cyberspace system. When you enter the system, you can choose from a number of fanciful avatars. Sophisticated 3-D avatars even change shape depending on what they are doing (e.g., walking, sitting, etc.). **2.** A common name for the superuser account on UNIX systems. The other common name is *root*.

⇒ See also CHAT; CYBERSPACE; MUD; VIRTUAL REALITY.

AVI Short for *A(udio) V(ideo) I(nterleave)*, the file format for Microsoft's Video for Windows standard.

⇒ See also VIDEO FOR WINDOWS.

awk An interpreted programming language that is included in most versions of UNIX. The name is derived from the initials of its creators—Alfred A(ho), Peter W(einberger), and Brian K(ernighan)—who developed the language in 1977 and 1978. The language is particularly designed for filtering and manipulating textual data. In this respect, it is similar to Perl, though Perl is more powerful.

There are many variants of *awk*, including *gawk*, which is the GNU version.

⇒ See also PERL; PROGRAMMING LANGUAGE.

AWT Short for *A(bstract) W(indows) T(oolkit)*, the Java API that enables programmers to develop Java applications with GUI components, such as windows, buttons, and scroll bars. The Java Virtual Machine (VM) is responsible for translating the AWT calls into the appropriate calls to the host operating system. Ideally, the AWT should enable any Java application to appear the same whether it's run in a Windows, Macintosh, or UNIX environment. In practice, however, most Java applications look slightly different depending on the platform on which they're executed.

⇒ See also AFC; GRAPHICAL USER INTERFACE; IFC; JAVA; VIRTUAL MACHINE.

Baby AT The form factor used by most PC motherboards prior to 1998. The original motherboard for the PC/AT measured 12 inches by 13 inches. Baby AT motherboards are a little smaller, 8.5 inches by 13 inches usually. The Baby AT is being replaced by the new ATX form factor.

⇒ See also ATX; FORM FACTOR; LPX; NLX.

backbone Another term for bus, the main wire that connects nodes. The term is often used to describe the main network connections composing the Internet.

⇒ See also BUS; HIPPI; MAE; NAP; NETWORK; NODE; NSP; T-3 CARRIER; vBNS.

back end See under FRONT END.

background 1. Multitasking computers are capable of executing several tasks, or programs, at the same time. In some multitasking systems, one of the processes is called the *foreground process*, and the others are called *background processes*.

The foreground process is the one that accepts input from the keyboard, mouse, or other input device. Background processes cannot accept interactive input from a user, but they can access data stored on a disk and write data to the video display. For example, some word processors print files in the background, enabling you to continue editing while files are being printed. This is called *print spooling*. In addition, many communications programs are designed to run in the background. Background processes generally have a lower priority than foreground processes so that they do not interfere with interactive applications.

Even though DOS is not a multitasking operating system, it can perform some specialized tasks, such as printing, in the background. Operating environments, such as Microsoft Windows and the Macintosh operating system, provide a more general multitasking environment. **2.** The area of a display screen not covered by characters and graphics. The background is like a canvas on top of which characters and graphics are placed. Some monitors allow you to control the color or shading of the background.

⇒ See also DISPLAY SCREEN; FOREGROUND; MICROSOFT WINDOWS; MONITOR; MULTITASKING; SPOOLING.

backlighting A technique used to make flat-panel displays easier to read. A backlit display is illuminated so that the foreground appears sharper in contrast with the background.

⇒ See also BACKGROUND; FLAT-PANEL DISPLAY; NOTEBOOK COMPUTER; SUPER-TWIST.

backplane A circuit board containing sockets into which other circuit boards can be plugged. In the context of PCs, the term *backplane* refers to the large circuit board that contains sockets for expansion cards.

Backplanes are often described as being either *active* or *passive*. Active backplanes contain, in addition to the sockets, logical circuitry that performs computing functions. In contrast, passive backplanes contain almost no computing circuitry.

Traditionally, most PCs have used active backplanes. Indeed, the terms *motherboard* and *backplane* have been synonymous. Recently, though, there has been a move toward passive backplanes, with the active components such as the CPU inserted on an additional card. Passive backplanes make it easier to repair faulty components and to upgrade to new components.

⇒ See also MOTHERBOARD; PRINTED CIRCUIT BOARD; VME BUS.

backslash The backslash character is \; a simple slash or *forward slash* is /. In DOS and Windows systems, the backslash represents the root directory and is also used to separate directory names and filenames in a *pathname*.

⇒ See also PATHNAME; ROOT DIRECTORY.

backspace A character that causes the cursor to move backward one character space, possibly deleting the preceding character. The backspace character has an ASCII value of 8. Most keyboards have a Backspace key that invokes this character. When inserted in a file, the character causes a printer or other device to move backward one space.

⇒ See also ASCII; BACKSPACE KEY; CURSOR; KEYBOARD; POINTER.

Backspace key A key that moves the cursor or insertion point backward one character space. In addition to moving the cursor backward, the Backspace key usually deletes the character to the left of the cursor or insertion point. It is particularly useful, therefore, for correcting typos. Note that PCs also have a Delete key, which deletes the character under the cursor (or to the right of the insertion point). To move the cursor or insertion point backward without deleting characters, use the arrow keys.

⇒ See also ARROW KEYS; BACKSPACE; DELETE KEY; KEYBOARD.

back up *v* To copy files to a second medium (a disk or tape) as a precaution in case the first medium fails. One of the cardinal rules in using computers is:

Back up your files regularly.
Even the most reliable computer is apt to break down eventually. Many professionals recommend that you make two, or even three, backups of all your files. To be especially safe, you should keep one backup in a different location from the others.

You can back up files using operating system commands, or you can buy a special-purpose backup utility. Backup programs often compress the data so that backups require fewer disks.

⇒ See also 3480, 3490; ARCHIVAL BACKUP; ARCHIVE; DATA COMPRESSION; DATA INTEGRITY; DMA; HSM.

backup *n* **1.** The act of backing up. **2.** A substitute or alternative. The term *backup* usually refers to a disk or tape that contain a copy of data.

backward compatible Compatible with earlier models or versions of the same product. A new version of a program is said to be backward compatible if it can use files and data created with an older version of the same program. A computer is said to be backward compatible if it can run the same software as the previous model of the computer.

Backward compatibility is important because it eliminates the need to start over when you upgrade to a newer product. A backward-compatible word processor, for instance, allows you to edit documents created with a previous version of the program. In general, manufacturers try to keep all their products backward compatible. Sometimes, however, it is necessary to sacrifice backward compatibility to take advantage of a new technology.

The flip side of backward compatibility is *upward compatibility.* Upward compatible is the same as backward compatible, except that it is from the point of view of the older model.

Another term for *backward compatible* is *downward compatible.*

⇒ See also COMPATIBLE; UPWARD COMPATIBLE.

bad sector A portion of a disk that cannot be used because it is flawed. When you format a disk, the operating system identifies any bad sectors on the disk and marks them so they will not be used. If a sector that already contains data becomes damaged, you will need special software to recover the data.

Almost all hard disks have sectors that are damaged during the manufacturing process, but these are usually replaced with spare sectors at the factory. By the time the disk is shipped, it should be free of bad sectors. If your disk utility starts showing bad sectors, therefore, this is a sign that there is something wrong with the disk or disk drive.

⇒ See also DISK; FORMAT; SECTOR.

BAK file In DOS systems, a file with a .BAK extension, indicating that the file is a backup. Many applications produce BAK files as part of their autosave procedure. Periodically, you may want to search for BAK files and delete old ones.

⇒ See also AUTOSAVE; EXTENSION.

ballistic tracking See under DYNAMIC ACCELERATION.

banding The presence of extraneous lines in a printed page. Banding generally occurs when a color printer needs to pass the print head over a
page multiple times to print each color. If the page isn't exactly lined up
for each pass, lines may appear. Such printers are called *multi-pass* printers. Because of the banding problem, *single-pass* printers—those that
print all the colors in one pass—are generally better.

⇒ See also COLOR PRINTER.

bandwidth The amount of data that can be transmitted in a fixed amount
of time. For digital devices, the bandwidth is usually expressed in bits
per second (bps) or bytes per second. For analog devices, the bandwidth
is expressed in cycles per second, or Hertz (Hz).
   The bandwidth is particularly important for I/O devices. For example, a
fast disk drive can be hampered by a bus with a low bandwidth. This is
the main reason that new buses, such as AGP, have been developed for
the PC.

⇒ See also BUS; CIR; EISA; I/O; LATENCY; PCI.

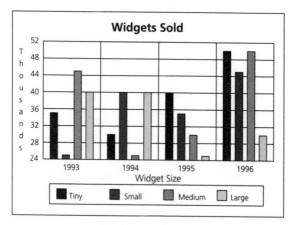

Figure 7: **bar chart**

bar chart In presentation graphics, a type of graph in which different
values are represented by rectangular bars.

⇒ See also PRESENTATION GRAPHICS.

barrel distortion See under PINCUSHION DISTORTION.

base address An address that serves as a reference point for other addresses. For example, a base address could indicate the beginning of a program. The address of every instruction in the program could then be specified by adding an offset to the base address. For example, the address of the fifth instruction would be the base address plus 5.

⇒ See also ADDRESS; OFFSET; RELATIVE ADDRESS.

baseband transmission A type of digital data transmission in which each medium (wire) carries only one signal, or channel, at a time. In contrast, broadband transmission enables a single wire to carry multiple signals simultaneously.

Most communications involving computers use baseband transmission. This includes communications from the computer to devices (printers, monitors, and so on), communications via modems, and the majority of networks. An exception is B-ISDN networks, which use broadband transmission.

⇒ See also 10BASE-2; BROADBAND ISDN (B-ISDN); BROADBAND TRANSMISSION; CHANNEL; COMMUNICATIONS; ISDN; LOCAL-AREA NETWORK; NETWORK.

baseline In typography, the imaginary line on which characters sit. The *x-height* of a font is measured from the baseline to the top of a lowercase *x*. The descender, for those characters that have one, is defined as the portion of the character that falls below the baseline.

⇒ See also ASCENDER; DESCENDER; FONT; TYPEFACE; X-HEIGHT.

base memory Same as CONVENTIONAL MEMORY.

BASIC Acronym for *B(eginner's) A(ll-purpose) S(ymbolic) I(nstruction) C(ode)*. Developed by John Kemeney and Thomas Kurtz in the mid-1960s at Dartmouth College, BASIC is one of the earliest and simplest high-level programming languages. During the 1970s, it was the principal programming language taught to students, and continues to be a popular choice among educators.

Despite its simplicity, BASIC is used for a wide variety of business applications. There is an ANSI standard for the BASIC language, but most versions of BASIC include many proprietary extensions. Microsoft's popular *Visual Basic*, for example, adds many object-oriented features to the standard BASIC.

Recently, many variations of BASIC have appeared as programming, or macro, languages within applications. For example, Microsoft Word and Excel both come with a version of BASIC with which users can write programs to customize and automate these applications.

⇒ See also GW-BASIC; HIGH-LEVEL LANGUAGE; INTERPRETER; MUMPS; PROGRAMMING LANGUAGE; QBASIC; VISUAL BASIC.

basic input/output system See BIOS.

Basic-Rate Interface See BRI.

batch file A file that contains a sequence, or batch, of commands. Batch files are useful for storing sets of commands that are always executed together because you can simply enter the name of the batch file instead of entering each command individually.

In DOS systems, batch files end with a .BAT extension. For example, the DOS batch file shown below prints the date and time and sets the prompt to *GO >*

Whenever you boot a DOS-based computer, the system automatically executes the batch file named AUTOEXEC.BAT, if it exists.

Many operating systems use the terms *command file* or *shell script* in place of *batch file*.

⇒ See also AUTOEXEC.BAT; BAT FILE; BATCH PROCESSING; DOS.

```
date
time
prompt [GO>]
```

batch processing Executing a series of noninteractive jobs all at one time. The term originated in the days when users entered programs on punch cards. They would give a batch of these programmed cards to the system operator, who would feed them into the computer.

Usually, batch jobs are stored up during working hours and then executed during the evening or whenever the computer is idle. Batch processing is particularly useful for operations that require the computer or a peripheral device for an extended period of time. Once a batch job begins, it continues until it is done or until an error occurs. Note that batch processing implies that there is no interaction with the user while the program is being executed.

The opposite of batch processing is *transaction processing* or *interactive processing.* In interactive processing, the application responds to commands as soon as you enter them.

⇒ See also BATCH FILE; INTERACTIVE; TRANSACTION PROCESSING.

BAT file In DOS systems, batch files are often called *BAT files* because their filenames end with a .BAT extension.

⇒ See also BATCH FILE; EXTENSION; FILENAME.

battery pack A rechargeable battery used in portable computer devices, such as notebook computers. The most common substances used in computer battery packs are nickel cadmium (NiCad), nickel metal hydride (NiMH), and Lithium Ion.

A new type of battery, called a *smart battery,* provides the computer with information about its power status so that the computer can conserve power intelligently. With a normal battery, the computer makes estimates about the battery's condition that are not always correct.

⇒ See also LITHIUM ION BATTERY; NICAD BATTERY PACK; NIMH BATTERY PACK; POWER MANAGEMENT.

baud Pronounced *bawd,* the number of *signaling elements* that occur each second. The term is named after J.M.E. Baudot, the inventor of the Baudot telegraph code.

At slow speeds, only one bit of information (signaling element) is encoded in each electrical change. The *baud,* therefore, indicates the number of bits per second that are transmitted. For example, *300 baud* means that 300 bits are transmitted each second (abbreviated *300 bps*). Assuming asynchronous communication, which requires 10 bits per character, this translates to 30 characters per second (cps). For slow rates (below 1,200 baud), you can divide the baud by 10 to see how many characters per second are sent.

At higher speeds, it is possible to encode more than one bit in each electrical change. 4,800 baud may allow 9,600 bits to be sent each second. At high data transfer speeds, therefore, data transmission rates are usually expressed in bits per second (bps) rather than baud. For example, a 9,600 bps modem may operate at only 2,400 baud.

⇒ See also BPS; MODEM.

baud rate See BAUD.

bay Short for *drive bay,* this refers to a site in a personal computer where a hard or floppy disk drive, CD-ROM drive, or tape drive can be installed. Thus, the number of drive bays in a computer determines how many mass storage devices can be internally installed.

For PCs, bays come in two basic sizes: 3.5-inch and 5.25-inch, representing the bay's height. In addition, bays are described as either *internal* or *exposed.* An internal bay cannot be used for drives that house removable media, such as floppy drives. Some manufacturers use the terms *hidden* and *accessible* in place of *internal* and *exposed,* respectively.

Do not confuse bays with *slots,* which are openings in the computer where *expansion boards* can be installed.

⇒ See also DISK DRIVE; EXPANSION BOARD; MASS STORAGE; SLOT.

BBS See BULLETIN BOARD SYSTEM.

BCD Short for *b(inary)-c(oded) d(ecimal),* a format for representing decimal numbers (integers) in which each digit is represented by four bits (a *nibble*). For example, the number 375 would be represented as:

0011 0111 0101

One advantage of BCD over binary representations is that there is no limit to the size of a number. To add another digit, you just need to add a new 4-bit sequence. In contrast, numbers represented in binary format are generally limited to the largest number that can be represented by 8, 16, 32, or 64 bits.

⇒ See also BINARY; BINARY FORMAT; DECIMAL; HEXADECIMAL; NIBBLE.

B-channel Short for *B(earer)*-**channel**, the main data channel in an ISDN connection. Basic Rate ISDN (BRI) service consists of two 64 Kbps B-channels, and one D-channel for transmitting control information. Primary ISDN service consists of 23 B-channels (in the U.S.) or 30 B-channels (in Europe).

⇒ See also BRI; CHANNEL; ISDN.

BEDO DRAM Short for *B(urst)* **EDO DRAM**, a new type of EDO DRAM that can process four memory addresses in one *burst*. Unlike SDRAM, however, BEDO DRAM can stay synchronized with the CPU clock for short periods (bursts) only. Also, it can't keep up with processors whose buses run faster than 66 MHz.

⇒ See also BURST MODE; DRAM; EDO DRAM; PIPELINE BURST CACHE; RDRAM; SDRAM; SLDRAM.

Bell 103 The de facto standard protocol in the United States for transmitting data over telephone lines at transmission rates of 300 baud. The Bell 103A standard defines asynchronous, full-duplex communication. Europe and Japan use the CCITT V.21 protocol.

⇒ See also ASYNCHRONOUS; BAUD; CCITT; COMMUNICATIONS PROTOCOL; FULL DUPLEX; PROTOCOL.

Bell 212A The de facto standard protocol in the United States for transmitting data over telephone lines at transmission rates of 1,200 bps. The Bell 212A standard defines asynchronous, full-duplex communications. Europe and Japan use the CCITT V.22 protocol.

⇒ See also ASYNCHRONOUS; BAUD; CCITT; COMMUNICATIONS PROTOCOL; FULL DUPLEX; PROTOCOL.

bells and whistles Fancy features provided by an application. Typically, the term refers to small features that are needed only in special cases or to features that make the program more visibly attractive (i.e., like real bells and whistles that are aimed at attracting your attention). Depending on the author, the term can be used either favorably or negatively. Many users and critics, for example, lament the increasing addition of bells and whistles that, they feel, make an application harder to learn and use without providing commensurate new functionality.

⇒ See also FEATURE.

benchmark A test used to compare performance of hardware and/or software. Many trade magazines have developed their own benchmark tests, which they use when reviewing a class of products. When comparing benchmark results, it is important to know exactly what the benchmarks are designed to test. A benchmark that tests graphics speed, for example, may be irrelevant to you if the type of graphical applications you use are different from those used in the test.

⇒ See also FLOPS; SPEC.

BeOS An operating system developed by Be, Inc., that runs on the PowerPC platform and Intel x86 processors. Despite being smaller than other modern operating systems, such as the Mac OS and Windows, BeOS nevertheless sports a modern graphical user interface (GUI), pre-emptive multitasking, multithreading, and built-in support for symmetric multiprocessing (SMP).

⇒ See also MAC OS; OPERATING SYSTEM; POWERPC; SMP.

Berkeley Internet Name Domain See BIND.

Bernoulli disk drive Named after a Swiss scientist who discovered the principle of aerodynamic lift, the Bernoulli disk drive was a special type of floppy disk drive from Iomega Corporation that was faster and had greater storage capacity than traditional floppy drives. It is no longer being produced.

⇒ See also DISK; HARD DISK DRIVE; MASS STORAGE.

beta Short for *beta test.*

beta test A test for a computer product prior to commercial release. Beta testing is the last stage of testing and normally involves sending the product to *beta test sites* outside the company for real-world exposure. Beta testing is often preceded by a round of testing called *alpha testing.*

⇒ See also ALPHA VERSION; APPLICATION.

Bézier curve Pronounced *bez-ee-ay,* curved lines (*splines*) defined by mathematical formulas. Nearly all draw programs support Bézier curves.
   Named after the French mathematician Pierre Bézier, Bézier curves employ at least three points to define a curve. The two endpoints of the curve are called *anchor points.* The other points, which define the shape of the curve, are called *handles, tangent points*, or *nodes.* Attached to each handle are two *control points.* By moving the handles themselves, or the control points, you can modify the shape of the curve.

⇒ See also DRAW PROGRAM; GRAPHICS; NURBS; SPLINE; VECTOR GRAPHICS.

BFT See BINARY FILE TRANSFER.

BGP Short for *B(order) G(ateway) P(rotocol),* an Internet protocol that enables groups of routers (called *autonomous systems*) to share routing information so that efficient, loop-free routes can be established. BGP is commonly used within and between internet service providers (ISPs). The protocol is defined in RFC 1771.

⇒ See also ROUTER; ROUTING.

Big Blue A slang name for International Business Machines Corporation (IBM). Blue is IBM's corporate color.

⇒ See also IBM PC.

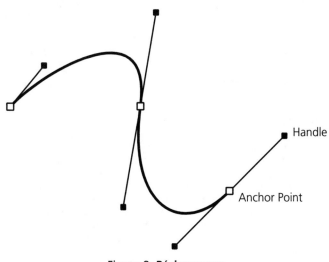

Figure 8: **Bézier curves**

big-endian Refers to which bytes are most significant in multibyte data types. In big-endian architectures, the leftmost bytes (those with a lower address) are most significant. In little-endian architectures, the rightmost bytes are most significant. For example, consider the number 1025 (2^{10} plus one) stored in a 4-byte integer

    00000000 00000000 00000100 00000001

Many mainframe computers, particularly IBM mainframes, use a big-endian architecture. Most modern computers, including PCs, use the little-endian system. The PowerPC system is *bi-endian* because it can understand both systems.

Converting data between the two systems is sometimes referred to as the *NUXI problem*. Imagine the word *UNIX* stored in two 2-byte words. In a big-endian system, it would be stored as *UNIX*. In a little-endian system, it would be stored as *NUXI*.

Note that the preceding example shows only big- and little-endian byte orders. The bit ordering within each byte can also be big- or little-endian, and some architectures actually use big-endian ordering for bits and little-endian ordering for bytes, or vice versa.

The terms *big-endian* and *little-endian* are derived from the Lilliputians of *Gulliver's Travels*, whose major political issue was whether soft-boiled eggs should be opened on the big side or the little side. Likewise, the big-/little-endian computer debate has much more to do with political issues than technological merits.

⇒ See also BYTE; DATA TYPE.

Address:	Big-Endian representation of 1025:	Little-Endian representation of 1025
00:	00000000:	00000001
01:	00000000:	00000100
02:	00000100:	00000000
03:	00000001:	00000000

bilevel printer A type of printer that can print only two levels of intensity for each dot—on or off. For monochrome printers, lightness and darkness (shading) are simulated through dithering. Bilevel color printers use dithering to produce a wide variety of colors. Most ink jet and laser printers are bilevel. In contrast, expensive color printers, such as thermal dye printers, can apply ink at various levels of intensity. Such printers are called continuous-tone printers. A third type of printer, called a *contone* or *multilevel printer,* can print at a few intensity levels (usually 8), but not as many as a true continuous-tone printer (usually 256). These printers use a combination of dithering and multilevel printing to produce different colors.

⇒ See also COLOR PRINTER; CONTINUOUS TONE; CONTONE PRINTER; DITHERING; PRINTER.

binary Pertaining to a number system that has just two unique digits. For most purposes, we use the decimal number system, which has ten unique digits, 0 through 9. All other numbers are then formed by combining these ten digits. Computers are based on the binary numbering system, which consists of just two unique numbers, 0 and 1. All operations that are possible in the decimal system (addition, subtraction, multiplication, division) are equally possible in the binary system.

We use the decimal system in everyday life because it seems more natural (we have ten fingers and ten toes). For the computer, the binary system is more natural because of its electrical nature (charged versus uncharged).

In the decimal system, each digit position represents a value of 10 to the position's power. For example, the number 345 means:

3   three 100s (10^2)
+
4   four 10s (10^1)
+
5   five 1s (10^0)

In the binary system, each digit position represents a power of 2. For example, the binary number 1011 equals:

1	one 8 (2^3)
+	
0	zero 4s (2^2)
+	
1	one 2 (2^1)
+	
1	one 1 (2^0)

So a binary 1011 equals a decimal 11.

Because computers use the binary number system, powers of 2 play an important role. This is why everything in computers seems to come in 8s (2^3), 64s (2^6), 128s (2^7), and 256s (2^8).

Programmers also use the octal (8 numbers) and hexadecimal (16 numbers) number systems because they map nicely onto the binary system. Each octal digit represents exactly three binary digits, and each hexadecimal digit represents four binary digits.

⇒ See also BINARY FORMAT; DECIMAL; HEXADECIMAL; OCTAL.

Table 7
Decimal and Binary Equivalents

Decimal	Binary
1	1
2	10
3	11
4	100
5	101
6	110
7	111
8	1000
9	1001
10	1010
16	10000
32	100000
64	1000000
100	1100100
256	10000000
512	100000000
1000	111111010
1024	1000000000

---

binary-coded decimal See BCD.

binary compatible Having the exact same data format, down to the binary level. That is, two files that are binary compatible will have the same pattern of zeroes and ones in the data portion of the file. The file header, however, may be different.

The term is used most commonly to state that data files produced by one application are exactly the same as data files produced by another application. For example, many software companies now produce applications for Windows and the Macintosh that are binary compatible, which means that a file produced in a Windows environment is interchangeable with a file produced on a Macintosh. This avoids many of the conversion problems caused by importing and exporting data.

⇒ See also BINARY FILE; COMPATIBLE; CROSS-PLATFORM; EXPORT; HETEROGENEOUS NETWORK; IMPORT.

binary digit See BIT.

binary file A file stored in binary format. A binary file is computer-readable but not human-readable. All executable programs are stored in binary files, as are most numeric data files. In contrast, text files are stored in a form (usually ASCII) that is human-readable.

⇒ See also ASCII; ASCII FILE; BINARY FORMAT; COFF; EXECUTABLE FILE; TEXT FILE.

Binary File Transfer (BFT) A standard for transmitting data files using fax modems. There are actually two standards, both of which are referred to as BFT: CCITT *T.434* and *Microsoft At Work (MAW)*.

⇒ See also CCITT; FAX MODEM; STANDARD.

binary format A format for representing data used by some applications. The other main formats for storing data are *text formats* (such as ASCII and EBCDIC), in which each character of data is assigned a specific code number.

Binary formats are used for executable programs and numeric data, whereas text formats are used for textual data. Many files contain a combination of binary and text formats. Such files are usually considered to be binary files even though they contain some data in a text format.

⇒ See also ASCII; BCD; BINARY; BINARY FILE; EBCDIC; EXECUTABLE FILE; TEXT FILE.

binary tree A special type of tree structure in which each node has at most two leaves. Binary trees are often used for sorting data, as in a heap sort.

⇒ See also HEAP; HEAP SORT; TREE STRUCTURE.

BIND Short for *B(erkeley) I(nternet) N(ame) D(omain)*, a domain name server (DNS). BIND is designed for UNIX systems based on BSD, the version of UNIX developed at the University of California's Berkeley campus.

⇒ See also DNS; DOMAIN NAME.

bind To assign a value to a symbolic placeholder. During compilation, for example, the compiler assigns symbolic addresses to some variables and instructions. When the program is bound, or *linked*, the binder replaces the symbolic addresses with real machine addresses. The moment at which binding occurs is called *bind time* or *link time*.

⇒ See also ADDRESS; COMPILE; LINK.

binder Same as LINKER.

BinHex An encoding scheme that converts binary data into ASCII characters. Any file, whether it is a graphics file, a text file, or a binary executable file, can be converted to BinHex. This format is particularly valuable for transferring files from one platform to another because nearly all computers can handle ASCII files. In fact, many e-mail programs include a BinHex encoder and decoder for sending and receiving attachments. BinHex is an especially common format for Macintosh files. Encoded files usually have a .HQX extension.

An alternative algorithm for converting binary files to ASCII is *Uuencode*.

⇒ See also E-MAIL; MIME; UUENCODE.

biometrics Generally, the study of measurable biological characteristics. In computer security, *biometrics* refers to authentication techniques that rely on measurable physical characteristics that can be automatically checked. Examples include computer analysis of fingerprints or speech.

Though the field is still in its infancy, many people believe that biometrics will play a critical role in future computers, and especially in electronic commerce. Personal computers of the future might include a *fingerprint scanner* on which you could place your index finger. The computer would analyze your fingerprint to determine who you are and, based on your identity, authorize you different levels of access. Access levels could include the ability to use credit card information to make electronic purchases.

⇒ See also AUTHENTICATION; ELECTRONIC COMMERCE; SECURITY.

BIOS Pronounced "bye-ose", an acronym for *b(asic) i(nput)/o(utput) s(ystem)*. The BIOS is built-in software that determines what a computer can do without accessing programs from a disk. On PCs, the BIOS contains all the code required to control the keyboard, display screen, disk drives, serial communications, and a number of miscellaneous functions.

The BIOS is typically placed in a ROM chip that comes with the computer (it is often called a *ROM BIOS*). This ensures that the BIOS will always be available and will not be damaged by disk failures. It also makes it possible for a computer to boot itself. Because RAM is faster than ROM, though, many computer manufacturers design systems so that the BIOS is copied from ROM to RAM each time the computer is booted. This is known as *shadowing*.

Many modern PCs have a *flash BIOS*, which means that the BIOS has been recorded on a flash memory chip, which can be updated if necessary.

The PC BIOS is fairly standardized, so all PCs are similar at this level (although there are different BIOS versions). Additional DOS functions are usually added through software modules. This means you can upgrade to a newer version of DOS without changing the BIOS.

PC BIOSes that can handle Plug-and-Play (PnP) devices are known as *PnP BIOSes*, or *PnP-aware BIOSes*. These BIOSes are always implemented with flash memory rather than ROM.

⇒ See also BOOT; CMOS; ESCD; FLASH MEMORY; I/O; NETBIOS; PHOENIX BIOS; PNP; POST; SHADOWING.

B-ISDN See BROADBAND ISDN.

bisync Short for *bi(nary) sync(hronous)*, a type of synchronous communications used primarily in mainframe networks. The de facto bisync standard is *Binary Synchronous Communications (BSC)*, developed by IBM. The *binary* part of the name signifies that the data are binary-coded. The *synchronous* part means that both the sender and receiver must be synchronized before the data transfer can begin.

⇒ See also ASYNCHRONOUS; SYNCHRONOUS.

bit Short for *bi(nary) digit*, the smallest unit of information on a machine. The term was first used in 1946 by John Tukey, a leading statistician and adviser to five presidents. A single bit can hold only one of two values: 0 or 1. More meaningful information is obtained by combining consecutive bits into larger units. For example, a byte is composed of 8 consecutive bits.

Computers are sometimes classified by the number of bits they can process at one time or by the number of bits they use to represent addresses. These two values are not always the same, which leads to confusion. For example, classifying a computer as a *32-bit machine* might mean that its data registers are 32 bits wide or that it uses 32 bits to identify each address in memory. Whereas larger registers make a computer faster, using more bits for addresses enables a machine to support larger programs.

Graphics are also often described by the number of bits used to represent each dot. A 1-bit image is monochrome; an 8-bit image supports 256 colors or grayscales; and a 24- or 32-bit graphic supports true color.

⇒ See also 32-BIT; ADDRESS SPACE; KILOBIT; MEGABIT; NIBBLE; REGISTER.

bit block transfer A transformation of a rectangular block of pixels. Typical transformations include changing the color or shade of all pixels or rotating the entire rectangle. Many modern video adapters include hardwired bit block transformations, which execute much faster than they do when executed by software routines.

⇒ See also GRAPHICS; PIXEL; VIDEO ADAPTER.

bitblt Pronounced *bit-blit,* see under **bit** *bl(ock) t(ransfer).*

bit map A representation, consisting of rows and columns of dots, of a graphics image in computer memory. The value of each dot (whether it is filled in or not) is stored in one or more bits of data. For simple monochrome images, one bit is sufficient to represent each dot, but for colors and shades of gray, each dot requires more than one bit of data. The more bits used to represent a dot, the more colors and shades of gray that can be represented.

The density of the dots, known as the *resolution,* determines how sharply the image is represented. This is often expressed in *dots per inch (dpi)* or simply by the number of rows and columns, such as 640 by 480.

To display a bit-mapped image on a monitor or to print it on a printer, the computer translates the bit map into pixels (for display screens) or ink dots (for printers). Optical scanners and fax machines work by transforming text or pictures on paper into bit maps.

Bit-mapped graphics are often referred to as *raster graphics.* The other method for representing images is known as *vector graphics* or *object-oriented graphics.* With *vector graphics,* images are represented as mathematical formulas that define all the shapes in the image. Vector graphics are more flexible than bit-mapped graphics because they look the same even when you scale them to different sizes. In contrast, bit-mapped graphics become ragged when you shrink or enlarge them.

Fonts represented with vector graphics are called *scalable fonts, outline fonts,* or *vector fonts.* The best-known example of a vector font system is PostScript. Bit-mapped fonts, also called *raster fonts,* must be designed for a specific device and a specific size and resolution.

⇒ See also BIT-MAPPED GRAPHICS; DIGITIZE; GRAPHICS; OPTICAL SCANNER; PIXEL; RESOLUTION.

Figure 9: **bit map**

bit-mapped font See under FONT.

bit-mapped graphics Refers to hardware and software that represent graphics images as bit maps. The other method for representing images is known as *vector graphics*.

⇒ See also BIT MAP; COMPUTER IMAGING; DIB; GRAPHICS; PNG; VECTOR GRAPHICS.

BITNET Short for *B(ecause) I(t)'s T(ime) Net(work)*, BITNET is one of the oldest and largest wide-area networks, used extensively by universities. A new version of BITNET, called BITNET-II, relies on the Internet network to transfer messages and files.

⇒ See also INTERNET; NETWORK; WIDE-AREA NETWORK.

bits per second See BPS.

bitwise operator An operator that manipulates individual bits. The operators that most people are familiar with, such as the addition operator (+), work with bytes or groups of bytes. Occasionally, however, programmers need to manipulate the bits within a byte. The C programming language supports the following bitwise operators:

> >> Shifts bits right
> << Shifts bits left
> & Does an AND compare on two groups of bits
> | Does an OR compare on two groups of bits
> ^ Does an XOR compare on two groups of bits
> ′ Complements a group of bits

Not all programming languages support bitwise operators.

⇒ See also OPERATOR.

blank character Also called a *space character*. A blank character is produced when you press the space bar.

bleed *n* **1.** Text or graphics that extends all the way to the edge of the paper. Bleeds are used for graphical effect and for printed tabs. Most printers cannot print all the way to the edge of the paper, so the only way to produce a bleed is to print on paper larger than the final page size and then trim the paper. —*v* **2.** To run to the edge of the paper, thereby producing a bleed.

⇒ See also DESKTOP PUBLISHING.

bloatware A sarcastic term that refers to software that has lots of features and requires considerable disk space and RAM. As the cost of RAM and disk storage has decreased, there has been a growing trend among software developers to disregard the size of applications. Some people refer to this trend as *creeping featuritis*. If creeping featuritis is the symptom, bloatware is the disease.

⇒ See also FEATURE; SOFTWARE; VAPORWARE.

BLOB Short for *b(inary) l(arge) ob(ject)*, a collection of binary data stored as a single entity in a database management system (DBMS). BLOBs are used primarily to hold multimedia objects such as images, videos, and sound, though they can also be used to store programs or even fragments of code. Not all DBMSs support BLOBs.

⇒ See also DATABASE MANAGEMENT SYSTEM; FIELD; OBJECT.

block *n* **1.** In word processing, a block is a group of characters that you have marked to perform some action on them. For example, to move a section of text, you must first block it. This is sometimes called a *block move*.

To specify a block of text, you press special function keys (or highlight with a mouse) at the beginning and end of the block, as by clicking and dragging. The function keys differ from one word processor to another. Word processors usually display blocks by highlighting them on the screen. **2.** In data management, a block is a group of records on a storage device. Blocks are manipulated as units. For example, disk drives often read and write data in 512-byte blocks. **3.** In communications, a block is a fixed-size chunk of data that is transferred together. For example, the Xmodem protocol transfers blocks of 128 bytes. In general, the larger the block size, the faster the data transfer rate. —*v* **4.** In word processing, to specify a section of text. See definition (1) above. Some applications call this *selecting*.

⇒ See also COMMUNICATIONS; SELECT; WORD PROCESSING; XMODEM.

block graphics Graphical images created in character mode.

⇒ See also CHARACTER MODE.

BMP The standard bit-mapped graphics format used in the Windows environment. By convention, graphics files in the BMP format end with a .BMP extension.

BMP files store graphics in a format called *device-independent bit map (DIB)*.

⇒ See also BIT MAP; DIB; EXTENSION; GRAPHICS FILE FORMATS.

BNC See BNC CONNECTOR.

BNC connector Short for *B(ritish) N(aval) C(onnector)* or *B(ayonet) N(ut) C(onnector)* or *B(ayonet) N(eill) C(oncelman)*, a type of connector used with coaxial cables such as the RG-58 A/U cable used with the 10Base-2 Ethernet system. The basic BNC connector is a male type mounted at each end of a cable. This connector has a center pin connected to the center cable conductor and a metal tube connected to the outer cable shield. A rotating ring outside the tube locks the cable to any female connector.

BNC T-connectors (used with the 10Base-2 system) are female devices for connecting two cables to a network interface card (NIC). A BNC barrel connector allows connecting two cables together.

BNC connectors can also be used to connect some monitors, which increases the accuracy of the signals sent from the video adapter.

⇒ See also 10Base-2; coaxial cable; connector; network interface card.

board Short for *printed circuit board* or *expansion board.*

⇒ See also expansion board; printed circuit board.

boilerplate Text or graphics elements designed to be used over and over. For example, you could create a boilerplate for a fax message that contains all the standard fax information that doesn't change, such as your name, address, and phone number. Then whenever you want to create a new fax, you need only insert the boilerplate rather than retype the information.

A boilerplate is similar to a template, but whereas a template holds layout and style information, a boilerplate contains actual text or graphics. Many applications, however, combine the two concepts.

⇒ See also template.

boldface A font that is darker than the regular face. For example, see below.

Most word processors allow you to mark text as boldface.

⇒ See also font; word processing.

normal font   **boldface font**

bomb To fail. The term *bomb* usually refers to a program's hanging or ending prematurely. Note that bombing is usually less serious than crashing, because bombing refers to a single program, whereas crashing refers to the entire system. The two terms, however, are not always used consistently.

The Apple Macintosh computer actually has a bomb message that sometimes appears just before the system crashes.

⇒ See also abort; bug; crash; hang; Macintosh computer.

bookmark *v* **1.** To mark a document or a specific place in a document for later retrieval. Nearly all Web browsers support a bookmarking feature that lets you save the address (URL) of a Web page so that you can easily revisit the page at a later time. —*n* **2.** A marker or address that identifies a document or a specific place in a document.

⇒ See also browser; Web page.

Boolean expression An expression that results in a value of either TRUE or FALSE. For example, the expression

2 < 5 (2 is less than 5)

is a Boolean expression because the result is TRUE. All expressions that contain *relational operators*, such as the *less than* sign (<), are Boolean. The operators—AND, OR, XOR, NOR, and NOT—are Boolean operators.

Boolean expressions are also called *comparison expressions, conditional expressions,* and *relational expressions.*

⇒ See also BOOLEAN LOGIC; BOOLEAN OPERATOR; EXPRESSION; RELATIONAL OPERATOR.

Boolean logic Named after the nineteenth-century mathematician George Boole, Boolean logic is a form of algebra in which all values are reduced to either TRUE or FALSE. Boolean logic is especially important for computer science because it fits nicely with the binary numbering system, in which each bit has a value of either 1 or 0. Another way of looking at it is that each bit has a value of either TRUE or FALSE.

⇒ See also BINARY; BOOLEAN EXPRESSION; BOOLEAN OPERATOR; LOGICAL.

Table 8
Boolean Operators

---

x AND y	Result is *TRUE* if both x and y are *TRUE*. Otherwise the result is *FALSE*.
x OR y	Result is *TRUE* if either x or y is *TRUE*. Otherwise the result is *FALSE*.
x XOR y	Result is *TRUE* only if x and y have different values. Otherwise the result is *FALSE*.
NOT x	Result is *TRUE* if x is *FALSE*. Result is *FALSE* if x is *TRUE*.

Boolean operator There are five Boolean operators that can be used to manipulate TRUE/FALSE values. These operators have the following meanings, where *x* and *y* represent values of TRUE or FALSE.

The OR operator is often called an *inclusive OR*, whereas XOR is an *exclusive OR*.

Boolean operators are used widely in programming and also in forming database queries. For example, the first query below

SELECT ALL WHERE LAST_NAME = 'Smith' AND FIRST_NAME = 'John'

finds all records with the name John Smith. But the second query

SELECT ALL WHERE LAST_NAME = 'Smith' OR FIRST_NAME = 'John'

finds all records with the last name 'Smith' *or* the first name 'John.'

⇒ See also BOOLEAN EXPRESSION; BOOLEAN LOGIC; OPERATOR; QUERY.

boot *v* **1.** To load the first piece of software that starts a computer. Because the operating system is essential for running all other programs, it is usually the first piece of software loaded during the boot process.

Boot is short for *bootstrap,* which in olden days was a strap attached to the top of your boot that you could pull to help get your boot on—hence the expression "pull oneself up by the bootstraps." Similarly, *bootstrap utilities* help the computer get started. —*n* **2.** Short for *bootstrap,* the starting up of a computer, which involves loading the operating system and other basic software. A cold boot is when you turn the computer on from an off position. A warm boot is when you reset a computer that is already on.

⇒ See also BIOS; BOOTABLE DISKETTE; BOOTP; CLEAN BOOT; COLD BOOT; LOAD; MBR; OPERATING SYSTEM; POST; WARM BOOT.

bootable diskette A diskette from which you can boot your computer. Normally, your computer boots from a hard disk, but if the hard disk is damaged (for example, by a virus), you can boot the computer from a bootable diskette. For this reason, it's a good idea to make sure you always have a bootable diskette on hand. In Windows 95, you can create a bootable diskette by following these steps:

Basic Steps

1. Insert a blank, formatted diskette in the floppy drive.
2. Select **Start->Settings->Control Panel**
3. Open **Add/Remove Programs**
4. Select the **Startup Disk** tab and press the **Create Disk...** button.

A bootable diskette is also called a *bootable floppy, boot disk,* and *startup disk.*

⇒ See also BOOT; MBR; VIRUS.

bootable floppy Same as BOOTABLE DISKETTE.

boot disk Same as BOOTABLE DISKETTE.

BOOTP Short for *Boot(strap) P(rotocol),* an Internet protocol that enables a diskless workstation to discover its own IP address, the IP address of a BOOTP server on the network, and a file to be loaded into memory to boot the machine. This enables the workstation to boot without requiring a hard or floppy disk drive. The protocol is defined by RFC 951.

⇒ See also BOOT; DISKLESS WORKSTATION.

boot sector See under MBR.

bootstrap See under BOOT.

Border Gateway Protocol See BGP.

Borland International A company providing programming and database tools. Borland was founded in 1983 and has its headquarters in Scotts Valley, California.
    Products include:

- **Delphi:** Windows development tool
- **Borland C++:** language
- **dBase** and **Visual:** database development tools
- **Paradox:** database development tools
- **InterBase:** a scalable SQL server database
- **IntraBuilder:** visual JavaScript toolset

⇒ See also C++; PASCAL; RDBMS; SPREADSHEET.

bot Short for *robot*, a computer program that runs automatically.

⇒ See also ROBOT.

box 1. In graphical user interfaces, a box is an enclosed area, resembling a window, on the screen. Unlike windows, however, you generally cannot move or resize boxes.
    There are many different types of boxes. For example, *dialog boxes* are boxes that request some type of information from you. *Alert boxes* are boxes that suddenly appear on the screen to give you information. Boxes can also be small rectangular icons that control windows. *Zoom boxes,* for example, enable you to make a window larger or smaller. **2.** Slang for *personal computer* or *workstation*.

⇒ See also ALERT BOX; BUTTON; DIALOG BOX; GRAPHICAL USER INTERFACE; ICON; WINDOW; ZOOM.

bps Abbreviation of *b(its) p(er) s(econd)*, the standard measure of data transmission speeds.

⇒ See also BAUD; CCITT; COMMUNICATIONS; MODEM.

branch In tree structures, a branch is a single line of the tree that ends with a *leaf*. The Windows 3.*x* File Manager, for example, has an *Expand Branch* command that shows all subdirectories of a specified directory.
    ⇒ See also DIRECTORY; TREE STRUCTURE.

Break key A special key on computer keyboards that temporarily interrupts the computer's communications line. This usually terminates an established modem connection. Not all keyboards have a Break key, and not all programs respond to it.

⇒ See also KEYBOARD.

BRI Short for *Basic-Rate Interface,* the basic ISDN configuration, which consists of two B-channels that can carry voice or data at rate of 64 Kbps, and one D-channel, which carries call-control information. Another type of ISDN configuration is called *Primary-Rate Interface (PRI),* which consists of 23 B-channels (30 in Europe) and one D-channel.

⇒ See also B-CHANNEL; ISDN.

bridge A device that connects two local-area networks (LANs), or two segments of the same LAN. The two LANs being connected can be alike or dissimilar. For example, a bridge can connect an Ethernet with a Token-Ring network.

Unlike routers, bridges are protocol independent. They simply forward packets without analyzing and re-routing messages. Consequently, they're faster than routers, but also less versatile.

⇒ See also BROUTER; HUB; INTERNETWORKING; LOCAL-AREA NETWORK; REPEATER; ROUTER; WIDE-AREA NETWORK.

British Naval Connector See BNC CONNECTOR.

broadband ISDN (B-ISDN) A standard for transmitting voice, video, and data at the same time over fiber optic telephone lines. Broadband ISDN can support data rates of 1.5 million bits per second (bps), but it has not been widely implemented.

⇒ See also BPS; BROADBAND TRANSMISSION; FIBER OPTICS; ISDN; SONET.

broadband transmission A type of data transmission in which a single medium (wire) can carry several channels at once. Cable TV, for example, uses broadband transmission. In contrast, baseband transmission allows only one signal at a time.

Most communications between computers, including the majority of local-area networks, use baseband communications. An exception is *B-ISDN* networks, which employ broadband transmission.

⇒ See also BASEBAND TRANSMISSION; BROADBAND ISDN (B-ISDN); CHANNEL; COMMUNICATIONS; LOCAL-AREA NETWORK; NETWORK.

broadcast To send the same message simultaneously to multiple recipients. Broadcasting is a useful feature in e-mail systems. It is also supported by some fax systems.

In networking, a distinction is made between *broadcasting* and *multicasting.* Broadcasting sends a message to everyone on the network whereas multicasting sends a message to a select list of recipients.

⇒ See also E-MAIL; FAX; MULTICAST; RTSP; WEBCASTING.

brouter Short for *bridge router,* and pronounced *brau-ter,* a device that functions as both a router and a bridge. A brouter understands how to route specific types of packets, such as TCP/IP packets. Any other packets it receives are simply forwarded to other network(s) connected to the device (this is the bridge function).

⇒ See also BRIDGE; ROUTER.

browse 1. In database systems, *browse* means to view data. Many database systems support a special *browse mode,* in which you can flip through fields and records quickly. Usually, you cannot modify data while you are in browse mode. **2.** In object-oriented programming languages, *browse* means to examine data structures. **3.** To view formatted documents. For example, you look at Web pages with a *Web browser.*

⇒ See also BROWSER; DATA STRUCTURE; DATABASE MANAGEMENT SYSTEM; FIELD; OBJECT ORIENTED; RECORD; SURF.

browser Short for *Web browser,* a software application used to locate and display Web pages. The two most popular browsers are Netscape Navigator and Microsoft Internet Explorer. Both of these are *graphical browsers,* which means that they can display graphics as well as text. In addition, most modern browsers can present multimedia information, including sound and video, though they require plug-ins for some formats.

⇒ See also ACTIVEX CONTROL; BROWSE; HTML; INTERNET EXPLORER; MOSAIC; NAVIGATOR; WORLD WIDE WEB; XML.

BSC See under BISYNC.

BSDI Short for *Berkeley Software Design, Inc.,* a commercial supplier of Internet and networking software based on the BSD (Berkeley) version of UNIX. In addition to providing a commercial version of the BSD operating system, BSDI also develops Internet server and gateway products.

⇒ See also UNIX; WEB SERVER.

bubble memory A type of nonvolatile memory composed of a thin layer of material that can be easily magnetized in only one direction. When a magnetic field is applied to a circular area of this substance that is not magnetized in the same direction, the area is reduced to a smaller circle, or bubble.

It was once widely believed that bubble memory would become one of the leading memory technologies, but these promises have not been fulfilled. Other nonvolatile memory types, such as EEPROM, are both faster and less expensive than bubble memory.

⇒ See also EEPROM; NONVOLATILE MEMORY.

bubble sort A simple but popular sorting algorithm. Bubble sorting is used frequently as a programming exercise because it is relatively easy to understand. It is not, however, particularly efficient. Other sorting algorithms, such as *heap sorts, merge sorts,* and *quicksorts,* are used more often in real applications.

⇒ See also ALGORITHM; HEAP SORT; PSEUDOCODE.

buffer *n* **1.** A temporary storage area, usually in RAM. The purpose of most buffers is to act as a holding area, enabling the CPU to manipulate data before transferring it to a device.

Because the processes of reading and writing data to a disk are relatively slow, many programs keep track of data changes in a buffer and then copy the buffer to a disk. For example, word processors employ a buffer to keep track of changes to files. Then when you *save* the file, the word processor updates the disk file with the contents of the buffer. This is much more efficient than accessing the file on the disk each time you make a change to the file.

Note that because your changes are initially stored in a buffer, not on the disk, all of them will be lost if the computer fails during an editing session. For this reason, it is a good idea to save your file periodically. Most word processors automatically save files at regular intervals.

Another common use of buffers is for printing documents. When you enter a PRINT command, the operating system copies your document to a print buffer (a free area in memory or on a disk) from which the printer can draw characters at its own pace. This frees the computer to perform other tasks while the printer is running in the background. Print buffering is called *spooling.*

Most keyboard drivers also contain a buffer so that you can edit typing mistakes before sending your command to a program. Many operating systems, including DOS, also use a *disk buffer* to temporarily hold data that they have read from a disk. The disk buffer is really a cache. —*v* **2.** To move data into a temporary storage area.

⇒ See also CACHE; COMMAND BUFFER; DISK CACHE; SAVE; SPOOLING.

bug An error or defect in software or hardware that causes a program to malfunction. According to the folklore, the term originated when a moth trapped in the electrical workings of the first digital computer, the ENIAC, was discovered by Lieutenant Grace Hopper.

⇒ See also BOMB; CRASH; GLITCH; HANG; MEMORY LEAK.

built-in font Same as RESIDENT FONT.

built-in function A function that is built into an application and can be accessed by end users. For example, most spreadsheet applications support a built-in SUM function that adds up all cells in a row or column.

⇒ See also FUNCTION.

bullet A small graphical element used to highlight or itemize a list.

⇒ See also DINGBAT.

● A round bullet.
■ A square bullet.
◆ A diamond bullet.
☛ A pointing-finger bullet.

bulletin board system An electronic message center. Most bulletin boards serve specific interest groups. They allow you to dial in with a modem, review messages left by others, and leave your own message if you want. Bulletin boards are a particularly good place to find free or inexpensive software products. In the United States alone, there are tens of thousands of BBSs.

⇒ See also COMMUNICATIONS SOFTWARE; E-MAIL; MODEM; NETWORK; ONLINE SERVICE.

bundled software Software that is sold with a computer or other hardware component as part of a package. As competition between computer manufacturers has intensified, bundling software has become a key strategy for attracting consumers. In some cases, the bundled software is even more valuable than the hardware.

Bundled software can also be part of a software package. For example, Microsoft Windows comes with many bundled software tools.

⇒ See also HARDWARE; SOFTWARE.

burst mode A data transmission mode in which data is sent faster than normal. There are a number of techniques for implementing burst modes. In a data bus, for example, a burst mode is usually implemented by allowing a device to seize control of the bus and not permitting other devices to interrupt. In RAM, burst modes are implemented by automatically fetching the next memory contents before they are requested. This is essentially the same technique used by disk caches.

The one characteristic that all burst modes have in common is that they are temporary and unsustainable. They allow faster data transfer rates than normal, but only for a limited period of time and only under special conditions.

⇒ See also BEDO DRAM; DATA TRANSFER RATE; PIPELINE BURST CACHE; WAIT STATE.

bus 1. A collection of wires through which data is transmitted from one part of a computer to another. You can think of a bus as a highway on which data travels within a computer. When used in reference to personal computers, the term *bus* usually refers to *internal bus*. This is a bus that connects all the internal computer components to the CPU and main memory. There's also an expansion bus that enables expansion boards to access the CPU and memory.

All buses consist of two parts—an address bus and a data bus. The data bus transfers actual data whereas the address bus transfers information about where the data should go.

The size of a bus, known as its *width*, is important because it determines how much data can be transmitted at one time. For example, a 16-bit bus can transmit 16 bits of data, whereas a 32-bit bus can transmit 32 bits of data.

Every bus has a clock speed measured in MHz. A fast bus allows data to be transferred faster, which makes applications run faster. On PCs, the old ISA bus is being replaced by faster buses such as PCI.

Nearly all PCs made today include a local bus for data that requires especially fast transfer speeds, such as video data. The local bus is a high-speed pathway that connects directly to the processor.

Several different types of buses are used on Apple Macintosh computers. Older Macs use a bus called NuBus, but newer ones use PCI. **2.** In networking, a bus is a central cable that connects all devices on a local-area network (LAN). It is also called the *backbone*.

⇒ See also 32-BIT; ACCESS.BUS; ADB; ADDRESS BUS; AT BUS; BUS MASTERING; CHANNEL; CLOCK SPEED; CONTROLLER; EISA; ETHERNET; EXPANSION BUS; FIBRE CHANNEL; INDUSTRY STANDARD ARCHITECTURE (ISA) BUS; LOCAL BUS; NETWORK; PCI; TOPOLOGY; USB; VME BUS; ZV PORT.

business graphics See under PRESENTATION GRAPHICS.

bus mastering Refers to a feature supported by some bus architectures that enables a controller connected to the bus to communicate directly with other devices on the bus without going through the CPU. Most modern bus architectures, including PCI, support bus mastering because it improves performance.

⇒ See also BUS; PCI.

bus mouse A mouse that connects to a computer via an expansion board. Another type of mouse is a *serial mouse*, which connects to a serial port. Serial mice are easier to install, but the advantage of bus mice is that they do not use up the serial port, so you can use the port for a different device (a modem, for example). A PS/2 mouse solves this problem by plugging into a special PS/2 port dedicated to the mouse. Bus mice are now obsolete.

⇒ See also BUS; MOUSE; SERIAL PORT.

bus network A network in which all nodes are connected to a single wire (the bus) that has two endpoints. Ethernet 10Base-2 and 10Base-5 networks, for example, are bus networks. Other common network types include star networks and ring networks.

⇒ See also ETHERNET; RING NETWORK; STAR NETWORK; TOKEN BUS NETWORK; TO-POLOGY.

bus topology See under TOPOLOGY.

button 1. In graphical user interfaces, a button is a small outlined area in a dialog box that you can click to select an option or command. **2.** A *mouse button* is a button on a mouse that you click to perform various functions, such as selecting an object.

⇒ See also CLICK; DIALOG BOX; GRAPHICAL USER INTERFACE; MOUSE; RADIO BUT-TONS.

byte Abbreviation for *binary term*, a unit of storage capable of holding a single character. On almost all modern computers, a byte is equal to 8 bits. Large amounts of memory are indicated in terms of kilobytes (1,024 bytes), megabytes (1,048,576 bytes), and gigabytes (1,073,741,824 bytes). A disk that can hold 1.44 megabytes, for example, is capable of storing approximately 1.4 million characters, or about 3,000 pages of information.

⇒ See also BIG-ENDIAN; GIGABYTE; KILOBYTE; MEGABYTE; NIBBLE.

bytecode The compiled format for Java programs. Once a Java program has been converted to bytecode, it can be transferred across a network and executed by Java Virtual Machine (VM). Bytecode files generally have a *.class* extension.

⇒ See also COMPILE; INTERPRETER; JAVA; JIT.

C A high-level programming language developed by Dennis Ritchie and Brian Kernighan at Bell Labs in the mid-1970s. Although originally designed as a systems programming language, C has proved to be a powerful and flexible language that can be used for a variety of applications, from business programs to engineering. C is a particularly popular language for personal-computer programmers because it is relatively small—it requires less memory than other languages.

The first major program written in C was the UNIX operating system, and for many years C was considered to be inextricably linked with UNIX. Now, however, C is an important language independent of UNIX.

Although it is a high-level language, C is much closer to assembly language than are most other high-level languages. This closeness to the underlying machine language allows C programmers to write very efficient code. The low-level nature of C, however, can make the language difficult to use for some types of applications.

⇒ See also ASSEMBLY LANGUAGE; C++; EIFFEL; HIGH-LEVEL LANGUAGE; MACHINE LANGUAGE; PROGRAMMING LANGUAGE; UNIX; VISUAL C++.

C++ A high-level programming language developed by Bjarne Stroustrup at Bell Labs. C++ adds object-oriented features to its predecessor, C. C++ is one of the most popular programming languages for graphical applications, such as those that run in Windows and Macintosh environments.

⇒ See also BORLAND INTERNATIONAL; C; HIGH-LEVEL LANGUAGE; JAVA; MFC; OBJECT ORIENTED; PROGRAMMING LANGUAGE; SMALLTALK; VISUAL C++.

CA Short for *Certificate Authority*.

cable modem A modem designed to operate over cable TV lines. Because the coaxial cable used by cable TV provides much greater bandwidth than telephone lines, a cable modem can be used to achieve extremely fast access to the World Wide Web. This, combined with the fact that millions of homes are already wired for cable TV, has made the cable modem something of a holy grail for Internet and cable TV companies.

There are a number of technical difficulties, however. One is that the cable TV infrastructure is designed to broadcast TV signals in just one direction—from the cable TV company to people's homes. The Internet, however, is a two-way system where data also needs to flow from the client to the server. In addition, it is still unknown whether the cable TV networks can handle the traffic that would ensue if millions of users began using the system for Internet access.

Despite these problems, cable modems that offer speeds up to 2 Mbps are already available in many areas.

⇒ See also WEBTV.

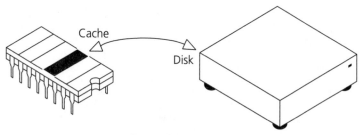

Figure 10: **disk cache**

cache Pronounced *cash*, a special high-speed storage mechanism. It can be either a reserved section of main memory or an independent high-speed storage device. Two types of caching are commonly used in personal computers: *memory caching* and *disk caching*.

A memory cache, sometimes called a *cache store* or *RAM cache*, is a portion of memory made of high-speed static RAM (SRAM) instead of the slower and cheaper dynamic RAM (DRAM) used for main memory. Memory caching is effective because most programs access the same data or instructions over and over. By keeping as much of this information as possible in SRAM, the computer avoids accessing the slower DRAM.

Some memory caches are built into the architecture of microprocessors. The Intel 80486 microprocessor, for example, contains an 8K memory cache, and the Pentium has a 16K cache. Such *internal caches* are often called *Level 1 (L1) caches*. Most modern PCs also come with external cache memory, called *Level 2 (L2) caches*. These caches sit between the CPU and the DRAM. Like L1 caches, L2 caches are composed of SRAM, but they are much larger.

Disk caching works under the same principle as memory caching, but instead of using high-speed SRAM, a disk cache uses conventional main memory. The most recently accessed data from the disk (as well as adjacent sectors) is stored in a memory buffer. When a program needs to access data from the disk, it first checks the disk cache to see if the data is there. Disk caching can dramatically improve the performance of applications, because accessing a byte of data in RAM can be thousands of times faster than accessing a byte on a hard disk.

When data is found in the cache, it is called a *cache hit*, and the effectiveness of a cache is judged by its *hit rate*. Many cache systems use a technique known as *smart caching*, in which the system can recognize certain types of frequently used data. The strategies for determining which information should be kept in the cache constitute some of the more interesting problems in computer science.

⇒ See also BUFFER; DISK CACHE; MAIN MEMORY; PIPELINE BURST CACHE; RAM DISK; TAG RAM; WRITE-BACK CACHE.

cache memory See under CACHE.

CAD Acronym for *c(omputer)-a(ided) d(esign)*. A CAD system is a combination of hardware and software that enables engineers and architects to design everything from furniture to airplanes. In addition to the software, CAD systems require a high-quality graphics monitor; a mouse, light pen, or digitizing tablet for drawing; and a special printer or plotter for printing design specifications.

CAD systems allow an engineer to view a design from any angle with the push of a button and to zoom in or out for close-ups and long-distance views. In addition, the computer keeps track of design dependencies so that when the engineer changes one value, all other values that depend on it are automatically changed accordingly.

Until the mid-1980s, all CAD systems were specially constructed computers. Now, you can buy CAD software that runs on general-purpose workstations and personal computers.

⇒ See also CAD/CAM; CAE; CAM; DIGITIZING TABLET; GRAPHICS; LIGHT PEN; MONITOR; MOUSE; PLOTTER; WORKSTATION.

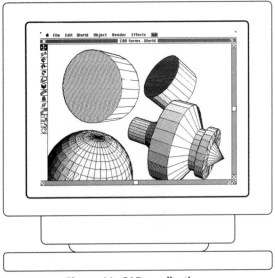

Figure 11: **CAD application**

CAD/CAM Acronym for *c(omputer)-a(ided) d(esign)/c(omputer)-a(ided) m(anufacturing)*, computer systems used to design and manufacture products. The term *CAD/CAM* implies that an engineer can use the system both for designing a product and for controlling manufacturing processes. For example, once a design has been produced with the CAD component, the design itself can control the machines that construct the part.

⇒ See also 3-D SOFTWARE; CAD; CADD; CAM; MODELING.

CADD Acronym for *c(omputer)-a(ided) d(esign) and d(rafting)*. CADD systems are CAD systems with additional drafting features. For example, CADD systems enable an engineer or architect to insert size annotations and other notes into a design.

⇒ See also CAD; CAD/CAM.

CAE Abbreviation of *c(omputer)-a(ided) e(ngineering)*, computer systems that analyze engineering designs. Most CAD systems have a CAE component, but there are also independent CAE systems that can analyze designs produced by various CAD systems. CAE systems are able to simulate a design under a variety of conditions to see if it actually works.

⇒ See also CAD; CASE.

calculator 1. A small hand-held computer that performs mathematical calculations. Some calculators even permit simple text editing and programming. **2.** A program on a computer that simulates a hand-held calculator. Calculator programs let you perform simple math calculations without leaving the computer. The Apple Macintosh comes with a calculator desk accessory. Likewise, Microsoft Windows includes a calculator accessory.

⇒ See also DESK ACCESSORY (DA); MICROSOFT WINDOWS; PROGRAM.

calendar A program that enables you to record events and appointments on an electronic calendar. Computer calendars act like datebooks, but they have several advantages over traditional datebooks:

automatic entries for regular events: You can specify, for example, that the first Thursday of every month is bridge night, and the calendar program will automatically fill in the appropriate days.
signaling of upcoming events: Most calendars will let you know that an event is approaching by issuing sounds.
clean deletion: With an electronic calendar, you can erase an appointment without leaving a trace.

Calendar software is part of a more general category of software known as *PIMs* (personal information managers). A special type of calendar, called a *scheduler*, enables groups of users connected to a network to coordinate their schedules.

⇒ See also PIM; SCHEDULER; UTILITY.

call *v* **1.** To invoke a routine in a programming language. Calling a routine consists of specifying the routine name and, optionally, parameters. For

example, the following is a *function call* in the C programming language:
printf("Hello")
The name of the function is *printf* and the parameter is "Hello." This
function call causes the computer to display the word *Hello* on the display screen.

A routine that invokes another routine is sometimes referred to as the
calling routine. The routine that is invoked is referred to as the *called
routine.* —*n* **2.** An invocation of a routine.

⇒ See also FUNCTION; ROUTINE.

CAM Acronym for *c(omputer)-a(ided) m(anufacturing)*, a type of computer
application that helps automate a factory. For example, the following are
types of CAM systems:

- real-time control
- robotics
- materials requirements

All these systems are concerned with automatically directing the manufacture and inventory of parts.

⇒ See also CAD; CAD/CAM; ROBOTICS.

camera-ready In desktop publishing, *camera-ready* refers to the final state
of a publication before it is printed. Historically, the term has meant that
the copy is ready to be photographed and turned into plates for offset
printing. Increasingly, however, it is possible to print directly from the
electronic version, either by sending it to a high-resolution laser printer
or to a special device that can generate plates directly from electronic
elements rather than from photographs. In these cases, therefore, *camera-ready* means merely that the document is ready to be printed.

⇒ See also DESKTOP PUBLISHING; IMAGESETTER; ISP; OFFSET PRINTING.

caps Short for *capital letters*. For example, "all caps" means all letters capitalized.

⇒ See also CASE SENSITIVE; UPPERCASE.

Caps Lock key A *toggle key* on computer keyboards that, when activated,
causes all subsequent alphabetic characters to be uppercase but has no
effect on other keys.

⇒ See also KEYBOARD; TOGGLE; UPPERCASE.

capture To save a particular state of a program. The term *capture* often refers to saving the information currently visible on a display screen. You
can capture the screen to a printer or to a file. The act of saving a display screen is called a *screen capture*. *Video capture* refers to storing
video images in a computer.

The term *capture* is also used to describe the recording of keystrokes during the definition of a *macro*.

⇒ See also LEARN MODE; SCREEN CAPTURE.

card 1. Same as EXPANSION BOARD. **2.** In hypertext systems such as Hyper-Card, a card is a single page of information.

⇒ See also HYPERCARD; HYPERTEXT.

CardBus The 32-bit version of the PCMCIA PC Card standard. In addition to supporting a wider bus (32 bits instead of 16 bits), CardBus also supports bus mastering and operation speeds up to 33 MHz.

⇒ See also PC CARD; PCMCIA.

caret A wedge-shaped symbol (^) generally found above the 6 on computer keyboards. In older technical documentation, the caret is often used to indicate the Control key. For example, "^C" would mean press the "C" key while holding down the Control key. Most modern documentation, however, would specify this key sequence as Ctrl + C.
　　The caret symbol is also called a *hat*.

⇒ See also CONTROL KEY.

carpal tunnel syndrome A common form of repetitive strain injury (RSI) produced by repeating the same small movements many times. As more and more people use computers, carpal tunnel syndrome and other forms of RSI have become more prevalent. Typical symptoms are numbness or burning in the fingers or wrist. If not addressed early on, the injury can cause permanent damage.
　　There are a number of ways to avoid carpal tunnel syndrome, including adjusting the height and angle of your chair and keyboard, and taking frequent breaks from typing. Modern office furniture, designed especially for computer use, can help considerably.

⇒ See also ERGONOMICS.

carriage The mechanism on a printer that feeds paper. A *wide-carriage printer* is a printer that can accept very wide paper. A *narrow-carriage printer* is a printer that accepts only standard-sized paper.

⇒ See also PAPER FEED; PRINTER.

carriage return Often abbreviated *CR,* a carriage return is a special code that moves the cursor (or print head) to the beginning of the current line. In the ASCII character set, a carriage return has a decimal value of 13.

⇒ See also LINE FEED; RETURN.

carrier Short for *carrier signal, carrier system,* or *carrier service provider:*

carrier signal: A frequency in a communications channel modulated to carry analog or digital signal information. For example, an FM radio transmitter modulates the frequency of a carrier signal and the receiver processes the carrier signal to extract the analog information. An AM radio transmitter modulates the amplitude of a carrier signal.

carrier system: A communications system providing a number of point-to-point channels through some type of multiplexing. T-1 and T-3 carrier services are examples of carrier systems that can be used between points in a wide-area network (WAN).

carrier service provider: A company offering telephone and data communications between points in a state or in one or more countries. The *Regional Bell Operating Companies (RBOCs)* are examples of carriers.

⇒ See also FDM; MULTIPLEX; T-1 CARRIER; T-3 CARRIER.

Carrier Sense Multiple Access/Collision Detection See CSMA/CD.

cartridge 1. A removable storage medium (tape, disk, or memory chip). Some printers have slots into which you can insert cartridges to load different fonts. A font loaded from a cartridge is called a *font cartridge* or *cartridge font.*

The term *removable cartridge* usually refers to a type of hard disk that you can remove. Removable cartridges offer the speed of hard disks along with the portability of floppy disks. **2.** For laser and ink jet printers, a *toner cartridge* is a metal container that holds the *toner.*

⇒ See also FONT CARTRIDGE; LASER PRINTER; REMOVABLE HARD DISK; SLOT; TONER.

cartridge font Same as FONT CARTRIDGE.

cascading delete See under REFERENTIAL INTEGRITY.

Cascading Style Sheets See CSS.

cascading update See under REFERENTIAL INTEGRITY.

cascading windows An arrangement of windows such that they overlap one another. Typically, the title bar remains visible so that you can always see which windows are open. Cascading windows are also called *overlaid windows.* An alternative arrangement of windows, in which every window is completely visible, is called *tiled windows.*

⇒ See also OVERLAID WINDOWS; TILED WINDOWS; WINDOW.

CASE Short for *C(omputer) A(ided) S(oftware) E(ngineering)*, a category of software that provides a development environment for programming teams. CASE systems offer tools to automate, manage, and simplify the development process. These can include tools for:

- Summarizing initial requirements
- Developing flow diagrams
- Scheduling development tasks
- Preparing documentation
- Controlling software versions
- Developing program code

Various companies offer CASE software capable of supporting some or all of these activities. While many CASE systems provide special support for object-oriented programming, the term *CASE* can apply to any type of software development environment.

⇒ See also CAE; PROGRAM.

case sensitive A program's ability to distinguish between uppercase (capital) and lowercase (small) letters. Programs that distinguish between uppercase and lowercase are said to be *case sensitive*.

A case-sensitive program that expects you to enter all commands in uppercase will not respond correctly if you enter one or more characters in lowercase. It will treat the command *RUN* differently from *run*. Programs that do not distinguish between uppercase and lowercase are said to be *case insensitive*.

⇒ See also LOWERCASE; UPPERCASE.

cathode ray tube See CRT.

CAV Short for *C(onstant) A(ngular) V(elocity)*, a technique for accessing data off of rotating disks. With CAV, the disk rotates at a constant speed regardless of what area of the disk is being accessed. This differs from *Constant Linear Velocity (CLV)*, which rotates the disk faster for inner tracks. Disk drives use CAV, whereas CD-ROMs generally use CLV, though some newer drives use a combination of CAV and CLV.

The advantage of CAV is that it is much simpler to design and produce because the motor doesn't need to change speed. In addition, CLV runs into problems for very high-speed CD-ROMs because there's a brief latency whenever the drive needs to change the rotational speed.

⇒ See also CD-ROM; CD-ROM PLAYER; CLV.

CBT Acronym for *c(omputer)-b(ased) t(raining)*, a type of education in which the student learns by executing special training programs on a computer. CBT is especially effective for training people to use computer applications because the CBT program can be integrated with the applications so that students can practice using the application as they learn.

Historically, CBT's growth has been hampered by the enormous resources required: human resources to create a CBT program and hardware resources needed to run it. However, the increase in PC computing power, and especially the growing prevalence of computers equipped with CD-ROMs, is making CBT a more viable option for corporations and individuals alike. Many PC applications now come with some modest

form of CBT, often called a *tutorial*.
CBT is also called *computer-assisted instruction (CAI)*.

⇒ See also COURSEWARE; DISTANCE LEARNING.

CCD Short for *charge-coupled device*, an instrument whose semiconductors are connected so that the output of one serves as the input of the next. Digital cameras, video cameras, and optical scanners all use CCD arrays.

⇒ See also DIGITAL CAMERA; OPTICAL SCANNER.

CCITT Abbreviation of *C(omit)é C(onsultatif) I(nternational) T(éléphonique et) T(élégraphique)*, an organization that sets international communications standards. CCITT, now known as ITU (the parent organization), has defined many important standards for data communications, including the following:

Group 3: The universal protocol for sending fax documents across telephone lines. The Group 3 protocol specifies CCITT T.4 data compression and a maximum transmission rate of 9,600 baud. There are two levels of resolution: 203 by 98 and 203 by 196.

Group 4: A protocol for sending fax documents over ISDN networks. The Group 400 protocol supports images of up to 400 dpi resolution.

V.21: The standard for full-duplex communication at 300 baud in Japan and Europe. In the United States, Bell 103 is used in place of V.21.

V.22: The standard for half-duplex communication at 1,200 bps in Japan and Europe. In the United States, the protocol defined by Bell 212A is more common.

V.22bis: The worldwide standard for full-duplex modems sending and receiving data across telephone lines at 1,200 or 2,400 bps.

V.29: The standard for half-duplex modems sending and receiving data across telephone lines at 1,200, 2,400, 4,800, or 9,600 bps. This is the protocol used by fax modems.

V.32: The standard for full-duplex modems sending and receiving data across phone lines at 4,800 or 9,600 bps. V.32 modems automatically adjust their transmission speeds based on the quality of the lines.

V.32bis: The V.32 protocol extended to speeds of 7,200, 12,000, and 14,400 bps.

V.34: The standard for full-duplex modems sending and receiving data across phone lines at up to 28,800 bps. V.34 modems automatically adjust their transmission speeds based on the quality of the lines.

V.42: An error-detection standard for high-speed modems. V.42 can be used with digital telephone networks. See MNP for a competing standard.

V.42bis: A data compression protocol that can enable modems to achieve a data transfer rate of 34,000 bps.

V.90: The standard for full-duplex modems sending and receiving data across phone lines at up to 56,600 bps.

X.25: The most popular packet-switching protocol for LANs. Ethernet, for example, is based on the X.25 standard.

X.400: The universal protocol for e-mail. X.400 defines the envelope for e-mail messages so all messages conform to a standard format.

X.500: An extension to X.400 that defines addressing formats so all e-mail systems can be linked together.

⇒ See also BAUD; BPS; COMMUNICATIONS PROTOCOL; DATA COMPRESSION; E-MAIL; FAX MACHINE; FAX MODEM; FULL DUPLEX; HALF DUPLEX; ISDN; ITU; MNP; MODEM; PROTOCOL; STANDARD; X.400; X.500.

CD See COMPACT DISC.

CD-DA See under RED BOOK.

CDDI Abbreviation of *C(opper) D(ata) D(istribution) I(nterface)*, a network technology capable of carrying data at 100 Mbps over unshielded twisted pair (UTP) cable. CDDI is a trade name of Crescendo Communications (acquired by Cisco Systems in 1993) and commonly used instead of the general term *Twisted Pair Physical Layer Medium (TP-PMD)*. TP-PMD is the general ANSI standard name for this FDDI-like service.

CDDI cable lengths are limited to 100 meters.

⇒ See also FDDI; LOCAL-AREA NETWORK; TWISTED-PAIR CABLE; UTP.

cdev Short for *c(ontrol) p(anel) dev(ice)*, and pronounced *see-dev*, a *cdev* is a special type of Macintosh utility that enables you to adjust basic system parameters. On newer Macs (System 7 and later) cdevs are called *control panels*.

⇒ See also CONTROL PANEL.

CDF Short for *c(hannel) d(efinition) f(ormat)*, a specification developed by Microsoft that allows Web publishers to *push* content at users. Once a user subscribes to a CDF channel, any software that supports the CDF format will automatically receive new content posted on the channel's Web server.

Announced in March 1997, CDF has received wide backing from the Internet community, with the notable exception of Netscape Communications. Microsoft has announced that Version 4.0 of its Internet Explorer browser will support CDF, and PointCast has also announced that it will support the CDF format. Microsoft has sent the specification to the World Wide Web Consortium (W3C) for standardization.

⇒ See also INTERNET EXPLORER; POINTCAST; PUSH.

CDFS Short for **CD***(-ROM) F(ile) S(ystem)*, the Windows 95 driver for CD-ROM players. CDFS replaces MSCDEX, which was used for DOS and Windows 3.x systems. Unlike MSCDEX, which is a 16-bit program that runs only in real mode, CDFS is a 32-bit program that runs in protected mode. In addition, it uses the VCACHE driver to control the CD-ROM

disk cache, which results in much smoother playback.
⇒ See also CD-ROM player; MSCDEX; VCACHE.

CD-I *C(ompact) D(isc)–I(nteractive)*, a software and hardware standard developed jointly by Philips International and Sony Corporation for storing video, audio, and binary data on compact optical disks. It supports 552MB (megabytes) of binary data and specifies several different types of video and audio encoding formats. Unlike conventional CD-ROM drives, CD-I drives have a built-in microprocessor to handle many of the computing functions. CD-I is sometimes referred to as the *Green Book* standard.

Although there are some CD-I devices and titles, the format has not become widely accepted.

⇒ See also CD-ROM; CD-ROM/XA; DVD; DVI; Green Book; optical disk; OS/9.

CDMA Short for *C(ode)-D(ivision) M(ultiple) A(ccess)*, a digital cellular technology that uses *spread-spectrum* techniques. Unlike competing systems, such as GSM, that use *time-division multiplexing (TDM)*, CDMA does not assign a specific frequency to each user. Instead, every channel uses the full available spectrum. Individual conversations are encoded with a pseudo-random digital sequence.

CDMA was developed by Qualcomm, Inc.

⇒ See also cellular; GSM; multiplex; PCS; TDM; TDMA.

CDPD Short for *C(ellular) D(igital) P(acket) D(ata)*, a data transmission technology developed for use on cellular phone frequencies. CDPD uses unused cellular channels (in the 800- to 900-MHz range) to transmit data in packets. This technology offers data transfer rates of up to 19.2 Kbps, quicker call setup, and better error correction than using modems on an analog cellular channel.

⇒ See also cell; packet switching.

CD-R See CD-R drive.

CD-R drive Short for *C(ompact) D(isk)-R(ecordable)* **drive,** a type of disk drive that can create CD-ROMs and audio CDs. This allows users to "master" a CD-ROM or audio CD for publishing. Until recently, CD-R drives were quite expensive, but prices have dropped dramatically.

A feature of many CD-R drives, called *multisession recording*, enables you to keep adding data to a CD-ROM over time. This is extremely important if you want to use the CD-R drive to create backup CD-ROMs.

To create CD-ROMs and audio CDs, you'll need not only a CD-R drive but also a CD-R software package. Often, it is the software package, not the drive itself, that determines how easy or difficult it is to create CD-ROMs.

CD-R drives can also read CD-ROMs and play audio CDs.

⇒ See also CD-ROM; CD-ROM PLAYER; CD-RW DISK; ORANGE BOOK.

CD-recordable drive See CD-R DRIVE.

CD-ROM Pronounced *see-dee-rom*, abbreviation of *C(ompact) D(isc)–R(ead)-O(nly) M(emory)*. A type of optical disk capable of storing large amounts of data—up to 1GB, although the most common size is 650MB (megabytes). A single CD-ROM has the storage capacity of 700 floppy disks, enough memory to store about 300,000 text pages.

CD-ROMs are *stamped* by the vendor, and once stamped, they cannot be erased and filled with new data. To read a CD, you need a CD-ROM player. All CD-ROMs conform to a standard size and format, so you can load any type of CD-ROM into any CD-ROM player. In addition, CD-ROM players are capable of playing audio CDs, which share the same technology.

CD-ROMs are particularly well-suited to information that requires large storage capacity. This includes color large software applications, graphics, sound, and especially video.

⇒ See also CAV; CD-I (COMPACT DISC-INTERACTIVE); CD-R DRIVE; CD-ROM PLAYER; CD-ROM/XA; CD-RW DISK; CLV; COMPACT DISC; DISK; ERASABLE OPTICAL DISK; MASS STORAGE; MULTIMEDIA; OPTICAL DISK; YELLOW_BOOK.

CD-ROM drive Same as CD-ROM PLAYER.

CD-ROM player Also called a *CD-ROM drive*, a device that can read information from a CD-ROM. CD-ROM players can be either internal, in which case they fit in a bay, or external, in which case they generally connect to the computer's SCSI interface or parallel port. Parallel CD-ROM players are easier to install, but they have several disadvantages: They're somewhat more expensive than internal players, they use up the parallel port which means that you can't use that port for another device such as a printer, and the parallel port itself may not be fast enough to handle all the data pouring through it.

There are a number of features that distinguish CD-ROM players, the most important of which is probably their speed. CD-ROM players are generally classified as single-speed or some multiple of single-speed. For example, a *4X* player accesses data at four times the speed of a single-speed player. Within these groups, however, there is some variation. Also, you need to be aware of whether the CD-ROM uses the CLV or CAV technology. The reported speeds of players that use CAV are generally not accurate because they refer only to the access speed for outer tracks. Inner tracks are accessed more slowly.

Two more precise measurements are the drive's *access time* and *data transfer rate*. The access time measures how long, on average, it takes the drive to access a particular piece of information. The data transfer rate measures how much data can be read and sent to the computer in a second.

Finally, you should consider how the player connects to your computer. Many CD-ROMs connect via a SCSI bus. If your computer doesn't already contain such an interface, you will need to install one. Other CD-ROMs connect to an *IDE* or *Enhanced IDE interface,* which is the one used by the hard disk drive; still others use a proprietary interface.

⇒ See also ACCESS TIME; BAY; CAV; CD-R DRIVE; CD-ROM; CDFS; CLV; IDE INTERFACE; MPC; MSCDEX; MULTIMEDIA KIT; MultiRead; PARALLEL PORT; PHOTOCD; SCSI.

Table 9
CD-ROM Drives

General Speed	Access Time (Milliseconds)	Data Transfer Rate
Single-Speed	600	150K per second
2X	320	300K per second
3X	250	450K per second
4X	135–180	600K per second
6X	135–180	900K per second
8X	135–180	1.2 MBps
10X	135–180	1.6 MBps
12X	100–150	1.8 MBps
16X	100–150	2.4 MBps (maximum)
24X	100–150	3.6 MBps (maximum)
32X	100–150	4.8 MBps (maximum)
40X	50–100	6.0 MBps (maximum)

CD-ROM/XA Short for **CD-ROM/***eX(tended) A(rchitecture),* a specification developed by Sony, Phillips, and Microsoft that enables many different types of data—audio, video, compressed video, and graphics—to be stored on a single CD-ROM.

⇒ See also CD-I (COMPACT DISC-INTERACTIVE); CD-ROM; YELLOW_BOOK.

CD-RW disk Short for **CD-***R(e)W(ritable)* **disk,** a type of CD disk that enables you to write onto it in multiple sessions. One of the problems with CD-R disks is that you can write to them only once. With CD-RW drives and disks, you can treat the optical disk just like a floppy or hard disk, writing data onto it multiple times.

The first CD-RW drives became available in mid-1997. They can read CD-ROMs and can write onto today's CD-R disks, but they cannot write on normal CD-ROMs. This means that disks created with a CD-RW drive can be read only by a CD-RW drive. However, a new standard called *MultiRead,* developed jointly by Philips Electronics and Hewlett-Packard, will enable CD-ROM players to read disks create by CD-RW drives.

Many experts believe that CD-RW disks will be a popular storage medium until DVD devices become widely available.

⇒ See also CD-R DRIVE; CD-ROM; DVD+RW; DVD-RAM; DVI; MULTIREAD.

cell 1. In spreadsheet applications, a cell is a box in which you can enter a single piece of data. The data is usually text, a numeric value, or a formula. The entire spreadsheet is composed of rows and columns of cells. A spreadsheet cell is analogous to a *field* in database management systems.

Individual cells are usually identified by a column letter and a row number. For example, *D12* specifies the cell in column D and row 12. **2.** In communications and networking, a fixed-size packet of data. **3.** In cellular telephone systems, a geographic area.

⇒ See also CDPD; CELL RELAY; CELLULAR; FIELD; FORMULA; SPREADSHEET.

cell relay A data transmission technology based on transmitting data in relatively small, fixed-size packets or cells. Each cell contains only basic path information that allows switching devices to route the cell quickly. Cell relay systems can reliably carry live video and audio because cells of fixed size arrive in a more predictable way than systems with packets or frames of varying size.

Asynchronous Transfer Mode (ATM) is the cell relay standard set by the CCITT organization. ATM uses a cell of 53 bytes.

⇒ See also ATM; CELL; FRAME RELAY; PACKET; PACKET SWITCHING.

Cells in Frames A specification that enables ATM cells to be carried in Ethernet packets. This makes it possible to implement the ATM protocol while using existing Ethernet equipment, especially network interface cards (NICs). CIF provides the advantages of ATM, such as Quality of Service (QoS), without the usual hardware expense.

cellular Refers to communications systems, especially the *Advance Mobile Phone Service (AMPS)*, that divide a geographic region into sections, called *cells*. The purpose of this division is to make the most use out of a limited number of transmission frequencies. Each connection, or conversation, requires its own dedicated frequency, and the total number of available frequencies is about 1,000. To support more than 1,000 simultaneous conversations, cellular systems allocate a set number of frequencies for each cell. Two cells can use the same frequency for different conversations so long as the cells are not adjacent to each other.

For digital communications, several competing cellular systems exist, including GSM and CDMA.

⇒ See also CDMA; CELL; GSM; PCS; TDMA.

cellular digital packet data See CDPD.

central processing unit See CPU.

centrex Short for *centr(al) (office) ex(change) (service)*, a new type of PBX service in which switching occurs at a local telephone station instead of at the company premises. Typically, the telephone company owns and manages all the communications equipment necessary to implement the PBX and then sells various services to the company.

⇒ See also PBX.

Centronics interface A standard interface for connecting printers and other parallel devices. Although Centronics Corporation designed the original standard, the Centronics interface used by modern computers was designed by Epson Corporation. For PCs, almost all parallel ports conform to the Centronics standard. Two new parallel port standards that are backward compatible with Centronics, but offer faster transmission rates, are *ECP (Extend Capabilities Port)* and *EPP (Enhanced Parallel Port)*.

⇒ See also ECP; EPP; INTERFACE; PARALLEL INTERFACE; STANDARD.

CERN Pronounced *sern,* and short for *European Laboratory for Particle Physics [C(onseil) E(uropeen) pour le R(echerche) N(ucleaire)* in French], a research laboratory headquartered in Geneva, Switzerland, and funded by many different countries. While most of its work deals with nuclear physics, the CERN is known for pioneering work in developing the World Wide Web portion of the Internet. The laboratory completed this work to improve the way scientists share information.

⇒ See also WEB SERVER; WORLD WIDE WEB.

Certificate Authority A trusted third-party organization or company that issues digital certificates used to create digital signatures and public-private key pairs. The role of the CA in this process is to guarantee that the individual granted the unique certificate is, in fact, who he or she claims to be. Usually, this means that the CA has an arrangement with a financial institution, such as a credit card company, which provides it with information to confirm an individual's claimed identity. CAs are a critical component in data security and electronic commerce because they guarantee that the two parties exchanging information are really who they claim to be.

⇒ See also DIGITAL CERTIFICATE; DIGITAL SIGNATURE; ELECTRONIC COMMERCE; PKI; PUBLIC-KEY ENCRYPTION.

CGA Abbreviation of *c(olor)/g(raphics) a(dapter)*, an old graphics system for PCs. Introduced in 1981 by IBM, CGA was the first color graphics system for IBM PCs. Designed primarily for computer games, CGA does not produce sharp enough characters for extended editing sessions. CGA's highest-resolution mode is 2 colors at a resolution of 640 by 200.

CGA has been superseded by VGA systems.

⇒ See also BACKWARD COMPATIBLE; EGA; GRAPHICS MODE; IBM PC; MCGA; PALETTE; RESOLUTION; SVGA; TEXT MODE; VGA; VIDEO ADAPTER; XGA.

CGI Abbreviation of *C(ommon) G(ateway) I(nterface)*, a specification for transferring information between a World Wide Web server and a CGI program. A CGI program is any program designed to accept and return data that conforms to the CGI specification. The program could be written in any programming language, including C, Perl, Java, or Visual Basic.

CGI programs are the most common way for Web servers to interact dynamically with users. Many HTML pages that contain forms, for example, use a CGI program to process the form's data once it's submitted. Another increasingly common way to provide dynamic feedback for Web users is to include scripts or programs that run on the user's machine rather than on the Web server. These programs can be Java applets, Java scripts, or ActiveX controls. These technologies are known collectively as *client-side* solutions, while the use of CGI is a *server-side* solution because the processing occurs on the Web server.

One problem with CGI is that each time a CGI script is executed, a new process is started. For busy Web sites, this can slow down the server noticeably. A more efficient solution, but one that it is also more difficult to implement, is to use the server's API, such as ISAPI or NSAPI. Another increasingly popular solution is to use Java servlets.

⇒ See also ACTIVE SERVER PAGES; DYNAMIC HTML; FORM; ISAPI; JAVA; NSAPI; PERL; SERVLET; WORLD WIDE WEB.

CGM Abbreviation of *C(omputer) G(raphics) M(etafile)*, a file format designed by several standards organizations and formally ratified by ANSI. It is designed to be the standard vector graphics file format and is supported by a wide variety of software and hardware products.

⇒ See also ANSI; GRAPHICS FILE FORMATS; VECTOR GRAPHICS.

Challenge Handshake Authentication Protocol See CHAP.

challenge-response A common authentication technique whereby an individual is prompted (the *challenge*) to provide some private information (the *response*). Most security systems that rely on smart cards are based on challenge-response. A user is given a code (the challenge) that he or she enters into the smart card. The smart card then displays a new code (the response) that the user can present to log in.

⇒ See also AUTHENTICATION; CHAP; SMART CARD.

channel 1. In communications, the term *channel* refers to a communications path between two computers or devices. It can refer to the physical medium (the wires) or to a set of properties that distinguishes one channel from another. For example, *TV channels* refer to particular frequencies at which radio waves are transmitted. *IRC channels* refer to specific discussions. **2.** For IBM PS/2 computers, a channel is the same as an expansion bus. **3.** In sales and marketing, the way in which a vendor communicates with and sells products to consumers.

⇒ See also B-CHANNEL; BUS; COMMUNICATIONS; IRC.

channel bonding A technology that combines two telephone lines into a single channel, effectively doubling the data transfer speeds. To take advantage of channel bonding, you need two modems and two telephone lines. If both modems offer 56 Kbps speeds, for example, bonding two modems together would give you a 112 Kbps Internet connection, comparable to an ISDN connection.

Modems that support channel bonding first emerged at the end of 1997. One stumbling block, however, is that there are many incompatible channel bonding systems, and your ISP must support the same system as your modems.

⇒ See also ISDN; K56FLEX; MODEM; X2.

channel definition format See CDF.

CHAP Short for *C(hallenge) H(andshake) A(uthentication) P(rotocol)*, a type of authentication in which the authentication agent (typically a network server) sends the client program a key to be used to encrypt the username and password. This enables the username and password to be transmitted in an encrypted form to protect them against eavesdroppers. Contrast with *PAP*.

⇒ See also AUTHENTICATION; CHALLENGE-RESPONSE; PAP.

character In computer software, any symbol that requires one byte of storage. This includes all the ASCII and extended ASCII characters, including the space character. In character-based software, everything that appears on the screen, including graphics symbols, is considered to be a character. In graphics-based applications, the term *character* is generally reserved for letters, numbers, and punctuation.

⇒ See also ALPHANUMERIC; ASCII; CHARACTER BASED; CPI; EXTENDED ASCII; GRAPHICS BASED.

character based Describes programs capable of displaying only ASCII (and extended ASCII) characters. Character-based programs treat a display screen as an array of boxes, each of which can hold one character. When in text mode, for example, PC screens are typically divided into 25 rows and 80 columns. In contrast, *graphics-based* programs treat the display screen as an array of millions of pixels. Characters and other objects are formed by illuminating patterns of pixels.

Because the IBM *extended ASCII* character set includes shapes for drawing pictures, character-based programs are capable of simulating some graphics objects. For example, character-based programs can display windows and menus, bar charts, and other shapes that consist primarily of straight lines. However, they cannot represent more complicated objects that contain curves.

Unlike PCs, the Macintosh computer is a graphics-based machine. All programs that run on a Macintosh computer are graphics based.

⇒ See also CHARACTER MODE; EXTENDED ASCII; GRAPHICAL USER INTERFACE; GRAPHICS BASED; TEXT MODE.

character mode Many video adapters support several different modes of resolution. All such modes are divided into two general categories: *character mode* (also called *text mode*) and *graphics mode*. In character mode, the display screen is treated as an array of blocks, each of which can hold one ASCII character. In graphics mode, the display screen is treated as an array of pixels, with characters and other shapes formed by turning on combinations of pixels.

Of the two modes, character mode is much simpler. Programs that run in character mode generally run much faster than those that run in graphics mode, but they are limited in the variety of fonts and shapes they can display. Programs that run entirely in character mode are called *character-based* programs.

⇒ See also ASCII; BLOCK GRAPHICS; CHARACTER BASED; PIXEL; VIDEO ADAPTER.

character recognition See OPTICAL CHARACTER RECOGNITION.

character set A defined list of characters recognized by the computer hardware and software. Each character is represented by a number. The ASCII character set, for example, uses the numbers 0 through 127 to represent all English characters as well as special control characters. European ISO character sets are similar to ASCII, but they contain additional characters for European languages.

⇒ See also ASCII; CHARACTER; CONTROL CHARACTER; UNICODE.

characters per inch See CPI.

characters per second See CPS.

character string A series of characters manipulated as a group. A character string differs from a name in that it does not represent anything—a name stands for some other object.

A character string is often specified by enclosing the characters in single or double quotes. For example, WASHINGTON would be a name, but 'WASHINGTON' and "WASHINGTON" would be character strings.

The length of a character string is usually the number of characters in it. For example, the character string 'WASHINGTON' has a length of 10 (the quote marks are not included). Some programs, however, mark the beginning or end of a character string with an invisible character, so the length might actually be one greater than the number of visible characters.

⇒ See also DATA TYPE; NAME.

charge-coupled device See under CCD.

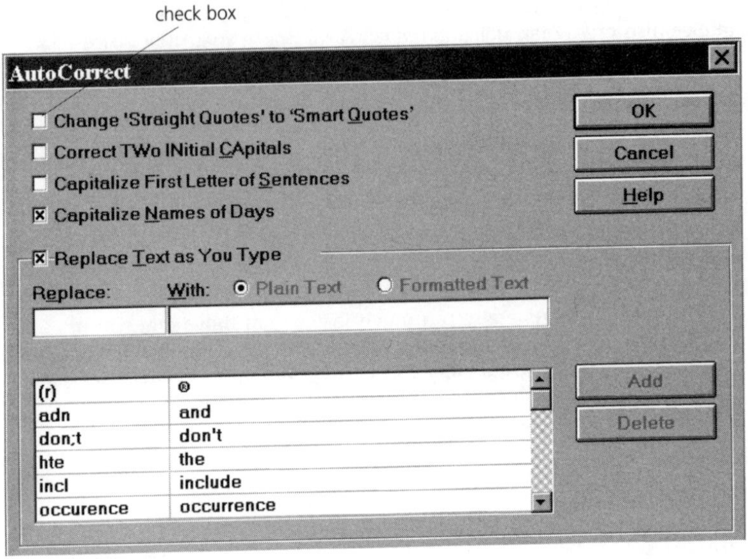

check box

Figure 12: **check box**

chassis Also called *case,* a metal frame that serves as the structural support for electronic components. Every computer system requires at least one chassis to house the circuit boards and wiring. The chassis also contains slots for expansion boards. If you want to insert more boards than there are slots, you will need an *expansion chassis,* which provides additional slots.

There are two basic flavors of chassis designs—*desktop models* and *tower models*—but there are many variations on these two basic types.

⇒ See also DESKTOP MODEL COMPUTER; EXPANSION BOARD; PRINTED CIRCUIT BOARD; SLOT; TOWER MODEL.

chat Real-time communication between two users via computer. Once a chat has been initiated, either user can enter text by typing on the keyboard, and the entered text will appear on the other user's monitor. Most networks and online services offer a chat feature.

⇒ See also AVATAR; CHAT ROOM; E-MAIL; INSTANT MESSAGING; IRC; NETMEETING; ONLINE SERVICE.

chat room A virtual room where a chat session takes place. Technically, a chat room is really a channel, but the term *room* is used to promote the chat metaphor.

⇒ See also ACRONYM; CHAT; IRC; LURK; MUD.

check box In graphical user interfaces, a box that you can click to turn an option on or off. When the option is on, an *x* appears in the box.

⇒ See also BOX; DIALOG BOX; GRAPHICAL USER INTERFACE; OPTION.

checksum A simple error-detection scheme in which each transmitted message is accompanied by a numerical value based on the number of set bits in the message. The receiving station then applies the same formula to the message and checks to make sure the accompanying numerical value is the same. If it is not, the receiver can assume that the message has been garbled.

⇒ See also COMMUNICATIONS; CRC; ECC MEMORY; ERROR DETECTION.

Chicago See under WINDOWS 95.

chip A small piece of semiconducting material (usually silicon) on which an integrated circuit is embedded. A typical chip is less than ¼ square inches and can contain millions of electronic components (transistors). Computers consist of many chips placed on electronic boards called *printed circuit boards.*

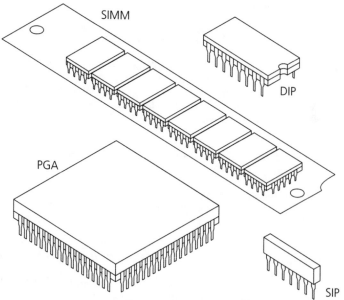

SIMM

DIP

PGA

SIP

Figure 13: **chips**

There are different types of chips. For example, CPU chips (also called *microprocessors*) contain an entire processing unit, whereas memory chips contain blank memory.

Chips come in a variety of packages. The three most common are:

DIPs: Dual in-line packages are the traditional buglike chips that have anywhere from 8 to 40 legs, evenly divided into two rows.

PGAs: Pin-grid arrays are square chips in which the pins are arranged in concentric squares.

SIPs: Single in-line packages are chips that have just one row of legs in a straight line like a comb.

In addition to these types of chips, there are also single in-line memory modules (SIMMs), which consist of up to nine chips packaged as a single unit.

⇒ See also ASIC; CHIPSET; CONTROLLER; CPU; INTEGRATED CIRCUIT; MICROPROCESSOR; MOORE'S LAW; PGA; PINOUT; PLD; PRINTED CIRCUIT BOARD; SEMICONDUCTOR; SIMM; TRANSISTOR.

chipset A number of integrated circuits designed to perform one or more related functions. For example, one chipset may provide the basic functions of a modem while another provides the CPU functions for a computer. Newer chipsets generally include functions provided by two or more older chipsets. In some cases, older chipsets that required two or more physical chips can be replaced with a chipset on one chip.

The term is often used to refer to the core functionality of a motherboard.

⇒ See also CHIP; CONTROLLER; MICROPROCESSOR; TRITON.

choose To pick a command or option. To choose a menu command or command button in a graphical user interface, you click on it. The terms *choose* and *select* are often used interchangeably, but some program developers make a distinction between choosing, which actually activates a command, and selecting, which merely highlights a command or other object.

⇒ See also CLICK; COMMAND; COMMAND KEY; GRAPHICAL USER INTERFACE; MENU; OPTION; SELECT.

Chooser A Macintosh desk accessory (DA) that enables you to select and configure printers and network devices, such as file servers.

⇒ See also DESK ACCESSORY (DA).

CHRP Pronounced *chirp*, and short for *C(ommon) H(ardware) R(eference) P(latform)*; a specification for PowerPC-based machines that can run the Mac OS, Windows NT, or AIX. First released in 1996, CHRP was supposed to make it possible for computer vendors to build Macintosh clones as well as PowerPC-based NT computers. However, Apple's purchase of the Next operating system has placed the future of CHRP in doubt.

CHRP is also called the *PowerPC Platform (PPCP)*.

⇒ See also MAC OS; MACINTOSH COMPUTER; POWERPC; PPCP.

CICS Short for *C(ustomer) I(nformation) C(ontrol) S(ystem)*, a TP monitor from IBM that was originally developed to provide transaction processing for IBM mainframes. It controls the interaction between applications and users and lets programmers develop screen displays without detailed knowledge of the terminals being used.

CICS is also available on nonmainframe platforms including the RS/6000, AS/400 and OS/2-based PCs.

⇒ See also COBOL; TP MONITOR; TRANSACTION PROCESSING.

CIDR Short for *C(lassless) I(nter)-D(omain) R(outing)*; a new IP addressing scheme that replaces the older system based on classes A, B, and C. With CIDR, a single IP address can be used to designate many unique IP addresses. A CIDR IP address looks like a normal IP address except that it ends with a slash followed by a number, called the *IP prefix*. For example:

172.200.0.0/16

The IP prefix specifies how many addresses are covered by the CIDR address, with lower numbers covering more addresses. An IP prefix of */12*, for example, can be used to address 4,096 former Class C addresses.

CIDR addresses reduce the size of routing tables and make more IP addresses available within organizations.

⇒ See also IP ADDRESS; ROUTING.

CIE color model A color model based on human perception developed by the CIE (Commission Internationale de l'Eclairage) committee. While widely regarded as the most accurate color model, CIE is unsuitable for many technologies, including color printing and color monitors. Consequently, these systems need to use other color models, such as CMYK and RGB. There is a growing trend, however, to make all color models relative to the CIE model. This would make it easier to translate from one model to another.

⇒ See also CMYK; COLOR MATCHING; RGB MONITOR.

CIF 1. Short for *Cells in Frames*. 2. Short for *Common Intermediate Format*.

Cinepak A popular codec (compression/decompression technology) for computer video developed by SuperMac Inc.

⇒ See also CODEC; INDEO.

cipher text Data that has been encrypted. Cipher text is unreadable until it has been converted into plain text (*decrypted*) with a key.

⇒ See also ENCRYPTION; PLAIN TEXT.

CIR Short for *c(ommitted) i(nformation) r(ate)*, a specified amount of guaranteed bandwidth (measured in bits per second) on a Frame Relay service. Typically, when purchasing a Frame Relay service, a company can specify the CIR level it wishes. The Frame Relay network vendor guarantees that frames not exceeding this level will be delivered. It's possible that additional traffic may also be delivered, but it's not guaranteed.

Some Frame Relay vendors offer inexpensive services with a CIR equal to zero. This essentially means that the network will deliver as many frames as it can, but it doesn't *guarantee* any bandwidth level.

⇒ See also BANDWIDTH; FRAME RELAY; QoS.

circuit board Short for *printed circuit board*.

circuit switching A type of communications in which a dedicated channel (or *circuit*) is established for the duration of a transmission. The best example of a circuit-switching network is the telephone system, which links together wire segments to create a single unbroken line for each telephone call.

The other common communications method is packet switching, which divides messages into packets and sends each packet individually. The packets may take different routes and may arrive out of order. The Internet is based on a packet-switching protocol, TCP/IP.

Circuit-switching systems are ideal for communications that require data to be transmitted in real time. Packet-switching networks are more efficient if some amount of delay is acceptable.

Circuit-switching networks are sometimes called *connection-oriented* networks. Note, however, that although packet switching is essentially connectionless, a packet-switching network can be made connection-oriented by the use of a higher-level protocol. TCP, for example, makes IP networks connection-oriented.

⇒ See also PACKET SWITCHING; PSTN.

CIS Short for *C(ompuServe) I(nformation) S(ervice)*. See under COMPUSERVE.

CISC Pronounced *sisk*, this acronym stands for *c(omplex) i(nstruction) s(et) c(omputer)*. Most personal computers use a CISC architecture, in which the CPU supports as many as 200 instructions. An alternative architecture, used by many workstations and also some personal computers, is *RISC r(educed) i(nstruction) s(et) c(omputer)*, which supports fewer instructions.

⇒ See also ARCHITECTURE; CPU; MACHINE LANGUAGE; RISC.

Cisco Systems One of the leading manufacturers of network equipment.

Cisco's primary business is in internetworking products, such as routers, bridges, and switches.

⇒ See also 3COM; BRIDGE; INTERNETWORKING; LAYER TWO FORWARDING; ROUTER; SWITCH; VLAN.

class In object-oriented programming, a category of objects. For example, there might be a class called "shape" containing objects that are circles, rectangles, and triangles. The class defines all the common properties of the different objects that belong to it.

⇒ See also AFC; IFC; MFC; OBJECT-ORIENTED PROGRAMMING; OVERLOADING; POLYMORPHISM.

Classless Inter-Domain Routing See CIDR.

clean boot Starting (booting) a computer as minimalistically as possible. Typically when you start your computer, it loads many files and programs to customize your environment. A clean boot eliminates these optional features and loads only those files and programs that are absolutely required by the operating system.

A clean boot is a troubleshooting technique that allows you to get the computer up and running so that you can perform diagnostic tests to determine which elements of the normal boot process are causing problems.

⇒ See also BOOT; OPERATING SYSTEM.

clear To erase. *Clear the screen*, for example, means to erase everything on the display screen. *Clear a variable* means to remove whatever data is currently stored in the variable. *Clear memory* means to erase all data currently stored in memory.

⇒ See also DISPLAY SCREEN; MEMORY; VARIABLE.

click *v* **1.** To tap on a mouse button, pressing it down and then immediately releasing it. Note that *clicking* a mouse button is different from *pressing* (or *dragging*) a mouse button, which implies that you hold the button down without releasing it. The phrase *to click on* means to select (a screen object) by moving the mouse pointer to the object's position and clicking a mouse button.

Some operations require a double click, meaning that you must click a mouse button twice in rapid succession. *Shift clicking* refers to clicking the mouse button while holding the Shift key down. —*n* **2.** The pressing down and rapid release of a mouse button. **3.** In the World Wide Web advertising industry, selection of a banner ad by a user. The effectiveness of Web advertisements are measured by their *click-through rate*—how often people who see the ad click on it.

⇒ See also CHOOSE; DOUBLE CLICK; DRAG; GRAPHICAL USER INTERFACE; MOUSE; SHIFT CLICKING.

client The client part of a *client-server architecture*. Typically, a client is an application that runs on a personal computer or workstation and relies on a server to perform some operations. For example, an *e-mail client* is an application that enables you to send and receive e-mail.

⇒ See also CLIENT-SIDE; CLIENT/SERVER ARCHITECTURE; E-MAIL CLIENT; SERVER; THIN CLIENT.

client/server architecture A network architecture in which each computer or process on the network is either a *client* or a *server*. Servers are powerful computers or processes dedicated to managing disk drives (*file servers*), printers (*print servers*), or network traffic (*network servers*). Clients are PCs or workstations on which users run applications. Clients rely on servers for resources, such as files, devices, and even processing power.
Another type of network architecture is known as a *peer-to-peer* architecture because each *node* has equivalent responsibilities. Both client/server and *peer-to-peer architectures* are widely used, and each has unique advantages and disadvantages.
Client-server architectures are sometimes called *two-tier architectures*.

⇒ See also ARCHITECTURE; CLIENT; CLIENT-SIDE; LOCAL-AREA NETWORK; NETWORK; NODE; PEER-TO-PEER ARCHITECTURE; PROCESS; SERVER; SERVER-SIDE; SYBASE; THIN CLIENT; THREE-TIER; TWO-TIER.

client-side Occurring on the client side of a client-server system. For example, on the World Wide Web, JavaScript scripts are client-side because they are executed by your browser (the client). In contrast, CGI scripts are server-side because they run on the Web server. Java applets can be either server-side or client-side depending on which computer (the server or the client) executes them.

⇒ See also CLIENT; CLIENT/SERVER ARCHITECTURE; SERVER-SIDE.

clip In computer graphics, to cut off a portion of a graphic at a defined boundary. Most bit-mapped graphics utilities provide a clip feature that enables you to draw a window around an object and clip everything outside of the window.

⇒ See also CROP; GRAPHICS; WINDOW.

clip art Electronic illustrations that can be inserted into a document. Many clip-art packages are available, some general and others specialized for a particular field. Most clip-art packages provide the illustrations in several file formats so that you can insert them into various word processing systems.

⇒ See also DESKTOP PUBLISHING.

clipboard A special file or memory area (*buffer*) where data is stored temporarily before being copied to another location. Many word processors, for example, use a clipboard for cutting and pasting. When you cut a block of text, the word processor copies the block to the clipboard; when you paste the block, the word processor copies it from the clipboard to its final destination. In Microsoft Windows and the Apple Macintosh operating system, the *Clipboard* (with a capital C) can be used to copy data from one application to another.

The Macintosh uses two types of clipboards. The one it calls the *Clipboard* can hold only one item at a time and is flushed when you turn the computer off. The other, called the *Scrapbook*, can hold several items at once and retains its contents from one working session to another.

⇒ See also COPY; CUT; PASTE.

Figure 14: **clip art**

Clipper chip An encryption chip designed under the auspices of the U.S. government. The government's idea was to enforce use of this chip in all devices that might use encryption, including computers, modems, telephones, and televisions. The government would control the encryption algorithm, thereby giving it the ability to decrypt any messages it recovered.

The purported goal of this plan was to enable the U.S. government to carry out surveillance on enemies of the state even if they used encryption to protect their messages. However, the Clipper chip created a fierce backlash from both public-interest organizations and the computer industry in general. The government eventually retracted its original plan but has since promoted two other plans called Clipper 2 and Clipper 3, respectively.

The Clipper 3 plan allows the use of any encryption technology but stipulates that government law-enforcement agencies be able to recover any keys exported out of the country.

⇒ See also CRYPTOGRAPHY; ELECTRONIC FRONTIER FOUNDATION; ENCRYPTION; SECURITY.

clock rate Same as CLOCK SPEED.

clock speed Also called *clock rate*, the speed at which a microprocessor executes instructions. Every computer contains an internal clock that regulates the rate at which instructions are executed and synchronizes all the various computer components. The CPU requires a fixed number of clock ticks (or *clock cycles*) to execute each instruction. The faster the clock, the more instructions the CPU can execute per second.

Clock speeds are expressed in megahertz (MHz), 1 MHz being equal to 1 million cycles per second. The CPUs of personal computers have clock speeds of anywhere from 33 MHz to more than 300 MHz.

The internal architecture of a CPU has as much to do with a CPU's performance as the clock speed, so two CPUs with the same clock speed will not necessarily perform equally. Whereas an Intel 80286 microprocessor requires 20 cycles to multiply two numbers, an Intel 80486 or later processor can perform the same calculation in a single clock tick. (Note that *clock tick* here refers to the system's clock, which runs at 66 MHz for all PCs.) These newer processors, therefore, would be 20 times faster than the older processors even if their clock speeds were the same. In addition, some microprocessors are *superscalar*, which means that they can execute more than one instruction per clock cycle.

Like CPUs, expansion buses also have clock speeds. Ideally, the CPU clock speed and the bus clock speed should be the same so that neither component slows down the other. In practice, the bus clock speed is often slower than the CPU clock speed, which creates a bottleneck. This is why new local buses, such as AGP, have been developed.

⇒ See also BUS; CPU; INSTRUCTION; MICROPROCESSOR; OVERCLOCK; SUPERSCALAR; WAIT STATE.

clone A computer, software product, or device that functions exactly like another, better-known product. In practice, the term refers to any PC not produced by one of the leading name-brand manufacturers, such as IBM and Compaq.

⇒ See also COMPATIBLE; IBM PC; PC.

close **1.** To finish work on a data file and save it. **2.** In graphical user interfaces, to close a window means to exit an application or file, thereby removing the window from the screen.

⇒ See also GRAPHICAL USER INTERFACE; OPEN; SAVE; WINDOW.

cluster A group of disk sectors. The operating system assigns a unique number to each cluster and then keeps track of files according to which clusters they use. Occasionally, the operating system marks a cluster as being used even though it is not assigned to any file. This is called a *lost cluster*. You can free up disk space by reassigning lost clusters, but you should first make sure that the clusters do not, in fact, contain valuable data. In DOS and Windows, you can find lost clusters with the ScanDisk utility.

DOS and Windows keep track of clusters with the file allocation table (FAT). The size of each cluster depends on the disk's partition size.

⇒ See also FILE ALLOCATION TABLE; FRAGMENTATION; PARTITION; ScanDisk; SECTOR; SLACK SPACE.

clustering Connecting two or more computers together in such a way that they behave like a single computer. Clustering is used for parallel processing, for load balancing, and for fault tolerance.

Clustering is a popular strategy for implementing parallel processing applications because it enables companies to leverage the investment already made in PCs and workstations. In addition, it's relatively easy to add new CPUs simply by adding a new PC to the network.

Microsoft's clustering solution for Windows NT systems is called *MSCS*.

⇒ See also FAULT TOLERANCE; LOAD BALANCING; MSCS; PARALLEL PROCESSING; WOLFPACK.

CLUT See under PALETTE.

CLV Short for *C(onstant) L(inear) V(elocity)*, a method used by most older CD-ROM players to access data. With CLV, the rotation speed of the disk changes based on how close to the center of the disk the data is. For tracks near the center, the disk rotates faster, and for data on the outside, the disk rotates slower.

The purpose of CLV is to ensure a constant data rate regardless of where on the disk the data is being accessed. Because less data can fit on the inside tracks, the disk needs to rotate faster for these areas.

An alternative technology, which is becoming increasingly popular, is *CAV (Constant Angular Velocity)*.

⇒ See also CAV; CD-ROM; CD-ROM PLAYER.

CMIP Short for *C(ommon) M(anagement) I(nformation) P(rotocol)*, and pronounced *see-mip*, an OSI standard protocol used with the *Common Management Information Services (CMIS)*. CMIS defines a system of network management information services. CMIP was proposed as a replacement for the less sophisticated Simple Network Management Protocol (SNMP) but has not been widely adopted. CMIP provides improved security and better reporting of unusual network conditions.

⇒ See also ISO; NETWORK MANAGEMENT.

CMOS Abbreviation of *c(omplementary) m(etal) o(xide) s(emiconductor)*. Pronounced **see**-*moss*, CMOS is a widely used type of semiconductor. CMOS semiconductors use both NMOS (negative polarity) and PMOS (positive polarity) circuits. Because only one of the circuit types is on at any given time, CMOS chips require less power than chips using just one type of transistor. This makes them particularly attractive for use in battery-powered devices, such as portable computers. Personal computers also contain a small amount of battery-powered CMOS memory to hold the date, time, and system setup parameters.

⇒ See also BIOS; SEMICONDUCTOR.

CMS See COLOR MANAGEMENT SYSTEM.

CMYK Short for *C(yan)-M(agenta)-Y(ellow)-B(lack)*, and pronounced as separate letters. CMYK is a color model in which all colors are described as a mixture of these four *process colors*. CMYK is the standard color model used in offset printing for full-color documents. Because such printing uses inks of these four basic colors, it is often called *four-color* printing.

In contrast, display devices generally use a different color model called *RGB*, which stands for *R(ed)-G(reen)-B(lue)*. One of the most difficult aspects of desktop publishing in color is color matching—properly converting the RGB colors into CMYK colors so that what gets printed looks the same as what appears on the monitor.

⇒ See also COLOR MATCHING; COLOR SEPARATION; DESKTOP PUBLISHING; INTEL MICROPROCESSORS; OFFSET PRINTING; RGB MONITOR; SPOT COLOR; WYSIWYP.

coaxial cable A type of wire that consists of a center wire surrounded by insulation and then a grounded shield of braided wire. The shield minimizes electrical and radio frequency interference.

Coaxial cabling is the primary type of cabling used by the cable television industry and is also widely used for computer networks. Although more expensive than standard telephone wire, it is much less susceptible to interference and can carry much more data. Because the cable television industry has already connected millions of homes with coaxial cable, many analysts believe that they are the best positioned to capitalize on the much-heralded information superhighway.

⇒ See also 10BASE-2; 10BASE5; AUI; BNC CONNECTOR; INFORMATION SUPER-HIGHWAY; NETWORK; UTP.

COBOL Acronym for *co(mmon) b(usiness) o(riented) l(anguage)*. Developed in the late 1950s and early 1960s, COBOL is the second-oldest high-level programming language (FORTRAN is the oldest). It is particularly popular for business applications that run on large computers.

COBOL is a wordy language; programs written in COBOL tend to be much longer than the same programs written in other languages. This can be annoying when you program in COBOL, but the wordiness makes it easy to understand programs because everything is spelled out. Although disparaged by many programmers for being outdated, COBOL is still the most widely used programming language in the world.

⇒ See also CICS; CODASYL; HIGH-LEVEL LANGUAGE; PROGRAMMING LANGUAGE.

CODASYL Short for *Co(nference) on Da(ta) Sy(stems) L(anguages)*, and pronounced *code-a-sill*. An organization founded in 1957 by the U.S. Department of Defense. Its mission was to develop computer programming languages.

CODASYL was responsible for developing COBOL. The organization is no longer extant, but the term CODASYL is still used sometimes to refer to COBOL.

⇒ See also COBOL.

code *n* **1.** A set of symbols for representing something. For example, most computers use ASCII codes to represent characters. **2.** Written computer instructions. The term *code* is somewhat colloquial. For example, a programmer might say: "I wrote a lot of code this morning" or "There's one piece of code that doesn't work."
  Code can appear in a variety of forms. The code that a programmer writes is called *source code*. After it has been compiled, it is called *object code*. Code that is ready to run is called *executable code* or *machine code*. —*v* **3.** Colloquial for *to program* (that is, *to write source code*).

⇒ See also ASCII; COMPILE; EXECUTABLE FILE; MACHINE LANGUAGE; OBJECT CODE; PROGRAM; PSEUDOCODE; SOURCE CODE.

codec **1.** Short for *co(mpressor)/dec(ompressor)*, a codec is any technology for compressing and decompressing data. Codecs can be implemented in software, hardware, or a combination of both. Some popular codecs for computer video include MPEG, Indeo, and Cinepak. **2.** In telecommunications, a device that encodes or decodes a signal. For example, telephone companies use codecs to convert binary signals transmitted on their digital networks to analog signals converted on their analog networks. **3.** The translation of a binary value into a voltage that can be transmitted over a wire.

⇒ See also CINEPAK; INDEO; MPEG; QUICKTIME; VIDEO FOR WINDOWS.

Code Division Multiple Access See CDMA.

coff Short for *C(ommon) O(bject) F(ile) F(ormat)*, a binary file format used in UNIX System V and Windows.

⇒ See also BINARY FILE; UNIX.

cold boot The start-up of a computer from a powered-down state.

⇒ See also BOOT.

collapse To compress a view of a hierarchy so that only the roots of each branch are visible. The opposite of collapse is *expand*, which makes the entire branch visible.

⇒ See also BRANCH; HIERARCHICAL; ROOT DIRECTORY.

color depth The number of distinct colors that can be represented by a piece of hardware or software. Color depth is sometimes referred to as *bit depth* because it is directly related to the number of bits used for each pixel. A 24-bit video adapter, for example, has a color depth of 2^{24} (about 16.7 million) colors. One would say that its color depth is 24 bits.

⇒ See also OPTICAL SCANNER; TRUE COLOR; VIDEO ADAPTER.

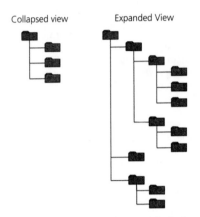

Collapsed view   Expanded View

Figure 15: **collapsed and expanded views**

color/graphics adapter See CGA.

Color Look-Up Table See under PALETTE.

color management system (CMS) A system for ensuring that colors remain the same regardless of the device or medium used to display the colors. This is extremely difficult because different devices use different technologies and models to produce colors. In addition, color is highly subjective; the same colors look different to different people.

⇒ See also CIE COLOR MODEL; CMYK; COLOR MATCHING; PANTONE MATCHING SYSTEM (PMS); PROCESS COLORS; RGB MONITOR; WYSIWYP.

color matching The process of ensuring that a color on one medium remains the same when converted to another medium. This is extremely difficult because different media use different color models. Color monitors, for example, use the RGB model, whereas process printing uses the CMYK model. As color desktop publishing matures, color matching is gaining more and more attention. The most recent Windows and Macintosh operating systems include a color management system (CMS) to assist in color matching.

⇒ See also CIE COLOR MODEL; CMYK; COLOR MANAGEMENT SYSTEM (CMS); RGB MONITOR.

color monitor A display monitor capable of displaying many colors. In contrast, a monochrome monitor can display only two colors—one for the background and one for the foreground. Color monitors implement the RGB color model by using three different phosphors that appear r(ed), g(reen), and b(lue) when activated. By placing the phosphors directly next to each other, and activating them with different intensities, color monitors can create an unlimited number of colors. In practice, however, the real number of colors that any monitor can display is controlled by the video adapter.

Color monitors based on CRT technology employ three different techniques to merge phosphor triplets into pixels:

Dot-trio shadow masks place a thin sheet of perforated metal in front of the screen. Since electrons can pass only through the holes in the sheet, each hole represents a single pixel.

Aperture-grille CRTs place a grid of wires between the screen and the electron guns.

Slot-mask CRTs uses a shadow mask but the holes are long and thin. It's sort of a cross between the dot-trio shadow mask and aperture-grill techniques.

⇒ See also CRT; DEGAUSS; DOT PITCH; LCD MONITOR; MASK PITCH; MONITOR; RGB MONITOR; VIDEO ADAPTER.

color printer A printer capable of printing more than one color. Most color printers are based on the CMYK color model, which prints in four basic colors: cyan, magenta, yellow, and black. By printing combinations of different colors close to each other (or, in the case of thermal dye transfer printers, on top of each other), the CMYK model can simulate most other colors (except for special colors such as fluorescent yellow). This is the same technique used in process color offset printing, which is the technology used to print most color books, magazines, and other paper materials. Some lower-price printers use only three colors—cyan, magenta, and yellow—but these printers cannot print true black and their colors tend to be a bit faded.

Color printers use a variety of techniques to lay down the different colors:

Thermal dye transfer printers, also called *dye sublimation printers,* heat ribbons containing dye and then diffuse the dyes onto specially coated paper or transparencies. These printers are the most expensive and slowest, but they produce continuous-tone images that mimic actual photographs. Note that you need special paper, which is quite expensive. A new breed of thermal dye transfer printers, called *snapshot printers,* produce small photographic snapshots and are much less expensive than their full-size cousins.

Thermal wax transfer printers use wax-based inks that are melted and then laid down on regular paper or transparencies. Unlike thermal dye transfer printers, these printers print images as dots, which means that images must be dithered first. As a result images are not quite photo-realistic, although they are very good. The big advantages of these printers over thermal dye transfer printers are that they don't require special paper and they are faster.

Solid ink-jet printers, also called *wax jet* or *phase change printers,* work by melting dyed wax and then spraying it on paper. This produces bright colors on virtually any type of paper. The downside to solid ink-jet printers is that they are slow and relatively expensive.

Color laser printers use the same principle as monochrome laser printers, but they include four toners rather than one. Although laser printers produce better quality output than ink-jet printers, they are also much more expensive.

Color ink-jet printers are the least expensive color printers. They contain three or four separate nozzles, each of which sprays a different color of ink.

Color printers are sometimes divided into the following categories:

Bi-level: Each of the ink colors is either on or off for each dot. Different colors are produced by dithering.

Continuous-tone: Each dot can contain a mixture of colors.

Contone: Provides more shades per dot than bi-level printers, but less than continuous-tone printers.

⇒ See also BANDING; BILEVEL PRINTER; CMYK; COLOR SEPARATION; CONTONE PRINTER; INK-JET PRINTER; LASER PRINTER; PRINTER; PROCESS COLORS; SNAPSHOT PRINTER.

color separation The act of decomposing a color graphic or photo into single-color layers. For example, to print full-color photos with an offset printing press, one must first separate the photo into the four basic ink colors: cyan, magenta, yellow, and black (CMYK). Each single-color layer is then printed separately, one on top of the other, to give the impression of infinite colors.

This type of color separation, mixing three or four colors to produce an infinite variety of colors, is called *process color separation.* Another type of color separation, called *spot color* separation, is used to separate colors that are not to be mixed. In this case, each spot color is represented by its own ink, which is specially mixed. Spot colors are effective for highlighting text, but they cannot be used to reproduce full-color images.

Traditionally, process color separation has been performed photographically with different-colored filters. However, many modern desktop publishing systems are now capable of producing color separations for graphics stored electronically. This capability is essential if you want to create full-color documents on your computer and then print them using an offset printer. You don't need to perform color separation if you are printing directly to a color printer because in this case the printer itself performs the color separation internally.

⇒ See also CMYK; COLOR MANAGEMENT SYSTEM (CMS); COLOR PRINTER; DESKTOP PUBLISHING; PROCESS COLORS.

Color Super Twisted Nematic See CSTN.

column 1. On a display screen in character mode, a column is a vertical line of characters extending from the top to the bottom of the screen. The size of a text display is usually measured in rows and columns. **2.** In spreadsheets, a column is a vertical row of cells. Spreadsheet columns are usually identified by letters. **3.** In database management systems, *column* is another name for *field*. **4.** In documents, a column is a vertical area reserved for text. Most newspapers, for example, contain four or more columns per page. Modern word processors and desktop publishing systems enable you to divide a page into columns automatically.

⇒ See also CELL; CHARACTER MODE; DATABASE MANAGEMENT SYSTEM; DESKTOP PUBLISHING; DISPLAY SCREEN; FIELD; SPREADSHEET; WORD PROCESSING.

column graph A type of presentation graphic in which numerical values are illustrated with horizontal columns. Column graphs are particularly effective for showing values that are categorized by two separate characteristics, such as year and sector.

⇒ See also PRESENTATION GRAPHICS.

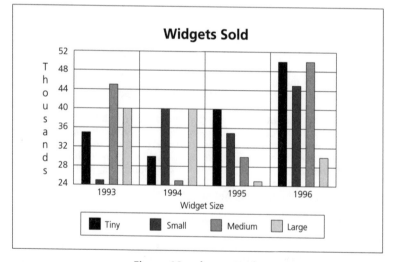

Figure 16: **column graph**

COM 1. In DOS systems, the name of a serial communications port. DOS supports four serial ports: *COM1, COM2, COM3,* and *COM4.* However, most software makes use of system interrupts to access the serial ports, and there are only two IRQ lines reserved. This means that the four COM ports share the same two IRQ lines. Typically, COM1 and COM3 use IRQ4, while COM2 and COM4 use IRQ3. So in general, if you have two devices, one of which is attached to COM1 and the other to COM3, you cannot use them simultaneously. **2.** Abbreviation of *Component Object Model*.

⇒ See also AUX; COMMUNICATIONS; PORT; SERIAL; WINDOWS DNA.

COM file In DOS environments, a *COM file* is an executable command file with a .COM filename extension. COM files can be directly executed and are usually slightly smaller than equivalent EXE files. However, COM files cannot exceed 64K, so large programs are usually stored in *EXE files*.

⇒ See also COMMAND; DOS; EXE FILE; EXECUTABLE FILE; EXTENSION; FILE.

Comité Consultatif International Téléphonique et Télégraphique
See under CCITT.

comma-delimited A data format in which each piece of data is separated by a comma. This is a popular format for transferring data from one application to another, because most database systems are able to import and export comma-delimited data.

⇒ See also EXPORT; IMPORT.

command An instruction to a computer or device to perform a specific task. Commands come in different forms. They can be:

- special words (*keywords*) that a program understands
- function keys
- choices in a menu
- buttons or other graphical objects on your screen

Every program that interacts with people responds to a specific set of commands. The set of commands and the syntax for entering them is called the *user interface* and varies from one program to another.

The DOS operating system makes a distinction between *internal* and *external commands*. Internal commands are commands, such as COPY and DIR, that can be handled by the COMMAND.COM program. External commands include the names of all other COM files, as well as EXE and BAT files.

Another word for *command* is *directive*.

⇒ See also BAT FILE; COM FILE; COMMAND DRIVEN; COMMAND LANGUAGE; COMMAND LINE; DOS; EXE FILE; EXTERNAL COMMAND; FUNCTION KEYS; INSTRUCTION; INTERNAL COMMAND; KEYWORD; MENU; USER INTERFACE.

command buffer A temporary storage area where commands are kept. (In DOS environments, the command buffer is called a *template*.) DOS and UNIX support several operations for manipulating the command buffer. For example, you can use the F3 function key in DOS to copy the template's contents to the display screen. This is useful for repeating a command or for correcting a mistake.

⇒ See also BUFFER; COMMAND; UNDO.

COMMAND.COM The DOS file that contains the DOS *command processor*.

⇒ See also COMMAND PROCESSOR; INTERNAL COMMAND.

command driven Refers to programs and operating systems that accept commands in the form of special words or letters. In contrast, programs that allow you to choose from a list of options in a menu are said to be *menu driven*. Command-driven software is often more flexible than menu-driven software, but it is more difficult to learn.

⇒ See also COMMAND; MENU DRIVEN; USER INTERFACE.

Command key Macintosh computers have a special command key marked by a four-leaf clover or an apple. The Command key is similar to a PC's Alt key—you hold it down while pressing another key to execute some operation. Typically, command-key combinations are shortcuts for menu choices. For example, on the desktop, pressing the Command key and O is equivalent to selecting the *open* option from the *file* menu.
  The Command key is sometimes called the Apple key or *Open Apple*.

⇒ See also APPLE KEY; CONTROL KEY; KEYBOARD.

command language The programming language through which a user communicates with the operating system or an application. For example, the DOS command language includes the commands DIR, COPY, and DEL, to name a few. The part of an operating system that responds to operating system commands is called the *command processor*.
  With graphical user interfaces, the command language consists of operations you perform with a mouse or similar input device.

⇒ See also COMMAND; COMMAND PROCESSOR; GRAPHICAL USER INTERFACE; OPERATING SYSTEM; SHELL.

command line The line on the display screen where a command is expected. Generally, the command line is the line that contains the most recently displayed *command prompt*.

⇒ See also COMMAND; PROMPT.

command line interpreter Same as COMMAND PROCESSOR.

command processor The part of the operating system that receives and executes operating system commands. Every operating system has a command processor. When the command prompt is displayed, the command processor is waiting for a command. After you enter a command, the command processor analyzes the syntax to make sure the command is valid and then either executes the command or issues an error warning. For operating systems with a graphical user interface, the command processor interprets mouse operations and executes the appropriate command.

Another term for command processor is *command-line interpreter*.

⇒ See also COMMAND LANGUAGE; OPERATING SYSTEM.

Commodore Amiga See AMIGA.

common carrier Same as PUBLIC CARRIER.

Common Gateway Interface See CGI.

Common Hardware Reference Platform See CHRP.

Common Intermediate Format A video format used in videoconferencing systems that easily supports both NTSC and PAL signals. CIF is part of the ITU H.261 videoconferencing standard. It specifies a data rate of 30 frames per second (fps), with each frame containing 288 lines and 352 pixels per line.

A related standard, *QCIF (Quarter CIF)*, transfers one-fourth the amount of data and is suitable for videoconferencing systems that use telephone lines.

CIF is sometimes called *Full CIF (FCIF)* to distinguish it from QCIF.

⇒ See also NTSC; PAL; QCIF; VIDEOCONFERENCING.

Common Management Information Protocol See CMIP.

Common Object Request Broker Architecture See CORBA.

Common User Access See CUA.

communications The transmission of data from one computer to another, or from one device to another. A *communications device*, therefore, is any machine that assists data transmission. For example, modems, cables, and ports are all communications devices. *Communications software* refers to programs that make it possible to transmit data.

⇒ See also BASEBAND TRANSMISSION; COMMUNICATIONS PROTOCOL; COMMUNICATIONS SOFTWARE; FLOW CONTROL; MODEM; NETWORK; PORT.

communications protocol All communications between devices require that the devices agree on the format of the data. The set of rules defining a format is called a *protocol*. At the very least, a communications protocol must define the following:

- rate of transmission (in baud or bps)
- whether transmission is to be *synchronous* or *asynchronous*
- whether data is to be transmitted in *half-duplex* or *full-duplex* mode

In addition, protocols can include sophisticated techniques for detecting and recovering from transmission errors and for encoding and decoding data.

The accompanying table lists the most commonly used protocols for communications via modems. These protocols are almost always implemented in the hardware—that is, they are built into modems.

In addition to the standard protocols listed in the table, there are a number of protocols that complement these standards by supplying additional functions such as file transfer capability, error detection and recovery, and data compression. The best-known are *Xmodem*, *Kermit*, *MNP*, and *CCITT V.42*. These protocols can be implemented either in hardware or software.

⇒ See also ASYNCHRONOUS; BELL 103; BELL 212A; BPS; CCITT; COMMUNICATIONS; FULL DUPLEX; HALF DUPLEX; HDLC; IPX; PROTOCOL.

Table 10
Communications Protocols

Protocol	Maximum Transmission Rate	Duplex Mode
Bell 103	300 bps	Full
CCITT V.21	300 bps	Full
Bell 212A	1,200 bps	Full
ITU V.22	1,200 bps	Half
ITU V.22bis	2,400 bps	Full
ITU V.29	9,600 bps	Half
ITU V.32	9,600 bps	Full
ITU V.32bis	14,400 bps	Full
ITU V.34	36,600 bps	Full
ITU V.90	56,000 bps	Full

communications software Software that makes it possible to send and receive data over telephone lines through modems.

⇒ See also AUTO-ANSWER; BATCH FILE; BULLETIN BOARD SYSTEM; COMMUNICATIONS; COMMUNICATIONS PROTOCOL; EDITOR; EMULATION; KERMIT; LOG ON; MACRO; MAINFRAME; MODEM; MULTITASKING; QUEUE; SCRIPT.

compact disc Known by its abbreviation, *CD*, a compact disc is a polycarbonate platter with one or more metal layers capable of storing digital information. The most prevalent types of compact discs are those used by the music industry to store digital recordings and CD-ROMs used to store computer data. Both of these types of compact disc are *read-only*, which means that once the data has been recorded onto them, they can be only read, or played.

Another type of compact disc, called *CD-Rs* and *CD-RWs*, can have their data erased and overwritten by new data. Currently, erasable optical storage is too slow to be used as a computer's main storage facility, but as the speed improves and the cost comes down, optical storage devices are becoming a popular alternative to tape systems as a backup method.

⇒ See also CD-ROM; DVD; ERASABLE OPTICAL DISK; MASS STORAGE; MULTI-READ; OPTICAL DISK; RED BOOK; WORM.

Compaq One of the leading PC manufacturers. Based in Houston, Texas, Compaq Computer Corporation was founded in 1982 by Rod Canion, Bill Murto, and Jim Harris. Its first product, released in 1983, was a portable computer. The following year it released a desktop PC.

Over the years, Compaq has built a reputation as a manufacturer of high-quality PCs. In 1991, it shook the PC world by dropping its prices dramatically, a move that made it the world's number one PC manufacturer.

Traditionally, Compaq machines have been available only through resellers. But in 1997, Compaq launched an aggressive strategy to manufacture "built-to-order" computers. The program allows corporations to specify the configurations they want and to purchase machines directly from Compaq. This puts Compaq in direct competition with mail-order vendors such as Gateway 2000 and Dell Computer.

In 1998, Compaq made an aggressive move into the high-end workstation market by acquiring Digital Equipment Corporation (DEC) for a reported $9.6 billion.

⇒ See also DEC; DELL COMPUTER; IBM; PC.

comparison operator Same as RELATIONAL OPERATOR.

compatible *n* **1.** Indicates that a product can work with or is equivalent to another, better-known product. The term is often used as a shorthand for *IBM-compatible PC*, a computer that is compatible with an IBM PC. Another term for a compatible is *clone.* —*adj* **2.** The ability of one device or program to work with another device or program. The term *compatible* implies different degrees of partnership. For example, a printer and a computer are said to be compatible if they can be connected to each other. An *IBM-compatible PC*, on the other hand, is a computer that can run the same software as an IBM PC.

Compatibility of two devices, such as printers, usually means that they react to software commands in the same way. Some printers achieve compatibility by tricking the software into believing that the printer is a different machine. This is called *emulation.*

Be aware, however, that hardware compatibility does not always extend to expansion slots. For example, two compatible printers may not accept the same font cartridges. Complete hardware compatibility is denoted by the term *plug compatible*.

Software products are compatible if they use the same data formats. For example, many programs are compatible with dBASE. This means that the files they produce can easily be transformed into a dBASE database or that they can *import* dBASE files.

⇒ See also BACKWARD COMPATIBLE; BINARY COMPATIBLE; CLONE; COMPATIBLE; dBASE; EMULATION; FONT CARTRIDGE; IBM PC; PC; PLUG COMPATIBLE; STANDARD; UPWARD COMPATIBLE.

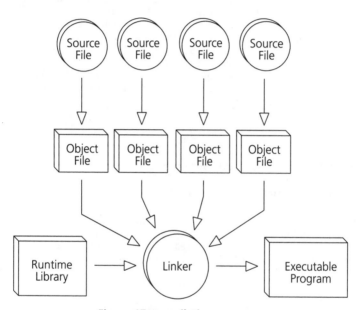

Figure 17: **compilation process**

compile To transform a program written in a high-level programming language from *source code* into *object code*. Programmers write programs in a form called source code. Source code must go through several steps before it becomes an executable program. The first step is to pass the source code through a *compiler*, which translates the high-level language instructions into object code.

The final step in producing an executable program—after the compiler has produced object code—is to pass the object code through a *linker*. The linker combines modules and gives real values to all symbolic addresses, thereby producing machine code.

⇒ See also ASSEMBLY LANGUAGE; BIND; BYTECODE; COMPILER; HIGH-LEVEL LANGUAGE; INTERPRETER; LINK; OBJECT CODE; PARSE; PROGRAMMING LANGUAGE; RUNTIME; SOURCE CODE.

compiler A program that translates *source code* into *object code*. The compiler derives its name from the way it works, looking at the entire piece of source code and collecting and reorganizing the instructions. Thus, a compiler differs from an *interpreter*, which analyzes and executes each line of source code in succession, without looking at the entire program. The advantage of interpreters is that they can execute a program immediately. Compilers require some time before an executable program emerges. However, programs produced by compilers run much faster than the same programs executed by an interpreter.

Every high-level programming language (except strictly interpretive languages) comes with a compiler. In effect, the compiler is the language, because it defines which instructions are acceptable.

Because compilers translate source code into object code, which is unique for each type of computer, many compilers are available for the same language. For example, there is a FORTRAN compiler for PCs and another for Apple Macintosh computers. In addition, the compiler industry is quite competitive, so there are actually many compilers for each language on each type of computer. More than a dozen companies develop and sell C compilers for the PC.

⇒ See also ASSEMBLY LANGUAGE; COMPILE; INTERPRETER; JIT; LINK; OBJECT CODE; PARSE; PROGRAMMING LANGUAGE; SOURCE CODE.

complementary metal oxide semiconductor See CMOS.

complex instruction set computer See CISC.

component 1. A small binary object or program that performs a specific function and is designed in such a way as to operate easily with other components and applications. Increasingly, the term is being used interchangeably with *applet*. **2.** A part of a device.

⇒ See also APPLET; COMPONENT OBJECT MODEL; COMPONENT SOFTWARE; OCX; VBX.

Component Object Model A model for binary code developed by Microsoft. The Component Object Model (COM) enables programmers to develop objects that can be accessed by any COM-compliant application. Both OLE and ActiveX are based on COM.

⇒ See also ACTIVEX; COMPONENT; COMPONENT SOFTWARE; DCOM; OLE; OPEN-DOC; SOM.

component software Sometimes called *componentware*, software designed to work as a component of a larger application. A good analogy is the way personal computers are built up from a collection of standard components: memory chips, CPUs, buses, keyboards, mice, disk drives, monitors, and so on. Because all of the interfaces between components are standardized, it is possible to mix components from different manufacturers in a single system.

Similarly, the goal of component software is to standardize the interfaces between software components so that they too can work together seamlessly. Two new standards—OLE and OpenDoc—are designed to help programmers develop components that can work together. Many analysts believe that component software is the natural extension of object-oriented programming and that it will become the standard programming paradigm for years to come.

⇒ See also COMPONENT; COMPONENT OBJECT MODEL; OBJECT-ORIENTED PROGRAMMING; OLE; OPENDOC; PLUG-IN.

componentware See under COMPONENT SOFTWARE.

COM port See COM.

composite video A type of video signal in which all information—the red, blue, and green signals (and sometimes audio signals as well)—is mixed together. This is the type of signal used by televisions in the United States (see *NTSC*).

In contrast, most computers use *RGB video*, which consists of three separate signals for red, green, and blue. In general, RGB video produces sharper images than composite video does.

⇒ See also NTSC; RGB MONITOR; S-VIDEO.

compound document A document that contains elements from a variety of computer applications. For example, a single compound document might include text from a word processor, graphics from a draw program, and a chart from a spreadsheet application. Most important, each element in the compound document is stored in such a way that it can be manipulated by the application that created it.

Many computer experts believe that compound documents represent the most useful metaphor for utilizing computers because they allow people to mix different forms of expression rather than artificially separate them. With the emergence of OLE as an important standard, compound documents are likely to become more and more a part of everyday computing.

⇒ See also DOCUMENT; OLE; OPENDOC.

compression See DATA COMPRESSION.

CompuServe Information Service One of the first and largest online services, CompuServe supports a wide array of *forums* and provides many types of electronic-mail services. In addition, it is connected to hundreds of different database systems. In 1997, the content portion of CompuServe was acquired by America Online and the network service was acquired by WorldCom.

⇒ See also AMERICA ONLINE; MSN; ONLINE SERVICE.

computer A programmable machine. The two principal characteristics of a computer are:

- It responds to a specific set of instructions in a well-defined manner.
- It can execute a prerecorded list of instructions (a program).

Modern computers are electronic and digital. The actual machinery—wires, transistors, and circuits—is called *hardware*; the instructions and data are called *software*.

All general-purpose computers require the following hardware components:

memory: Enables a computer to store, at least temporarily, data and programs.

mass storage device: Allows a computer to permanently retain large amounts of data. Common mass storage devices include disk drives and tape drives.

input device: Usually a keyboard and mouse, the input device is the conduit through which data and instructions enter a computer.

output device: A display screen, printer, or other device that lets you see what the computer has accomplished.

central processing unit (CPU): The heart of the computer, this is the component that actually executes instructions.

In addition to these components, many others make it possible for the basic components to work together efficiently. For example, every computer requires a bus that transmits data from one part of the computer to another.

Computers can be generally classified by size and power as follows, though there is considerable overlap:

personal computer: A small, single-user computer based on a microprocessor. In addition to the microprocessor, a personal computer has a keyboard for entering data, a monitor for displaying information, and a storage device for saving data.

workstation: A powerful, single-user computer. A workstation is like a personal computer, but it has a more powerful microprocessor and a higher-quality monitor.

minicomputer: A multi-user computer capable of supporting from 10 to hundreds of users simultaneously.

mainframe: A powerful multi-user computer capable of supporting many hundreds or thousands of users simultaneously.

supercomputer: An extremely fast computer that can perform hundreds of millions of instructions per second.

⇒ See also CPU; HARDWARE; MAINFRAME; MICROPROCESSOR; MINICOMPUTER; PERSONAL COMPUTER; SOFTWARE; SUPERCOMPUTER; WORKSTATION.

computer-aided design See CAD.

computer-aided engineering See CAE.

computer-aided instruction Same as COMPUTER-BASED TRAINING. See under CBT.

computer-aided manufacturing See CAM.

Computer-Aided Software Engineering See CASE.

Computer-Aided Systems Engineering See CASE.

computer-based training See CBT.

Computer Graphics Metafile See CGM.

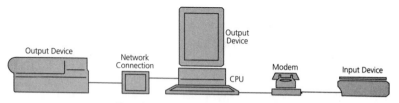

Figure 18: **computer peripherals**

computer imaging A field of computer science covering digital images—images that can be stored on a computer, particularly bit-mapped images. Computer imaging is a wide field that includes digital photography, scanning, and composition and manipulation of bit-mapped graphics.

Computer imaging is often called *digital imaging.*

⇒ See also BIT-MAPPED GRAPHICS; DIGITAL PHOTOGRAPHY; FlashPix; OPTICAL SCANNER.

computer literacy The level of expertise and familiarity someone has with computers. *Computer literacy* generally refers to the ability to use applications rather than to program. Individuals who are very computer literate are sometimes called *power users.*

⇒ See also POWER USER.

computer science The study of computers, including both hardware and software design. Computer science is composed of many broad disciplines, including artificial intelligence and software engineering. Most universities now offer bachelor's, master's, and doctorate degrees in computer science.

⇒ See also ARTIFICIAL INTELLIGENCE; IT; PROGRAM; SOFTWARE ENGINEERING.

computer system A complete, working computer. The computer system includes not only the computer but also any software and peripheral devices that are necessary to make the computer function. Every computer system, for example, requires an operating system.

⇒ See also COMPUTER; OPERATING SYSTEM.

computer-telephony-integration See CTI.

computer virus See VIRUS.

concatenate To link together or join. For example, concatenating the three words *in, as,* and *much* yields the single word *inasmuch.* Computer manuals often refer to the process of *concatenating strings,* a string being any series of characters. You can also concatenate files by appending one to another.

⇒ See also APPEND; CHARACTER STRING.

concatenation The act of linking together two or more objects.

⇒ See also CONCATENATE.

concentrator A type of multiplexor that combines multiple channels onto a single transmission medium in such a way that all the individual channels can be simultaneously active. For example, ISPs use concentrators to combine their dial-up modem connections onto faster T-1 lines that connect to the Internet.

Concentrators are also used in local-area networks (LANs) to combine transmissions from a cluster of nodes. In this case, the concentrator is often called a *hub* or *MAU.*

⇒ See also HUB; MULTIPLEXOR.

conditional Referring to an action that takes place only if a specific condition is met. Conditional expressions are one of the most important components of programming languages because they enable a program to act differently each time it is executed, depending on the input. Most programming languages use the word *if* for conditional expressions. For example, the conditional statement

if x equals 1 exit

directs the program to exit if the variable x is equal to 1.

⇒ See also EXPRESSION; PROGRAMMING LANGUAGE.

conference Same as *forum,* an area in a bulletin board or online service in which participants can meet to discuss a topic of common interest.

⇒ See also BULLETIN BOARD SYSTEM; FORUM; LURK; ONLINE SERVICE.

CONFIG.SYS The configuration file for DOS systems. Whenever a DOS computer boots up, it reads the CONFIG.SYS file (if it exists) and executes any commands in it. The most common commands are *BUFFERS =* and *FILES =* , which enable you to specify the buffer size and the number of files that can be open simultaneously. In addition, you can enter commands that install drivers for devices.

⇒ See also BOOT; CONFIGURATION; DRIVER; HIMEM.SYS.

configuration The way a system is set up, or the assortment of components that make up the system. Configuration can refer to either hardware or software, or the combination of both. For instance, a typical configuration for a PC consists of 32MB (megabytes) of main memory, a floppy drive, a hard disk, a modem, a CD-ROM drive, a VGA monitor, and the Windows operating system.

Many software products require that the computer have a certain *minimum configuration.* For example, the software might require a graphics display monitor and a video adapter, a particular microprocessor, and a minimum amount of main memory.

When you install a new device or program, you sometimes need to configure it, which means to set various switches and jumpers (for hardware) and to define values of parameters (for software). For example, the device or program may need to know what type of video adapter you have and what type of printer is connected to the computer. Thanks to new technologies, such as Plug-and-Play, much of this configuration is performed automatically.

⇒ See also CONFIG.SYS; CONFIGURATION FILE; CONTROL PANEL; DIP SWITCH; JUMPER; MIF; PARAMETER; REGISTRY.

configuration file A file that contains configuration information for a particular program. When the program is executed, it consults the configuration file to see what parameters are in effect. The configuration file for DOS is called CONFIG.SYS. Older versions of the Windows operating system stores configuration information in files with a .INI extension. The two most important configuration files are *WIN.INI* and *SYS.INI.* Starting with Windows 95, most configuration information is stored in MIF files and in the Registry.

⇒ See also .INI FILE; CONFIG.SYS; CONFIGURATION.

configure To set up a program or computer system for a particular application.

⇒ See also CONFIGURATION.

connectionless Refers to network protocols in which a host can send a message without establishing a connection with the recipient. That is, the host simply puts the message onto the network with the destination address and hopes that it arrives. Examples of connectionless protocols include Ethernet, IPX, and UDP.

In contrast, *connection-oriented* protocols require a channel to be established between the sender and receiver before any messages are transmitted. Examples of connection-oriented protocols include the telephone, TCP, and HTTP.

⇒ See also IPX; PROTOCOL; UDP.

connectivity A computer buzzword that refers to a program or device's ability to link with other programs and devices. For example, a program that can *import* data from a wide variety of other programs and can *export* data in many different formats is said to have *good connectivity*. On the other hand, computers that have difficulty linking into a network (many laptop computers, for example) have *poor connectivity*.

⇒ See also EXPORT; IMPORT.

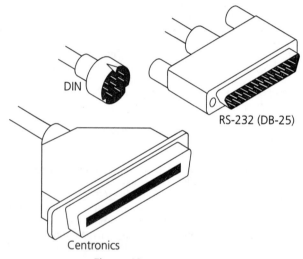

DIN

RS-232 (DB-25)

Centronics

Figure 19: **connectors**

connector The part of a cable that plugs into a port or interface to connect one device to another. Most connectors are either *male* (containing one or more exposed pins) or *female* (containing holes into which the male connector can be inserted).

⇒ See also BNC CONNECTOR; DIN CONNECTOR; INTERFACE; PINOUT; PORT; RJ-45.

connect time The amount of time a computer is logged in to a remote computer. Many online services charge users per connect time. Other services offer unlimited connect time for a flat monthly fee.

⇒ See also ONLINE SERVICE.

console 1. The combination of display monitor and keyboard (or other device that allows input). Another term for console is *terminal.* The term *console* usually refers to a terminal attached to a minicomputer or mainframe and used to monitor the status of the system. **2.** Another term for *monitor* or *display screen.* **3.** A bank of meters and lights indicating a computer's status, and switches that allow an operator to control the computer in some way.

⇒ See also DISPLAY SCREEN; KEYBOARD; TERMINAL.

constant In programming, a constant is a value that never changes. The other type of values that programs use is *variables*, symbols that can represent different values throughout the course of a program.
A constant can be

- a number, like 25 or 3.6
- a character, like *a* or *$*
- a character string, like "this is a string"

Constants are also used in spreadsheet applications to place nonchanging values in cells. In contrast, a spreadsheet formula can produce a different value each time the spreadsheet is opened or changed.

⇒ See also ABSOLUTE CELL REFERENCE; CHARACTER STRING; FORMULA; LITERAL; VARIABLE.

Constant Linear Velocity See CLV.

contact manager An application that enables you easily to store and find contact information, such as names, addresses, and telephone numbers. Sophisticated contact managers provide reporting functions and allow several people in a workgroup to access the same database of contacts. Some also provide calendar functions, which blurs the line between contact managers and personal information managers (PIMs).

⇒ See also PIM.

contention 1. Competition for resources. The term is used especially in networks to describe the situation where two or more nodes attempt to transmit a message across the same wire at the same time. **2.** A type of network protocol that allows nodes to *contend* for network access. That is, two or more nodes may try to send messages across the network simultaneously. The contention protocol defines what happens when this occurs. The most widely used contention protocol is CSMA/CD, used by Ethernet.

⇒ See also CSMA/CD; ETHERNET.

context sensitive Refers to a program feature that changes depending on what you are doing in the program. For example, *context-sensitive help* provides documentation for the particular feature that you are in the process of using.

⇒ See also HELP.

context switching Same as TASK SWITCHING.

contiguous Immediately adjacent. For example, contiguous sectors on a disk are sectors that come one after the other. Frequently, a file stored on disk can become fragmented, which means that it is stored on noncontiguous sectors.

⇒ See also FRAGMENTATION.

continuous-form paper A type of printing paper that consists of a single sheet or roll of paper, normally perforated at regular intervals so that sheets can be easily separated. Most continuous-form paper has holes punched along each side so that the paper can be pulled through the printer by a tractor-feed mechanism.

⇒ See also PAPER FEED; TRACTOR FEED.

continuous tone Refers to images that have a virtually unlimited range of color or shades of grays. Photographs and television images, for example, are continuous-tone images. In contrast, computer hardware and software are digital, which means that they can represent only a limited number of colors and gray levels. Converting a black-and-white continuous-tone image into a computer image is known as *gray scaling*.

Continuous-tone printers can print each dot at many different shades of lightness and darkness. Though this isn't true continuous-tone because the level of shades is limited, there are enough shades (256 or more) so that the difference between one shade and the next is imperceptible to the human eye.

⇒ See also BILEVEL PRINTER; CONTONE PRINTER; DIGITAL; GRAY SCALING; HALF-TONE.

contone printer A type of printer that uses a combination of dithering and printing at different levels of intensity to produce different colors and different shades of lightness and darkness. Unlike a true continuous-tone printer, contone printers can lay down ink at only a few different levels of intensity (usually 8). To produce the full range of colors that can be perceived by the human eye, they must also use dithering techniques. Many of the newer color laser printers are contone printers.

⇒ See also BILEVEL PRINTER; COLOR PRINTER; CONTINUOUS TONE; DITHERING.

control 1. An object in a window or dialog box. Examples of controls include push-buttons, scroll bars, radio buttons, and pull-down menus. **2.**

An OLE or ActiveX object.

⇒ See also ACTIVEX CONTROL; GRAPHICAL USER INTERFACE; OCX; OLE; VBX.

control character A special, nonprinting character. The ASCII character set defines 32 control characters, as shown in the table. Originally, these codes were designed to control teletype machines. Now, however, they are often used to control display monitors, printers, and other modern devices.

⇒ See also ASCII; BREAK KEY; CONTROL KEY; KEYBOARD.

Control key A key on PC keyboards labeled *Ctrl*. You use the Control key in the same way that you use the Shift key—keeping it pressed down while pressing another character. The result is a *control key combination*, which can have different meanings depending on which program is running. On Macintoshes, the Control key is called an *Apple key* or *Command key*.

⇒ See also APPLE KEY; COMMAND KEY; CONTROL KEY COMBINATION.

Control key combination A command issued by pressing a keyboard character in conjunction with the Control key. Manuals usually represent control key commands with the prefix *CTRL-* or *CNTL-*. For example, CTRL-N means the Control key and *N* pressed at the same time. Sometimes a control character is represented by a caret (for example, ^N is the same as CTRL-N).

What happens after you enter a Control key combination depends on what application is active. Certain Control key combinations are semi-standardized. For example, in Windows applications, CTRL-X usually copies the selected text.

⇒ See also COMMAND; CONTROL KEY.

controller A device that controls the transfer of data from a computer to a peripheral device and vice versa. For example, disk drives, display screens, keyboards, and printers all require controllers.

In personal computers, the controllers are often single chips. When you purchase a computer, it comes with all the necessary controllers for standard components, such as the display screen, keyboard, and disk drives. If you attach additional devices, however, you may need to insert new controllers that come on expansion boards.

Controllers must be designed to communicate with the computer's expansion bus. There are three standard bus architectures for PCs—the AT bus, PCI (Peripheral Component Interconnect), and SCSI. When you purchase a controller, therefore, you must ensure that it conforms to the bus architecture that your computer uses.

⇒ See also ADAPTER; AT BUS; ATA; BUS; CHIP; CPU; DRIVER; EISA; EXPANSION BOARD; MICROCONTROLLER; PCI; PERIPHERAL DEVICE; PRINTED CIRCUIT BOARD; SCSI.

Table 11
ASCII Control Characters

Oct	Dec	Hex	Char	Symbol	Meaning
0	0	0	^@	NUL	Null
1	1	1	^A	SOH	Start of Heading
2	2	2	^B	STX	Start of Text
3	3	3	^C	ETX	End of Text
4	4	4	^D	EQT	End of Transmit
5	5	5	^E	ENQ	Enquiry
6	6	6	^F	ACK	Acknowledge
7	7	7	^G	BEL	Bell
10	8	8	^H	BS	Backspace
11	9	9	^I	HT	Horizontal Tab
12	10	A	^J	LF	Line Feed
13	11	B	^K	VT	Vertical Tab
14	12	C	^L	FF	Form Feed
15	13	D	^M	CR	Carriage Return
16	14	E	^N	SO	Shift Out
17	15	F	^O	SI	Shift In
20	16	10	^P	DLE	Data Link Escape
21	17	11	^Q	DC1	Device Control 1
22	18	12	^R	DC2	Device Control 2
23	19	13	^S	DC3	Device Control 3
24	20	14	^T	DC4	Device Control 4
25	21	15	^U	NAK	Negative Acknowledge
26	22	16	^V	SYN	Synchronous Idle
27	23	17	^W	ETB	End Transmit Block
30	24	18	^X	CAN	Cancel
31	25	19	^Y	EM	End of Medium
32	26	1A	^Z	SUB	Substitution
33	27	1B	^[	ESC	Escape
34	28	1C	^|	FS	Figures Shift
35	29	1D	^]	GS	Group Separator
36	30	1E	^^	RS	Record Separator
37	31	1F	^	US	Unit Separator

control panel A Macintosh utility that permits you to set many of the system parameters. For example, you can control the type of beeps the Mac makes and the sensitivity of the mouse. On older Macs (System 6 and earlier), control panels are called *cdevs*.

The Windows operating system has a Control Panel program that offers many of the same features as the Macintosh control panels.

⇒ See also CDEV.

control panel device See CDEV.

control program 1. A program that enhances an operating system by creating an environment in which you can run other programs. Control programs generally provide a graphical interface and enable you to run several programs at once in different windows.

Control programs are also called *operating environments*. **2.** Another term for *operating system*.

⇒ See also GRAPHICAL USER INTERFACE; MICROSOFT WINDOWS; OPERATING ENVIRONMENT; OPERATING SYSTEM.

conventional memory On DOS systems, *conventional memory* refers to the portion of memory that is available to standard DOS programs. DOS systems have an *address space* of 1MB (megabyte), but the top 384K (called *high memory*) is reserved for system use. This leaves 640K of conventional memory. Everything above 1MB is either *extended* or *expanded memory*.

⇒ See also EXPANDED MEMORY; EXTENDED MEMORY; MAIN MEMORY.

convergence 1. The coming together of two or more disparate disciplines or technologies. For example, the so-called fax revolution was produced by a convergence of telecommunications technology, optical scanning technology, and printing technology. **2.** In graphics, *convergence* refers to how sharply an individual color pixel on a monitor appears. Each pixel is composed of three dots—red, blue, and green. If the dots are badly misconverged, the pixel will appear blurry. All monitors have some convergence errors, but they differ in degree.

⇒ See also GRAPHICS; MONITOR; PIXEL; RGB MONITOR.

convert To change data from one format to another.

⇒ See also EXPORT; IMPORT.

cookie A message given to a Web browser by a Web server. The browser stores the message in a text file called *cookie.txt*. The message is then sent back to the server each time the browser requests a page from the server.

The main purpose of cookies is to identify users and possibly prepare customized Web pages for them. When you enter a Web site using cookies, you may be asked to fill out a form providing such information as your name and interests. This information is packaged into a cookie and sent to your Web browser, which stores it for later use. The next time you go to the same Web site, your browser will send the cookie to the Web server. The server can use this information to present you with custom Web pages. So, for example, instead of seeing just a generic welcome page you might see a welcome page with your name on it.

The name *cookie* derives from UNIX objects called *magic cookies*. These are tokens that are attached to a user or program and change depending on the areas entered by the user or program. Cookies are also sometimes called *persistent cookies* because they typically stay in the browser for long periods of time.

⇒ See also BROWSER; DYNAMIC HTML; LOG FILE; STATELESS; WEB SERVER; WORLD WIDE WEB.

CoolTalk An Internet telephone (Voice on the Net) tool built into Netscape Navigator 3.0. Like NetMeeting, which is included with Microsoft's Internet Explorer, CoolTalk supports audio conferencing, a whiteboard, and a chat tool.

⇒ See also INTERNET TELEPHONY; NETMEETING.

cooperative multitasking A type of multitasking in which the process currently controlling the CPU must offer control to other processes. It is called *cooperative* because all programs must cooperate for it to work. If one program does not cooperate, it can hog the CPU. In contrast, *preemptive multitasking* forces applications to share the CPU whether they want to or not. Both the Macintosh and Windows 3.x operating systems are based on cooperative multitasking, whereas UNIX, Windows 95 and 98, Windows NT, and OS/2 are based on preemptive multitasking.

⇒ See also MICROSOFT WINDOWS; MULTITASKING; UNIX.

Copper Distributed Data Interface See CDDI.

coprocessor A special-purpose processing unit that assists the CPU in performing certain types of operations. For example, a *math coprocessor* performs mathematical computations, particularly floating-point operations. Math coprocessors are also called *numeric* and *floating-point* coprocessors.

Most computers come with a floating-point coprocessor built in. Note, however, that programs themselves must be written to take advantage of the coprocessor. If a program contains no coprocessor instructions, the coprocessor will never be utilized.

In addition to math coprocessors, there are also *graphics coprocessors* for manipulating graphic images. These are often called *accelerator boards*.

⇒ See also ACCELERATOR BOARD; CPU; FLOATING-POINT NUMBER.

copy *v* **1.** To copy a piece of data to a temporary location. In word processing, for example, *copying* refers to duplicating a section of a document and placing it in a *buffer* (sometimes called a *clipboard*). The term *copy* differs from *cut*, which refers to actually removing a section of a document and placing it in a buffer. After cutting or copying, you can paste the contents of the buffer somewhere else. **2.** In file management, the term *copy* refers to making a duplicate of a file. —*n* **3.** A duplicate of a piece of data, such as a file or a directory.

⇒ See also BUFFER; CLIPBOARD; CUT; FILE MANAGEMENT SYSTEM; PASTE.

copy protection Any of the programming techniques used to prevent the unauthorized copying of software. The idea of copy-protected software was created by software manufacturers who wanted to prevent *software piracy*—users copying programs and giving them to friends and colleagues free of charge.

As enticing an idea as it may be, copy protection has not proved to be a viable strategy. For one, it is practically impossible to create software that cannot be copied by a knowledgeable programmer. Second, many consumers shy away from copy-protected software because backup copies are difficult to make. Thus, if their original copy of the software is damaged, the user must contact the manufacturer for a new copy. Finally, some copy-protection techniques can actually damage other software on the system. For these reasons, copy-protected software is becoming less common.

Most software producers now protect their programs by issuing registration numbers with each package. When you install the software, you must enter the registration number. This does not prevent all piracy, but it limits it. In addition, users cannot get updates to a product unless they own the original diskettes and documentation.

An alternative strategy for dealing with the problem of software piracy is *shareware*, where users are actually encouraged to copy and disseminate programs. Shareware publishers rely on people's honesty to pay for the products used.

⇒ See also DIGITAL WATERMARK; DONGLE; DVD-VIDEO; SHAREWARE; SOFTWARE LICENSING; SOFTWARE PIRACY; WAREZ.

CORBA Short for *C(ommon) O(bject) R(equest) B(roker) A(rchitecture)*, an architecture that enables pieces of programs, called objects, to communicate with one another regardless of what programming language they were written in or what operating system they're running on. CORBA was developed by an industry consortium known as the Object Management Group (OMG).

There are several implementations of CORBA, the most widely used being IBM's SOM and DSOM architectures. CORBA has also been embraced by Netscape as part of its Netscape ONE (Open Network Environment) platform. Two competing models are Microsoft's COM and DCOM and Sun Microsystems' RMI.

⇒ See also DCOM; DISTRIBUTED COMPUTING; IIOP; OBJECT; OMG; ORB; RMI; RPC; SOM.

core memory The old term for main memory, which was composed of doughnut-shaped magnets called cores.

⇒ See also MAIN MEMORY.

corrupted Refers to data that have been damaged in some way.

Courier font A common monospaced (*fixed-pitch*) font, supported by most printers and most word-processing software.

⇒ See also FIXED PITCH; FONT; MONOSPACING.

This sentence is in Courier font.

courseware Software designed to be used in an educational program.

⇒ See also CBT.

cpi Short for *c(haracters) p(er) i(nch)*, a typographic measurement specifying the number of characters that can fit on a printed line one inch long. The measurement really makes sense only for fixed-pitch fonts, where every character has the same width. For proportionally spaced fonts, the cpi represents an average number rather than an absolute number.

⇒ See also CHARACTER; FIXED PITCH; FONT; MONOSPACING; PITCH; PROPORTIONAL SPACING.

CP/M Abbreviation of *C(ontrol) P(rogram) for M(icroprocessors)*. Created by Digital Research Corporation, CP/M was one of the first operating systems for personal computers. However, Digital Research Corporation made a critical strategic error by not agreeing to produce an operating system for the first IBM PC. According to the folklore, the president of Digital Research was flying his airplane when IBM came to call. IBM marched out and never looked back.

Instead, IBM turned to Microsoft Corporation, which developed MS-DOS. By the mid-1980s, MS-DOS had become the standard operating system for IBM-compatible personal computers. CP/M is now obsolete.

⇒ See also DOS; OPERATING SYSTEM.

cps Abbreviation of *c(haracters) p(er) s(econd)*, a unit of measure used to describe the speed of dot-matrix and daisy-wheel printers. The speed of laser and ink jet printers is described in terms of pages per minute (ppm).

⇒ See also PRINTER.

CPU Abbreviation of *c(entral) p(rocessing) u(nit)*, and pronounced as separate letters. The CPU is the brains of the computer. Sometimes referred to simply as the *processor* or *central processor*, the CPU is where most calculations take place. In terms of computing power, the CPU is the most important element of a computer system.

On large machines, CPUs require one or more printed circuit boards. On personal computers and small workstations, the CPU is housed in a single chip called a *microprocessor*.

Two typical components of a CPU are: (1) The *arithmetic logic unit (ALU)*, which performs arithmetic and logical operations and (2) the *control unit*, which extracts instructions from memory and decodes and executes them, calling on the ALU when necessary.

⇒ See also ALU; CHIP; CISC; CLOCK SPEED; COPROCESSOR; INTEL MICROPROCESSORS; MICROPROCESSOR; MMU; PowerPC; RISC.

CPU time The amount of time the CPU is actually executing instructions. During the execution of most programs, the CPU sits idle much of the time while the computer fetches data from the keyboard or disk, or sends data to an output device. The CPU time of an executing program, therefore, is generally much less than the total execution time of the program. Multitasking operating systems take advantage of this by sharing the CPU among several programs.

CPU times are used for a variety of purposes: to compare the speed of two different processors, to gauge how CPU-intensive a program is, and to measure the amount of processing time being allocated to different programs in a multitasking environment.

⇒ See also CPU; MULTITASKING.

crack 1. To break into a computer system. The term was coined in the mid-1980s by hackers who wanted to differentiate themselves from individuals whose sole purpose is to sneak through security systems. Whereas *crackers'* sole aim is to break into secure systems, hackers are more interested in gaining knowledge about computer systems and possibly using this knowledge for playful pranks. Although hackers still argue that there's a big difference between what they do and what crackers do, the mass media have failed to understand the distinction, so the two terms—*hack* and *crack*—are often used interchangeably. **2.** To copy commercial software illegally by breaking (cracking) the various copy-protection and registration techniques present in the software.

⇒ See also HACKER; PHREAKING; SMURF.

cracker See under CRACK.

crash *n* **1.** A serious computer failure. A computer crash means that the computer itself stops working or that a program *aborts* unexpectedly. A crash signifies either a hardware malfunction or a very serious software bug.

If your computer crashes, it is not your fault. If the program is good and your hardware is functioning properly, there is nothing you can do to make your system crash. —*v* **2.** To fail or break. Other terms for *crash* include *hang* and *bomb*.

⇒ See also ABORT; BOMB; BUG; FATAL ERROR; GPF; HANG; HEAD CRASH; INVALID PAGE FAULT; SMART.

CRC Abbreviation of *c(yclic) r(edundancy) c(heck)*, a common technique for detecting data transmission errors. A number of file transfer protocols, including Zmodem, use CRC in addition to *checksum*.

⇒ See also CHECKSUM; COMMUNICATIONS PROTOCOL; ERROR DETECTION; ZMODEM.

crippled version A demonstration version of a piece of software that has one or more critical features disabled. Many software companies distribute crippled versions of their applications free with the hope that users will get hooked and buy the full version.

⇒ See also BETA TEST.

crop In computer graphics, to cut off the edges of an image to make it the proper size or to remove unwanted parts. Most graphics applications allow you to crop images with a *clip* feature.

⇒ See also CLIP.

crop marks Printed or drawn lines indicating where the paper should be cut to produce the correct page size. Crop marks are necessary for offset printing because the original paper that goes through the printing press is usually larger than the final page size. Many desktop publishing systems are capable of automatically printing crop marks for camera-ready copy.

⇒ See also CAMERA-READY; DESKTOP PUBLISHING; OFFSET PRINTING.

cross-platform Refers to the capability of software or hardware to run identically on different platforms. Many applications for Windows and the Macintosh, for example, now produce binary-compatible files, which means that users can switch from one platform to the other without converting their data to a new format.

Cross-platform computing is becoming increasingly important as local-area networks become better at linking machines of different types.

⇒ See also BINARY COMPATIBLE; LOCAL-AREA NETWORK; PLATFORM.

CRT Abbreviation of *c(athode)-r(ay) t(ube)*, the technology used in most televisions and computer display screens. A CRT works by moving an electron beam back and forth across the back of the screen. Each time the electron beam makes a pass across the screen, it lights up phosphor dots on the inside of the glass tube, thereby illuminating the active portions of the screen. By drawing many such lines from the top or the screen to the bottom, it creates an entire screenful of images.

⇒ See also COLOR MONITOR; DEGAUSS; DISPLAY SCREEN; LCD MONITOR; MONITOR; PINCUSHION DISTORTION; REFRESH.

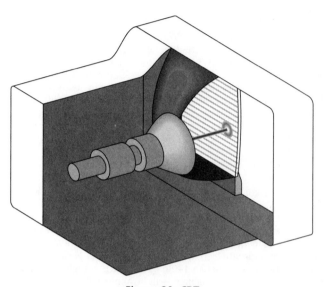

Figure 20: **CRT**

cryptography The art of protecting information by transforming it (*encrypting* it) into an unreadable format, called *cyphertext*. Only those who possess a secret *key* can decipher (or *decrypt*) the message into *plaintext*. Encrypted messages can sometimes be broken by cryptanalysis, also called *codebreaking*, although modern cryptography techniques are virtually unbreakable.

As the Internet and other forms of electronic communication become more prevalent, electronic security is becoming increasingly important. Cryptography is used to protect e-mail messages, credit card information, and corporate data. One of the most popular cryptography systems used on the Internet is *Pretty Good Privacy* because it's effective and free.

Cryptography systems can be broadly classified into *symmetric-key* systems that use a single key that both the sender and recipient have, and *public-key* systems that use two keys, a public key known to everyone and a private key that only the recipient of messages uses.

⇒ See also CLIPPER CHIP; DES; PRETTY GOOD PRIVACY; PUBLIC-KEY ENCRYPTION; SECURITY; SYMMETRIC-KEY CRYPTOGRAPHY.

CSMA/CD Short for *C(arrier) S(ense) M(ultiple) A(ccess)/C(ollision) D(etection)*, a set of rules determining how network devices respond when two devices attempt to use a data channel simultaneously (called a *collision*). Standard Ethernet networks use CSMA/CD. This standard enables devices to detect a collision. After detecting a collision, a device waits a random delay time and then attempts to re-transmit the message.

CSMA/CD is a type of contention protocol.

⇒ See also 100Base-T; CONTENTION; ETHERNET.

CSS Short for *C(ascading) S(tyle) S(heets)*, a new feature being added to HTML that gives both Web site developers and users more control over how pages are displayed. With CSS, designers and users can create style sheets that define how different elements, such as headers and links, appear. These style sheets can then be applied to any Web page.

The term *cascading* derives from the fact that multiple style sheets can be applied to the same Web page. CSS was developed by the *W3C*. The specification is still evolving and is not fully supported by any current Web browsers.

⇒ See also HTML; STYLE SHEET.

CSTN Short for *c(olor) s(uper)-t(wist) n(ematic)*, an LCD technology developed by Sharp Electronics Corporation. Unlike TFT, CSTN is based on a passive matrix, which is less expensive to produce. The original CSTN displays developed in the early 1990s suffered from slow response times and ghosting. Recent advances in the technology, however, have made CSTN a viable alternative to active-matrix displays. New CSTN displays offer 100ms response times, a 140-degree viewing angle, and high-quality color rivaling that of TFT displays—all at about half the cost.

A newer passive-matrix technology called High-Performance Addressing (HPA) offers even better response times and contrast than CSTN.

⇒ See also DSTN; LCD; PASSIVE-MATRIX DISPLAY; SUPER-TWIST; TFT.

CSU See under CSU/DSU.

CSU/DSU Short for *C(hannel) S(ervice) U(nit)/D(ata) S(ervice) U(nit)*. The DSU is a device that performs protective and diagnostic functions for a telecommunications line. The CSU is a device that connects a terminal to a digital line. Typically, the two devices are packaged as a single unit. You can think of it as a very high-powered and expensive modem. Such a device is required for both ends of a T-1 or T-3 connection, and the units at both ends must be from the same manufacturer.

⇒ See also SMDS; T-1 CARRIER; T-3 CARRIER; V.35.

CTI Short for *c(omputer)-t(elephony)-i(ntegration)*, which refers to systems that enable a computer to act as a call center, accepting incoming calls and routing them to the appropriate device or person. Today's CTI systems are quite sophisticated and can handle all sorts of incoming and outgoing communications, including phone calls, faxes, and Internet messages.

⇒ See also TELEPHONY.

Ctrl See under CONTROL KEY COMBINATION.

CUA Short for *C(ommon) U(ser) A(ccess)*, a set of standards for user interfaces developed by IBM. CUA is one component of the *System Application Architecture (SAA)* standards introduced in 1987.

The CUA standards deal with interface appearance, programming conventions, and communications.

⇒ See also SAA; USER INTERFACE.

current Refers to an object that is acting as a reference point. For example, the *current directory* is the same as the *working directory* or *default directory*. The *current drive* is the *default mass storage device*. In a spreadsheet application, the *current cell* is the *active cell*, the cell that you are manipulating at the moment.

⇒ See also ACTIVE; DEFAULT; WORKING DIRECTORY.

cursor 1. A special symbol, usually a solid rectangle or a blinking underline character, that signifies where the next character will be displayed on the screen. To type in different areas of the screen, you need to move the cursor. You can do this with the arrow keys, or with a mouse if your program supports it.

If you are running a graphics-based program, the cursor may appear as a small arrow, called a *pointer*. (The terms *cursor* and *pointer* are often used interchangeably.) In text processing, a cursor sometimes appears as an *I-beam pointer*, a special type of pointer that always appears between two characters. Note also that programs that support a mouse may use two cursors: a *text cursor*, which indicates where characters from the keyboard will be entered, and a *mouse cursor* for selecting items with the mouse. **2.** A device, similar in appearance to a mouse, that is used to sketch lines on a digitizing tablet. Cursors for digitizing tablets are sometimes called *pucks*. **3.** In some database languages, short for *cur(rent) s(et) o(f) r(ecords)*, the currently selected set of records.

⇒ See also ARROW KEYS; DIGITIZING TABLET; MOUSE; POINTER.

cursor control keys Special keys on computer keyboards that move the cursor. The arrow keys, for example, move the cursor up, down, right, and left. In addition, most keyboards have *End, Home, Page Up, Page Down*, and *Backspace keys*.

⇒ See also ARROW KEYS; CURSOR; KEYBOARD.

cursor position The position of the cursor on the display screen. While in text mode, a display screen is capable of displaying a certain number of lines and a certain number of characters on each line. The cursor position is represented by the *line number* and the *character number* and signifies where the next character will be displayed. For example, cursor position 1,1 always indicates the upper-leftmost corner position on the terminal. Cursor position 10,30 indicates the 30th character position on the

10th line.

⇒ See also CURSOR; DISPLAY SCREEN; TEXT MODE.

CU-SeeMe A videoconferencing program that uses the Internet to transmit audio and video signals. There is a freeware version of CU-SeeMe, which was developed at Cornell University, and an enhanced commercial version sold by WhitePine, Inc. You can use the program for *point-to-point* videoconferencing (just two people) or *multipoint* videoconferencing. You'll need a computer equipped with a sound card and speakers, and a video camera.

⇒ See also VIDEOCONFERENCING.

Customer Information Control System See CICS.

customer support Service that computer and software manufacturers, and third-party service companies, offer to customers. For personal computer products, the following are common customer-support options:

mail-in service: The manufacturer will repair your equipment if you mail it in. Typical turnaround time is about four days. In some service plans, the manufacturer charges you for shipping expenses.

carry-in service: The manufacturer will repair your equipment, but you must deliver it to a local service site. This is sometimes called *depot service.*

on-site contract: For a monthly or annual fee, a repair person will come to your site to fix problems. (The fee is included in the purchase price of some machines.) Most on-site contracts guarantee that the service will be rendered within a fixed number of hours from when you report a problem.

hot lines: Many software manufacturers provide a phone number that you can call for advice and trouble-shooting. Often the number is toll-free. The quality of this type of support varies considerably from one company to another. Some hot lines are so good that they enable you to solve most problems yourself. Others are so bad that you are unable even to get through.

bulletin board system: Some companies maintain electronic bulletin boards (or forums within online services) staffed by service engineers. If you have a modem, you can report a problem to the bulletin board and a technician will respond. This can be convenient because bulletin boards are usually open 24 hours a day. Also, bulletin boards enable you to download software updates that correct known bugs.

Customer support is also called *technical support.*

⇒ See also BULLETIN BOARD SYSTEM; DOWNLOAD.

cut To remove an object from a document and place it in a *buffer*. In word processing, for example, *cut* means to move a section of text from a document to a temporary buffer. This is one way to delete text. However, because the text is transferred to a buffer, it is not lost forever. You can copy the buffer somewhere else in the document or in another document, which is called *pasting*. To move a section of text from one place to another, therefore, you need to first cut it and then paste it. This is often called *cut-and-paste*.

Most applications have only one buffer, sometimes called a *clipboard*. If you make two cuts in succession, the text from the original cut will be replaced by the text from the second cut.

Graphical user interfaces, such as MS-Windows and the Macintosh interface, allow you to cut and paste graphics as well as text.

⇒ See also BUFFER; CLIPBOARD; COPY; DELETE; PASTE.

cut-sheet feeder See under SHEET FEEDER.

cyber A prefix used in a growing number of terms to describe new things that are being made possible by the spread of computers. Cyberphobia, for example, is an irrational fear of computers. Cyberpunk is a genre of science fiction that draws heavily on computer science ideas. Cyberspace is the nonphysical terrain created by computer systems. Anything related to the Internet also falls under the cyber category.

⇒ See also CYBERSPACE; VIRTUAL REALITY.

cybernetics Originally the study of biological and artificial control systems, cybernetics has evolved into many disparate areas of study, with research in many disciplines, including computer science, social philosophy, and epistemology. In general, cybernetics is concerned with discovering what mechanisms control systems and, in particular, how systems regulate themselves.

The term was coined by Norbert Weiner in 1943.

⇒ See also ARTIFICIAL INTELLIGENCE; ROBOTICS.

cyberspace A metaphor for describing the non-physical terrain created by computer systems. Online systems, for example, create a cyberspace within which people can communicate with one another (via e-mail), do research, or simply window shop. Like physical space, cyberspace contains *objects* (files, mail messages, graphics, etc.) and different modes of transportation and delivery. Unlike real space, though, exploring cyberspace does not require any physical movement other than pressing keys on a keyboard or moving a mouse.

Some programs, particularly computer games, are designed to create a special cyberspace, one that resembles physical reality in some ways but defies it in others. In its extreme form, called *virtual reality*, users are presented with visual, auditory, and even tactile feedback that makes cyberspace feel real.

⇒ See also AVATAR; INFORMATION SUPERHIGHWAY; MUD; ONLINE SERVICE; VIRTUAL REALITY; VRML.

cycle time A measurement of how quickly two back-to-back accesses of a memory chip can be made. Note that a DRAM chip's cycle time is usually much longer than its access time, which measures only a single access. This is because there is a latency between successive memory accesses.

⇒ See also ACCESS TIME; DRAM; SRAM.

cyclic redundancy check See under CRC.

cylinder A single track location on all the *platters* making up a hard disk. For example, if a hard disk has four platters, each with 600 tracks, then there will be 600 cylinders, and each cylinder will consist of 8 tracks (assuming that each platter has tracks on both sides).

⇒ See also HARD DISK; PLATTER; TRACK.

Cyrix A U.S. corporation founded in 1988 that manufactures Intel-compatible microprocessors. Its 6x86 line of processors is comparable to Intel's line of Pentium chips. In 1997, Cyrix was acquired by National Semiconductor.

⇒ See also AMD; INTEL; INTEL MICROPROCESSORS; MICROPROCESSOR; PENTIUM MICROPROCESSOR.

D3D See Direct3D.

DA Pronounced as separate letters, *DA* stands for *desk accessory*. See under DESK ACCESSORY.

DAC Short for *d(igital)-to-a(nalog) c(onverter)*, a device (usually a single chip) that converts digital data into analog signals. Modems require a DAC to convert data to analog signals that can be carried by telephone wires. Video adapters also require DACs, called *RAMDACs*, to convert digital data to analog signals that the monitor can process.

⇒ See also ANALOG; DIGITAL; RAMDAC.

daemon Pronounced *demon* or *damon*, a process that runs in the background and performs a specified operation at predefined times or in response to certain events. Although the term *daemon* is a UNIX term, many other operating systems provide support for daemons, sometimes under other names. Windows, for example, refers to daemons as *System Agents* and *services.*

Typical daemon processes include print spoolers, e-mail handlers, and other programs that perform administrative tasks for the operating system. The term comes from Greek mythology, where daemons were guardian spirits.

⇒ See also AGENT; PROCESS; UNIX.

daisy chain *n* **1.** A hardware configuration in which devices are connected one to another in a series. The *SCSI interface*, for example, supports a daisy chain of up to 7 devices. —*v* **2.** To connect devices in a daisy chain pattern.

⇒ See also SCSI.

daisy-wheel printer A type of printer that produces letter-quality type. A daisy-wheel printer works on the same principle as a ball-head typewriter. The daisy wheel is a disk made of plastic or metal on which characters stand out in relief along the outer edge. To print a character, the printer rotates the disk until the desired letter is facing the paper. Then a hammer strikes the disk, forcing the character to hit an ink ribbon, leaving an impression of the character on the paper. You can change the daisy wheel to print different fonts.

Daisy-wheel printers cannot print graphics, and in general they are noisy and slow, printing from 10 to about 75 characters per second. As the price of laser and ink jet printers has declined, and the quality of dot-matrix printers has improved, daisy-wheel printers have become obsolete.

⇒ See also IMPACT PRINTER; PRINTER.

DAO 1. Short for *d(ata) a(ccess) o(bjects)*, objects that work with the Jet database engine. DAO objects are generally created with Visual Basic. Once created, a DAO object can be accessed and manipulated by any application that can use the Jet engine. This includes all of the applications in Microsoft Office, such as MS-Word, MS-Access, and Excel. **2.** Short for *d(isk) a(t) o(nce)*, a method of recording to CD-R disks in which all data are written in a single session.

⇒ See also ADO; JET; VISUAL BASIC.

DASD Short for *D(irect) A(ccess) S(torage) D(evice)*, and pronounced *daz-dee*, another name for disk drive in the world of mainframes.

⇒ See also DISK DRIVE; RANDOM ACCESS.

DAT Acronym for *d(igital) a(udio) t(ape)*, a type of magnetic tape that uses a scheme called *helical scan* to record data. A DAT cartridge is slightly larger than a credit card in width and height and contains a magnetic tape that can hold from 2 to 24 GB of data. It can support data transfer rates of about 2 MBps. Like other types of tapes, DATs are *sequential-access* media.

The most common format for DAT cartridges is *DDS (digital data storage)*.

⇒ See also GIGABYTE; HELICAL-SCAN CARTRIDGE; MASS STORAGE; MEGABYTE; SEQUENTIAL ACCESS; TAPE.

data 1. Distinct pieces of information, usually formatted in a special way. All software is divided into two general categories: *data* and *programs*. Programs are collections of instructions for manipulating data.

Data can exist in a variety of forms—as numbers or text on pieces of paper, as bits and bytes stored in electronic memory, or as facts stored in a person's mind.

Strictly speaking, data is the plural of *datum*, a single piece of information. In practice, however, people use *data* as both the singular and plural form of the word. As a singular noun, it means "information." **2.** The term *data* is often used to distinguish binary machine-readable information from textual human-readable information. For example, some applications make a distinction between *data files* (files that contain binary data) and *text files* (files that contain ASCII data). **3.** In database management systems, data files are the files that store the database information, whereas other files, such as index files and data dictionaries, store administrative information, known as metadata.

⇒ See also ASCII; BINARY; DATA DICTIONARY; DATA INTEGRITY; DATABASE MANAGEMENT SYSTEM; METADATA; PROGRAM; SOFTWARE.

database 1. A collection of information organized in such a way that a computer program can quickly select desired pieces of data. You can think of a database as an electronic filing system.

Traditional databases are organized by *fields*, *records*, and *files*. A field is a single piece of information; a record is one complete set of fields; and a file is a collection of records. For example, a telephone book is analogous to a file. It contains a list of records, each of which consists of three fields: name, address, and telephone number.

An alternative concept in database design is known as *Hypertext*. In a Hypertext database, any object, whether it be a piece of text, a picture, or a film, can be linked to any other object. Hypertext databases are particularly useful for organizing large amounts of disparate information, but they are not designed for numerical analysis.

To access information from a database, you need a *database management system (DBMS)*. This is a collection of programs that enables you to enter, organize, and select data in a database. **2.** Increasingly, the term *database* is used as shorthand for *database management system*.

⇒ See also DATA MINING; DATA WAREHOUSE; DATABASE MANAGEMENT SYSTEM; DISTRIBUTED DATABASE; FIELD; FILE; HYPERTEXT; METADATA; OLAP; RDBMS; RECORD; REPLICATION.

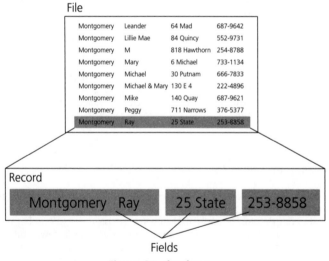

Figure 21: **database**

DATABASE 2 See DB2.

database management system A collection of programs that enables you to store, modify, and extract information from a database. There are many different types of DBMSs, ranging from small systems that run on personal computers to huge systems that run on mainframes. The following are examples of database applications:

- computerized library systems
- automated teller machines
- flight reservation systems
- computerized parts inventory systems

From a technical standpoint, DBMSs can differ widely. The terms *relational, network, flat,* and *hierarchical* all refer to the way a DBMS organizes information internally. The internal organization can affect how quickly and flexibly you can extract information.

Requests for information from a database are made in the form of a *query,* which is a stylized question. For example, the query

SELECT ALL WHERE NAME = "SMITH" AND AGE > 35

requests all records in which the NAME field is SMITH and the AGE field is greater than 35. The set of rules for constructing queries is known as a *query language.* Different DBMSs support different query languages, although there is a semi-standardized query language called *SQL (structured query language).* Sophisticated languages for managing database systems are called *fourth-generation languages,* or *4GLs* for short.

The information from a database can be presented in a variety of formats. Most DBMSs include a *report writer program* that enables you to output data in the form of a report. Many DBMSs also include a graphics component that enables you to output information in the form of graphs and charts.

⇒ See also BLOB; DATA DICTIONARY; DATA MART; DATABASE; DB2; DISTRIBUTED DATABASE; FLAT-FILE DATABASE; FOURTH-GENERATION LANGUAGE; HYPERTEXT; INFORMIX; ISAM; MULTIDIMENSIONAL DBMS; OLAP; ORACLE; PROGRESS SOFTWARE; QUERY; RDBMS; REPORT WRITER; SQL; STORED PROCEDURE.

data bus See under BUS.

data communications See COMMUNICATIONS.

data compression Storing data in a format that requires less space than usual. *Compressing* data is the same as *packing* data.

Data compression is particularly useful in communications because it enables devices to transmit the same amount of data in fewer bits. There are a variety of data compression techniques, but only a few have been standardized. The *CCITT* has defined a standard data compression technique for transmitting faxes (Group 3 standard) and a compression standard for data communications through modems (CCITT V.42 *bis*). In addition, there are file compression formats, such as ARC and ZIP.

Data compression is also widely used in backup utilities, spreadsheet applications, and database management systems. Certain types of data, such as bitmapped graphics, can be compressed to a small fraction of their normal size.

⇒ See also ARC; CCITT; DCT; DISK COMPRESSION; DSP; JPEG; LOSSLESS COMPRESSION; LOSSY COMPRESSION; LZW; MNP; MP3; MPEG; ZIP.

data dictionary In database management systems, a file that defines the basic organization of a database. A data dictionary contains a list of all files in the database, the number of records in each file, and the names and types of each field. Most database management systems keep the data dictionary hidden from users to prevent them from accidentally destroying its contents.

Data dictionaries do not contain any actual data from the database, only bookkeeping information for managing it. Without a data dictionary, however, a database management system cannot access data from the database.

⇒ See also DATABASE MANAGEMENT SYSTEM.

data encryption See under ENCRYPTION.

Data Encryption Standard See DES.

data entry The process of entering data into a computerized database or spreadsheet. Data entry can be performed by an individual typing at a keyboard or by a machine entering data electronically.

⇒ See also DATABASE; SPREADSHEET.

datagram Same as PACKET.

data integrity Refers to the validity of data. Data integrity can be compromised in a number of ways:

- Human errors when data is entered
- Errors that occur when data is transmitted from one computer to another
- Software bugs or viruses
- Hardware malfunctions, such as disk crashes
- Natural disasters, such as fires and floods

There are many ways to minimize these threats to data integrity. These include:

- Backing up data regularly
- Controlling access to data via security mechanisms
- Designing user interfaces that prevent the input of invalid data
- Using error detection and correction software when transmitting data

⇒ See also BACKUP; DATA; ERROR DETECTION.

data mart A database, or collection of databases, designed to help managers make strategic decisions about their business. Whereas a data warehouse combines databases across an entire enterprise, data marts are usually smaller and focus on a particular subject or department. Some data marts, called *dependent data marts,* are subsets of larger data warehouses.

⇒ See also DATA WAREHOUSE; DATABASE MANAGEMENT SYSTEM.

data mining A hot buzzword for a class of database applications that look for hidden patterns in a group of data. For example, data mining software can help retail companies find customers with common interests. The term is commonly misused to describe software that presents data in new ways. True data mining software doesn't just change the presentation but actually discovers previously unknown relationships among the data.

⇒ See also DATABASE.

data processing 1. Refers to a class of programs that organize and manipulate data, usually large amounts of numeric data. Accounting programs are the prototypical examples of data processing applications. In contrast, word processors, which manipulate text rather than numbers, are not usually referred to as data processing applications. **2.** Same as Information Technology (IT). Refers to all computing functions within an enterprise.

⇒ See also ACCOUNTING SOFTWARE; APPLICATION.

data rate Short for *data transfer rate.*

data recovery Salvaging data stored on damaged media, such as magnetic disks and tapes. There are a number of software products that can help recover data damaged by a disk crash or virus. In addition, there are companies that specialize in data recovery. Of course, not all data is recoverable, but data recovery specialists can often restore a surprisingly high percentage of the data on damaged media.

⇒ See also HEAD CRASH; VIRUS.

data structure In programming, the term *data structure* refers to a scheme for organizing related pieces of information. The basic types of data structures include:

- files
- lists
- arrays
- records
- trees
- tables

Each of these basic structures has many variations and allows different operations to be performed on the data.

⇒ See also ARRAY; FILE; HEAP; LIST; RECORD; STACK; TREE STRUCTURE.

data transfer rate The speed with which data can be transmitted from one device to another. Data rates are often measured in *megabits* (million bits) or *megabytes* (million bytes) *per second*. These are usually abbreviated as *Mbps* and *MBps,* respectively.

Another term for data transfer rate is *throughput.*

⇒ See also ACCESS TIME; BURST MODE; KBPS; MBPS; MBPS; STREAMING.

data type In programming, classification of a particular type of information. It is easy for humans to distinguish between different types of data. We can usually tell at a glance whether a number is a percentage, a time, or an amount of money. We do this through special symbols—%, :, and $—that indicate the data's *type*. Similarly, a computer uses special internal codes to keep track of the different types of data it processes.

Most programming languages require the programmer to declare the data type of every data object, and most database systems require the user to specify the type of each data field. The available data types vary from one programming language to another, and from one database application to another, but the following usually exist in one form or another:

integer: In more common parlance, *whole number*; a number that has no fractional part.
floating-point: A number with a decimal point. For example, 3 is an integer, but 3.5 is a floating-point number.
character (text): Readable text

⇒ See also BIG-ENDIAN; CHARACTER; DATABASE; DECLARE; FIELD; FLOATING-POINT NUMBER; INTEGER; OVERLOADING; POLYMORPHISM; VARIABLE.

data warehouse A collection of data designed to support management decision making. Data warehouses contain a wide variety of data that present a coherent picture of business conditions at a single point in time.

Development of a data warehouse includes development of systems to extract data from operating systems plus installation of a warehouse database system that provides managers flexible access to the data.

The term *data warehousing* generally refers to the combining of many different databases across an entire enterprise. Contrast with *data mart.*

⇒ See also DATA MART; DATABASE; METADATA.

data warehousing See under DATA WAREHOUSE.

daughtercard A printed circuit board that plugs into another circuit board (usually the motherboard). A daughtercard is similar to an expansion board, but it accesses the motherboard components (memory and CPU) directly instead of sending data through the slower expansion bus.

A daughtercard is also called a *daughterboard.*

⇒ See also EXPANSION BOARD; MOTHERBOARD; PRINTED CIRCUIT BOARD.

DB2 Short for *D(ata)b(ase)* **2**, a family of relational database products offered by IBM. DB2 provides an open database environment that runs on a wide variety of computing platforms. A DB2 database can grow from a small single-user application to a large multi-user system. Using SQL, users can obtain data simultaneously from DB2 and other databases. DB2 includes a range of application development and management tools.

⇒ See also DATABASE MANAGEMENT SYSTEM; RDBMS.

dBASE A popular database management system produced by Ashton-Tate Corporation. The original version, called *Vulcan,* was created by Wayne Ratliff. In 1981, Ashton-Tate bought Vulcan and marketed it as dBASE II. Subsequent versions with additional features are known as dBASE III, dBASE III + , and dBASE IV, all of which are currently owned and developed by Borland Corporation.

The dBASE format for storing data has become a de facto standard and is supported by nearly all database management and spreadsheet systems. Even systems that do not use the dBASE format internally are able to import and export data in dBASE format.

⇒ See also DATABASE MANAGEMENT SYSTEM; EXPORT; IMPORT.

DBMS See DATABASE MANAGEMENT SYSTEM.

DCC Short for *D(irect) C(able) C(onnection),* a Windows 95 feature that enables two computers to be connected via a serial or parallel cable. Once connected, the two computers function as if they were on a local-area network (LAN). Either computer can access files on the other computer. But because DCC does not require network interface cards (NICs), it is less expensive and simpler. The limitations are that it can connect only two PCs, and the data transfer rate is slower than with a true LAN.

⇒ See also ECP; LOCAL-AREA NETWORK; NETWORK NEIGHBORHOOD; NULL-MODEM CABLE.

DCE 1. Short for *Distributed Computing Environment,* a suite of technology services developed by The Open Group for creating distributed applications that run on different platforms. DCE services include:

- Remote Procedure Calls (RPC)
- Security Service
- Directory Service
- Time Service
- Threads Service
- Distributed File Service

DCE is a popular choice for very large systems that require robust security and fault tolerance. **2.** Short for *D(ata) C(ommunications) E(quipment)*, a device that communicates with a *Data Terminal Equipment (DTE)* device in RS-232C communications. See DTE for more information.

⇒ See also DISTRIBUTED PROCESSING; DTE; FAULT TOLERANCE; MIDDLEWARE; MODEM; OSF; THE OPEN GROUP.

DCI See under DIRECTDRAW.

DCOM Short for *D(istributed) C(omponent) O(bject) M(odel)*, an extension of the Component Object Model (COM) to support objects distributed across a network. DCOM was developed by Microsoft and has been submitted to the *IETF* as a draft standard. Since 1996, it has been part of Windows NT and is also available for Windows 95 and 98.

DCOM serves the same purpose as IBM's DSOM protocol, which is the most popular implementation of CORBA. Unlike CORBA, which runs on many operating systems, DCOM is currently implemented only for Windows.

⇒ See also COMPONENT OBJECT MODEL; CORBA; DISTRIBUTED COMPUTING; DSOM; RMI.

DCT Short for *D(iscrete) C(osine) T(ransform)*, a technique for representing waveform data as a weighted sum of cosines. DCT is commonly used for data compression, as in JPEG. This use of DCT results in lossy compression. DCT itself does not lose data; rather, data compression technologies that rely on DCT approximate some of the coefficients to reduce the amount of data.

⇒ See also DATA COMPRESSION; JPEG; LOSSY COMPRESSION.

DDC Short for *D(isplay) D(ata) C(hannel)*, a VESA standard for communication between a monitor and a video adapter. Using DDC, a monitor can inform the video card about its properties, such as maximum resolution and color depth. The video card can then use this information to ensure that the user is presented with valid options for configuring the display.

⇒ See also MONITOR; VESA; VIDEO ADAPTER.

DDE Abbreviation for *D(ynamic) D(ata) E(xchange)*, an *interprocess communication (IPC)* system built into the Macintosh, Windows, and OS/2 operating systems. DDE enables two running applications to share the same data. For example, DDE makes it possible to insert a spreadsheet chart into a document created with a word processor. Whenever the spreadsheet data changes, the chart in the document changes accordingly.

Although the DDE mechanism is still used by many applications, it is being supplanted by OLE, which provides greater control over shared data.

⇒ See also INTERPROCESS COMMUNICATION (IPC); OLE.

DDR-SDRAM Short for *D(ouble) D(ata) R(ate)-S(ynchronous)* **DRAM**, a type of SDRAM that supports data transfers on both edges of each clock cycle, effectively doubling the memory chip's data throughput. DDR-SDRAM is also called *SDRAM II.*

⇒ See also SDRAM.

DDS Abbreviation of *D(igital) D(ata) S(torage)*, the industry standard for digital audio tape (DAT) formats. The latest format, *DDS-3*, specifies tapes that can hold 24 GB (the equivalent of over 40 CD-ROMs) and support data transfer rates of 2 MBps.

⇒ See also DAT.

deadlock A condition that occurs when two processes are each waiting for the other to complete before proceeding. The result is that both processes hang. Deadlocks occur most commonly in multitasking and client/server environments. Ideally, the programs that are deadlocked, or the operating system, should resolve the deadlock, but this doesn't always happen.
  A deadlock is also called a *deadly embrace.*

⇒ See also HANG.

deadly embrace Same as DEADLOCK.

debug To find and remove errors (*bugs*) from a program or design.

⇒ See also ALPHA VERSION; BUG; TWEAK.

debugger A special program used to find errors (*bugs*) in other programs. A debugger allows a programmer to stop a program at any point and examine and change the values of variables.

⇒ See also BUG.

DEC Pronounced *deck,* and short for *D(igital) E(quipment) C(orporation).* One of leading producers of workstations, servers, and high-end PCs. DEC also developed one of the leading Internet search engines, Alta Vista.
  In January, 1998, DEC agreed to be acquired by Compaq for a reported $9.6 billion.

⇒ See also ALTA VISTA; COMPAQ; IBM; SERVER; SGI; SUN MICROSYSTEMS; VAX; WORKSTATION.

decimal Refers to numbers in base 10 (the numbers we use in everyday life). For example, the following are decimal numbers:

9
100,345,000
-256

Note that a decimal number is not necessarily a number with a decimal point in it. Numbers with decimal points (that is, numbers with a fractional part) are called *fixed-point* or *floating-point numbers.*

In addition to the decimal format, computer data are often represented in binary, octal, and hexadecimal formats.

⇒ See also BCD; BINARY; FLOATING-POINT NUMBER; HEXADECIMAL; INTEGER; OCTAL.

declare In programming, *to declare* is to define the name and data type of a variable or other programming construct. Many programming languages, including C and Pascal, require you to declare variables before using them.

⇒ See also DATA TYPE; PROGRAMMING LANGUAGE; VARIABLE.

decrement To subtract. For example, if you count down consecutively from 10 to 0, you decrement by 1. If you count down by twos, you decrement by 2. The opposite of decrementing is *incrementing.*

⇒ See also INCREMENT.

decryption The process of decoding data that has been *encrypted* into a secret format. Decryption requires a secret *key* or *password.*

⇒ See also CRYPTOGRAPHY; ENCRYPTION; SECURITY.

dedicated Reserved for a specific use. In communications, a *dedicated channel* is a line reserved exclusively for one type of communication. This is the same as a *leased line* or *private line.*

A *dedicated server* is a single computer in a network reserved for serving the needs of the network. For example, some networks require that one computer be set aside to manage communications between all the other computers. A dedicated server could also be a computer that manages printer resources. Note, however, that not all servers are dedicated. In some networks, it is possible for a computer to act as a server and to perform other functions as well.

The opposite of dedicated is *general purpose.*

⇒ See also CHANNEL; EXPANSION SLOT; NETWORK; SERVER.

de facto standard A format, language, or protocol that has become a standard not because it has been approved by a standards organization but because it is widely used and recognized by the industry as being standard. Some examples of de facto standards include:

• Hayes command set for controlling modems

- Kermit Communications Protocol
- Xmodem Communications Protocol
- Hewlett-Packard Printer Control Language (PCL) for laser printers
- PostScript page description language for laser printers

⇒ See also HAYES COMPATIBLE; KERMIT; PCL; POSTSCRIPT; STANDARD; XMODEM.

default A value or setting that a device or program automatically selects if you do not specify a substitute. For example, word processors have default margins and default page lengths that you can override or reset.

The *default drive* is the disk drive the computer accesses unless you specify a different disk drive. Likewise, the *default directory* (or *folder*) is the directory the operating system searches unless you specify a different one.

The default can also be an action that a device or program will take. For example, some word processors generate backup files *by default*.

⇒ See also MODE.

Defrag A DOS and Windows utility that defragments your hard disk. In Windows 95, you run Defrag by selecting **Start->Programs->Accessories->System Tools->Disk Defragmenter**.

⇒ See also DISK OPTIMIZER; FRAGMENTATION; SCANDISK.

defragment To optimize a disk by unfragmenting files. See under FRAGMENTATION.

⇒ See also FRAGMENTATION.

defragmentation See under FRAGMENTATION.

degauss To remove magnetism from a device. The term is usually used in reference to color monitors and other display devices that use a cathode ray tube (CRT). These devices aim electrons onto the display screen by creating magnetic fields inside the CRT. External magnetic forces—such as a magnet placed close to the monitor or the earth's natural magnetism—can magnetize the shadow mask, causing distorted images and colors.

To remove this external magnetic forces, most monitors automatically *degauss* the CRT whenever you turn on the monitor. In addition, many monitors have a manual *degauss button* that performs a more thorough degaussing of the CRT. You can also use an external *degausser* that degausses the monitor from the outside. Since it may be impossible to remove the external magnetic force, degaussing works by re-aligning the magnetic fields inside the CRT to compensate for the external magnetism.

You can also degauss magnetic media, such as disks, which removes all data from the media.

⇒ See also COLOR MONITOR; CRT; MONITOR; PINCUSHION DISTORTION.

degausser See under DEGAUSS.

delete To remove or erase. For example, deleting a character means removing it from a file or erasing it from the display screen. Deleting a file means erasing it from a disk. Note that, unlike *cutting*, deleting does not necessarily place the removed object in a buffer from which it can be recovered.

⇒ See also CUT; RECYCLE BIN.

Delete key Often abbreviated as *Del*, the Delete key is used to remove characters and other objects. On PCs, the Delete key generally removes the character immediately under the cursor (or to the right of the insertion point), or the highlighted text or object. Note the difference between the Delete key, which deletes the character under the cursor, and the Backspace key, which deletes the character to the left of the cursor or insertion point. On Macintoshes, the Delete key generally acts like a PC's Backspace key, deleting the character immediately in front of the insertion point.

⇒ See also BACKSPACE; BACKSPACE KEY; INSERTION POINT; KEYBOARD.

delimiter A punctuation character or group of characters that separates two names or two pieces of data or marks the beginning or end of a programming construct. Delimiters are used in almost every computer application. For example, in specifying DOS *pathnames*, the backslash (\) is the delimiter that separates directories and filenames. Other common delimiters include the comma (,), semicolon (;), quotes ("), and braces ({}).

⇒ See also PATHNAME.

Dell Computer The world's largest mail-order computer vendor. Founded by Michael Dell in 1984, Dell Computer has built a reputation for delivering quality PCs at competitive prices.

⇒ See also COMPAQ; PC.

Delphi A rapid application development (RAD) system developed by Borland International, Inc. Delphi is similar to Visual Basic from Microsoft, but whereas Visual Basic is based on the BASIC programming language, Delphi is based on Pascal.

⇒ See also PASCAL; RAPID APPLICATION DEVELOPMENT; VISUAL BASIC.

demand paging In virtual memory systems, demand paging is a type of *swapping* in which pages of data are not copied from disk to RAM until they are needed. In contrast, some virtual memory systems use *anticipatory paging*, in which the operating system attempts to anticipate which piece of data will be needed next and copies it to RAM before it is actually required.

⇒ See also PAGING; RAM; SWAP; VIRTUAL MEMORY.

demodulate See under MODULATE.

demodulation See under MODULATE.

density How tightly information is packed together on a storage medium (tape or disk). A higher density means that data are closer together, so the medium can hold more information. Floppy disks can be *single-density*, *double-density*, *high-density*, or *extra-high-density*. To use a double-density, high-density, or extra-high-density disk, you must have a disk drive that supports the density level. *Density*, therefore, can refer both to the media and the device.

The table shows the storage capacities of double- and high-density floppies on the PC and the Apple Macintosh.

⇒ See also AREAL DENSITY; DISK; DISK DRIVE; DOUBLE-DENSITY DISK; FDHD; FLOPPY DISK; HIGH-DENSITY DISK.

Table 12 Floppy Disk Densities			
5 ¼-inch			
	Single	*Double*	*High*
PC	360K	720K	1.2MB
Mac	NA	NA	NA
3 ½-inch			
	Single	*Double*	*High*
PC	NA	720K	1.44MB
Mac	400K	800K	1.2MB

DES Short for *D(ata) E(ncryption) S(tandard)*, a popular symmetric-key encryption method developed in 1975 and standardized by ANSI in 1981 as ANSI X.3.92. DES uses a 56-bit key and is illegal to export from the U.S. or Canada.

⇒ See also CRYPTOGRAPHY; SYMMETRIC-KEY CRYPTOGRAPHY.

descender In typography, the portion of a lowercase letter that falls below the baseline. In the English alphabet, 5 letters have descenders: *g, j, p, q,* and *y*.

⇒ See also ASCENDER; BASELINE; X-HEIGHT.

Deschutes One of Intel's Pentium II microprocessors. Unlike previous Pentium IIs manufactured with a 0.35-micron process, the Deschutes processors have transistor sizes of 0.25 microns. The smaller size will enable Intel to produce smaller chips with lower power consumption. The first series of Deschutes chips ran at 333 MHz.

⇒ See also PENTIUM II; PENTIUM MICROPROCESSOR.

desk accessory (DA) On Apple Macintoshes, a utility—that is, a small, stand-alone program designed to perform one small task. For example, Apple's Calculator is a desk accessory.

⇒ See also UTILITY.

desktop 1. In graphical user interfaces, a *desktop* is the metaphor used to portray file systems. Such a desktop consists of pictures, called *icons*, that show cabinets, files, folders, and various types of documents (that is, letters, reports, pictures). You can arrange the icons on the electronic desktop just as you can arrange real objects on a real desktop —moving them around, putting one on top of another, reshuffling them, and throwing them away. **2.** Short for *desktop model computer.*

⇒ See also GRAPHICAL USER INTERFACE; SHORTCUT.

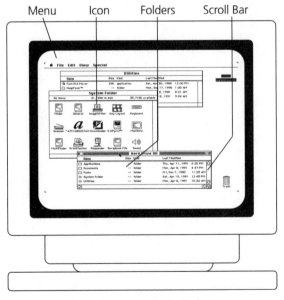

Figure 22: **Macintosh desktop**

Desktop Management Interface See DMI.

desktop model computer A computer designed to fit comfortably on top of a desk, typically with the monitor sitting on top of the computer. Desktop model computers are broad and low, whereas *tower model* computers are narrow and tall. Because of their shape, desktop model computers are generally limited to three internal mass storage devices. Desktop models designed to be very small are sometimes referred to as *slimline models*.

⇒ See also CHASSIS; PERSONAL COMPUTER; TOWER MODEL.

desktop publishing Using a personal computer or workstation to produce high-quality printed documents. A desktop publishing system allows you to use different typefaces, specify various margins and justifications, and embed illustrations and graphs directly into the text. The most powerful desktop publishing systems enable you to create illustrations, while less powerful systems let you insert illustrations created by other programs.

As word processing programs become more and more powerful, the line separating such programs from desktop publishing systems is becoming blurred. In general, though, desktop publishing applications give you more control over typographical characteristics, such as kerning, and provide more support for full-color output.

A particularly important feature of desktop publishing systems is that they enable you to see on the display screen exactly how the document will appear when printed. Systems that support this feature are called *WYSIWYGs (what you see is what you get)*.

Until recently, hardware costs made desktop publishing systems impractical for most uses. But as the prices of personal computers and printers have fallen, desktop publishing systems have become increasingly popular for producing newsletters, brochures, books, and other documents that formerly required a typesetter.

Once you have produced a document with a desktop publishing system, you can output it directly to a printer or you can produce a PostScript file that you can then take to a service bureau. The service bureau has special machines that convert the PostScript file to film, which can then be used to make plates for offset printing. Offset printing produces higher-quality documents, especially if color is used, but is generally more expensive than laser printing.

⇒ See also ADOBE PHOTOSHOP; COLOR SEPARATION; ISP; OFFSET PRINTING; PAGE LAYOUT PROGRAM.

desktop system Same as DESKTOP MODEL COMPUTER.

destination Many computer commands move data from one file to another or from one storage device to another. This is referred to as moving the data from the *source* to the *destination* (or *target*). The term is also used as an adjective, as in *destination file* or *destination device*.

⇒ See also SOURCE.

device Any machine or component that attaches to a computer. Examples of devices include disk drives, printers, mice, and modems. These particular devices fall into the category of peripheral devices because they are separate from the main computer. Display monitors and keyboards are also devices, but because they are integral parts of the computer, they are not considered peripheral.

Most devices, whether peripheral or not, require a program called a *device driver* that acts as a translator, converting general commands from an application into specific commands that the device understands.

⇒ See also COMPUTER; CONFIG.SYS; DRIVER; INPUT DEVICE.

Device Bay A specification developed by Intel, Compaq, and Microsoft that would standardize the size, shape, and connection of computer components, such as disk drives, modems, and audio devices. This would enable computer owners to exchange and upgrade these components easily. The Device Bay specification is similar to the PCMCIA standard but is designed for larger, faster devices. Device Bay components would connect to a computer using either the USB or IEEE 1394 (FireWire) interfaces.

Although the original specification was worked out in early 1997, computer manufacturers have not yet adopted it. Some analysts expect the first computers supporting Device Bay to appear sometime in 1999.

⇒ See also IEEE 1394; PCMCIA; USB.

device dependent Like *machine dependent, device dependent* refers to programs that can run only on a certain type of hardware.

⇒ See also MACHINE DEPENDENT.

device driver See DRIVER.

DHCP Short for *D(ynamic) H(ost) C(onfiguration) P(rotocol)*, a protocol for assigning dynamic IP addresses to devices on a network. With dynamic addressing, a device can have a different IP address every time it connects to the network. In some systems, the device's IP address can even change while it is still connected. DHCP also supports a mix of static and dynamic IP addresses.

Dynamic addressing simplifies network administration because the software keeps track of IP addresses rather than requiring an administrator to manage the task. This means that a new computer can be added to a network without the hassle of manually assigning it a unique IP address. Many ISPs use dynamic IP addressing for dial-up users.

DHCP client support is built into Windows 95 and NT workstation. NT 4 server includes both client and server support.

⇒ See also WINS.

DHTML Short for *Dynamic HTML*.

dialog box A box that appears on a display screen to present information or request input. Typically, dialog boxes are temporary — they disappear once you have entered the requested information.

In the Macintosh and Microsoft Windows interfaces, there is a convention that any menu option followed by ellipsis points (...) will, when selected, bring up a dialog box. Options without ellipsis points are executed directly.

⇒ See also BOX; GRAPHICAL USER INTERFACE; POP-UP WINDOW; WINDOW.

Dialog Box

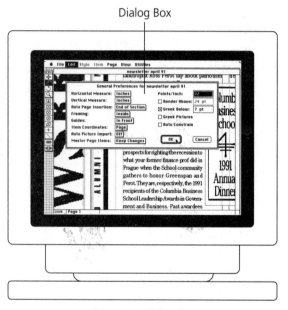

Figure 23: **dialog box**

dial-up access Refers to connecting a device to a network via a modem and a public telephone network. Dial-up access is really just like a phone connection, except that the parties at the two ends are computer devices rather than people. Because dial-up access uses normal telephone lines, the quality of the connection is not always good and data rates are limited. In the past, the maximum data rate with dial-up access was 28.8 Kbps (28,800 bits per second), but new technologies such as ISDN are providing faster rates.

An alternative way to connect two computers is through a *leased line*, which is a permanent connection between two devices. Leased lines provide faster throughput and better-quality connections, but they are also more expensive.

⇒ See also DIAL-UP NETWORKING; FRACTIONAL T-1; INTERNET; ISP; L2TP; LEASED LINE; MODEM; POP; RADIUS.

Dial-Up Networking A component in Windows 95 that enables you to connect your computer to a network via a modem. If your computer is not connected to a LAN and you want to connect to the Internet, you need to configure Dial-Up Networking (DUN) to dial a Point of Presence (POP) and log into your internet service provider (ISP). Your ISP will need to provide certain information, such as the gateway address and your computer's IP address.

You access DUN through the **My Computer** icon. You can configure a different profile (called a *connectoid*) for each different online service you use. Once it is configured, you can copy a connectoid shortcut to your desktop so that all you need to do to make a connection is double-click the connectoid icon.

⇒ See also DIAL-UP ACCESS; POP; RAS; WINDOWS 95.

DIB 1. Short for *D(ual) I(ndependent) B(us)*, a new bus architecture that is part of Intel's Pentium Pro and Pentium II microprocessors. As its name implies, DIB uses two buses: one from the processor to main memory, and the other from the processor to the L2 cache. The processor can access both buses simultaneously, which increases throughput. **2.** Short for *d(evice)-i(ndependent) b(itmap)*, the bit-mapped graphics format used by Windows. Graphics stored in DIB format generally end with a .BMP extension. It's called device independent because colors are represented in a format independent of the final output device. When a DIB image is output (to a monitor or printer), the device driver translates the DIB colors into actual colors that the output device can display.

⇒ See also BIT-MAPPED GRAPHICS; BMP; GRAPHICS FILE FORMATS; NETWORK MANAGEMENT; PENTIUM PRO; RMON.

digital Describes any system based on discontinuous data or events. Computers are digital machines because at their most basic level they can distinguish between just two values, 0 and 1, or off and on. There is no simple way to represent all the values in between, such as 0.25. All data that a computer processes must be encoded digitally, as a series of zeroes and ones.

The opposite of digital is *analog*. A typical analog device is a clock in which the hands move continuously around the face. Such a clock is capable of indicating every possible time of day. In contrast, a digital clock is capable of representing only a finite number of times (every tenth of a second, for example).

In general, humans experience the world analogically. Vision, for example, is an analog experience because we perceive infinitely smooth gradations of shapes and colors. Most analog events, however, can be simulated digitally. Photographs in newspapers, for instance, consist of an array of dots that are either black or white. From afar, the viewer does not see the dots (the digital form) but only lines and shading, which appear to be continuous. Although digital representations are approximations of analog events, they are useful because they are relatively easy to store and manipulate electronically. The trick is in converting from analog to digital, and back again.

This is the principle behind compact discs (CDs). The music itself exists in an analog form, as waves in the air, but these sounds are then translated into a digital form that is encoded onto the disk. When you play a compact disc, the CD player reads the digital data, translates it back into its original analog form, and sends it to the amplifier and eventually the speakers.

Internally, computers are digital because they consist of discrete units called bits that are either on or off. But by combining many bits in complex ways, computers simulate analog events. In one sense, this is what computer science is all about.

⇒ See also ANALOG; DAC; DIGITAL AUDIO; DIGITIZE; MODEM.

digital audio Refers to the reproduction and transmission of sound stored in a digital format. This includes CDs as well as any sound files stored on a computer. In contrast, the telephone system (but not ISDN) is based on an analog representation of sound.

⇒ See also AU; DIGITAL; DIGITAL VIDEO; DOLBY DIGITAL; MIDI; MP3; WAV.

digital audio tape See DAT.

digital camera A camera that stores images digitally rather than recording them on film. Once a picture has been taken, it can be downloaded to a computer system and then manipulated with a graphics program and printed. Unlike film photographs, which have an almost infinite resolution, digital photos are limited by the amount of memory in the camera, the optical resolution of the digitizing mechanism, and, finally, by the resolution of the final output device. Even the best digital cameras connected to the best printers cannot produce film-quality photos. However, if the final output device is a laser printer, it doesn't really matter whether you take a real photo and then scan it, or take a digital photo. In both cases, the image must eventually be reduced to the resolution of the printer.

The big advantage of digital cameras is that making photos is both inexpensive and fast because there is no film processing. Interestingly, one of the biggest boosters of digital photography is Kodak, the largest producer of film. Kodak developed the Kodak PhotoCD format, which has become the de facto standard for storing digital photographs.

Most digital cameras use CCDs to capture images, though some of the newer, less expensive cameras use CMOS chips instead.

⇒ See also DIGITAL; DIGITAL PHOTOGRAPHY; FlashPix; OPTICAL RESOLUTION; PhotoCD.

digital cash A system that allows a person to pay for goods or services by transmitting a number from one computer to another. Like the serial numbers on real dollar bills, the digital cash numbers are unique. Each one is issued by a bank and represents a specified sum of real money. One of the key features of digital cash is that, like real cash, it is anonymous and reusable. That is, when a digital cash amount is sent from a buyer to a vendor, there is no way to obtain information about the buyer. This is one of the key differences between digital cash and credit card systems. Another key difference is that a digital cash certificate can be reused.

Digital cash transactions are expected to become commonplace by the year 2000. However, there a number of competing protocols, and it is unclear which ones will become dominant. Most digital cash systems start with a participating bank that issues cash numbers or other unique identifiers that carry a given value, such as five dollars. To obtain such a certificate, you must have an account at the bank; when you purchase digital cash certificates, the money is withdrawn from your account. You transfer the certificate to the vendor to pay for a product or service, and the vendor deposits the cash number in any participating bank or retransmits it to another vendor. For large purchases, the vendor can check the validity of a cash number by contacting the issuing bank.

⇒ See also ELECTRONIC COMMERCE; INTERNET; SMART CARD.

digital certificate An attachment to an electronic message used for security purposes. The most common use of a digital certificate is to verify that a user sending a message is who he or she claims to be, and to provide the receiver with the means to encode a reply.

An individual wishing to send an encrypted message applies for a digital certificate from a *Certificate Authority (CA)*. The CA issues an encrypted digital certificate containing the applicant's public key and a variety of other identification information. The CA makes its own public key readily available through print publicity or perhaps on the Internet.

The recipient of an encrypted message uses the CA's public key to decode the digital certificate attached to the message, verifies it as issued by the CA, and then obtains the sender's public key and identification information held within the certificate. With this information, the recipient can send an encrypted reply.

The most widely used standard for digital certificates is X.509.

⇒ See also CERTIFICATE AUTHORITY; ENCRYPTION; PUBLIC-KEY ENCRYPTION; SSL; X.509.

Digital Data Storage See DDS.

Digital Electronics Corporation See DEC.

digital envelope A type of security that uses two layers of encryption to protect a message. First, the message itself is encoded using symmetric encryption, and then the key to decode the message is encrypted using public-key encryption. This technique overcomes one of the problems of public-key encryption, which is that it is slower than symmetric encryption. Because only the key is protected with public-key encryption, there is very little overhead.

⇒ See also ENCRYPTION; PUBLIC-KEY ENCRYPTION; SYMMETRIC ENCRYPTION.

digital imaging Same as COMPUTER IMAGING.

Digital Light Processing See DLP.

digital monitor A monitor that accepts digital rather than analog signals. All monitors (except flat-panel displays) use CRT technology, which is essentially analog. The term *digital*, therefore, refers only to the type of input received from the video adapter. A digital monitor then translates the digital signals into analog signals that control the actual display.

Although digital monitors are fast and produce clear images, they cannot display continuously variable colors. Consequently, only low-quality video standards, such as *MDA, CGA*, and *EGA*, specify digital signals. *VGA* and *SVGA*, on the other hand, require an analog monitor. Some monitors are capable of accepting either analog or digital signals.

⇒ See also ANALOG; ANALOG MONITOR; DIGITAL; MONITOR; VIDEO ADAPTER.

digital nervous system See DNS.

digital photography The art and science of producing and manipulating digital photographs—photographs that are represented as bit maps. Digital photographs can be produced in a number of ways:

- Directly with a digital camera
- By capturing a frame from a video
- By scanning a conventional photograph

Once a photograph is in digital format, you can apply a wide variety of special effects to it with image enhancing software. You can then print the photo out on a normal printer or send it to a developing studio which will print it out on photographic paper.

Although the resolution of digital photos is not nearly as high as photos produced from film, digital photography is ideal when you need instant, low-resolution pictures. It's especially useful for photos that will be displayed on the World Wide Web because Web graphics need to be low resolution anyway so that they can be downloaded quickly.

⇒ See also COMPUTER IMAGING; DIGITAL CAMERA; FlashPix; IMAGE ENHANCEMENT; IMAGE PROCESSING; SNAPSHOT PRINTER.

Digital Service Unit/Channel Service Unit See CSU/DSU.

digital signal processing See DSP.

digital signature A digital code that can be attached to an electronically transmitted message that uniquely identifies the sender. Like a written signature, the purpose of a digital signature is to guarantee that the individual sending the message really is who he or she claims to be. Digital signatures are especially important for electronic commerce and are a key component of most authentication schemes. To be effective, digital signatures must be unforgeable. A number of different encryption techniques are available to guarantee this level of security.

⇒ See also AUTHENTICATION; CERTIFICATE AUTHORITY; ELECTRONIC COMMERCE; SSL.

Digital Simultaneous Voice and Data See DSVD.

digital-to-analog converter See DAC.

digital versatile disk See DVD.

digital video Refers to the capturing, manipulation, and storage of video in digital formats. A digital video (DV) camcorder, for example, is a video camera that captures and stores images on a digital medium such as a DAT.

⇒ See also DIGITAL AUDIO; DIGITAL PHOTOGRAPHY; DOLBY DIGITAL; MOTION-JPEG; VIDEO CAPTURE; VIDEO EDITING.

Digital Video Interactive See DVI.

digital watermark A pattern of bits inserted into a digital image or an audio or video file that identifies the file's copyright information (author, rights, etc.). The name comes from the faintly visible watermarks imprinted on stationery that identify the manufacturer of the stationery. The purpose of digital watermarks is to provide copyright protection for intellectual property that's in digital format.

Unlike printed watermarks, which are intended to be somewhat visible, digital watermarks are designed to be completely invisible, or in the case of audio clips, inaudible. Moreover, the actual bits representing the watermark must be scattered throughout the file in such a way that they cannot be identified and manipulated. Finally, the digital watermark must be robust enough so that it can withstand normal changes to the file, such as reductions from lossy compression algorithms.

Satisfying all these requirements is no easy feat, but there are a number of companies offering competing technologies. All of them work by making the watermark appear as *noise*—that is, random data that exists in most digital files anyway. To view a watermark, you need a special program that knows how to extract the watermark data.

⇒ See also COPY PROTECTION; FLASHPIX; SOFTWARE PIRACY.

digitize To translate into a digital form. For example, optical scanners digitize images by translating them into bit maps. It is also possible to digitize sound, video, and any type of movement. In all these cases, digitization is performed by sampling at discrete intervals. To digitize sound, for example, a device measures pitch and volume many times per second. These numeric values can then be recorded digitally.

⇒ See also BIT MAP; DIGITAL; OPTICAL SCANNER; PCM; SAMPLING.

digitizing tablet An input device that enables you to enter drawings and sketches into a computer. A digitizing tablet consists of an electronic tablet and a *cursor* or pen. A cursor (also called a *puck*) is similar to a mouse, except that it has a window with cross hairs for pinpoint placement, and it can have as many as 16 buttons. A pen (also called a *stylus*) looks like a simple ballpoint pen but uses an electronic head instead of ink. The tablet contains electronics that enable it to detect movement of the cursor or pen and translate the movements into digital signals that it sends to the computer.

For digitizing tablets, each point on the tablet represents a point on the display screen in a fixed manner. This differs from mice, in which all movement is relative to the current cursor position. The static nature of digitizing tablets makes them particularly effective for tracing drawings. Most modern digitizing tablets also support a *mouse emulation mode*, in which the pen or cursor acts like a mouse.

Digitizing tablets are also called *digitizers, graphics tablets, touch tablets,* or simply *tablets.*

⇒ See also CURSOR; INPUT DEVICE; MOUSE.

Figure 24: **dingbats**

DIMM Short for *d(ual) i(n)-line m(emory) m(odule)*, a small circuit board that holds memory chips. A *single in-line memory module (SIMM)* has a 32-bit path to the memory chips, whereas a DIMM has a 64-bit path. Because the Pentium processor requires a 64-bit path to memory, you need to install SIMMs two at a time. With DIMMs, you can install memory one DIMM at a time.

⇒ See also DRAM; SIMM.

DIN connector *DIN* is an acronym for *D(eutsche) I(ndustri)n(orm)*, the standards-setting organization for Germany. A DIN connector is one that conforms to one of the many standards defined by DIN. DIN connectors are used widely in personal computers. For example, the keyboard connector for PCs is a DIN connector.

DIN 41612 connectors are used widely to connect network equipment, such as routers and switches.

⇒ See also CONNECTOR.

dingbat A small picture, such as a star or a pointing finger, that can be inserted into a document. Many sets of dingbats are available as a special font. One of the most popular is *Zapf dingbats*, named after its creator, Hermann Zapf.

⇒ See also BULLET; FONT.

DIP Acronym for *d(ual) i(n)-line p(ackage)*, a type of *chip* housed in a rectangular casing with two rows of connecting pins on either side.

⇒ See also CHIP; PGA.

DIP switch Any in a series of tiny switches built into circuit boards. The housing for the switches, which has the same shape as a chip, is the DIP.

DIP switches enable you to configure a circuit board for a particular type of computer or application. The installation instructions should tell you how to set the switches. DIP switches are always toggle switches, which means they have two possible positions—on or off. (Instead of on and off, you may see the numbers 1 and 0.)

One of the historic advantages of the Macintosh over the PC was that it allowed you to configure circuit boards by entering software commands instead of setting DIP switches. However, the new Plug-and-Play standard developed by Microsoft makes DIP switches obsolete for PC expansion cards too.

⇒ See also CHIP; CONFIGURATION; EXPANSION BOARD; PRINTED CIRCUIT BOARD; TOGGLE.

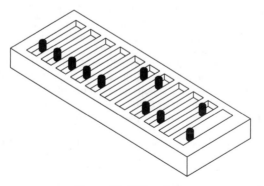

Figure 25: **DIP switches**

DirecPC A service offered by Hughes Network Systems that provides Internet access through private satellite dishes. Requests for Web pages go through a normal modem connection, but pages are delivered through the satellite link at up to 400 Kbps (about 15 times faster than a 28.8 Kbps modem, and 4 times faster than an ISDN connection).

To install the DirecPC system, you need to purchase a small satellite dish from Hughes, plus an ISA card to install in your computer. You'll also need a normal Internet connection via an ISP for *upstream* traffic (e.g., requests for Web pages).

⇒ See also ISDN; ISP.

Direct3D An Application Programming Interface (API) for manipulating and displaying three-dimensional objects. Developed by Microsoft, Direct3D provides programmers with a way to develop 3-D programs that can utilize whatever graphics acceleration device is installed in the machine. Virtually all 3-D accelerator cards for PCs support Direct3D.

Another 3-D standard offering similar functionality is *OpenGL*.

⇒ See also 3-D SOFTWARE; DIRECTDRAW; DIRECTX; GRAPHICS ACCELERATOR; OPENGL.

direct access Same as RANDOM ACCESS.

Direct Access Storage Device See DASD.

Direct Cable Connection See DCC.

direct-connect modem A modem that connects directly to a telephone line via modular connectors rather than requiring an acoustic coupler. Almost all modern modems are direct-connect.

⇒ See also ACOUSTIC COUPLER; MODEM.

DirectDraw A software interface standard for transferring video processing from a PC's CPU to the video adapter. The standard was first developed by Intel and called the *Display Control Interface (DCI)* and is now supported by Microsoft with the name *DirectDraw* as a registered trademark.

When the CPU is not busy, the Windows Graphics Display Interface (GDI) updates the video display. If the CPU is busy, the DCI driver allows an application to send update information directly to the video adapter. DirectDraw can also provide applications, such as games, direct access to features of particular display devices.

⇒ See also DIRECT3D; GDI; GRAPHICS ACCELERATOR; VIDEO ADAPTER.

directive Same as COMMAND.

direct memory access See DMA.

directory 1. A special kind of file used to organize other files into a hierarchical structure. Directories contain bookkeeping information about files that are, figuratively speaking, beneath them. You can think of a directory as a folder or cabinet that contains files and perhaps other folders. In fact, many graphical user interfaces use the term *folder* instead of *directory*.

Computer manuals often describe directories and file structures in terms of an *inverted tree*. The files and directories at any level are contained in the directory above them. To access a file, you may need to specify the names of all the directories above it. You do this by specifying a *path*.

The topmost directory in any file is called the *root directory*. A directory that is below another directory is called a *subdirectory*. A directory above a subdirectory is called the *parent directory*. Under DOS and Windows, the root directory is represented by a forward slash (/).

To read information from, or write information into, a directory, you must use an operating system command. You cannot directly edit directory files. For example, the DIR command in DOS reads a directory file and displays its contents. **2.** In networks, a database of network resources, such as e-mail addresses. See under DIRECTORY SERVICE.

⇒ See also FILE; FILE MANAGEMENT SYSTEM; FOLDER; HIERARCHICAL; PATH; ROOT DIRECTORY; TREE STRUCTURE.

Root Directory

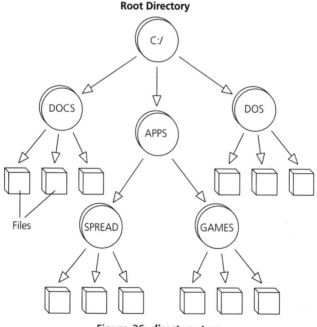

Figure 26: **directory tree**

directory service A network service that identifies all resources on a network and makes them accessible to users and applications. Resources include e-mail addresses, computers, and peripheral devices such as printers. Ideally, the directory service should make the physical network topology and protocols transparent so that a user on a network can access any resource without knowing where or how it is physically connected.

A number of directory services are used widely. Two of the most important ones are LDAP, which is used primarily for e-mail addresses, and *Netware Directory Service (NDS)*, which is used on Novell Netware networks. Virtually all directory services are based on the X.500 ITU standard, although the standard is so large and complex that no vendor complies with it fully.

⇒ See also ACTIVE DIRECTORY; LDAP; NDS; UNC; X.500.

DirectX A set of APIs developed by Microsoft that enables programmers to write programs that access hardware features of a computer without knowing exactly what hardware will be installed on the machine on which the program eventually runs. DirectX achieves this by creating an intermediate layer that translates generic hardware commands into specific commands for particular pieces of hardware. In particular, DirectX lets multimedia applications take advantage of hardware acceleration features supported by graphics accelerators.

DirectX 2, released in 1996, supports the Direct3D architecture. DirectX 5, released in 1998, adds new layers to the DirectX API. In addition to the low-level layer that communicates directly with multimedia hardware, DirectX 5 also includes a *Media layer* that enables programmers to manipulate multimedia objects and streams. DirectX 5 also supports USB and IEEE 1394 buses, AGP, and MMX.

⇒ See also ACTIVEX; DIRECT3D; GRAPHICS ACCELERATOR.

disc Alternative spelling of *disk*. *Disc* is often used for optical discs, whereas *disk* generally refers to magnetic discs, but there is no real rule.

⇒ See also DISK; OPTICAL DISK.

discretionary hyphen See under HYPHENATION.

disk A round plate on which data can be encoded. There are two basic types of disks: *magnetic disks* and *optical disks*.

On magnetic disks, data is encoded as microscopic magnetized *needles* on the disk's surface. You can record and erase data on a magnetic disk any number of times, just as you can with audio tape. Magnetic disks come in a number of different forms:

floppy disk: A typical 5¼-inch floppy disk can hold 360K, or 1.2MB (megabytes). 3½-inch floppies normally store 720K, 1.2MB, or 1.44MB of data.

hard disk: Hard disks can store anywhere from 20MB to more than 10GB. Hard disks are also from 10 to 100 times faster than floppy disks.

removable cartridge: Removable cartridges are hard disks encased in a metal or plastic cartridge, so you can remove them just like a floppy disk. Removable cartridges are very fast, though usually not as fast as fixed hard disks.

Optical disks record data by burning microscopic holes in the surface of the disk with a laser. To read the disk, another laser beam shines on the disk and detects the holes by changes in the reflection pattern. Optical disks come in three basic forms:

CD-ROM: Most optical disks are read-only. When you purchase them, they are already filled with data. You can read the data from a CD-ROM, but you cannot modify, delete, or write new data.
WORM: Stands for *w(rite)-o(nce), r(ead)-m(any)*. WORM disks can be written on once and then read any number of times; however, you need a special WORM disk drive to write data onto a WORM disk.
erasable optical (EO): EO disks can be read to, written to, and erased just like magnetic disks.

The machine that spins a disk is called a disk drive. Within each disk drive is one or more *heads* (often called *read/write heads*) that actually read and write data.

Accessing data from a disk is not as fast as accessing data from main memory, but disks are much cheaper. And unlike RAM, disks hold on to data even when the computer is turned off. Consequently, disks are the storage medium of choice for most types of data. Another storage medium is magnetic tape. But tapes are used only for backup and archiving because they are *sequential-access* devices (to access data in the middle of a tape, the tape drive must pass through all the preceding data).

A new disk, called a *blank disk,* has no data on it. Before you can store data on a blank disk, however, you must *format* it. Some disks are preformatted when you purchase them.

⇒ See also AREAL DENSITY; CD-ROM; DISK DRIVE; ERASABLE OPTICAL DISK; FLOPPY DISK; FORMAT; HARD DISK; HEAD; MASS STORAGE; OPTICAL DISK; REMOVABLE HARD DISK.

disk cache A portion of RAM used to speed up access to data on a disk. The RAM can be part of the disk drive itself (sometimes called a hard disk *cache* or *buffer*), or it can be general-purpose RAM in the computer that is reserved for use by the disk drive (sometimes called a *soft disk cache*). *Hard disk caches* are more effective, but they are also much more expensive, and therefore smaller. Nearly all modern disk drives include a small amount of internal cache.

A soft disk cache works by storing the most recently accessed data in the RAM cache. When a program needs to access new data, the operating system first checks to see if the data is in the cache before reading it from the disk. Because computers can access data from RAM much faster than from a disk, disk caching can significantly increase performance. Many cache systems also attempt to predict what data will be requested next so they can place that data in the cache ahead of time.

Although caching improves performance, there is some risk involved. If the computer crashes (because of a power failure, for example), the system may not have time to copy the cache back to the disk. In this case, whatever changes you made to the data will be lost. Usually, however, the cache system updates the disk frequently so that even if you lose some data, it will not be much. Caches that work in this manner are called *write-back caches*. Another type of disk cache, called a *write-thru cache*, removes the risk of losing data because it caches only data for read operations; write operations are always sent directly to the disk.

⇒ See also ACCESS TIME; BUFFER; CACHE; DISK DRIVE; RAM; SMARTDRIVE; VC-ACHE.

disk compression A type of data compression that works by storing compressed versions of files on the hard disk. A disk compression utility sits between the operating system and the disk drive. Whenever the operating system attempts to save a file to disk, the utility intercepts it and compresses it. Likewise, when the operating system attempts to open a file, the disk compression utility intercepts the file, decompresses it, and then passes it to the operating system. Because all applications access files through the operating system, disk compression utilities work with all applications. The entire process is transparent to the user, though opening and closing files may take a little longer. On the other hand, a disk compression utility can double the amount of disk space available.

Windows comes with a built-in disk compression utility called *Drive-Space*. You can also purchase third-party disk compression utilities for Windows and other operating systems.

⇒ See also DATA COMPRESSION; HARD DISK DRIVE; PACKED FILE.

disk controller A chip and associated circuitry that is responsible for controlling a disk drive. There are different controllers for different interfaces. For example, an IDE interface requires an IDE controller, and a SCSI interface requires a SCSI controller. On Macintosh computer systems, the disk controller is built into the motherboard.

A controller for a hard disk is called a *hard disk controller (HDC)*, and a controller for a floppy disk is called a *floppy disk controller (FDC)*.

⇒ See also CONTROLLER; DISK DRIVE; EISA; IDE INTERFACE; SCSI.

disk crash See under HEAD CRASH.

disk drive A machine that reads data from and writes data onto a disk. A disk drive rotates the disk very fast and has one or more heads that read and write data.

There are different types of disk drives for different types of disks. For example, a *hard disk drive* (HDD) reads and writes hard disks, and a *floppy drive* (FDD) accesses floppy disks. A *magnetic disk* drive reads magnetic disks, and an *optical drive* reads optical disks.

Disk drives can be either *internal* (housed within the computer) or *ex-*

ternal (housed in a separate box that connects to the computer).

⇒ See also ATA; DISK; DISK STRIPING; FLOPPY DISK; HARD DISK; MASS STORAGE; OPTICAL DISK; RAID; SMART.

diskette Same as FLOPPY DISK.

diskless workstation A workstation or PC on a *local-area network (LAN)* that does not have its own disk. Instead, it stores files on a network file server. Diskless workstations can reduce the overall cost of a LAN because one large-capacity disk drive is usually less expensive than several low-capacity drives. In addition, diskless workstations can simplify backups and security because all files are in one place—on the file server. Also, accessing data from a large remote file server is often faster than accessing data from a small local-storage device.

One disadvantage of diskless workstations, however, is that they are useless if the network fails.

When the workstation is a PC, it is often called a *diskless PC* or a *Net PC*.

⇒ See also BOOTP; DISK DRIVE; LOCAL-AREA NETWORK; NET PC; NETWORK COMPUTER; SERVER; WORKSTATION.

disk mirroring A technique in which data is written to two duplicate disks simultaneously. This way if one of the disk drives fails, the system can instantly switch to the other disk without any loss of data or service. Disk mirroring is used commonly in on-line database systems where it's critical that the data be accessible at all times.

⇒ See also FAULT TOLERANCE; RAID; SERVER MIRRORING.

disk operating system See DOS.

disk optimizer A program that makes a disk more efficient. Disk optimizers use a variety of techniques, including defragmenting the disk. Fragmentation occurs naturally when a disk is used often.

⇒ See also DEFRAG; FRAGMENTATION.

disk pack A stack of removable hard disks encased in a metal or plastic container.

⇒ See also HARD DISK; REMOVABLE HARD DISK.

disk striping A technique for spreading data over multiple disk drives. Disk striping can speed up operations that retrieve data from disk storage. The computer system breaks a body of data into units and spreads these units across the available disks. Systems that implement disk striping generally allow the user to select the data unit size or *stripe width.*

Disk striping is available in two types. *Single-user striping* uses relatively large data units and improves performance on a single-user workstation by allowing parallel transfers from different disks. *Multi-user striping* uses smaller data units and improves performance in a multi-user environment by allowing simultaneous (or overlapping) read operations on multiple disk drives.

Disk striping stores each data unit in only one place and does not offer protection from disk failure.

⇒ See also RAID.

dispatch table Same as INTERRUPT VECTOR TABLE.

display *v* **1.** To make data or images appear on a monitor. —*n* **2.** Short for DISPLAY SCREEN or MONITOR.

display adapter Same as VIDEO ADAPTER.

Display Control Interface See under DIRECTDRAW.

Display Data Channel See DDC.

display screen The display part of a monitor. Most display screens work under the same principle as a television, using a *cathode ray tube (CRT)*. Consequently, the term *CRT* is often used in place of *display screen*.

⇒ See also CAD/CAM; DESKTOP PUBLISHING; FLAT-PANEL DISPLAY; GRAPHICS; MONITOR; NOTEBOOK COMPUTER; PINCUSHION DISTORTION; RASTER; RESOLUTION.

distance learning A type of education in which students work on their own at home or at the office and communicate with faculty and other students via e-mail, electronic forums, videoconferencing, and other forms of computer-based communication. Distance learning is becoming especially popular with companies that need to regularly re-train their employees because it is less expensive than bringing all the students together in a traditional classroom setting.

Most distance learning programs include a computer-based training (CBT) system and communications tools to produce a *virtual classroom*. Because the Internet and World Wide Web are accessible from virtually all computer platforms, they serve as the foundation for many distance learning systems.

⇒ See also CBT; FORUM; VIDEOCONFERENCING.

Distributed Component Object Model See DCOM.

distributed computing A type of computing in which different components and objects constituting an application can be located on different computers connected to a network. So, for example, a word processing application might consist of an editor component on one computer, a spell-checker object on a second computer, and a thesaurus on a third computer. In some distributed computing systems, each of the three computers could even be running a different operating system.

Distributed computing is a natural outgrowth of object-oriented programming. Once programmers began creating objects that could be combined to form applications, it was a natural extension to develop systems that allowed these objects to be physically located on different computers.

One of the requirements of distributed computing is a set of standards that specify how objects communicate with one another. There are currently two chief distributed computing standards: CORBA and DCOM.

⇒ See also CORBA; DCOM; OBJECT-ORIENTED PROGRAMMING; OMG.

Distributed Computing Environment See DCE.

distributed database A database that consists of two or more data files located at different sites on a computer network. Because the database is distributed, different users can access it without interfering with one another. However, the database management system must periodically synchronize the scattered databases to make sure that they all have consistent data.

⇒ See also DATABASE; DATABASE MANAGEMENT SYSTEM; DISTRIBUTED PROCESSING; NETWORK; TWO-PHASE COMMIT.

distributed processing Refers to any of a variety of computer systems that use more than one computer, or processor, to run an application. This includes *parallel processing*, in which a single computer uses more than one *CPU* to execute programs. More often, however, *distributed processing* refers to *local-area networks (LANs)* designed so that a single program can run simultaneously at various sites. Most distributed processing systems contain sophisticated software that detects idle CPUs on the network and parcels out programs to utilize them.

Another form of distributed processing involves *distributed databases*, databases in which the data is stored across two or more computer systems. The database system keeps track of where the data is so that the distributed nature of the database is not apparent to users.

⇒ See also DATABASE MANAGEMENT SYSTEM; DCE; DISTRIBUTED DATABASE; LOCAL-AREA NETWORK; PARALLEL PROCESSING.

Distributed System Object Model See DSOM.

dithering Creating the illusion of new colors and shades by varying the pattern of dots. Newspaper photographs, for example, are dithered. If you look closely, you can see that different shades of gray are produced by varying the patterns of black and white dots. There are no gray dots at all. The more dither patterns that a device or program supports, the more shades of gray it can represent. In printing, dithering is usually called *halftoning,* and shades of gray are called *halftones.*

Note that *dithering* differs from *gray scaling.* In gray scaling, each individual dot can have a different shade of gray.

⇒ See also BILEVEL PRINTER; CONTONE PRINTER; GRAY SCALING; HALFTONE.

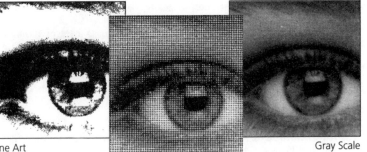

Line Art

Dithering

Gray Scale

Figure 27: **dithering**

Divx Short for *Di(gital) v(ideo) (e)x(press)*, a new DVD-ROM format being promoted by several large Hollywood companies, including Disney, Dreamworks SKG, Paramount, and Universal. With Divx, a movie (or other data) loaded onto a DVD-ROM is playable only during a specific time frame, typically two days. As soon as you begin playing a Divx disc, the counter starts. Each Divx player is connected to a telephone outlet and communicates with a central server to exchange billing information.

Divx discs have the potential to replace video tapes. They're especially convenient for video rentals because there are no late fees. Once you purchase a Divx title, you never need to return it. However, Divx has thrown a monkey wrench in the DVD market because the Divx format is not backward compatible with current DVD-ROM players. This means that you need to buy a new Divx player to play Divx titles. Understandably, people and companies that have already invested in non-Divx players are not pleased.

⇒ See also DVD; DVD-ROM.

DLC Short for *D(ata) L(ink) C(ontrol)*, the second lowest layer in the OSI Reference Model. Every network interface card (NIC) has a *DLC address* or *DLC identifier (DLCI)* that uniquely identifies the node on the network. Some network protocols, such as Ethernet and Token-Ring, use the DLC addresses exclusively. Other protocols, such as TCP/IP, use a logical address at the Network Layer to identify nodes. Ultimately, however, all network addresses must be translated to DLC addresses. In TCP/IP networks, this translation is performed with the Address Resolution Protocol (ARP).

For networks that conform to the IEEE 802 standards (e.g., Ethernet), the DLC address is usually called the *Media Access Control (MAC) address*.

⇒ See also ARP; IEEE 802 STANDARDS; MAC ADDRESS; NETWORK INTERFACE CARD; NODE; OSI.

DLL Short for *D(ynamic) L(ink) L(ibrary)*, a library of executable functions or data that can be used by a Windows application. Typically, a DLL provides one or more particular functions, and a program accesses the functions by creating either a static or dynamic link to the DLL. A static link remains constant during program execution, while a dynamic link is created by the program as needed. DLLs can also contain just data. DLL files usually end with the extension *.dll, .exe, .drv,* or *.fon.*

A DLL can be used by several applications at the same time. Some DLLs are provided with the Windows operating system and available to any Windows application. Other DLLs are written for a particular application and are loaded with the application.

⇒ See also LIBRARY; LINK; OLE; VBX.

DLP Short for *Digital Light Processing,* a new technology developed by Texas Instruments, used for projecting images from a monitor onto a large screen for presentations. Prior to the development of DLP, most computer projection systems were based on LCD technology, which tends to produce faded and blurry images. DLP uses tiny mirrors housed on a special kind of microchip called a *Digital Micromirror Device (DMD).* The result is sharp images that can be clearly seen even in a normally lit room.

⇒ See also LCD; MONITOR; TEXAS INSTRUMENTS.

DLT Short for *D(igital) L(inear) T(ape),* a type of magnetic tape storage device originally developed by DEC and now marketed by several companies. DLTs are ½-inch wide and the cartridges come in several sizes ranging from 20 to more than 40 GB. DLT drives are faster than most other types of tape drives, achieving transfer rates of 2.5 MBps.

⇒ See also TAPE; TAPE DRIVE.

DMA Abbreviation of *d(irect) m(emory) a(ccess),* a technique for transferring data from main memory to a device without passing it through the CPU. Computers that have DMA channels can transfer data to and from devices much more quickly than computers without a DMA channel can. This is useful for making quick backups and for *real-time* applications.

Some expansion boards, such as CD-ROM cards, are capable of accessing the computer's DMA channel. When you install the board, you must specify which DMA channel is to be used, which sometimes involves setting a jumper or DIP switch.

⇒ See also BACKUP; CHANNEL; CPU; DIP SWITCH; EXPANSION BOARD; JUMPER; MAIN MEMORY; REAL TIME.

DMI Short for *D(esktop) M(anagement) I(nterface),* an API to enable software to collect information about a computer environment. For example, using DMI, a program can determine what software and expansion boards are installed on a computer.

DMI is designed to be platform-independent and operating system-independent so that programs can make the same function calls to collect information no matter what system they're running in. This system independence is implemented by collecting information from MIF files, which are plain text files containing information about a software or hardware component.

DMI was designed by the *Desktop Management Task Force (DMTF),* a consortium of hardware manufacturers led by Intel. Version 2.0 allows a central computer not only to gather information about computers connected to a network but also to configure them. PCs that comply with DMI 2.0 are sometimes called *managed PCs.*

⇒ See also MIF.

DNA See WINDOWS DNA.

DNS 1. Short for *Domain Name System* (or *Service*), an Internet service that translates *domain names* into IP addresses. Because domain names are alphabetic, they're easier to remember. The Internet, however, is really based on IP addresses. Every time you use a domain name, therefore, a DNS service must translate the name into the corresponding IP address. For example, the domain name *www.example.com* might translate to *198. 105.232.4.*

The DNS system is, in fact, its own network. If one DNS server doesn't know how to translate a particular domain name, it asks another one, and so on, until the correct IP address is returned. **2.** Short for **d**igital n(ervous) s(ystem), a term coined by Bill Gates to describe a network of personal computers that make it easier to obtain and understand information.

⇒ See also BIND; DOMAIN; DOMAIN NAME; IAHC; INTERPROCESS COMMUNICATION (IPC); WINS.

docking station A platform into which you can install a portable computer. The docking station typically contains slots for expansion cards, bays for storage devices, and connectors for peripheral devices, such as printers and monitors. Once inserted in a docking station, the portable computer essentially becomes a desktop model computer. When it is taken out, it becomes a portable computer again. Most important, the same data is accessible in both modes because it resides on the portable computer's drives. The idea behind docking stations is to let you simultaneously enjoy the expansion possibilities of desktop model computers with the portability of notebook computers. In addition, the docking station enables you to use a full-size keyboard and monitor when you're not traveling.

There is no standard for docking stations, so you must purchase one that is made specifically for your type of portable computer.

⇒ See also BAY; DESKTOP MODEL COMPUTER; EXPANSION BOARD; NOTEBOOK COM-
PUTER; PORT REPLICATOR; PORTABLE; SLOT.

document n **1.** In the PC world, a file created with a word processor. In
addition to text, documents can contain graphics, charts, and other objects.

Increasingly, the line separating word processing files from files produced by other applications is becoming blurred. A word processing application can produce graphics and a graphics application can produce
words. This trend is accelerating with new technologies such as OLE and
OpenDoc that allow an application to combine many components. Consequently, the term *document* is used more and more to describe any file
produced by an application. Interestingly, this is the way the term has always been used in Macintosh environments. —v **2.** To enter written ex-
planations. For example, programmers are always exhorted to document
their code by inserting comments.

⇒ See also COMPOUND DOCUMENT; DOCUMENTATION; FILE.

documentation Instructions for using a computer device or program. Documentation can appear in a variety of forms, the most common being
manuals. When you buy a computer product (hardware or software), it
almost always comes with one or more manuals that describe how to install and operate the product. In addition, many software products include an online version of the documentation that you can display on
your screen or print out on a printer. A special type of online documentation is a *help system*, which has the documentation embedded into the
program. Help systems are often called *context-sensitive* because they display different information depending on the user's position (context) in
the application.

Documentation is often divided into the following categories:

installation: Describes how to install a program or device but not how
  to use it.
reference: Detailed descriptions of particular items presented in alphabetical order. Reference documentation is designed for people who
  are already somewhat familiar with the product but need reminders
  or very specific information about a particular topic.
tutorial: Teaches a user how to use the product. Tutorials move at a
  slower pace than reference manuals and generally contain less detail.

A frequent lament from computer users is that their documentation is
inscrutable. Fortunately, this situation is improving, thanks largely to
advances in help systems and online tutorials. These forms of documentation make it much easier to deliver the specific information a user
needs when he or she needs it.

⇒ See also HELP; MAN PAGE; README FILE.

document management The computerized management of electronic as
  well as paper-based documents. Document-management systems generally include the following components: (1) An optical scanner and OCR

system to convert paper documents into an electronic form, (2) a database system to organize stored documents, and (3) a search mechanism to find specific documents quickly.

Document-management systems are becoming more important as it becomes increasingly obvious that the paperless office is an ideal that may never be achieved. Instead, document-management systems strive to create systems that can handle paper and electronic documents together.

⇒ See also OPTICAL CHARACTER RECOGNITION; PAPERLESS OFFICE.

Document Object Model See DOM.

Dolby Digital A standard for high-quality digital audio that is used for the sound portion of video stored in digital format, especially videos stored on DVD-ROMs. Dolby Digital delivers 6 channels in the so-called "5:1" configuration: left, right, and center screen channels, separate left and right sounds, and a subwoofer channel. This is sometimes called *surround sound* or *3-D sound*.

⇒ See also AC-3; DIGITAL AUDIO; DIGITAL VIDEO; DVD.

DOM Short for *D(ocument) O(bject) M(odel)*, the specification for how objects in a Web page (text, images, headers, links, etc.) are represented. The DOM defines what attributes are associated with each object and how the objects and attributes can be manipulated. Dynamic HTML (DHTML) relies on the DOM to change the appearance of Web pages dynamically after they have been downloaded to a user's browser.

Unfortunately, the two leading browsers—Netscape Navigator and Microsoft Internet Explorer—use different DOMs. This is one reason why their respective implementations of DHTML are so different. Both companies have submitted their DOMs to the World Wide Web Consortium (W3C) for standardization, which now has the daunting task of specifying a standard DOM without alienating either of the browser giants. The W3C's DOM specification will support both HTML and XML.

⇒ See also DYNAMIC HTML; HTML; JAVASCRIPT; WEB PAGE; XML.

domain A group of computers and devices on a network that are administered as a unit with common rules and procedures. Within the Internet, domains are defined by the *IP address*. All devices sharing a common part of the IP address are said to be in the same domain.

⇒ See also DNS; DOMAIN NAME; INTERNET.

domain name A name that identifies one or more *IP addresses*. For example, the domain name *microsoft.com* represents about a dozen IP addresses. Domain names are used in URLs to identify particular Web pages. For example, in the URL *http://www.pcwebopedia.com/index.html,* the domain name is *pcwebopedia.com.*

Every domain name has a suffix that indicates which *top-level domain*

(TLD) it belongs to. There are only a limited number of such domains. For example:

- **gov** - Government agencies
- **edu** - Educational institutions
- **org** - Organizations (nonprofit)
- **mil** - Military
- **com** - commercial business
- **net** - Network organizations
- **ca** - Canada
- **th** - Thailand

Because of a shortage of domain names at the top level, the *Internet Ad Hoc Committee (IAHC)* has proposed six new top-level domains, to start being used in 1998:

- **store** - merchants
- **web** - parties emphasizing Web activities
- **arts** - arts and cultural-oriented entities
- **rec** - recreation/entertainment sources
- **info** - information services
- **nom** - individuals

Because the Internet is based on IP addresses, not domain names, every Web server requires a Domain Name System (DNS) server to translate domain names into IP addresses.

⇒ See also DNS; DOMAIN; IAHC; INTERNIC; IP ADDRESS; TLD; WHOIS.

Domain Name Server See DNS.

Domain Name Service (DNS) See DNS.

dongle A device that attaches to a computer to control access to a particular application. Dongles provide the most effective means of copy protection. Typically, the dongle attaches to a PC's parallel port. On Macintoshes, the dongle sometimes attaches to the ADB port. The dongle passes through all data coming through the port so it does not prevent the port from being used for other purposes. In fact, it's possible to attach several dongles to the same port.

⇒ See also COPY PROTECTION.

DOS Acronym for *d(isk) o(perating) s(ystem)*. The term *DOS* can refer to any operating system, but it is most often used as a shorthand for *MS-DOS* [*(M(icro)s(oft) d(isk) o(perating) s(ystem)*]. Originally developed by Microsoft for IBM, MS-DOS was the standard operating system for IBM-compatible personal computers.

The initial versions of DOS were very simple and resembled another operating system called CP/M. Subsequent versions have became increasingly sophisticated as they incorporated features of minicomputer operating systems. However, DOS is still a 16-bit operating system and does not support multiple users or multitasking.

For some time, it has been widely acknowledged that DOS is insufficient for modern computer applications. Microsoft Windows helped alleviate some problems, but until Windows 95, it sat on top of DOS and relied on DOS for many services. Newer operating systems, including Windows 95 and 98, Windows NT, and OS/2 Warp, do not rely on DOS to the same extent, although they can execute DOS-based programs. It is expected that as these operating systems gain market share, DOS will eventually disappear. In the meantime, Caldera, Inc., markets a version of DOS called *DR-OpenDOS* that extends MS-DOS in significant ways.

⇒ See also MICROSOFT; MICROSOFT WINDOWS; OPERATING SYSTEM; OS/2; PC; PIF FILE.

dot 1. Same as the period character (.). In DOS, Windows, and OS/2 systems, the dot is used to separate a filename from its extension. For example, the filename CONFIG.SYS is pronounced *config-dot-sys*. **2.** In bit-mapped representations, a dot is a single point, the smallest identifiable part of an image. Laser printers, for example, create characters and images by printing patterns of dots. Likewise, monitors display images as arrays of dots. The resolutions of devices are often measured in *dots per inch (dpi)*.

⇒ See also BIT MAP; DPI; EXTENSION; FILENAME; RESOLUTION.

dot-matrix printer A type of printer that produces characters and illustrations by striking pins against an ink ribbon to print closely spaced dots in the appropriate shape. Dot-matrix printers are relatively expensive and do not produce high-quality output. However, they can print to multi-page forms (that is, carbon copies), something laser and ink-jet printers cannot do.

Dot-matrix printers vary in two important characteristics:

speed: Given in *characters per second (cps)*, the speed can vary from about 50 to more than 500 cps. Most dot-matrix printers offer different speeds depending on the quality of print desired.
print quality: Determined by the number of pins (the mechanisms that print the dots), it can vary from 9 to 24. The best dot-matrix printers (24 pins) can produce near letter-quality type, although you can still see a difference if you look closely.

In addition to these characteristics, you should also consider the noise factor. Compared with laser and ink-jet printers, dot-matrix printers are notorious for making a racket.
⇒ See also IMPACT PRINTER; OKIDATA; PRINTER.

dot pitch A measurement that indicates the diagonal distance between like-colored phosphor dots on a display screen. Measured in millimeters, the dot pitch is one of the principal characteristics that determine the quality of display monitors. The lower the number, the crisper the image.

The dot pitch of color monitors for personal computers ranges from about 0.15 mm to 0.30 mm.

Another term for *dot pitch* is *phosphor pitch.*

⇒ See also COLOR MONITOR; MASK PITCH; MONITOR; PIXEL.

dots per inch See DPI.

double click Tapping a mouse button twice in rapid succession. Note that the second click must immediately follow the first; otherwise, the program will interpret them as two separate clicks rather than one double click.

In Microsoft Windows and the Macintosh interface, you can use a double click to open files and applications. Both systems let you set the double-click speed (the longest acceptable interval between each click).

⇒ See also CLICK; MOUSE.

double-density disk A floppy disk that has twice the storage capacity of a single-density floppy. Single-density disks are now obsolete. Double-density 5¼-inch disks for PCs can hold 360K of data. Double-density 3½-inch disks can hold 720K.

⇒ See also DENSITY; FLOPPY DISK.

double precision Refers to a type of floating point number that has more precision (that is, more digits to the right of the decimal point) than a *single-precision* number. The term *double precision* is something of a misnomer because the precision is not really double. The word *double* derives from the fact that a double-precision number uses twice as many bits as a regular floating-point number. For example, if a single-precision number requires 32 bits, its double-precision counterpart will be 64 bits long.

The extra bits increase not only the precision but also the range of magnitudes that can be represented. The exact amount by which the precision and range of magnitudes are increased depends on what format the program is using to represent floating-point values. Most computers use a standard format known as the *IEEE floating-point format.*

⇒ See also FLOATING-POINT NUMBER; IEEE.

double-scan display Same as DUAL-SCAN DISPLAY.

double-sided disk A floppy disk with both sides prepared for recording data. You can store twice as much data on a double-sided disk, but you need to use a double-sided disk drive. All modern disks and disk drives are double-sided.

⇒ See also DISK DRIVE; FLOPPY DISK.

double-speed CD-ROM See under CD-ROM.

double supertwist See under SUPERTWIST.

down Not working. A computer system is said to be down when it is not available to users. This can occur because it is broken (that is, it has crashed), or because it has been made temporarily unavailable to users so that routine servicing can be performed.

⇒ See also CRASH.

download To copy data (usually an entire file) from a main source to a peripheral device. The term is often used to describe the process of copying a file from an online service or *bulletin board service (BBS)* to one's own computer. Downloading can also refer to copying a file from a network file server to a computer on the network.

In addition, the term is used to describe the process of loading a font into a laser printer. The font is first copied from a disk to the printer's local memory. A font that has been downloaded like this is called a *soft font* to distinguish it from the *hard fonts* that are permanently in the printer's memory.

The opposite of download is *upload*, which means to copy a file from your own computer to another computer.

⇒ See also ANONYMOUS FTP; BULLETIN BOARD SYSTEM; FONT; ONLINE SERVICE; UPLOAD.

downloadable font Same as SOFT FONT.

downward compatible Same as BACKWARD COMPATIBLE.

DP See DATA PROCESSING.

dpi Abbreviation of *d(ots) p(er) i(nch)*, which indicates the resolution of images. The more dots per inch, the higher the resolution. A common resolution for laser printers is 600 dots per inch. This means 600 dots across and 600 dots down, so there are 360,000 dots per square inch.

⇒ See also DOT; LASER PRINTER; RESOLUTION.

draft mode A printing mode in which the printer prints text as fast as possible without regard to the print quality. Most dot-matrix printers support two modes: draft mode and either *letter-quality (LQ)* or *near letter quality (NLQ)* mode. In addition, many word processors support a draft mode in which they display and print pages without all the formatting detail specified for the document.

⇒ See also DOT-MATRIX PRINTER; LETTER QUALITY (LQ); NEAR LETTER QUALITY.

draft quality Describes print whose quality is less than *near letter quality*. Most 9-pin dot-matrix printers produce draft-quality print.

⇒ See also DOT-MATRIX PRINTER; DRAFT MODE; LETTER QUALITY (LQ); NEAR LETTER QUALITY.

drag In graphical user interfaces, *drag* refers to moving an icon or other image on a display screen. To drag an object across a display screen, you usually select the object with a mouse button ("grab" it) and then move the mouse while keeping the mouse button pressed down.

The term *drag* is also used more generally to refer to any operation in which the mouse button is held down while the mouse is moved. For example, you would drag the mouse to select a block of text.

⇒ See also DRAG-AND-DROP; GRAPHICAL USER INTERFACE; MOUSE; SELECT.

drag-and-drop Describes applications that allow you to drag objects to specific locations on the screen to perform actions on them. For example, in the Macintosh environment, you can drag a document to the trashcan icon to delete it. This is a classic case of drag-and-drop functionality.

When implemented well, drag-and-drop functionality is both faster and more intuitive than alternatives, such as selecting options from a menu or typing in commands.

Modern operating systems, including Windows and the Mac OS, even allow you to drag and drop *between* applications. You can, for example, create a picture with a draw program, select it, and then drag it into a document that you are editing with a word processor.

⇒ See also DRAG; GRAPHICAL USER INTERFACE.

drag-n-drop Same as DRAG-AND-DROP.

DRAM Pronounced **dee**-ram, DRAM stands for *d(ynamic) r(andom) a(ccess) m(emory)*, a type of memory used in most personal computers.

⇒ See also BEDO DRAM; DIMM; DYNAMIC RAM; EDO DRAM; MDRAM; PIPELINE BURST CACHE; RDRAM; SDRAM; SGRAM; SLDRAM.

drawing tablet Same as DIGITIZING TABLET.

draw program A graphics program that enables you to draw pictures, then store the images in files, merge them into documents, and print them. Unlike paint programs, which represent images as bit maps, draw programs use *vector graphics*, which makes it easy to scale images to different sizes. In addition, graphics produced with a draw program have no inherent resolution. Rather, they can be represented at any resolution, which makes them ideal for high-resolution output.

⇒ See also GRAPHICS; PAINT PROGRAM; VECTOR GRAPHICS.

drive Short for *disk drive*.

drive bay An area of reserved space in a personal computer where hard or floppy disk drives (or tape drives) can be installed. The number of drive bays in a computer determines the total number of internal mass storage devices it can handle.

⇒ See also BAY; DISK DRIVE; MASS STORAGE.

driver A program that controls a device. Every device, whether a printer, disk drive, or keyboard, must have a driver program. Many drivers, such as the keyboard driver, come with the operating system. For other devices, you may need to load a new driver when you connect the device to your computer. In DOS systems, drivers are files with a .SYS extension. In Windows environments, drivers often have a .DRV extension.

A driver acts like a translator between the device and programs that use the device. Each device has its own set of specialized commands that only its driver knows. In contrast, most programs access devices by using generic commands. The driver, therefore, accepts generic commands from a program and then translates them into specialized commands for the device.

⇒ See also CONFIG.SYS; CONTROLLER; DEVICE; ODI; VIRTUAL DEVICE DRIVER.

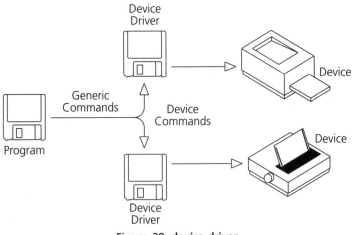

Figure 28: **device driver**

drop cap In desktop publishing, the first letter of a paragraph that is enlarged to "drop" down two or more lines, as in the accompanying paragraph.

⇒ See also DESKTOP PUBLISHING.

D rop caps are used to make a page more visually interesting and to draw the reader's eyes to the beginning of a section.

drop-down menu Same as PULL-DOWN MENU.

DS-1 Same as T-1.

DS-3 Same as T-3.

DSL See under xDSL.

DSOM Short for *D(istributed) S(ystem) O(bject) M(odel)*, a version of *SOM* that supports sharing binary objects across networks. DSOM is similar to Microsoft's competing standard called DCOM.

⇒ See also CORBA; DCOM; SOM.

DSP Short for *d(igital) s(ignal) p(rocessing)*, which refers to manipulating analog information, such as sound or photographs, that has been converted into a digital form. DSP also implies the use of a data compression technique.

When used as a noun, *DSP* stands for *d(igital) s(ignal) p(rocessor)*, a special type of coprocessor designed for performing the mathematics involved in DSP. Most DSPs are programmable, which means that they can be used for manipulating different types of information, including sound, images, and video.

⇒ See also COPROCESSOR; DATA COMPRESSION; DIGITIZE; GRAPHICS ACCELERATOR; MMX; SOUND CARD.

DSS Short for *d(igital) s(atellite) s(ystem)*, a network of satellites that broadcast digital data. An example of a DSS is *DirecTV*, which broadcasts digital television signals. DSSs are expected to become more important as the TV and computer converge into a single medium for information and entertainment.

⇒ See also HDTV.

DSTN Short for *d(ouble)-layer s(uper)t(wist) n(ematic)*, a passive-matrix LCD technology that uses two display layers to counteract the color shifting that occurs with conventional supertwist displays.
⇒ See also CSTN; LCD; PASSIVE-MATRIX DISPLAY; SUPERTWIST.

DSU See under CSU/DSU.

DSVD Short for *D(igital) S(imultaneous) V(oice) and D(ata)*, an all-digital technology for concurrent voice and data (SVD) transmission over a single analog telephone line. DSVD is endorsed by Intel, Hayes, U.S. Robotics, and others and has been submitted to the ITU (*International Telecommunication Union*) for possible standardization. DSVD modems became available in the first half of 1995.

⇒ See also ITU; MODEM; POTS.

DTE Short for *D(ata) T(erminal) E(quipment)*, a device that controls data flowing to or from a computer. The term is most often used in reference to serial communications defined by the RS-232C standard. This standard defines the two ends of the communications channel as being a DTE and Data Communications Equipment (DCE) device. In practical terms, the DCE is usually a modem and the DTE is the computer itself, or, more precisely, the computer's UART chip. For internal modems, the DCE and DTE are part of the same device.

⇒ See also DCE; RS-232C; UART.

DTMF Short for *D(ual) T(one) M(ulti)-F(requency)*, the system used by touch-tone telephones. DTMF assigns a specific frequency, or tone, to each key so that it can easily be identified by a microprocessor.

⇒ See also TELEPHONY.

DTP See DESKTOP PUBLISHING.

dual in-line memory module See DIMM.

dual in-line package See DIP.

dual-scan display A type of passive-matrix LCD display that provides faster refresh rates than conventional passive-matrix displays by dividing the screen into two sections that are refreshed simultaneously. Dual-scan displays are not as sharp or bright as active-matrix displays, but they consume less power.

⇒ See also ACTIVE-MATRIX DISPLAY; FLAT-PANEL DISPLAY; LCD; PASSIVE-MATRIX DISPLAY.

dual supertwist See under SUPERTWIST.

Dual Tone Multi-Frequency See DTMF.

dumb terminal A display monitor that has no processing capabilities. A dumb terminal is simply an output device that accepts data from the CPU. In contrast, a *smart terminal* is a monitor that has its own processor for special features, such as bold and blinking characters. Dumb terminals are not as fast as smart terminals, and they do not support as many display features, but they are adequate for most applications.

⇒ See also DISPLAY SCREEN; INTELLIGENT TERMINAL; SMART TERMINAL; TERMINAL; WINDOWS TERMINAL.

dummy A placeholder. A *dummy variable*, for example, is a variable that doesn't contain any useful data, but it does reserve space that a real variable will use later.

⇒ See also VARIABLE.

dump *n* **1.** The act of copying raw data from one place to another with little or no formatting for readability. Usually, *dump* refers to copying data from main memory to a display screen or a printer. Dumps are useful for diagnosing bugs. After a program fails, you can study the dump and analyze the contents of memory at the time of the failure. Dumps are usually output in a difficult-to-read form (that is, binary, octal, or hexadecimal), so a dump will not help you unless you know exactly what to look for. —*v* **2.** To output an image of computer memory.

DUN See DIAL-UP NETWORKING.

duplex Same as FULL DUPLEX.

DV Short for *digital video*.

DVD Short for *d(igital) v(ersatile) d(isc)* or *d(igital) v(ideo) d(isc)*, a new type of CD-ROM that holds a minimum of 4.7GB, enough for a full-length movie. Many experts believe that DVDs, called *DVD-ROMs*, will eventually replace CD-ROMs, as well as VHS video cassettes and laser discs.
   The DVD specification supports disks with capacities of from 4.7GB to 17GB and access rates of 600KBps to 1.3 MBps. One of the best features of DVD drives is that they are backward-compatible with CD-ROMs. This means that DVD players can play old CD-ROMs, CD-I disks, and video CDs, as well as new DVD-ROMs. Newer DVD players can also read CD-R disks.
   DVD uses MPEG-2 to compress video data.

⇒ See also CD-I (COMPACT DISC–INTERACTIVE); CD-ROM; COMPACT DISC; DIVX; DOLBY DIGITAL; DVD+RW; DVD-RAM; DVD-ROM; DVD-VIDEO; DVI; MPEG; MULTIMEDIA.

DVD-RAM A new type of rewritable compact disc that provides much greater data storage than today's CD-RW systems. The specifications for DVD-RAMs are still being hammered out by the DVD Consortium. Meanwhile, a competing group of manufacturers led by Hewlett-Packard, Philips, and Sony have come up with a competing standard called DVD + RW. Whereas the DVD-RAM standard supports 2.6 GB per disk side, DVD + RW supports 3 GB per side.

⇒ See also CD-RW DISK; DVD; DVD+RW; DVD-ROM; DVD-VIDEO.

DVD-ROM A new type of read-only compact disc that can hold a minimum of 4.7GB, enough for a full-length movie. Many experts believe that DVD-ROMs will eventually replace CD-ROMs, as well as VHS video cassettes and laser discs. Currently, however, DVD-ROMs are more promise than reality. There are only a few DVD-ROM devices currently on the market and even fewer DVD-ROM titles.

The DVD-ROM specification supports disks with capacities of from 4.7GB to 17GB and access rates of 600 KBps to 1.3 MBps. One of the best features of DVD-ROM drives is that they are backward-compatible with CD-ROMs. This means that DVD-ROM players can play old CD-ROMs, CD-I disks, and video CDs, as well as new DVD-ROMs. Newer DVD players can also read CD-R disks.

DVD-ROMs use MPEG-2 to compress video data.

⇒ See also Divx; DVD; DVD-RAM; MPEG.

DVD+RW A new standard for rewritable DVD disks being promoted by Hewlett-Packard, Philips, and Sony. It is competing with another standard, called DVD-RAM, developed by the DVD Consortium. The two standards are incompatible. DVD + RW disks have a slightly higher capacity—3 GB per side, versus 2.6 GB per side for DVD-RAM disks.

⇒ See also CD-RW DISK; DVD; DVD-RAM.

DVD-Video A video format for displaying full-length digital movies. A number of manufacturers are just beginning to sell DVD-Video players, which attach to a television just like a video cassette player. Unlike DVD-ROMs, the Digital-Video format includes a *Content Scrambling System (CSS)* to prevent users from copying discs. This means that today's DVD-ROM players cannot play DVD-Video discs without a software or hardware upgrade to decode the encrypted discs.

⇒ See also COPY PROTECTION; DVD; DVD-ROM.

DVI 1. Abbreviation of *D(igital) V(ideo) I(nteractive)*, a technology developed by General Electric that enables a computer to store and display moving video images like those on television. The most difficult aspect of displaying TV-like images on a computer is overcoming the fact that each frame requires an immense amount of storage. A single frame can require up to 2MB of storage. Televisions display 30 frames per second, which can quickly exhaust a computer's mass storage resources. It is also difficult to transfer so much data to a display screen at a rate of 30 frames per second.

DVI overcomes these problems by using specialized processors to compress and decompress the data. DVI is a hardware-only *codec (compression/decompression)* technology. A competing hardware codec, which has become much more popular, is MPEG. Intel has developed a software version of the DVI algorithms, which it markets under the name *Indeo*. **2.** Short for *D(e)v(ice) I(ndependent)*, a file format used by the TeX typography system.

⇒ See also CD-I (COMPACT DISC–INTERACTIVE); CD-RW DISK; CODEC; DVD; INDEO; INTEL; MPEG.

Dvorak keyboard A keyboard designed for speed typing. The Dvorak keyboard was designed in the 1930s by August Dvorak, a professor of education, and his brother-in-law, William Dealy. Unlike the traditional QWERTY keyboard, the Dvorak keyboard is designed so that the middle row of keys includes the most common letters. In addition, common letter combinations are positioned in such a way that they can be typed quickly.

It has been estimated that in an average eight-hour day, a typist's hands travel 16 miles on a QWERTY keyboard, but only 1 mile on a Dvorak keyboard.

In addition to the standard Dvorak keyboard, there are two additional Dvorak keyboards, a left-handed keyboard and a right-handed keyboard. These keyboards are designed for people who have only one hand for typing.

⇒ See also KEYBOARD; MACRO; QWERTY KEYBOARD.

Figure 29: **Dvorak keyboard**

DW Short for *data warehousing.*

DXF Abbreviation of *D(ata) Ex(change) F(ile)*, a two-dimensional graphics file format supported by virtually all PC-based CAD products. It was created by AutoDesk for the AutoCAD system.

⇒ See also CAD; GRAPHICS; GRAPHICS FILE FORMATS.

dynamic Refers to actions that take place at the moment they are needed rather than in advance. For example, many programs perform *dynamic memory allocation,* which means that they do not reserve memory ahead of time but seize sections of memory when needed. In general, such programs require less memory, although they may run a little more slowly.
The opposite of dynamic is *static.*

⇒ See also DYNAMIC VARIABLE; STATIC VARIABLE.

dynamic acceleration A feature supported by some mice drivers that causes the mouse resolution to depend on how fast the mouse is moved. When you move the mouse fast, the cursor moves proportionally farther (the resolution is low). This is useful for jumping across the screen. Without this feature, you might need to sweep the mouse several times to move the cursor from one side of the display screen to the other. When you move the mouse slowly, the resolution increases to enable you to pinpoint specific pixels.
Dynamic resolution is also called *ballistic tracking, automatic acceleration, variable acceleration,* and *dynamic acceleration.*

⇒ See also MOUSE; RESOLUTION.

Dynamic Data Exchange See DDE.

Dynamic Host Configuration Protocol See DHCP.

dynamic HTML 1. Refers to Web content that changes each time it is viewed. For example, the same URL could result in a different page depending on any number of parameters, such as:

• Geographic location of the reader
• Time of day
• Previous pages viewed by the reader
• Profile of the reader

There are many technologies for producing dynamic HTML, including CGI scripts, Server-Side Includes (SSI), cookies, Java, JavaScript, and ActiveX. **2.** When capitalized, *Dynamic HTML* refers to new HTML extensions that will enable a Web page to react to user input without sending requests to the Web server. Microsoft and Netscape have submitted competing Dynamic HTML proposals to W3C, which is producing the final specification.

⇒ See also ActiveX CONTROL; CGI; COOKIE; DOM; JAVA; JAVASCRIPT; SSI; W3C; WINDOWS DNA.

dynamic link library See DLL.

dynamic RAM A type of physical memory used in most personal computers. The term *dynamic* indicates that the memory must be constantly *refreshed* (reenergized) or it will lose its contents. *RAM (random-access memory)* is sometimes referred to as *DRAM* (pronounced **dee**-ram) to distinguish it from *static RAM (SRAM)*. Static RAM is faster and less volatile than dynamic RAM, but it requires more power and is more expensive.

⇒ See also MAIN MEMORY; RAM; REFRESH; SRAM.

dynamic variable In programming, a dynamic variable is a variable whose address is determined when the program is run. In contrast, a *static variable* has memory reserved for it at compilation time.

⇒ See also STATIC VARIABLE; VARIABLE.

easter egg A secret message or screen buried in an application. Typically, easter eggs are used to display the credits for the development team or to display a humorous message. To see an easter egg, you need to know a special procedure or sequence of keystrokes. For example, in Windows 95, follow these steps to see the members of the product team:

1. Right Click on the Desktop.
2. Select New... then Folder.
3. Name the folder "and now, the moment you've all been waiting for" (Do not type the quotation marks.)
4. Right Click on the folder and rename it to "we proudly present for your viewing pleasure".
5. Rename it again to "The Microsoft Windows 95 Product Team!"
6. Open the folder and the Windows 95 credits will be displayed.

The folder will remain around so anytime you want to view the credits again, all you have to do is re-open the folder.

⇒ See also APPLICATION; PROGRAM.

EBCDIC Abbreviation of *E(xtended) B(inary)-C(oded) D(ecimal) I(nter-change) C(ode)*. Pronounced **eb**-sih-dik, EBCDIC is an IBM code for representing characters as numbers. Although it is widely used on large IBM computers, most other computers, including PCs and Macintoshes, use ASCII codes.

⇒ See also ASCII.

ECC See under ECC MEMORY.

ECC memory Short for *E(rror)-C(orrecting) C(ode) memory*, a type of memory that includes special circuitry for testing the accuracy of data as it passes in and out of memory.

⇒ See also CHECKSUM; MEMORY.

e-commerce Short for *e(lectronic)* **commerce**.

ECP Short for *E(xtended) C(apabilities) P(ort)*, a parallel-port standard for PCs that supports bi-directional communication between the PC and attached devices (such as a printer). ECP is about 10 times faster than the older Centronics standard.

Table 13
EBCDIC Codes

Decimal	Hexidecimal	Character	Decimal	Hexidecimal	Character
129	81	a	194	C2	B
130	82	b	195	C3	C
131	83	c	196	C4	D
132	84	d	197	C5	E
133	85	e	198	C6	F
134	86	f	199	C7	G
135	87	g	200	C8	H
136	88	h	201	C9	I
137	89	i	209	D1	J
145	91	j	210	D2	K
146	92	k	211	D3	L
147	93	l	212	D4	M
148	94	m	213	D5	N
149	95	n	214	D6	O
150	96	o	215	D7	P
151	97	p	216	D8	Q
152	98	q	217	D9	R
153	99	r	226	E2	S
162	A2	s	227	E3	T
163	A3	t	228	E4	U
164	A4	u	229	E5	V
165	A5	v	230	E6	W
166	A6	w	231	E7	X
167	A7	x	232	E8	Y
168	A8	y	233	E9	Z
169	A9	z	64	40	blank
240	F0	0	75	4B	.
241	F1	1	76	4C	<
242	F2	2	77	4D	(
243	F3	3	78	4E	+
244	F4	4	79	4F	I
245	F5	5	80	50	&
246	F6	6	90	5A	!
247	F7	7	91	5B	$
248	F8	8	92	5C	*
249	F9	9	93	5D	)
122	7A	:	94	5E	;
123	7B	#	96	60	-
124	7C	@	97	61	/
125	7D	'	107	6B	,
126	7E	=	108	6C	%
127	7F	"	109	6D	_
193	C1	A	110	6E	>
			111	6F	?

Another modern parallel port for PCs that offers similar performance is the EPP (Enhanced Parallel Port).

⇒ See also CENTRONICS INTERFACE; DCC; EPP; PARALLEL PORT.

edge connector The part of a printed circuit board that plugs into a computer or device. The edge connector generally has a row of broad metallic tracks that provide the electrical connection.

⇒ See also PRINTED CIRCUIT BOARD.

EDI Short for *E(lectronic) D(ata) I(nterchange)*, the transfer of data beween different companies using networks, such as the Internet. As more and more companies get connected to the Internet, EDI is becoming increasingly important as an easy mechanism for companies to buy, sell, and trade information. ANSI has approved a set of EDI standards known as the *X12 standards*.

⇒ See also ELECTRONIC COMMERCE.

editor Sometimes called *text editor,* a program that enables you to create and edit text files. There are many different types of editors, but they all fall into two general categories:

line editors: A primitive form of editor that requires you to specify a specific line of text before you can make changes to it.
screen-oriented editors: Also called *full-screen editors,* these editors enable you to modify any text that appears on the display screen by moving the cursor to the desired location.

The distinction between editors and word processors is not clear-cut, but in general, word processors provide many more formatting features. Nowadays, the term editor usually refers to source code editors that include many special features for writing and editing source code.

⇒ See also SOURCE CODE; WORD PROCESSING.

EDO DRAM Short for *E(xtended) D(ata) O(utput) D(ynamic) R(andom) A(ccess) M(emory)*, a type of DRAM that is faster than conventional DRAM. Unlike conventional DRAM which can only access one block of data at a time, EDO DRAM can start fetching the next block of memory at the same time that it sends the previous block to the CPU.

⇒ See also ACCESS TIME; BEDO DRAM; CYCLE TIME; DRAM; FPM RAM; RDRAM; SDRAM; SLDRAM.

EEMS Abbreviation of *E(nhanced) E(xpanded) M(emory) S(pecification)*, an enhanced version of the original EMS, which enables DOS applications to use more than 1MB (megabyte) of memory. EEMS was developed by AST, Quadram, and Ashton-Tate to improve the performance of the original version of EMS. Subsequently, Lotus, *Intel*, and Microsoft developed the LIM 4.0 version of EMS, which supports both the original EMS and EEMS.

⇒ See also EXPANDED MEMORY; LIM MEMORY.

EEPROM Acronym for *e(lectrically) e(rasable) p(rogrammable) r(ead)-o(nly) m(emory)*. Pronounced *double-ee-prom* or *e-e-prom*, an EEPROM is a special type of PROM that can be erased by exposing it to an electrical charge. Like other types of PROM, EEPROM retains its contents even when the power is turned off. Also like other types of ROM, EEPROM is not as fast as RAM.

EEPROM is similar to *flash memory* (sometimes called *flash EEPROM*). The principal difference is that EEPROM requires data to be written or erased one byte at a time whereas flash memory allows data to be written or erased in blocks. This makes flash memory faster.

⇒ See also BUBBLE MEMORY; EPROM; FLASH MEMORY; MEMORY; NVRAM; PROM; RAM; ROM.

EGA Abbreviation of *e(nhanced) g(raphics) a(dapter)*, a graphics display system for PCs introduced by IBM in 1984. EGA supports 16 colors from a palette of 64 and provides a resolution of 640 by 350. This is better than CGA but not as good as VGA. EGA is now obsolete.

⇒ See also CGA; VIDEO ADAPTER.

EIA Short for *Electronic Industries Association*.

EIA (Electronic Industries Association) interface Same as RS-232C.

EIDE Short for *E(nhanced)* **IDE**, a newer version of the IDE mass storage device interface standard developed by Western Digital Corporation. It supports data rates of between 4 and 16.6 MBps, about three to four times faster than the old IDE standard. In addition, it can support mass storage devices of up to 8.4 gigabytes, whereas the old standard was limited to 528MB. Because of its lower cost, enhanced EIDE has replaced SCSI in many areas.

EIDE is sometimes referred to as *Fast ATA* or *Fast IDE*, which is essentially the same standard, developed and promoted by Seagate Technologies. It is also sometimes called *ATA-2*.

There are four EIDE modes defined. The most common is Mode 4, which supports transfer rates of 16.6MBps. There is also a new mode, called *ATA-3* or *Ultra ATA*, that supports transfer rates of 33 MBps.

⇒ See also ATA; ESDI; IDE INTERFACE; SCSI.

Eiffel An advanced programming language created by Bertrand Meyer and developed by his company, Interactive Software Engineering (ISE). The language was introduced in 1986 and a basic Windows compiler is available at no charge.

Eiffel encourages object-oriented program development and supports a systematic approach to software development. The Eiffel compiler generates C code, which you can then modify and re-compile with a C compiler.

⇒ See also C; OBJECT-ORIENTED PROGRAMMING.

8088 See under INTEL MICROPROCESSORS.

8086 Short for the *Intel 8086 microprocessor*.

⇒ See also INTEL MICROPROCESSORS.

8514/A A high-resolution video standard for PCs developed by IBM in 1987. It is designed to extend the capabilities of VGA. The 8514/A standard provides a resolution of 1,024 by 768 pixels, which gives it about 2.5 times the pixels of VGA (640 by 480). Like VGA, 8514/A provides a palette of 262,000 colors, of which 256 can be displayed at one time. On monochrome displays, 8514/A provides 64 shades of gray.

In its original version, 8514/A relies on *interlacing*, a technique that makes it possible to provide resolution at low cost. Interlacing, however, carries a performance penalty, so many manufacturers produce *noninterlaced* 8514/A clones.

In 1990, IBM released the Extended Graphics Array *(XGA)* standard, which supersedes 8514/A.

⇒ See also INTERLACING; MONOCHROME; PALETTE; RESOLUTION; SVGA; VIDEO ADAPTER; XGA.

80486 See under INTEL MICROPROCESSORS.

80386 See under INTEL MICROPROCESSORS.

80286 See under INTEL MICROPROCESSORS.

EISA Acronym for *E(xtended) I(ndustry) S(tandard) A(rchitecture)*, a bus architecture designed for PCs using an Intel 80386, 80486, or Pentium microprocessor. EISA buses are 32 bits wide and support multiprocessing.

The EISA bus was designed by nine IBM competitors (sometimes called the *Gang of Nine*): AST Research, Compaq Computer, Epson, Hewlett-Packard, NEC, Olivetti, Tandy, WYSE, and Zenith Data Systems. They designed the architecture to compete with IBM's own high-speed bus architecture called the *Micro Channel architecture (MCA)*.

The principal difference between EISA and MCA is that EISA is backward compatible with the ISA bus (also called the *AT bus*), while MCA is not. This means that computers with an EISA bus can use new EISA expansion cards as well as old AT expansion cards. Computers with an MCA bus can use only MCA expansion cards.

EISA and MCA are not compatible with each other. This means that the type of bus in your computer determines which expansion cards you can install.

Neither EISA nor MCA has been very successful. Instead, a new tech-

nology called local bus (PCI) is being used in combination with the old
ISA bus.

⇒ See also BUS; EXPANSION BOARD; INDUSTRY STANDARD ARCHITECTURE (ISA)
BUS; LOCAL BUS; MICRO CHANNEL ARCHITECTURE (MCA); MULTIPROCESSING; PCI;
VL-BUS.

ELD See ELECTROLUMINESCENT DISPLAY.

electrically erasable programmable read-only memory See EEPROM.

electroluminescent display (ELD) A technology used to produce a very
thin display screen, called a *flat-panel display*, used in some portable
computers. An ELD works by sandwiching a thin film of phosphorescent
substance between two plates. One plate is coated with vertical wires and
the other with horizontal wires, forming a grid. When an electrical current is passed through a horizontal and vertical wire, the phosphorescent
film at the intersection glows, creating a point of light, or *pixel*.
    Other types of flat-panel displays include *LCD displays* and *gas-plasma
displays*, both of which are more common than ELDs.

⇒ See also ACTIVE MATRIX DISPLAY; FLAT-PANEL DISPLAY; GAS-PLASMA DISPLAY;
LCD; NOTEBOOK COMPUTER.

electronic commerce Conducting business on-line. This includes, for example, buying and selling products with digital cash and via Electronic
Data Interchange (EDI).

⇒ See also BIOMETRICS; CERTIFICATE AUTHORITY; DIGITAL CASH; DIGITAL SIGNA-
TURE; EDI; ESD; PKI; SET.

Electronic Data Interchange See EDI.

Electronic Frontier Foundation A non-profit organization dedicated to
protecting civil liberties in the modern communications age. Its emphasis
is on ensuring that the general public has equal access to new
communications channels such as the Internet. It sponsors court cases
and acts as an information clearinghouse. It has taken the lead in fighting
efforts, such as the Clipper chip, to restrict Internet access.

⇒ See also CLIPPER CHIP.

Electronic Industries Association (EIA) A trade association representing
the U.S. high technology community. It began in 1924 as the Radio Manufacturers Association. The EIA sponsors a number of activities on behalf
of its members, including conferences and trade shows. In addition, it
has been responsible for developing some important standards, such as
the RS-232, RS-422 and RS-423 standards for connecting serial devices.

⇒ See also RS-232C; RS-422 AND RS-423; RS-485; STANDARD.

electronic mail See under E-MAIL.

electronic publishing Publishing information in an electronic form. This includes publishing CD-ROMs as well as making information available through online services.

⇒ See also CD-ROM; MULTIMEDIA; ONLINE SERVICE.

electrostatic discharge See ESD.

elevator Same as SCROLL BOX. See under SCROLL BAR.

ELF emission ELF stands for *e(xtremely) l(ow) f(requency)*, and ELF emissions are magnetic fields generated by common electrical appliances. There is considerable debate about whether ELF emissions from computer monitors pose a threat. Some European countries have adopted regulations controlling the amount of allowable emission. The most well-know regulation is Sweden's *MPR II* standard. You can play it safe by buying MPR II-compliant monitors.

⇒ See also MONITOR.

e-mail Short for *e(lectronic)* **mail**, the transmission of messages over communications networks. The messages can be notes entered from the keyboard or electronic files stored on disk. Most mainframes, minicomputers, and computer networks have an e-mail system. Some electronic-mail systems are confined to a single computer system or network, but others have gateways to other computer systems, enabling users to send electronic mail anywhere in the world. Companies that are fully computerized make extensive use of e-mail because it is fast, flexible, and reliable.

Most e-mail systems include a rudimentary text editor for composing messages, but many allow you to edit your messages using any editor you want. You then send the message to the recipient by specifying the recipient's address. You can also send the same message to several users at once. This is called *broadcasting*.

Sent messages are stored in electronic mailboxes until the recipient fetches them. To see if you have any mail, you may have to check your electronic mailbox periodically, although many systems alert you when mail is received. After reading your mail, you can store it in a text file, forward it to other users, or delete it. Copies of memos can be printed out on a printer if you want a paper copy.

All online services and Internet Service Providers (ISPs) offer e-mail, and most also support gateways so that you can exchange mail with users of other systems. Usually, it takes only a few seconds or minutes for mail to arrive at its destination. This is a particularly effective way to communicate with a group because you can broadcast a message or document to everyone in the group at once.

Although different e-mail systems use different formats, some emerging standards are making it possible for users on all systems to exchange messages. In the PC world, an important e-mail standard is MAPI. The

CCITT standards organization has developed the X.400 standard, which attempts to provide a universal way of addressing messages. To date, though, the de facto addressing standard is the one used by the Internet system because almost all e-mail systems have an Internet gateway.

In recent years, the use of e-mail has exploded. By some estimates, there are now 25 million e-mail users sending 15 billion messages per year.

Another common spelling for e-mail is *email*.

⇒ See also ACRONYM; ATTACHMENT; BINHEX; CCITT; E-MAIL ADDRESS; FINGER; GATEWAY; IMAP; INSTANT MESSAGING; MAILBOX; MAILING LIST; MAPI; MIME; NETWORK; ONLINE SERVICE; POP; SNAILMAIL; SNMP; SPAM; USERNAME; UUENCODE; WORKGROUP COMPUTING.

e-mail address A name that identifies an electronic post office box on a network where e-mail can be sent. Different types of networks have different formats for e-mail addresses. On the Internet, all e-mail addresses have the form:

< name > @ < domain name >
For example,

webmaster@sandybay.com
Every user on the Internet has a unique e-mail address.

⇒ See also ADDRESS; E-MAIL; X.400.

e-mail client An application that runs on a personal computer or workstation and enables you to send, receive and organize e-mail. It's called a *client* because e-mail systems are based on a client-server architecture. Mail is sent from many clients to a central server, which re-routes the mail to its intended destination.

⇒ See also CLIENT; EUDORA; FINGER; MAILING LIST; PINE; TNEF.

embedded command In word processing, an embedded command is a sequence of special characters inserted into a document that affects the formatting of the document when it is printed. For example, when you change fonts in a word processor (by specifying bold type), the word processor inserts an embedded command that causes the printer to change fonts. Embedded commands can also control the display screen, causing it to display blinking characters or produce other special effects.

Embedded commands are usually invisible when you edit a file, but many word processors support a special mode that lets you see these commands.

⇒ See also COMMAND; FONT; WORD PROCESSING.

embedded computer Same as EMBEDDED SYSTEM.

embedded object An object created with one application and embedded into a document created by another application. *Embedding* the object, rather than simply inserting or pasting it, ensures that the object retains its original format. In fact, you can modify the embedded object with the original program. In Windows environments, embedding objects is made possible by a technology called OLE.

⇒ See also DOCUMENT; OLE.

embedded system A specialized computer system that is part of a larger system or machine. Typically, an embedded system is housed on a single microprocessor board with the programs stored in ROM. Virtually all appliances that have a digital interface—watches, microwaves, VCRs, cars—utilize embedded systems. Some embedded systems include an operating system, but many are so specialized that the entire logic can be implemented as a single program.

⇒ See also MICROCONTROLLER; SYSTEM.

emoticon Short for *emot(ion)* **icon**, a small icon composed of punctuation characters that indicates how an e-mail message should be interpreted (that is, the writer's mood). For example, a :-) emoticon indicates that the message is meant as a joke and shouldn't be taken seriously.
An emoticon is also called a *smiley*.

⇒ See also E-MAIL.

Table 14	
Emoticons	
Emoticon	**Meaning**
:-)	Joking
:-0	Bored
;-)	Winking
:-(	Sad
:-<	Frowning

EMS Abbreviation of *E(xpanded) M(emory) S(pecification)*.

⇒ See also EXPANDED MEMORY.

emulation The ability of a program or device to imitate another program or device. Many printers, for example, are designed to emulate Hewlett-Packard LaserJet printers because so much software is written for HP printers. By emulating an HP printer, a printer can work with any software written for a real HP printer. Emulation tricks the software into believing that a device is really some other device.

Communications software packages often include *terminal emulation drivers*. This enables your PC to emulate a particular type of terminal so that you can log on to a mainframe.

It is also possible for a computer to emulate another type of computer. For example, there are programs that enable an Apple Macintosh to emulate a PC.

⇒ See also COMMUNICATIONS SOFTWARE; COMPATIBLE; LOG ON; MAINFRAME; TERMINAL.

Encapsulated PostScript See EPS.

encapsulation 1. In programming, the process of combining elements to create a new entity. For example, a procedure is a type of encapsulation because it combines a series of computer instructions. Likewise, a complex data type, such as a record or class, relies on encapsulation. Object-oriented programming languages rely heavily on encapsulation to create high-level objects. Encapsulation is closely related to abstraction and information hiding. **2.** In networking, same as *tunneling*.

⇒ See also TUNNELING.

encryption The translation of data into a secret code. Encryption is the most effective way to achieve data security. To read an encrypted file, you must have access to a secret key or password that enables you to *decrypt* it. Unencrypted data is called *plain text;* encrypted data is referred to as *cipher text*.

There are two main types of encryption: asymmetric encryption (also called public-key encryption) and symmetric encryption.

⇒ See also CIPHER TEXT; CLIPPER CHIP; CRYPTOGRAPHY; DECRYPTION; DIGITAL CERTIFICATE; DIGITAL ENVELOPE; PASSWORD; PLAIN TEXT; PUBLIC-KEY ENCRYPTION; RSA; SECURITY; SYMMETRIC ENCRYPTION.

endian See under BIG-ENDIAN.

End key A special cursor control key on PC keyboards and Macintosh extended keyboards. The End key has different meanings depending on which program is running. For example, it might move the cursor to the end of the line, the end of the page, or the end of the file.

⇒ See also KEYBOARD.

end of file See EOF.

end of line See EOL MARK.

end user The final or ultimate user of a computer system. The end user is the individual who uses the product after it has been fully developed and marketed. The term is useful because it distinguishes two classes of users, users who require a bug-free and finished product (end users), and users who may use the same product for development purposes. The term *end user* usually implies an individual with a relatively low level of computer expertise. Unless you are a programmer or engineer, you are almost certainly an end user.

⇒ See also EULA; USER.

Energy Star A voluntary labeling program of the U.S. Environmental Protection Agency (EPA) and the U.S. Department of Energy that identifies energy efficient products. Qualified products exceed minimum federal standards for energy consumption by a certain amount, or where no federal standards exist, have certain energy saving features. Such products may display the Energy Star label.

⇒ See also GREEN PC.

Enhanced Data Output DRAM See EDO DRAM.

Enhanced Expanded Memory Specification See EEMS.

enhanced graphics adapter See EGA.

Enhanced IDE See under EIDE.

Enhanced Keyboard 1. A 101- or 102-key keyboard from IBM that supersedes the keyboard for the PC /AT computer. The most significant difference between the enhanced keyboard and previous models is that the enhanced keyboard has a row of 12 function keys at the top instead of 10 function keys grouped on the left side of the keyboard. Nearly all PCs made today come with an Enhanced Keyboard. **2.** For Macintoshes, see under *extended keyboard*.

⇒ See also EXTENDED KEYBOARD; FUNCTION KEYS; KEYBOARD.

Enhanced Small Device Interface See ESDI.

Enter key A key that moves the cursor (or insertion point) to the beginning of the next line, or returns control to whatever program is currently running. After a program requests information from you (by displaying a prompt), it will usually not respond to your input until you have pressed the Enter or Return key. This allows you to correct typing mistakes or to reconsider your entry before it is too late. In many applications, pressing the Enter key moves the cursor to the next field. In graphical user interfaces, pressing Enter activates the currently selected button or option.

⇒ See also RETURN KEY.

enterprise Literally, a business organization. In the computer industry, the term is often used to describe any large organization that utilizes comput-

ers. An intranet, for example, is a good example of an enterprise computing system.

⇒ See also ERP; INTRANET.

enterprise resource planning See ERP.

environment 1. The state of a computer, usually determined by which
programs are running and basic hardware and software characteristics.
For example, when one speaks of running a program in a UNIX environment, it means running a program on a computer that has the UNIX operating system.

   One ingredient of an environment, therefore, is the operating system.
But operating systems include a number of different parameters. For example, many operating systems allow you to choose your command
prompt or a default command path. All these parameters taken together
constitute the environment.

   Another term for environment in this sense is *platform*. **2.** In DOS systems, the environment is an area in memory that the operating system
and other programs use to store various types of miscellaneous information. For example, your word processor may use the environment area to
store the location of backup files. You can view or modify the environment with the SET command.

⇒ See also DOS; OPERATING SYSTEM; PARAMETER; PLATFORM.

EO See ERASABLE OPTICAL DISK.

EOF mark Short for *e(nd)-o(f)-f(ile) mark*, a special character or sequence
of characters that marks the end of a file. Operating systems need to
keep track of where every file ends. There are two techniques for doing
this: One is to put a special end-of-file mark at the end of each file. The
other is to keep track of how many characters are in the file.

   In many operating systems, including DOS and OS/2, the end-of-file
mark is CTRL-Z. In UNIX, the end-of-file mark is CTRL-D.

⇒ See also EOL MARK.

EOL mark Short for *e(nd)-o(f)-l(ine) mark*, a special character or sequence
of characters that marks the end of a line. For many programs, the EOL
character is CTRL-M (carriage return) or CTRL-J (new line). End-of-line
can also be abbreviated *EOLN*.

⇒ See also EOF MARK.

EPOC An operating system from Psion Software, designed specifically for
mobile, ROM-based computing devices. *EPOC16* is a 16-bit version of the
operating system that has been available for several years and is embedded in many handheld devices. *EPOC32* is a newer, 32-bit operating system that supports preemptive multitasking. EPOC is competing head-to-

head with Windows CE in the growing PDA market.

⇒ See also HAND-HELD COMPUTER; OPERATING SYSTEM; PDA; WINDOWS CE.

EPP Short for *E(nhanced) P(arallel) P(ort)*, a parallel port standard for PCs that supports bi-directional communication between the PC and attached devices (such as a printer). EPP is about 10 times faster than the older Centronics standard.

Another modern parallel port for PCs that offers similar performance is the ECP (Extended Capabilities Port).

⇒ See also CENTRONICS INTERFACE; ECP; PARALLEL PORT.

EPROM Acronym for *e(rasable) p(rogrammable) r(ead)-o(nly) m(emory)*, and pronounced *ee-prom*. EPROM is a special type of memory that retains its contents until it is exposed to ultraviolet light. The ultraviolet light clears its contents, making it possible to reprogram the memory. To write to and erase an EPROM, you need a special device called a *PROM programmer* or *PROM burner*.

An EPROM differs from a PROM in that a PROM can be written to only once and cannot be erased. EPROMs are used widely in personal computers because they enable the manufacturer to change the contents of the PROM before the computer is actually shipped. This means that bugs can be removed and new versions installed shortly before delivery.

⇒ See also EEPROM; MEMORY; PROM.

EPS Abbreviation of *E(ncapsulated) P(ost)S(cript)*, and pronounced as separate letters. EPS is the graphics file format used by the PostScript language.

EPS files can be either binary or ASCII. The term *EPS* usually implies that the file contains a bit-mapped representation of the graphics for display purposes. In contrast, *PostScript files* include only the PostScript commands for printing the graphic.

⇒ See also GRAPHICS; GRAPHICS FILE FORMATS; POSTSCRIPT.

erasable optical disk A type of optical disk that can be erased and loaded with new data. In contrast, most optical disks, called CD-ROMs, are read-only.

⇒ See also ACCESS TIME; CD-ROM; DISK; FLOPPY DISK; MASS STORAGE; OPTICAL DISK.

erasable programmable read-only memory See EPROM.

ergonomics The science concerned with designing safe and comfortable machines for use by humans. For example, one branch of ergonomics deals with designing furniture that avoids causing backaches and muscle cramps. In the computer field, ergonomics plays an important role in the design of monitors and keyboards.

Another term for ergonomics is *human engineering*.

⇒ See also CARPAL TUNNEL SYNDROME.

ERP Short for *e(nterprise) r(esource) p(lanning)*, a business management system that integrates all facets of the business, including planning, manufacturing, sales, and marketing. As the ERP methodology has become more popular, software applications have emerged to help business managers implement ERP.

⇒ See also ENTERPRISE.

error checking and correcting See ECC.

Error-Correcting Code memory See ECC MEMORY.

error detection In communications, *error detection* refers to a class of techniques for detecting garbled messages. Two of the simplest and most common techniques are called *checksum* and *CRC*. More sophisticated strategies include *MNP* and *CCITT V.42*.

⇒ See also CCITT; CHECKSUM; CRC; DATA INTEGRITY; KERMIT; MNP; XMODEM.

ESC Short for *Escape key*. For example, *ESC-Q* means *press the Escape key and then the Q key*.

⇒ See also ESCAPE CHARACTER; ESCAPE KEY.

escape character A special character that can have many different functions. It is often used to abort the current command and return to a previous place in the program. It is also used to send special instructions to printers and other devices. An escape character is generated with the *Escape key*, a special key that exists on most computer keyboards.

When the escape character is combined with other characters, it is called an *escape sequence*.

⇒ See also ESCAPE SEQUENCE; KEYBOARD.

Escape key A key on computer keyboards, usually labeled *Esc*. In DOS and Windows environments, pressing the Escape key usually cancels or aborts the current operation.

⇒ See also ABORT; ESC; KEYBOARD.

escape sequence A sequence of special characters that sends a command to a device or program. Typically, an escape sequence begins with an *escape character*, but this is not universally true.

⇒ See also ESCAPE CHARACTER.

ESCD Short for *E(xtended) S(ystem) C(onfiguration) D(ata)*, a format for storing information about Plug-and-Play (PnP) devices in the BIOS. Windows and the BIOS access the ESCD area each time you re-boot your computer.

⇒ See also BIOS; PLUG-AND-PLAY; PNP.

ESD 1. Short for *E(lectronic) S(oftware) D(istribution)*, a system for selling software over a network. ESD systems provide secure communications that customers use to download and pay for software. These systems can operate over the Internet or on a direct modem-to-modem connection. ESD systems can also allow users to use software for a trial period before purchasing. **2.** Short for *e(lectro)s(tatic) d(ischarge)*, the rapid discharge of static electricity from one conductor to another of a different potential. An electrostatic discharge can damage integrated circuits found in computer and communications equipment.

⇒ See also ELECTRONIC COMMERCE; UPGRADE.

ESDI Abbreviation of *E(nhanced) S(mall) D(evice) I(nterface)*, an interface standard developed by a consortium of the leading personal-computer manufacturers for connecting disk drives to PCs. ESDI is two to three times faster than the older ST-506 standard. To use an ESDI drive, your computer must have an ESDI controller.

Introduced in the early 1980s, ESDI is already obsolete. Instead, modern computers use a SCSI, IDE, or EIDE interface.

⇒ See also DISK DRIVE; EIDE; IDE INTERFACE; SCSI; ST-506 INTERFACE.

Ethernet A local-area network (LAN) protocol developed by Xerox Corporation in cooperation with DEC and Intel in 1976. Ethernet uses a bus or star topology and supports data transfer rates of 10 Mbps. The Ethernet specification served as the basis for the IEEE 802.3 standard, which specifies the physical and lower software layers. Ethernet uses the CSMA/CD access method to handle simultaneous demands. It is one of the most widely implemented LAN standards.

A newer version of Ethernet, called *100Base-T* (or *Fast Ethernet*), supports data transfer rates of 100 Mbps. And the newest version, *Gigabit Ethernet*, supports data rates of 1 gigabit (1,000 megabits) per second.

⇒ See also 100BASE-T; 10BASE-2; 10BASE5; 10BASET; ATM; AUI; BUS NETWORK; CSMA/CD; GIGABIT ETHERNET; IEEE; IEEE 802 STANDARDS; LOCAL-AREA NETWORK; NETWORK; PROTOCOL; SHARED ETHERNET; SWITCHED ETHERNET; TOPOLOGY.

Eudora A popular e-mail client developed by QUALCOMM, Inc.

⇒ See also E-MAIL CLIENT.

EULA Short for *E(nd)-U(ser) L(icense) A(greement)*, the type of *license* used for most software.

⇒ See also END USER; SOFTWARE LICENSING.

even header In word processing, a header that appears only on even-numbered pages.

⇒ See also HEADER.

even parity Refers to the parity-checking mode in which each set of transmitted bits must have an even number of set bits. The parity-checking system on the sending side ensures even parity by setting the extra *parity bit* if necessary.

⇒ See also PARITY CHECKING.

event An action or occurrence detected by a program. Events can be user actions, such as clicking a mouse button or pressing a key, or system occurrences, such as running out of memory. Most modern applications, particularly those that run in Macintosh and Windows environments, are said to be *event-driven*, because they are designed to respond to events.

⇒ See also INTERRUPT.

exabyte 1. 2^{60} (1,152,921,504,606,846,976) bytes. An exabyte is equal to 1,024 petabytes. **2.** When capitalized, the name of a manufacturer of mass storage devices.

⇒ See also PETABYTE; TERABYTE; YOTTABYTE; ZETTABYTE.

Excite A World Wide Web search engine developed by Excite, Inc. In addition to providing a full-text index of approximately 50 million Web pages, Excite enables you to search from its list of over 60,000 reviewed sites. Sites are rated with a 5-star rating system.

⇒ See also ALTA VISTA; HOTBOT; INFOSEEK; LYCOS; MAGELLAN; OPEN TEXT; SEARCH ENGINE; WEBCRAWLER; YAHOO!.

exclusive OR A Boolean operator that returns a value of TRUE only if both its operands have different values. Contrast with the *inclusive OR operator*, which returns a value of TRUE if *either* of its operands is TRUE. Whereas an inclusive OR can be translated "this, that, or both," an exclusive OR means "this or that, but not both."
     An exclusive OR is often called an *XOR* or *EOR*.

⇒ See also BOOLEAN OPERATOR.

executable file A file in a format that the computer can directly execute. Unlike source files, executable files cannot be read by humans. To transform a source file into an executable file, you need to pass it through a compiler or assembler.
     In DOS systems, executable files have either a .COM or .EXE extension

and are called *COM files* and *EXE files*, respectively.

⇒ See also ASSEMBLER; BINARY FILE; BINARY FORMAT; COM FILE; COMPILER; EXE FILE; FILE; SOURCE CODE.

execute Same as RUN. *Execute* means to perform an action, as in executing a program or a command.

⇒ See also LAUNCH.

EXE file Pronounced *ee-ex-ee file*, in DOS and Windows systems, an EXE file is an executable file with a .EXE extension.

⇒ See also COM FILE; EXECUTABLE FILE; EXTENSION; PROGRAM.

expanded memory Also known as *EMS [E(xpanded) M(emory) S(pecification)]*, expanded memory is a technique for utilizing more than 1MB (megabyte) of main memory in DOS-based computers. The limit of 1MB is built into the DOS operating system. The upper 384K is reserved for special purposes, leaving just 640K of conventional memory for programs.

There are several versions of EMS. The original versions, called *EMS 3.0* and *3.2*, enable programs to use an additional 8MB of memory, but for data only. An improved version developed by AST, Quadram, and Ashton-Tate is known as *EEMS (Extended EMS)*. EEMS enables programs to use extra memory for code as well as for data. The most recent version of EMS (created in 1987) is known as *EMS 4.0* or *LIM 4.0*, LIM being the initials of the three companies that developed the specification: Lotus, Intel, and Microsoft. EMS 4.0 raises the available amount of memory to 32MB.

Until the release of Microsoft Windows 3.0 in 1990, expanded memory was the preferred way to add memory to a PC. The alternative method, called *extended memory*, was less flexible and could be used only by special programs such as RAM disks. Windows 3.0 and all later versions of Windows, however, contain an *extended memory manager* that enables programs to use extended memory without interfering with one another. In addition, Windows can simulate expanded memory for those programs that need it (by using the EMM368.EXE driver).

⇒ See also CONVENTIONAL MEMORY; EEMS; EXTENDED MEMORY; LOW MEMORY; MAIN MEMORY; RAM DISK.

expansion board A printed circuit board that you can insert into a computer to give it added capabilities. For example, all of the following are expansion boards:

• video adapters
• graphics accelerators
• sound cards
• accelerator boards
• internal modems

Expansion boards for PCs can be *half-size* (also *half-length*) or *full-size* (also *full-length*). Most PCs have slots for each type of board. A half-size board is sometimes called an *8-bit board* because it can transmit only 8 bits at a time. A full-size board is called a *16-bit board*. In addition, some expansion boards are designed to operate with a local bus, such as PCI.

Expansion boards are also called *adapters, cards, add-ins*, and *add-ons*.

⇒ See also ACCELERATOR BOARD; ADAPTER; ADD-IN; ADD-ON; CPU; DAUGHTER-CARD; EXPANSION SLOT; GRAPHICS ACCELERATOR; PCI; PRINTED CIRCUIT BOARD; SOUND CARD; TELEVISION BOARD; VIDEO ADAPTER.

expansion bus A collection of wires and protocols that allows the expansion of a computer by the insertion of printed circuit boards (*expansion boards*). Traditionally, PCs have utilized an expansion bus called the *ISA bus*. In recent years, however, the ISA bus has become a bottleneck, so nearly all new PCs have a *PCI* bus for performance as well as an ISA bus for backward compatibility.

⇒ See also BUS; EISA; EXPANSION BOARD; LOCAL BUS; PCI; PROTOCOL; VL-BUS.

expansion card Same as EXPANSION BOARD.

expansion slot An opening in a computer where a circuit board can be inserted to add new capabilities to the computer. Nearly all personal computers except portables contain expansion slots for adding more memory, graphics capabilities, and support for special devices. The boards inserted into the expansion slots are called *expansion boards, expansion cards, cards, add-ins*, and *add-ons*.

Expansion slots for PCs come in two basic sizes: *half-* and *full-size*. Half-size slots are also called 8-bit slots because they can transfer 8 bits at a time. Full-size slots are sometimes called 16-bit slots. In addition, modern PCs include PCI slots for expansion boards that connect directly to the PCI bus.

⇒ See also EXPANSION BOARD; LOCAL BUS; PRINTED CIRCUIT BOARD.

expert system A computer application that performs a task that would otherwise be performed by a human expert. For example, there are expert systems that can diagnose human illnesses, make financial forecasts, or schedule routes for delivery vehicles. Some expert systems are designed to take the place of human experts, while others are designed to aid them.

Expert systems are part of a general category of computer applications known as *artificial intelligence*. To design an expert system, one needs a *knowledge engineer*, an individual who studies how human experts make decisions and translates the rules into terms that a computer can understand.

⇒ See also ARTIFICIAL INTELLIGENCE; HEURISTIC PROGRAMMING; PROLOG.

exploded view A picture or diagram that shows the components of an object slightly separated, as if there had been a neat explosion in the middle of the object. Many spreadsheet applications can automatically create exploded diagrams such as exploded pie charts.

⇒ See also SPREADSHEET.

export To format data in such a way that it can be used by another application. An application that can export data can create a file in a format that another application understands, enabling the two programs to share the same data. The two programs might be different types of word processors, or one could be a word processor while the other could be a database management system.

The flip side of exporting is *importing*. Importing refers to the ability of an application to read and use data produced by a different application. Exporting implies that the sending application reformats the data for the receiving application, whereas importing implies that the receiving application does the reformatting.

⇒ See also COMMA-DELIMITED; CONVERT; FILTER; IMPORT; MIDDLEWARE.

expression In programming, an expression is any legal combination of symbols that represents a value. Each programming language and application has its own rules for what is legal and illegal. For example, in the C language $x + 5$ is an expression, as is the character string *"MONKEYS."*

Every expression consists of at least one *operand* and can have one or more *operators*. Operands are values, whereas operators are symbols that represent particular actions. In the expression

    x + 5

x and 5 are operands, and + is an operator.

Expressions are used in programming languages, database systems, and spreadsheet applications. For example, in database systems, you use expressions to specify which information you want to see. These types of expressions are called *queries*.

Expressions are often classified by the type of value that they represent. For example:

Boolean expressions: Evaluate to either TRUE or FALSE
Integer expressions: Evaluate to whole numbers, like 3 or 100
Floating point expressions: Evaluate to real numbers, like 3.141 or -0. 005
String expressions: Evaluate to character strings

⇒ See also ARITHMETIC EXPRESSION; BOOLEAN EXPRESSION; CHARACTER STRING; DATA TYPE; FLOATING POINT NUMBER; FORMULA; INTEGER; OPERAND; OPERATOR; QUERY.

extended ASCII A set of codes that extends the basic ASCII set. The basic ASCII set uses 7 bits for each character, giving it a total of 128 unique symbols. The extended ASCII character set uses 8 bits, which gives it an additional 128 characters. The extra characters represent characters from foreign languages and special symbols for drawing pictures.

⇒ See also ASCII; CHARACTER BASED; ISO LATIN 1.

Extended Binary-Coded Decimal Interchange Code See EBCDIC.

Extended Capabilities Port See ECP.

extended graphics array See XGA.

Extended Industry Standard Architecture See EISA.

extended keyboard A keyboard for Macintosh computers that contains up to 15 function keys above the alphanumeric keys, and a numeric keypad. It is sometimes called an *enhanced keyboard* because of its similarity to the PC enhanced keyboard.

⇒ See also ENHANCED KEYBOARD.

extended memory Memory above and beyond the standard 1MB (megabyte) of main memory that DOS supports. Extended memory is available only in PCs with an Intel 80286 or later microprocessor.
  Two types of memory can be added to a PC to increase memory beyond 1MB: *expanded memory* and *extended memory*. Expanded memory conforms to a published standard called *EMS* that enables DOS programs to take advantage of it. Extended memory, on the other hand, is not configured in any special manner and is therefore unavailable to most DOS programs. However, MS-Windows and OS/2 can use extended memory.

⇒ See also CONVENTIONAL MEMORY; EXPANDED MEMORY; HIGH MEMORY AREA; HIMEM.SYS; LOW MEMORY; PROTECTED MODE; RAM DISK; VCPI; XMS.

Extended Memory Specification See XMS.

extended VGA See SVGA.

eXtensible Markup Language See XML.

extension 1. An extra feature added to a standard programming language or system. **2.** In DOS and some other operating systems, one or several letters at the end of a filename. Filename extensions usually follow a period (dot) and indicate the type of information stored in the file. For example, in the filename *EDIT.COM*, the extension is *COM*, which indicates that the file is a command file. (Depending on the operating system, the punctuation separating the extension from the rest of the filename may or may not be considered part of the extension itself.) **3.** In Macintosh environments, a program that extends the system's capabilities. When they reside in the Extensions folder, extensions are loaded into memory when the system starts. On older Macs (System 6 and earlier), extensions were called *inits.* **4.** Same as PLUG-IN.

⇒ See also ASSOCIATE; BAK FILE; BAT FILE; COM FILE; DOT; FTS FILE; GID FILE; INIT; MEMORY RESIDENT.

external bus A bus that connects a computer to peripheral devices. Two examples are the Universal Serial Bus (USB) and IEEE 1394.

⇒ See also IEEE 1394; PERIPHERAL DEVICE.

external cache Same as L2 CACHE.

external command In DOS systems, any command that does not reside in the COMMAND.COM file. This includes all other COM files, as well as EXE and BAT files. Commands in the COMMAND.COM file are called *internal commands.*

⇒ See also COMMAND; COMMAND.COM; INTERNAL COMMAND.

external modem A modem that resides in a self-contained box outside the computer system. Contrast with an *internal modem,* which resides on a printed circuit board inserted into the computer.

External modems tend to be slightly more expensive than internal modems. Many experts consider them superior because they contain lights that indicate how the modem is functioning. In addition, they can easily be moved from one computer to another. However, they do use up one COM port.

⇒ See also INTERNAL MODEM; MODEM.

extranet A new buzzword that refers to an intranet that is partially accessible to authorized outsiders. Whereas an intranet resides behind a firewall and is accessible only to people who are members of the same company or organization, an extranet provides various levels of accessibility to outsiders. You can access an extranet only if you have a valid username and password, and your identity determines which parts of the extranet you can view.

Extranets are becoming a very popular means for business partners to exchange information.

⇒ See also AUTHORIZATION; FIREWALL; INTRANET.

extremely low-frequency (ELF) emission See ELF EMISSION.

e-zine Short for *e(lectronic) magazine,* the name for a web site that is modeled after a print magazine. Some e-zines are simply electronic versions of existing print magazines, whereas others exist only in their digital format. Most e-zines are advertiser-supported, but a few charge a subscription.

⇒ See also WEB SITE.

F1, F2 . . . F15 The names of the function keys. See under FUNCTION KEYS.

facsimile machine See FAX MACHINE.

FAQ Pronounced as separate letters or as *fak,* and short for *f(requently) a(sked) q(uestions),* a FAQ is a document that answers questions about some topic, often a technical one. Frequently, FAQs are formatted as help files or hypertext documents.

⇒ See also HELP; HYPERTEXT.

Fast AT Attachment (ATA) See under EIDE.

Fast Ethernet See 100BASE-T.

fast IDE Short for *Fast AT Attachment (ATA).* See under EIDE.

Fast Page Mode RAM See FPM RAM.

FAT See FILE ALLOCATION TABLE.

fatal error An error that causes a program to abort. Sometimes a fatal error returns you to the operating system. When a fatal error occurs, you may lose whatever data the program was currently processing.

⇒ See also ABORT; CRASH; GPF; RUNTIME ERROR.

FAT32 A new version of the file allocation table (FAT) available in Windows 95 OSR 2 and in Windows 98. FAT32 increases the number of bits used to address clusters and also reduces the size of each cluster. The result is that it can support larger disks (up to 2 terabytes) and better storage efficiency (less slack space).

⇒ See also CLUSTER; FILE ALLOCATION TABLE; FILE MANAGEMENT SYSTEM; OSR 2; SLACK SPACE.

fault tolerance The ability of a system to respond gracefully to an unexpected hardware or software failure. There are many levels of fault tolerance, the lowest being the ability to continue operation in the event of a power failure. Many fault-tolerant computer systems *mirror* all operations—that is, every operation is performed on two or more duplicate systems, so if one fails another can take over.

⇒ See also CLUSTERING; DISK MIRRORING; RAID; SERVER MIRRORING.

fax *v* **1.** To send a document via a fax machine. —*n* **2.** A document that has been sent, or is about to be sent, via a fax machine. **3.** Short for *facs(imile) machine.*

⇒ See also FAX MACHINE.

fax board See FAX MODEM.

fax machine Abbreviation of *facs(imile) machine,* a fax machine is a device that can send or receive pictures and text over a telephone line. Fax machines work by digitizing an image—dividing it into a grid of dots. Each dot is either on or off, depending on whether it is black or white. Electronically, each dot is represented by a bit that has a value of either 0 (off) or 1 (on). In this way, the fax machine translates a picture into a series of zeros and ones (called a bit map) that can be transmitted like normal computer data. On the receiving side, a fax machine reads the incoming data, translates the zeros and ones back into dots, and reprints the picture.

The idea of fax machines has been around since 1842, when Alexander Bain invented a machine capable of receiving signals from a telegraph wire and translating them into images on paper. In 1850, a London inventor named F. C. Blakewell received a patent for a similar machine, which he called a *copying telegraph.*

But while the idea of fax machines has existed since the 1800s, fax machines did not become popular until the mid 1980s. The spark igniting the fax revolution was the adoption in 1983 of a standard protocol for sending faxes at rates of 9,600 bps. The standard was created by the CCITT standards organization and is known as the *Group 3* standard. Now, faxes are commonplace in offices of all sizes. They provide an inexpensive, fast, and reliable method for transmitting correspondence, contracts, résumés, handwritten notes, and illustrations.

A fax machine consists of an optical scanner for digitizing images on paper, a printer for printing incoming fax messages, and a telephone for making the connection. The optical scanner generally does not offer the same quality of resolution as stand-alone scanners. Some printers on fax machines are *thermal,* which means they require a special kind of paper.

All fax machines conform to the CCITT Group 3 protocol. (There is a new protocol called *Group 4,* but it requires ISDN lines.) The Group 3 protocol supports two classes of resolution: 203 by 98 dpi and 203 by 196 dpi. The protocol also specifies a data-compression technique and a maximum transmission speed of 9,600 bps.

Some of the features that differentiate one fax machine from another include the following:

speed: Fax machines transmit data at different rates, from 4,800 bps to 28,800 bps. A 9,600-bps fax machine typically requires 10 to 20 seconds to transmit one page.
printer type: Many fax machines use a thermal printer that requires

special paper which tends to turn yellow or brown after a period. More expensive, plain-paper fax machines have printers that can print on regular bond paper.

paper size: The thermal paper used in fax machines comes in two basic sizes: 8.5-inches wide and 10.1-inches wide. Some machines accept only the narrow-sized paper.

paper cutter: Many fax machines include a paper cutter because the thermal paper that they use comes in rolls. The least expensive models and portable faxes, however, may not include a paper cutter.

paper feed: Most fax machines have paper feeds so that you can send multiple-page documents without manually feeding each page into the machine. Plain-paper fax machines allow you to load several sheets of paper at once.

autodialing: fax machines come with a variety of dialing features. Some enable you to program the fax to send a document at a future time so that you can take advantage of the lowest telephone rates.

As an alternative to stand-alone fax machines, you can also put together a fax system by purchasing separately a fax modem and an optical scanner. You may not even need the optical scanner if the documents you want to send are already in electronic form.

⇒ See also BPS; DIGITIZE; FAX MODEM; MFP; OPTICAL SCANNER; THERMAL PRINTER.

fax modem A device you can attach to a personal computer that enables you to transmit and receive electronic documents as faxes. A fax modem is like a regular modem except that it is designed to transmit documents to a fax machine or to another fax modem. Some, but not all, fax modems do double duty as regular modems. As with regular modems, fax modems can be either *internal* or *external.* Internal fax modems are often called *fax boards.*

Documents sent through a fax modem must already be in an electronic form (that is, in a disk file). The documents you receive are stored in files on your disk or received as hard copy on a fax machine. To create fax documents from images on paper, you need an optical scanner.

Fax modems come with communications software similar to communications software for regular modems. This software can give the fax modem many capabilities that are not available with stand-alone fax machines. For example, you can broadcast a fax document to several sites at once. In addition, fax modems offer the following advantages over fax machines:

price: fax modems are less expensive. In addition, they require less maintenance because there are no moving parts. However, if you need to purchase an optical scanner in addition to the fax modem, there is no price advantage.

convenience: fax modems are more convenient if the documents you want to send are already in electronic form. With a fax machine, you first need to print the document. A fax modem lets you send it directly.

speed: fax modems can almost always transmit documents at the maximum speed of 9,600 bps, whereas not all fax machines support such high data transmission rates.

image quality: The image quality of documents transmitted by fax modems is usually superior because the documents remain in electronic form.

The principal disadvantage of fax modems is that you cannot fax paper documents unless you buy a separate optical scanner, which eliminates any cost and convenience advantages of fax modems. Another problem with fax modems is that each document you receive requires a large amount of disk storage (about 100K per page). Not only does this eat up disk storage, but it takes a long time to print such files.

⇒ See also BROADCAST; FAX MACHINE; MODEM; OPTICAL SCANNER.

FC-AL See under FIBRE CHANNEL.

FCC Abbreviation of *F(ederal) C(ommunications) C(ommission)*. Among other duties, the FCC is responsible for rating personal computers and other equipment as either Class A or Class B. The ratings indicate how much radiation a personal computer emits. Almost all personal computers satisfy Class A requirements, which means that they are suitable for office use. Class B machines, which are suitable for use anywhere (including the home), must pass more stringent tests. Class B indicates that the machine's radio frequency (RF) emissions are so low that they do not interfere with other devices such as radios and TVs.

FCIF See under COMMON INTERMEDIATE FORMAT.

FDC See under DISK CONTROLLER.

FDD Short for *floppy disk drive.*

FDDI Abbreviation of *F(iber) D(istributed) D(ata) I(nterface)*, a set of ANSI protocols for sending digital data over fiber optic cable. FDDI networks are token-passing networks and support data rates of up to 100 Mbps (100 million bits) per second. FDDI networks are typically used as backbones for wide-area networks.

An extension to FDDI, called *FDDI-2*, supports the transmission of voice and video information as well as data. Another variation of FDDI, called *FDDI Full Duplex Technology (FFDT)*, uses the same network infrastructure but can potentially support data rates up to 200 Mbps.

⇒ See also ATM; CDDI; FIBER OPTICS; NETWORK; PROTOCOL.

FDHD Short for *f(loppy) d(rive), h(igh) d(ensity)*, and pronounced *fud-hud.* FDHD refers to 3½-inch disk drives for Macintosh computers that can accept double-density or high-density 3½-inch floppy disks. FDHDs can

also read DOS-formatted floppy disks, which enables Macintosh computers and PCs to share data. FDHD drives are often called *SuperDrives*.

⇒ See also DENSITY; DOS; FLOPPY DISK; MACINTOSH COMPUTER; SUPERDRIVE.

fdisk A DOS and Windows utility that prepares a hard disk for formatting
by creating one or more partitions on the disk.

⇒ See also FORMAT; PARTITION.

FDM Abbreviation of *F(requency) D(ivision) M(ultiplexing)*, a multiplexing
technique that uses different frequencies to combine multiple streams of
data for transmission over a communications medium. FDM assigns a
discrete carrier frequency to each data stream and then combines many
modulated carrier frequencies for transmission. For example, television
transmitters use FDM to broadcast several channels at once.

⇒ See also CARRIER; MULTIPLEX; TDM; WDM.

feathering In desktop publishing, feathering is the process of adding space
between all lines on a page or in a column to force vertical justification.

⇒ See also JUSTIFICATION; VERTICAL JUSTIFICATION.

feature A notable property of a device or software application. Many analysts bemoan the advent of *featuritis*—the seemingly endless addition of
more and more features onto what was once a simple application. One of
the principal challenges of modern applications is to offer a multitude of
features without making the application complex.

⇒ See also BELLS AND WHISTLES; BLOATWARE; OVERHEAD; VANILLA.

Federal Communications Commission See FCC.

female connector See under CONNECTOR.

FF See FORM FEED.

Fiber Distributed Data Interface See FDDI.

fiber optics A technology that uses glass (or plastic) threads (fibers) to
transmit data. A fiber optic cable consists of a bundle of glass threads,
each of which is capable of transmitting messages modulated onto light
waves.
   Fiber optics has several advantages over traditional metal
communications lines:

• Fiber optic cables have a much greater bandwidth than metal cables. This means that they can carry more data.
• Fiber optic cables are less susceptible than metal cables to interference.

- Fiber optic cables are much thinner and lighter than metal wires.
- Data can be transmitted digitally (the natural form for computer data) rather than analogically.

The main disadvantage of fiber optics is that the cables are expensive to install. In addition, they are more fragile than wire and are difficult to split.

Fiber optics is a particularly popular technology for local area networks. In addition, telephone companies are steadily replacing traditional telephone lines with fiber optic cables. In the future, almost all communications will employ fiber optics.

⇒ See also FDDI; ISDN; LOCAL AREA NETWORK; SDH; SONET; UTP; WDM.

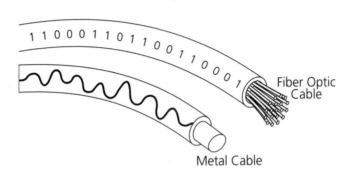

Figure 30: **fiber optics**

Fibre Channel A serial data transfer architecture developed by a consortium of computer and mass storage device manufacturers and now being standardized by ANSI. The most prominent Fibre Channel standard is *Fibre Channel Arbitrated Loop (FC-AL)*.

FC-AL was designed for new mass storage devices and other peripheral devices that require very high bandwidth. Using optical fiber to connect devices, FC-AL supports full-duplex data transfer rates of 100MBps. FC-AL is compatible with, and is expected to eventually replace, SCSI for high-performance storage systems.

⇒ See also BUS; HIPPI; SCSI.

field 1. A space allocated for a particular item of information. A tax form, for example, contains a number of fields: one for your name, one for your Social Security number, one for your income, and so on. In database systems, fields are the smallest units of information you can access. In spreadsheets, fields are called *cells*.

Most fields have certain attributes associated with them. For example, some fields are numeric whereas others are textual; some are long, while others are short. In addition, every field has a name called the *field name*.

In database management systems, a field can be *required, optional,* or *calculated.* A *required field* is one in which you must enter data, while an *optional field* is one you may leave blank. A calculated field is one whose value is derived from some formula involving other fields. You do not enter data into a calculated field; the system automatically determines the correct value.

A collection of fields is called a *record.* **2.** The phrase *in the field* refers to any geographical location other than the factory or office where a product was created. Similarly, a *field representative* is an employee who represents a company in distant locations.

⇒ See also ATTRIBUTE; BLOB; CELL; DATA TYPE; DATABASE; DATABASE MANAGEMENT SYSTEM; FORM; RECORD.

file A collection of data or information that has a name, called the *filename.* Almost all information stored in a computer must be in a file. There are many different types of files: *data files, text files, program files, directory files,* and so on. Different types of files store different types of information. For example, program files store programs, whereas text files store text.

⇒ See also DIRECTORY; DOCUMENT; EXECUTABLE FILE; FILENAME; FOLDER; LIBRARY.

Table 15
File Types

File Type	Description
Batch file	Same as command file—contains operating system commands
Binary file	Contains data or instructions in binary format
Command file	Contains operating system commands
Data file	Contains data
Directory file	Contains bookkeeping information about files that are below it
Executable file	Contains a program or commands in an executable format
Library file	Contains functions in object format
Map file	Contains a map of a program
Object file	Contains code that has been compiled
Text file	Contains textual data (that is, data that can be read by humans), including files you create with a text editor and any file in ASCII format.

---

file allocation table A table that the operating system uses to locate files on a disk. Because of fragmentation, a file may be divided into many sections that are scattered around the disk. The FAT keeps track of all these pieces.

In DOS systems, FATs are stored in *hidden files,* called *FAT files.*

The FAT system for older versions of Windows 95 is called *VFAT,* and the one for new versions of Windows 95 and Windows 98 is called *FAT32.*

⇒ See also CLUSTER; DISK; FAT32; FILE; FILE MANAGEMENT SYSTEM; FRAGMENTA-TION; PARTITION; SLACK SPACE; VFAT.

file attribute See under ATTRIBUTE.

file compression See under DATA COMPRESSION and *packed file.*

⇒ See also DATA COMPRESSION; PACKED FILE.

file defragmentation See under FRAGMENTATION.

file extension See EXTENSION.

file format A format for encoding information in a file. Each different type of file has a different file format. The file format specifies first whether the file is a binary or ASCII file, and second, how the information is organized.

⇒ See also FILE; FORMAT; GRAPHICS FILE FORMATS; PDF.

file fragmentation See FRAGMENTATION.

file locking See under LOCK.

file management system The system that an operating system or program uses to organize and keep track of files. For example, a *hierarchical file system* is one that uses directories to organize files into a tree structure.

Although the operating system provides its own file management system, you can buy separate file management systems. These systems interact smoothly with the operating system but provide more features, such as improved backup procedures and stricter file protection.

⇒ See also DIRECTORY; FAT32; FILE ALLOCATION TABLE; HIERARCHICAL; NFS; NTFS; VFAT; VSAM.

filename The name of a file. All files have names. Different operating systems impose different restrictions on filenames. Most operating systems, for example, prohibit the use of certain characters in a filename and impose a limit on the length of a filename. In addition, many systems, including DOS and UNIX, allow a filename extension that consists of one or more characters following the proper filename. The *filename extension* usually indicates what type of file it is.

Within a single directory or folder, filenames must be unique. However, two files in different directories may have the same name. Some operating systems, such as UNIX and the Macintosh operating system, allow a file to have more than one name, called an *alias*. (In Unix, aliases are called *links* or *symbolic links*.)

⇒ See also ALIAS; DIRECTORY; EXTENSION; FILE; WILDCARD CHARACTER.

filename extension See EXTENSION.

file server See under SERVER.

file system Same as FILE MANAGEMENT SYSTEM.

File Transfer Protocol See FTP.

File Transport Protocol See FTP.

fill 1. In graphics applications, to paint the inside of an enclosed object. Typically, you can choose a color and pattern, and then paint the object with a *fill tool*. The area that is painted is called the *fill area*. **2.** In spreadsheet applications, to copy the contents of one cell to an entire range of cells—that is, to *fill* the range with a formula or value.

⇒ See also GRAPHICS; SPREADSHEET.

White Fill   Gray Fill   Fountain Fill

Figure 31: fills

filter 1. A program that accepts a certain type of data as input, transforms it in some manner, and then outputs the transformed data. For example, a program that sorts names is a filter because it accepts the names in unsorted order, sorts them, and then outputs the sorted names.

Utilities that allow you to import or export data are also sometimes called filters. **2.** A pattern through which data is passed. Only data that match the pattern are allowed to pass through the filter. **3.** In paint programs and image editors, a filter is an effect that can be applied to a bit map. Some filters mimic conventional photographic filters, but many transform images in unusual ways. A *pointillism filter*, for example, can make a digitized photograph look like a pointillistic painting.

⇒ See also EXPORT; IMAGE EDITOR; IMAGE ENHANCEMENT; IMPORT; PHOTO ILLUSTRATION.

Original photo   Photo with pointillism filter applied

Figure 32: **Pointillism filter**

Finder The desktop management and file management system for Apple Macintosh computers. In addition to managing files and disks, the Finder is responsible for managing the Clipboard and Scrapbook and all desktop icons and windows.

⇒ See also CLIPBOARD; DESKTOP; FILE MANAGEMENT SYSTEM; MAC OS; MULTIFINDER; MULTITASKING.

finger A UNIX program that takes an e-mail address as input and returns information about the user who owns that e-mail address. On some systems, finger reports only whether the user is currently logged on. Other systems return additional information, such as the user's full name, address, and telephone number. Of course, the user must first enter this information into the system. Many e-mail programs now have a finger utility built into them.

⇒ See also E-MAIL; E-MAIL CLIENT; INSTANT MESSAGING; WHOIS.

firewall A system designed to prevent unauthorized access to or from a private network. Firewalls can be implemented in both hardware and software, or a combination of both. Firewalls are frequently used to prevent unauthorized Internet users from accessing private networks connected to the Internet, especially *intranets*. All messages entering or leaving the intranet pass through the firewall, which examines each message and blocks those that do not meet the specified security criteria.

There are several types of firewall techniques:

Packet filter: Looks at each packet entering or leaving the network and accepts or rejects it based on user-defined rules. Packet filtering is fairly effective and transparent to users, but it is difficult to configure. In addition, it is susceptible to *IP spoofing.*

Application gateway: Applies security mechanisms to specific applications, such as FTP and Telnet servers. This is very effective but can impose a performance degradation.

Circuit-level gateway: Applies security mechanisms when a TCP or UDP connection is established. Once the connection has been made, packets can flow between the hosts without further checking.

Proxy server: Intercepts all messages entering and leaving the network. The proxy server effectively hides the true network addresses.

In practice, many firewalls use two or more of these techniques in concert.

A firewall is considered a first line of defense in protecting private information. For greater security, data can be encrypted.

⇒ See also EXTRANET; INTRANET; IP SPOOFING; NAT; NETWORK; PROXY SERVER; SECURITY.

FireWire See under IEEE 1394.

firmware Software (programs or data) that has been written onto read-only memory (ROM). Firmware is a combination of software and hardware. ROMs, PROMs, and EPROMs that have data or programs recorded on them are firmware.

⇒ See also HARDWARE; PROM; ROM; SOFTWARE.

first normal form See under NORMALIZATION.

fixed disk Same as HARD DISK.

fixed-frequency monitor A monitor that can accept signals in only one frequency range. In contrast, *multiscanning monitors* automatically adjust themselves to the frequency at which data is being sent.

⇒ See also MONITOR; MULTISCANNING MONITOR.

fixed length Having a set length that never varies. In database systems, a field can have a *fixed* or a *variable length*. A variable-length field is one whose length can be different in each record, depending on what data is stored in the field.

The terms *fixed length* and *variable length* can also refer to the entire record. A fixed-length record is one in which every field has a fixed length. A variable-length record has at least one variable-length field.

⇒ See also DATABASE MANAGEMENT SYSTEM; FIELD; RECORD; VARIABLE LENGTH.

fixed pitch Refers to fonts in which every character has the same width. Most typewriters and inexpensive printers use fixed-pitch fonts. Newspapers, magazines, and books, however, usually use *proportional fonts*, in which different characters have different widths.

The use of a fixed-pitch font is called *monospacing*.

⇒ See also COURIER FONT; CPI; FONT; MONOSPACING; PITCH; PROPORTIONAL SPACING.

fixed width Same as FIXED PITCH.

flag *n* **1.** A software or hardware mark that signals a particular condition or status. A flag is like a switch that can be either on or off. The flag is said to be *set* when it is turned on. **2.** A special mark indicating that a piece of data is unusual. For example, a record might contain an *error flag* to indicate that the record consists of unusual, probably incorrect, data. —*v* **3.** To mark an object to indicate that a particular event has occurred or that the object marked is unusual in some way.

⇒ See also SEMAPHORE.

flame *n* **1.** A searing e-mail or newsgroup message in which the writer attacks another participant in overly harsh, and often personal, terms. Flames are an unfortunate, but inevitable, element of unmoderated conferences. —*v* **2.** To post a flame.

⇒ See also CONFERENCE; E-MAIL; FORUM; MODERATED NEWSGROUP; ONLINE SERVICE.

flash BIOS See under BIOS.

flash EEPROM See FLASH MEMORY.

flash memory A special type of *EEPROM* that can be erased and reprogrammed in blocks instead of one byte at a time. Many modern PCs have their BIOS stored on a flash memory chip so that it can easily be updated if necessary. Such a BIOS is sometimes called a *flash BIOS*. Flash memory is also popular in modems because it enables the modem manufacturer to support new protocols as they become standardized.

⇒ See also BIOS; EEPROM.

FlashPix A format for storing digital images, especially digital photographs, developed by Eastman Kodak Company. FlashPix offers a number of unique features, including:
the ability to store various resolutions of an image in a single file
use of Microsoft's OLE structured storage format, which enables developers to extend the format
built-in linking support so that different applications can link to the same image in different ways
built-in support for digital watermarks
Currently, FlashPix is not supported by most imaging software.

⇒ See also COMPUTER IMAGING; DIGITAL CAMERA; DIGITAL PHOTOGRAPHY; DIGITAL WATERMARK.

flash ROM Same as FLASH MEMORY.

flatbed scanner A type of *optical scanner* that consists of a flat surface on which you lay documents to be scanned. Flatbed scanners are particularly effective for bound documents.

⇒ See also OPTICAL SCANNER.

flat-file database A relatively simple database system in which each database is contained in a single table. In contrast, *relational database* systems can use multiple tables to store information, and each table can have a different record format. Relational systems are more suitable for large applications, but flat databases are adequate for many small applications.

⇒ See also DATABASE MANAGEMENT SYSTEM; RDBMS.

flat-panel display A very thin display screen used in portable computers and increasingly as a replacement for a CRT with desktop computers. Nearly all modern flat-panel displays use LCD technologies. Most LCD screens are backlit to make them easier to read in bright environments.

⇒ See also ACTIVE-MATRIX DISPLAY; BACKLIGHTING; DISPLAY SCREEN; DUAL-SCAN DISPLAY; ELECTROLUMINESCENT DISPLAY (ELD); GAS-PLASMA DISPLAY; LCD; LCD MONITOR; NOTEBOOK COMPUTER; TFT; VIRTUAL DESKTOP.

flat screen Same as FLAT-PANEL DISPLAY.

flat technology monitor Often abbreviated as *FTM*, flat technology monitors are monitors that have a flat display screen to reduce glare. Conventional display screens are curved, which makes them more susceptible to reflections from external light sources.

Do not confuse flat technology monitors with *flat-panel displays*. Flat-panel displays are the display screens used in laptops and other portable computers.

⇒ See also CRT; FLAT-PANEL DISPLAY; MONITOR.

flicker See SCREEN FLICKER.

floating In graphical user interfaces, *floating* refers to application elements that you can move to different places. Many applications support *floating toolbars*, which are collections of icons that represent tools. By moving them wherever you want on the screen, you can create your own customized working environment. In addition to toolbars, many graphics programs support *floating palettes*.

⇒ See also PALETTE.

floating point See FLOATING-POINT NUMBER.

floating-point number A real number (that is, a number that can contain a fractional part). The following are floating-point numbers:

3.0
-111.5
½
3E-5

The last example is a computer shorthand for scientific notation. It means 3*10-5 (or 10 to the negative 5th power multiplied by 3).

In essence, computers are integer machines and are capable of representing real numbers only by using complex codes. The most popular code for representing real numbers is called the *IEEE Floating-Point Standard*.

The term *floating point* is derived from the fact that there is no fixed number of digits before and after the decimal point; that is, the decimal point can float. There are also representations in which the number of digits before and after the decimal point is set, called *fixed-point* representations. In general, floating-point representations are slower and less accurate than fixed-point representations, but they can handle a larger range of numbers.

Note that most floating-point numbers a computer can represent are just approximations. One of the challenges in programming with floating-point values is ensuring that the approximations lead to reasonable results. If the programmer is not careful, small discrepancies in the approximations can snowball to the point where the final results become meaningless.

Because mathematics with floating-point numbers requires a great deal of computing power, many microprocessors come with a chip, called a *floating point unit (FPU)*, specialized for performing floating-point arithmetic. FPUs are also called *math coprocessors* and *numeric coprocessors*.

⇒ See also DATA TYPE; DOUBLE PRECISION; FLOPS; FPU; NORMALIZATION; PRECISION; SCIENTIFIC NOTATION.

floating-point unit See FPU.

floppy Short for *floppy disk*.

floppy disk A soft magnetic disk. It is called *floppy* because it flops if you wave it (at least, the 5¼-inch variety does). Unlike most hard disks, floppy disks (often called *floppies* or *diskettes*) are portable, because you can remove them from a disk drive. Disk drives for floppy disks are called *floppy drives*. Floppy disks are slower to access than hard disks and have less storage capacity, but they are much less expensive. And, most important, they are portable.

Floppies come in two basic sizes:

5¼-inch: The common size for PCs made before 1987. This type of floppy is generally capable of storing between 100K and 1.2MB (megabytes) of data. The most common sizes are 360K and 1.2MB.

3½-inch: *Floppy* is something of a misnomer for these disks, as they are encased in a rigid envelope. Despite their small size, microfloppies have a larger storage capacity than their cousins—from 400K to 1.4MB of data. The most common sizes for PCs are 720K (double-density) and 1.44MB (high-density). Macintoshes support disks of 400K, 800K, and 1.2MB.

⇒ See also DENSITY; DISK; FDHD; FLOPPY DRIVE; HIFD; SUPERDISK; ZIP DRIVE.

Write Protect Switch

1 MB 3.5-inch disk

Figure 33: floppy disk

floppy disk drive See FLOPPY DRIVE.

floppy drive Short for floppy disk drive (FDD), a disk drive that can read and write to floppy disks.

⇒ See also DISK DRIVE; FLOPPY DISK; HIFD; ZIP DRIVE.

FLOPS Short for *fl(oating)-point op(erations) per s(econd)*, a common benchmark measurement for rating the speed of microprocessors. Floating-point operations include any operations that involve fractional numbers. Such operations, which take much longer to compute than integer operations, occur often in some applications.

Most modern microprocessors include a floating-point unit (FPU), which is a specialized part of the microprocessor responsible for executing floating-point operations. The FLOPS measurement, therefore, actually measures the speed of the FPU. One of the most common benchmark tests used to measure FLOPS is called *Linpack*.

Many experts feel that FLOPS is not a relevant measurement because it fails to take into account factors such as the condition under which the microprocessor is running (e.g., heavy or light loads) and which exact operations are included as floating-point operations. For this reason, a consortium of vendors created the *Standard Performance Evaluation Corporation (SPEC)*, which provides more meaningful benchmark values.

A *megaFLOPS (MFLOPS)* is equal to one million floating-point operations per second, and a *gigaFLOPS (GFLOPS)* is equal to one billion floating-point operations per second.

⇒ See also BENCHMARK; FLOATING-POINT NUMBER; FPU; MIPS; SPEC.

floptical A type of disk drive technology that uses a combination of magnetic and optical techniques to achieve greater storage capacity than normal floppy disks without sacrificing access speeds.

⇒ See also OPTICAL DISK.

flow In desktop publishing, to insert a body of text into a document such that it wraps (or *flows*) around any objects on the page.

⇒ See also DESKTOP PUBLISHING.

flow control 1. In communications, the process of adjusting the flow of data from one device to another to ensure that the receiving device can handle all of the incoming data. This is particularly important where the sending device is capable of sending data much faster than the receiving device can receive it.

There are many flow control mechanisms. One of the most common flow control protocols for asynchronous communication is called *xon-xoff*. In this case, the receiving device sends a an *xoff* message to the sending device when its buffer is full. The sending device then stops sending data. When the receiving device is ready to receive more data, it sends an *xon* signal.

Flow control can be implemented in hardware or software, or a combination of both. **2.** In programming, the statements and other constructs that control the order in which operations are executed. For example, common looping statements such as **for...next** and **while** are known as flow control statements. Branching statements, such as **if...then**, are also part of a programming language's flow control mechanism.

⇒ See also ASYNCHRONOUS; COMMUNICATIONS; LOOP; PROGRAM; PROGRAMMING LANGUAGE.

flush *adj* **1.** Aligned along a margin. For example, text that is *flush left* is aligned along the left margin. *Flush-right* text is aligned along the right margin. The opposite of flush is *ragged*. Text that is both flush left and flush right is said to be *justified*. —*v* **2.** To copy data from a temporary storage area such as RAM to a more permanent storage medium such as a disk.

⇒ See also JUSTIFY; MARGINS; RAGGED.

This text	This text
is flush	is flush
left.	right.

folder In graphical user interfaces such as Windows and the Macintosh environment, a folder is an object that can contain multiple documents or other folders. Folders are used to organize information. In the DOS and UNIX worlds, folders are called directories.

⇒ See also DESKTOP; DIRECTORY; FILE; GRAPHICAL USER INTERFACE.

font A design for a set of characters. A font is the combination of typeface and other qualities, such as size, pitch, and spacing. For example, Times Roman is a typeface that defines the shape of each character. Within Times Roman, however, there are many fonts to choose from—different sizes, italic, bold, and so on. (The term *font* is often used incorrectly as a synonym for *typeface*.)

The height of characters in a font is measured in *points*, each point being approximately 1/72 inch. The width is measured by *pitch*, which refers to how many characters can fit in an inch. Common pitch values are 10 and 12. A font is said to be *fixed pitch* if every character has the same width. If the widths vary depending on the shape of the character, it is called a *proportional font*.

Most applications that support text enable you to choose from among many fonts. Laser, ink-jet, and dot-matrix printers offer the widest selection of fonts. These printers support a certain set of resident fonts, but you can expand this set by loading different fonts from software (*soft fonts*) or from font cartridges.

Computers and devices use two methods to represent fonts. In a *bit-mapped font*, every character is represented by an arrangement of dots. To print a bit-mapped character, a printer simply locates the character's bit-mapped representation stored in memory and prints the corresponding dots. Each different font, even when the typeface is the same, requires a different set of bit maps.

The other method utilizes a *vector graphics system* to define fonts. In vector graphics systems, the shape or outline of each character is defined geometrically. The typeface can be displayed in any size, so a single font description really represents innumerable fonts. For this reason, vector fonts are called *scalable fonts*—they can be any size (scale). Other terms for vector fonts are *object-oriented fonts* or *outline fonts*. The most widely used scalable-font systems are PostScript and TrueType.

Aside from the scalability of vector fonts, their other main advantage over bit-mapped fonts is that they make the most of high-resolution devices. Bit-mapped fonts look almost the same whether printed on a 300-dpi printer or a 1,200-dpi printer. Vector fonts look better, the higher the resolution.

Despite the advantages of vector fonts, bit-mapped fonts are still widely used. One reason for this is that small vector fonts do not look very good on low-resolution devices, such as display monitors (which are low-resolution when compared with laser printers). Many computer systems, therefore, use bit-mapped fonts for screen displays. These are sometimes called *screen fonts*. In addition, some professionals prefer to use bit-mapped fonts on high-resolution printers because characters can be individually tailored to the printing device.

An additional drawback of vector fonts is that every character must be generated as it is needed. This is a computation-intensive process that requires a powerful microprocessor to make it acceptably fast.

⇒ See also BIT-MAPPED GRAPHICS; CPI; FIXED PITCH; FONT CARTRIDGE; FONT FAMILY; KERNING; PAGE DESCRIPTION LANGUAGE (PDL); PITCH; POINT; POSTSCRIPT; PROPORTIONAL SPACING; SCALABLE FONT; SOFT FONT; TRUETYPE; TYPEFACE; VECTOR GRAPHICS.

Frutiger
ABCDEFGHIJKLMNOPQRSTUVWXYZ
Fonts are designed for a set of characters. A font is the combination of

Slimbach
ABCDEFGHIJKLMNOPQRSTUVWXYZ
Fonts are designed for a set of characters. A font is the combination of

Helvetica
ABCDEFGHIJKLMNOPQRSTUVWXYZ
Fonts are designed for a set of characters. A font is the combination of typeface

Courier
ABCDEFGHIJKLMNOPQRSTUVWXYZ
Fonts are designed for a set
of characters. A font is the

Figure 34: Popular fonts

font card Same as FONT CARTRIDGE.

font cartridge A ROM cartridge that contains one or more fonts. By inserting the cartridge into a laser printer, you give the printer the ability to print different fonts. Another way to load fonts into a printer is to download them from the computer's storage device.

⇒ See also CARTRIDGE; DOWNLOAD; FONT; LASER PRINTER; SOFT FONT.

font family A set of fonts all with the same typeface, but with different sizes, weights, and slants.

⇒ See also FONT; TYPEFACE.

footer One or more lines of text that appear at the bottom of every page of a document. Once you specify what text should appear in the footer, the application automatically inserts it.
   Most applications allow you to use special symbols in the footer that

represent changing values. For example, you can enter a symbol for the page number, and the application will replace the symbol with the correct number on each page. If you enter the date symbol, the application will insert the current date, which will change if necessary each time you print the document.

You can usually specify at least two different footers, one for odd-numbered pages (*odd footer*) and one for even-numbered pages (*even footer*).

A footer is sometimes called a *running foot*.

⇒ See also HEADER.

footprint The amount of floor or desk space required by a device. For example, a *small-footprint* computer is a computer whose dimensions (width and depth) are relatively small.

⇒ See also DESKTOP MODEL COMPUTER; TOWER MODEL.

forced page break A page break that you explicitly insert. The application cannot override a forced page break. Forced page breaks are sometimes called *hard page breaks*.

⇒ See also HARD; PAGE BREAK; SOFT.

foreground 1. In multiprocessing systems, the process that is currently accepting input from the keyboard or other input device is sometimes called the *foreground process*. **2.** On display screens, the foreground consists of the characters and pictures that appear on the screen. The background is the uniform canvas behind the characters and pictures.

⇒ See also BACKGROUND; MULTIPROCESSING.

foreign key See under KEY.

form A formatted document containing blank fields that users can fill in with data. With paper forms, it is usually necessary for someone to transfer the data from the paper to a computer database, where the results can then be statistically analyzed. Some OCR systems can do this automatically, but they're generally limited to forms containing just check boxes. They can't handle handwritten text.

Electronic forms solve this problem by entirely skipping the paper stage. Instead, the form appears on the user's display screen and the user fills it in by selecting options with a pointing device or typing in text from the computer keyboard. The data is then sent directly to a forms processing application, which enters the information into a database.

Electronic forms are especially common on the World Wide Web because the HTML language has built-in codes for displaying form elements such as text fields and check boxes. Typically, the data entered into a Web-based form is processed by a CGI program.

⇒ See also CGI; FIELD; OPTICAL CHARACTER RECOGNITION.

format *v* **1.** To prepare a storage medium, usually a disk, for reading and writing. When you format a disk, the operating system erases all book-keeping information on the disk, tests the disk to make sure all sectors are reliable, marks bad sectors (that is, those that are scratched), and creates internal address tables that it later uses to locate information. You must format a disk before you can use it.

Note that reformatting a disk does not erase the data on the disk, only the address tables. Do not panic, therefore, if you accidentally reformat a disk that has useful data. A computer specialist should be able to recover most, if not all, of the information on the disk. You can also buy programs that enable you to recover a disk yourself.

The previous discussion, however, applies only to *high-level* formats, the type of formats that most users execute. In addition, hard disks have a *low-level format*, which sets certain properties of the disk such as the interleave factor. The low-level format also determines what type of disk controller can access the disk (e.g., *RLL* or *MFM*).

Almost all hard disks that you purchase have already had a low-level format. It is not necessary, therefore, to perform a low-level format yourself unless you want to change the interleave factor or make the disk accessible by a different type of disk controller. Performing a low-level format erases all data on the disk. **2.** To specify the properties, particularly visible properties, of an object. For example, word processing applications allow you to format text, which involves specifying the font, alignment, margins, and other properties. —*n* **3.** A particular arrangement. Almost everything associated with computers has a format.

⇒ See also CONTROLLER; DISK; FDISK; HARD DISK; INITIALIZE; INTERLEAVE; LOW-LEVEL FORMAT; MFM; RLL; SECTOR; TAG.

form factor The physical size and shape of a device. It is often used to describe the size of circuit boards.

⇒ See also ATX; BABY AT; LPX; NLX; PRINTED CIRCUIT BOARD.

form feed **1.** Printers that use continuous paper normally have a form feed button or command that advances the paper to the beginning of the next page. **2.** A special character that causes the printer to advance one page length or to the top of the next page. In systems that use the ASCII character set, a form feed has a decimal value of 12. *Form feed* is sometimes abbreviated *FF*.

⇒ See also ASCII.

forms software A type of program that enables you to design and fill in forms on a computer. Most forms packages contain a number of sample forms that you can modify for your own purposes. Newer forms software packages enable you to publish a form on the Internet so that anyone with Internet access can fill it out.

formula **1.** An equation or expression. **2.** In spreadsheet applications, a formula is an expression that defines how one cell relates to other cells.

For example, you might define cell C5 (column C, row 5) with the formula

   $= A4*D7$

which means to multiply the value in cell A4 by the value in cell D7.

⇒ See also CELL; CONSTANT; EXPRESSION; SPREADSHEET.

FORTRAN Acronym for *for(mula) tran(slator)*, FORTRAN is the oldest high-level programming language. Designed by John Backus for IBM in the late 1950s, it is still popular today, particularly for scientific applications that require extensive mathematical computations.

The two most common versions of FORTRAN are FORTRAN IV and FORTRAN 77. FORTRAN IV was approved as a USASI standard in 1966. FORTRAN 77 is a version of FORTRAN that was approved by ANSI in 1978 (they had expected to approve it in 1977, hence the name). FORTRAN 77 includes a number of features not available in older versions of FORTRAN. A new ISO and ANSI standard for FORTRAN, called FORTRAN-90, was developed in the early 1990s.

⇒ See also ANSI; HIGH-LEVEL LANGUAGE; ISO; MUMPS; PROGRAMMING LANGUAGE.

forum An online discussion group. Online services and bulletin board services (BBSs) provide a variety of forums, in which participants with common interests can exchange open messages. Forums are sometimes called *newsgroups* (in the Internet world) or conferences.

⇒ See also BULLETIN BOARD SYSTEM; CONFERENCE; DISTANCE LEARNING; NEWSGROUP; ONLINE SERVICE; USENET.

486 Short for the *Intel 80486 microprocessor*.

⇒ See also INTEL MICROPROCESSORS.

4GL See FOURTH-GENERATION LANGUAGE.

fourth-generation language Often abbreviated *4GL*, fourth-generation languages are programming languages closer to human languages than typical high-level programming languages. Most 4GLs are used to access databases. For example, a typical 4GL command is

   FIND ALL RECORDS WHERE NAME IS "SMITH"

The other three generations of computer languages are

first generation: machine language
second generation: assembly language
third generation: high-level programming languages, such as C, C + +, and Java.

⇒ See also DATABASE MANAGEMENT SYSTEM; NATURAL LANGUAGE; PROGRAMMING LANGUAGE; QUERY; QUERY LANGUAGE.

FPM RAM Short for *F(ast) P(age) M(ode)* **RAM**, a type of Dynamic RAM (DRAM) that allows faster access to data in the same row or page. Page-mode memory works by eliminating the need for a row address if data is located in the row previously accessed. It is sometimes called *page-mode memory*.

FPM RAM is being replaced by newer types of memory, such as SDRAM.

⇒ See also CPU; EDO DRAM; INTERLEAVED MEMORY; MEMORY; RAM; RDRAM; SLDRAM; WAIT STATE.

fps Stands for *f(rames) p(er) s(econd)*, a measure of how much information is used to store and display motion video. The term applies equally to film video and digital video. Each frame is a still image; displaying frames in quick succession creates the illusion of motion. The more frames per second (fps), the smoother the motion appears. Television in the U.S., for example, is based on the NTSC format, which displays 30 interlaced frames per second (60 *fields per second*). In general, the minimum fps needed to avoid jerky motion is about 30. Some computer video formats, such as AVI, provide only 15 frames per second.

⇒ See also AVI; NTSC.

FPU Short for *f(loating)-p(oint) u(nit)*, a specially designed chip that performs *floating-point* calculations. Computers equipped with an FPU perform certain types of applications much faster than computers that lack one. In particular, graphics applications are faster with an FPU.

Some microprocessors, such as the Intel 80486 and Pentium, have a built-in FPU. With other microprocessors, you can usually add an FPU by inserting the FPU chip on the *motherboard*.

Floating-point units are also called numeric coprocessors, *math coprocessors*, and *floating-point processors*.

⇒ See also COPROCESSOR; FLOATING-POINT NUMBER; FLOPS; INTEL MICROPROCESSORS.

fractal A word coined by Benoit Mandelbrot in 1975 to describe shapes that are "self-similar"—that is, shapes that look the same at different magnifications. To create a fractal, you start with a simple shape and duplicate it successively according to a set of fixed rules. Oddly enough, such a simple formula for creating shapes can produce very complex structures, some of which have a striking resemblance to objects that appear in the real world. For example, graphics designers use fractals to generate images of mountainous landscapes, coastlines, and flowers. In fact, many of the computer-generated images that appear in science fiction films utilize fractals.

⇒ See also GRAPHICS.

fractional T-1 One or more channels of a T-1 service. A complete T-1 carrier contains 24 channels, each of which provides 64 Kbps. Most phone companies, however, also sell fractional T-1 lines, which provide less bandwidth but are also less expensive. Typically, fractional T-1 lines are sold in increments of 56 Kbps (the extra 8 Kbps per channel are used for data management).

⇒ See also DIAL-UP ACCESS; LEASED LINE; T-1 CARRIER.

FRAD Short for *F(rame) R(elay) A(ssembler)/D(isassembler),* a communications device that breaks a data stream into frames for transmission over a Frame Relay network and recreates a data stream from incoming frames. A Frame Relay router serves the same purpose but provides more intelligence in avoiding congestion.

⇒ See also FRAME RELAY.

Figure 35: **fractal image of moon, mountains and lake.**

fragmentation **1.** Refers to the condition of a disk in which files are divided into pieces scattered around the disk. Fragmentation occurs naturally when you use a disk frequently, creating, deleting, and modifying files. At some point, the operating system needs to store parts of a file in noncontiguous clusters. This is entirely invisible to users, but it can slow down the speed at which data is accessed because the disk drive must search through different parts of the disk to put together a single file.

  In DOS 6.0 and later systems, you can defragment a disk with the DE-

FRAG command. You can also buy software utilities, called disk optimizers or *defragmenters,* that defragment a disk. **2.** Fragmentation can
also refer to RAM that has small, unused holes scattered throughout it.
This is called *external fragmentation.* With modern operating systems
that use a paging scheme, a more common type of RAM fragmentation is
internal fragmentation. This occurs when memory is allocated in frames
and the frame size is larger than the amount of memory requested.

⇒ See also CLUSTER; DEFRAG; DISK OPTIMIZER; FILE ALLOCATION TABLE.

frame 1. In graphics and desktop publishing applications, a rectangular
area in which text or graphics can appear. **2.** In communications, a
packet of transmitted information. **3.** In video and animation, a single
image in a sequence of images. See under FPS. **4.** In HTML, refers to dividing the browser display area into separate sections, each of which is
really a different Web page. See under FRAMES.

⇒ See also FPS.

Frame Relay A packet-switching protocol for connecting devices on a
Wide Area Network (WAN). Frame Relay networks in the U.S. support
data transfer rates at T-1 (1.544 Mbps) and T-3 (45 Mbps) speeds. In
fact, you can think of Frame Relay as a way of utilizing existing T-1 and
T-3 lines owned by a service provider. Most telephone companies now
provide Frame Relay service for customers who want connections at 56
Kbps to T-1 speeds. (In Europe, Frame Relay speeds vary from 64 Kbps
to 2 Mbps.)
    In the U.S., Frame Relay is quite popular because it is relatively inex-
pensive. However, it is being replaced in some areas by faster technologies, such as ATM.

⇒ See also ATM; CELL RELAY; CIR; FRAD; PACKET SWITCHING; PVC.

Frame Relay Assembler/Dissassembler See FRAD.

frames A feature supported by most modern Web browsers that enables
the Web author to divide the browser display area into two or more sections (frames). The contents of each frame are taken from a different
Web page. Frames provide great flexibility in designing Web pages, but
many designers avoid them because they are supported unevenly by current browsers.

⇒ See also HTML.

frames per second See FPS.

FreeBSD A popular and free version of UNIX that runs on Intel microprocessors. FreeBSD is distributed in executable and source code form. The
source code enables ambitious users to extend the operating system.
    Another popular and free version of UNIX is Linux.

⇒ See also Linux; UNIX.

freeware Copyrighted software given away for free by the author. Although it is available for free, the author retains the copyright, which means that you cannot do anything with it that is not expressly allowed by the author. Usually, the author allows people to use the software but not sell it.

⇒ See also PUBLIC-DOMAIN SOFTWARE; SHAREWARE; WAREZ.

Frequency Division Multiplexing See FDM.

friction feed A method of feeding paper through a printer. Friction-feed printers use plastic or rubber rollers to squeeze a sheet of paper and pull it through the printer.

The other principal form of feeding paper into a dot-matrix or daisy-wheel printer is through a *tractor feed*, in which sprocketed wheels on either side of the printer fit into holes in the paper. As the wheels revolve, the paper is pulled through the printer.

Tractor-feed printers require special paper, whereas friction-feed printers can handle most types of cut-sheet paper, including envelopes. Many printers support both types of feeding mechanisms.

⇒ See also PRINTER; SHEET FEEDER; TRACTOR FEED.

front end 1. For software applications, *front end* is the same as *user interface*. **2.** In client/server applications, the client part of the program is often called the *front end* and the server part is called the *back end*. **3.** Compilers, the programs that translate source code into object code, are often composed of two parts: a *front end* and a *back end*. The front end is responsible for checking syntax and detecting errors, whereas the back end performs the actual translation into object code.

⇒ See also CLIENT/SERVER ARCHITECTURE; COMPILER; DISTRIBUTED PROCESSING; USER INTERFACE.

frozen Unresponsive. The term is used to describe a monitor, keyboard, or the entire computer when it no longer reacts to input because of a malfunction.

⇒ See also CRASH.

FTM See FLAT TECHNOLOGY MONITOR.

FTP Abbreviation of *F(ile) T(ransfer) T(ransport) P(rotocol)* or *F(ile) T(ransport) P(rotocol)*, the protocol used on the Internet for sending files.

⇒ See also ANONYMOUS FTP; COMMUNICATIONS; INTERNET; TFTP; UUCP.

.fts extension See FTS FILE.

FTS file A hidden index file ending in a **.FTS** [*f(ull)-t(ext) s(earch)*] extension used by the Windows 95 and NT Help system. The first time you select the **Find** tab in a Windows help file, the system displays a dialog box asking what type of index you want to create. After you make a selection, the system creates an index and stores it in an FTS file.

You can delete an FTS file without harming your system. The help system will recreate the file next time it's needed.

⇒ See also EXTENSION; GID FILE; HELP.

full duplex Refers to the transmission of data in two directions simultaneously. For example, a telephone is a full-duplex device because both parties can talk at once. In contrast, a walkie-talkie is a *half-duplex* device because only one party can transmit at a time.

Most modems have a switch that lets you choose between full-duplex and half-duplex modes. The choice depends on which communications program you are running.

In full-duplex mode, data you transmit does not appear on your screen until it has been received and sent back by the other party. This enables you to validate that the data has been accurately transmitted. If your display screen shows two of each character, it probably means that your modem is set to half-duplex mode when it should be in full-duplex mode.

⇒ See also COMMUNICATIONS; HALF DUPLEX; MODEM; SIMPLEX.

full-length See under EXPANSION BOARD and *expansion slot.*

function 1. In programming, a named section of a program that performs a specific task. In this sense, a function is a type of procedure or routine. Some programming languages make a distinction between a *function*, which returns a value, and a *procedure*, which performs some operation but does not return a value.

Most programming languages come with a prewritten set of functions that are kept in a library. You can also write your own functions to perform specialized tasks. **2.** The term *function* is also used synonymously with *operation* and command. For example, you execute the delete *function* to erase a word.

⇒ See also COMMAND; LIBRARY; PROCEDURE; PROGRAM; ROUTINE.

functional spec Short for *functional specification.*

functional specification A formal description of a software system that is used as a blueprint for implementing the program. At minimum, a functional specification should precisely state the purpose (e.g., the *function*) of the software. Depending on the software engineering methodology used, the functional specification might also provide implementation details, such as how the project is divided into modules and how the different modules interact. In addition, a functional specification often describes the software from the user's perspective—how the user interface appears and how a user would use the program to perform specific functions.

A functional specification is often called a *functional spec,* or just *spec.*

⇒ See also ARCHITECTURE; SOFTWARE ENGINEERING; USER INTERFACE.

function keys Special keys on the keyboard that have different meanings depending on which program is running. Function keys are normally labeled F1 to F10 or F12 (or F15 on Macintoshes). On older PCs, for example, ten function keys are grouped on the left side of the keyboard; new PCs have the enhanced keyboard, with twelve function keys aligned along the top of the keyboard.

⇒ See also ALT KEY; ENHANCED KEYBOARD; F1, F2...F15; KEYBOARD.

fuzzy logic A type of logic that recognizes more than simple true and false values. With fuzzy logic, propositions can be represented with degrees of truthfulness and falsehood. For example, the statement *today is sunny* might be 100 percent true if there are no clouds, 80 percent true if there are a few clouds, 50 percent true if it's hazy, and 0 percent true if it rains all day.

Fuzzy logic has proved to be particularly useful in expert system and other artificial intelligence applications. It is also used in some spell checkers to suggest a list of probable words to replace a misspelled one.

⇒ See also ARTIFICIAL INTELLIGENCE; BOOLEAN LOGIC; EXPERT SYSTEM; SPELL CHECKER.

G The symbol used for *giga* or *gigabyte.*

⇒ See also GIGA (G).

garbage in, garbage out Often abbreviated as GIGO, this is a famous computer axiom meaning that if invalid data is entered into a system, the resulting output will also be invalid. Although originally applied to computer software, the axiom holds true for all systems, including, for example, decision-making systems.

gas-plasma display A type of thin display screen, called a *flat-panel display,* used in some older portable computers. A gas-plasma display works by sandwiching neon gas between two plates. Each plate is coated with a conductive print. The print on one plate contains vertical conductive lines and the other plate has horizontal lines. Together, the two plates form a grid. When electric current is passed through a horizontal and vertical line, the gas at the intersection glows, creating a point of light, or *pixel.* You can think of a gas-plasma display as a collection of very small neon bulbs. Images on gas-plasma displays generally appear as orange objects on top of a black background.

Although gas-plasma displays produce very sharp monochrome images, they require much more power than the more common LCD displays.

⇒ See also FLAT-PANEL DISPLAY; LCD; NOTEBOOK COMPUTER.

gateway In networking, a combination of hardware and software that links two different types of networks. Gateways between e-mail systems, for example, allow users on different e-mail systems to exchange messages.

⇒ See also NETWORK.

GB Short for *gigabyte.*

Gbps Short for *G(iga)b(its) p(er) s(econd),* a data transfer speed measurement for high-speed networks such as Gigabit Ethernet. When used to describe data transfer rates, a gigabit equals 1,000,000,000 bits.

⇒ See also GIGABIT; GIGABIT ETHERNET; MBPS.

GDI Short for *G(raphical) D(evice) I(nterface),* a Windows standard for representing graphical objects and transmitting them to output devices, such as monitors and printers.

⇒ See also DirectDraw; GDI printer; host-based printer.

GDI printer A printer that has built-in support for Windows Graphical Device Interface (GDI). GDI is used by most Windows applications to display images on a monitor, so when printing from a Windows application to a GDI printer, there is no need to convert the output to another format such as PostScript or PCL.

GDI printers are sometimes called *host-based printers* because they rely on the host computer to rasterize pages.

⇒ See also GDI; host-based printer; PCL; PostScript; printer; Windows.

geek Short for *computer geek,* an individual with a passion for computers, to the exclusion of other normal human interests. Depending on the context, it can be used in either a derogatory or affectionate manner. Basically, *geek* and *nerd* are synonymous.

⇒ See also hacker.

GEM A graphical user interface developed by Digital Research that is built into personal computers made by Atari and is also used as an interface for some DOS programs. Like the Macintosh interface and Microsoft Windows, GEM provides a windowed environment for running programs.

GEM also refers to a special graphics file format used in GEM-based applications.

⇒ See also graphical user interface; Macintosh computer; Microsoft Windows.

general protection fault See GPF.

genetic programming A type of programming that utilizes the same properties of natural selection found in biological evolution. The general idea behind genetic programming is to start with a collection of functions and randomly combine them into programs; then run the programs and see which gives the best results; keep the best ones (natural selection), mutate some of the others, and test the new generation; repeat this process until a clear best program emerges.

LISP is a popular language for genetic programming.

⇒ See also artificial intelligence; LISP.

genlock Short for *gen(erator) lock(ing) device,* a genlock is a device that enables a composite video machine, such as a TV, to accept two signals simultaneously. A genlock locks one set of signals while it processes the second set. This enables you to combine graphics from a computer with video signals from a second source such as a video camera.

⇒ See also composite video.

Geoport A serial port for Apple computers that provides an interface between a telephone line and the computer. The *GeoPort Telecom Adapter Kit* announced in late 1996 supports modem speeds of up to 28.8 Kbps and provides enhanced fax and telephone services when used with the Apple Telecom 3.0 suite of communications applications.

⇒ See also SERIAL PORT; VIDEOCONFERENCING.

GFLOPS See under FLOPS.

.gid extension See GID FILE.

GID file A hidden Windows 95 configuration file, ending with a **.GID** extension, used by the Windows Help system. The first time you open a Windows help file, the Help system analyzes the file and creates an associated GID file that helps speed up access to help file topics. You can delete a GID file without harming your system, but Windows will automatically recreate the file next time you open the corresponding help file.

⇒ See also EXTENSION; FTS FILE; HELP.

GIF Pronounced *jiff* or *giff* (hard *g*), stands for *g(raphics) i(nterchange) f(ormat)*, a bit-mapped graphics file format used by the World Wide Web, CompuServe, and many BBSs. GIF supports color and various resolutions. It also includes data compression, making it especially effective for scanned photos.

⇒ See also ANIMATED GIF; DATA COMPRESSION; GRAPHICS FILE FORMATS; IMAGE MAP; LZW; PNG.

gigabit 1. When used to describe data storage, 1,024 megabits. **2.** When used to described data transfer rates, it refers to one 10^9 (1,000,000,000) bits.

⇒ See also GBPS; GIGABYTE; MEGABIT.

Gigabit Ethernet The newest version of Ethernet, which supports data transfer rates of 1 Gigabit (1,000 megabits) per second. The first Gigabit Ethernet standard (802.3z) was ratified by the IEEE 802.3 Committee in 1998.

⇒ See also 100BASE-T; ETHERNET; HIPPI; IEEE.

gigabyte 2^{30} (1,073,741,824) bytes. One gigabyte is equal to 1,024 megabytes. Gigabyte is often abbreviated as *G* or *GB*.

⇒ See also BYTE; GIGA (G); GIGABIT; MEGABYTE; PETABYTE.

GigaFLOPS See under FLOPS.

giga (G) 1. When decimal notation is used, *giga* stands for 10^9. For example, a *gigavolt* is 1,000,000,000 volts. **2.** When applied to computers, which use the binary notation system, *giga* represents 2^{30}, which is 1,073,741,824, a little more than 1 billion. A gigabyte, therefore, is about 1.073 billion bytes.

⇒ See also BINARY; MASS STORAGE; MEGABYTE.

GIGO See GARBAGE IN, GARBAGE OUT.

glitch A malfunction. *Glitch* is sometimes used as a synonym for bug, but more often it refers to a hardware problem.

⇒ See also BUG.

GNU Self-referentially, short for *GNU's not UNIX,* a UNIX-compatible software system developed by the Free Software Foundation (FSF). The philosophy behind GNU is to produce software that is non-proprietary. Anyone can download, modify, and redistribute GNU software. The only restriction is that they cannot limit further redistribution. The GNU project was started in 1983 by Richard Stallman at the Massachusetts Institute of Technology.

Linux systems rely heavily on GNU software, and in the past, GNU systems used the Linux kernel. This close connection has led some people mistakenly to equate GNU with Linux. They are actually quite separate. In fact, the FSF is developing a new kernel called HURD to replace the Linux kernel in GNU systems.

⇒ See also LINUX; UNIX.

Gopher A system that predates the World Wide Web for organizing and displaying files on Internet servers. A Gopher server presents its contents as a hierarchically structured list of files. With the ascendance of the Web, most Gopher databases are being converted to Web sites, which can be more easily accessed via Web search engines.

Gopher was developed at the University of Minnesota and named after the school's mascot. Two systems, *Veronica* and *Jughead,* let you search global indices of resources stored in Gopher systems.

⇒ See also ARCHIE; INTERNET; JUGHEAD; VERONICA; WORLD WIDE WEB.

GPF Short for *G(eneral) P(rotection) F(ault),* a computer condition that causes a Windows application to crash. The most common cause of a GPF is two applications trying to use the same block of memory, or more specifically, one application trying to use memory assigned to another application.

The following situations can also cause GPFs:

- Running an application with insufficient resources
- Using improper hardware device drivers
- Corrupted or missing Windows files

- Applications exchanging data that cannot be read

  GPFs are often preceded by an *invalid page fault*.

⇒ See also CRASH; FATAL ERROR; INVALID PAGE FAULT; RUNTIME ERROR.

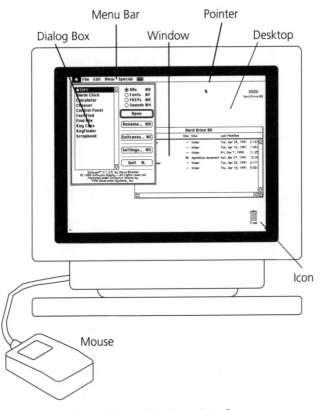

Figure 36: **graphical user interface**

gppm Abbreviation for *g(raphics) p(ages) p(er) m(inute)*, the speed with which laser printers can print nontext pages. Typically, laser printers are rated in terms of *pages per minute (ppm)*, but this refers only to the speed with which they print text pages. The gppm is always much less and may be the more important figure if you are using the printer to print graphics-intensive documents.

⇒ See also LASER PRINTER; PPM.

grabber 1. A device that captures data. The term is used most often to describe devices that can capture full-motion video from a television or video camera and convert it to digital form for storage on a computer's disk. **2.** In some applications, a special tool or cursor that enables you to grab objects on the screen and move them or manipulate them in some other way. A grabber cursor is often represented by a hand icon.

⇒ See also CURSOR.

Graphical Device Interface See GDI.

graphical user interface A program interface that takes advantage of the computer's graphics capabilities to make the program easier to use. Well-designed graphical user interfaces can free the user from having to learn complex command languages. On the other hand, many users find that they work more effectively with a command-driven interface, especially if they already know the command language.

Graphical user interfaces, such as Microsoft Windows and the one used by the Apple Macintosh, feature the following basic components:

pointer: A symbol that appears on the display screen and that you move to select objects and commands. Usually, the pointer appears as a small angled arrow. Text-processing applications, however, use an *I-beam pointer* that is shaped like a capital *I*.

pointing device: A device, such as a mouse or trackball, that enables you to select objects on the display screen.

icons: Small pictures that represent commands, files, or windows. By moving the pointer to the icon and pressing a mouse button, you can execute a command or convert the icon into a window. You can also move the icons around the display screen as if they were real objects on your desk.

desktop: The area on the display screen where icons are grouped is often referred to as the desktop because the icons are intended to re-present real objects on a real desktop.

windows: You can divide the screen into different areas. In each window, you can run a different program or display a different file. You can move windows around the display screen, and change their shape and size at will.

menus: Most graphical user interfaces let you execute commands by selecting a choice from a drop-down menu.

The first graphical user interface was designed by Xerox Corporation's Palo Alto Research Center in the 1970s, but it was not until the 1980s and the emergence of the Apple Macintosh that graphical user interfaces became popular. One reason for their slow acceptance was the fact that they require considerable CPU power and a high-quality monitor, which until recently were prohibitively expensive.

In addition to their visual components, graphical user interfaces also make it easier to move data from one application to another. A true GUI includes standard formats for representing text and graphics. Because the formats are well defined, different programs that run under a common GUI can share data. This makes it possible, for example, to copy a graph created by a spreadsheet program into a document created by a word processor.

Many DOS programs include some features of GUIs, such as menus, but are not *graphics based*. Such interfaces are sometimes called *graphical character-based user interfaces* to distinguish them from true GUIs.

⇒ See also AWT; CHARACTER BASED; DESKTOP; DRAG-AND-DROP; ICON; MACINTOSH COMPUTER; MDI; MICROSOFT WINDOWS; POINTER; POINTING DEVICE; USER INTERFACE; XEROX.

graphics Pertains to any computer device or program that makes a computer capable of displaying and manipulating pictures. For example, laser printers and plotters are *graphics devices* because they permit the computer to output pictures. A *graphics monitor* is a display monitor that can display pictures. A *graphics board* (or *graphics card*) is a printed circuit board that, when installed in a computer, permits the computer to display pictures.

Many software applications include graphics components. Such programs are said to *support* graphics. For example, certain word processors support graphics because they let you draw or import pictures. All CAD/CAM systems support graphics. Some database management systems and spreadsheet programs support graphics because they let you display data in the form of graphs and charts. Such applications are often referred to as *business graphics.*

The following are also considered *graphics applications:*

paint programs: Allow you to create rough freehand drawings. The images are stored as bitmaps and can easily be edited.

illustration/design programs: Support more advanced features than paint programs, particularly for drawing curved lines. The images are usually stored in vector-based formats. Illustration/design programs are often called *draw programs.*

presentation graphics software: Lets you create bar charts, pie charts, graphics, and other types of images for slide shows and reports. The charts can be based on data imported from spreadsheet applications.

animation software: Enables you to chain and sequence a series of images to simulate movement. Each image is like a frame in a movie.

CAD software: Enables architects and engineers to draft designs.

desktop publishing: Provides a full set of word processing features as well as fine control over placement of text and graphics, so that you can create newsletters, advertisements, books, and other types of documents.

In general, applications that support graphics require a powerful CPU and a large amount of memory. Until recently, many graphics applications—for example, computer animation systems—required more computing power than was available on personal computers and would run only on powerful workstations or specially designed graphics computers. This was true of all three-dimensional computer graphics applications. However, with the advent of more powerful processors, personal computers are catching up as graphic workstations.

In addition to the CPU and memory, graphics software requires a graphics monitor and support for one of the many graphics standards. Most PC programs, for instance, require VGA graphics. If your computer does not have built-in support for a specific graphics system, you can insert a video adapter card.

The quality of most graphics devices is determined by their *resolution*—how many points per square inch they can represent—and their color capabilities.

⇒ See also ALPHA CHANNEL; BIT MAP; BIT-MAPPED GRAPHICS; CAD; CAD/CAM; CHARACTER BASED; CLIP ART; CPU; DESKTOP PUBLISHING; DISPLAY SCREEN; GRAPHICS FILE FORMATS; IMAGE PROCESSING; LASER PRINTER; MICROSOFT WINDOWS; MONITOR; PERSONAL COMPUTER; PLOTTER; 3-D GRAPHICS.

graphics accelerator A type of video adapter that contains its own processor to boost performance levels. These processors are specialized for computing graphical transformations, so they achieve better results than the general-purpose CPU used by the computer. In addition, they free up the computer's CPU to execute other commands while the graphics accelerator is handling graphics computations.

The popularity of graphical applications, and especially multimedia applications, has made graphics accelerators not only a common enhancement, but a necessity. Most computer manufacturers now bundle a graphics accelerator with their mid-range and high-end systems.

Aside from the graphics processor used, the other characteristics that differentiate graphics accelerators are:

memory: Graphics accelerators have their own memory, which is reserved for storing graphical representations. The amount of memory determines how much resolution and how many colors can be displayed. Some accelerators use conventional DRAM, but others use a special type of video RAM (VRAM), which enables both the video circuitry and the processor to access the memory simultaneously.

bus: Each graphics accelerator is designed for a particular type of video bus. As of 1995, most are designed for the PCI bus.

register width: The wider the register, the more data the processor can manipulate with each instruction. 64-bit accelerators are already becoming common, and we can expect 128-bit accelerators in the near future.

⇒ See also 3-D GRAPHICS; ACCELERATOR BOARD; AGP; CPU; DIRECT3D; DIRECTDRAW; DIRECTX; DRAM; GRAPHICS; MDRAM; MULTIMEDIA; PCI; SGRAM; VIDEO ADAPTER; VIDEO MEMORY; VRAM.

graphics adapter Same as VIDEO ADAPTER.

graphics based Refers to software and hardware that treat objects on a display screen as bit maps or geometrical shapes rather than as characters. In contrast, character-based systems treat everything as ASCII or extended ASCII characters.

All graphics software is by definition graphics based. Systems that manipulate text can also be graphics based; for example, desktop publishing systems are essentially graphics-based word processors.

Traditionally, most DOS applications—word processors, spreadsheets, and database management systems—have been character based. Windows and the Mac OS are graphics-based.

⇒ See also CHARACTER BASED.

graphics card Same as VIDEO ADAPTER.

graphics character A character that represents a shape. By combining graphics characters, even character-mode programs can display rudimentary graphics, known as block graphics. Many of the characters in the extended ASCII character set are graphics characters.

⇒ See also BLOCK GRAPHICS; CHARACTER MODE; EXTENDED ASCII.

Table 16
Bit-Mapped Graphics File Formats

Format	Description
BMP	The bit-mapped file format used by Microsoft Windows.
GIF	The bit-mapped file format used by CompuServe and many other BBSs.
PCX	Originally developed by ZSOFT for its PC Paintbrush program, PCX is a common graphics file format supported by many graphics programs, as well as most optical scanners and fax modems.
TIFF (Tagged Image File Format)	A standard file format for storing images as bit maps. It is used especially for scanned images because it can support any size, resolution, and color depth.

graphics coprocessor A microprocessor specially designed for handling graphics computations. Most graphics accelerators include a graphics coprocessor.

⇒ See also COPROCESSOR; GRAPHICS ACCELERATOR.

graphics display system The combination of monitor and video adapter that makes a computer capable of displaying graphics.

⇒ See also GRAPHICS; MONITOR; VIDEO ADAPTER.

Table 17
Vector Graphics File Formats

Format	Description
CGM (Computer Graphics Metafile)	A format developed by several standards organizations, CGM is supported by many PC software products.
DXF (Data Exchange File)	A format created by AutoDesk. Almost all PC-based CAD systems support DXF.
EPS (Encapsulated PostScript)	The file format for the PostScript language. EPS uses a combination of PostScript commands and TIFF or PICT formats.
GEM	The graphics file format used by GEM-based applications. GEM is a graphical user interface (GUI) developed by Digital Research.
HPGL (Hewlett-Packard Graphics Language)	One of the oldest file formats. Although it is not very sophisticated, it is supported by many PC-based graphics products.
IGES (Initial Graphics Exchange Specification)	An ANSI standard for three-dimensional wire frame models. IGES is supported by most PC-based CAD systems.
PIC (Lotus Picture File)	A relatively simple file format developed by Lotus for representing graphs generated by Lotus 1-2-3. PIC is supported by a wide variety of PC applications.
PICT	Developed by Apple Computer in 1984 as the standard format for storing and exchanging graphics files. It is supported by all graphics programs that run on a Macintosh.
WMF (Windows Metafile Format)	A file format for exchanging graphics between Microsoft Windows applications. WMF files can also hold bit-mapped images.

---

graphics file formats A file format designed specifically for representing graphical images. Graphics file formats can be broadly categorized into bitmapped formats and vector formats.

⇒ See also BMP; CGM; DIB; DXF; EPS; GEM; GIF; GRAPHICS; HPGL; IGES; PCX; PIC; PICT FILE FORMAT; TIFF; WMF.

graphics mode Many video adapters support several different modes of resolution, all of which are divided into two general categories: character mode and *graphics mode*. In character mode, the display screen is treated as an array of blocks, each of which can hold one ASCII character. In graphics mode, the display screen is treated as an array of pixels. Characters and other shapes are formed by turning on combinations of pixels.

Of the two modes, graphics mode is the more sophisticated. Programs that run in graphics mode can display an unlimited variety of shapes and fonts, whereas programs running in character mode are severely limited. Programs that run entirely in graphics mode are called *graphics-based* programs.

⇒ See also CHARACTER BASED; GRAPHICS BASED; PIXEL; VIDEO ADAPTER.

graphics monitor A monitor capable of displaying graphics—that is, any monitor that supports a graphics mode in addition to text modes. Nearly all modern monitors are graphics monitors.

⇒ See also GRAPHICS; MONITOR.

graphics pages per minute See GPPM.

graphics tablet Same as DIGITIZING TABLET.

gray scaling The use of many shades of gray to represent an image. *Continuous-tone* images, such as black-and-white photographs, use an almost unlimited number of shades of gray. Conventional computer hardware and software, however, can represent only a limited number of shades of gray (typically 16 or 256). Gray scaling is the process of converting a continuous-tone image to an image that a computer can manipulate.

While gray scaling is an improvement over monochrome, it requires larger amounts of memory because each dot is represented by from 4 to 8 bits. At a resolution of 300 dpi, you would need more than 8 megabytes to represent a single 8½ by 11–inch page using 256 shades of gray. This can be reduced considerably through data compression techniques, but gray scaling still requires a great deal of memory.

Many optical scanners are capable of gray scaling, using from 16 to 256 different shades of gray. However, gray scaling is useful only if you have an output device—monitor or printer—that is capable of displaying all the shades. Most color monitors are capable of gray scaling, but the images are generally not as good as on dedicated gray-scaling monitors.

Note that gray scaling is different from dithering. Dithering simulates shades of gray by altering the density and pattern of black and white dots. In gray scaling, each individual dot can have a different shade of gray.

⇒ See also CONTINUOUS TONE; DATA COMPRESSION; DITHERING; MONITOR; OPTI-
CAL SCANNER.

greeking 1. The approximation of text characters on a screen display.
Greeking is often used by word processors that support a *preview* function. In preview mode, the word processor attempts to show what a document will look like when printed. Frequently, however, the graphics display capabilities of the monitor are not sufficient to show text at a small
size. To give a general idea of what the text will look like and how page
layout will appear, the word processor uses graphics symbols to approximate the text. These symbols suggest Greek letters, hence the term *greeking*. **2.** The term *greeking* is also used to describe nonsense text inserted
in a document to check a layout. This allows a layout artist to concentrate on the overall appearance of a page without worrying about the actual text that will be inserted later.

⇒ See also LAYOUT; PREVIEW.

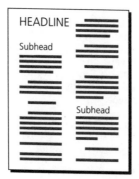

Figure 37: **greeking**

Green Book The specification covering CD-I.

⇒ See also CD-I (COMPACT DISC–INTERACTIVE); ORANGE BOOK; RED BOOK;
WHITE BOOK; YELLOW_BOOK.

green PC A PC specially designed to minimize power consumption. Green
PCs draw less power than normal PCs and support *sleep modes*, in which
the computer powers down all unnecessary components when it is inac-
tive.

⇒ See also ENERGY STAR; SLEEP MODE.

Group 3 protocol The universal protocol defined by the CCITT for sending faxes.

⇒ See also CCITT; FAX MACHINE.

Group 4 protocol A protocol defined by CCITT for sending faxes over ISDN networks.

⇒ See also CCITT; FAX MACHINE; ISDN.

groupware A class of software that helps groups of colleagues (*workgroups*) attached to a local-area network organize their activities. Typically, groupware supports the following operations:

- scheduling meetings and allocating resources
- e-mail
- password protection for documents
- telephone utilities
- electronic newsletters
- file distribution

Groupware is sometimes called *workgroup productivity software.*

⇒ See also E-MAIL; LOCAL-AREA NETWORK; LOTUS NOTES; SCHEDULER; TEAMWARE; WORKGROUP COMPUTING.

GSM Short for *G(lobal) S(ystem) for M(obile) Communications,* one of the leading digital cellular systems. GSM uses narrowband TDMA, which allows eight simultaneous calls on the same radio frequency.

GSM was first introduced in 1991. As of the end of 1997, GSM service was available in more than 100 countries and has become the *de facto* standard in Europe and Asia.

⇒ See also CDMA; CELLULAR; PCS; TDMA.

GUI Pronounced **goo**-ee, acronym for *graphical user interface.* See under *graphical user interface.*

⇒ See also *graphical user interface.*

gutter In desktop publishing, the space between columns in a multiple-column document.

⇒ See also DESKTOP PUBLISHING.

GW-BASIC A dialect of the BASIC programming language that comes with many versions of the DOS operating system.

⇒ See also BASIC; QBASIC.

H.323 A standard approved by the International Telecommunication Union (ITU) that defines how audiovisual conferencing data is transmitted across networks. In theory, H.323 should enable users to participate in the same conference even though they are using different videoconferencing applications. Although most videoconferencing vendors have announced that their products will conform to H.323, it's too early to say whether such adherence will actually result in interoperability.

⇒ See also H.324; ITU; RTSP; VIDEOCONFERENCING.

H.324 A suite of standards approved by the International Telecommunications Union (ITU) that defines videoconferencing over analog (POTS) telephone wires. A main component of H.234 is the V.80 protocol that specifies how modems should handle streaming audio and video data.

⇒ See also H.323; ITU; STREAMING; VIDEOCONFERENCING.

hack *n* **1.** An inelegant and usually temporary solution to a problem. —*v* **2.** To modify a program, often in an unauthorized manner, by changing the code itself.

⇒ See also HACKER; KLUDGE.

hacker A slang term for a computer enthusiast. Among professional programmers, the term *hacker* implies an amateur or a programmer who lacks formal training. Depending on how it used, the term can be either complimentary or derogatory, although it is developing an increasingly derogatory connotation. The pejorative sense of *hacker* is becoming more prominent largely because the popular press has co-opted the term to refer to individuals who gain unauthorized access to computer systems for the purpose of stealing and corrupting data. Hackers, themselves, maintain that the proper term for such individuals is *cracker*.

⇒ See also CRACK; GEEK; IP SPOOFING; PHREAKING; PROGRAMMER; SNIFFER.

half duplex Refers to the transmission of data in just one direction at a time. For example, a walkie-talkie is a half-duplex device because only one party can talk at a time. In contrast, a telephone is a *full-duplex* device because both parties can talk simultaneously.

Most modems contain a switch that lets you select between half-duplex and full-duplex modes. The correct choice depends on which program you are using to transmit data through the modem.

In half-duplex mode, each character transmitted is immediately displayed on your screen. (For this reason, it is sometimes called *local echo*—characters are echoed by the local device). In full-duplex mode, transmitted data is not displayed on your monitor until it has been received and returned (remotely echoed) by the other device. If you are running a communications program and every character appears twice, it probably means that your modem is in half-duplex mode when it should be in full-duplex mode, and every character is being both locally and remotely echoed.

⇒ See also COMMUNICATIONS; FULL DUPLEX; MODEM; SIMPLEX.

half height Some older PCs supported both full-height and half-height bays for disk drives and other mass storage devices. Today, all bays are half-height.

⇒ See also BAY.

halftone In printing, a continuous-tone image, such as a photograph, that has been converted into a black-and-white image. Halftones are created through a process called dithering, in which the density and pattern of black-and-white dots are varied to simulate different shades of gray.

In conventional printing, halftones are created by photographing an image through a screen. The *screen frequency,* measured in lines per inch, determines how many dots are used to make each spot of gray. In theory, the higher the screen frequency (the more lines per inch), the more accurate the halftone will be. However, actual screen frequencies are limited by the technology because higher screen frequencies create smaller, more tightly packed dots. If you are printing on a low-resolution device, therefore, you may get better results with a lower screen frequency.

Modern desktop publishing systems can create halftones by simulating the conventional photographic process. This is why some programs allow you to specify a screen frequency even when no actual screen is used.

⇒ See also CONTINUOUS TONE; DESKTOP PUBLISHING; DITHERING; MOIRÉ.

hand-held computer A portable computer that is small enough to be held in one's hand. Although extremely convenient to carry, handheld computers have not replaced notebook computers because of their small keyboards and screens. The most popular hand-held computers are those that are specifically designed to provide PIM (personal information manager) functions, such as a calendar and address book.

Some manufacturers are trying to solve the small-keyboard problem by replacing the keyboard with an electronic pen. However, these pen-based devices rely on handwriting recognition technologies, which are still in their infancy.

⇒ See also EPOC; HANDWRITING RECOGNITION; NOTEBOOK COMPUTER; PALMTOP; PDA; PIM; WINDOWS CE.

Handheld PC See HPC.

handle 1. In many applications, when you select a graphical object, an outline of the object appears with small boxes. Each box is a handle. By dragging the handles, you can change the shape and size of the object. **2.** In programming, a handle is a token, typically a pointer, that enables the program to access a resource, such as a library function. **3.** When communicating via an online service, your handle is the name that you use to identify yourself. It could be your real name, a nickname, or a completely fictitious name.

⇒ See also CHAT; GRAPHICS; ONLINE SERVICE; POINTER.

handshaking The process by which two devices initiate communications. Handshaking begins when one device sends a message to another device indicating that it wants to establish a communications channel. The two devices then send several messages back and forth that enable them to agree on a communications protocol.

⇒ See also COMMUNICATIONS; PROTOCOL.

handwriting recognition The technique by which a computer system can recognize characters and other symbols written by hand. In theory, handwriting recognition should free us from our keyboards, allowing us to write and draw in a more natural way. It is considered one of the key technologies that will determine the ultimate success or failure of PDAs and other handheld devices. To date, however, the technology has had only limited success. This is partly because it is still a young technology and is not as fast or accurate as it needs to be. Another reason for its slow acceptance, however, is that the keyboard is in fact more convenient in many situations. Many people can write much faster with a keyboard than they can by hand.

⇒ See also HAND-HELD COMPUTER; PDA; PEN COMPUTER.

hang To crash in such a way that the computer does not respond to input from the keyboard or mouse. If your computer is hung, you usually need to reboot it, although sometimes hitting the correct sequence of control characters will free it up.

⇒ See also ABORT; BOMB; BUG; CRASH; DEADLOCK.

hanging indent In word processing, a paragraph that has all lines but the first indented. See below for example.

With many word processors, you can create hanging indents by specifying a negative indentation for the first line of each paragraph.

> This is an example of a hanging indent.
> A hanging indent is also known as
> a hanging paragraph.

⇒ See also WORD PROCESSING.

hanging paragraph Same as HANGING INDENT.

hard The term *hard* is used to describe anything that is permanent or physically exists. In contrast, the term *soft* refers to concepts, symbols, and other intangible and changeable objects.

⇒ See also HARDWARE; HARDWIRED; SOFTWARE.

hard card A hard disk drive and controller on an expansion card. Unlike most disk drives that are either external to the computer or that fit in one of the disk drive bays, a hard card slips into an expansion slot. Hard cards are often faster than conventional disk drives, and easier to install. Their storage capacities, however, are more limited.

⇒ See also BAY; CONTROLLER; EXPANSION BOARD; EXPANSION SLOT; HARD DISK.

hard coded Unchangeable. Hard-coded features are built into the hardware or software in such a way that they cannot be modified.

⇒ See also HARD.

hard copy A printout of data stored in a computer. It is considered *hard* because it exists physically on paper, whereas a *soft* copy exists only electronically.

⇒ See also HARD; SOFT.

hard disk A magnetic disk on which you can store computer data. The term *hard* is used to distinguish it from a soft, or *floppy*, disk. Hard disks hold more data and are faster than floppy disks. A hard disk, for example, can store anywhere from 10 megabytes to several gigabytes, whereas most floppies have a maximum storage capacity of 1.44 megabytes.

A single hard disk usually consists of several *platters*. Each platter requires two read/write heads, one for each side. All the read/write heads are attached to a single access arm so that they cannot move independently. Each platter has the same number of *tracks*, and a track location that cuts across all platters is called a cylinder. For example, a typical 84MB hard disk for a PC might have two platters (four sides) and 1,053 cylinders.

In general, hard disks are less portable than floppies, although it is possible to buy removable hard disks.

⇒ See also CACHE; CYLINDER; DISK DRIVE; DISK PACK; EIDE; FLOPPY DISK; HARD CARD; HARD DISK TYPE; IDE INTERFACE; INTERLEAVE; MASS STORAGE; PLATTER; REMOVABLE HARD DISK; ScanDisk; SMART; TRACK.

hard disk drive The mechanism that reads and writes data on a hard disk. Hard disk drives (HDDs) for PCs generally have seek times of about

12 milliseconds or less. Many disk drives improve their performance through a technique called *caching*.

There are several interface standards for passing data between a hard disk and a computer. The most common are IDE and SCSI.

Hard disk drives are sometimes called *Winchester drives,* Winchester being the name of one of the first popular hard disk drive technologies, developed by IBM in 1973.

⇒ See also DISK COMPRESSION; DISK DRIVE; HARD DISK.

hard disk type A number that indicates important features of a hard disk, such as the number of platters and cylinders. However, the numbering scheme has broken down over the past few years and is no longer used by most disk drive manufacturers.

⇒ See also BIOS; HARD DISK.

hard drive Same as HARD DISK DRIVE.

hard hyphen See under HYPHENATION.

hard return A *return* is the process of jumping from the end of one line of text to the beginning of the next line. Word processors utilize two types of returns: *hard returns* and *soft returns*.

A hard return is an actual symbol inserted into the text. The hard-return symbol is usually invisible, but most word processors support a mode that lets you see them. Whenever you press the Return or Enter key while editing a document, the word processor inserts a hard return.

Hard returns cause the word processor to start a new line regardless of how margins are set. Therefore, if a document contains hard returns, the lines will end at the same place even if you change the margins. In contrast, soft returns, inserted by the program rather than by the user, depend on how the margins are set.

⇒ See also RETURN; SOFT RETURN.

hardware Refers to objects that you can actually touch, like disks, disk drives, display screens, keyboards, printers, boards, and chips. In contrast, software is untouchable. Software exists as ideas, concepts, and symbols, but it has no substance.

Books provide a useful analogy. The pages and the ink are the hardware, while the words, sentences, paragraphs, and the overall meaning are the software. A computer without software is like a book full of blank pages—you need software to make the computer useful just as you need words to make a book meaningful.

⇒ See also FIRMWARE; HARD; SOFTWARE.

hardwired Refers to elements of a program or device that cannot be changed. Originally, the term was used to describe functionality that was built into the circuitry (i.e., the wires) of a device. Nowadays, however, the term is also used to describe constants built into software.

⇒ See also CONSTANT; HARD.

hash See under HASHING.

hashing Producing *hash values* for accessing data or for security. A hash value (or simply *hash*) is a number generated from a string of text. The hash is substantially smaller than the text itself and is generated by a formula in such a way that it is extremely unlikely that some other text will produce the same hash value.

Hashes play a role in security systems where they're used to ensure that transmitted messages have not been tampered with. The sender generates a hash of the message, encrypts it, and sends it with the message itself. The recipient then decrypts both the message and the hash, produces another hash from the received message, and compares the two hashes. If they're the same, there is a very high probability that the message was transmitted intact.

Hashing is also a common method of accessing data records. Consider, for example, a list of names:

- John Smith
- Sarah Jones
- Roger Adams

To create an index, called a *hash table,* for these records, you would apply a formula to each name to produce a unique numeric value. So you might get something like:

- 1345873 John Smith
- 3097905 Sarah Jones
- 4060964 Roger Adams

Then to search for the record containing *Sarah Jones,* you just need to reapply the formula, which directly yields the index key to the record. This is much more efficient than searching through all the records until the matching record is found.

⇒ See also INDEX; KEY.

hash search See under HASHING.

hash table See under HASHING.

Hayes compatible Hayes Microcomputer Products is one of the leading manufacturers of modems and has developed a language called the AT command set for controlling modems that has become the de facto standard. Any modem that recognizes Hayes modem commands is said to be *Hayes compatible.* This is very useful because most communications programs use Hayes modem commands. Virtually all modems manufactured today are Hayes compatible.

⇒ See also AT COMMAND SET; COMMUNICATIONS; DE FACTO STANDARD; MODEM.

HDC See under DISK CONTROLLER.

HDD Short for *hard disk drive.*

HDLC Short for *H(igh)-level D(ata) L(ink) C(ontrol)*, a transmission protocol used at the data link layer (layer 2) of the OSI seven-layer model for data communications. The HDLC protocol embeds information in a data frame that allows devices to control data flow and correct errors. HDLC is an ISO standard developed from the *Synchronous Data Link Control (SDLC)* standard proposed by IBM in the 1970s.

For any HDLC communications session, one station is designated primary and the other secondary. A session can use one of the following connection modes, which determine how the primary and secondary stations interact.

Normal unbalanced: The secondary station responds only to the primary station.
Asynchronous: The secondary station can initiate a message.
Asynchronous balanced: Both stations send and receive over its part of a duplex line. This mode is used for X.25 packet-switching networks.

The *Link Access Procedure-Balanced (LAP-B)* and *Link Access Procedure D-channel (LAP-D)* protocols are subsets of HDLC.

⇒ See also COMMUNICATIONS PROTOCOL; FRAME; OSI.

HDTV Short for *High-Definition Television,* a new type of television that provides much better resolution than current televisions based on the NTSC standard. There are a number of competing HDTV standards, which is one reason that the new technology has not been widely implemented. All of the standards support a wider screen than NTSC and roughly twice the resolution. To pump this additional data through the narrow TV channels, images are digitized and then compressed before they are transmitted and then decompressed when they reach the TV.

⇒ See also DSS; NTSC.

head The mechanism that reads data from or writes data to a magnetic disk or tape. If the head becomes dirty, it will not work properly. This is one of the first things to check if your disk drive or tape drive begins to malfunction.

The head is sometimes called a *read/write head.* Double-sided floppy disk drives have two heads, one for each side of the disk. Hard disk drives have many heads, usually two for each *platter.*

⇒ See also DISK DRIVE; HEAD CRASH; PLATTER.

head crash A serious disk drive malfunction. A head crash usually means that the head has scratched or burned the disk. In a hard disk drive, the head normally hovers a few microinches from the disk. If the head becomes misaligned or if dust particles come between it and the disk, it can touch the disk. When this happens, you usually lose much of the data on the hard disk and will need to replace both the head and the disk. For this reason, it is important to operate disk drives, particularly hard disk drives, in as clean an environment as possible. Even smoke particles can cause a head crash.

Head crashes are less common for floppy disks because the head touches the disk anyway under normal operation.

Another term for *head crash* is *disk crash*.

⇒ See also CRASH; DATA RECOVERY; DISK; DISK DRIVE; HEAD.

header 1. In word processing, one or more lines of text set up to appear at the top of each page of a document. Once you specify the text that should appear in the header, the word processor automatically inserts it.

Most word processors allow you to use special symbols in the header that represent changing values. For example, you can enter a symbol for the page number, and the word processor will automatically replace the symbol with the correct number on each page. If you enter the date symbol, the word processor will insert the current date, which will change if necessary each time you print the document.

Most word processors allow you to specify different headers—for example, one for odd-numbered pages (*odd headers*) and another for even-numbered pages (*even headers*). Headers are also called *running heads*. **2.** In many disciplines of computer science, a header is a unit of information that precedes a data object. In file management, for example, a header is a region at the beginning of each file where bookkeeping information is kept. The file header may contain the date the file was created, the date it was last updated, and the file's size. The header can be accessed only by the operating system or by specialized programs.

⇒ See also FOOTER; WORD PROCESSING.

head-mounted display See HMD.

heap 1. In programming, an area of memory reserved for data that is created at runtime—that is, when the program actually executes. In contrast, the *stack* is an area of memory used for data whose size can be determined when the program is compiled. **2.** A special type of binary tree in which the value of each node is greater than the values of its leaves. A heap sort algorithm works by first organizing a list of data into a heap.

⇒ See also BINARY TREE; DATA STRUCTURE; STACK.

heap sort A sorting algorithm that works by first organizing the data to be sorted into a special type of binary tree called a *heap*. The heap itself has, by definition, the largest value at the top of the tree, so the heap sort algorithm must also reverse the order. It does this with the following

steps:
  1. Remove the topmost item (the largest) and replace it with the right-most leaf. The topmost item is stored in an array.
  2. Reestablish the heap.
  3. Repeat steps 1 and 2 until there are no more items left in the heap. The sorted elements are now stored in an array.
  A heap sort is especially efficient for data that is already stored in a binary tree. In most cases, however, the *quick sort* algorithm is more efficient.

⇒ See also ALGORITHM; BINARY TREE; BUBBLE SORT.

heat sink A component designed to lower the temperature of an electronic device by dissipating heat into the surrounding air. All modern CPUs require a heat sink. Some also require a fan. A heat sink without a fan is called a *passive heat sink;* a heat sink with a fan is called an *active heat sink.* Heat sinks are generally made of a zinc alloy and often have fins.

⇒ See also MOTHERBOARD; VOLTAGE REGULATOR.

helical-scan cartridge A type of magnetic tape that uses the same technology as VCR tapes. The term *helical scan* usually refers to 8 mm tapes, although 4 mm tapes (called DAT *tapes*) use the same technology. The 8 mm helical-scan tapes have data capacities up to 40 GB.

⇒ See also DAT; MASS STORAGE; TAPE.

Help Online documentation. Many programs come with the instruction manual, or a portion of the manual, integrated into the program. If you encounter a problem or forget a command while running the program, you can summon the documentation by pressing a designated *Help key* or entering a *HELP command.* In Windows, the Help key is the function key labeled *F1.*
  Once you summon the Help system, the program often displays a menu of Help topics. You can choose the appropriate topic for whatever problem you are currently encountering. The program will then display a *help screen* that contains the desired documentation.
  Some programs are more sophisticated, displaying different Help messages depending on where you are in the program. Such systems are said to be context sensitive.
  The Macintosh Help system is often referred to as *Balloon Help* because the help messages appear in a cartoonlike balloon. Newer Macs (starting with System 7.5) also have something called *Interactive Help,* which contains tutorials that show you how to perform different operations.
  In Windows systems, help files end with a **.HLP** extension.

⇒ See also CONTEXT SENSITIVE; DOCUMENTATION; FAQ; FTS FILE; GID FILE; HELP DESK; MAN PAGE.

help desk A department within a company that responds to user's technical questions. Most large software companies have help desks to answer user questions. Questions and answers can be delivered by telephone, e-mail, BBS, or fax. There is even help desk software that makes it easier for the people running the help desk to find answers to common questions quickly.

⇒ See also HELP.

Hercules graphics A graphics display system for PCs developed by Van Suwannukul, founder of Hercules Computer Technology. Suwannukul developed the system so that he could produce his doctoral thesis on PC equipment using his native Thai alphabet.

First offered in 1982, the original Hercules system filled a void left by IBM's MDA (*monochrome display adapter*) system. MDA produces high-resolution monochrome text but cannot generate graphics. Hercules systems generate both high-resolution text and graphics for monochrome monitors. The resolution is 720 by 348.

Hercules has been supplanted by other standards, such as VGA, and is now obsolete.

⇒ See also MDA; VIDEO ADAPTER.

heterogeneous network A network that includes computers and other devices from different manufacturers. For example, local-area networks (LANs) that connect PCs with Apple Macintosh computers are heterogeneous.

⇒ See also LOCAL-AREA NETWORK; NETWORK.

heuristic programming A branch of artificial intelligence, that uses *heuristics*—common-sense rules drawn from experience—to solve problems. This is in contrast to *algorithmic programming*, which is based on mathematically provable procedures. Heuristic programming is characterized by programs that are self-learning; they get better with experience. Heuristic programs do not always reach the very best result but usually produce a good result. Many expert systems use heuristic programming.

⇒ See also ALGORITHM; ARTIFICIAL INTELLIGENCE; EXPERT SYSTEM.

Hewlett-Packard See HP.

Hewlett-Packard Graphics Language See HPGL.

hex Short for *hexadecimal*.

hexadecimal Refers to the base-16 number system, which consists of 16 unique symbols: the numbers 0 to 9 and the letters A to F. For example, the decimal number 15 is represented as F in the hexadecimal numbering system. The hexadecimal system is useful because it can represent every byte (8 bits) as two consecutive hexadecimal digits. It is easier for humans to read hexadecimal numbers than binary numbers.

To convert a value from hexadecimal to binary, you merely translate each hexadecimal digit into its 4-bit binary equivalent. Hexadecimal numbers have either an *0x* prefix or an *h* suffix. For example, the hexadecimal number

0x3F7A

translates to the following binary number:

0011 1111 0111 1010

⇒ See also BCD; BINARY; DECIMAL; NIBBLE; OCTAL.

Table 18
Table of Hexadecimal Values

Decimal	Hexadecimal	Binary
0	0	0000
1	1	0001
2	2	0010
3	3	0011
4	4	0100
5	5	0101
6	6	0110
7	7	0111
8	8	1000
9	9	1001
10	A	1010
11	B	1011
12	C	1100
13	D	1101
14	E	1110
15	F	1111

hidden file A file with a special *hidden attribute* turned on, so that the file is not normally visible to users. For example, hidden files are not listed when you execute the DOS DIR command. However, most file management utilities allow you to view hidden files.

DOS hides some files, such as MSDOS.SYS and IO.SYS, so that you will not accidentally corrupt them. You can also turn on the hidden attribute for any normal file, thereby making it invisible to casual snoopers. On a Macintosh, you can hide files with the ResEdit utility.

⇒ See also ATTRIBUTE; FILE MANAGEMENT SYSTEM.

hierarchical Refers to systems that are organized in the shape of a pyramid, with each row of objects linked to objects directly beneath it. Hierarchical systems pervade everyday life. The army, for example, which has generals at the top of the pyramid and privates at the bottom, is a hierarchical system. Similarly, the system for classifying plants and animals according to species, family, genus, and so on is also hierarchical.

Hierarchical systems are as popular in computer systems as they are in other walks of life. The most obvious example of a hierarchical system in computers is a file system, in which directories have files and subdirectories beneath them. Such a file organization is, in fact, called a *hierarchical file system*.

In addition to file systems, many data structures for storing information are hierarchical in form. Menu-driven programs are also hierarchical, because they contain a *root menu* at the top of the pyramid and *submenus* below it.

⇒ See also DIRECTORY; FILE MANAGEMENT SYSTEM; TREE STRUCTURE.

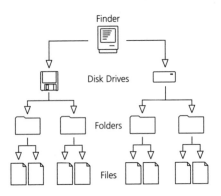

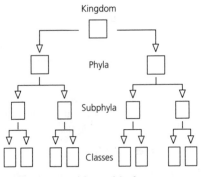

Figure 38: **hierarchical systems**

Hierarchical Storage Management See HSM.

HiFD Short for *Hi(gh) F(loppy) D(isk),* a type of high-density floppy disk developed by Sony that can hold 200 MB of data. Like the competing SuperDisk disk drive from Imation, HiFD disk drives can read and write old 1.44 MB floppy disks in addition to the new high-density disks. HiFD drives support data transfer rates of up to 3.6 MBps.

⇒ See also FLOPPY DISK; FLOPPY DRIVE; SuperDISK; ZIP DRIVE.

high ASCII Same as EXTENDED ASCII.

High Definition Television See HDTV.

high-density disk A high-quality floppy disk capable of holding more data than a double-density disk. High-density 5¼-inch disks for PCs can hold 1.2MB (megabytes) of data. High-density 3½-inch disks can store 1. 44MB.

⇒ See also DENSITY; FLOPPY DISK.

High-level Data Link Control See HDLC.

high-level language A programming language such as C, FORTRAN, or Pascal that enables a programmer to write programs that are more or less independent of a particular type of computer. Such languages are considered high level because they are closer to human languages and further from machine languages. In contrast, assembly languages are considered low level because they are very close to machine languages.

The main advantage of high-level languages over low-level languages is that they are easier to read, write, and maintain. Ultimately, programs written in a high-level language must be translated into machine language by a compiler or interpreter.

The first high-level programming languages were designed in the 1950s. Now there are dozens of different languages, including Ada, Algol, BASIC, COBOL, C, C + +, FORTRAN, LISP, Pascal, and Prolog.

⇒ See also ADA; ASSEMBLY LANGUAGE; BASIC; C; C++; COBOL; COMPILE; FORTRAN; LISP; LOW-LEVEL LANGUAGE; MACHINE LANGUAGE; OBJECT-ORIENTED PROGRAMMING; PASCAL; PROGRAMMING LANGUAGE.

High Level Language Application Program Interface See HLLAPI.

highlight To make an object on a display screen stand out by displaying it in a different mode from that of other objects. Typical highlighted objects include menu options, command buttons, and selected blocks of text.

⇒ See also SELECT.

high memory In DOS-based systems, *high memory* refers to the memory area between the first 640K and 1 megabyte. It is also called the *upper memory area (UMA).*

⇒ See also CONVENTIONAL MEMORY; DOS; EXPANDED MEMORY; EXTENDED MEMORY; LOW MEMORY; TSR.

high memory area In DOS-based systems, the high memory area refers to the first 64K of extended memory.

⇒ See also EXTENDED MEMORY.

High Performance Computing A branch of computer science that concentrates on developing supercomputers and software to run on supercomputers. A main area of this discipline is developing parallel processing algorithms and software—programs that can be divided into little pieces so that each piece can be executed simultaneously by separate processors.

⇒ See also HPCC; PARALLEL PROCESSING; SUPERCOMPUTER.

High Performance Computing and Communications (HPCC) See HPCC.

high resolution See under RESOLUTION.

himem.sys An extended memory (XMS) driver included with DOS, Windows 3.1, Windows for Workgroups, Windows 95, and Windows 98. Windows 95 automatically loads himem.sys during startup. With older versions of Windows, and with DOS, himem.sys must be explicitly loaded by placing a command in CONFIG.SYS.

⇒ See also CONFIG.SYS; EXTENDED MEMORY; XMS.

HIPPI Short for *Hi(gh) P(erformance) P(arallel) I(nterface)*, a standard technology for physically connecting devices at short distances and high speeds. The basic flavor of HIPPI transfers 32 bits in parallel for a data transfer speed of 0.8 Gbps. *Wide HIPPI* transfers 64 bits at a time to yield 1.6 Gbps. New HIPPI standards supporting rates of 6.4 Gbps are under development.

HIPPI became an official ANSI standard in 1990 and is used primarily to connect supercomputers and to provide high-speed backbones for local-area networks (LANs).

⇒ See also BACKBONE; FIBRE CHANNEL; GIGABIT ETHERNET; SUPERCOMPUTER.

HLLAPI Short for *High Level Language Application Program Interface*, an IBM API that allows a PC application to communicate with a mainframe computer. HLLAPI requires a PC to run emulation software and then defines an interface between a PC application and the emulation software. This API is also called *screen-scraping* because the approach uses characters that would otherwise be displayed on a terminal screen.

⇒ See also API; MAINFRAME; TERMINAL; TERMINAL EMULATION.

HMD Short for *h(ead)-m(ounted) d(isplay)*, a headset used with virtual reality systems. An HMD can be a pair of goggles or a full helmet. In front of each eye is a tiny monitor. Because there are two monitors, images appear as three-dimensional. In addition, most HMDs include a *head tracker* so that the system can respond to head movements. For example, if you move your head left, the images in the monitors will change to make it seem as if you're actually looking at a different part of the virtual reality.

⇒ See also VIRTUAL REALITY.

home computer A personal computer specially configured for use in a home rather than an office. Typically, home computers have only medium-power microprocessors but are equipped with a full complement of multimedia devices. In addition, manufacturers often bundle recreational and educational software with home computers.

⇒ See also MULTIMEDIA; PERSONAL COMPUTER.

Home key A key on PC and newer Macintosh keyboards that controls cursor movement. Usually, the Home key moves the cursor to the top left corner of the screen or to the beginning of the file, but it can have other meanings depending on which program is running.

⇒ See also KEYBOARD.

home page The main page of a Web site. Typically, the home page serves as an index or table of contents to other documents stored at the site.

⇒ See also WEB SITE.

home PC Same as HOME COMPUTER.

hop An intermediate connection in a string of connections linking two network devices. On the Internet, for example, most data packets need to go through several routers before they reach their final destination. Each time the packet is forwarded to the next router, a hop occurs. The more hops, the longer it takes for data to go from source to destination. You can see how many hops it takes to get to another Internet host by using the PING or traceroute utilities.

Some Internet Service Providers (ISPs) advertise how many hops away from Internet backbone they are. Theoretically, the fewer hops it takes to get your data onto the backbone, the faster your access will be.

⇒ See also PING; ROUTER; TRACEROUTE; TTL.

host *n* **1.** A computer system that is accessed by a user working at a remote location. Typically, the term is used when there are two computer systems connected by modems and telephone lines. The system that contains the data is called the host, while the computer at which the user sits is called the remote terminal. **2.** A computer that is connected to a TCP/IP network, including the Internet. Each host has a unique IP address. —*v* **3.** To provide the infrastructure for a computer service. For example, there are many companies that host Web servers. This means that they provide the hardware, software, and communications lines required by the server, but the content on the server may be controlled by someone else.

⇒ See also HOST-BASED; REMOTE CONTROL; REMOTE CONTROL SOFTWARE; TELNET.

host-based Refers to any device that relies on the host computer (that is, the computer the device is attached to) to handle some operations. Two common examples are *host-based printers* and *host-based modems.*

⇒ See also HOST; HOST-BASED MODEM; HOST-BASED PRINTER.

host-based modem A modem that uses the computer's processor to handle some operations. Because host-based modems require less processing power of their own, they should be less expensive than conventional modems. There are also *software modems*, in which there's no modem device at all. Instead, all of the modem's functions are handled by the computer's processor.

In the PC world, host-based modems are sometimes called *Winmodems.*

⇒ See also HOST-BASED; MODEM; SOFTWARE MODEM.

host-based printer A printer that relies on the host computer's processor to generate printable pages. Most host-based printers on the market today use the GDI interface built into Windows. Because they don't need a powerful processor of their own, host-based printers tend to be less expensive than conventional printers. But because they share your computer's processor, they may be slow and they may slow down your other computer work. How fast these printers operate depends on how powerful the host computer is and how occupied it is with other operations.

⇒ See also GDI; GDI PRINTER; HOST-BASED; PRINTER.

HotBot A World Wide Web search engine developed collaboratively by Inktomi Corporation and HotWired, Inc., the publisher of *Wired* magazine. Rather than using a few mainframes or supercomputers to search and index Web pages, HotBot uses many workstations working in parallel, what it calls a *Network of Workstations (NOW).* HotBot claims that this strategy allows it to keep up with the exponential growth of the Web better than competing search engines.

⇒ See also ALTA VISTA; EXCITE; INFOSEEK; LYCOS; SEARCH ENGINE; YAHOO!.

HotJava A set of products developed by Sun Microsystems that utilize Java technology. Currently, HotJava products include a set of libraries for building Java-aware applications and a Java-enabled Web browser. Other Java-enabled Web browsers include the newest versions of Netscape

Navigator and Microsoft Internet Explorer.
⇒ See also BROWSER; JAVA.

hot key A user-defined key sequence that executes a command or causes the operating system to switch to another program. In DOS systems, for example, you can use hot keys to open memory-resident programs (*TSRs*). In Windows environments, you can often press a hot key to execute common commands. For example, Ctrl + C usually copies the selected objects.

⇒ See also CONTROL CHARACTER; FUNCTION KEYS; MEMORY RESIDENT; TSR.

hot link *n* **1.** A link between two applications such that changes in one affect the other. For example, some desktop publishing systems let you establish hot links between documents and databases or spreadsheets. When data in the spreadsheet changes, the corresponding charts and graphs in the document change accordingly. —*v* **2.** To establish a link between two applications.

⇒ See also DATABASE; LINK; OLE; SPREADSHEET.

hot plugging The ability to add to and remove devices from a computer while the computer is running and have the operating system automatically recognize the change. Two new external bus standards—*Universal Serial Bus (USB)* and *IEEE 1394*—support hot plugging. This is also a feature of PCMCIA.
  Hot plugging is also called *hot swapping*.

⇒ See also IEEE 1394; PCMCIA; PLUG-AND-PLAY; USB.

hot spot An area of a graphics object, or a section of text, that activates a function when selected. Hot spots are particularly common in multimedia applications, where selecting a hot spot can make the application display a picture, run a video, or open a new window of information.

⇒ See also IMAGE MAP; MULTIMEDIA.

hot swap See under HOT PLUGGING.

hot swapping Same as HOT PLUGGING.

HP Short for *H(ewlett)-P(ackard)*, one of the world's largest computer and electronics companies. Founded in 1939 by William Hewlett and David Packard, HP is best known today for its line of LaserJet and DeskJet printers. However, it produces more than 10,00 different products, ranging from computer systems to specialized electronic devices.

⇒ See also HP-COMPATIBLE PRINTER; PCL; PRINTER.

HPC 1. Short for *H(igh) P(erformance) C(omputing)*. **2.** Short for *H(and-*

held) **PC**, Microsoft's name for a *personal digital assistant (PDA)*.
⇒ See also PDA; WINDOWS CE.

HPCC The U.S. government's term for *High Performance Computing*. There are a number of U.S. agencies conducting HPCC research.

⇒ See also HIGH PERFORMANCE COMPUTING.

HP-compatible printer Hewlett-Packard was one of the first companies to produce a laser printer for PCs, and most software products include drivers for HP printers. The drivers control the printers through a language called *PCL (printer control language)*. Other manufacturers of laser printers design their printers so that they, too, understand PCL, making them able to emulate HP printers. In this way, their printers are HP compatible and are thus automatically supported by many software products.

No non-HP printer, however, is 100 percent HP compatible. Manufacturers claim HP compatibility even if their printers recognize only a subset of PCL commands. Note also that there are different versions of PCL. A printer may be able to emulate an HP LaserJet Plus but not a LaserJet II. Finally, HP laser printers support font cartridges, and not all HP-compatible printers can accept the same cartridges.

⇒ See also COMPATIBLE; DRIVER; EMULATION; FONT CARTRIDGE; HP; LASER PRINTER; PCL; POSTSCRIPT.

HPGL Abbreviation of *H(ewlett)-P(ackard) G(raphics) L(anguage)*, a set of commands for controlling plotters and printers. HPGL is part of Hewlett-Packard's PCL Level 5 page description language.

⇒ See also PCL; PLOTTER.

.hqx See under BINHEX.

hqx See under BINHEX.

HSM Short for *H(ierarchical) S(torage) M(anagement)*. A data storage system that automatically moves data between high-cost and low-cost storage media. HSM systems exist because high-speed storage devices, such as hard disk drives, are more expensive (per byte stored) than slower devices, such as optical discs and magnetic tape drives. While it would be ideal to have all data available on high-speed devices all the time, this is prohibitively expensive for many organizations. Instead, HSM systems store the bulk of the enterprise's data on slower devices, and then copy data to faster disk drives when needed. In effect, HSM turns the fast disk drives into caches for the slower mass storage devices. The HSM system monitors the way data is used and makes best guesses as to which data can safely be moved to slower devices and which data should stay on the hard disks.

⇒ See also BACKUP; MASS STORAGE; STORAGE; STORAGE DEVICE.

HTML Short for *H(yper)T(ext) M(arkup) L(anguage),* the authoring language used to create documents on the World Wide Web. HTML is similar to SGML, although it is not a strict subset.

⇒ See also BROWSER; CSS; DOM; FRAMES; HTTP; HYPERTEXT; JAVASCRIPT; SGML; SSI; TAG; VRML; W3C; WORLD WIDE WEB; XML.

HTTP Short for *H(yper)T(ext) T(ransfer) P(rotocol),* the underlying protocol used by the World Wide Web. HTTP defines how messages are formatted and transmitted, and what actions Web servers and browsers should take in response to various commands. For example, when you enter a URL in your browser, this actually sends an HTTP command to the Web server directing it to fetch and transmit the requested Web page.

The other main standard that controls how the World Wide Web works is HTML, which covers how Web pages are formatted and displayed.

HTTP is called a *stateless* protocol because each command is executed independently, without any knowledge of the commands that came before it. This is the main reason that it is difficult to implement Web sites that react intelligently to user input. This shortcoming of HTTP is being addressed in a number of new technologies, including ActiveX, Java, JavaScript, and cookies.

Currently, most Web browsers and servers support HTTP 1.1. One of the main features of HTTP 1.1 is that it supports *persistent connections.* This means that once a browser connects to a Web server, it can receive multiple files through the same connection. This should improve performance by as much as 20 percent.

⇒ See also HTML; S-HTTP; STATELESS; W3C; WORLD WIDE WEB.

hub A common connection point for devices in a network. Hubs are commonly used to connect segments of a LAN. A hub contains multiple ports. When a packet arrives at one port, it is copied to the other ports so that all segments of the LAN can see all packets.

A *passive hub* serves simply as a conduit for the data, enabling it to go from one device (or segment) to another. So-called *intelligent hubs* include additional features that enable an administrator to monitor the traffic passing through the hub and to configure each port in the hub. Intelligent hubs are also called *manageable hubs.*

A third type of hub, called a *switching hub,* actually reads the destination address of each packet and then forwards the packet to the correct port.

⇒ See also 10BASET; 3COM; BRIDGE; CONCENTRATOR; MAU; REPEATER; STAR NETWORK; SWITCHING HUB.

human engineering Same as ERGONOMICS.

HyperCard A hypertext programming environment for the Macintosh introduced by Apple in 1987. The HyperCard model consists of cards, and collections of cards, called *stacks.* You can connect the cards in various ways, and leaf through them the way you would with a set of Rolodex cards. In addition to data, each card can contain graphics and buttons that trigger other events, such as sound or video.

Each object in a HyperCard system—stack, card, text field, button, or background—can have a *script* associated with it. A script is a set of instructions that specify what actions should take place when a user selects an object with the mouse or when some other event occurs.

Writing HyperCard applications is known as *authoring*.

⇒ See also AUTHORING TOOL; HYPERTEXT.

hyperlink An element in an electronic document that links to another place in the same document or to an entirely different document. Typically, you click on the hyperlink to follow the link. Hyperlinks are the most essential ingredient of all hypertext systems, including the World Wide Web.

⇒ See also HYPERMEDIA; HYPERTEXT.

hypermedia An extension to hypertext that supports linking graphics, sound, and video elements in addition to text elements. The World Wide Web is a partial hypermedia system because it supports graphical hyperlinks and links to sound and video files. New hypermedia systems under development will allow objects in computer videos to be hyperlinked.

⇒ See also HYPERLINK; HYPERTEXT; MULTIMEDIA; WORLD WIDE WEB.

Hypertext A special type of database system, invented by Ted Nelson in the 1960s, in which objects (text, pictures, music, programs, and so on) can be creatively linked to each other. When you select an object, you can see all the other objects that are linked to it. You can move from one object to another even though they might have very different forms. For example, while reading a document about Mozart, you might click on the phrase *Violin Concerto in A Major,* which could display the written score or perhaps even invoke a recording of the concerto. Clicking on the name *Mozart* might cause various illustrations of Mozart to appear on the screen. The icons that you select to view associated objects are called *Hypertext links* or buttons.

Hypertext systems are particularly useful for organizing and browsing through large databases that consist of disparate types of information. There are several Hypertext systems available for Apple Macintosh computers and PCs that enable you to develop your own databases. Such systems are often called *authoring systems*. HyperCard software from Apple Computer is the most well known.

⇒ See also AUTHORING TOOL; HELP; HTML; HYPERCARD; HYPERLINK; HYPERMEDIA; MULTIMEDIA; SGML.

Hypertext Markup Language See HTML.

HyperText Transfer Protocol See HTTP.

HyperText Transport Protocol See HTTP.

hyphenation In word processing, *hyphenation* refers to splitting a word that would otherwise extend beyond the right margin. Not all word processors support hyphenation, and of those that do support it, not all perform it correctly.

Word processors use two basic techniques to perform hyphenation. The first employs an internal dictionary of words that indicates where hyphens may be inserted. The second uses a set of logical formulas to make hyphenation decisions. The dictionary method is more accurate but is usually slower. The most sophisticated programs use a combination of both methods.

Most word processors allow you to override their own hyphenation rules and define for yourself where a word should be divided.

Hyphens inserted automatically by a hyphenation utility are called *discretionary* or *soft hyphens*. Hyphens that you add explicitly by entering the dash character are called *hard hyphens*.

⇒ See also WORD PROCESSING; WORD WRAP.

I2 Short for *I(nternet)* **2**, a new global network being developed cooperatively by about 100 universities. The goal of I2 is to develop the technologies necessary to support high bandwidths required by applications such as live video. I2 is expected to be 100 to 1,000 times faster than the current Internet.

In addition to being fast, I2 will also support *Quality-of-Service (QoS)*. This will allow two hosts to establish a connection with a guaranteed bandwidth.

⇒ See also INTERNET; NGI INITIATIVE; vBNS.

I2O Also called *Intelligent I/O*, a new I/O architecture being developed by a consortium of computer companies called the *I2O special Interest Group (SIG)*. I2O is designed to eliminate I/O bottlenecks by utilizing special I/O processors (IOPs) that handle the nitty-gritty details of interrupt handling, buffering and data transfer. In addition, an I2O driver consists of an OS-specific module (OSM) that deals with higher-level operating system details (such as accessing files) and a hardware device module (HDM), that understands how to communicate with specific devices. Because the OSM and HDM are autonomous, they can perform a number of tasks independently, without sending data over the I/O bus.

I2O is being designed to work with PCI but isn't expect to be widely available until 1998 or later.

⇒ See also I/O; PCI.

IA-64 See under MERCED.

IAB Short for *Internet Architecture Board.*

IAC Short for *I(nternet) A(ccess) C(oalition)*, a consortium of companies involved in the Internet, including AT&T, Microsoft, and MCI. The IAC's stated purpose is to maintain the affordability of Internet access over telephone lines and accelerate the availability of inexpensive digital telephone network connections to the Internet.

⇒ See also INTERNET; POTS.

IAHC Short for *I(nternet) International A(d) H(oc) C(ommittee)*, the international organization responsible for managing the Internet's domain name system (DNS).
⇒ See also DNS; DOMAIN NAME.

IANA Short for *I(nternet) A(ssigned) N(umbers) A(uthority),* an organization working under the auspices of the Internet Architecture Board (IAB)
that is responsible for assigning new Internet-wide IP addresses.

⇒ See also INTERNET ARCHITECTURE BOARD; IP ADDRESS.

I-beam pointer A pointer shaped like a capital I used in graphics-based
text processing applications. Many desktop publishing systems and word
processors use an I-beam pointer to mark blocks of text and move the insertion point. Note that the I-beam pointer is not the same as the selection pointer, which is usually shaped like an arrow.

⇒ See also INSERTION POINT; POINTER.

IBM Short for *I(nternational) B(usiness) M(achines),* the largest computer
company in the world. IBM started in 1911 as a producer of punch card
tabulating machines. In 1953, it introduced its first computer, the *701.*
During the 1960s and 1970s, IBM came to dominate the new field of
mainframe and minicomputers. In 1981, IBM launched its first personal
computer, called the *IBM PC,* which quickly became the standard. However, IBM underestimated the market for PCs and lost market share to
vendors of PC compatibles, such as Compaq.

Over the past six or seven years, IBM has had to make some difficult
adjustments as the market for mainframe computers has declined. While
not the juggernaut it once was, IBM is still the most powerful company
in the computer industry.

⇒ See also AS/400; COMPAQ; DEC; IBM PC; MAINFRAME; PC; SGI; SUN
MICROSYSTEMS.

IBM compatible See under IBM PC.

IBM PC Refers to a family of personal computers produced by IBM. The
term can also refer to computers that conform to set of loosely controlled
standards. These are also called *IBM clones, IBM compatibles,* or simply
compatibles. These terms are actually misnomers because many of the
PCs produced by IBM do not conform to industry standards. For example, IBM attempted to change the expansion bus to MCA in its PS/2 line
of PCs, but the industry did not follow suit.

⇒ See also COMPATIBLE; IBM; PC.

ICC See under SMART CARD.

ICMP Short for *I(nternet) C(ontrol) M(essage) P(rotocol),* an extension to
the Internet Protocol (IP) defined by RFC 792. ICMP supports packets
containing error, control, and informational messages. The PING command, for example, uses ICMP to test an Internet connection.
⇒ See also IP; PING.

icon A small picture that represents an object or program. Icons are very useful in applications that use windows, because with the click of a mouse button you can shrink an entire window into a small icon. (This is sometimes called *minimizing*.) To redisplay the window, you merely move the pointer to the icon and click (or double click) a mouse button. (This is sometimes called *restoring* or *maximizing*.)

Icons are a principal feature of graphical user interfaces.

⇒ See also GRAPHICAL USER INTERFACE.

IDE 1. See under IDE INTERFACE. 2. See under INTEGRATED DEVELOPMENT ENVIRONMENT.

⇒ See also APPLICATION; IDE INTERFACE; INTEGRATED; PROGRAMMING LANGUAGE; VISUAL C++.

IDE interface Abbreviation of either *I(ntelligent) D(rive) E(lectronics)* or *I(ntegrated) D(rive) E(lectronics)*, depending on whom you ask. An IDE interface is an interface for mass storage devices, in which the controller is integrated into the disk or CD-ROM drive.

Although it really refers to a general technology, most people use the term to refer the ATA specification, which uses this technology. Refer to *ATA* for more information.

⇒ See also ATA; EIDE; HARD DISK DRIVE; INTERFACE; SCSI; ST-506 INTERFACE.

identifier Same as NAME. The term *identifier* is usually used for variable names.

⇒ See also NAME; VARIABLE.

IE Short for *Internet Explorer*.

IEEE Abbreviation of *I(nstitute) of E(lectrical) and E(lectronics) E(ngineers)*, pronounced *I-triple-E*. Founded in 1884, the IEEE is an organization composed of engineers, scientists, and students. The IEEE is best known for developing standards for the computer and electronics industry. In particular, the IEEE 802 standards for local-area networks are widely followed.

⇒ See also ETHERNET; FLOATING-POINT NUMBER; GIGABIT ETHERNET; IEEE 802 STANDARDS; NETWORK; TOKEN-RING NETWORK.

IEEE 1394 A new, very fast external bus standard that supports data transfer rates of up to 400 Mbps (400 million bits per second). Products supporting the 1394 standard go under different names, depending on the company. Apple, which originally developed the technology, uses the trademarked name *FireWire*. Other companies use other names, such as *I-link* and *Lynx*, to describe their 1394 products.

A single 1394 port can be used to connect up 63 external devices. In addition to its high speed, 1394 also supports *isochronous data*—delivering data at a guaranteed rate. This makes it ideal for devices that need to transfer high levels of data in real-time, such as video devices.

Although extremely fast and flexible, 1394 is also expensive. Like USB, 1394 supports both Plug-and-Play and hot plugging, and also provides power to peripheral devices. The main difference between 1394 and USB is that 1394 supports faster data transfer rates and is more expensive. For this reason, it is expected to be used mostly for devices that require large throughputs, such as video cameras, whereas USB will be used to connect most other peripheral devices.

⇒ See also DEVICE BAY; HOT PLUGGING; PCMCIA; PLUG-AND-PLAY; SERIAL PORT; USB.

IEEE 802 See IEEE 802 STANDARDS.

IEEE 802 standards A set of network standards developed by the IEEE. They include:

IEEE 802.1: Standards related to network management.
IEEE 802.2: General standard for the data link layer in the OSI Reference Model. The IEEE divides this layer into two sublayers—the *data link control (DLC) layer* and the *media access control (MAC) layer*. The MAC layer varies for different network types and is defined by standards IEEE 802.3 through IEEE 802.5.
IEEE 802.3: Defines the MAC layer for bus networks that use CSMA/CD. This is the basis of the Ethernet standard.
IEEE 802.4: Defines the MAC layer for bus networks that use a token-passing mechanism (token bus networks).
IEEE 802.5: Defines the MAC layer for token-ring networks.
IEEE 802.6: Standard for Metropolitan Area Networks (MANs).

⇒ See also DLC; ETHERNET; IEEE; LOCAL-AREA NETWORK; MAN; TOKEN BUS NETWORK; TOKEN-RING NETWORK.

IETF Short for *I(nternet) E(ngineering) T(ask) F(orce)*, the main standards organization for the Internet. The IETF is a large, open international community of network designers, operators, vendors, and researchers concerned with the evolution of the Internet architecture and the smooth operation of the Internet. It is open to any interested individual.

⇒ See also INTERNET; INTERNET ARCHITECTURE BOARD; INTERNET SOCIETY; RFC; SSL; STANDARD.

IFC Short for *I(nternet) F(oundation) C(lasses)*, a set of Java classes developed by Netscape that enables programmers to easily add GUI elements, such as windows, menus, and buttons.

Netscape and Sun Microsystems have announced that the next version of the Java Development Kit (JDK) will combine the Abstract Window Toolkit (AWT) with the IFC. This combination of classes will be called the *Java Foundation Classes (JFC)*.

The IFC is similar to Microsoft's Application Foundation Classes (AFC).

⇒ See also AFC; AWT; CLASS; JAVA; JDK.

IGES Acronym for *I(nitial) G(raphics) E(xchange) S(pecification)*, an ANSI graphics file format for three-dimensional wire frame models.

⇒ See also ANSI; GRAPHICS FILE FORMATS.

IIOP Short for *I(nternet) I(nter)-O(RB) P(rotocol)*, a protocol developed by the Object Management Group (OMG) to implement CORBA solutions over the World Wide Web. IIOP enables browsers and servers to exchange integers, arrays, and more complex objects, unlike HTTP, which supports only transmission of text.

⇒ See also CORBA; OMG.

IIS Short for *I(nternet) I(nformation) S(erver)*, Microsoft's Web server that runs on Windows NT platforms. In fact, IIS comes bundled with Windows NT 4.0. Because IIS is tightly integrated with the operating system, it is relatively easy to administer. However, currently IIS is available only for the Windows NT platform, whereas Netscape's Web servers run on all major platforms, including Windows NT, OS/2, and UNIX.

⇒ See also ISAPI; WEB SERVER.

illegal page fault See under PAGING.

image editor A graphics program that provides a variety of special features for altering bit-mapped images. The difference between image editors and paint programs is not always clear-cut, but in general image editors are specialized for *modifying* bit-mapped images, such as scanned photographs, whereas paint programs are specialized for *creating* images.
  In addition to offering a host of filters and image transformation algorithms, image editors also enable you to create and superimpose layers.

⇒ See also IMAGE ENHANCEMENT; PAINT PROGRAM; PHOTO ILLUSTRATION.

image enhancement In computer graphics, the process of improving the quality of a digitally stored image by manipulating the image with software. It is quite easy, for example, to make an image lighter or darker, or to increase or decrease contrast. Advanced image-enhancement software also supports many filters for altering images in various ways. Programs specialized for image enhancement are sometimes called *image editors*.

⇒ See also ADOBE PHOTOSHOP; DIGITAL PHOTOGRAPHY; IMAGE EDITOR; IMAGE PROCESSING; PHOTO ILLUSTRATION; PHOTO SCANNER.

image map A single graphic image containing more than one hot spot. For example, imagine a graphic of a bowl of fruit. When you click on a banana, the system displays the number of calories in a banana and when you click on an apple, it displays the number of calories in an apple.

Image maps are used extensively on the World Wide Web. Each hot spot in a Web image map takes you to a different Web page or to another area of the same Web page.

Image map is sometimes spelled as one word: *imagemap.*

⇒ See also GIF; HOT SPOT.

image processing Analyzing and manipulating images with a computer. Image processing generally involves three steps:

1. Import an image with an optical scanner or directly through digital photography.

2. Manipulate or analyze the image in some way. This stage can include image enhancement and data compression, or the image may be analyzed to find patterns that aren't visible to the human eye. For example, meteorologists use image processing to analyze satellite photographs.

3. Output the result. The result might be the image altered in some way or it might be a report based on analysis of the image.

⇒ See also DIGITAL PHOTOGRAPHY; GRAPHICS; IMAGE ENHANCEMENT; PHOTO SCANNER.

imagesetter A typesetting device that produces very high-resolution output on paper or film. Imagesetters are too expensive for homes or most offices, but you can obtain imagesetter output by bringing a PostScript file to a service bureau. One reason that PostScript has become the standard for desktop publishing is that nearly all imagesetters support it. This means that you can produce drafts on an inexpensive PostScript laser printer with high assurance that the final output from an imagesetter will look the same, but with higher resolution (up to 3,540 dots per inch).

⇒ See also DESKTOP PUBLISHING; ISP; LaTeX; LINOTRONIC; POSTSCRIPT.

ImageWriter Refers to any in a family of dot-matrix printers that Apple offers for the Macintosh computer. Laser printers for the Macintosh are called *LaserWriters.*

⇒ See also DOT-MATRIX PRINTER; LASERWRITER; LETTER QUALITY (LQ); MACINTOSH COMPUTER; PRINTER.

IMAP Short for *I(nternet) M(essage) A(ccess) P(rotocol),* a protocol for retrieving e-mail messages. The latest version, *IMAP4,* is similar to *POP3* but supports some additional features. For example, with IMAP4, you can search through your e-mail messages for keywords while the messages are still on the mail server. You can then choose which messages to download to your machine. Like POP, IMAP uses SMTP for communication between the e-mail client and server.

IMAP was developed at Stanford University in 1986.

⇒ See also POP; SMTP.

impact printer Refers to a class of printers that work by banging a head or needle against an ink ribbon to make a mark on the paper. This includes dot-matrix printers, daisy-wheel printers, and line printers. In contrast, laser and ink-jet printers are *nonimpact printers*. The distinction is important because impact printers tend to be considerably noisier than nonimpact printers but are useful for multipart forms such as invoices.

⇒ See also DAISY-WHEEL PRINTER; DOT-MATRIX PRINTER; INK-JET PRINTER; LASER PRINTER; LINE PRINTER; NON-IMPACT PRINTER; PRINTER.

import To use data produced by another application. The ability to import data is very important in software applications because it means that one application can complement another. Many programs, for example, are designed to be able to import graphics in a variety of formats.

The opposite of importing is *exporting*, which refers to the ability of one application to format data for another application.

⇒ See also COMMA-DELIMITED; CONVERT; EXPORT; FILTER; MIDDLEWARE.

in-betweening See under TWEENING.

inclusive OR operator A Boolean operator that returns a value of TRUE if *either or both* of its operands is TRUE. Contrast with the *exclusive OR operator*, which returns a value of TRUE only if just one of the operands is TRUE.

⇒ See also BOOLEAN OPERATOR.

increment *v* **1.** To add a fixed amount. For example, if you count consecutively from 1 to 10, you increment by one. If you count by twos, you increment by two. A large proportion of computer software consists of loops of instructions in which one or more values are incremented each time the loop is executed. —*n* **2.** An amount that is added. For example, if you count by threes, the increment is three.

⇒ See also DECREMENT; LOOP.

incremental backup A backup procedure that backs up only those files that have been modified since the previous backup. Contrast with an archival backup, in which all files are backed up regardless of whether or not they have been modified since the last backup.

⇒ See also ARCHIVAL BACKUP; BACKUP.

Indeo A codec (compression/decompression technology) for computer video developed by Intel Corporation. Although it is a software-only codec, Indeo is based on the DVI, which is a hardware-only codec. Competing video standards include Cinepak and MPEG.

⇒ See also CINEPAK; CODEC; DVI; MPEG.

index *n* **1.** In database design, a list of keys (or keywords), each of which identifies a unique record. Indices make it faster to find specific records and to sort records by the index field—that is, the field used to identify each record. —*v* **2.** To create an index for a database, or to find records using an index.

⇒ See also HASHING; ISAM; KEY; KEYWORD.

Indexed Sequential Access Method See ISAM.

Industry Standard Architecture (ISA) bus The bus architecture used in the IBM PC/XT and PC/AT. It's often abbreviated as ISA (pronounced as separate letters or as *eye-sa*) bus. The AT version of the bus is called the AT bus and became a de facto industry standard. Starting in the early 1990s, ISA began to be replaced by the PCI local bus architecture. Most computers made today include both an AT bus for slower devices and a PCI bus for devices that need better bus performance.

In 1993, Intel and Microsoft introduced a new version of the ISA specification called Plug and Play ISA. Plug and Play ISA enables the operating system to configure expansion boards automatically so that users do not need to fiddle with DIP switches and jumpers.

⇒ See also AT BUS; BUS; EISA; LOCAL BUS; PCI; PLUG-AND-PLAY.

Information Services See IS.

information superhighway A popular buzzword to describe the Internet, bulletin board services, online services, and other services that enable people to obtain information from telecommunications networks. In the U.S., there is currently a national debate about how to shape and control these avenues of information. Many people believe that the information superhighway should be designed and regulated by the government, just the way conventional highway systems are. Others argue that government should adopt a more laissez-faire attitude. Nearly everyone agrees that accessing the information superhighway is going to be a normal part of everyday life in the near future.

⇒ See also BULLETIN BOARD SYSTEM; ONLINE SERVICE; TELECOMMUNICATIONS.

Information Systems See IS.

Information Technology See IT.

Informix Founded in 1980, Informix is one of the fastest-growing DBMS software companies. Though still a much smaller company than its chief rival, Oracle, Informix has been able to make large market-share gains recently due to its innovative technology.

⇒ See also DATABASE MANAGEMENT SYSTEM; ORACLE; SYBASE.

Infoseek A World Wide Web search engine developed by Infoseek Corporation. In addition to providing a full-text search engine, Infoseek also provides categorized lists of Web sites. This is similar to Yahoo!'s approach, though Infoseek's categorization is not as detailed or complete.

⇒ See also ALTA VISTA; EXCITE; HOTBOT; LYCOS; OPEN TEXT; SEARCH ENGINE; WEBCRAWLER; YAHOO!.

Infrared Data Association See IRDA.

INI See under .INI FILE.

.INI file Pronounced *dot-in-ee file*, a file that has a .INI extension and contains configuration information for MS-Windows. Two .INI files, WIN.INI and SYSTEM.INI, are required by MS-Windows. In addition, many applications have their own .INI files. In Windows 95, Windows 98, and Windows NT, .INI files have been replaced by the Registry, though many applications still include .INI files for backward compatibility.

⇒ See also EXTENSION.

init 1. On Macintoshes, an old term (before System 7) for *System extensions.* See under EXTENSION. **2.** Short for *initialize* or *initialization.*

⇒ See also EXTENSION.

Initial Graphics Exchange Specification See IGES.

initialize 1. On Apple Macintosh computers, *initializing* a disk means *formatting* it. **2.** In programming, *initialize* means to assign a starting value to a variable. **3.** *Initialize* can refer to the process of starting up a program or system.

⇒ See also ASSIGN; FORMAT; VARIABLE.

ink-jet printer A type of printer that works by spraying ionized ink at a sheet of paper. Magnetized plates in the ink's path direct the ink onto the paper in the desired shapes. Ink-jet printers are capable of producing high-quality print approaching that produced by laser printers. A typical ink-jet printer provides a resolution of 300 dots per inch, although some newer models offer higher resolutions.

In general, the price of ink-jet printers is lower than that of laser printers. However, they are also considerably slower. Another drawback of ink-jet printers is that they require a special type of ink that is apt to smudge on inexpensive copier paper.

Because ink-jet printers require smaller mechanical parts than laser printers, they are especially popular as portable printers. In addition, color ink-jet printers provide an inexpensive way to print full-color documents.

⇒ See also COLOR PRINTER; DOWNLOAD; DPI; FONT; FONT CARTRIDGE; LASER PRINTER; PRINTER; SOLID INK-JET PRINTER.

input *n* **1.** Whatever goes into the computer. Input can take a variety of forms, from commands you enter from the keyboard to data from another computer or device. A device that feeds data into a computer, such as a keyboard or mouse, is called an input device. —*v* **2.** The act of entering data into a computer.

⇒ See also I/O; OUTPUT.

input device Any machine that feeds data into a computer. For example, a keyboard is an input device, whereas a display monitor is an output device. Input devices other than the keyboard are sometimes called *alternate input devices*. Mice, trackballs, and light pens are all alternate input devices.

⇒ See also DEVICE; I/O; LIGHT PEN; MOUSE; OUTPUT; TRACKBALL.

input/output See I/O.

insert To place an object between two other objects. Inserting characters, words, paragraphs, and documents is common in word processing. Note that *insert* differs from append, which means to add at the end.
  Most computer keyboards have an *Insert key*, which turns *insert mode* on and off.

⇒ See also APPEND; INS KEY; INSERT MODE.

insertion point In graphics-based programs, the insertion point is the point where the next characters typed from the keyboard will appear on the display screen. The insertion point is usually represented by a blinking vertical line. You can reposition the insertion point by pressing arrow keys or by moving the I-beam pointer.

⇒ See also I-BEAM POINTER; INSERT MODE; POINTER.

Insert key A key on computer keyboards that turns insert mode on and off. The Insert key does not work for all programs, but most word processors and text editors support it.

⇒ See also INSERT MODE.

insert mode Most text editors and word processors have two text-entry modes from which you can choose. In *insert mode,* the editor inserts all characters you type at the cursor position (or to the right of the insertion point). With each new insertion, the editor pushes over characters to the right of the cursor or pointer to make room for the new character.
  If insert mode is turned off, the editor overwrites existing characters in-

stead of inserting the new ones before the old ones. This is often called *overstrike* (or *overwrite*) *mode*. Most PC keyboards have an *Ins key* that lets you switch back and forth between insert and overwrite modes.

For most programs, the default text-entry mode is insert mode.

⇒ See also INS KEY; INSERTION POINT; OVERSTRIKE; WORD PROCESSING.

Ins key Another name for the Insert key.

⇒ See also INSERT KEY.

instant messaging A type of communications service that enables you to create a private chat room with another individual. Typically, the instant messaging system alerts you whenever somebody on your private list is online. You can then initiate a chat session with that particular individual.

There are several competing instant messaging systems. Unfortunately, there's no standard, so anyone you want to send instant messages to must use the same instant messaging system that you use.

⇒ See also CHAT; E-MAIL; FINGER.

Institute of Electrical and Electronic Engineers See IEEE.

instruction A basic command. The term *instruction* is often used to describe the most rudimentary programming commands. For example, a computer's *instruction set* is the list of all the basic commands in the computer's machine language.

⇒ See also CISC; COMMAND; MACHINE LANGUAGE; MICROCODE; RISC; SUPERSCALAR.

integer A whole number. The following are integers:

0
1
-125
144457

In contrast, the following are *not* integers:

5.34
-1.0
1.3E4
"string"

The first three are *floating-point numbers*; the last is a character string. Integers, floating-point numbers, and character strings constitute the basic data types that most computers support. There are often different sizes of integers available; for example, PCs support short integers, which are 2 bytes, and long integers, which are 4 bytes.

⇒ See also CHARACTER STRING; DATA TYPE; FLOATING-POINT NUMBER.

integrated 1. A popular computer buzzword that refers to two or more components merged together into a single system. For example, any software product that performs more than one task can be described as *integrated*. **2.** Increasingly, the term *integrated software* is reserved for applications that combine word processing, database management, spreadsheet functions, and communications into a single package.

⇒ See also IDE; MIDDLEWARE.

integrated circuit Another name for a chip, an IC is a small electronic device made out of a semiconductor material. The first integrated circuit was developed in the 1950s by Jack Kilby of Texas Instruments and Robert Noyce of Fairchild Semiconductor.

Integrated circuits are used for a variety of devices, including microprocessors, audio and video equipment, and automobiles. Integrated circuits are often classified by the number of transistors and other electronic components they contain:

SSI (small-scale integration): Up to 100 electronic components per chip
MSI (medium-scale integration): From 100 to 3,000 electronic components per chip
LSI (large-scale integration): From 3,000 to 100,000 electronic components per chip
VLSI (very large-scale integration): From 100,000 to 1,000,000 electronic components per chip
ULSI (ultra large-scale integration): More than 1 million electronic components per chip

⇒ See also ASIC; CHIP; MOORE'S LAW; NANOTECHNOLOGY; PLD; SEMICONDUCTOR; TEXAS INSTRUMENTS; TRANSISTOR.

integrated development environment A programming environment integrated into an application. For example, Microsoft Office applications support various versions of the BASIC programming language. You can develop a WordBasic application while running Microsoft Word.

⇒ See also POWERBUILDER.

Integrated Drive Electronics See IDE.

integrated services digital network See ISDN.

Intel The world's largest manufacturer of computer chips. Although it has been challenged in recent years by newcomers AMD and Cyrix, Intel still dominates the market for PC microprocessors. Nearly all PCs are based on Intel's x86 architecture.

Intel was founded in 1968 by Bob Noyce and Gordon Moore. Strategically, it is closely allied with Microsoft because the Windows 3.x and 95/98 operating systems are designed for x86 microprocessors. The popularity of Windows creates a demand for Intel or Intel-compatible microprocessors. Many people refer to this alliance as *Wintel* (short for *W(indows)*-**Intel**).

⇒ See also AMD; Cyrix; DVI; Intel microprocessors; NEC; PCI; Wintel.

Intellifont A *scalable font* technology that is part of Hewlett-Packard's *PCL 5* page description language.

⇒ See also Page Description Language (PDL); PCL; scalable font.

Intelligent Drive Electronics See IDE.

Intelligent I/O Same as I2O.

intelligent terminal A terminal (monitor and keyboard) that contains processing power. Intelligent terminals include memory and a processor to perform special display operations. In contrast, a *dumb terminal* has no processing capabilities; it must rely entirely on the central computer. A *smart terminal* has some processing capabilities, but not as many as an intelligent terminal.

⇒ See also display screen; dumb terminal; monitor; smart terminal; terminal.

Intel microprocessors Microprocessors made by Intel Corporation form the foundation of all PCs.

Models after the 8086 are often referred to by the last three digits (for example, the *286, 386,* and *486*). Many of the microprocessors come in different varieties that run at various clock rates. The 80486 architecture, for example, supports clock rates of from 33 to 66 MHz. Because Intel discovered that it couldn't trademark its CPU numbers, it shifted to a naming scheme, starting with the Pentium processors. Intel's sixth-generation chip was called the Pentium Pro, followed by the Pentium with MMX and the Pentium II.

All Intel microprocessors are backward compatible, which means that they can run programs written for a less powerful processor. The 80386, for example, can run programs written for the 8086, 8088, and 80286. The 80386 and later models, however, offer special programming features not available on previous models. Software written specifically for these processors, therefore, may not run on older microprocessors. The common architecture behind all Intel microprocessors is known as the *x86 architecture*.

Until the late 1980s, Intel was essentially the only producer of PC microprocessors. Increasingly, however, Intel is facing competition from other manufacturers who produce "Intel-compatible" chips. These chips support the Intel instruction set and are often less expensive than Intel chips. In some cases, they also offer better performance. Two of the lead-

Table 19
Intel Microprocessors

Microprocessor	Date	Estimated Power (in Mips)	Register Width (Bits)	Bus Width (Bits)	Clock Rates (in MHz)	Notes
8086	1978	0.5	16	16	5, 8, and 10	
8088	1979	0.5	16	8	5 and 8	Used in the original IBM PC and PC/XT.
80286	1982	1.5	16	16	8, 10, and 12	Supports virtual memory and an address space of 16MB (megabytes); is 5 to 20 times faster than the 8086.
80386DX	1985	10	32	32	16, 20, 25, and 33	Built-in multitasking and virtual memory, has an address space of 4GB; is 2 to 4 times faster than the 80286.
80386SX	1988	2.5	32	16	16, 20, 25, and 33	Compatible with both the 80286 and the 80386.
80386SL	1990	5	32	32	20 and 25	Same architecture as the 80386DX, but with added power management features; popular in portable computers that rely on a battery for power.
80486DX	1989	30	32	32	25, 33 and 50	Similar to the 386 but much faster; uses a built-in memory cache to avoid wait states and includes a numeric coprocessor; uses pipelining techniques.
80486SX	1991	20	32	32	16, 20, 25, and 33	An inexpensive variety of the 80486DX that runs at low speeds and lacks a numeric coprocessor.

Table 19 (continued)
Intel Microprocessors

Microprocessor	Date	Estimated Power (in Mips)	Register Width (Bits)	Bus Width (Bits)	Clock Rates (in MHz)	Notes
80486SL	1992	20	32	32	20, 25, and 33	Based on 80486DX architecture, with power management features for battery-operated computers.
80486DX2 and OverDrive	1992	50	32	32	50 and 66	Same architecture as the 80486DX, but with the internal clock speed doubled.
486DX4	1994	70	32	32	75 and 100	Same architecture as the 80486DX, but with the internal clock rate tripled.
Pentium	1993	125	32	64	60, 66, 75, 100, 120, 133, 150, 166 and 200	Although basically a CISC architecture, the Pentium chip includes many RISC features, such as pipelining and super-scaling; contains more than 3 million transistors.
Pentium OverDrive	1995		32	64	60, 66, and 100	A Pentium chip that can be installed in a 486-based computer that has an OverDrive socket.
Pentium Pro	1995		32	64	150, 166, 180 and 200	More than 5 million transistors.
Pentium with MMX	1997		32	64	166 and 200	Pentium processor with the MMX chip for faster multimedia processing.
MMX Overdrive	1997		32	64		MMX upgrade for Pentium processors.
Pentium II	1997		32	64	233, 266, 300, 333, 350, 400 and 450	Uses DIB and SEC packaging; supports AGP.

ing manufacturers of Intel-compatible chips are Cyrix and AMD.

⇒ See also Alpha Processor; AMD; bus; clock speed; Cyrix; Intel; Merced; microprocessor; MMX; multitasking; OverDrive; Pentium II; Pentium microprocessor; Pentium Pro; register; RISC; Triton; virtual memory; Wintel.

interactive Accepting input from a human. Interactive computer systems are programs that allow users to enter data or commands. Most popular programs, such as word processors and spreadsheet applications, are interactive.

A noninteractive program is one that, when started, continues without requiring human contact. A compiler is a noninteractive program, as are all batch processing applications.

⇒ See also batch processing.

interface *n* **1.** Something that connects two separate entities. For example, a *user interface* is the part of a program that connects the computer with a human operator (user).

There are also interfaces to connect programs, to connect devices, and to connect programs to devices. An interface can be a program or a device, such as an electrical connector. —*v* **2.** To communicate. For example, two devices that can transmit data between each other are said to *interface with each other.* This use of the term is scorned by language purists because *interface* has historically been used as a noun.

⇒ See also user interface.

interlacing 1. A display technique that enables a monitor to provide more resolution inexpensively. With interlacing monitors, the electron guns draw only half the horizontal lines with each pass (for example, all odd lines on one pass and all even lines on the next pass). Because an interlacing monitor refreshes only half the lines at one time, it can display twice as many lines per refresh cycle, giving it greater resolution. Another way of looking at it is that interlacing provides the same resolution as noninterlacing, but less expensively.

A shortcoming of interlacing is that the reaction time is slower, so programs that depend on quick refresh rates (animation and video, for example) may experience flickering or streaking. Given two display systems that offer the same resolution, the noninterlacing one will generally be better. **2.** Preparing a graphic image so that alternating rows are displayed in separate passes. Interlaced images give a nice effect because the entire image is displayed quickly and then details are filled in gradually. They are especially prevalent on the World Wide Web because of the slow transmission speed. Web pages with interlaced GIFs appear in a browser more quickly than pages with normal GIF images. The interlaced GIFs look blurry at first but then become sharp as the rows are filled in.

⇒ See also CRT; monitor; refresh; resolution.

interleave To arrange data in a noncontiguous way to increase performance. When used to describe disk drives, the term refers to the way *sectors* on a disk are organized. In one-to-one interleaving, the sectors are placed sequentially around each track. In two-to-one interleaving, sectors are staggered so that consecutively numbered sectors are separated by an intervening sector.

The purpose of interleaving is to make the disk drive more efficient. The disk drive can access only one sector at a time, and the disk is constantly spinning beneath the read/write head. This means that by the time the drive is ready to access the next sector, the disk may have already spun beyond it. If a data file spans more than one sector and if the sectors are arranged sequentially, the drive will need to wait a full rotation to access the next chunk of the file. If instead the sectors are staggered, the disk will be perfectly positioned to access sequential sectors.

The optimum interleaving factor depends on the speed of the disk drive, the operating system, and the application. The only way to find the best interleaving factor is to experiment with various factors and various applications.

Memory can also be interleaved. See INTERLEAVED MEMORY for more information.

⇒ See also DISK; DISK DRIVE; SECTOR; TRACK.

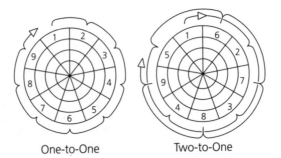

One-to-One   Two-to-One

Figure 39: **interleaving**

interleaved memory Main memory divided into two or more sections. The CPU can access alternate sections immediately, without waiting for memory to catch up (through wait states). Interleaved memory is one technique for compensating for the relatively slow speed of dynamic RAM (DRAM). Other techniques include page-mode memory and memory caches.

⇒ See also ACCESS TIME; CACHE; CLOCK SPEED; CPU; DYNAMIC RAM; FPM RAM; MEMORY; WAIT STATE.

internal bus Same as EXPANSION BUS.

internal cache Same as L1 CACHE.

internal command In DOS systems, an internal command is any command that resides in the COMMAND.COM file. This includes the most common DOS commands, such as COPY and DIR. Commands that reside in other COM files, or in EXE or BAT files, are called external commands.

⇒ See also COMMAND; DOS; EXTERNAL COMMAND.

internal font Same as RESIDENT FONT.

internal modem A modem that resides on an expansion board that plugs into a computer. In contrast, an *external modem* is a box that attaches to a computer's COM port via cables.

⇒ See also EXPANSION BOARD; EXTERNAL MODEM; MODEM.

International Business Machines See IBM.

International Standards Organization See ISO.

International Telecommunication Union See ITU.

Internet A global network connecting millions computers. As of this writing, the Internet has more than 100 million users worldwide, and that number is growing rapidly. More than 100 countries are linked into exchanges of data, news, and opinions.

Unlike online services, which are centrally controlled, the Internet is decentralized by design. Each Internet computer, called a *host*, is independent. Its operators can choose which Internet services to use and which local services to make available to the global Internet community. Remarkably, this anarchy by design works exceedingly well.

There are a variety of ways to access the Internet. Most online services, such as America Online, offer access to some Internet services. It is also possible to gain access through a commercial internet service provider (ISP).

⇒ See also ARPANET; ATM; DIAL-UP ACCESS; DOMAIN; FTP; GOPHER; I2; IAC; IETF; INTERNIC; INTRANET; IP ADDRESS; MBONE; MOSAIC; NAP; NGI INITIATIVE; ONLINE SERVICE; USENET; vBNS; WORLD WIDE WEB.

Internet2 See I2.

Internet Access Coalition See IAC.

Internet Ad Hoc Committee See IAHC.

Internet appliance Same as NETWORK COMPUTER.

Internet Architecture Board A technical advisory group of the Internet Society, whose responsibilities include:

- Overseeing the Internet Engineering Task Force (IETF)
- Overseeing the Internet standards process
- Publishing and managing Request for Comments (RFCs)

⇒ See also IANA; IETF; INTERNET SOCIETY; RFC.

Internet Assigned Numbers Authority See IANA.

Internet box Same as NETWORK COMPUTER.

Internet Engineering Task Force See IETF.

Internet Explorer Microsoft's Web browser. Like Netscape Navigator, Internet Explorer enables you to view Web pages. Both browsers support Java and JavaScript. Internet Explorer also supports ActiveX.

⇒ See also ACTIVEX CONTROL; BROWSER; CDF; MICROSOFT; NAVIGATOR; VB-SCRIPT; WINDOWS 98.

Internet Foundation Classes See IFC.

Internet Information Server See IIS.

Internet Inter-ORB Protocol See IIOP.

Internet Message Access Protocol See IMAP.

Internet Phone A popular *Voice on the Net (VON)*. There are actually two different products called *Internet Phone*, one produced by Intel and the other developed by VocalTec Ltd.

⇒ See also INTERNET TELEPHONY; NETMEETING; TELEPHONY.

Internet Protocol See IP.

Internet Relay Chat See IRC.

Internet Service Provider See ISP.

Internet Society A nongovernmental, nonprofit organization dedicated to maintaining and enhancing the Internet. Through its committees, such as the Internet Advisory Board and the Internet Engineering Task Force, the Internet Society is responsible for developing and approving new Internet standards and protocols.

⇒ See also IETF; INTERNET ARCHITECTURE BOARD; STANDARD.

Internet telephony A category of hardware and software that enables people to use the Internet as the transmission medium for telephone calls. For users who have free, or fixed-price Internet access, Internet telephony software essentially provides free telephone calls anywhere in the world. To date, however, Internet telephony does not offer the same quality of telephone service as direct telephone connections.

There are many Internet telephony applications available. Some, like CoolTalk and NetMeeting, come bundled with popular Web browsers. Others are stand-alone products. Internet telephony products are sometimes called *IP telephony, Voice over the Internet (VOI)*, or *Voice over IP (VOIP)* products.

⇒ See also COOLTALK; INTERNET; INTERNET PHONE; TELEPHONY.

internetworking The art and science of connecting individual local area networks (LANs) to create wide-area networks (WANs), and connecting WANs to form even larger WANs. Internetworking can be extremely complex because it generally involves connecting networks that use different protocols. Internetworking is accomplished with routers, bridges, and gateways.

⇒ See also BRIDGE; CISCO SYSTEMS; LOCAL-AREA NETWORK; ROUTER; WIDE-AREA NETWORK.

Internetwork Packet eXchange See IPX.

InterNIC A collaborative project between AT&T and Network Solutions, Inc. (NSI), supported by the National Science Foundation. The project currently offers the following four services to users of the Internet.

(1) InterNIC Directory and Database Services: on-line white pages directory and directory of publicly accessible databases managed by AT&T.

(2) Registration Services: domain name and IP address assignment managed by NSI.

(3) Support Services: outreach, education, and information services for the Internet community managed by NSI.

(4) Net Scout Services: online publications that summarize recent happenings of interest to Internet users (managed by NSI).

⇒ See also DOMAIN NAME; INTERNET; IP ADDRESS.

interpolated resolution See under OPTICAL RESOLUTION.

interpreter A program that executes instructions written in a high-level language. There are two ways to run programs written in a high-level language. The most common is to compile the program; the other method is to pass the program through an interpreter.

An interpreter translates high-level instructions into an intermediate form, which it then executes. In contrast, a compiler translates high-level instructions directly into machine language. Compiled programs generally run faster than interpreted programs. The advantage of an interpreter, however, is that it does not need to go through the compilation stage during which machine instructions are generated. This process can be time consuming if the program is long. The interpreter, on the other hand, can immediately execute high-level programs. For this reason, interpreters are sometimes used during the development of a program, when a programmer wants to add small sections at a time and test them quickly. In addition, interpreters are often used in education because they allow students to program interactively.

Both interpreters and compilers are available for most high-level languages. However, BASIC and LISP are especially designed to be executed by an interpreter. In addition, page description languages, such as PostScript, use an interpreter. Every PostScript printer, for example, has a built-in interpreter that executes PostScript instructions.

⇒ See also BASIC; BYTECODE; COMPILE; COMPILER; JAVA; LISP; PAGE DESCRIPTION LANGUAGE (PDL); PERL; POSTSCRIPT; PROGRAMMING LANGUAGE; TCL.

interprocess communication (IPC) A capability supported by some operating systems that allows one *process* to communicate with another process. The processes can be running on the same computer or on different computers connected through a network.

IPC enables one application to control another application, and for several applications to share the same data without interfering with one another. IPC is required in all multiprocessing systems, but it is not generally supported by single-process operating systems such as DOS. OS/2 and MS-Windows support an IPC mechanism called DDE.

⇒ See also DDE; MULTIPROCESSING; NAMED PIPES; NETWORK; OPERATING SYSTEM; PROCESS; SEMAPHORE.

interrupt *n* **1.** A signal informing a program that an event has occurred. When a program receives an interrupt signal, it takes a specified action (which can be to ignore the signal). Interrupt signals can cause a program to suspend itself temporarily to service the interrupt.

Interrupt signals can come from a variety of sources. For example, every keystroke generates an interrupt signal. Interrupts can also be generated by other devices, such as a printer, to indicate that some event has occurred. These are called *hardware interrupts*. Interrupt signals initiated by programs are called *software interrupts*. A software interrupt is also called a *trap* or an *exception*.

PCs support 256 types of software interrupts and 15 hardware interrupts. Each type of software interrupt is associated with an *interrupt handler*—a routine that takes control when the interrupt occurs. For example, when you press a key on your keyboard, this triggers a specific interrupt handler. The complete list of interrupts and associated interrupt handlers is stored in a table called the *interrupt vector table*, which resides in the first 1 K of addressable memory. —*v* **2.** To send an interrupt signal.

⇒ See also EVENT; INTERRUPT VECTOR TABLE; IRQ.

interrupt request line See IRQ.

interrupt vector table A table of *interrupt vectors* (pointers to routines that handle interrupts). On PCs, the interrupt vector table consists of 256 4-byte pointers and resides in the first 1 K of addressable memory. Each interrupt number is reserved for a specific purpose. For example, 16 of the vectors are reserved for the 16 IRQ lines.

An interrupt vector table is also called a *dispatch table.*

⇒ See also INTERRUPT; IRQ.

intranet A network based on TCP/IP protocols (an internet) belonging to an organization, usually a corporation, accessible only by the organization's members, employees, or others with authorization. An intranet's Web sites look and act just like any other Web sites, but the *firewall* surrounding an intranet prevents unauthorized access.

Like the Internet itself, intranets are used to share information. Secure intranets are now the fastest-growing segment of the Internet because they are much less expensive to build and manage than private networks based on proprietary protocols.

⇒ See also ENTERPRISE; EXTRANET; FIREWALL; INTERNET; LOTUS NOTES; NET-WORK.

invalid page fault A page fault that produces an error. Page fault errors can occur for any of the following reasons:

(1) The virtual memory system becomes unstable due to a shortage of physical memory (RAM).

(2) The virtual memory system becomes unstable due to a shortage of free disk space.

(3)The virtual memory area is corrupted by a misbehaving application.

(4) An application attempts to access data that is being modified by another running application.

The first two causes are the most common. These conditions can also cause a general protection fault (GPF).

An invalid page fault is also called a *page fault error (PFE).*

⇒ See also CRASH; GPF; PAGE FAULT.

inverse video Same as REVERSE VIDEO.

inverted tree See under TREE STRUCTURE.

invisible file Same as HIDDEN FILE.

invocation The execution of a program or function.

⇒ See also INVOKE.

invoke To activate. One usually speaks of *invoking* a function or routine in a program. In this sense, the term *invoke* is synonymous with *call.*

⇒ See also CALL; FUNCTION; ROUTINE.

I/O Short for *i(nput)/o(utput)*, and pronounced *eye-oh.* I/O refers to any operation, program, or device whose purpose is to enter data into a computer or to extract data from a computer.

One usually uses the term *I/O* to distinguish noncomputational parts of a program from other parts that are strictly computational, or to distinguish certain devices from other devices. For example, a printer is an I/O device, whereas a CPU is a computational device.

All computer applications contain both I/O and computational parts. A word processing system, for instance, contains I/O components (for entering, displaying, and printing text) as well as non-I/O components (for checking spelling, searching for words, and so on).

⇒ See also I2O; INPUT; OUTPUT.

IP Abbreviation of *I(nternet) P(rotocol)*, pronounced as two separate letters. IP specifies the format of packets, also called *datagrams,* and the addressing scheme. Most networks combine IP with a higher-level protocol called *Transmission Control Protocol (TCP)*, which establishes a virtual connection between a destination and a source.

IP by itself is something like the postal system. It allows you to address a package and drop it in the system, but there's no direct link between you and the recipient. TCP/IP, on the other hand, establishes a connection between two hosts so that they can send messages back and forth for a period of time.

The current version of IP is *IPv4*. A new version, called *IPv6* or IPng, is under development.

⇒ See also ICMP; IPNG; IPSEC; PACKET; TCP; TCP/IP; UDP.

IP address An identifier for a computer or device on a TCP/IP network. Networks using the TCP/IP protocol route messages based on the IP address of the destination. The format of an IP address is a 32-bit numeric address written as four numbers separated by periods. Each number can be 0 to 255. For example, 1.160.10.240 could be an IP address.

Within an isolated network, you can assign IP addresses at random as long as each one is unique. However, connecting a private network to the Internet requires using registered IP addresses (called Internet addresses) to avoid duplicates.

The four numbers in an IP address are used in different ways to identify a particular network and a host on that network. The InterNIC Registration Service assigns Internet addresses from the following three classes.

- Class A: supports 16 million hosts on each of 127 networks
- Class B: supports 65,000 hosts on each of 16,000 networks
- Class C: supports 254 hosts on each of 2 million networks

The number of unassigned Internet addresses is running out, so a new classless scheme called CIDR is gradually replacing the system based on classes A, B, and C and is tied to adoption of IPv6.

⇒ See also ARP; CIDR; DNS; DOMAIN NAME; IANA; INTERNET; INTERNIC; IP SPOOFING; NAT; PING; ROUTING; SUBNET; TCP/IP; TLD; WHOIS; WINS.

IPC See INTERPROCESS COMMUNICATION.

IP Multicast Sending out data to distributed servers on the MBone (Multicast Backbone). For large amounts of data, IP Multicast is more efficient than normal Internet transmissions because the server can broadcast a message to many recipients simultaneously. Unlike traditional Internet traffic that requires separate connections for each source-destination pair, IP Multicasting allows many recipients to share the same source. This means that just one set of packets is transmitted for all the destinations.

⇒ See also MBONE; MULTICAST; REALVIDEO.

IPng Short for *I(nternet) P(rotocol) n(ext) g(eneration)*, a new version of the Internet Protocol (IP) currently being reviewed in IETF standards committees. The official name of IPng is *IPv6,* where the *v6* stands for *version 6.* The current version of IP is version 4, so it is sometimes referred to as *IPv4.*

IPng is designed as an evolutionary upgrade to the Internet Protocol and will, in fact, coexist with the older IPv4 for some time. IPng is designed to allow the Internet to grow steadily, both in terms of the number of hosts connected and the total amount of data traffic transmitted.

⇒ See also IP.

IPsec Short for **IP** *Sec(urity)*, a set of protocols being developed by the IETF to support secure exchange of packets at the IP layer. Once it's completed, IPsec is expected to be deployed widely to implement virtual private networks (VPNs).

IPsec supports two encryption modes: Transport and Tunnel. Transport mode encrypts only the data portion (*payload*) of each packet but leaves the header untouched. The more secure Tunnel mode encrypts both the header and the payload. On the receiving side, an IPsec-compliant device decrypts each packet.

For IPsec to work, the sending and receiving devices must share a public key. This is accomplished through a protocol known as *Internet Security Association and Key Management Protocol/Oakley (ISAKMP/Oakley),* which allows the receiver to obtain a public key and authenticate the sender using digital certificates.

⇒ See also IP; L2TP; SSL.

IP spoofing A technique used to gain unauthorized access to computers, whereby the intruder sends messages to a computer with an IP address indicating that the message is coming from a trusted port. To engage in IP spoofing, a hacker must first use a variety of techniques to find an IP address of a trusted port and then modify the packet headers so that it appears that the packets are coming from that port.

Newer routers and firewall arrangements can offer protection against IP spoofing.

⇒ See also FIREWALL; HACKER; IP ADDRESS; ROUTER; SMURF; SPOOF.

IP switch See under IP SWITCHING.

IP switching A new type of IP routing developed by Ipsilon Networks, Inc. Unlike conventional routers, IP switching routers use ATM hardware to speed packets through networks. This new technology appears to be considerably faster than older router techniques.

⇒ See also ATM; ROUTER; ROUTING; ROUTING SWITCH.

IPv6 See under IPNG.

IPX Short for *I(nternetwork) P(acket) Ex(change)*, a networking protocol used by the Novell NetWare operating systems. Like UDP/IP, IPX is a datagram protocol used for connectionless communications. Higher-level protocols, such as SPX and NCP, are used for additional error recovery services.

The successor to IPX is the *NetWare Link Services Protocol (NLSP)*.

⇒ See also COMMUNICATIONS PROTOCOL; CONNECTIONLESS; NETWARE; SPX; UDP.

IPX/SPX See under SPX.

IRC Short for *I(nternet) R(elay) C(hat)*, a *chat system* developed by Jarkko Oikarinen in Finland in the late 1980s. IRC has become very popular as more people get connected to the Internet because it enables people connected anywhere on the Internet to join in live discussions. Unlike older chat systems, IRC is not limited to just two participants.

To join an IRC discussion, you need an *IRC client* and Internet access. The IRC client is a program that runs on your computer and sends and receives messages to and from an IRC *server*. The IRC server, in turn, is responsible for making sure that all messages are broadcast to everyone participating in a discussion. There can be many discussions going on at once; each one is assigned a unique *channel*.

⇒ See also CHANNEL; CHAT; CHAT ROOM; INTERNET.

IrDA Short for *I(nfra)r(ed) D(ata) A(ssociation)*, a group of device manufacturers that developed a standard for transmitting data via infrared light waves. Increasingly, computers and other devices (such as printers) come with IrDA ports. This enables you to transfer data from one device to another without any cables. For example, if both your laptop computer and printer have IrDA ports, you can simply put your computer in front of the printer and output a document, without needing to connect the two with a cable.

IrDA ports support roughly the same transmission rates as traditional parallel ports. The only restrictions on their use is that the two devices must be within a few feet of each other and there must be a clear line of sight between them.

⇒ See also PARALLEL PORT.

IRMA board A popular expansion board for PCs and Macintoshes that enables these personal computers to emulate IBM 3278 and 3279 mainframe terminals. In other words, personal computers with IRMA boards can function as both stand-alone computers and as terminals connected to a mainframe computer. IRMA boards are made by a company called DCA.

⇒ See also EMULATION; EXPANSION BOARD; MAINFRAME; STAND-ALONE; TERMINAL.

IRQ Abbreviation of *i(nterrupt) r(equest) l(ine)*, and pronounced *I-R-Q*. IRQs are hardware lines over which devices can send interrupt signals to the microprocessor. When you add a new device to a PC, you sometimes need to set its IRQ number by setting a DIP switch. This specifies which interrupt line the device may use. IRQ conflicts used to be a common problem when adding expansion boards, but the Plug-and-Play specification has removed this headache in most cases.

⇒ See also DIP SWITCH; EXPANSION BUS; INDUSTRY STANDARD ARCHITECTURE (ISA) BUS; INTERRUPT; INTERRUPT VECTOR TABLE; PLUG-AND-PLAY.

IS Pronounced as separate letters, and short for *I(nformation) S(ystems)* or *I(nformation) S(ervices)*. For many companies, *IS* is the name of the department responsible for computers, networking, and data management. Other companies refer to the department as *IT (Information Technology)* and *MIS (Management Information Services)*.

⇒ See also IT; MIS; SYSTEM MANAGEMENT.

ISA Abbreviation of *I(ndustry) S(tandard) A(rchitecture)* and pronounced *eye-sa*. See under INDUSTRY STANDARD ARCHITECTURE (ISA) BUS.

ISA bus See under INDUSTRY STANDARD ARCHITECTURE (ISA) BUS.

ISAM Abbreviation for *I(ndexed) S(equential) A(ccess) M(ethod)*, a method for managing how a computer accesses records and files stored on a hard disk. While storing data sequentially, ISAM provides direct access to specific records through an index. This combination results in quick data access regardless of whether records are being accessed sequentially or randomly.

There are a number of products that provide basic ISAM access for different operating systems and program languages.

⇒ See also DATABASE-MANAGEMENT SYSTEM; INDEX; RANDOM ACCESS; SEQUENTIAL ACCESS.

ISAPI Short for *I(nternet) S(erver) API*, an API for Microsoft's IIS (Internet Information Server) Web server. ISAPI enables programmers to develop Web-based applications that run much faster than conventional CGI programs because they're more tightly integrated with the Web server. In addition to IIS, several Web servers from companies other than Microsoft support ISAPI.

⇒ See also CGI; IIS; NSAPI; STATELESS.

ISDN Abbreviation of *i(ntegrated) s(ervices) d(igital) n(etwork)*, an international communications standard for sending voice, video, and data over digital telephone lines. ISDN requires special metal wires and supports data transfer rates of 64 Kbps (64,000 bits per second). Most ISDN lines offered by telephone companies give you two lines at once, called *B channels*. You can use one line for voice and the other for data, or you can use both lines for data to give you data rates of 128 Kbps, three times the data rate provided by today's fastest modems.

The original version of ISDN employs baseband transmission. Another version, called B-ISDN, uses broadband transmission and is able to support transmission rates of 1.5 Mbps. B-ISDN requires fiber optic cables and is not widely available.

⇒ See also ADSL; B-CHANNEL; BRI; BROADBAND ISDN (B-ISDN); CHANNEL BONDING; DirecPC; FDDI; FIBER OPTICS; GROUP 4 PROTOCOL; NDIS; SDSL; SPID; TERMINAL ADAPTER; xDSL.

ISO Short for *I(nternational) O(rganization) for S(tandardization)*. Note that ISO is not an acronym; instead, the name derives from the greek word *iso*, which means equal. Founded in 1946, ISO is an international organization composed of national standards bodies from more than 75 countries. For example, ANSI (American National Standards Institute) is a member of ISO. ISO has defined a number of important computer standards, the most significant of which is perhaps OSI (Open Systems Interconnection), a standardized architecture for designing networks.

⇒ See also ANSI; CMIP; ISO 9000; NETWORK; OSI; STANDARD.

ISO 9000 A family of standards approved by the International Standards Organization (ISO) that define a quality assurance program. Companies that conform to these standards can receive *ISO 9000 certification*. This doesn't necessarily mean that the company's products have a high quality; it means only that the company follows well-defined procedures for ensuring quality products. Increasingly, software buyers are requiring ISO 9000 certification from their suppliers.

⇒ See also ISO; STANDARD.

ISOC Short for *Internet Society*.

isochronous Time dependent. Pronounced *eye-sock-ra-nuss*, it refers to processes where data must be delivered within certain time constraints. For example, multimedia streams require an isochronous transport mechanism to ensure that data is delivered as fast as it is displayed and to ensure that the audio is synchronized with the video.

Isochronous can be contrasted with *asynchronous*, which refers to processes in which data streams can be broken by random intervals, and *synchronous* processes, in which data streams can be delivered only at specific intervals. Isochronous service is not as rigid as synchronous service and not as lenient as asynchronous service.

Certain types of networks, such as ATM, are said to be isochronous because they can guarantee a specified throughput. Likewise, new bus architectures, such as IEEE 1394, support isochronous delivery.

⇒ See also ASYNCHRONOUS; ATM; IEEE 1394; REAL TIME; SYNCHRONOUS; THROUGHPUT.

ISO Latin 1 Officially named *ISO-8859-1*, a standard character set developed by the International Standards Organization (ISO). ISO Latin-1 is a superset of the ASCII character set and is very similar to the ANSI character set used in Windows, though the two are not identical. Both the HTTP and HTML protocols used on the World Wide Web are based on ISO Latin-1. This means that to represent non-ASCII characters on a Web page, you need to use the corresponding ISO Latin-1 code.

⇒ See also ANSI CHARACTER SET; ASCII; EXTENDED ASCII.

ISP Short for *I(nternet) S(ervice) P(rovider)*, a company that provides access to the Internet. For a monthly fee, the service provider gives you a software package, username, password, and access phone number. Equipped with a modem, you can then log on to the Internet and browse the World Wide Web and USENET, and send and receive e-mail.

In addition to serving individuals, ISPs also serve large companies, providing a direct connection from the company's networks to the Internet. ISPs themselves are connected to one another through *Network Access Points (NAPs)*.

ISPs are also called *IAPs (Internet Access Providers)*.

⇒ See also DIAL-UP ACCESS; DirecPC; E-MAIL; INTERNET; MAE; NAP; NSP; RADIUS; T-1 CARRIER; T-3 CARRIER; USENET; WORLD WIDE WEB.

ISV Short for *I(ndependent) S(oftware) V(endor)*, a company that produces software.

⇒ See also SOFTWARE.

IT Short for *I(nformation) T(echnology)*, and pronounced as separate letters, the broad subject concerned with all aspects of managing and processing information, especially within a large organization or company. Because computers are central to information management, computer departments within companies and universities are often called *IT departments*. Some companies refer to this department as *IS (Information Services)* or *MIS (Management Information Services)*.

⇒ See also COMPUTER SCIENCE; IS; MIS; SYSTEM MANAGEMENT.

italic In typography, *italic* refers to fonts with characters slanted to the right. An italic font, however, often includes one or more character shapes, such as the *a* and the *f*, that differ from those in the roman font of the same family. Slanted versions of fonts without the special shapes are often called oblique.

⇒ See also FONT.

Roman
abcdefghijklmnopqrstuvwxyz
Slanted
abcdefghijklmnopqrstuvwxyz
Italic
abcdefghijklmnopqrstuvwxyz

Figure 40: roman, slanted, and italic versions of the Times Roman font.

iteration A single pass through a group of instructions. Most programs contain loops of instructions that are executed over and over again. The computer *iterates* through the loop, which means that it repeatedly executes the loop.

⇒ See also LOOP.

ITU Short for *I(nternational) T(elecommunication) U(nion)*, an intergovernmental organization through which public and private organizations develop telecommunications. The ITU was founded in 1865 and became a United Nations agency in 1947. It is responsible for adopting international treaties, regulations, and standards governing telecommunications. The standardization functions were formerly performed by a group within the ITU called CCITT, but after a 1992 reorganization the CCITT no longer exists as a separate body.

⇒ See also CCITT; DSVD; H.323; STANDARD; TELECOMMUNICATIONS; V.35; V.90; X.500.

IVT Short for *i(nterrupt) v(ector) t(able)*.

jaggies Stairlike lines that appear where there should be smooth curves or smooth, straight diagonal lines. Jaggies can occur for a variety of reasons, the most common being that the output device (display monitor or printer) does not have enough resolution to portray a smooth line. In addition, jaggies often occur when a bit-mapped image is converted to a different resolution. This is one of the advantages that vector graphics has over bit-mapped graphics—the output looks the same regardless of the resolution of the output device.

The effect of jaggies can be reduced somewhat by a graphics technique known as antialiasing. Antialiasing smoothes out jagged lines by surrounding the jaggies with shaded pixels. In addition, some printers can reduce jaggies with a technique known as *smoothing*.

⇒ See also ANTIALIASING; SMOOTHING.

Java A high-level programming language developed by Sun Microsystems. Java was originally called *Oak* and was designed for handheld devices and set-top boxes. Oak was unsuccessful so in 1995 Sun changed the name to Java and modified the language to take advantage of the burgeoning World Wide Web.

Java is an object-oriented language similar to C++, but simplified to eliminate language features that cause common programming errors. Java source code files (files with a *.java* extension) are compiled into a format called *bytecode* (files with a *.class* extension), which can then be executed by a Java interpreter. Compiled Java code can run on most computers because Java interpreters and runtime environments, known as *Java Virtual Machines (VMs)*, exist for most operating systems, including UNIX, the Macintosh OS, and Windows. Bytecode can also be converted directly into machine language instructions by a just-in-time compiler (JIT).

Java is a general-purpose programming language with a number of features that make the language well suited for use on the World Wide Web. Small Java applications are called Java applets and can be downloaded from a Web server and run on your computer by a Java-compatible Web browser, such as Netscape Navigator or Microsoft Internet Explorer.

⇒ See also ACTIVEX; APPLET; AWT; BYTECODE; C++; CGI; DYNAMIC HTML; HOTJAVA; IFC; INTERPRETER; JAVABEANS; JAVASCRIPT; JDBC; JDK; JIT; OBJECT-ORIENTED PROGRAMMING; PROGRAMMING LANGUAGE; RMI; SMALLTALK; SUN MICROSYSTEMS; THIN CLIENT; VIRTUAL MACHINE.

JavaBeans A specification developed by Sun Microsystems that defines how Java objects interact. An object that conforms to this specification is called a *JavaBean* and is similar to an ActiveX control. It can be used by any application that understands the JavaBeans format.

The principal differences between ActiveX controls and JavaBeans are that ActiveX controls can be developed in any programming language but executed only on a Windows platform, whereas JavaBeans can be developed only in Java but can run on any platform.

⇒ See also ActiveX control; Java; JDK.

Java Database Connectivity See JDBC.

Java Development Kit See JDK.

JavaScript A scripting language developed by Netscape to enable Web authors to design interactive sites. Although it shares many of the features and structures of the full Java language, it was developed independently. Javascript can interact with HTML source code, enabling Web authors to spice up their sites with dynamic content. JavaScript is endorsed by a number of software companies and is an open language that anyone can use without purchasing a license. It is supported by recent browsers from Netscape and Microsoft, though Internet Explorer supports only a subset, which Microsoft calls *Jscript*.

⇒ See also DOM; dynamic HTML; HTML; Java; JScript; script; VBScript.

JavaSoft The business unit of Sun Microsystems that is responsible for Java technology.

⇒ See also HotJava; Java; JDBC; JDK; Sun Microsystems.

Java VM See under virtual machine.

Jaz drive A removable disk drive developed by Iomega Corporation. The Jaz drive has a 12-ms average seek time and a transfer rate of 5.5 Mbps. The removable cartridges hold up to 2 GB of data. The fast data rates and large storage capacity make it a viable alternative for backup storage as well as everyday use.

⇒ See also removable hard disk.

JDBC Short for *J(ava) D(ata)b(ase) C(onnectivity)*, a Java API that enables Java programs to execute SQL statements. This allows Java programs to interact with any SQL-compliant database. Because nearly all relational database management systems (DBMSs) support SQL, and because Java itself runs on most platforms, JDBC makes it possible to write a single database application that can run on different platforms and interact with different DBMSs.

JDBC is similar to ODBC but is designed specifically for Java programs, whereas ODBC is language independent.

JDBC was developed by JavaSoft, a subsidiary of Sun Microsystems.

⇒ See also Java; JavaSoft; JDK; ODBC; SQL.

JDK Short for *J(ava) D(evelopment) K(it)*, a software development kit (SDK) for producing Java programs. The JDK is developed by Sun Microsystem's JavaSoft division. The most recent version, 1.1, includes the JavaBeans component architecture and support for JDBC.

⇒ See also AFC; IFC; Java; JavaBeans; JavaSoft; JDBC; SDK.

Jet Short for *J(oint) e(ngine) t(echnology)*, the database engine used by Microsoft Office and Visual Basic.

⇒ See also DAO; Visual Basic.

JIT Short for *j(ust)-i(n)-t(ime) compiler*, a code generator that converts Java bytecode into machine language instructions. Some Java Virtual Machines (VMs), including the VM in the Netscape Navigator browser, include a JIT in addition to a Java interpreter. Java programs compiled by a JIT generally run much faster than when the bytecode is executed by an interpreter.

⇒ See also bytecode; compiler; Java; virtual machine.

job A task performed by a computer system. For example, printing a file is a job. Jobs can be performed by a single program or by a collection of programs.

⇒ See also program; task.

join In relational databases, a *join operation* matches records in two tables. The two tables must be *joined* by at least one common field. That is, the *join field* is a member of both tables. Typically, a join operation is part of a SELECT query.

⇒ See also database; field; query; RDBMS.

Joint Photographic Experts Group See JPEG.

joystick A lever that moves in all directions and controls the movement of a pointer or some other display symbol. A joystick is similar to a mouse, except that with a mouse the cursor stops moving as soon as you stop moving the mouse. With a joystick, the pointer continues moving in the direction the joystick is pointing. To stop the pointer, you must return the joystick to its upright position. Most joysticks include two buttons called *triggers*.

Joysticks are used mostly for computer games, but they are also used occasionally for CAD/CAM systems and other applications.

⇒ See also mouse; pointer.

JPEG Short for *J(oint) P(hotographic) E(xperts) G(roup)*, and pronounced *jay-peg*. JPEG is a *lossy compression* technique for color images. Although it can reduce files sizes to about 5 percent of their normal size, some detail is lost in the compression.

⇒ See also DATA COMPRESSION; DCT; MOTION-JPEG; MPEG.

jpg See under JPEG.

.jpg See under JPEG.

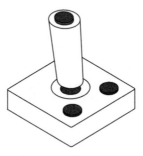

Figure 41: **joystick**

JScript Microsoft's version of JavaScript, which is built into Internet Explorer (IE) browsers. Unfortunately, Netscape's JavaScript and JScript are not entirely compatible, so Web pages containing JavaScript/JScript code may run properly in a Navigator browser, but not in an IE browser, or vice versa.

⇒ See also JAVASCRIPT; VBSCRIPT.

Jughead A search engine for Gopher sites. Jughead is similar to Veronica but has fewer options and indexes fewer Gopher sites.

⇒ See also GOPHER; SEARCH ENGINE; VERONICA.

jumper A metal bridge that closes an electrical circuit. Typically, a jumper consists of a plastic plug that fits over a pair of protruding pins. Jumpers are sometimes used to configure expansion boards. By placing a jumper plug over a different set of pins, you can change a board's parameters.

⇒ See also CONFIGURATION; CONFIGURE; EXPANSION BOARD.

justification Alignment of text along a margin. To produce good-looking justification, the word processor and printer must be capable of microspacing; that is, they must be able to separate letters by less than a full space. In addition, justified text always looks better when a *proportional font* is used (see examples below).

Vertical justification refers to adjusting the vertical space between lines so that columns and pages have an even bottom margin. One vertical justification technique, called *feathering*, inserts an even amount of space between each line so that the page or column has a specified vertical length.

⇒ See also ALIGNMENT; FEATHERING; LEADING; MICROSPACING; VERTICAL JUSTIFI-CATION.

```
This text  is left- and right-jus-
tified  because  the  left  and
right  margins  are  aligned.  The
justification does not look  very
good because the text is  printed
with a fixed-pitch font.
```

This text is left- and right-justified, and microspacing is in effect. Compare this to the previous example, which did not use microspacing.

justify In word processing, to align text along the left and right margins.

⇒ See also FLUSH; JUSTIFICATION.

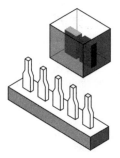

Figure 42: **jumper**

just-in-time compiler See JIT.

K Short for *kilo* or *kilobyte*. See under KILOBYTE.

⇒ See also KB; M.

K56flex A technology developed by Lucent Technologies and Rockwell International for delivering data rates up to 56 Kbps over plain old telephone service (POTS). It was long believed that the maximum data transmission rate over copper telephone wires was 33.6 Kbps, but K56flex achieves higher rates by taking advantage of the fact that most phone switching stations are connected by high-speed digital lines. K56flex bypasses the normal digital-to-analog conversion and sends the digital data over the telephone wires directly to your modem, where it is decoded.

Lucent and Rockwell have announced that future K56flex modems will conform to the new V.90 standard approved by the ITU. And users with older K56flex modems may upgrade their modems to support V.90.

While K56flex offers faster Internet access than normal modems, there are several caveats to using an K56flex modem:

1. The high speeds are available only with downstream traffic (e.g., data sent to your computer). Upstream traffic is delivered using normal techniques, with a maximum speed of 33.6 Kbps.

2. To connect to the Internet at K56flex speeds, your internet service provider (ISP) must have a modem at the other end that supports V.90.

3. Even if your ISP supports V.90, you might not achieve maximum transmission rates due to noisy lines.

⇒ See also CHANNEL BONDING; MODEM; V.90; X2.

K6 A new microprocessor from AMD that supports the MMX instruction set. The K6 is completely compatible with Intel's Pentium processors.

⇒ See also AMD; MMX; PENTIUM MICROPROCESSOR; SOCKET 7.

KB Short for kilobyte. When used to decribe data storage, *KB* usually represents 1,024 bytes. When used to describe data transfer rates, *KB* represents 1,000 bytes.

⇒ See also KILOBYTE.

Kbps Short for *k(ilo)b(its) p(er) s(econd)*, a measure of data transfer speed. Modem speeds, for example, are measured in Kbps. Note that one Kbps is 1,000 bits per second, whereas a KB (kilobyte) is 1,024 bytes. Data transfer rates are measured using the decimal meaning of *K*, whereas data storage is measured using the powers-of-2 meaning of *K*. Technically, *kbps* should be spelled with a lowercase *k* to indicate that it is decimal, but almost everyone spells it with a capital *K*.

⇒ See also DATA TRANSFER RATE; KILOBIT; MODEM.

Table 20
Special Keys on PC Keyboards

Alt key	Short for Alternate, this key is like a second Control key.
Arrow keys	Most keyboards have four arrow keys that enable you to move the cursor (or insertion point) up, down, right, or left. Used in conjunction with the Shift or Alt keys, the arrow keys can move the cursor more than one position at a time, but this depends on which program is running.
Backspace key	Deletes the character just to the left of the cursor (or insertion point) and moves the cursor to that position.
Caps Lock Key	A toggle key that, when activated, causes all alphabetic characters to be uppercase.
Ctrl key	Short for Control, this key is used in conjunction with other keys to produce control characters. The meaning of each control character depends on which program is running.
Delete key	Sometimes labeled Del, deletes the character at the current cursor position, or the selected object, but does not move the cursor. For graphics-based applications, the Delete key deletes the character to the right of the insertion point.
Enter key	Used to enter commands or to move the cursor to the beginning of the next line. Sometimes labeled Return instead of Enter.
Esc key	Short for Escape, this key is used to send special codes to devices and to exit (or escape) from programs and tasks.
Fn key	Short for Function, this key is used in conjunction with other keys to produce special actions that vary depending on which program is running. This key is found most frequently on portable computers that do not have full-size keyboards.
Function Keys	Special keys labeled F1 to Fx, x being the number of function keys on the keyboard. These keys have different meanings depending on which program is running.
Return key	Another name for the Enter key.

Kerberos An authentication system developed at the Massachusetts Institute of Technology (MIT). Kerberos is designed to enable two parties to exchange private information across an otherwise open network. It works by assigning a unique key, called a *ticket*, to each user who logs on to the network. The ticket is then embedded in messages to identify the sender of the message.

⇒ See also AUTHENTICATION; SECURITY.

Kermit A communications *protocol* and set of associated software utilities developed at Columbia University. Kermit can be used to transfer files or for terminal emulation. It is frequently used with modem connections, although it also supports communications via other transport mechanisms such as TCP/IP.

Kermit is noted for its transmission accuracy and slow transmission speeds due to its default settings that optimize for accuracy. However, Kermit can also be tuned to transfer data as quickly as any other data transfer protocol.

Kermit is not in the public domain, but Columbia University allows people to use the protocol for free, so almost all communications products support it. However, not all implementations support the full protocol. This has led some people to refer to an advanced version of Kermit as *Super Kermit*. Actually, there is only one version of the Kermit protocol, which supports all the advanced features usually attributed to Super Kermit, such as sliding windows and long packets.

Other file transfer protocols used by modems include Xmodem and Zmodem.

⇒ See also CCITT; COMMUNICATIONS; COMMUNICATIONS SOFTWARE; FTP; FULL DUPLEX; MNP; MODEM; PROTOCOL; TERMINAL EMULATION; XMODEM; ZMODEM.

kernel The central module of an operating system. It is the part of the operating system that loads first, and it remains in main memory. Because it stays in memory, it is important for the kernel to be as small as possible while still providing all the essential services required by other parts of the operating system and applications. Typically, the kernel is responsible for memory management, process and task management, and disk management.

⇒ See also OPERATING SYSTEM.

kerning In typography, *kerning* refers to adjusting the space between characters, especially by placing two characters closer together than normal. Kerning makes certain combinations of letters, such as WA, MW, TA, and VA, look better.

Only the most sophisticated word processors and desktop publishing systems perform kerning. Normally, you can activate or deactivate kerning for particular fonts.

⇒ See also DESKTOP PUBLISHING; FONT; WORD PROCESSING.

OCTAVE

Before

OCTAVE

After

Figure 43: kerning

key 1. A button on a keyboard. **2.** In database management systems, a key is a field that you use to sort data. It can also be called a *key field, sort key, index,* or *key word.* For example, if you sort records by age, then the age field is a key. Most database management systems allow you to have more than one key so that you can sort records in different ways. One of the keys is designated the *primary key* and must hold a unique value for each record. A key field that identifies records in a different table is called a *foreign key.* **3.** A password or table needed to decipher encoded data.

⇒ See also DATABASE MANAGEMENT SYSTEM; ENCRYPTION; FIELD; HASHING; IN-DEX; NORMALIZATION; PASSWORD; REFERENTIAL INTEGRITY; SYMMETRIC-KEY CRYP-TOGRAPHY.

keyboard The set of typewriter-like keys that enables you to enter data into a computer. Computer keyboards are similar to electric-typewriter keyboards but contain additional keys. The keys on computer keyboards are often classified as follows:

alphanumeric keys — letters and numbers
punctuation keys — comma, period, semicolon, and so on.
special keys — function keys, control keys, arrow keys, Caps Lock key, and so on.

The standard layout of letters, numbers, and punctuation is known as a *QWERTY keyboard* because the first six keys on the top row of letters spell *QWERTY.* The QWERTY keyboard was designed in the 1800s for mechanical typewriters and was actually designed to slow typists down to avoid jamming the keys. Another keyboard design, which has letters positioned for speed typing, is the *Dvorak keyboard.*

There is no standard computer keyboard, although many manufacturers imitate the keyboards of PCs. There are actually three different PC keyboards: the original PC keyboard, with 84 keys; the AT keyboard, also with 84 keys; and the *enhanced keyboard*, with 101 keys. The three differ somewhat in the placement of function keys, the Control key, the Return key, and the Shift keys.

In addition to these keys, IBM keyboards contain the following keys: Page Up, Page Down, Home, End, Insert, Pause, Num Lock, Scroll Lock, Break, Caps Lock, Print Screen.

Various keyboard designs have emerged in the past few years that attempt to provide the user with a more ergonomic shape by positioning keys at a more natural angle for the user. In addition, many modern PC keyboards have three extra keys (bringing the total to 104) that are used for switching between windows and scrolling within windows.

There are several different types of keyboards for the Apple Macintosh. All of them are called *ADB keyboards* because they connect to the Apple Desktop bus (*ADB*). The two main varieties of Macintosh keyboards are the *standard* keyboard and the *extended keyboard*, which has 15 additional special-function keys.

⇒ See also ADB; ALPHANUMERIC; ALT KEY; ARROW KEYS; BACKSPACE KEY; BREAK KEY; CAPS LOCK KEY; CONTROL KEY; CURSOR; DELETE KEY; DVORAK KEYBOARD; END KEY; ENHANCED KEYBOARD; ENTER KEY.

keyboard buffer See under BUFFER.

keyboard template See under TEMPLATE.

key field See under KEY.

keypad See under NUMERIC KEYPAD.

keystroke The pressing of a key. The efficiency of software programs is sometimes measured by the number of keystrokes required to perform a specific function. The fewer the keystrokes, claim some software producers, the faster and more efficient the program. The number of keystrokes, however, is generally less important than other characteristics of the software.

⇒ See also KEY; KEYBOARD.

keyword 1. In text editing and database management systems, a *keyword* is an index entry that identifies a specific record or document. **2.** In programming, a *keyword* is a word that is reserved by a program because the word has a special meaning. Keywords can be commands or parameters. Every programming language has a set of keywords that cannot be used as variable names. Keywords are sometimes called *reserved names*.

⇒ See also COMMAND; INDEX; PARAMETER; VARIABLE.

killer app See under APP.

⇒ See also APPLICATION.

kilobit 1,024 bits. Data transfer rates are often measured in kilobits per second, abbreviated as *Kbps*.

⇒ See also BIT; KBPS; MEGABIT.

XT Keyboard

AT (Standard)

AT (Enhanced)

Figure 44: **keyboards**

kilobyte In decimal systems, *kilo* stands for 1,000, but in binary systems, a *kilo* is 1,024 (2^{10}). Technically, therefore, a kilobyte is 1,024 bytes, but it is often used loosely as a synonym for 1,000 bytes. For example, a computer that has 256K main memory can store approximately 256,000 bytes (or characters) in memory at one time.

A megabyte is 2^{20} (approximately 1 million) and a gigabyte is 2^{30} (approximately 1 billion).

In computer literature, *kilobyte* is usually abbreviated as *K* or *Kb*. To distinguish between a decimal K (1,000) and a binary K (1,024), the IEEE has suggested following the convention of using a small k for a decimal kilo and a capital K for a binary kilo, but this convention is by no means strictly followed.

⇒ See also BINARY; BYTE; GIGA (G); MEGABYTE; MEMORY.

kiosk A booth providing a computer-related service, such as an *automated teller machine (ATM)*. Another type of kiosk offers tourist information. Kiosks providing Internet access are expected to be popular in the near future.

A kiosk requires a simple user interface that can be used without training or documentation, and the hardware must be rugged and capable of operating unattended for long periods of time. Touch screens can provide some of these features because they enable a user to enter and display information on the same device and eliminate the need for keyboards, which are prone to break.

⇒ See also TOUCH SCREEN.

kludge Pronounced *klooj*, a derogatory term that refers to a poor design. Like *hacks*, kludges use nonstandard techniques. But, whereas a hack can connote a clever solution to a problem, a kludge always implies that the solution is inelegant.

⇒ See also HACK.

ABCDEFGHIJK **L** MNOPQRSTUVWXYZ

L1 cache Short for *L(evel)* **1 cache**, a memory cache built into the micro-processor. See under *cache*.
The L1 cache is also called the *primary cache*.

⇒ See also CACHE.

L2 cache Short for *L(evel)* **2 cache**, cache memory that is external to the microprocessor. In general, L2 cache memory, also called the *secondary cache*, resides on a separate chip from the microprocessor chip. The Pentium Pro, however, has an L2 cache on the same chip as the microproc-essor.

⇒ See also CACHE; L1 CACHE; PENTIUM MICROPROCESSOR; PENTIUM PRO; TAG RAM.

L2F Short for LAYER TWO FORWARDING.

L2TP Short for *L(ayer) T(wo) T(unneling) P(rotocol)*, an extension to the PPP protocol that enables ISPs to operate Virtual Private Networks (VPNs). L2TP merges the best features of two other tunneling protocols: PPTP from Microsoft and L2F from Cisco Sysyems.

⇒ See also DIAL-UP ACCESS; IPSEC; LAYER TWO FORWARDING; PPTP; TUNNEL-ING; VPN.

label 1. A name. **2.** For mass storage devices, a label is the name of a stor-age volume. It is sometimes referred to as a *volume label*. Each operating system has its own set of rules for labeling volumes. The label provides a mnemonic name that indicates what type of information is stored on the media. **3.** In spreadsheet programs, a label is any descriptive text placed in a cell. **4.** In programming languages, a label refers to a particular loca-tion in a program, usually a particular line of source code. **5.** The term *label* is also commonly used to mean a small, sticky piece of paper that you can place on an object to identify it. For example, you can paste la-bels on floppy disks to indicate what data are stored on them.

⇒ See also CELL; DISK; MASS STORAGE; NAME; SPREADSHEET; VOLUME.

LAN See LOCAL-AREA NETWORK.

landscape In word processing and desktop publishing, the terms *portrait* and *landscape* refer to whether the document is oriented vertically or horizontally. A page with landscape orientation is wider than it is tall.

Not all printers are capable of generating text in landscape mode. Of those that are, some require special landscape versions of their fonts; others can rotate the standard portrait fonts 90 degrees.

Orientation is also a characteristic of monitors.

⇒ See also MONITOR; PORTRAIT; PRINTER; WORD PROCESSING.

Landscape　　　　　　　Portrait

Figure 45: **landscape vs. portrait**

language A system for communicating. Written languages use symbols (that is, characters) to build words. The entire set of words is the language's *vocabulary*. The ways in which the words can be meaningfully combined is defined by the language's *syntax* and *grammar*. The actual meaning of words and combinations of words is defined by the language's *semantics*.

In computer science, human languages are known as *natural languages*. Unfortunately, computers are not sophisticated enough to understand natural languages. As a result, we must communicate with computers using special computer languages. There are many different classes of computer languages, including *machine languages*, *programming languages*, and *fourth-generation languages*.

⇒ See also ARTIFICIAL INTELLIGENCE; FOURTH-GENERATION LANGUAGE; MACHINE LANGUAGE; NATURAL LANGUAGE; PROGRAMMING LANGUAGE; SYNTAX.

laptop computer A small, portable computer—small enough that it can sit on your lap. Nowadays, laptop computers are more frequently called *notebook computers*.

⇒ See also NOTEBOOK COMPUTER; PORTABLE; ZV PORT.

large-scale integration (LSI) Refers to the placement of thousands of electronic components on a single integrated circuit.

⇒ See also CHIP; INTEGRATED CIRCUIT; VLSI.

laser printer A type of printer that utilizes a laser beam to produce an image on a drum. The light of the laser alters the electrical charge on the drum wherever it hits. The drum is then rolled through a reservoir of toner, which is picked up by the charged portions of the drum. Finally, the toner is transferred to the paper through a combination of heat and pressure. This is also the way copy machines work.

Because an entire page is transmitted to a drum before the toner is applied, laser printers are sometimes called *page printers*. There are two other types of page printers that fall under the category of *laser printers* even though they do not use lasers at all. One uses an array of *LEDs* to expose the drum, and the other uses *LCDs*. Once the drum is charged, however, they both operate like a real laser printer.

One of the chief characteristics of laser printers is their resolution—how many dots per inch (dpi) they lay down. The available resolutions range from 300 dpi at the low end to 1,200 dpi at the high end. By comparison, offset printing usually prints at 1,200 or 2,400 dpi. Some laser printers achieve higher resolutions with special techniques known generally as *resolution enhancement*.

In addition to the standard monochrome laser printer, which uses a single toner, there also exist color laser printers that use four toners to print in full color. Color laser printers tend to be about five to ten times as expensive as their monochrome siblings.

Laser printers produce very high-quality print and are capable of printing an almost unlimited variety of fonts. Most laser printers come with a basic set of fonts, called *internal* or *resident fonts*, but you can add additional fonts in one of two ways:

font cartridges: Laser printers have slots in which you can insert font cartridges, ROM boards on which fonts have been recorded. The advantage of font cartridges is that they use none of the printer's memory.

soft fonts: All laser printers come with a certain amount of RAM memory, and you can usually increase the amount of memory by adding memory boards in the printer's expansion slots. You can then copy fonts from a disk to the printer's RAM. This is called *downloading* fonts. A font that has been downloaded is often referred to as a *soft font*, to distinguish it from the *hard fonts* available on font cartridges. The more RAM a printer has, the more fonts can be downloaded at one time.

In addition to text, laser printers are very adept at printing graphics. However, you need significant amounts of memory in the printer to print high-resolution graphics. To print a full-page graphic at 300 dpi, for example, you need at least 1 MB (megabyte) of printer RAM. For a 600-dpi graphic, you need at least 4 MB RAM.

Because laser printers are *nonimpact* printers, they are much quieter than dot-matrix or daisy-wheel printers. They are also relatively fast, although not as fast as some dot-matrix printers. The speed of laser printers ranges from about 4 to 20 pages of text per minute (ppm). A typical rate of 6 ppm is equivalent to about 40 characters per second (cps).

Laser printers are controlled through *page description languages (PDLs)*. There are two de facto standards for PDLs:

PCL: Hewlett-Packard (HP) was one of the pioneers of laser printers and has developed a Printer Control Language (PCL) to control output. There are several versions of PCL, so a printer may be compatible with one but not another. In addition, many printers that claim compatibility cannot accept HP font cartridges.

PostScript: This is the de facto standard for Apple Macintosh printers and for all desktop publishing systems.

Most software can print using either of these PDLs. PostScript tends to be a bit more expensive, but it has some features that PCL lacks and it is the standard for desktop publishing. Some printers support both PCL and PostScript.

⇒ See also COLOR PRINTER; FONT CARTRIDGE; HP-COMPATIBLE PRINTER; INK-JET PRINTER; LCD PRINTER; OFFSET PRINTING; OKIDATA; PAGE DESCRIPTION LANGUAGE (PDL); PCL; POSTSCRIPT; PRINTER; RESIDENT FONT; RESOLUTION ENHANCEMENT; SMOOTHING; SOFT FONT; TONER.

LaserWriter A family of Apple laser printers designed to run with a Macintosh computer.

⇒ See also IMAGEWRITER; LASER PRINTER; MACINTOSH COMPUTER; POSTSCRIPT; PRINTER; QUICKDRAW.

latency 1. In general, the period of time that one component in a system is spinning its wheels waiting for another component. Latency, therefore, is wasted time. For example, in accessing data on a disk, latency is defined as the time it takes to position the proper sector under the read/write head. **2.** In networking, the amount of time it takes a packet to travel from source to destination. Together, latency and bandwidth define the speed and capacity of a network.

⇒ See also BANDWIDTH; QoS; WAIT STATE.

LaTeX A typesetting system based on the TeX programming language developed by Donald E. Knuth. Most people who use TeX, however, utilize one of several macro packages that provide an easier interface. The two most popular are *LaTeX*, originally written by Leslie Lamport, and *plain TeX*, written by Knuth. LaTeX provides higher-level macros, which makes it easier to format documents but sacrifices some of the flexibility of TeX.

⇒ See also IMAGESETTER; MACRO; MuTeX; TeX.

launch To start a program.

⇒ See also EXECUTE; LOAD; RUN.

LAWN See LOCAL-AREA WIRELESS NETWORK.

layer-3 switch Same as ROUTING SWITCH.

Layer Two Forwarding Often abbreviated as *L2F,* a tunneling protocol developed by Cisco Systems. L2F is similar to the PPTP protocol developed by Microsoft, enabling organizations to set up virtual private networks (VPNs) that use the Internet backbone to move packets.

Recently, Microsoft and Cisco agreed to merge their respective protocols into a single, standard protocol called *Layer Two Tunneling Protocol (L2TP).*

⇒ See also Cisco Systems; L2TP; PPTP; tunneling; VPN.

layout 1. In word processing and desktop publishing, *layout* refers to the arrangement of text and graphics. The layout of a document can determine which points are emphasized, and whether the document is aesthetically pleasing.

While no computer program can substitute for a professional layout artist, a powerful desktop publishing system can make it easier to lay out professional-looking documents. WYSIWYG helps layout considerably because it allows you to lay out a document on the display screen and see what it will look like when printed. **2.** In database management systems, *layout* refers to the way information is displayed. You can change the layout by selecting different fields.

⇒ See also database management system; desktop publishing; field; report writer; word processing; WYSIWYG.

LBA Short for *l(ogical) b(lock) a(ddressing),* a method used with SCSI and IDE disk drives to translate the cylinder, head, and sector specifications of the drive into addresses that can be used by an enhanced BIOS. LBA is used with drives that are larger than 528 MB.

⇒ See also cylinder; disk drive; head; sector.

LCD Abbreviation of *l(iquid) c(rystal) d(isplay),* a type of display used in digital watches and many portable computers. LCD displays utilize two sheets of polarizing material with a liquid crystal solution between them. An electric current passed through the liquid causes the crystals to align so that light cannot pass through them. Each crystal, therefore, is like a shutter, either allowing light to pass through or blocking the light.

Monochrome LCD images usually appear as blue or dark gray images on top of a grayish-white background. Color LCD displays use two basic techniques for producing color. *Passive matrix* is the less expensive of the two technologies. The other technology, called *thin film transistor* (TFT) or *active-matrix,* produces color images that are as sharp as those of traditional CRT displays, but the technology is expensive. Recent passive-matrix displays using new CSTN and DSTN technologies produce sharp colors rivaling those of active-matrix displays.

Most LCD screens used in notebook computers are backlit to make them easier to read.

⇒ See also active-matrix display; backlighting; CSTN; DLP; DSTN; elec-

TROLUMINESCENT DISPLAY (ELD); FLAT-PANEL DISPLAY; GAS-PLASMA DISPLAY; LCD MONITOR; LCD PRINTER; LED; NOTEBOOK COMPUTER; SUPERTWIST; TFT.

LCD monitor A monitor that uses LCD technologies rather than the conventional CRT technologies used by most desktop monitors. Until recently, LCD panels were used exclusively on notebook computers and other portable devices. In 1997, however, several manufacturers began offering full-size LCD monitors as alternatives to CRT monitors. The main advantage of LCD displays is that they take up less desk space and are lighter. Currently, however, they are also much more expensive.

⇒ See also COLOR MONITOR; CRT; FLAT-PANEL DISPLAY; LCD; MONITOR.

LCD printer A type of printer similar to a laser printer. Instead of using a laser to create an image on the drum, however, it shines a light through a liquid crystal panel. Individual pixels in the panel either let the light pass or block the light, thereby creating an image composed of dots on the drum.

Liquid crystal shutter printers produce print quality equivalent to that of laser printers.

⇒ See also LASER PRINTER; LCD; PIXEL.

LDAP Short for *L(ightweight) D(irectory) A(ccess) P(rotocol)*, a set of protocols for accessing information directories. LDAP is based on the standards contained within the X.500 standard, but is significantly simpler. And unlike X.500, LDAP supports TCP/IP, which is necessary for any type of Internet access. Because it's a simpler version of X.500, LDAP is sometimes called *X.500-lite.*

Although not yet widely implemented, LDAP should eventually make it possible for almost any application running on virtually any computer platform to obtain directory information, such as e-mail addresses and public keys. Because LDAP is an open protocol, applications need not worry about the type of server hosting the directory.

⇒ See also ACTIVE DIRECTORY; DIRECTORY SERVICE; NDS; PUBLIC-KEY ENCRYPTION; TCP/IP.

leader Rows of dots, dashes, or other characters that lead your eye from one text element to another. Leaders are used commonly in tables of contents. For example:

Chapter 5 233

leading Pronounced *ledd-ing*, a typographical term that refers to the vertical space between lines of text. The word derives from the fact that typographers once used thin strips of lead to separate lines. Now, the leading value also includes the size of the font. For example, 10-point text with 2 points of spacing between lines would mean a leading of 12 points.

Many word processors and all desktop publishing systems allow you to specify the leading. In addition, some systems automatically adjust leading so that columns and pages have even bottom margins. This feature is called *vertical justification*.

Leading is also called *line spacing*.

⇒ See also FONT; JUSTIFICATION; POINT; VERTICAL JUSTIFICATION.

leading zero A zero that appears in the leftmost digit(s) of a number. Many programs that display numbers in columns allow you to specify whether the number should be preceded with spaces or leading zeros, as shown below.

LEADING ZEROS	SPACES
0003.45	3.45
0148.70	148.70
0002.01	2.01

leaf Items at the very bottom of a hierarchical tree structure. In hierarchical file systems, files are leaves because they can have nothing below them. Directories, on the other hand, are *nodes*.

⇒ See also HIERARCHICAL; NODE; TREE STRUCTURE.

learn mode A mode in which a program learns. The term is usually used to describe a process of defining *macros*. Once you switch the program into learn mode, it will record all subsequent keystrokes you make. You can then assign these keystrokes to a function key to create a macro.

⇒ See also MACRO.

leased line A permanent telephone connection between two points set up by a telecommunications common carrier. Typically, leased lines are used by businesses to connect geographically distant offices. Unlike normal dial-up connections, a leased line is always active. The fee for the connection is a fixed monthly rate. The primary factors affecting the monthly fee are distance between end points and the speed of the circuit. Because the connection doesn't carry anybody else's communications, the carrier can assure a given level of quality.

For example, a T-1 channel is a type of leased line that provides a maximum transmission speed of 1.544 Mbps. You can divide the connection into different lines for data and voice communication or use the channel for one high-speed data circuit. Dividing the connection is called *multiplexing*.

Increasingly, leased lines are being used by companies, and even individuals, for Internet access because they afford faster data transfer rates and are cost effective if the Internet is used heavily.

⇒ See also DIAL-UP ACCESS; FRACTIONAL T-1; T-1 CARRIER; T-3 CARRIER; TDM; TELECOMMUNICATIONS.

LED Abbreviation of *l(ight) e(mitting) d(iode)*, an electronic device that lights up when electricity is passed through it. LEDs are usually red. They are good for displaying images because they can be relatively small, and they do not burn out. However, they require more power than LCDs.

⇒ See also LASER PRINTER; LCD.

LED printer See under LASER PRINTER.

left justify To align text along the left margin. *Left-justified* text is the same as *flush-left* text.

⇒ See also FLUSH; JUSTIFY.

legacy application An application in which a company or organization has already invested considerable time and money. Typically, legacy applications are database management systems (DBMSs) running on mainframes or minicomputers. An important feature of new software products is the ability to work with a company's legacy applications, or at least be able to import data from them.

⇒ See also APPLICATION; MAINFRAME; MINICOMPUTER; VSAM.

legend In presentation graphics, text that describes the meaning of colors and patterns used in the chart.

⇒ See also PRESENTATION GRAPHICS.

letter quality (LQ) Refers to print that has the same quality as that produced by a typewriter. Computer printers are sometimes divided into two classes: those that produce letter-quality type, such as laser, ink-jet, and daisy-wheel printers; and those that do not, including most dot-matrix printers.

The term *letter quality* is really something of a misnomer now, because laser printers produce print that is considerably better than that produced by a typewriter.

Many dot-matrix printers produce a high-quality print known as *near letter quality*. You have to look closely to see that the print is not really letter quality. A lower classification of print quality is called *draft quality*.

Draft Quality   Near Letter Quality   Letter Quality

Figure 46: **letter quality vs. draft quality**

⇒ See also DAISY-WHEEL PRINTER; DOT-MATRIX PRINTER; DRAFT QUALITY; INK-JET PRINTER; LASER PRINTER; NEAR LETTER QUALITY; PRINTER.

Level 2 cache See L2 CACHE.

library 1. A collection of files. **2.** In programming, a library is a collection of precompiled routines that a program can use. The routines, sometimes called *modules*, are stored in object format. Libraries are particularly useful for storing frequently used routines because you do not need to explicitly link them to every program that uses them. The linker automatically looks in libraries for routines that it does not find elsewhere. In MS-Windows environments, library files have a .DLL extension.

⇒ See also DLL; LINKER; MODULE; OBJECT CODE; ROUTINE; RUNTIME.

light bar On a display screen, a highlighted region that indicates a selected component in a menu. The light bar can be produced by using a different color or by reversing the image so that black-on-white text becomes white-on-black.

⇒ See also HIGHLIGHT; MENU; REVERSE VIDEO.

light-emitting diode See LED.

light pen An input device that utilizes a light-sensitive detector to select

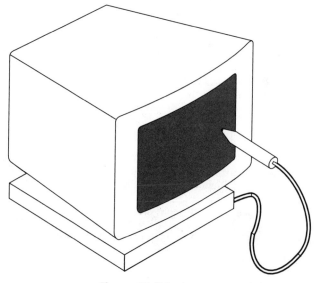

Figure 47: **light pen**

objects on a display screen. A light pen is similar to a mouse, except that with a light pen you can move the pointer and select objects on the display screen by directly pointing to the objects with the pen.

⇒ See also CAD/CAM; DISPLAY SCREEN; INPUT DEVICE; MOUSE; PIXEL; POINTER.

Lightweight Directory Access Protocol See LDAP.

Li-ion Short for LITHIUM ION BATTERY.

LIM See LIM MEMORY.

LIM memory A technique for adding memory to DOS systems. LIM memory lets you exceed the 1MB (megabyte) memory limit imposed by DOS. The name derives from the initials of the three companies that designed the technique—L(otus), Intel, and M(icrosoft)—and is sometimes referred to as *LIM 4.0*, which is its official name.
  LIM memory has been superseded by extended memory.

⇒ See also EEMS; EXPANDED MEMORY; EXTENDED MEMORY.

line 1. A hardware circuit connecting two devices. **2.** In programming, a single program statement. **3.** In caches, a single data entry. A cache line can contain data from one or more addresses. Modern PC motherboards, for example, generally have an L2 cache where each line is 32 bytes wide.

⇒ See also CHANNEL.

line art A type of graphic consisting entirely of lines, without any shading. Most art produced on computers is *not* line art because the computer makes it so easy to add subtle shadings.

⇒ See also GRAPHICS.

line editor A primitive type of editor that allows you to edit only one line of a file at a time.

⇒ See also EDITOR.

line feed Often abbreviated *LF*, a line feed is a code that moves the cursor on a display screen down one line. In the ASCII character set, a line feed has a decimal value of 10.
  On printers, a line feed advances the paper one line. Some printers have a button labeled *LF* that executes a line feed when pressed. (Note, however, that the printer must be in *off-line mode* to execute a line feed.)

⇒ See also ASCII; CARRIAGE RETURN; OFF-LINE.

line graph A type of graph that highlights trends by drawing connecting lines between data points. Compare with *bar chart* and *pie graph.*

⇒ See also BAR CHART; PIE CHART; PRESENTATION GRAPHICS.

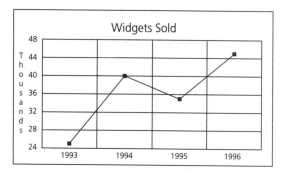

Figure 48: **line graph**

line-interactive UPS See under UPS.

line printer A high-speed printer capable of printing an entire line at one time. A fast line printer can print as many as 3,000 lines per minute. The disadvantages of line printers are that they cannot print graphics, the print quality is low, and they are very noisy.

⇒ See also IMPACT PRINTER; PRINTER.

line spacing See under LEADING.

lines per inch See under HALFTONE.

link *v* **1.** To bind together. **2.** In programming, the term *link* refers to execution of a *linker.* **3.** To paste a copy of an object into a document in such a way that it retains its connection with the original object. Updates to the original object can be reflected in the duplicate by *updating* the link. **4.** In spreadsheet programs, *linking* refers to the ability of a worksheet to take its data for particular cells from another worksheet. Two or more files are thus *linked* by common cells. —*n* **5.** In communications, a link is a line or channel over which data is transmitted. **6.** In data management systems, a link is a pointer to another record. You can connect one or more records by inserting links into them. **7.** In some operating systems (UNIX, for example), a link is a pointer to a file. Links make it possible to reference a file by several different names and to access a file without specifying a full *path.* **8.** In hypertext systems, such as the World Wide Web, a link is a reference to another document. Such links are sometimes called *hot links* because they take you to other documents when you click on them.

⇒ See also BIND; CELL; CHANNEL; COMMUNICATIONS; COMPILE; DATABASE MANAGEMENT SYSTEM; DLL; FILENAME; HOT LINK; LINKER; OLE; PATH; RECORD; SPREADSHEET; UNIX.

link edit To run a linker.

⇒ See also LINKER.

linker Also called *link editor* and *binder,* a linker is a program that combines object modules to form an executable program. Many programming languages allow you to write different pieces of code, called *modules,* separately. This simplifies the programming task because you can break a large program into small, more manageable pieces. Eventually, though, you need to put all the modules together. This is the job of the linker.

In addition to combining modules, a linker also replaces symbolic addresses with real addresses. Therefore, you may need to link a program even if it contains only one module.

⇒ See also ADDRESS; COMPILE; EXECUTABLE FILE; MODULE; OBJECT CODE.

Lino Short for *Linotronic,* a type of imagesetter. Although Linotronic is a brand name, the terms *Lino* and *Linotronic* are often used to refer to any imagesetter.

⇒ See also IMAGESETTER; LINOTRONIC.

Linotronic A common type of high-quality printer, called an *imagesetter,* capable of printing at resolutions of up to 2,540 dots per inch. Linotronic printers are too expensive for homes or most offices, but you can obtain Linotronic output by taking a PostScript file to a service bureau.

⇒ See also IMAGESETTER; ISP; POSTSCRIPT.

Linux Pronounced *lee-nucks,* a freely distributable implementation of UNIX that runs on a number of hardware platforms, including Intel and Motorola microprocessors. It was developed mainly by Linus Torvalds. Because it's free, and because it runs on many platforms, including PCs, Macintoshes, and Amigas, Linux has become extremely popular over the last couple of years.

Another popular, free version of UNIX that runs on Intel microprocessors is *FreeBSD.*

⇒ See also APACHE WEB SERVER; FREEBSD; GNU; UNIX.

liquid crystal display See LCD.

liquid crystal shutter printer See under LCD PRINTER.

LISP Acronym for *lis(t) p(rocessor),* a high-level programming language especially popular for artificial intelligence applications. LISP was developed in the early 1960s by John McCarthy at MIT.

⇒ See also ARTIFICIAL INTELLIGENCE; GENETIC PROGRAMMING; HIGH-LEVEL LANGUAGE; INTERPRETER; PROGRAMMING LANGUAGE; PROLOG.

list *v* **1.** To display data in an ordered format. For example, the LIST command in BASIC displays lines of a program. —*n* **2.** Any ordered set of data.

⇒ See also DATA; DATA STRUCTURE.

listing A printout of text, usually a source program.

⇒ See also PRINTOUT; SOURCE CODE.

LISTSERV An automatic mailing list server developed by Eric Thomas for BITNET in 1986. When e-mail is addressed to a LISTSERV mailing list, it is automatically broadcast to everyone on the list. The result is similar to a newsgroup or forum, except that the messages are transmitted as e-mail and are therefore available only to individuals on the list.
   LISTSERV is currently a commercial product marketed by L-Soft International. Although LISTSERV refers to a specific mailing list server, the term is sometimes used incorrectly to refer to any mailing list server. Another popular mailing list server is Majordomo, which is freeware.

⇒ See also MAILING LIST SERVER; MAJORDOMO.

list server See MAILING LIST SERVER.

literal In programming, a value written exactly as it's meant to be interpreted. In contrast, a *variable* is a name that can represent different values during the execution of the program. And a *constant* is a name that represents the same value throughout a program. But a literal is not a name—it is the value itself.
   A literal can be a number, a character, or a string. For example, in the expression,

x = 3

x is a variable, and **3** is a literal.

⇒ See also CONSTANT; NAME; VARIABLE.

Lithium-Ion battery A type of a battery composed of Lithium, the lightest metal and the metal that has the highest electrochemical potential. Lithium, however, is an unstable metal, so Lithium-Ion batteries are made from Lithium ions from chemicals. Because of its lightness and high energy density, Lithium-Ion batteries are ideal for portable devices, such as notebook computers. In addition, Lithium-Ion batteries have no memory effect and do not use poisonous metals, such as lead, mercury, or cadmium. The only disadvantage to Lithium-Ion batteries is that they are currently more expensive than NiCad and NiMH battery packs.

⇒ See also BATTERY PACK; NiCad BATTERY PACK; NiMH BATTERY PACK.

little-endian See under BIG-ENDIAN.

load 1. To install. For example, to load a disk means to mount it in a disk drive. **2.** To copy a program from a storage device into memory. Every program must be loaded into memory before it can be executed. Usually the loading process is performed invisibly by a part of the operating system called the *loader*. You simply enter the name of the program you want to run, and the operating system loads it and executes it for you. **3.** In programming, *load* means to copy data from main memory into a data register. —*n.* **4.** In networking, *load* refers to the amount of data (traffic) being carried by the network.

⇒ See also LOADER; MAIN MEMORY; OPERATING SYSTEM; PROGRAM; REGISTER; TRAFFIC.

load balancing Distributing processing and communications activity evenly across a computer network so that no single device is overwhelmed. Load balancing is especially important for networks where it's difficult to predict the number of requests that will be issued to a server. Busy Web sites typically employ two or more Web servers in a load-balancing scheme. If one server starts to get swamped, requests are forwarded to another server with more capacity. *Load balancing* can also refer to the communications channels themselves.

⇒ See also CLUSTERING; SERVER; THREE-TIER; TP MONITOR.

loader An operating system utility that copies programs from a storage device to main memory, where they can be executed. In addition to copying a program into main memory, the loader can also replace virtual addresses with physical addresses.

Most loaders are invisible: that is, you cannot directly execute them, but the operating system uses them when necessary.

⇒ See also LOAD; MAIN MEMORY; PROGRAM; UTILITY; VIRTUAL MEMORY.

local In networks, *local* refers to files, devices, and other resources at your workstation. Resources located at other *nodes* on the networks are *remote*.

⇒ See also LOCAL-AREA NETWORK; NETWORK; NODE; REMOTE; REMOTE CONTROL SOFTWARE; WORKSTATION.

local-area network A computer network that spans a relatively small area. Most LANs are confined to a single building or group of buildings. However, one LAN can be connected to other LANs over any distance via telephone lines and radio waves. A system of LANs connected in this way is called a *wide-area network (WAN)*.

Most LANs connect workstations and personal computers. Each *node* (individual computer) in a LAN has its own CPU with which it executes programs, but it is also able to access data and devices anywhere on the LAN. This means that many users can share expensive devices, such as laser printers, as well as data. Users can also use the LAN to communicate with one another, by sending e-mail or engaging in chat sessions.

There are many different types of LANs, *Ethernets* being the most common for PCs. Most Apple Macintosh networks are based on Apple's AppleTalk network system, which is built into Macintosh computers.

The following characteristics differentiate one LAN from another:

topology: The geometric arrangement of devices on the network. For example, devices can be arranged in a ring or in a straight line.

protocols: The rules and encoding specifications for sending data. The protocols also determine whether the network uses a peer-to-peer or client/server architecture.

media: Devices can be connected by twisted-pair wire, coaxial cables, or fiber optic cables. Some networks do without connecting media altogether, communicating instead via radio waves.

LANs are capable of transmitting data at very fast rates, much faster than data can be transmitted over a telephone line; but the distances are limited, and there is also a limit on the number of computers that can be attached to a single LAN.

⇒ See also APPLETALK; ARCNET; BRIDGE; CLIENT/SERVER ARCHITECTURE; DCC; E-MAIL; ETHERNET; IEEE 802 STANDARDS; INTERNETWORKING; MAN; NETWARE; NETWORK; NETWORK INTERFACE CARD; NETWORK OPERATING SYSTEM; NODE; NOVELL; PEER-TO-PEER ARCHITECTURE; PERSONAL COMPUTER; PROTOCOL; SNMP; SWITCHING HUB; TOKEN BUS NETWORK; TOKEN-RING NETWORK; TOPOLOGY; TOPS; VLAN; WIDE-AREA NETWORK.

local-area wireless network (LAWN) A type of local-area network that uses high-frequency radio waves rather than wires to communicate between nodes.

⇒ See also LOCAL-AREA NETWORK.

local bus A data bus that connects directly, or almost directly, to the microprocessor. Although local buses can support only a few devices, they provide very fast throughput. Modern PCs include both a PCI local bus and a more general ISA expansion bus for devices that do not require such fast data throughput.

⇒ See also BUS; EXPANSION BUS; PCI; VL-BUS.

local echo Same as HALF DUPLEX.

LocalTalk The cabling scheme supported by the AppleTalk network protocol for Macintosh computers. Most local-area networks that use AppleTalk, such as *TOPS*, also conform to the LocalTalk cable system. Such networks are sometimes called *LocalTalk networks*.

Although LocalTalk networks are relatively slow, they are popular because they are easy and inexpensive to install and maintain. An alternative cabling scheme that is faster is Ethernet.

⇒ See also AppleTalk; Ethernet; local-area network; Macintosh computer; TOPS.

lock 1. To make a file or other piece of data inaccessible. *File locking* is a critical component of all multi-user computer systems, including local-area networks. When users share files, the operating system must ensure that two or more users do not attempt to modify the same file simultaneously. It does this by *locking* the file as soon as the first user opens it. All subsequent users may read the file, but they cannot write to it until the first user is finished.

In addition to file locking, many database management systems support *record locking*, in which a single record, rather than an entire file, is locked. This enables different users to access different records within the same file without interfering with one another. **2.** In Macintosh environments, locking a diskette means write-protecting it.

⇒ See also DATABASE MANAGEMENT SYSTEM; FILE; LOCAL-AREA NETWORK; MULTI-USER; OPERATING SYSTEM; RECORD; WRITE-PROTECT.

log *v* **1.** To record an action. For example, to enter a record into a log file. —*n* **2.** Same as LOG FILE.

⇒ See also LOG FILE.

log file A file that lists actions that have occurred. For example, Web servers maintain log files listing every request made to the server. With log file analysis tools, it's possible to get a good idea of where visitors are coming from, how often they return, and how they navigate through a site. Using cookies enables Webmasters to log even more detailed information about how individual users are accessing a site.

⇒ See also AUDIT TRAIL; COOKIE; LOG.

logical 1. Refers to a user's view of the way data or systems are organized. The opposite of logical is *physical*, which refers to the real organization of a system. For example, a logical description of a file is that it is a collection of data stored together. This is the way files appear to users. Physically, however, a single file can be divided into many pieces scattered across a disk. **2.** Refers to any Boolean logic operation.

⇒ See also BOOLEAN LOGIC; FRAGMENTATION; PHYSICAL.

logical block address See LBA.

logical operator Same as BOOLEAN OPERATOR.

log in Same as LOG ON.

login See under LOG ON.

log off Same as LOG OUT.

log on To make a computer system or network recognize you so that you can begin a computer session. Most personal computers have no log-on procedure—you just turn the machine on and begin working. For larger systems and networks, however, you usually need to enter a *username* and *password* before the computer system will allow you to execute programs.

Alternative spellings for log on are *log in* and *login*.

⇒ See also ACCESS CODE; LOG OUT; PASSWORD; USERNAME.

log out To end a session at the computer. For personal computers, you can log out simply by exiting applications and turning the machine off. On larger computers and networks, where you share computer resources with other users, there is generally an operating system command that lets you log off.

⇒ See also LOG ON.

look-and-feel Refers to the general appearance and operation of a user interface. This is a hot legal issue because some software companies are claiming that competitors who copy the look-and-feel of their products are infringing on their copyright protection. To date, the courts have not ruled definitively on this matter.

⇒ See also USER INTERFACE.

loop In programming, a loop is a series of instructions that is repeated until a certain condition is met. Each pass through the loop is called an *iteration*. Loops constitute one of the most basic and powerful programming concepts.

⇒ See also FLOW CONTROL; ITERATION.

lossless compression Refers to data compression techniques in which no data is lost. The PKZIP compression technology is an example of lossless compression. For most types of data, lossless compression techniques can reduce the space needed by only about 50 percent. For greater compression, one must use a *lossy compression* technique. Note, however, that only certain types of data—graphics, audio, and video—can tolerate lossy compression. You must use a lossless compression technique when compressing data and programs.

⇒ See also DATA COMPRESSION; LOSSY COMPRESSION; PKZIP.

lossy compression Refers to data compression techniques in which some amount of data is lost. Lossy compression technologies attempt to eliminate redundant or unnecessary information. Most video compression technologies, such as MPEG, use a lossy technique.

⇒ See also DATA COMPRESSION; DCT; JPEG; LOSSLESS COMPRESSION.

Lotus 1-2-3 A spreadsheet program designed for IBM-compatible personal computers by Lotus Corporation in 1982. Lotus 1-2-3 was the first publicly available program to combine graphics, spreadsheet functions, and data management (three functions, hence the name). Its relative ease of use and flexibility made it an enormous success and contributed to the acceptance of personal computers in business.

⇒ See also SPREADSHEET; VISICALC.

Lotus Notes A groupware application developed by Lotus, now part of IBM. Notes was one of the first applications to support a distributed database of documents that could be accessed by users across a LAN or WAN. Its sophisticated replication features enable users to work with local copies of documents and have their modifications propagated throughout an entire Notes network.

For many years, Notes was the only full-featured groupware solution. With the sudden popularity of the World Wide Web, and intranets in particular, new groupware solutions are emerging. However, the replication model at the heart of Notes is still more robust than any of the Web-based solutions. In addition, IBM has moved quickly to integrate Web support into Notes to stay ahead of the competition.

⇒ See also GROUPWARE; INTRANET; REPLICATION.

lowercase Small letters, as opposed to capital letters. The word *yes*, for example, is in lowercase, while the word *YES* is in uppercase. For many programs, this distinction is very important. Programs that distinguish between lowercase and uppercase are said to be case sensitive.

⇒ See also CASE SENSITIVE; UPPERCASE.

low-level format Hard disks must be formatted twice before they can be used. The first format, called a *low-level* or *physical* format, sets the interleave factor and prepares the disk for a particular type of disk controller. This is generally performed at the factory.

Floppy disks must also undergo a low-level and high-level format, but these two formats are generally performed at the same time. On PCs, for example, the FORMAT command performs both a low-level and high-level format the first time a floppy is formatted.

⇒ See also CONTROLLER; FORMAT; INTERLEAVE.

low-level language A machine language or an assembly language. Low-level languages are closer to the hardware than are high-level programming languages, which are closer to human languages.

⇒ See also ASSEMBLY LANGUAGE; HIGH-LEVEL LANGUAGE; LANGUAGE; MACHINE LANGUAGE; PROGRAMMING LANGUAGE.

low memory In DOS systems, the first 640K of memory. This portion of memory is reserved for applications, device drivers, and memory-resident programs (TSRs).

Low memory is also called *conventional memory*.

⇒ See also EXPANDED MEMORY; EXTENDED MEMORY; HIGH MEMORY; TSR.

low resolution See under RESOLUTION.

LPT A name frequently used by operating systems to identify a printer. Although LPT originally stood for *l(ine) p(rinter) t(erminal)*, it is now used more generally to identify any type of printer.

⇒ See also PRINTER.

LPX A motherboard form factor used in some desktop model PCs. The distinguishing characteristic of LPX is that expansion boards are inserted into a *riser* that contains several slots. The expansion boards are therefore parallel to the motherboard rather than perpendicular to it as in other common form factors, such as AT and ATX. The LPX design allows for smaller cases, but the number of expansion boards is usually limited to two or three.

The LPX form factor is gradually being replaced by NLX.

⇒ See also ATX; BABY AT; FORM FACTOR; MOTHERBOARD; NLX.

LQ See LETTER QUALITY.

LS-120 See under SUPERDISK.

LSI See LARGE-SCALE INTEGRATION.

luggable Same as TRANSPORTABLE.

lurk To eavesdrop on a chat room, newsgroup, or conference. In most on-line areas, lurking is perfectly acceptable behavior and is, in fact, encouraged so that you get the feel of the area before posting your own comments. However, some on-line areas, particularly ones where participants are discussing personal issues, frown on lurking.

⇒ See also CHAT ROOM; CONFERENCE; NEWSGROUP; SURF.

Lycos A popular World Wide Web search engine and directory. Like Excite, Lycos offers a full-text search engine, a directory of Web sites organized by category, and reviews of selected sites.

⇒ See also ALTA VISTA; EXCITE; HOTBOT; INFOSEEK; OPEN TEXT; SEARCH ENGINE; WEBCRAWLER; YAHOO!.

LZW Short for *L(empel-)Z(if-)W(elsh)*, a popular data compression technique developed in 1977 by J. Ziv and A. Lempel, and later refined by T. Welsh. It is the compression algorithm used in the GIF graphics file format, which is one of the standard graphic formats used by CompuServe and the World Wide Web.

The patent for LZW is owned by Unisys, which for many years allowed anyone to use the algorithm for free. Then in 1995, Unisys suddenly decided to charge a license fee. There was an uproar from the CompuServe and Web communities, and Unisys backed down somewhat, though it still enforces the licensing requirement for commercial applications.

⇒ See also DATA COMPRESSION; GIF; PNG; ZIP.

M 1. Abbreviation for *m(ega)* or megabyte. **2.** Same as MUMPS.

⇒ See also K; MEGABYTE.

Mac Short for *Macintosh computer.*

MAC address Short for *Me(dia) A(ccess) C(ontrol)* **address**, a hardware
address that uniquely identifies each node of a network. In IEEE 802 networks, the Data Link Control (DLC) layer of the OSI Reference Model is
divided into two sublayers: the *Logical Link Control (LLC) layer* and the
Media Access Control (MAC) layer. The MAC layer interfaces directly with
the network media. Consequently, each different type of network media
requires a different MAC layer.

On networks that do not conform to the IEEE 802 standards but do
conform to the OSI Reference Model, the node address is called the *Data
Link Control (DLC) address.*

⇒ See also ADDRESS; DLC; NETWORK INTERFACE CARD; NODE.

machine address Same as ABSOLUTE ADDRESS.

⇒ See also ADDRESS.

machine code See under MACHINE LANGUAGE.

machine dependent Refers to a software application that runs only on a
particular type of computer. Programs that run on a variety of different
types of computers are called *machine independent.*

Almost all programs have some machine dependencies (that is, they
run somewhat differently on different types of computers), but the degree
of independence can vary widely. Machine-independent programs give
you more flexibility: If you buy a new type of computer, you can continue using the same software package instead of learning a new one. On
the other hand, machine-dependent programs often take advantage of
special hardware features of a particular computer, making the programs
faster.

Another term for *machine dependent* is *device dependent,* but whereas
machine dependent usually refers to the computer, *device dependent* can
refer to a dependency on any device, like a printer.

⇒ See also APPLICATION.

machine independent Able to run on a variety of computers.

⇒ See also MACHINE DEPENDENT.

machine language The lowest-level programming language (except for computers that utilize programmable microcode). Machine languages are the only languages understood by computers. While easily understood by computers, machine languages are almost impossible for humans to use because they consist entirely of numbers. Programmers, therefore, use either a high-level programming language or an assembly language. An assembly language contains the same instructions as a machine language, but the instructions and variables have names instead of being just numbers.

Programs written in high-level languages are translated into assembly language or machine language by a compiler. Assembly language programs are translated into machine language by a program called an assembler.

Every CPU has its own unique machine language. Programs must be rewritten or recompiled, therefore, to run on different types of computers.

⇒ See also ASSEMBLY LANGUAGE; INSTRUCTION; LOW-LEVEL LANGUAGE; MICROCODE.

machine readable In a form that a computer can accept. Machine-readable data includes files stored on disk or tape, or data that comes from a device connected to a computer. Even typewritten pages can be considered machine readable if you have an optical character recognition (OCR) system.

⇒ See also OPTICAL CHARACTER RECOGNITION.

Macintosh computer A popular model of computer made by Apple Computer. Introduced in 1984, the Macintosh features a graphical user interface (GUI) that utilizes windows, icons, and a mouse to make it relatively easy for novices to use the computer productively. Rather than learning a complex set of commands, you need only point to a selection on a menu and click a mouse button.

Moreover, the GUI is embedded into the operating system. This means that all applications that run on a Macintosh computer have a similar user interface. Once a user has become familiar with one application, he or she can learn new applications relatively easily. The success of the Macintosh GUI led heralded a new age of graphics-based applications and operating systems. The Windows interface copies many features from the Mac.

There are many different Macintosh models, with varying degrees of speed and power. All models are available in many different configurations. All models since 1994 are based on the PowerPC microprocessor.

⇒ See also APPLE COMPUTER; CHRP; GRAPHICAL USER INTERFACE; POWERPC.

Mac OS The official name of the Macintosh operating system. Earlier versions were called *System x.x,* where *x.x* were the version numbers. With its latest release, *Mac OS 8,* however, Apple has dropped the *System* designation.

⇒ See also AppleScript; BeOS; CHRP; Finder; MultiFinder; operating system; System.

macro 1. A symbol, name, or key that represents a list of commands, actions, or keystrokes. Many programs allow you to create macros so that you can enter a single character or word to perform a whole series of actions. Suppose, for example, that you are editing a file and want to indent every third line five spaces. If your word processor supports macros, you can create one that consists of the following keystrokes:

Move Cursor to Beginning of Line
Move Cursor Down 1 Line
Move Cursor Down 1 Line
Move Cursor Down 1 Line
Insert 5 Spaces

Now you can enter the name of the macro, and the word processor will perform all these commands at once.

You can also use macros to enter words or phrases that you use frequently. For example, you could define a macro to contain all the keystrokes necessary to begin a letter—your name, address, and a code that inserts the current date. Then, whenever you write a letter, you just press the macro key to include the letter header.

In a way, macros are like simple programs or batch files. Some applications support sophisticated macros that even allow you to use variables and flow control structures such as loops. **2.** In dBASE programs, a macro is a variable that points to another variable where the data is actually stored. In most other applications, this would be called a *link.*

⇒ See also AppleScript; batch file; command; dBASE; link; loop; macro virus; program.

macro virus A type of computer virus that is encoded as a macro embedded in a document. Many applications, such as Microsoft Word and Excel, support powerful macro languages. These applications allow you to embed a macro in a document, and have the macro execute each time the document is opened.

According to some estimates, 75 percent of all viruses today are macro viruses. Once a macro virus gets onto your machine, it can embed itself in all future documents you create with the application. Antivirus programs can protect your system against most macro viruses, although new ones are always being created that slip by the antivirus filters.

⇒ See also antivirus program; macro; Microsoft Word; virus.

MAE Short for *M(etropolitan) A(rea) E(thernet),* a Network Access Point (NAP) where internet service providers (ISPs) can connect with each other. The original MAE was set up by a company called MFS and is based in Washington, D.C. Later, MFS built another one in Silicon Valley, dubbed *MAE-West*. In addition to the MAEs from MFS, there are many other NAPs. Although MAE refers really only to the NAPs from MFS, the two terms are often used interchangeably.

⇒ See also BACKBONE; ISP; NAP.

Magellan A Web directory published by the McKinley Group, now owned by Excite, Inc. Magellan takes its name from Ferdinand Magellan, a Portuguese explorer who navigated the Strait of Magellan in 1520.

⇒ See also ALTA VISTA; EXCITE; YAHOO!.

magic cookie See under COOKIE.

magnetic disk See under DISK.

magnetic tape See under TAPE.

magneto-optical (MO) drive A type of disk drive that combines magnetic disk technologies with CD-ROM technologies. Like magnetic disks, MO disks can be read and written to. And like floppy disks, they are removable. However, their storage capacity can be more than 200 megabytes, much greater than that of magnetic floppies. In terms of data access speed, they are faster than floppies but not as fast as hard disk drives.

⇒ See also CD-ROM; HARD DISK; MASS STORAGE; PHASE CHANGE DISK.

mail See E-MAIL.

mailbox An area in memory or on a storage device where e-mail is placed. In e-mail systems, each user has a private mailbox. When the user receives e-mail, the mail system automatically puts it in the mailbox.

The mail system allows you to scan mail that is in your mailbox, copy it to a file, delete it, print it, or forward it to another user. If you want to save mail, it is a good idea to copy it to a file, because files tend to be more stable than mailboxes.

⇒ See also E-MAIL.

mail client See E-MAIL CLIENT.

mailing list A list of e-mail addresses identified by a single name, such as *mail-list@sandybay.com*. When an e-mail message is sent to the mailing list name, it is automatically forwarded to all the addresses in the list.

Most e-mail clients support mailing lists, which enables you to broadcast e-mail messages to groups that you define. In addition, there are *mailing list servers* that manage centralized mailing lists for groups of users.

⇒ See also E-MAIL; E-MAIL CLIENT; MAILING LIST SERVER.

mailing list server A server that manages mailing lists for groups of users. Two of the most popular mailing list server systems for the Internet are LISTSERV and Majordomo.

⇒ See also LISTSERV; MAILING LIST; MAJORDOMO.

mail merge A feature supported by many word processors that enables you to generate form letters. To use a mail-merge system, you first store a set of information, like a list of names and addresses, in one file. In another file, you write a letter, substituting special symbols in place of names and addresses (or whatever other information will come from the first file). For example, you might write:

Dear NAME:
Our records show that your address is:
STREET
CITY, STATE ZIP
If this is incorrect,

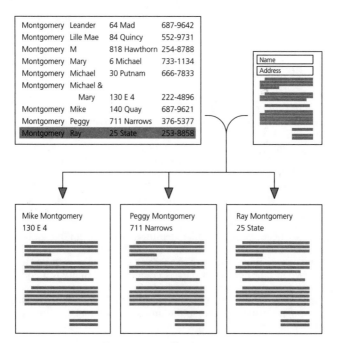

Figure 49: **mail merge**

When you execute the merge command, the word processor automatically generates letters by replacing symbols (NAME, STREET, CITY, STATE, and ZIP) in the second file with the appropriate data from the first file.

The power and flexibility of mail-merge systems vary considerably from one word processor to another. Some word processors support a full set of logical operators that enable you to specify certain conditions under which information should be merged. Also, some merge systems allow you to merge data from several files at once.

Mail merge is sometimes called *print merge*.

⇒ See also MERGE.

mainboard Same as MOTHERBOARD.

mainframe A very large and expensive computer capable of supporting hundreds, or even thousands, of users simultaneously. In the hierarchy that starts with a simple microprocessor (in watches, for example) at the bottom and moves to supercomputers at the top, mainframes are just below supercomputers. In some ways, mainframes are more powerful than supercomputers because they support more simultaneous programs. But supercomputers can execute a single program faster than a mainframe. The distinction between small mainframes and minicomputers is vague, depending really on how the manufacturer wants to market its machines.

Unisys and IBM are the largest manufacturers of mainframes.

⇒ See also COMPUTER; HLLAPI; IBM; LEGACY APPLICATION; MICROPROCESSOR; MINICOMPUTER; MVS; SNA; SUPERCOMPUTER; VSAM.

main memory Refers to physical memory that is internal to the computer. The word *main* is used to distinguish it from the memory available on external mass storage devices such as disk drives. Another term for main memory is *RAM*.

The computer can manipulate only data that is in main memory. Therefore, every program you execute and every file you access must be copied from a storage device into main memory. The amount of main memory on a computer is crucial because it determines how many programs can be executed at one time and how much data can be readily available to a program.

Because computers often have too little main memory to hold all the data they need, computer engineers invented a technique called *swapping*, in which portions of data are copied into main memory as they are needed. Swapping occurs when there is no room in memory for needed data. When one portion of data is copied into memory, an equal-sized portion is copied (swapped) out to make room.

Now, most PCs come with a minimum of 32 megabytes of main memory. You can usually increase the amount of memory by inserting extra memory in the form of chips.

⇒ See also ADDRESS SPACE; CACHE; CHIP; CONVENTIONAL MEMORY; DYNAMIC

RAM; EXPANDED MEMORY; EXPANSION BOARD; EXTENDED MEMORY; L2 CACHE; LOADER; MEGABYTE; MEMORY; RAM; SWAP; VIDEO MEMORY; VIRTUAL MEMORY.

Majordomo A free mailing list server that runs under UNIX. When e-mail is addressed to a Majordomo mailing list, it is automatically broadcast to everyone on the list. The result is similar to a newsgroup or forum, except that the messages are transmitted as e-mail and are therefore available only to individuals on the list.
   Another popular mailing list server is LISTSERV.

⇒ See also LISTSERV; MAILING LIST SERVER.

male connector See under CONNECTOR.

MAN Short for *M(etropolitan) A(rea) N(etwork)*, a data network designed for a town or city. In terms of geographic breadth, MANs are larger than local-area networks (LANs) but smaller than wide-area networks (WANs). MANs are usually characterized by very high-speed connections using fiber optical cable or other digital media.

⇒ See also IEEE 802 STANDARDS; LOCAL-AREA NETWORK; NETWORK; WIDE-AREA NETWORK.

Management Information Base See MIB.

management information system See under MIS.

man page Short for *man(ual) page*, a page of on-line documentation in UNIX systems. Every UNIX command, utility, and library function has an associated man page that you can view by entering the command:
   > man *< command name >*
For example, to find out about the **man** command itself, you would enter:
   > man man
If you don't know the name of the command, but only the general topic, you can use the **apropos** command,
   > apropos *< topic >*
which lists all the man pages related to the specified topic.
   Man pages are stored as *nroff* files.

⇒ See also DOCUMENTATION; HELP.

manual recalculation In spreadsheet programs, a mode in which formulas are not recalculated until you explicitly (manually) run the recalculation function. Compare with *automatic recalculation*, where cells containing formulas are automatically reevaluated whenever necessary.

⇒ See also RECALCULATE.

map *n* **1.** A file showing the structure of a program after it has been compiled. The *map file* lists every variable in the program along with its memory address. This information is useful for debugging purposes. Normally a compiler will not produce a map file unless you explicitly ask for it by specifying the appropriate compiler option. —*v* **2.** To make logical connections between two entities. Because programs cannot translate directly from human concepts to computer numbers, they translate incrementally through a series of layers. Each layer contains the same amount of information as the layer above but in a form somewhat closer to the form that the computer understands. This activity of translating from one layer to another is called *mapping.*

The term *map* is often used to describe characteristics of programming languages. For example, C is an efficient programming language because it *maps well* onto the machine language. What this means is that it is relatively easy to translate from the C language to machine languages. **3.** To copy a set of objects from one place to another while preserving the objects' organization. For example, when loaded, programs on a disk are mapped into memory. Graphics images in memory are mapped onto a display screen.

⇒ See also COMPILE; DEBUG; LOAD; OPTION; PROGRAMMING LANGUAGE.

map file See under MAP.

MAPI Abbreviation of *M(essaging) A(pplication) P(rogramming) I(nterface),* a system built into Microsoft Windows that enables different e-mail applications to work together to distribute mail. As long as both applications are *MAPI-enabled,* they can share mail messages with each other.

⇒ See also API; E-MAIL.

margins In word processing, the strips of white space around the edge of the paper. Most word processors allow you to specify the widths of margins. The wider the left and right margins, the narrower the page. The wider the top and bottom margins, the shorter the page.

If your word processor performs *word wrap,* it will automatically adjust the length of the lines when you change the widths of the margins.

⇒ See also FLUSH; WORD PROCESSING; WORD WRAP.

marquee 1. On Web pages, a scrolling area of text. Starting with Version 2, Microsoft Internet Explorer supports a special < MARQUEE > tag for creating these areas. Netscape Navigator, however, does not support this tag. You can also create marquees with Java applets and Dynamic HTML. **2.** In graphics software, a sizable and movable frame that identifies a selected portion of a bit-mapped image. The marquee frame can be rectangular in shape or, in some cases, irregular. A *lasso* tool, for example, enables you to select all contiguous portions of an image that share the same color.

The marquee frame is usually displayed with a flashing dashed line. In fact, that explains the origin of the name, since the dashed lines look a little like the flashing lights around a theater entrance, which is also called a *marquee.*

⇒ See also PAINT PROGRAM; SCROLL; SELECT; TAG.

mask A filter that selectively includes or excludes certain values. For example, when defining a database field, it is possible to assign a mask that indicates what sort of value the field should hold. Values that do not conform to the mask cannot be entered.

⇒ See also FIELD; SUBNET MASK.

mask pitch In color monitors, the distance between holes in the shadow mask. The mask pitch is essentially the same as the dot pitch, but it's measured on the mask rather than on the screen. The mask pitch is generally about .30 millimeters (mm). The tighter the mask pitch, the sharper the image.

⇒ See also COLOR MONITOR; DOT PITCH; RGB MONITOR.

massively parallel processing See MPP.

mass storage Refers to various techniques and devices for storing large amounts of data. The earliest storage devices were punched paper cards, which were used as early as 1804 to control silk-weaving looms. Modern mass storage devices include all types of disk drives and tape drives. Mass storage is distinct from *memory*, which refers to temporary storage areas within the computer. Unlike main memory, mass storage devices retain data even when the computer is turned off.
   The main types of mass storage are:

floppy disks: Relatively slow and have a small capacity, but they are portable, inexpensive, and universal. A relatively new type of floppy disk called a SuperDisk can store up to 120 MB per disk.
hard disks: Very fast and with more capacity than floppy disks, but also more expensive. Some hard disk systems are portable (removable cartridges), but most are not. The popular Zip disks from Iomega, for example, are removable hard disks.
optical disks: Unlike floppy and hard disks, which use electromagnetism to encode data, optical disk systems use a laser to read and write data. Optical disks have very large storage capacity, but they are not as fast as hard disks. In addition, the inexpensive optical disk drives are read-only. Read/write varieties (CD-R and CD-RW disks) are more expensive.
tapes: Relatively inexpensive and can have very large storage capacities, but they do not permit random access of data.

   Mass storage is measured in kilobytes (1,024 bytes), megabytes (1,024 kilobytes), gigabytes (1,024 megabytes), and terabytes (1,024 gigabytes). Mass storage is sometimes called *auxiliary storage.*

⇒ See also DAT; DISK; DISK DRIVE; ERASABLE OPTICAL DISK; FLOPPY DISK; GIGA-

BYTE; HARD DISK; HSM; KILOBYTE; MAGNETO-OPTICAL (MO) DRIVE; MAIN MEMORY; MEGABYTE; MEMORY; OPTICAL DISK; RANDOM ACCESS; STORAGE DEVICE; TAPE.

Master Boot Record See MBR.

master/slave Refers to an architecture in which one device (the master) controls one or more other devices (the slaves).

⇒ See also DEVICE.

math coprocessor See under COPROCESSOR.

mathematical expression Any expression that represents a numeric value.

⇒ See also EXPRESSION.

matrix 1. A two-dimensional array; that is, an array of rows and columns. **2.** The background area of color display.

⇒ See also ARRAY; BACKGROUND.

MAU 1. Short for *M(edia) A(ccess) U(nit)*, an Ethernet transceiver. **2.** Short for *M(ultistation) A(ccess) U(nit)* (also abbreviated as *MSAU*), a token-ring network device that physically connects network computers in a star topology while retaining the logical ring structure. One of the problems with the token-ring topology is that a single non-operating node can break the ring. The MAU solves this problem because it has the ability to short out non-operating nodes and maintain the ring structure. A MAU is a special type of hub.

⇒ See also HUB; TOKEN-RING NETWORK; TRANSCEIVER.

maximize In graphical user interfaces, to enlarge a window to its maximum size. In Windows 3.x and Macintosh environments, the buttons for minimizing and maximizing windows are located in the top right corner of the window.

⇒ See also GRAPHICAL USER INTERFACE; WINDOW; ZOOM.

Figure 50: **minimize and maximize buttons**

MB Short for *megabyte* (1,000,000 or 1,048,576 bytes depending on the context).

⇒ See also MEGABYTE.

Mbone Short for *M(ulticast Back)* **bone** *on the Internet,* MBone is an extension to the Internet to support *IP multicasting*—two-way transmission of data between multiple sites. The TCP/IP protocol used by the Internet divides messages into packets and sends each packet independently. Packets can travel different routes to their destination which means that they can arrive in any order and with sizable delays between the first and last packets. In addition, each recipient of the data requires that separate packets be sent from the source to the destination. This works fine for static information, such as text and graphics, but it doesn't work well for real-time audio and video.

With Mbone, a single packet can have multiple destinations and isn't split up until the last possible moment. This means that it can pass through several routers before it needs to be divided to reach its final destinations. This leads to much more efficient transmission and also ensures that packets reach multiple destinations at roughly the same time.

The MBone is an experiment to upgrade the Internet to handle live multimedia messages. MBone servers have special Class D IP addresses. As of March 1997, there were more than 3,000 MBone servers on the Internet.

The Mbone was developed by Steve Deering at Xerox PARC and adopted by the Internet Engineering Task Force (IETF) in March 1992.

⇒ See also INTERNET; IP MULTICAST; MULTIMEDIA.

MBps Short for *m(ega)b(ytes) p(er) s(econd),* a measure of data transfer speed. Mass storage devices are generally measured in MBps.

⇒ See also DATA TRANSFER RATE.

Mbps Short for *m(ega)b(its) p(er) s(econd),* a measure of data transfer speed. Networks, for example, are generally measured in Mbps.

⇒ See also DATA TRANSFER RATE; GBPS; MEGABIT.

MBR Short for *M(aster) B(oot) R(ecord),* a small program that is executed when a computer boots up. Typically, the MBR resides on the first sector of the hard disk. The program begins the boot process by looking up the partition table to determine which partition to use for booting. It then transfers program control to the *boot sector* of that partition, which continues the boot process. In DOS and Windows systems, you can create the MBR with the FDISK /MBR command.

An *MBR virus* is a common type of virus that replaces the MBR with its own code. Since the MBR executes every time a computer is started, this type of virus is extremely dangerous. MBR viruses normally enter a system through a floppy disk that is installed in the floppy drive when the computer is started up. Even if the floppy disk is not bootable, it can infect the MBR.

⇒ See also BOOT; BOOTABLE DISKETTE; PARTITION; VIRUS.

Mbyte Short for *megabyte.*

MCA See MICRO CHANNEL ARCHITECTURE.

MCGA Abbreviation of *m(ulti)c(olor)/g(raphics) a(rray)* [or *m(emory) c(ontroller) g(ate) a(rray)*], the graphics system built into some older PCs. It provides graphics capabilities equal to or greater than MDA and CGA, but it is not as powerful as VGA. Like VGA, MCGA uses analog signals.

⇒ See also CGA; EGA; GRAPHICS; MDA; MONITOR; VGA; VIDEO STANDARDS.

MCI 1. Short for *M(edia) C(ontrol) I(nterface),* a high-level API developed by Microsoft and IBM for controlling multimedia devices, such as CD-ROM players and audio controllers. Both OS/2 and Windows support MCI. **2.** A large telecommunications company.

⇒ See also API; MULTIMEDIA.

MDA Abbreviation of *m(onochrome) d(isplay) a(dapter),* an old monochrome video standard for PCs. MDA supports high-resolution monochrome text but does not support graphics or colors. The resolution for text is 720 by 350 pixels.

⇒ See also GRAPHICS; HERCULES GRAPHICS; MONITOR; MONOCHROME; PIXEL; RESOLUTION; VGA; VIDEO STANDARDS.

MDI Short for *M(ultiple) D(ocument) I(nterface),* a Windows API that enables programmers to easily create applications with multiple windows. Each MDI application has a single *main window,* and any number of *child windows.* All child windows are displayed within the main window.
    Although many programmers still use MDI, Microsoft recommends using a newer API called *Single Document Interface (SDI).*

⇒ See also GRAPHICAL USER INTERFACE; WINDOW.

MDRAM Short for *M(ultibank)* **DRAM,** a relatively new memory technology developed by MoSys Inc. MDRAM utilizes small banks of DRAM (32 KB each) in an array, where each bank has its own I/O port that feeds into a common internal bus. Because of this design, data can be read or written to multiple banks simultaneously, which makes it much faster than conventional DRAM.
    Another advantage of MDRAM is that memory can be configured in smaller increments, which can reduce the cost of some components. For example, it's possible to produce MDRAM chips with 2.5 MB, which is what is required by video adapters for 24-bit color at a resolution of 1,024 by 768. With conventional memory architectures, it's necessary to

jump all the way to 4 MB. Currently, MDRAM is used only in some video adapters and graphics accelerators.

⇒ See also DRAM; GRAPHICS ACCELERATOR; MEMORY; SDRAM; VIDEO ADAPTER; VRAM.

mean time between failures See MTBF.

media 1. Objects on which data can be stored. These include hard disks, floppy disks, CD-ROMs, and tapes. **2.** In computer networks, *media* refers to the cables linking workstations together. There are many different types of transmission media, the most popular being twisted-pair wire (normal electrical wire), coaxial cable (the type of cable used for cable television), and fiber optic cable (cables made out of glass). **3.** The form and technology used to communicate information. Multimedia presentations, for example, combine sound, pictures, and videos, all of which are different types of media.

⇒ See also DISK; FIBER OPTICS; LOCAL-AREA NETWORK; MASS STORAGE; MULTIME-DIA; NETWORK.

Media Control Interface See MCI.

meg Short for *megabyte.*

mega In decimal systems, the prefix *mega* means one million, but in binary systems, *mega* stands for 2^{20}, or 1,048,576. One megabyte, therefore, is either 1,000,000 or 1,048,576 bytes (this is equivalent to 1,024K), depending on the context.

⇒ See also GIGA (G); KILOBYTE; MEGABYTE.

megabit 1. When used to describe data storage, 1,024 kilobits. **2.** When used to described data transfer rates, it refers to one million bits. Networks are often measured in megabits per second, abbreviated as *Mbps*.

⇒ See also BIT; GIGABIT; KILOBIT; MBPS.

megabyte 1. When used to describe data storage, 1,048,576 (2^{20}) bytes. *Megabyte* is frequently abbreviated as *M* or *MB*. **2.** When used to describe data transfer rates, as in *MBps*, it refers to one million bytes.

⇒ See also BYTE; GIGABYTE; KILOBYTE.

megaflop See MFLOP.

megaFLOPS See under FLOPS.

megahertz See MHz.

membrane keyboard A type of keyboard in which the keys are covered by a transparent, plastic shell. The keys have very little movement, but are sensitive to pressure applied on them. The advantage of membrane keyboards is that the covering protects the components from dirt, but it is difficult to type accurately and quickly.

⇒ See also KEYBOARD.

memory Internal storage areas in the computer. The term *memory* identifies data storage that comes in the form of chips, and the word *storage* is used for memory that exists on tapes or disks. Moreover, the term *memory* is usually used as a shorthand for *physical memory*, which refers to the actual chips capable of holding data. Some computers also use virtual memory, which expands physical memory onto a hard disk.

Every computer comes with a certain amount of physical memory, usually referred to as *main memory* or *RAM*. You can think of main memory as an array of boxes, each of which can hold a single byte of information. A computer that has 1 megabyte of memory, therefore, can hold about 1 million bytes (or characters) of information.

There are several different types of memory:

RAM (random-access memory): This is the same as main memory. When used by itself, the term *RAM* refers to *read and write* memory; that is, you can both write data into RAM and read data from RAM. This is in contrast to ROM, which permits you only to read data. Most RAM is *volatile*, which means that it requires a steady flow of electricity to maintain its contents. As soon as the power is turned off, whatever data was in RAM is lost.

ROM (read-only memory): Computers almost always contain a small amount of read-only memory that holds instructions for starting up the computer. Unlike RAM, ROM cannot be written to.

PROM (programmable read-only memory): A PROM is a memory chip on which you can store a program. But once the PROM has been used, you cannot wipe it clean and use it to store something else. Like ROMs, PROMs are nonvolatile.

EPROM (erasable programmable read-only memory): An EPROM is a special type of PROM that can be erased by exposing it to ultraviolet light.

EEPROM (electrically erasable programmable read-only memory): An EEPROM is a special type of PROM that can be erased by exposing it to an electrical charge.

⇒ See also ADDRESS; CHIP; EEPROM; EPROM; MAIN MEMORY; MDRAM; MEMORY LEAK; NVRAM; PROM; RAM; RDRAM; ROM; VIRTUAL MEMORY; VRAM.

memory cache See under CACHE.

memory controller gate array See MCGA.

memory dump See under DUMP.

memory effect The property of nickel-cadmium (NiCad) batteries that causes them to lose their capacity for full recharging if they are discharged repeatedly the same amount and then recharged without overcharge before they have fully drained. The term derives from the fact that the battery appears to have a *memory* for the amount of charging it can sustain.

The effect was first noticed in aerospace applications and has been widely misunderstood with regard to the batteries used in portable computer devices. The memory effect is very rare in computer NiCad batteries, especially modern ones.

⇒ See also NiCad BATTERY PACK.

memory leak A bug in a program that prevents it from freeing up memory that it no longer needs. As a result, the program grabs more and more memory until it finally crashes because there is no more memory left.

⇒ See also BUG; MEMORY.

memory management unit See MMU.

memory resident Permanently in memory. Normally, a computer does not have enough memory to hold all the programs you use. When you want to run a program, therefore, the operating system is obliged to free some memory by copying data or programs from main memory to a disk. This process is known as *swapping*.

Certain programs, however, can be marked as being *memory resident*, which means that the operating system is not permitted to swap them out to a storage device; they will always remain in memory.

The programs and data used most frequently are the ones that should be memory resident. This includes central portions of the operating system and special programs, such as calendars and calculators, that you want to be able to access immediately.

Another term for *memory resident* is *RAM resident*. In DOS systems, memory-resident programs are called *pop-up utilities* or *TSRs* (terminate and stay resident).

⇒ See also MEMORY; OPERATING SYSTEM; SWAP; TSR.

menu A list of commands or options from which you can choose. Most applications now have a menu-driven component. You can choose an item from the menu by highlighting it and then pressing the Enter or Return key, or by simply pointing to the item with a mouse and clicking one of the mouse buttons.

The antithesis of a menu-driven program is a command-driven system, in which you must explicitly enter the command you want rather than choose from a list of possible commands. Menu-driven systems are simpler and easier to learn but are generally not as flexible as command-driven systems, which lend themselves more naturally to interaction with programs.

There are several different types of menus:

pop-up menu: A menu that appears temporarily when you click the mouse button on a selection. Once you make a selection from a pop-up menu, the menu usually disappears.

cascading menu: A submenu that opens when you select a choice from another menu.

pull-down menu: Also called a *drop-down menu,* a special type of pop-up menu that appears directly beneath the command you selected.

moving-bar menu: A menu in which options are highlighted by a bar that you can move from one item to another. Most menus are moving-bar menus.

menu bar: A menu arranged horizontally. Each menu option is generally associated with another pull-down menu that appears when you make a selection.

tear-off menu: A pop-up menu that you can move around the screen like a window.

⇒ See also CHOOSE; COMMAND DRIVEN; GRAPHICAL USER INTERFACE; USER INTERFACE.

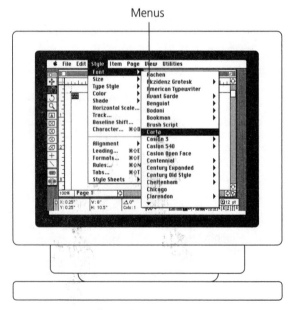

Figure 51: **menus**

menu bar A horizontal menu that appears on top of a window. Usually, each option in a menu bar is associated with a pull-down menu.

⇒ See also MENU; WINDOW.

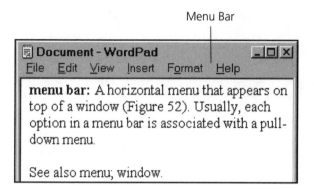

Figure 52: **menu bar**

menu driven Refers to programs whose user interface employs menus. The antithesis of a menu-driven program is a command-driven program.

⇒ See also COMMAND DRIVEN; MENU; USER INTERFACE.

Merced The code name for a new 64-bit microprocessor being developed jointly by Intel and Hewlett-Packard. Although Merced will be able to run software written for the x86 architecture, it will utilize a new architecture, officially known as *Intel Architecture-64 (IA-64)*. IA-64 will employ many cutting-edge microprocessor techniques, including *long instruction words (LIW), instruction predication, branch elimination,* and *speculative loading.*
    Merced chips are expected to be available in late 1999. They will be manufactured with a new 0.18-micron process technology and will contain tens of millions of transistors. The Merced chip is designed primarily for use in servers and workstations.

⇒ See also INTEL MICROPROCESSORS; MICROPROCESSOR; PENTIUM MICROPROCESSOR.

merge 1. To combine two files in such a way that the resulting file has the same organization as the two individual files. For example, if two files contain a list of names in alphabetical order, merging the two files results in one large file with all the names still in alphabetical order. Note that *merge* is different from *append. Append* means to combine two files by adding one of them to the end of the other. **2.** In word processing, *mail merge* refers to generating form letters by combining one file containing a list of names, addresses, and other information with a second file containing the text of the letter.

⇒ See also MAIL MERGE.

message box Same as ALERT BOX.

Messaging Application Programming Interface See MAPI.

meta In computer science, a common prefix that means *about*. So, for example, *metadata* is data that describes other data (*data about data*). A *metalanguage* is a language used to describe other languages. A *metafile* is a file that contains other files. The HTML **META** tag is used to describe the contents of a Web page.

⇒ See also META TAG; METADATA.

metadata Data about data. *Metadata* describes how and when and by whom a particular set of data was collected, and how the data is formatted. Metadata is essential for understanding information stored in data warehouses.

⇒ See also DATA; DATA WAREHOUSE; DATABASE; META.

meta tag A special HTML tag that provides information about a Web page. Unlike normal HTML tags, meta tags do not affect how the page is displayed. Instead, they provide information such as who created the page, how often it is updated, what the page is about, and which keywords represent the page's content. Many search engines use this information when building their indices.

⇒ See also META; SEARCH ENGINE; TAG.

MFC Short for *M(icrosoft) Fo(undation) C(lasses)*, a large library of C++ classes developed by Microsoft. For Windows-based applications written in C++, MFC provides an enormous headstart. One of the hardest parts of developing C++ programs is designing a logical hierarchy of classes. With MFC, this work has already been done.

MFC is bundled with several C++ compilers and is also available as part of the Microsoft Developer's Network (MSDN).

⇒ See also AFC; C++; CLASS; VISUAL C++.

MFLOP Short for *m(ega) f(loating)-point o(perations) p(er) s(econd)*, MFLOPs are a common measure of the speed of computers used to perform *floating-point* calculations. Another common measure of computer speed and power is *MIPS* [m(illion) i(nstructions) p(er) s(econd)], which indicates integer performance.

⇒ See also FLOATING-POINT NUMBER; MIPS.

MFLOPS See under FLOPS.

MFM Abbreviation of *m(odified) f(requency) m(odulation)*, an encoding scheme used by PC floppy disk drives and older hard drives. A competing scheme, known as RLL (run length limited), produces faster data access speeds and can increase a disk's storage capacity by up to 50 percent. RLL is used on most newer hard drives.

⇒ See also CONTROLLER; DISK DRIVE; MODULATE; RLL; ST-506 INTERFACE.

MFP Short for *m(ulti)f(unction) p(eripheral)*, a single device that serves several functions, including printing. Typically, multifunction printers can act as a printer, a scanner, a fax machine, and a photocopier. These devices are becoming a popular option for SOHO users because they're less expensive than buying three or four separate devices. The downsides to combining all these functions in one device are:
   (1) If the device breaks, you may lose all of its functions at the same time.
   (2) You can do only one operation at a time. For example, you can't print a document and receive a fax simultaneously.
   MFPs are also known as *multifunction printers*.

⇒ See also FAX MACHINE; OPTICAL SCANNER; PRINTER; SOHO.

MHz Abbreviation for *m(ega)h(ert)z*. One MHz represents one million cycles per second. The speed of microprocessors, called the clock speed, is measured in megahertz. For example, a microprocessor that runs at 200 MHz executes 200 million cycles per second. Each computer instruction requires a fixed number of cycles, so the clock speed determines how many instructions per second the microprocessor can execute. To a large degree, this controls how powerful the microprocessor is. Another chief factor in determining a microprocessor's power is its data width (that is, how many bits it can manipulate at one time).
   In addition to microprocessors, the speeds of buses and interfaces are also measured in MHz.

⇒ See also BUS; CLOCK SPEED; MICROPROCESSOR; OVERCLOCK.

MIB Short for *M(anagement) I(nformation) B(ase)*, a database of objects that can be monitored by a network management system. Both SNMP and RMON use standardized MIB formats that allows any SNMP and RMON tools to monitor any device defined by a MIB.

⇒ See also NETWORK MANAGEMENT; SNMP.

micro 1. Short for *microprocessor*. **2.** Short for *personal computer*. **3.** A prefix meaning *one millionth*. For example, a *microsecond* is one millionth of a second. **4.** Something very small. For example, a *microfloppy* is a small floppy disk.

⇒ See also MICROFLOPPY DISK.

Micro Channel Architecture (MCA) A bus architecture for older PCs. It is called a bus *architecture* because it defines how peripheral devices and internal components communicate across the computer's expansion bus. Introduced by IBM in 1987, MCA was designed to take the place of the older AT bus, the architecture used on IBM PC-ATs and compatibles. For a variety of reasons, however, the industry never accepted the new architecture.

⇒ See also AT BUS; BUS; LOCAL BUS.

microcode 1. The lowest-level instructions that directly control a microprocessor. A single machine-language instruction typically translates into several microcode instructions.

In modern PC microprocessors, the microcode is hardwired and can't be modified. Some RISC designs go one step further by completely eliminating the microcode level so that machine instructions directly control the processor. At the other end of the spectrum, some mainframe and minicomputer architectures utilize *programmable* microcode. In this case, the microcode is stored in EEPROM, which can be modified. This is called *microprogramming*. **2.** Some people use *microcode* as a synonym for *firmware*.

⇒ See also INSTRUCTION; MACHINE LANGUAGE; MICROPROCESSOR.

Microcom Networking Protocol See MNP.

microcomputer Same as PERSONAL COMPUTER.

microcontroller A highly integrated chip that contains all the components making up a controller. Typically this includes a CPU, RAM, some form of ROM, I/O ports, and timers. Unlike a general-purpose computer, which also includes all of these components, a microcontroller is designed for a very specific task—to control a particular system. As a result, the parts can be simplified and reduced, which cuts down on production costs.

Microcontrollers are sometimes called *embedded microcontrollers,* which just means that they are part of an embedded system—that is, one part of a larger device or system.

⇒ See also CONTROLLER; EMBEDDED SYSTEM; MICROPROCESSOR.

microfloppy disk An old name for the small, 3.5-inch floppy disks. PCs support two types of microfloppies:

- Double-density microfloppies hold 720K (kilobytes).
- High-density microfloppies can store 1.44MB (megabytes).

For Macintosh computers, which have always used microfloppies, there are three sizes:

- **Single-sided** standard microfloppies hold 400K.
- **Double-sided** standard microfloppies hold 800 K.

* **Double-sided, high-density** microfloppies hold 1.44MB.

⇒ See also DENSITY; DISK; FLOPPY DISK.

micro-justification Refers to the use of microspacing to justify text.

⇒ See also MICROSPACING.

microprocessor A silicon chip that contains a CPU. In the world of personal computers, the terms *microprocessor* and *CPU* are used interchangeably. At the heart of all personal computers and most workstations sits a microprocessor. Microprocessors also control the logic of almost all digital devices, from clock radios to fuel-injection systems for automobiles.
   Three basic characteristics differentiate microprocessors:

Instruction set: The set of instructions that the microprocessor can execute.
bandwidth: The number of bits processed in a single instruction.
clock speed: Given in megahertz (MHz), the clock speed determines how many instructions per second the processor can execute.

In both cases, the higher the value, the more powerful the CPU. For example, a 32-bit microprocessor that runs at 50 MHz is more powerful than a 16-bit microprocessor that runs at 25 MHz.
   In addition to bandwidth and clock speed, microprocessors are classified as being either RISC (reduced instruction set computer) or CISC (complex instruction set computer).

⇒ See also ALPHA PROCESSOR; AMD; BANDWIDTH; CHIP; CISC; CLOCK SPEED; CPU; CYRIX; INTEL MICROPROCESSORS; MERCED; MICROCODE; MICROCONTROLLER; MOORE'S LAW; MOTOROLA MICROPROCESSORS; OVERCLOCK; PENTIUM MICROPROCESSOR; PENTIUM PRO; POWERPC; RISC; SUPERSCALAR; VOLTAGE REGULATOR.

microprogramming See under MICROCODE.

Microsoft Founded in 1975 by Paul Allen and Bill Gates, Microsoft Corporation is the largest and most influential company in the personal computer industry. In addition to developing the de facto standard operating systems — DOS and Windows — Microsoft has a strong presence in almost every area of computer software, from programming tools to end-user applications.
   In recent years, Microsoft has broadened its product categories to include different types of media, such as CD-ROMs and its TV news network (together with NBC) called *MSNBC*. In the mid-1990s, Microsoft was caught somewhat by surprise by the sudden explosion of the Internet, but it quickly re-created itself to make the Internet the core element of its product line. Most observers were amazed by how quickly such a large company could adapt.
   Many people have accused Microsoft of monopolistic policies and it has been investigated several times by the U.S. Justice Department. Currently, it is in a fierce battle with Netscape Communications and other

companies for control of the corporate desktop. Microsoft wants Windows to retain its role as the standard operating system for PCs, whereas Netscape and some of its allies, such as Sun Microsystems, would like to see Windows give way to a new model of computing in which PCs run small Java applets locally, with the bulk of the operating system functionality performed by Internet servers.

⇒ See also ActiveX; DOS; Internet Explorer; Microsoft Word; Netscape; ODBC; Visual Basic; Windows; Windows NT; Wintel.

Microsoft Cluster Server See MSCS.

Microsoft Foundation Classes See MFC.

Microsoft Internet Explorer See Internet Explorer.

Microsoft Network See MSN.

Microsoft Windows A family of operating systems for personal computers. Windows dominates the personal computer world, running, by some estimates, on 90 percent of all personal computers. The remaining 10 percent are mostly Macintosh computers. Like the Macintosh operating environment, Windows provides a graphical user interface (GUI), virtual memory management, multitasking, and support for many peripheral devices.

In addition to Windows 3.x, Windows 95, and Windows 98, which run on Intel-based machines, Microsoft also sells Windows NT, a more advanced operating system that runs on a variety of hardware platforms.

⇒ See also DOS; graphical user interface; Intel microprocessors; operating system; OS/2; Windows 95; Windows NT.

Microsoft Word A powerful word processor from Microsoft.

⇒ See also macro virus; Microsoft; word processing.

microspacing The insertion of variable-sized spaces between letters to justify text. Some word processors are capable of microspacing. To print microspaced text, however, you need an ink-jet or laser printer. Most

This text is right- and left-justified and is microspaced. Compare with the following example, which is not microspaced.

```
This text  is right-   and left-jus-
tified  and   is   not  microspaced.
Compare with  the   previous   exam-
ple, which  is microspaced.
```

daisy-wheel printers and inexpensive dot-matrix printers are not capable of microspacing. (See examples below of text with and without microspacing.)

⇒ See also JUSTIFICATION; PRINTER.

middleware Software that connects two otherwise separate applications. For example, there are a number of middleware products that link a database system to a Web server. This allows users to request data from the database using forms displayed on a Web browser, and it enables the Web server to return dynamic Web pages based on the user's requests and profile.

The term *middleware* is used to describe separate products that serve as the glue between two applications. It is, therefore, distinct from import and export features that may be built into one of the applications. Middleware is sometimes called *plumbing* because it connects two sides of an application and passes data between them. In a three-tier architecture, middleware occupies the middle tier. Common middleware categories include:

- TP monitors
- DCE environments
- RPC systems
- Object Request Brokers (ORBs)
- Database access systems
- Message Passing

⇒ See also DCE; EXPORT; IMPORT; INTEGRATED; ORB; RPC; THREE-TIER; TP MONITOR.

MIDI Pronounced *middy*, an acronym for *m(usical) i(nstrument) d(igital) i(nterface)*, a standard adopted by the electronic music industry for controlling devices, such as synthesizers and sound cards, that emit music. At minimum, a MIDI representation of a sound includes values for the note's pitch, length, and volume. It can also include additional characteristics, such as attack and delay time.

The MIDI standard is supported by most synthesizers, so sounds created on one synthesizer can be played and manipulated on another. Computers that have a MIDI interface can record sounds created by a synthesizer and then manipulate the data to produce new sounds. For example, you can change the key of a composition with a single keystroke.

A number of software programs are available for composing and editing music that conforms to the MIDI standard. They offer a variety of functions: for instance, when you play a tune on a keyboard connected to a computer, a music program can translate what you play into a written score.

⇒ See also AMIGA; AU; MACINTOSH COMPUTER; SOUND CARD; WAVE TABLE SYNTHESIS.

MIF Short for *M(anagement) I(nformation) F(ormat)*, a format used to describe a hardware or software component. MIF files are used by DMI to report system configuration information. Although MIF is a system-independent format, it is used primarily by Windows systems. To install a new device in a Windows 95 system, you need the corresponding MIF file.

⇒ See also CONFIGURATION; DMI.

millennium bug See under YEAR 2000 PROBLEM.

million instructions per second See MIPS.

millisecond One thousandth of a second. Access times of hard disk drives are measured in milliseconds, usually abbreviated as *ms*.

⇒ See also ACCESS TIME.

MIME Short for *M(ultipurpose) I(nternet) M(ail) E(xtensions)*, a specification for formatting non-ASCII messages so that they can be sent over the Internet. Many e-mail clients now support MIME, which enables them to send and receive graphics, audio, and video files via the Internet mail system. In addition, MIME supports messages in character sets other than ASCII.

There are many predefined MIME types, such as GIF graphics files and PostScript files. It is also possible to define your own MIME types.

In addition to e-mail applications, Web browsers also support various MIME types. This enables the browser to display or output files that are not in HTML format.

MIME was defined in 1992 by the Internet Engineering Task Force (IETF). A new version, called *S/MIME*, supports encrypted messages.

⇒ See also BINHEX; E-MAIL; S/MIME; UUENCODE.

mini Short for *minicomputer.*

minicomputer A midsized computer. In size and power, minicomputers lie between *workstations* and *mainframes*. In the past decade, the distinction between large minicomputers and small mainframes has blurred, how-ever, as has the distinction between small minicomputers and worksta-tions. But in general, a minicomputer is a multiprocessing system capable of supporting from 4 to about 200 users simultaneously.

⇒ See also AS/400; COMPUTER; LEGACY APPLICATION; MAINFRAME; MULTI-USER; VAX; WORKSTATION.

minifloppy A 5¼-inch floppy disk.

⇒ See also FLOPPY DISK.

minimize In graphical user interfaces, to convert a window into an icon.

⇒ See also GRAPHICAL USER INTERFACE; ICON; WINDOW.

minitower See under TOWER MODEL.

MIPS Acronym for *m(illion) i(nstructions) p(er) s(econd)*. A old measure of a computer's speed and power, MIPS measures roughly the number of machine instructions that a computer can execute in one second. However, different instructions require more or less time than others, and there is no standard method for measuring MIPS. In addition, MIPS refers only to the CPU speed, whereas real applications are generally limited by other factors, such as I/O speed. A machine with a high MIPS rating, therefore, might not run a particular application any faster than a machine with a low MIPS rating. For all these reasons, MIPS ratings are not used often anymore. In fact, some people jokingly claim that MIPS really stands for *M(eaningless) I(ndicator) of P(erformance)*.

Despite these problems, a MIPS rating can give you a general idea of a computer's speed. The IBM PC/XT computer, for example, is rated at ¼ MIPS, while Pentium-based PCs run at over 100 MIPS.

⇒ See also CPU; FLOPS; MFLOP; SPEC.

MIS Short for *m(anagement) i(nformation) s(ystem)* or *m(anagement) i(nformation) s(ervices)*, and pronounced as separate letters, MIS refers to a class of software that provides managers with tools for organizing and evaluating their department. Typically, MIS systems are written in COBOL and run on mainframes or minicomputers.

Within companies and large organizations, the department responsible for computer systems is sometimes called the MIS department. Other names for MIS include *IS (Information Services)* and *IT (Information Technology)*.

⇒ See also COBOL; IS; IT; MAINFRAME; MINICOMPUTER; SYSTEM ADMINISTRATOR; SYSTEM MANAGEMENT.

M-JPEG Short for *Motion-JPEG*.

MMU Short for *m(emory) m(anagement) u(nit)*, the hardware component that manages virtual memory systems. Typically, the MMU is part of the CPU, though in some designs it is a separate chip. The MMU includes a small amount of memory that holds a table matching virtual addresses to physical addresses. This table is called the *Translation Look-aside Buffer (TLB)*. All requests for data are sent to the MMU, which determines whether the data is in RAM or needs to be fetched from the mass storage device. If the data is not in memory, the MMU issues a page fault interrupt.

⇒ See also CPU; PAGE FAULT; VIRTUAL MEMORY.

MMX A set of 57 multimedia instructions built into Intel's newest microprocessors and other x86-compatible microprocessors. MMX-enabled microprocessors can handle many common multimedia operations, such as digital signal processing (DSP), that are normally handled by a separate sound or video card. However, only software especially written to call MMX instructions — so-called *MMX-enabled software* — can take advantage of the MMX instruction set.

The first generation of computers with MMX chips hit the market in January, 1997.

⇒ See also AMD; DSP; INTEL MICROPROCESSORS; K6; MULTIMEDIA.

MMX processor See MMX.

MMX Technology See MMX.

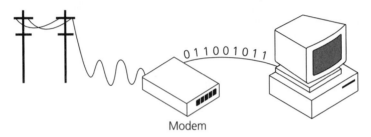

011001011

Modem

Figure 53: **modem**

MNP Abbreviation of *M(icrocom) N(etworking) P(rotocol)*, a communications protocol developed by Microcom, Inc., that is used by many high-speed modems. MNP supports several different classes of communication, each higher class providing additional features. Modems can support one or more classes. Class 4 provides error detection and automatically varies the transmission speed based on the quality of the line. Class 5 provides data compression. Class 6 attempts to detect the highest transmission speed of the modem at the other end of the connection and transmit at that speed.

The most common levels of MNP support are Class 4 and Class 5, frequently called *MNP-4* and *MNP-5*. Using the data compression techniques provided by MNP-5, devices can double normal transmission speeds.

Because MNP is usually built into the modem hardware, it affects all data transmission. In contrast, software protocols, such as *Xmodem* and *Kermit*, affect only file transfer operations.

⇒ See also COMMUNICATIONS PROTOCOL; DATA COMPRESSION; ERROR DETECTION; KERMIT; MODEM; XMODEM.

mode The state or setting of a program or device. For example, when a word processor is in *insert mode*, characters that you type are inserted at the cursor position. In *overstrike mode*, characters typed replace existing characters.

The term *mode* implies a choice—that you can change the setting and put the system in a different mode.

⇒ See also INSERT MODE; OVERSTRIKE.

modeling Generally, the process of representing a real-world object or phenomenon as a set of mathematical equations. More specifically, the term is used to describe the process of representing three-dimensional objects in a computer. All 3-D applications, including CAD/CAM and animation software, perform modeling.

⇒ See also 3-D SOFTWARE; ANIMATION; CAD/CAM; NURBS; RENDER; TEXTURE; VRML.

modem Acronym for *mo(dulator)-dem(odulator)*. A modem is a device or program that enables a computer to transmit data over telephone lines. Computer information is stored digitally, whereas information transmitted over telephone lines is transmitted in the form of analog waves. A modem converts between these two forms.

Fortunately, there is one standard interface for connecting external modems to computers called *RS-232*. Consequently, any external modem can be attached to any computer that has an RS-232 port, which almost all personal computers have. There are also modems that come as an expansion board that you can insert into a vacant expansion slot. These are sometimes called *onboard* or *internal modems*.

While the modem interfaces are standardized, a number of different protocols for formatting data to be transmitted over telephone lines exist. Some, like CCITT V.34, are official standards, while others have been developed by private companies. Most modems have built-in support for the more common protocols—at slow data transmission speeds at least, most modems can communicate with each other. At high transmission speeds, however, the protocols are less standardized.

Aside from the transmission protocols that they support, the following characteristics distinguish one modem from another:

bps: How fast the modem can transmit and receive data. At slow rates, modems are measured in terms of baud rates. The slowest rate is 300 baud (about 25 cps). At higher speeds, modems are measured in terms of bits per second (bps). The fastest modems run at 57,600 bps, although they can achieve even higher data transfer rates by compressing the data. Obviously, the faster the transmission rate, the faster you can send and receive data. Note, however, that you cannot receive data any faster than it is being sent. If, for example, the device sending data to your computer is sending it at 2,400 bps, you must receive it at 2,400 bps. It does not always pay, therefore, to have a very fast modem. In addition, some telephone lines are unable to transmit data reliably at very high rates.

voice/data: Many modems support a switch to change between voice and data modes. In data mode, the modem acts like a regular modem. In voice mode, the modem acts like a regular telephone. Modems that support a voice/data switch are connected to a loudspeaker and microphone for voice communication.

auto-answer: An auto-answer modem enables your computer to receive calls in your absence. This is necessary only if you are offering some type of computer service that people can call in to use.

data compression: Some modems perform data compression, which enables them to send data at faster rates. However, the modem at the receiving end must be able to decompress the data using the same compression technique.

flash memory: Some modems come with *flash memory* rather than conventional ROM, which means that the communications protocols can be easily updated if necessary.

Fax capability: Most modern modems are fax modems, which means that they can send and receive faxes.

To get the most out of a modem, you should have a communications software *package,* a program that simplifies the task of transferring data.

⇒ See also BPS; CCITT; CHANNEL BONDING; COMMUNICATIONS; COMMUNICATIONS PROTOCOL; COMMUNICATIONS SOFTWARE; DATA COMPRESSION; DIAL-UP ACCESS; DSVD; FLASH MEMORY; HAYES COMPATIBLE; HOST-BASED MODEM; K56FLEX; MNP; MODULATE; RJ-11; RS-232C; SOFTWARE MODEM; TELEPHONY; TERMINAL ADAPTER; V.90; WIRELESS MODEM; X2.

moderated newsgroup A newsgroup monitored by an individual or group (the *moderator*) who has the authority to block messages deemed inappropriate. Moderated newsgroups have fewer flames and less spam than unmoderated forums.

⇒ See also FLAME; NEWSGROUP; SPAM.

moderator See under MODERATED NEWSGROUP.

modified frequency modulation See MFM.

modifier key A key on a keyboard that has a meaning only when combined with another key. Examples of modifier keys include the Shift, Control, and Alt keys.

⇒ See also KEYBOARD.

MO drive See MAGNETO-OPTICAL (MO) DRIVE.

Modula-2 A programming language designed by Niklaus Wirth, the author of Pascal. Wirth created Modula-2 in the late 1970s to answer many of the criticisms leveled at Pascal, which he had created ten years earlier. In particular, Modula-2 addresses Pascal's lack of support for separate compilation of modules and multitasking. Although Modula-2 found support in academia, it is not often used for applications.

⇒ See also COMPILE; MULTITASKING; PASCAL; PROGRAMMING LANGUAGE.

modular architecture Refers to the design of any system composed of separate components that can be connected together. The beauty of modular architecture is that you can replace or add any one component (module) without affecting the rest of the system. The opposite of a modular architecture is an *integrated* architecture, in which no clear divisions exist between components.

The term *modular* can apply to both hardware and software. *Modular software design,* for example, refers to a design strategy in which a system is composed of relatively small and autonomous routines that fit together.

⇒ See also ARCHITECTURE; INTEGRATED; MODULE.

modulate To blend data into a carrier signal. At the receiving side, a device *demodulates* the signals by separating the constant carrier signals from the variable data signals. For example, radio uses two types of modulation — amplitude modulation (AM) and frequency modulation (FM) — to mix audio signals with an AM or FM carrier signal. A modem modulates data by converting it to audible tones that can be transmitted on a telephone wire and demodulates received signals to get the data.

⇒ See also ADPCM; MFM; MODEM; PCM; TDM.

modulation See under MODULATE.

module 1. In software, a module is a part of a program. Programs are composed of one or more independently developed modules that are not combined until the program is linked. A single module can contain one or several routines. **2.** In hardware, a module is a self-contained component.

⇒ See also LINK; MODULAR ARCHITECTURE; PROGRAM; ROUTINE.

moiré An undesirable pattern that appears when a graphic image is displayed or printed with an inappropriate resolution. Moiré patterns are difficult to predict because they result from a complex combination of parameters: the size of the image, resolution of the image, resolution of the output device, halftone screen angle, and so on.

If you're planning to print a graphic image (particularly a bit-mapped image) on a high-resolution printer, it's a good idea to print a test page first to see if there are any moiré patterns. If there are, you can sometimes eliminate them by changing the resolution of the printout, resizing the image, or changing the angle of the halftone screen.

⇒ See also HALFTONE.

monitor 1. Another term for display screen. The term *monitor,* however, usually refers to the entire box, whereas *display screen* can mean just the screen. In addition, the term *monitor* often implies graphics capabilities.

There are many ways to classify monitors. The most basic way is in terms of color capabilities, which separate monitors into three classes:

monochrome: Monochrome monitors actually display two colors, one for the background and one for the foreground. The colors can be black and white, green and black, or amber and black.

grayscale: A grayscale monitor is a special type of monochrome monitor capable of displaying different shades of gray.

color: Color monitors can display anywhere from 16 million to more than 1 million different colors. Color monitors are sometimes called *RGB monitors* because they accept three separate signals—red, green, and blue.

After this classification, the most important aspect of a monitor is its screen size. Like televisions, screen sizes are measured in inches, the distance from one corner to the opposite corner diagonally. A typical size for small *VGA* monitors is 14 inches. Monitors that are 16 or more inches diagonally are often called *full-page* monitors. In addition to their size, monitors can be either *portrait* (height greater than width) or *landscape* (width greater than height). Larger landscape monitors can display two full pages, side by side. The screen size is sometimes misleading because, with *CRTs*, there is always an area around the edge of the screen that can't be used. Therefore, monitor manufacturers must now also state the viewable area—that is, the area of screen that is actually used.

The resolution of a monitor indicates how densely packed the pixels are. In general, the more pixels (often expressed in dots per inch), the sharper the image. Most modern monitors can display 1024 by 768 pixels, the SVGA standard. Some high-end models can display 1280 by 1024, or even 1600 by 1200.

Another common way of classifying monitors is in terms of the type of signal they accept: analog or digital. Nearly all modern monitors accept analog signals, which is required by the VGA, SVGA, 8514/A, and other high-resolution color standards.

A few monitors are *fixed frequency*, which means that they accept input at only one frequency. Most monitors, however, are *multiscanning*, which means that they automatically adjust themselves to the frequency of the signals being sent to it. This means that they can display images at different resolutions, depending on the data being sent to them by the video adapters.

Other factors that determine a monitor's quality include the following:

bandwidth: The range of signal frequencies the monitor can handle. This determines how much data it can process and therefore how fast it can refresh at higher resolutions.

refresh rate: How many times per second the screen is refreshed (redrawn). To avoid flickering, the refresh rate should be at least 72 Hz.

interlaced or noninterlaced: Interlacing is a technique that enables a monitor to have more resolution, but it reduces the monitor's reaction speed.

dot pitch: The amount of space between each pixel. The smaller the dot pitch, the sharper the image.

convergence: The clarity and sharpness of each pixel.

2. A program that *observes* a computer. For example, some monitor programs report how often another program accesses a disk drive or how much CPU time it uses.

⇒ See also ANALOG MONITOR; BACKGROUND; BANDWIDTH; COLOR MONITOR; CONVERGENCE; DDC; DIGITAL MONITOR; DISPLAY SCREEN; DLP; DOT PITCH; DPI; ELF EMISSION; FIXED-FREQUENCY MONITOR; FLAT TECHNOLOGY MONITOR; GRAY SCALING; INTERLACING; LCD MONITOR; MONOCHROME; MULTISCANNING MONITOR; NEC; PINCUSHION DISTORTION; PIXEL; RAMDAC; RASTER; REFRESH.

monochrome One color. Monitors, for example, can be monochrome, grayscale, or color. Monochrome monitors actually use two colors, one for the display image (the foreground) and one for the background. Graphic images can also be monochrome, grayscale, or color.

⇒ See also BACKGROUND; FOREGROUND; GRAPHICS; GRAYSCALING; MONITOR.

monochrome display adapter See MDA.

monospacing Refers to fonts in which each character has the same width. The opposite of monospacing is *proportional spacing*, in which different characters have different widths. For example, in a proportionally spaced font, the letter *o* is wider than the letter *i*. Proportionally spaced fonts look more professional, but monospaced fonts are often superior for tabular data because the uniform width of each character makes alignment of columns easier.

Most printed matter, including this book, uses proportional spacing.

⇒ See also COURIER FONT; CPI; FONT; PROPORTIONAL SPACING.

MOO Short for *M(ud), O(bject) O(riented)*, a specific implementation of a MUD system developed by Stephen White. MOO is in the public domain and can be freely downloaded and executed.

⇒ See also MUD; OBJECT ORIENTED.

Moore's Law The observation made in 1965 by Gordon Moore, cofounder of Intel, that the number of transistors per square inch on integrated circuits had doubled every year since the integrated circuit was invented. Moore predicted that this trend would continue for the foreseeable future. In subsequent years, the pace slowed down a bit, but data density has doubled approximately every 18 months, and this is the current definition of Moore's Law, which Moore himself has blessed. Most experts, including Moore himself, expect Moore's Law to hold for at least another two decades.

⇒ See also CHIP; INTEGRATED CIRCUIT; MICROPROCESSOR; NANOTECHNOLOGY; TRANSISTOR.

morphing Short for *metamorphosing, morphing* refers to an animation technique in which one image is gradually turned into another. Many advanced animation programs support some type of morphing feature.

⇒ See also ANIMATION.

Mosaic An application that simplifies accessing documents on the World Wide Web. Originally produced by the National Center for Supercomputing Applications (NCSA), Mosaic has always been distributed as freeware. In 1994, however, the NCSA turned over commercial development of the program to a company called Spyglass. There are now several varieties of Mosaic, some free and some for sale.

⇒ See also BROWSER; INTERNET; WORLD WIDE WEB.

motherboard The main circuit board of a microcomputer. The motherboard contains the connectors for attaching additional boards. Typically, the motherboard contains the CPU, BIOS, memory, mass storage interfaces, serial and parallel ports, expansion slots, and all the controllers required to control standard peripheral devices, such as the display screen, keyboard, and disk drive. Collectively, all these chips that reside on the motherboard are known as the motherboard's chipset.

On most PCs, it is possible to add memory chips directly to the motherboard. You may also be able to upgrade to a faster CPU by replacing the CPU chip. To add additional core features, you may need to replace the motherboard entirely.

⇒ See also ADD-ON; ATX; BACKPLANE; BIOS; BUS; CONTROLLER; CPU; DAUGHTERCARD; EXPANSION BOARD; EXPANSION SLOT; HEAT SINK; LPX; MICROPROCESSOR; NLX; OVERCLOCK; PORT; PRINTED CIRCUIT BOARD; VOLTAGE REGULATOR.

motion-JPEG JPEG stands for the *J(oint) P(hotographic) E(xperts) G(roup)* standard, a standard for storing and compressing digital images. Motion-JPEG extends this standard by supporting videos. In motion-JPEG, each frame in the video is stored with the JPEG format.

⇒ See also JPEG; MPEG.

Motorola microprocessors Motorola Inc. is one of the leading manufacturers of microprocessors. Until the early 1990s, Motorola microprocessors were used in all Apple Macintosh computers and in many workstations. Following the development of its 68040 chip in 1989, however, Motorola changed its focus from the 680x0 line of CISC chips to RISC technologies. In 1993, Motorola joined Apple Computer and IBM in designing a new RISC architecture that would form the basis of the next generation of personal computers. This effort culminated in the introduction of the PowerPC architecture in 1994.

There are five main chips in the 680x0 family: the 6800, 68020, 68030, 68040, and 68060. Many people refer to them by their last three digits. For example, the "oh-forty" refers to the 68040 chip.

⇒ See also CISC; MICROPROCESSOR; POWERPC; RISC.

mount 1. To make a mass storage device available. In Macintosh environments, for example, inserting a floppy disk into the drive is called *mounting* the floppy. **2.** To install a device, such as a disk drive or expansion board.

⇒ See also MASS STORAGE.

mouse A device that controls the movement of the cursor or pointer on a display screen. A mouse is a small object you can roll along a hard, flat surface. Its name is derived from its shape, which looks a bit like a mouse, its connecting wire that one can imagine to be the mouse's tail, and the fact that one must make it scurry along a surface. As you move the mouse, the pointer on the display screen moves in the same direction. Mice contain at least one button and sometimes as many as three, which have different functions depending on what program is running. Some newer mice also include a *scroll wheel* for scrolling through long documents.

Invented by Douglas Engelbart of Stanford Research Center in 1963 and pioneered by Xerox in the 1970s, the mouse is one of the great breakthroughs in computer ergonomics because it frees the user to a large extent from using the keyboard. In particular, the mouse is important for graphical user interfaces because you can simply point to options and objects and click a mouse button. Such applications are often called *point-and-click* programs. The mouse is also useful for graphics programs that allow you to draw pictures by using the mouse like a pen, pencil, or paintbrush.

There are three basic types of mice:

mechanical: Has a rubber or metal ball on its underside that can roll in all directions. Mechanical sensors within the mouse detect the direction the ball is rolling and move the screen pointer accordingly.
optomechanical: Same as a mechanical mouse, but uses optical sensors to detect motion of the ball.
optical: Uses a laser to detect the mouse's movement. You must move the mouse along a special mat with a grid so that the optical mechanism has a frame of reference. Optical mice have no mechanical moving parts. They respond more quickly and precisely than mechanical and optomechanical mice, but they are also more expensive.

Mice connect to PCs in one of three ways:

Serial mice connect directly to an RS-232C serial port or a PS/2 port. This is the simplest type of connection.
PS/2 mice connect to a PS/2 port.
Cordless mice aren't physically connected at all. Instead they rely on infrared or radio waves to communicate with the computer. Cordless mice are more expensive than both serial and bus mice, but they do eliminate the cord, which can sometimes get in the way.

Mice connect to Macintosh computers through the ADB (Apple Desktop bus) port.

⇒ See also ADB; BUS; BUS MOUSE; CLICK; CURSOR; DOUBLE CLICK; ERGONOMICS; EXPANSION BOARD; GRAPHICAL USER INTERFACE; MENU DRIVEN; POINTER; SERIAL PORT; TRACKBALL.

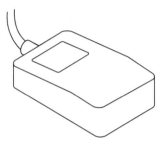

Figure 54: **mouse**

mousepad A pad over which you can move a mouse. Mousepads provide more traction than smooth surfaces such as glass and wood, so they make it easier to move a mouse accurately.

For mechanical mice, mousepads are optional. Optical mice, however, require special mousepads that have grids drawn on them.

⇒ See also MOUSE.

mouse pointer See under POINTER.

mouse port Same as PS/2 PORT.

moving-bar menu A common type of menu in which options are selected by moving a highlighted bar over them. You can move the bar with a mouse or with arrow keys, or sometimes with the Tab key.

⇒ See also MENU.

Moving Picture Experts Group See MPEG.

Mozilla The original name for Netscape's browser, now called Navigator. Some people claim that the term is a contraction of *Mo(saic God)zilla* (e.g., Mosaic killer), since Mosaic was the number-one Web browser at the time Netscape began developing its product. The term *Mozilla* is still used by many Web developers and appears in server log files that identify the browsers being used.

In 1998, Netscape decided to make the source code for Navigator freely available to the public. The Netscape group responsible for releasing the code is called *mozilla.org*, and its Web site is www.mozzila.org.

MP3 Short for *MP(EG) Layer* **3**, a type of audio data compression that can reduce digital sound files by a 12:1 ratio with virtually no loss in quality.

⇒ See also DATA COMPRESSION; DIGITAL AUDIO; MPEG.

MPC Abbreviation of *M(ultimedia) P(ersonal) C(omputer)*, a software and hardware standard developed by a consortium of computer firms led by Microsoft. There are three MPC standards, called *MPC*, *MPC2*, and MPC3, respectively. Each specifies a minimum hardware configuration for running multimedia software.

To run MPC-2 software, you need at least an Intel 486SX microprocessor with a clock speed of 25 MHz, 4 MB (megabytes) of RAM, a VGA display, and a double-speed CD-ROM drive.

MPC3 specifies the following minimum configuration:

- 8 MB RAM
- 540 MB disk drive
- 75 MHz Pentium processor
- 4X CD-Rom
- MPEG support

⇒ See also CD-ROM; CD-ROM PLAYER; INTEL MICROPROCESSORS; MULTIMEDIA.

MPEG Short for *M(oving) P(icture) E(xperts) G(roup)*, and pronounced *m-peg*, a working group of ISO. The term also refers to the family of digital video compression standards and file formats developed by the group. MPEG generally produces better-quality video than competing formats, such as Video for Windows, Indeo, and QuickTime. MPEG files can be decoded by special hardware or by software.

MPEG achieves high compression rates by storing only the changes from one frame to another, instead of each entire frame. The video information is then encoded using a technique called *DCT*. MPEG uses a type of *lossy compression,* because some data is removed. But the diminishment of data is generally imperceptible to the human eye.

There are two major MPEG standards: MPEG-1 and MPEG-2. The most common implementations of the MPEG-1 standard provide a video resolution of 352 by 240 at 30 frames per second (fps). This produces video quality slightly below the quality of conventional VCR videos.

A newer standard, *MPEG-2*, offers resolutions of 720 by 480 and 1280 by 720 at 60 fps, with full CD-quality audio. This is sufficient for all the major TV standards, including NTSC, and even HDTV. MPEG-2 is used by DVD-ROMs. MPEG-2 can compress a two-hour video into a few gigabytes. While decompressing an MPEG-2 data stream requires only modest computing power, encoding video in MPEG-2 format requires significantly more processing power.

The ISO standards body is currently working on a new version of MPEG called *MPEG-4* (there is no MPEG-3). MPEG-4 will be based on the QuickTime file format.

⇒ See also CODEC; DATA COMPRESSION; DVD; DVD-ROM; DVI; FPS; INDEO; JPEG; MP3; QUICKTIME; VIDEO EDITING.

MPEG-1 See under MPEG.

MPEG-2 See under MPEG.

MPP Short for *m(assively) p(arallel) p(rocessing)*, a type of computing that uses many separate CPUs running in parallel to execute a single program. MPP is similar to symmetric processing (SMP), with the main difference being that in SMP systems all the CPUs share the same memory, whereas in MPP systems, each CPU has its own memory. MPP systems are therefore more difficult to program because the application must be divided in such a way that all the executing segments can communicate with one another. On the other hand, MPP systems don't suffer from the bottleneck problems inherent in SMP systems when all the CPUs attempt to access the same memory at once.

⇒ See also NUMA; SMP.

ms Short for *m(illi)s(econd)*, one thousandth of a second. Access times of mass storage devices are often measured in milliseconds.

⇒ See also MASS STORAGE.

MSAU See MAU.

MSCDEX Short for *M(icro)s(oft) CD-ROM Ex(tension)*, a driver that enables DOS and Windows 3.x systems to recognize and control CD-ROM players. The driver is located in a file called *MSCDEX.EXE*. Windows 95 and 98 replace MSCDEX with a 32-bit, dynamically loadable driver called CDFS.

⇒ See also CD-ROM PLAYER; CDFS.

MSCS Short for *M(icro)s(oft) C(luster) S(erver)*, a clustering technology built into Windows NT 4.0 and later versions. MSCS supports clustering of two NT servers to provide a single fault-tolerant server.
    During its development stage, MSCS was code-named *Wolfpack*.

⇒ See also CLUSTERING; WINDOWS NT.

MS-DOS Pronounced *em-ess-doss*. See under DOS.

MSN Short for *M(icro)s(oft) N(etwork)*, Microsoft's online service. Like competing services such as America Online, MSN offers e-mail, topic-related forums, and full access to the World Wide Web.

⇒ See also AMERICA ONLINE; COMPUSERVE INFORMATION SERVICE; ONLINE SERVICE.

MS-TNEF See TNEF.

MS-Windows Pronounced *emm-ess-windows*. See MICROSOFT WINDOWS.

MS-Word Short for *Microsoft Word*.

MTBF Short for *m(ean) t(ime) b(etween) f(ailures)*. MTBF ratings are measured in hours and indicate the sturdiness of hard disk drives and printers.

Typical disk drives for personal computers have MTBF ratings of about 300,000 hours. This means that of all the drives tested, one failure occurred every 300,000 hours of testing. However, this is rather meaningless since most disk drives are tested for only a few hours, so it would be unlikely for a failure to occur during this short testing period. A more useful gauge of a device's lifetime is how long a warranty the manufacturer offers.

⇒ See also DISK DRIVE; SMART.

MTU Short for *M(aximum) T(ransmission) U(nit)*, the largest physical packet size, measured in bytes, that a network can transmit. Any messages larger than the MTU are divided into smaller packets before being sent.

Every network has a different MTU, which is set by the network administrator. On Windows 95, you can also set the MTU of your machine. This defines the maximum size of the packets sent from your computer onto the network. Ideally, you want the MTU to be the same as the smallest MTU of all the networks between your machine and a message's final destination. Otherwise, if your messages are larger than one of the intervening MTUs, they will get broken up (fragmented), which slows down transmission speeds.

Trial and error is the only sure way of finding the optimal MTU, but there are some guidelines that can help. For example, the MTU of many PPP connections is 576, so if you connect to the Internet via PPP, you might want to set your machine's MTU to 576 too. Most Ethernet networks, on the other hand, have an MTU of 1500, which is the default MTU setting for Windows 95.

⇒ See also PACKET; WINSOCK.

MUCK Short for *M(ulti)-U(ser) C(hat) K(ingdom)*, a text-based MUD system. MUCK is similar to MUSH, though it uses different software.

⇒ See also MUD; MUSH.

MUD Short for *M(ulti)-U(ser) D(ungeon)* [or *M(ulti)-U(ser) D(imension)*], a cyberspace where users can take on an identity in the form of an avatar and interact with one another. Originally, MUDs tended to be adventure games played within enormous old castles with hidden rooms, trapdoors, exotic beasts, and magical items. Nowadays, the term is used more generically to refer to any cyberspace. MUDs are also known as *3-D worlds* and *chat worlds*.

⇒ See also AVATAR; CHAT ROOM; CYBERSPACE; MOO; MUCK; MUSH; VIRTUAL REALITY.

multicast To transmit a message to a select group of recipients. A simple example of multicasting is sending an e-mail message to a mailing list. Teleconferencing and videoconferencing also use multicasting but require more robust protocols and networks.

Standards are being developed to support multicasting over a TCP/IP network such as the Internet. These standards, IP Multicast and Mbone, will allow users to join multicast groups easily.

Note that *multicasting* refers to sending a message to a select group whereas *broadcasting* refers to sending a message to everyone connected to a network.

The terms *multicast* and *narrowcast* are often used interchangeably, although *narrowcast* usually refers to the business model whereas *multicast* refers to the actual technology used to transmit the data.

⇒ See also BROADCAST; IP MULTICAST; RTSP; TELECONFERENCE.

Multicast Backbone (MBone) See MBONE.

multicolor/graphics array See MCGA.

multidimensional DBMS A database management system (DBMS) organized around groups of records that share a common field value. Multidimensional databases are often generated from relational databases. Whereas relational databases make it easy to work with individual records, multidimensional databases are designed for analyzing large groups of records.

The term *OLAP (On-Line Analytical Processing)* has become almost synonymous with multidimensional databases, whereas *OLTP (On-Line Transaction Processing)* generally refers to relational DBMSs.

⇒ See also DATABASE MANAGEMENT SYSTEM; OLAP; RDBMS.

MultiFinder The multitasking version of *Finder* for Apple Macintosh computers. This is the part of the operating system responsible for managing the desktop—locating documents and folders and handling the Clipboard and Scrapbook. For System 6, and earlier versions of the Mac OS, Multi-Finder was optional. Since System 7, MultiFinder has replaced the older Finder.

⇒ See also CLIPBOARD; DESKTOP; FINDER; MAC OS; MACINTOSH COMPUTER; MULTITASKING; OPERATING SYSTEM.

multifrequency monitor A type of video monitor capable of accepting signals at more than one frequency range. This enables the monitor to support several different resolutions. Multifrequency monitors differ somewhat from *multiscanning monitors*. Multiscanning monitors can support video signals at any frequency level within their range, whereas multifrequency monitors support only a select number of frequency levels. However, because almost all video signals conform to one of a handful of video standards, the greater potential of multiscanning monitors is generally not utilized.

⇒ See also MONITOR; MULTISCANNING MONITOR; VIDEO ADAPTER.

multifunction peripheral See MFP.

multifunction printer Same as MULTIFUNCTION PERIPHERAL (MFP).

multilevel printer Same as CONTONE PRINTER.

multimedia The use of computers to present text, graphics, video, animation, and sound in an integrated way. Long touted as the future revolution in computing, multimedia applications were, until the mid-1990s, uncommon due to the expensive hardware required. With increases in performance and decreases in price, however, multimedia is now commonplace. Nearly all PCs are capable of displaying video, though the resolution available depends on the power of the computer's video adapter and CPU.

Because of the storage demands of multimedia applications, the most effective media are CD-ROMs.

⇒ See also 3DO; ACTIVEMOVIE; ANIMATION; AUTHORING TOOL; CD-ROM; HYPERMEDIA; HYPERTEXT; MBONE; MEDIA; MMX; MPC; SHOCKWAVE; STREAMING; WAV.

multimedia kit A package of hardware and software that adds multimedia capabilities to a computer. Typically a multimedia kit includes a CD-ROM or DVD player, a sound card, speakers, and a bundle of CD-ROMs.

⇒ See also CD-ROM; MULTIMEDIA.

Multimedia Personal Computer See MPC.

Multiple Document Interface See MDI.

multiplex To combine multiple signals (analog or digital) for transmission over a single line or medium. A common type of multiplexing combines several low-speed signals for transmission over a single high-speed connection. The following are examples of different multiplexing methods:

Frequency Division Multiplexing (FDM): each signal is assigned a different frequency
Time Division Multiplexing (TDM): each signal is assigned a fixed time slot in a fixed rotation
Statistical Time Division Multiplexing (STDM): time slots are assigned to signals dynamically to make better use of bandwidth
Wavelength Division Multiplexing (WDM): each signal is assigned a

particular wavelength; used on optical fiber.

⇒ See also CARRIER; CDMA; FDM; MULTIPLEXOR; TDM; WDM.

multiplexor A communications device that multiplexes (combines) several signals for transmission over a single medium. A *demultiplexor* completes the process by separating multiplexed signals from a transmission line. Frequently a multiplexor and demultiplexor are combined into a single device capable of processing both outgoing and incoming signals.

A multiplexor is sometimes called a *mux.*

⇒ See also CONCENTRATOR; MULTIPLEX.

multiprocessing 1. Refers to a computer system's ability to support more than one process (program) at the same time. Multiprocessing operating systems enable several programs to run concurrently. UNIX is one of the most widely used multiprocessing systems, but there are many others, including OS/2 for high-end PCs. Multiprocessing systems are much more complicated than single-process systems because the operating system must allocate resources to competing processes in a reasonable manner. **2.** Refers to the utilization of multiple CPUs in a single computer system. This is also called *parallel processing.*

⇒ See also CPU; DISTRIBUTED PROCESSING; INTERPROCESS COMMUNICATION (IPC); MULTITASKING; OS/2; PARALLEL PROCESSING; PROCESS; SMP; UNIX.

Multipurpose Internet Mail Extensions (MIME) See MIME.

MultiRead A new specification for CD-ROM and compact disc players that enables them to read discs created by CD-RW drives. The specification was developed jointly by Philips Electronics and Hewlett-Packard and has been approved by the Optical Storage Technology Association (OSTA).

⇒ See also CD-ROM PLAYER; CD-RW DISK; COMPACT DISC.

multiscanning monitor A type of monitor that automatically adjusts to the signal frequency of the video display board to which it is connected. Consequently, multiscanning monitors can display images based on almost any graphics display system, including MDA, Hercules, EGA, VGA, and SVGA.

In contrast, fixed-frequency monitors respond to only one, or a few, frequencies, so they can connect to a limited number of video display boards. However, fixed-frequency monitors are less expensive than multiscanning monitors and sometimes produce sharper images.

Multiscanning monitors are also called *multisync, multifrequency*, and *variable-frequency* monitors. Increasingly, however, the term *multifrequency monitor* is reserved for monitors that support a fixed number of video frequencies. In contrast, multiscanning monitors scan the incoming signals and set themselves to whatever frequency range they are receiving. In practice, there is little difference between the two types of monitors because most video signals conform to one of a handful of video standards.

⇒ See also ANALOG MONITOR; DIGITAL MONITOR; FIXED-FREQUENCY MONITOR; MULTIFREQUENCY MONITOR; VIDEO ADAPTER; VIDEO STANDARDS.

Multi-station Access Unit See MAU.

Multistation Access Unit See MAU.

multisync monitor Same as MULTISCANNING MONITOR.

multitasking The ability to execute more than one *task* at the same time, a task being a program. The terms *multitasking* and *multiprocessing* are often used interchangeably, although multiprocessing sometimes implies that more than one CPU is involved.

In multitasking, only one CPU is involved, but it switches from one program to another so quickly that it gives the appearance of executing all of the programs at the same time.

There are two basic types of multitasking: *preemptive* and *cooperative.* In preemptive multitasking, the operating system parcels out CPU *time slices* to each program. In cooperative multitasking, each program can control the CPU for as long as it needs it. If a program is not using the CPU, however, it can allow another program to use it temporarily. OS/2, Windows 95 and 98, Windows NT, the Amiga operating system, and UNIX use preemptive multitasking, whereas Microsoft Windows 3.x and the MultiFinder (for Macintosh computers) use cooperative multitasking.

⇒ See also COOPERATIVE MULTITASKING; MULTIFINDER; MULTIPROCESSING; OPERATING SYSTEM; OS/2; UNIX.

multithreading The ability of an operating system to execute different parts of a program, called *threads,* simultaneously. The programmer must carefully design the program in such a way that all the threads can run at the same time without interfering with one another.

⇒ See also MULTITASKING; SMP.

multi-user Refers to computer systems that support two or more simultaneous users. All mainframes and minicomputers are multi-user systems, but most personal computers and workstations are not. Another term for *multi-user* is *time sharing.*

⇒ See also MAINFRAME; MINICOMPUTER.

MUMPS Short for *M(assachusetts) General Hospital U(tility) M(ulti) P(rogramming) S(ystem),* a general-purpose programming language developed in the late 1960s. MUMPS is similar to other procedural languages developed in this period, such as BASIC, FORTRAN, and C. A MUMPS standard was approved by ANSI in 1977.

Although MUMPS has never achieved the popularity level of other languages such as C and BASIC, there is still an active community of

MUMPS developers. Since about 1993, there has been a growing trend to change the name from MUMPS to *M* or *M-Technology*.

⇒ See also BASIC; FORTRAN.

MUSH Short for *M(ulti)-U(ser) S(hared) H(allucination)*, a text-based MUD system. There are many MUSH worlds that have been evolving for years.

⇒ See also MUCK; MUD.

musical instrument digital interface See MIDI.

MuTeX A package of macros for the TeX typesetting system that supports musical notation. MuTeX was written by Andrea Steinbach and Angelika Schofer, as a master's thesis at Rheinische Friedrich-Wilhelms University.

⇒ See also LaTeX; MACRO; TeX.

mux Short for *mu(ltiple)x(or)*.

MVS Short for *M(ultiple) V(irtual) S(torage)*, the operating system for older IBM mainframes. MVS was first introduced in 1974 and continues to be used, though it has been largely superseded by IBM's newer operating system, *OS/390*.

⇒ See also MAINFRAME; OPERATING SYSTEM; VSAM.

name A sequence of one or more characters that uniquely identifies a file, variable, account, or other entity. Computer systems impose various rules about naming objects. For example, there is often a limit to the number of characters you can use, and not all characters are allowed.

Names are sometimes called *identifiers*.

⇒ See also ALIAS; DOMAIN NAME; EXTENSION; FILENAME; IDENTIFIER; LABEL; LITERAL; VARIABLE.

Named Pipes An interprocess control (IPC) protocol for exchanging information between two applications, possibly running on different computers in a network. Named Pipes are supported by a number of network operating systems (NOSs), including Netware and LAN Manager.

⇒ See also INTERPROCESS COMMUNICATION (IPC).

name server A program that translates names from one form into another. For example, the Internet relies on domain name servers (DNSs) that translate domain names into IP addresses.

⇒ See also DNS; SERVER.

nanosecond A billionth of a second. Many computer operations, such as the speed of memory chips, are measured in nanoseconds. *Nanosecond* is often abbreviated as *ns*.

⇒ See also ACCESS TIME.

nanotechnology A field of science whose goal is to control individual atoms and molecules to create computer chips and other devices that are thousands of times smaller than current technologies permit. Current manufacturing processes use lithography to imprint circuits on semiconductor materials. While lithography has improved dramatically over the last two decades—to the point where some manufacturing plants can produce circuits smaller than one micron (1,000 nanometers)—it still deals with aggregates of millions of atoms. It is widely believed that lithography is quickly approaching its physical limits. To continue reducing the size of semiconductors, new technologies that juggle individual atoms will be necessary. This is the realm of nanotechnology.

Although research in this field dates back to Richard P. Feynman's classic talk in 1959, the term nanotechnology was first coined by K. Eric Drexler in 1986 in the book *Engines of Creation*.

In the popular press, the term nanotechnology is sometimes used to refer to any sub-micron process, including lithography. Because of this, many scientists are beginning to use the term *molecular nanotechnology* when talking about true nanotechnology at the molecular level.

⇒ See also INTEGRATED CIRCUIT; MOORE'S LAW.

NAP Short for *N(etwork) A(ccess) P(oint)*, a public network exchange facility where internet service providers (ISPs) can connect with one another in *peering* arrangements. The NAPs are a key component of the Internet backbone because the connections within them determine how traffic is routed. They are also the points of most Internet congestion.

⇒ See also BACKBONE; INTERNET; ISP; MAE; NSP.

NAT Short for *N(etwork) A(ddress) T(ranslation)*, an Internet standard that enables a local-area network (LAN) to use one set of IP addresses for internal traffic and a second set of addresses for external traffic. A *NAT box* located where the LAN meets the Internet makes all necessary IP address translations.

NAT serves three main purposes:

• Provides a type of firewall by hiding internal IP addresses
• Enables a company to use more internal IP addresses. Because they're used internally only, there's no possibility of conflict with IP addresses used by other companies and organizations.
• Allows a company to combine multiple ISDN connections into a single Internet connection.

NAT is an official IETF standard, specified in RFC 1631.

⇒ See also FIREWALL; IP ADDRESS.

National Television Standards Committee See NTSC.

native Referring to an original form. For example, many applications can work with files in a variety of formats, but an application's *native file format* is the one it uses internally. For all other formats, the application must first convert the file to its native format.

⇒ See also EXPORT; IMPORT.

natural language A human language. For example, English, French, and Chinese are natural languages. Computer languages, such as FORTRAN and C, are not.

Probably the single most challenging problem in computer science is to develop computers that can understand natural languages. So far, the complete solution to this problem has proved elusive, although a great deal of progress has been made. Fourth-generation languages are the programming languages closest to natural languages.

⇒ See also ARTIFICIAL INTELLIGENCE; FOURTH-GENERATION LANGUAGE; LANGUAGE.

navigation keys Same as CURSOR CONTROL KEYS.

Navigator Netscape Communication's popular Web browser. There are
many versions of Navigator, and it runs on all the major platforms
—Windows, Macintoshes, and UNIX.

⇒ See also BROWSER; INTERNET EXPLORER; NETSCAPE.

NC A type of network computer designed to execute Java programs locally.
NCs do not contain any storage devices, so they must be connected to a
network server that holds the data to be processed. However, unlike thin
clients and Windows terminals, NCs do have a microprocessor so that
they can execute programs locally.

⇒ See also NET PC; NETWORK COMPUTER; THIN CLIENT; WINDOWS TERMINAL.

NDIS Short for *N(etwork) D(evice) I(nterface) S(pecification)*, a Windows
device driver interface that enables a single network interface card (NIC)
to support multiple network protocols. For example, with NDIS a single
NIC can support both TCP/IP and IPX connections. NDIS can also be
used by some ISDN adapters.
   NDIS includes a protocol manager that accepts requests from the network driver (at the *transport layer*) and passes these requests to the NIC
(at the *data link layer*). So multiple NDIS-conforming network drivers can
coexist. Also, if a computer contains multiple NICs because it is connected to more than one network, NDIS can route traffic to the correct
card.
   NDIS was developed by Microsoft and 3COM. Novell offers a similar
device driver for NetWare called *Open Data-Link Interface (ODI)*.

⇒ See also ISDN; NETWORK INTERFACE CARD; PROTOCOL.

NDS Short for *N(ovell) D(irectory) S(ervices)*, the directory services for Novell Netware networks. NDS complies with the X.500 standard and provides a logical tree-structure view of all resources on the network so that
users can access them without knowing where they're physically located.
NDS also inter-operates with other types of networks.

⇒ See also ACTIVE DIRECTORY; DIRECTORY SERVICE; LDAP; NETWARE; X.500.

near letter quality A quality of print that is not quite letter quality but is
better than draft quality. Many dot-matrix printers produce near-letter-
quality print.
   Near letter quality is often abbreviated *NLQ*.

⇒ See also DOT-MATRIX PRINTER; DRAFT MODE; DRAFT QUALITY; LETTER QUALITY
(LQ); PRINTER.

NEC One of the world's largest computer and electronics manufacturers. NEC Technologies is the second largest producers of semiconductors (Intel is first), and its line of monitors has set the standard for many years. It also produces PCs and notebook computers and controls half the PC market in Japan.

⇒ See also INTEL; MONITOR; SEMICONDUCTOR.

nesting Embedding one object in another object of the same type. Nesting is quite common in programming. It also occurs in applications. For example, many word processing applications allow you to embed (nest) one document inside another.

Net Short for *Internet*, as in *"I found this on file on the Net."*

⇒ See also INTERNET.

Netbeui Pronounced *net-booey*, Netbeui is short for *NetB(ios) E(nhanced) U(ser) Interface.* It is an enhanced version of the NetBIOS protocol used by network operating systems such as LAN Manager, LAN Server, Windows for Workgroups, Windows 95, Windows 98, and Windows NT.
    Netbeui was originally designed by IBM for its Lan Manager server and later extended by Microsoft and Novell.

⇒ See also NETBIOS.

NetBIOS Short for *Net(work) B(asic) I(nput) O(utput) S(ystem),* an application programming interface (API) that augments the DOS BIOS by adding special functions for local-area networks (LANs). Almost all LANs for PCs are based on the NetBIOS. Some LAN manufacturers have even extended it, adding additional network capabilities.
    NetBIOS relies on a message format called *Server Message Block (SMB).*

⇒ See also API; BIOS; LOCAL-AREA NETWORK; NETBEUI; SMB.

netiquette Contraction of *Internet etiquette,* the etiquette guidelines for posting messages to online services, and particularly Internet newsgroups. Netiquette covers not only rules to maintain civility in discussions (e.g., avoiding flames) but also special guidelines unique to the electronic nature of forum messages. For example, netiquette advises users to use simple formats because complex formatting may not appear correctly for all readers. In most cases, netiquette is enforced by fellow users who will vociferously object if you break a rule of netiquette.

⇒ See also FORUM; INTERNET.

NetMeeting A product developed by Microsoft Corporation that enables groups to teleconference using the Internet as the transmission medium. NetMeeting supports Voice on the Net, chat sessions, a whiteboard, and application sharing. It's built into Microsoft's Internet Explorer Web browser.

⇒ See also CHAT; COOLTALK; INTERNET PHONE; TELECONFERENCE.

Net PC A type of network computer designed cooperatively by Microsoft and Intel. In some respects, the Net PC is really just a scaled-down PC able to execute Windows applications locally. However, it also includes features to simplify connecting it to a network and to administer it remotely.

Net PCs are based on the Wintel platform but are configured to be as inexpensive as possible and to discourage users from configuring the machines themselves. Consequently, they have no floppy disk drive or CD-ROM drive. They do have a hard disk though it's meant to be used as a temporary cache to improve performance rather than for permanently storing data. Configuration and management of a Net PC is performed through a network server and Microsoft's Zero Administration Windows (ZAW) system.

⇒ See also DISKLESS WORKSTATION; NC; NETWORK COMPUTER; SMS; WINDOWS TERMINAL; ZAW.

Netscape Officially called *Netscape Communications Corporation*, Netscape was founded by James H. Clark and Marc Andreessen in 1994. It revolutionized the computer software market by giving away for free its popular Navigator Web browser until it had acquired an overwhelming market share for this category of software.

This strategy is now used by many other software companies, including Microsoft, which also distributes its Web browser, *Internet Explorer,* for free.

In addition to its browsers, Netscape also produces Web servers and tools for building intranets. Indeed, it is from the server category that Netscape gets most of its revenue.

Netscape's headquarters are located in Mountain View, California.

⇒ See also MICROSOFT; NAVIGATOR; SUN MICROSYSTEMS.

Netscape Navigator See NAVIGATOR.

Netscape Server API See NSAPI.

NetShow A specification developed by Microsoft for streaming multimedia content over the World Wide Web. A competing specification backed by Netscape is *RTSP.*

⇒ See also RTSP; STREAMING.

NetWare A popular local-area network (LAN) operating system developed by Novell Corporation. NetWare is a software product that runs on a variety of different types of LANs, from Ethernets to IBM token-ring networks. It provides users and programmers with a consistent interface that is independent of the actual hardware used to transmit messages.

⇒ See also ETHERNET; IPX; LOCAL-AREA NETWORK; NDS; NOVELL; OPERATING SYSTEM; SAP; SPX; TOKEN-RING NETWORK.

NetWare Loadable Module Known as an *NLM*, it is software that enhances or provides additional functions in a NetWare 3.x or higher server. Support for database engines, workstations, network protocols, and fax and print servers are examples. The NetWare 2.x counterpart is a VAP.

network A group of two or more computer systems linked together. There are many types of computer networks, including:

local-area networks (LANs): The computers are geographically close together (that is, in the same building).
wide-area networks (WANs): The computers are farther apart and are connected by telephone lines or radio waves.

In addition to these types, the following characteristics are also used to categorize different types of networks:

topology: The geometric arrangement of a computer system. Common topologies include a bus, star, and ring.
protocol: The protocol defines a common set of rules and signals that computers on the network use to communicate. One of the most popular protocols for LANs is called *Ethernet*. Another popular LAN protocol for PCs is the *IBM token-ring network*.
architecture: Networks can be broadly classified as using either a *peer-to-peer* or *client/server architecture*.

Computers on a network are sometimes called *nodes*. Computers and devices that allocate resources for a network are called *servers*.

⇒ See also BACKBONE; CLIENT/SERVER ARCHITECTURE; COMMUNICATIONS; ETHERNET; FIREWALL; HETEROGENEOUS NETWORK; INTRANET; LOCAL-AREA NETWORK; MAN; NETWORK MANAGEMENT; PACKET SWITCHING; PROTOCOL; SERVER; SNA; SNMP; TOKEN-RING NETWORK; TOPOLOGY; WIDE-AREA NETWORK.

network adapter Same as NETWORK INTERFACE CARD.

Network Address Translation See NAT.

Network Basic Input/Output System See NETBIOS.

network card Same as NETWORK INTERFACE CARD.

network computer A computer with minimal memory, disk storage, and processor power designed to connect to a network, especially the Internet. The idea behind network computers is that many users who are connected to a network don't need all the computer power they get from a typical personal computer. Instead, they can rely on the power of the network servers.

This is really a variation on an old idea — *diskless workstations* — which are computers that contain memory and a processor but no disk storage. Instead, they rely on a server to store data. Network computers take this idea one step further by also minimizing the amount of memory and processor power required by the workstation. Network computers designed to connect to the Internet are sometimes called *Internet boxes, Net PCs,* and *Internet appliances.*

One of the strongest arguments behind network computers is that they reduce the *total cost of ownership (TCO)* — not only because the machines themselves are less expensive than PCs, but also because network computers can be administered and updated from a central network server.

⇒ See also DISKLESS WORKSTATION; INTERNET; NC; NET PC; ORACLE; SMS; SUN MICROSYSTEMS; TCO; THIN CLIENT; WINDOWS TERMINAL; WORKSTATION; ZAW.

Network Device Interface Specification See NDIS.

Network Directory Services See NDS.

Network File System See NFS.

network interface card Often abbreviated as *NIC,* an *expansion board* you insert into a computer so the computer can be connected to a network. Most NICs are designed for a particular type of network, protocol, and media, although some can serve multiple networks.

⇒ See also AUI; BNC CONNECTOR; DLC; EXPANSION BOARD; LOCAL-AREA NETWORK; MAC ADDRESS; MEDIA; NDIS; NETWORK; ODI; PROTOCOL; PROTOCOL STACK; TRANSCEIVER.

network management Refers to the broad subject of managing computer networks. There exists a wide variety of software and hardware products that help network system administrators manage a network. Network management covers a wide area, including:

Security: Ensuring that the network is protected from unauthorized users.

Performance: Eliminating bottlenecks in the network.

Reliability: Making sure the network is available to users and responding to hardware and software malfunctions.

⇒ See also CMIP; DIB; MIB; NETWORK; RMON; SECURITY; SNIFFER; SNMP; SPOOF.

Network Neighborhood A Windows 95 and 98 folder that lists computers, printers, and other resources connected to your local-area network (LAN). By default, a Network Neighborhood icon appears on your desktop, and the folder is also accessible from within the Windows 95 Explorer. The Network Neighborhood is designed to replace the *drive map-*

ping older system, which associates a letter with each shared disk drive. Many programs, however, still require drive mapping.

The Network Neighborhood serves no purpose if your computer is not connected to a LAN, except that it is required to link two computers using Windows 95's Direct Cable Connection (DCC) feature.

⇒ See also DCC; LOCAL-AREA NETWORK; WINDOWS 95.

Network News Transfer Protocol See NNTP.

network operating system An operating system that includes special functions for connecting computers and devices into a local-area network (LAN). Some operating systems, such as UNIX and the Mac OS, have networking functions built in. The term *network operating system*, however, is generally reserved for software that enhances a basic operating system by adding networking features. For example, some popular NOSs for DOS and Windows systems include Novell Netware, Artisoft's LANtastic, Microsoft LAN Manager, and Windows NT.

⇒ See also LOCAL-AREA NETWORK; OPERATING SYSTEM.

network PC Same as NETWORK COMPUTER.

Network Service Provider See NSP.

network topology See TOPOLOGY.

neural network A type of artificial intelligence that attempts to imitate the way a human brain works. Rather than using a digital model, in which all computations manipulate zeros and ones, a neural network works by creating connections between *processing elements*, the computer equivalent of neurons. The organization and weights of the connections determine the output.

Neural networks are particularly effective for predicting events when the networks have a large database of prior examples to draw on. Strictly speaking, a neural network implies a nondigital computer, but neural networks can be simulated on digital computers.

The field of neural networks was pioneered by Bernard Widrow of Stanford University in the 1950s. To date, there are very few commercial applications of neural networks, but the approach is beginning to prove useful in certain areas that involve recognizing complex patterns, such as voice recognition.

⇒ See also ARTIFICIAL INTELLIGENCE; DIGITAL; VOICE RECOGNITION.

newbie Slang term for someone who is a new user on an online service, particularly the Internet.

⇒ See also ONLINE SERVICE.

newsgroup Same as FORUM, an on-line discussion group. On the Internet, there are literally thousands of newsgroups covering every conceivable interest. To view and post messages to a newsgroup, you need a *news reader*, a program that runs on your computer and connects you to a news server on the Internet.

⇒ See also ACRONYM; FORUM; LURK; MODERATED NEWSGROUP; NEWS READER.

news reader Sometimes spelled as one word, a news reader is a client application that enables you to read messages posted to Internet newsgroups, and to post your own messages. Both Microsoft Internet Explorer and Netscape Navigator come with news readers, but there are also freeware, shareware, and commercial stand-alone news readers.

⇒ See also NEWSGROUP; NNTP.

Next Generation Internet Initiative See NGI INITIATIVE.

NEXTSTEP An object-oriented operating system developed by Next Inc., a company started in 1985 by Steven Jobs, one of the cofounders of Apple Computer. In 1997, Apple Computer acquired Next, with the idea of making NEXTSTEP the foundation of its new Macintosh operating system.

⇒ See also APPLE COMPUTER; OBJECT ORIENTED; OPERATING SYSTEM.

NFS Abbreviation of *N(etwork) F(ile) S(ystem),* an open operating system designed by Sun Microsystems that allows all network users to access shared files stored on computers of different types. NFS provides access to shared files through an interface called the *Virtual File System (VFS)* that runs on top of TCP/IP. Users can manipulate shared files as if they were stored locally on the user's own hard disk.

With NFS, computers connected to a network operate as clients while accessing remote files, and as servers while providing remote users access to local shared files. The NFS standards are publicly available and widely used.

⇒ See also FILE MANAGEMENT SYSTEM; UNIX.

NGI Initiative Short for *N(ext) G(eneration) I(nternet)* **Initiative,** a U.S. program designed to fund and coordinate federal agencies and academia to design and build the next generation of Internet services. The program was first proposed by President Bill Clinton in 1996 and has not yet been formally specified or funded by Congress. It is still unclear how the NGI Initiative will complement other initiatives, such as the NSF's very high-speed Backbone Network Service (vNBS) and Internet2 (I2).

⇒ See also I2; INTERNET; vBNS.

nibble Half a byte — four bits. Nibbles are important in hexadecimal and BCD representations.

The term is sometimes spelled *nybble.*

⇒ See also BCD; BIT; BYTE; HEXADECIMAL.

NIC See NETWORK INTERFACE CARD.

NiCad battery pack NiCad stands for *ni(ckel)-cad(mium)*, the materials used in the battery packs for many notebook computers. NiCad batteries can provide considerable power, but they need to be recharged every three or four hours. Full recharging can take as much as twelve hours, although newer batteries can be recharged in just a few hours.

Older NiCad batteries suffer from a phenomenon known as the *memory effect*. If they were only partially drained and then recharged, they lost their capacity to be fully charged. This is not such a problem with modern NiCad batteries.

Even with full drainage (called *deep discharging*), all batteries have a limit to the number of times they can be recharged. The maximum for most NiCad batteries is about 1,000 recharges.

⇒ See also BATTERY PACK; LITHIUM-ION BATTERY; MEMORY EFFECT; NiMH BATTERY PACK; NOTEBOOK COMPUTER.

NiMH battery pack NiMH stands for *Ni(ckel)-M(etal) H(ydride)*, the materials used in some battery packs. Unlike NiCad batteries, NiMH batteries do not use heavy metals that may have toxic effects. In addition, they can store up to 50 percent more power than NiCad batteries and do not suffer from memory effects.

⇒ See also BATTERY PACK; LITHIUM-ION BATTERY; MEMORY EFFECT; NiCad BATTERY PACK.

NLM See NETWARE LOADABLE MODULE.

NLQ Stands for *near letter quality*.

NLX A new form factor designed by Intel for PC motherboards. The NLX form factor features a number of improvements over the current LPX form factor and is expected to be widely implemented. Its features include:

- Support for larger memory modules and DIMMs
- Support for the newest microprocessors, including the Pentium II using SEC packaging
- Support for AGP video cards
- Better access to motherboard components
- Support for *dockable* designs in which the motherboard can be removed without tools

⇒ See also AGP; BABY AT; FORM FACTOR; MOTHERBOARD; LPX.

NNTP Short for *N(etwork) N(ews) T(ransport) P(rotocol)*, the protocol used to post, distribute, and retrieve USENET messages. The official specification is RFC 977.

⇒ See also NEWS READER; USENET.

node 1. In networks, a processing location. A node can be a computer or some other device, such as a printer. Every node has a unique network address, sometimes called a *Data Link Control (DLC) address* or *Media Access Control (MAC) address*. **2.** In tree structures, a point where two or more lines meet.

⇒ See also DLC; LEAF; MAC ADDRESS; NETWORK; TREE STRUCTURE.

noise 1. In communications, interference (static) that destroys the integrity of signals on a line. Noise can come from a variety of sources, including radio waves, nearby electrical wires, lightning, and bad connections. One of the major advantages of fiber optic cables over metal cables is that they are much less susceptible to noise. **2.** In general, anything that prevents a clear signal or message from being transmitted. For example, you might hear someone complain of a lot of noise in a newsgroup, meaning that there are many superfluous messages that don't add anything to the discussion.

⇒ See also COMMUNICATIONS; FIBER OPTICS.

non-impact printer A type of printer that does not operate by striking a head against a ribbon. Examples of nonimpact printers include laser and ink-jet printers. The term *nonimpact* is important primarily in that it distinguishes quiet printers from noisy (impact) printers.

⇒ See also IMPACT PRINTER; INK-JET PRINTER; LASER PRINTER; PRINTER.

noninterlaced Refers to monitors and video standards that do not use interlacing techniques to improve resolution. Although interlacing increases resolution, it also increases screen flicker and reduces reaction time.

⇒ See also INTERLACING; MONITOR; SCREEN FLICKER.

Non-Uniform Memory Access See NUMA.

nonvolatile memory Types of memory that retain their contents when power is turned off. ROM is nonvolatile, whereas RAM is *volatile*. This term often refers to the CMOS memory in PCs that holds the BIOS.

⇒ See also BUBBLE MEMORY; MEMORY; NVRAM; RAM; ROM.

normalization 1. In relational database design, the process of organizing data to minimize duplication. Normalization usually involves dividing a database into two or more tables and defining relationships between the tables. The objective is to isolate data so that additions, deletions, and modifications of a field can be made in just one table and then propagated through the rest of the database via the defined relationships.

There are three main normal forms, each with increasing levels of normalization:

- **First Normal Form (1NF):** Each field in a table contains different information. For example, in an employee list, each table would contain only one birthdate field.
- **Second Normal Form (2NF):** No field values can be derived from another field. For example, if a table already included a birthdate field, it could not also include a birth year field, because this information would be redundant.
- **Third Normal Form (3FN):** No duplicate information is permitted. So, for example, if two tables both required a birthdate field, the birthdate information would be separated into a separate table, and the two other tables would then access the birthdate information via an index field in the birthdate table. Any change to a birthdate would automatically be reflected in all tables that link to the birthdate table.

There are additional normalization levels, such as *Boyce Codd Normal Form (BCNF), fourth normal form (4NF),* and *fifth normal form (5NF).* While normalization makes databases more efficient to maintain, they can also make them more complex because data are separated into so many different tables. **2.** In data processing, a process applied to all data in a set that produces a specific statistical property. For example, each expenditure for a month can be divided by the total of all expenditures to produce a percentage. **3.** In programming, changing the format of a floating-point number so the left-most digit in the mantissa is not a zero.

⇒ See also FLOATING-POINT NUMBER; KEY; RDBMS; REFERENTIAL INTEGRITY.

normalize See under NORMALIZATION.

NOR operator A Boolean operator that returns a value of TRUE only if both operands are FALSE.

⇒ See also BOOLEAN OPERATOR.

NOS See NETWORK OPERATING SYSTEM.

notebook computer An extremely lightweight personal computer. Notebook computers typically weigh less than 6 pounds and are small enough to fit easily in a briefcase. Aside from size, the principal difference between a notebook computer and a personal computer is the display screen. Notebook computers use a variety of techniques, known as *flat-panel technologies,* to produce a lightweight and non-bulky display screen.

The quality of notebook display screens varies considerably. Many notebook display screens are limited to VGA resolution. Active-matrix screens produce very sharp images, but they do not refresh as rapidly as full-size monitors.

In terms of computing power, modern notebook computers are nearly equivalent to personal computers. They have the same CPUs, memory capacity, and disk drives. However, all this power in a small package is expensive. Notebook computers cost about twice as much as equivalent regular-sized computers.

Notebook computers come with battery packs that enable you to run them without plugging them in. However, the batteries need to be recharged every few hours.

⇒ See also ACTIVE-MATRIX DISPLAY; BACKLIGHTING; BATTERY PACK; HAND-HELD COMPUTER; PDA; PORT REPLICATOR; SLATE PC; SUBNOTEBOOK COMPUTER; VGA; VIRTUAL DESKTOP; ZV PORT.

Figure 55: **notebook computer**

Notes See under LOTUS NOTES.

NOT operator A Boolean operator that returns TRUE if its operand is FALSE, and FALSE if its operand is TRUE.

⇒ See also BOOLEAN OPERATOR.

Novell The world's largest network software company. Its flagship product, Netware, has been a corporate standard for building local-area networks (LANs) for more than a decade.

Like all software companies, Novell has been scrambling to respond to the sudden emergence of the Internet and intranets. Recently, it joined with Netscape to form a new company called Novonyx that will integrate Netscape's intranet products with Novell's networking software.

Novell was founded in 1983 and is headquartered in Utah.

⇒ See also LOCAL-AREA NETWORK; NETWARE.

Novell NetWare See under NETWARE.

ns Short for *nanosecond.*

NSAPI Short for *N(etscape) S(erver)* **API**, an API for Netscape's Web servers. NSAPI enables programmers to create Web-based applications that are more sophisticated and run much faster than applications based on CGI scripts.

⇒ See also CGI; ISAPI; STATELESS.

NSFnet A wide-area network developed under the auspices of the National Science Foundation (NSF). NSFnet replaced ARPANET as the main government network linking universities and research facilities. In 1995, however, the NSF dismantled NSFnet and replaced it with a commercial Internet backbone. At the same time, the NSF implemented a new backbone called very high-speed Backbone Network Service (vBNS), which serves as a testing ground for the next generation of Internet technologies.

⇒ See also ARPANET; NETWORK; WIDE-AREA NETWORK.

NSP Short for *N(etwork) S(ervice) P(rovider)*, a company that provides Internet access to ISPs. Sometimes called *backbone providers*, NSPs offer direct access to the Internet backbone and the Network Access Points (NAPs).

⇒ See also BACKBONE; ISP; NAP.

NT See under WINDOWS NT.

NT File System See NTFS.

NTFS Short for **NT** *F(ile) S(ystem)*, one of the file systems for the Windows NT operating system (Windows NT also supports the FAT file system). NTFS has features to improve reliability, such as transaction logs to help recover from disk failures. To control access to files, you can set permissions for directories and/or individual files. NTFS files are not accessible from other operating systems such as DOS.

For large applications, NTFS supports spanning volumes, which means that files and directories can be spread out across several physical disks.

⇒ See also FILE MANAGEMENT SYSTEM; UNICODE; VOLUME; WINDOWS NT.

NTSC Abbreviation of *National Television Standards Committee*. The NTSC is responsible for setting television and video standards in the United States (in Europe and the rest of the world, the dominant television standards are PAL and SECAM). The NTSC standard for television defines a composite video signal with a refresh rate of 60 half-frames (interlaced) per second. Each frame contains 525 lines and can contain 16 million different colors.

The NTSC standard is incompatible with most computer video standards, which generally use *RGB* video signals. However, you can insert special video adapters into your computer that convert NTSC signals into computer video signals and vice versa.

A new digital television standard being developed is called *HDTV (High-Definition Television)*.

⇒ See also COMMON INTERMEDIATE FORMAT; COMPOSITE VIDEO; HDTV; INTERLACING; PAL; QCIF; RGB MONITOR; S-VIDEO; SAP; TELEVISION BOARD; VIDEO ADAPTER; VIDEO OVERLAY.

NuBus The expansion bus for versions of the Macintosh computers starting with the Macintosh II and ending with the Performa. Current Macs use the PCI bus.

⇒ See also EXPANSION BUS; MACINTOSH COMPUTER; PCI.

null character A character that has all its bits set to 0. A null character, therefore, has a numeric value of 0, but it has a special meaning when interpreted as text. In some programming languages, notably C, a null character is used to mark the end of a character string. In database and spreadsheet applications, null characters are often used as padding and are displayed as spaces.

⇒ See also CHARACTER STRING; PADDING.

null modem Same as NULL-MODEM CABLE.

null-modem cable A specially designed cable that allows you to connect two computers directly to each other via their communications ports (RS-232 ports). Null modems are particularly useful with portable computers because they enable the portable computer to exchange data with a larger system.

⇒ See also DCC; MODEM; PORT; RS-232C.

NUMA Short for *N(on)-U(niform) M(emory) A(ccess)*, a type of parallel processing architecture in which each processor has its own local memory but can also access memory owned by other processors. It's called *non-uniform* because the memory access times are faster when a processor accesses its own memory than when it borrows memory from another processor.

NUMA computers offer the scalability of MPP and the programming ease of SMP.

⇒ See also MPP; PARALLEL PROCESSING; SMP.

number cruncher 1. A computer whose dominant characteristic is its ability to perform large amounts of numerical computations quickly. Supercomputers, for example, are sometimes called number crunchers. In addition, the term *number cruncher* is often applied to powerful workstations. **2.** The term *number cruncher* is sometimes applied to programs. For example, statistical programs are number crunchers because their main task is to perform mathematical calculations. **3.** Less frequently, the term *number cruncher* refers to individuals who use a computer primarily for analyzing numbers.

⇒ See also SUPERCOMPUTER; WORKSTATION.

numeric coprocessor See under COPROCESSOR.

numeric keypad A separate set of keys on some keyboards that contains the numbers 0 through 9 and a decimal point arranged as on an adding machine. Numeric keypads make it easier to enter large amounts of numeric data.

Frequently, the keys on the numeric keyboard also serve as cursor control keys. Their meanings, therefore, depend on what mode the numeric keypad is in. In *numeric mode*, they represent numbers; in *cursor control mode*, they are like arrow keys. Keyboards that support these dual functions contain an additional key that enables you to switch modes. The name of this key varies—on many keyboards it is labeled *Num Lock*.

⇒ See also ARROW KEYS; KEYBOARD; MODE; NUM LOCK KEY.

Figure 56: **numeric keypad**

Num Lock key A key that switches the numeric keypad from numeric mode to cursor control mode, and vice versa. In numeric mode, the keys represent numbers even when they are combined with the Shift key,

Function key, or Control key. Otherwise these combinations may have different meanings.

The Num Lock key is a toggle key, meaning that it changes the current mode. If the numeric keypad is already locked in numeric mode, pressing the Num Lock key releases it.

⇒ See also CURSOR CONTROL KEYS; NUMERIC KEYPAD; TOGGLE.

NURB See NURBS.

NURBS Short for *N(on)-U(niform) R(ational)* **B**-*S(pline)*, a mathematical representation of a three-dimensional object. Most CAD/CAM applications support NURBS, which can be used to represent analytic shapes, such as cones, as well as free-form shapes, such as car bodies.

⇒ See also 3-D SOFTWARE; BÉZIER CURVE; MODELING; SPLINE.

NVRAM Abbreviation of *N(on)-V(olatile) R(andom) A(ccess) M(emory)*, a type of memory that retains its contents when power is turned off. One type of NVRAM is SRAM that is made *nonvolatile* by connecting it to a constant power source such as a battery. Another type of NVRAM uses EEPROM chips to save its contents when power is turned off. In this case, NVRAM is composed of a combination of SRAM and EEPROM chips.

⇒ See also EEPROM; MEMORY; NONVOLATILE MEMORY; RAM; SRAM.

OA Short for *office automation.*

object Generally, any item that can be individually selected and manipulated. This can include shapes and pictures that appear on a display screen as well as less tangible software entities. In object-oriented programming, for example, an object is a self-contained entity that consists of both data and procedures to manipulate the data.

⇒ See also BLOB; CORBA; OBJECT ORIENTED; OBJECT-ORIENTED GRAPHICS; OBJECT-ORIENTED PROGRAMMING; OLE; OMG.

object code The code produced by a compiler. Programmers write programs in a form called source code. The source code consists of instructions in a particular language, like C or FORTRAN. Computers, however, can execute only instructions written in a low-level language called *machine language.*

To get from source code to machine language, the programs must be transformed by a compiler. The compiler produces an intermediary form called object code. Object code is often the same as or similar to a computer's machine language. The final step in producing an executable program is to transform the object code into machine language, if it is not already in this form. This can be done by a number of different types of programs, called *assemblers, binders, linkers,* and *loaders.*

⇒ See also ASSEMBLER; ASSEMBLY LANGUAGE; CODE; COMPILE; LIBRARY; LINK; LOAD; MACHINE LANGUAGE.

Object Linking and Embedding See OLE.

Object Management Group See OMG.

object oriented A popular buzzword that can mean different things depending on how it is used. *Object-oriented programming (OOP)* refers to a special type of programming that combines data structures with functions to create reusable objects (see under *object-oriented programming*). Object-oriented graphics is the same as *vector graphics.*

Otherwise, the term *object-oriented* is generally used to describe a system that deals primarily with different types of objects, and where the actions you can take depend on what type of object you are manipulating. For example an object-oriented draw program might enable you to draw many types of objects, such as circles, rectangles, triangles, and so on. Applying the same action to each of these objects, however, would produce different results. If the action is *Make 3D*, for instance, the result would be a sphere, box, and pyramid, respectively.

⇒ See also OBJECT-ORIENTED PROGRAMMING; SMALLTALK; VECTOR GRAPHICS.

object-oriented graphics The representation of graphical objects, such as lines, arcs, circles, and rectangles, with mathematical formulas. This method of describing objects enables the system to manipulate the objects more freely. In an object-oriented system, for example, you can overlap objects but still access them individually, which is difficult in a bit-mapped system. Also, object-oriented images profit from high-quality output devices. The higher the resolution of a monitor or printer, the sharper an object-oriented image will look. In contrast, bit-mapped images always appear the same regardless of a device's resolution.

One of the most widely used formats for object-oriented graphics is PostScript. PostScript is a page description language (PDL) that makes it possible to describe objects and manipulate them in various ways. For example, you can make objects smaller or larger, turn them at various angles, and change their shading and color. A font described in PostScript, therefore, can easily be transformed into another font by changing its size or weight. Object-oriented fonts are called *outline fonts*, *scalable fonts*, or *vector fonts*.

Object-oriented graphics is also called *vector graphics*, whereas bit-mapped graphics is sometimes called *raster graphics*.

⇒ See also BIT-MAPPED GRAPHICS; GRAPHICS; POSTSCRIPT; SCALABLE FONT; VECTOR GRAPHICS.

object-oriented programming A type of programming in which programmers define not only the data type of a data structure but also the types of operations (functions) that can be applied to the data structure. In this way, the data structure becomes an *object* that includes both data and functions. In addition, programmers can create relationships between one object and another. For example, objects can *inherit* characteristics from other objects.

One of the principal advantages of object-oriented programming techniques over procedural programming techniques is that they enable programmers to create modules that do not need to be changed when a new type of object is added. A programmer can simply create a new object that inherits many of its features from existing objects. This makes object-oriented programs easier to modify.

To perform object-oriented programming, one needs an *object-oriented programming language (OOPL)*. C++ and Smalltalk are two of the more popular languages, and there are also object-oriented versions of Pascal.

⇒ See also C++; CLASS; COMPONENT SOFTWARE; DISTRIBUTED COMPUTING; EIFFEL; ENCAPSULATION; JAVA; OBJECT ORIENTED; OMG; OVERLOADING; POLYMORPHISM; SMALLTALK; UML; VISUAL C++.

Object Request Broker See ORB.

OC Short for *O(ptical) C(arrier),* used to specify the speed of fiber optic networks conforming to the SONET standard. The following table shows the speeds for common OC levels.

OC Level: Speed

OC-1: 51.85 Mbps Mbps
OC-3: 155.52 Mbps
OC-12: 622.08 Mbps
OC-24: 1.244 Gbps
OC-48: 2.488 Gbps

⇒ See also SDH; SONET; T-1 CARRIER; T-3 CARRIER.

OC-1 See under OC.

OC-12 See under OC.

OC-24 See under OC.

OC-3 See under OC.

OC-48 See under OC.

OCR See OPTICAL CHARACTER RECOGNITION.

octal Refers to the base-8 number system, which uses just eight unique symbols (0, 1, 2, 3, 4, 5, 6, and 7). Programs often display data in octal

Table 21
Octal and Binary Equivalents

Octal	Binary
0	000
1	001
2	010
3	011
4	100
5	101
6	110
7	111

format because it is relatively easy for humans to read and can easily be translated into binary format, which is the most important format for computers. By contrast, decimal format is the easiest format for humans to read because it is the one we use in everyday life, but translating between decimal and binary formats is relatively difficult.

In octal format, each digit represents three binary digits, as shown in the accompanying table:

With this table it is easy to translate between octal and binary. For example, the octal number 3456 is 011 100 101 110 in binary.

⇒ See also BINARY; DECIMAL; HEXADECIMAL.

OCX Short for *O(LE) C(ustom) control*, an independent program module that can be accessed by other programs in a Windows environment. OCX controls end with a .OCX extension. OCX controls represent Microsoft's second generation of control architecture, the first being VBX controls written in Visual Basic.

Both VBX and OCX controls have now been superseded by ActiveX controls. However, ActiveX is backward compatible with OCX controls, which means that ActiveX containers, such as Microsoft's Internet Explorer, can execute OCX components.

⇒ See also ACTIVEX CONTROL; COMPONENT; CONTROL; OLE; VBX.

ODBC Abbreviation of *O(pen) D(ata)B(ase) C(onnectivity)*, a standard database access method developed by Microsoft Corporation. The goal of ODBC is to make it possible to access any data from any application, regardless of which database management system (DBMS) is handling the data. ODBC manages this by inserting a middle layer, called a database *driver*, between an application and the DBMS. The purpose of this layer is to translate the application's data queries into commands that the DBMS understands. For this to work, both the application and the DBMS must be *ODBC-compliant* —that is, the application must be capable of issuing ODBC commands and the DBMS must be capable of responding to them. Since version 2.0, the standard supports SAG SQL.

⇒ See also ADO; DATABASE MANAGEMENT SYSTEM; DRIVER; JDBC; MICROSOFT; QUERY; SQL.

odd header In word processing, a header that appears only on odd-numbered pages.

⇒ See also HEADER.

odd parity The mode of parity checking in which each 9-bit combination of a data byte plus a parity bit contains an odd number of set bits.

⇒ See also PARITY CHECKING.

ODI Short for *O(pen) D(ata)-link I(nterface)*, an application programming interface (API) developed by Novell for writing network drivers. ODI separates the physical network layer (the Data-Link Layer in the OSI model) from the network protocol layer (the Transport Layer). As a result, the same network interface card (NIC) can be used to carry data for different protocols. For example, ODI allows a computer with just one NIC to be simultaneously connected to both an IPX/SPX network and a TCP/IP network.

⇒ See also API; DRIVER; NETWORK INTERFACE CARD; OSI.

OEM *n* **1.** Stands for *o(riginal) e(quipment) m(anufacturer)*, which is a misleading term for a company that has a special relationship with computer producers. OEMs buy computers in bulk and customize them for a particular application. They then sell the customized computer under their own name. The term is really a misnomer because OEMs are not the *original* manufacturers—they are the customizers.

Another term for OEM is *VAR (value-added reseller).* —*v* **2.** To provide equipment to another company, an OEM, which customizes and markets the equipment.

⇒ See also VAR.

office automation The use of computer systems to execute a variety of office operations, such as word processing, accounting, and e-mail. Office automation almost always implies a network of computers with a variety of available programs.

⇒ See also E-MAIL; NETWORK; WORD PROCESSING.

off-line **1.** Not connected. For example, all printers have a switch that allows you to turn them off-line. While the printer is off-line, you can perform certain commands like advancing the paper *(form feed)*, but you cannot print documents sent from the computer. The opposite of off-line is *on-line.* **2.** Aside from its technical meaning, *off-line* is used frequently in a more general sense to describe events that occur outside of a standard procedure. For example, if somebody at a meeting says, "Let's continue this discussion off-line," it means "Let's discuss it informally at another time."

⇒ See also FORM FEED; ON-LINE.

offset **1.** Refers to a value added to a base address to produce a second address. For example, if B represents address 100, then the expression

B + 5

signifies the address 105. The 5 in the expression is the offset.

Specifying addresses using an offset is called *relative addressing* because the resulting address is relative to some other point. Another word for *offset* is *displacement.* **2.** In desktop publishing, the offset is the amount of space along the edge of the paper. Its purpose is to allow room for the binding. The offset is sometimes called the *gutter.*

⇒ See also ADDRESS; BASE ADDRESS; DESKTOP PUBLISHING; GUTTER; RELATIVE AD-
DRESS.

offset printing A printing technique whereby ink is spread on a metal
plate with etched images, then transferred to an intermediary surface
such as a rubber blanket, and finally applied to paper by pressing the paper against the intermediary surface. Most print shops use offset printing
to produce large volumes of high-quality documents. Although the equipment and set-up costs are relatively high, the actual printing process is
relatively inexpensive.

Desktop publishing generally involves producing documents on the
computer, printing out drafts on a laser printer, and then offset printing
the final version. To produce the plates used in offset printing, a print
shop requires either film or high-resolution paper output, which the
printer can then photograph. You can obtain either by taking a PostScript
file to a service bureau.

⇒ See also DESKTOP PUBLISHING; POSTSCRIPT.

Okidata One of the leading producers of printers, especially dot-matrix and
LED printers. Okidata, based in New Jersey, is a subsidiary of OKI Electric Industry Company, a huge Japanese conglomerate.

⇒ See also DOT-MATRIX PRINTER; LASER PRINTER.

OLAP Short for *O(n)l(ine) A(nalytical) P(rocessing)*, a category of software
tools that provides analysis of data stored in a database. OLAP tools enable users to analyze different dimensions of multidimensional data. For
example, it provides time series and trend analysis views.

The chief component of OLAP is the OLAP server, which sits between
a client and a database management systems (DBMS). The OLAP server
understands how data is organized in the database and has special functions for analyzing the data. There are OLAP servers available for nearly
all the major database systems.

⇒ See also DATABASE; DATABASE MANAGEMENT SYSTEM; MULTIDIMENSIONAL
DBMS; OLTP.

OLE Abbreviation of *O(bject) L(inking) and E(mbedding)*, pronounced as
separate letters or as *oh-leh*. OLE is a compound document *standard* developed by Microsoft Corporation. It enables you to create objects with
one application and then link or embed them in a second application.
Embedded objects retain their original format and links to the application
that created them.

Support for OLE is built into the Windows and Macintosh operating
systems. A competing compound document standard developed jointly by
IBM, Apple Computer, and other computer firms is called *OpenDoc*.

⇒ See also ACTIVEX; APPLET; COMPONENT OBJECT MODEL; COMPONENT SOFT-

WARE; DDE; DLL; EMBEDDED OBJECT; HOT LINK; LINK; OBJECT ORIENTED; OCX; OpenDoc.

OLTP Short for *O(n)-L(ine) T(ransaction) P(rocessing)*. Same as TRANSACTION PROCESSING.

⇒ See also OLAP; TRANSACTION PROCESSING.

OMG Short for *O(bject) M(anagement) G(roup)*, a consortium with a membership of more than 700 companies. The organization's goal is to provide a common framework for developing applications using object-oriented programming techniques. OMG is responsible for the CORBA specification.

⇒ See also CORBA; DISTRIBUTED COMPUTING; IIOP; OBJECT; OBJECT-ORIENTED PROGRAMMING.

on-board Literally, on a circuit board. *On-board memory,* for example, refers to memory chips on the motherboard. *On-board modems* are modems that are on expansion boards.

⇒ See also EXPANSION BOARD; MOTHERBOARD; ON-BOARD MODEM; PRINTED CIRCUIT BOARD.

on-board modem Another term for an *internal modem* — that is, a modem that comes as an expansion board you can insert into a computer.

⇒ See also MODEM.

100Base-T A networking standard that supports data transfer rates up to 100 Mbps (100 megabits per second). 100Base-T is based on the older Ethernet standard. Because it is 10 times faster than Ethernet, it is often referred to as *Fast Ethernet*. Officially, the 100BASE-T standard is *IEEE 802.3u*.
  Like Ethernet, 100BASE-T is based on the CSMA/CD LAN access method. There are several different cabling schemes that can be used with 100BASE-T, including:

100BASE-TX: two pairs of high-quality twisted-pair wires
100BASE-T4: four pairs of normal-quality twisted-pair wires
100BASE-FX: fiber optic cables

⇒ See also 10BASET; CSMA/CD; ETHERNET; GIGABIT ETHERNET; SWITCHED ETHERNET.

1-2-3 See LOTUS 1-2-3.

on-line Turned on and connected. For example, printers are on-line when they are ready to receive data from the computer. You can also turn a printer *off-line*. While the printer is off-line, you can perform certain tasks such as advancing the paper, but you cannot send data to it. Most printers have an on-line button you can press to turn the machine on- or off-line.

Users are considered *on-line* when they are connected to a computer service through a modem. That is, they are actually *on the line.*

Increasingly, the term is being spelled as one word, *online.*

⇒ See also OFF-LINE; PRINTER.

online See ON-LINE.

OnLine Analytical Processing See OLAP.

online help See under HELP.

online service A business that provides its subscribers with a wide variety of data transmitted over telecommunications lines. Online services provide an infrastructure in which subscribers can communicate with one another, either by exchanging e-mail messages or by participating in online conferences (forums). In addition, the service can connect users with an almost unlimited number of third-party information providers. Subscribers can get up-to-date stock quotes, news stories hot off the wire, articles from many magazines and journals — in fact, almost any information that has been put in electronic form. Of course, accessing all this data carries a price.

The difference between an online service and a bulletin board service is one of scale and profits. Online services provide a variety of information and services, whereas BBSs normally concentrate on a single theme. In addition, BBSs are often operated on a nonprofit basis whereas online services are always for profit. Three of the largest online services are America Online, CompuServe, and MSN.

One online service that defies classification is the Internet. In terms of users, it is the largest service, but it is not centrally controlled by any one organization, nor is it operated for profit.

⇒ See also AMERICA ONLINE; BULLETIN BOARD SYSTEM; CHAT; CompuServe INFORMATION SERVICE; FORUM; INTERNET; MSN.

On-Line Transaction Processing See OLTP.

OOP See OBJECT-ORIENTED PROGRAMMING.

OOPL Stands for *object-oriented programming language.*

open *v* **1.** To make an object accessible. Whenever you access a file (that is, you edit a text file or run a program file), the operating system opens the file. Opening a file can be simple or complex depending on the operating system. For example, in a multiprocessing operating system, in which different users can share the same resources, the operating system must decide whether the file can be accessed simultaneously by more than one user, and, if so, it must ensure that different users do not try to modify the file's contents at the same time. —*adj* **2.** Accessible. When

used to describe designs or architectures, *open* means public. See under
OPEN ARCHITECTURE.

⇒ See also CLOSE; FILE; OPERATING SYSTEM.

open architecture An architecture whose specifications are public. This
includes officially approved standards as well as privately designed architectures whose specifications are made public by the designers. The opposite of *open* is *closed* or *proprietary*.

The great advantage of open architectures is that anyone can design
add-on products for them. By making an architecture public, however, a
manufacturer allows others to duplicate its product. The IBM PC, for example, was based on open architectures and has spawned an entire industry of IBM clones. In contrast, the Macintosh architecture and operating system have been predominantly closed.

⇒ See also ADD-ON; ARCHITECTURE; CLONE; PROPRIETARY; STANDARD; THE OPEN
GROUP.

Open Data-Link Interface See ODI.

OpenDoc A standard and application programming interface (API) that
makes it possible to design independent programs (components) that can
work together on a single document. OpenDoc is being developed by a
loose alliance of companies, including Apple Computer, IBM, and Lotus.
Notably absent from this list is Microsoft, which is pushing an alternative
standard and API called Object Linking and Embedding (OLE).

⇒ See also COMPONENT OBJECT MODEL; COMPONENT SOFTWARE; COMPOUND
DOCUMENT; OLE.

OpenGL A 3-D graphics language developed by Silicon Graphics. There are
two main implementations:

* *Microsoft OpenGL,* developed by Microsoft
* *Cosmo OpenGL,* developed by Silicon Graphics

Microsoft OpenGL is built into Windows NT and is designed to improve performance on hardware that supports the OpenGL standard.
Cosmo OpenGL, on the other hand, is a software-only implementation
specifically designed for machines that do not have a graphics accelerator.

Another standard that is popular for rendering 3-D images is Direct3D.

⇒ See also 3-D SOFTWARE; DIRECT3D; SGI.

Open Graphics Language See OPENGL.

Open Shortest Path First See OSPF.

Open Software Foundation (OSF) See under THE OPEN GROUP.

Open System Interconnection See OSI.

Open Text A popular Internet search engine developed by Open Text Corporation. Though not the most complete Web index, Open Text is considered by many to be the most sophisticated because it provides powerful ways to fine-tune a query. Open Text Corporation licenses its search engine software as a product called *LiveLink*.

⇒ See also ALTA VISTA; EXCITE; INFOSEEK; LYCOS; SEARCH ENGINE; WEB-CRAWLER.

operand In all computer languages, expressions consist of two types of components: *operands* and *operators*. Operands are the objects that are manipulated and operators are the symbols that represent specific actions. For example, in the expression

$5 + x$

x and 5 are operands and + is an operator. All expressions have at least one operand.

⇒ See also EXPRESSION; OPERATOR; OVERLOADING.

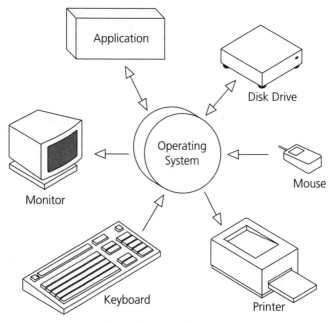

Figure 57: **operating system**

operating environment The environment in which users run programs.

For example, the DOS environment consists of all the DOS commands available to users. The Macintosh environment, on the other hand, is a graphical user interface that uses icons and menus instead of commands.

There is a thin line between operating environments and shells. Historically, shells are the interfaces to operating systems. They do not actually add any new capabilities; they simply provide a better user interface. So-called intelligent shells, however, actually extend an operating system's capabilities, so there is little difference between intelligent shells and operating environments.

Operating environments are sometimes called control programs.

⇒ See also CONTROL PROGRAM; ENVIRONMENT; GRAPHICAL USER INTERFACE; MICROSOFT WINDOWS; OPERATING SYSTEM; SHELL; VIRTUAL MACHINE.

operating system The most important program that runs on a computer. Every general-purpose computer must have an operating system to run other programs. Operating systems perform basic tasks, such as recognizing input from the keyboard, sending output to the display screen, keeping track of files and directories on the disk, and controlling peripheral devices such as disk drives and printers.

For large systems, the operating system has even greater responsibilities and powers. It is like a traffic cop—it makes sure that different programs and users running at the same time do not interfere with each other. The operating system is also responsible for *security*, ensuring that unauthorized users do not access the system.

Operating systems can be classified as follows:

multi-user: Allows two or more users to run programs at the same time. Some operating systems permit hundreds or even thousands of concurrent users.

multiprocessing: Supports running a program on more than one CPU.

multitasking: Allows more than one program to run concurrently.

multithreading: Allows different parts of a single program to run concurrently.

real-time: Responds to input instantly. General-purpose operating systems, such as DOS and UNIX, are not real-time.

Operating systems provide a software platform on top of which other programs, called *application programs,* can run. The application programs must be written to run on top of a particular operating system. Your choice of operating system, therefore, determines to a great extent the applications you can run. For PCs, the most popular operating systems are DOS, OS/2, and Windows, but others are available, such as Linux.

As a user, you normally interact with the operating system through a set of commands. For example, the DOS operating system contains commands such as COPY and RENAME for copying files and changing the names of files, respectively. The commands are accepted and executed by a part of the operating system called the command processor or command line interpreter. Graphical user interfaces allow you to enter commands by pointing and clicking at objects that appear on the screen.

⇒ See also APPLICATION; BeOS; BIOS; COMMAND PROCESSOR; DOS; FILE MANAGEMENT SYSTEM; KERNEL; MAC OS; MICROSOFT WINDOWS; MULTI-USER; MULTIPROCESSING; MULTITASKING; MULTITHREADING; MVS; OS/2; UNIX; VMS; WINDOWS CE.

operator 1. A symbol that represents a specific action. For example, a plus sign (+) is an operator that represents addition. The basic mathematic operators are

Operator: Action

+ :   addition
-:   subtraction
*:   multiplication
/:   division

In addition to these operators, many programs and programming languages recognize other operators that allow you to manipulate numbers and text in more sophisticated ways. For example, Boolean operators enable you to test the truth or falsity of conditions, and *relational operators* let you compare one value to another. **2.** A computer operator is an individual who is responsible for mounting tapes and disks, making backups, and generally ensuring that a computer runs properly.

⇒ See also BITWISE OPERATOR; BOOLEAN OPERATOR; EXPRESSION; OPERAND; OVERLOADING; PRECEDENCE; RELATIONAL OPERATOR.

Table 22
Mathematical Operators

Operator	Action
+	addition
−	subtraction
*	multiplication
/	division

optical character recognition Often abbreviated *OCR*, optical character recognition refers to the branch of computer science that involves reading text from paper and translating the images into a form that the computer can manipulate (for example, into ASCII codes). An OCR system enables you to take a book or a magazine article, feed it directly into an electronic computer file, and then edit the file using a word processor.

All OCR systems include an optical scanner for reading text, and sophisticated software for analyzing images. Most OCR systems use a combination of hardware (specialized circuit boards) and software to recognize characters, although some inexpensive systems do it entirely through software. Advanced OCR systems can read text in a large variety of fonts, but they still have difficulty with handwritten text.

The potential of OCR systems is enormous because they enable users to harness the power of computers to access printed documents. OCR is already being used widely in the legal profession, where searches that once required hours or days can now be accomplished in a few seconds.

⇒ See also ASCII; DOCUMENT MANAGEMENT; FONT; FORM; OPTICAL SCANNER; PRINTED CIRCUIT BOARD.

optical disk A storage medium from which data is read and to which it is written by lasers. Optical disks can store much more data—up to 6 gigabytes (6 billion bytes)—than most portable magnetic media, such as floppies. There are three basic types of optical disks:

CD-ROM: Like audio CDs, CD-ROMs come with data already encoded onto them. The data is permanent and can be read any number of times, but CD-ROMs cannot be modified.

WORM: Stands for *write-once, read -many*. With a WORM disk drive, you can write data onto a WORM disk, but only once. After that, the WORM disk behaves just like a CD-ROM.

erasable: Optical disks that can be erased and loaded with new data, just like magnetic disks. These are often referred to as *EO* (e(rasable) o(ptical)) disks.

These three technologies are not compatible with one another; each requires a different type of disk drive and disk. Even within one category, there are many competing formats, although CD-ROMs are relatively standardized.

⇒ See also AREAL DENSITY; CD-I (COMPACT DISC-INTERACTIVE); CD-ROM; COMPACT DISC; DISK; ERASABLE OPTICAL DISK; MASS STORAGE; PHASE CHANGE DISK; ROM; WORM.

optical fiber See under FIBER OPTICS.

optical mouse See under MOUSE.

optical resolution The physical resolution at which a device can capture an image. The term is used most frequently in reference to optical scanners and digital cameras. In contrast, the *interpolated resolution* indicates the resolution that the device can yield through *interpolation* —the process of generating intermediate values based on known values. For example, most scanners offer an optical resolution of 300 dpi, but an interpolated resolution of up to 4,800 dpi. This means that the scanner can actually capture 90,000 pixels per square inch. Then, based on the values of these pixels, it can add 15 additional pixels in-between each pair of known values to yield a higher resolution.

⇒ See also DIGITAL CAMERA; OPTICAL SCANNER; RESOLUTION.

optical scanner A device that can read text or illustrations printed on paper and translate the information into a form the computer can use. A scanner works by digitizing an image—dividing it into a grid of boxes and representing each box with either a zero or a one, depending on whether the box is filled in. (For color and gray scaling, the same principle applies, but each box is then represented by up to 24 bits.) The resulting matrix of bits, called a bit map, can then be stored in a file, displayed on a screen, and manipulated by programs.

Optical scanners do not distinguish text from illustrations; they represent all images as bit maps. Therefore, you cannot directly edit text that has been scanned. To edit text read by an optical scanner, you need an *optical character recognition (OCR)* system to translate the image into ASCII characters. Most optical scanners sold today come with OCR packages.

Scanners differ from one another in the following respects:

scanning technology: Most scanners use charge-coupled device (CCD) arrays, which consist of tightly packed rows of light receptors that can detect variations in light intensity and frequency. The quality of the CCD array is probably the single most important factor affecting the quality of the scanner. Industry-strength drum scanners use a different technology that relies on a photomultiplier tube (PMT), but this type of scanner is much more expensive than the more common CCD -based scanners.

resolution: The denser the bit map, the higher the resolution. Typically, scanners support resolutions of from 72 to 600 dpi.

bit depth: The number of bits used to represent each pixel. The greater the bit depth, the more colors or grayscales can be represented. For example, a 24-bit color scanner can represent 2^{24} (16.7 million) colors. Note, however, that a large color range is useless if the CCD arrays are capable of detecting only a small number of distinct colors.

size and shape: Some scanners are small hand-held devices that you move across the paper. These hand-held scanners are often called *half-page* scanners because they can only scan 2 to 5 inches at a time. Hand-held scanners are adequate for small pictures and photos, but they are difficult to use if you need to scan an entire page of text or graphics.

Larger scanners include machines into which you can feed sheets of paper. These are called *sheet-fed* scanners. Sheet-fed scanners are excellent for loose sheets of paper, but they are unable to handle bound documents.

A second type of large scanner, called a *flatbed scanner*, is like a photocopy machine. It consists of a board on which you lay books, magazines, and other documents that you want to scan.

Overhead scanners (also called *copyboard* scanners) look somewhat like overhead projectors. You place documents face-up on a scanning bed, and a small overhead tower moves across the page.

⇒ See also ASCII; BIT MAP; CCD; COLOR DEPTH; COMPUTER IMAGING; FAX MACHINE; FLATBED SCANNER; FONT; GRAY SCALING; MFP; OPTICAL CHARACTER RECOGNITION; OPTICAL RESOLUTION; PHOTO SCANNER; RESOLUTION; TWAIN.

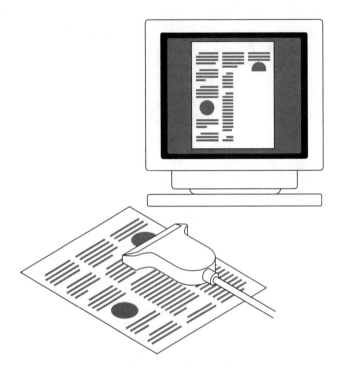

Figure 58: **optical scanner**

optimization See under OPTIMIZE.

optimize 1. In programming, to fine-tune a program so that it runs more quickly or takes up less space. **2.** When applied to disks, the term means the same as defragment. See under FRAGMENTATION. **3.** To configure a device or application so that it performs better.

⇒ See also FRAGMENTATION; PROGRAM.

option 1. In command-driven interfaces, an option is an addition to a command that changes or refines the command in a specified manner. As the term implies, options are just that—they are not required.

In the DOS operating system, options are preceded by a slash (/). For example the DIR command supports the /P option, which causes the system to pause between screenfuls of data. Other operating systems and applications have different rules for specifying options.

Other words for option are *switch* and *parameter.* **2.** In graphical user interfaces, an option is a choice in a menu or dialog box.

⇒ See also COMMAND; COMMAND DRIVEN; DIALOG BOX; GRAPHICAL USER INTERFACE; MENU.

Option key A key on Macintosh keyboards that you use in concert with other keys to generate special characters and commands. On PCs, the corresponding key is the Alt key.

⇒ See also ALT KEY; KEYBOARD; MACINTOSH COMPUTER.

opto-mechanical mouse See under MOUSE.

Oracle Based in Redwood, California, Oracle Corporation is the largest software company whose primary business is database products. Historically, Oracle has targeted high-end workstations and minicomputers as the server platforms to run its database systems. Its relational database was the first to support the SQL language, which has since become the industry standard.

Along with Sun Microsystems, Oracle has been one of the leading champions of network computers.

⇒ See also DATABASE MANAGEMENT SYSTEM; INFORMIX; NETWORK COMPUTER; SQL; SYBASE.

Orange Book The specification covering writable CDs, including CD-R.

⇒ See also CD-R DRIVE; GREEN BOOK; RED BOOK; WHITE BOOK; YELLOW_ BOOK.

ORB Short for *O(bject) R(equest) B(roker),* a component in the CORBA programming model that acts as the middleware between clients and servers. In the CORBA model, a client can request a service without knowing anything about what servers are attached to the network. The various ORBs receive the requests, forward them to the appropriate servers, and then hand the results back to the client.

⇒ See also CORBA; MIDDLEWARE.

orientation See under LANDSCAPE and PORTRAIT.

original equipment manufacturer See OEM.

OR operator A Boolean operator that returns a value of TRUE if either (or both) of its operands is TRUE. This is called an *inclusive OR operator.* There is also an *exclusive OR operator* (often abbreviated *XOR*) that returns a value of TRUE only if just one of the operands is TRUE.

⇒ See also BOOLEAN OPERATOR.

orphan In word processing, an orphan is the first line of a paragraph that appears as the last line of a page, or the last line of a paragraph that appears as the first line of a page (this is sometimes called a *widow*). Orphans are considered bad form in page layout, so most word processors allow you to avoid them.

⇒ See also PAGINATION; WIDOW; WORD PROCESSING.

OS Short for *operating system*.

OS/2 An operating system for PCs developed originally by Microsoft Corporation and IBM but sold and managed solely by IBM. OS/2 is compatible with DOS and Windows, which means that it can run all DOS and Windows programs. However, programs written specifically to run under OS/2 will not run under DOS or Windows.

Since its introduction in the late 1980s, OS/2 has traveled a particularly rocky road. The first releases were hampered by a number of technical and marketing problems. Then Microsoft abandoned the project in favor of its own operating system solution, Microsoft Windows. That break spawned a feud between the two computer giants that is still being played out in many arenas.

⇒ See also DOS; GRAPHICAL USER INTERFACE; MICROSOFT WINDOWS; MULTITASKING; OPERATING SYSTEM; PC.

OS-9 A real-time, multi-user, multitasking operating system developed by Microware Systems Corporation. Originally, OS-9 was a joint effort between Microware and Motorola. In the 1980s, Microware ported OS-9 to the Motorola 680x0 family of microprocessors, creating OS-9/68000, which is used in a variety of industrial and commercial arenas, including Philips' CD-I and, most recently, WebTV boxes.

⇒ See also CD-I (COMPACT DISC–INTERACTIVE); REAL TIME; WEBTV.

OSF Short for *Open Software Foundation*, now part of *The Open Group*.

⇒ See also DCE.

OSI Short for *O(pen) S(ystem) I(nterconnection)*, an ISO standard for worldwide communications that defines a networking framework for implementing protocols in seven layers. Control is passed from one layer to the next, starting at the application layer in one station, proceeding to the bottom layer, over the channel to the next station and back up the hierarchy.

At one time, most vendors agreed to support OSI in one form or another, but OSI was too loosely defined and proprietary standards were too entrenched. Except for the OSI-compliant X.400 and X.500 e-mail and directory standards, which are widely used, what was once thought to become the universal communications standard now serves as the teaching model for all other protocols.

Most of the functionality in the OSI model exists in all communications systems, although two or three OSI layers may be incorporated into one.

OSI is also referred to as the *OSI Reference Model* or just the *OSI Model*.

⇒ See also DLC; ISO; PROTOCOL STACK.

Table 23
OSI Model

Layer	Name	Function
7	Application Layer	Program-to-program communication.
6	Presentation Layer	Manages data representation conversions. For example, the Presentation Layer would be responsible for converting from EBCDIC to ASCII.
5	Session Layer	Responsible for establishing and maintaining communications channels. In practice, this layer is often combined with the Transport Layer.
4	Transport Layer	Responsible for end-to-end integrity of data transmission.
3	Network Layer	Routes data from one node to another.
2	Data Link Layer	Responsible for physical passing data from one node to another.
1	Physical Layer	Manages putting data onto the network media and taking the data off.

OSI Reference Model See OSI.

OSPF Short for *O(pen) S(hortest) P(ath) F(irst)*, a new protocol that defines how routers share routing information. Unlike the older Routing Information Protocol (RIP), which transfers entire routing tables, OSPF transfers only routing information that has changed since the previous transfer. As a result, it doesn't need to transfer as much data, which conserves bandwidth.

OSPF Version 2 is defined in RFC 1583. It is rapidly replacing RIP on the Internet.

⇒ See also ROUTER; ROUTING; ROUTING INFORMATION PROTOCOL.

OSR 2 Short for *OEM Service Release 2*, a new version of Windows 95 released at the end of 1996. Also called *Windows 95b,* OSR 2 provides a number of new features and bug fixes. Probably the most important new feature is FAT32, a new version of the file allocation table. FAT32 supports disk drives up to 2 terabytes and yields better storage efficiency due to smaller clusters.

OSR 2 is available only bundled in new computers. You cannot obtain it as an upgrade to older versions of Windows 95.

⇒ See also FAT32; Windows 95.

outline font A *scalable font* in which the outlines of each character are geometrically defined. The most popular languages for defining outline fonts are *PostScript* and *TrueType.*

An outline font is *scalable* because, given a geometrical description of a typeface, a printer or other display device can generate the characters at any size (scale). Aside from offering innumerable sizes of each font, outline fonts have the added advantage that they make the most of an output device's resolution. The more resolution a printer or monitor offers, the better an outline font will look.

⇒ See also bit map; font; PostScript; resolution; scalable font; TrueType; typeface; vector graphics.

output *n* **1.** Anything that comes out of a computer. Output can be meaningful information or gibberish, and it can appear in a variety of forms —as binary numbers, as characters, as pictures, and as printed pages. Output devices include display screens, loudspeakers, and printers. —*v* **2.** To give out. For example, display screens output images, printers output print, and loudspeakers output sounds.

⇒ See also I/O.

output device Any machine capable of representing information from a computer. This includes display screens, printers, plotters, and synthesizers.

⇒ See also device; output.

overclock To run a microprocessor faster than the speed for which it has been tested and approved. Overclocking is a popular technique for eking out a little more performance from a system. In many cases, you can force your CPU to run faster than it was intended simply by setting a jumper on the motherboard. Overclocking does come with some risks, however, such as overheating, so you should become familiar with all the pros and cons before you attempt it.

Overclocking is sometimes called *speed margining.*

⇒ See also clock speed; MHz; microprocessor; motherboard.

OverDrive A user-installable microprocessor from Intel for the 486 microprocessor. Many 486-based PCs are built with an OverDrive socket, which allows the owner to upgrade to a faster microprocessor simply by inserting an OverDrive chip.

⇒ See also Intel microprocessors.

overflow error An error that occurs when the computer attempts to handle a number that is too large for it. Every computer has a well-defined range of values that it can represent. If during execution of a program it arrives at a number outside this range, it will experience an overflow error. Overflow errors are sometimes referred to as *overflow conditions*.

⇒ See also floating-point number.

overhead Use of computer resources for performing a specific feature. Typically, the term is used to describe a function that is optional, or an enhancement to an existing application. For example, maintaining an audit trail might result in 10 percent overhead, meaning that the program will run 10 percent slower when the audit trail is turned on. Programmers often need to weigh the overhead of new features before implementing them.

⇒ See also feature.

overlaid windows Windows arranged so that they overlap one another. Overlaid windows resemble a stack of pieces of paper lying on top of one another; only the topmost window is displayed in full. You can move a window to the top or bottom of the stack by clicking one of the mouse buttons. This is known as *popping* or *pushing,* respectively.
　　Overlaid windows are also called cascading windows. Windows that do not overlap are called *tiled windows.*

⇒ See also pop; push; tiled windows; window.

overloading In programming languages, a feature that allows an object to have different meanings depending on its context. The term is used most often in reference to operators that can behave differently depending on the data type, or class, of the operands. For example, $x + y$ can mean different things depending on whether x and y are simple integers or complex data structures.
　　Not all programming languages support overloading, but it is a feature of most object-oriented languages, including C + + and Java. Overloading is one type of *polymorphism.*

⇒ See also class; data type; object-oriented programming; operand; operator; polymorphism.

oversampling Same as antialiasing.

overstrike To print one character directly on top of another. In older printers, this was one way to create unusual characters or bold characters, but it is not necessary with modern printers.

overwrite mode Most word processors and text editors allow you to choose between two modes: *overwrite* and *insert*. In overwrite mode, every character you type is displayed at the cursor position. If a character is already at that position, it is replaced. In insert mode, each character you type is inserted at the cursor position. This means that existing characters are moved over to make room for the new character and are not replaced.

Overwrite mode is sometimes called *overtype mode.*

⇒ See also INSERT MODE.

pack To compress data.

⇒ See also DATA COMPRESSION; PACKED FILE.

packed file A file in a compressed format. Many operating systems and applications contain commands that enable you to pack a file so that it takes up less memory. For example, suppose you have a text file containing ten consecutive space characters. Normally, this would require ten bytes of storage. However, a program that packs files would replace the space characters by a special *space-series* character followed by the number of spaces being replaced. In this case, the ten spaces would require only two bytes. This is just one packing technique—there are many others. One disadvantage of packed files, however, is that they can be read only by the program that packed them because they contain special codes.

Some modems automatically pack data before transmitting it across communications lines. This can produce faster communication because fewer bytes need to be sent. However, the modem on the receiving side must be capable of *unpacking* the data.

Packing is often referred to as data compression, particularly when it involves data communications.

⇒ See also DATA COMPRESSION; DISK COMPRESSION; MODEM.

packet A piece of a message transmitted over a packet-switching network. See under PACKET SWITCHING. One of the key features of a packet is that it contains the destination address in addition to the data. In IP networks, packets are often called *datagrams*.

⇒ See also CELL RELAY; IP; MTU; PACKET SWITCHING; ROUTER; ROUTING; TRACEROUTE.

packet switching Refers to protocols in which messages are divided into packets before they are sent. Each packet is then transmitted individually and can even follow different routes to its destination. Once all the packets forming a message arrive at the destination, they are recompiled into the original message.

Most modern wide-area network (WAN) protocols, including TCP/IP, X.25, and Frame Relay, are based on packet-switching technologies. In contrast, normal telephone service is based on a circuit-switching technology, in which a dedicated line is allocated for transmission between two parties. Circuit-switching is ideal when data must be transmitted quickly and must arrive in the same order in which they are sent. This is the case with most real-time data, such as live audio and video. Packet switching is more efficient and robust for data that can withstand some delays in transmission, such as e-mail messages and Web pages.

A new technology, ATM, attempts to combine the best of both worlds —the guaranteed delivery of circuit-switched networks and the robustness and efficiency of packet-switching networks.

⇒ See also CDPD; CELL RELAY; CIRCUIT SWITCHING; FRAME RELAY; NETWORK; SVC; TCP/IP; WIDE-AREA NETWORK; X.25.

pad character A character used to fill empty space. Many applications have fields that must be a particular length. For example, in a database application, you may have a field that is ten characters in length. If you use only four of the allotted characters, the program itself must fill in the remaining six characters with pad characters.

Some applications allow you to choose the character to be used as padding.

⇒ See also DATABASE; FIELD; NULL CHARACTER.

padding Filling in unused space.

⇒ See also PAD CHARACTER.

page *n* **1.** A fixed amount of data. **2.** In word processing, a page of text. Most text-processing applications recognize a hierarchy of components, starting with a character at the lowest level, followed by a *word*, a *line*, a *paragraph*, and a *page*. Applications permit certain operations for each type of component; for example, you can delete a character, a word, a line, and sometimes an entire page. For pages, you can also specify formatting characteristics (for example, page size, margins, and number of columns). **3.** In virtual memory systems, a page is a fixed number of bytes recognized by the operating system. **4.** Short for Web page. —*v* **5.** To display one page (or screenful) of a document at a time. To contrast, see *scroll.* **6.** To copy a page of data from main memory to a mass storage device, or vice versa. Paging is one form of swapping.

⇒ See also FPM RAM; MAIN MEMORY; PAGING; SEGMENT; SWAP; VIRTUAL MEMORY.

page break The end of a page of text. In word-processing systems, you can enter special codes, called *hard page breaks* or *forced page breaks*, that cause the printer to advance to the next page. Without hard page breaks, the word processor automatically begins a new page after a page has been filled (this depends on the number of lines per page). In this case, the page break is called a *soft page break.*

⇒ See also HARD; SOFT; WORD PROCESSING.

Page Description Language (PDL) A language for describing the layout and contents of a printed page. The best-known PDLs are Adobe Post-Script and Hewlett-Packard PCL (Printer Control Language), both of which are used to control laser printers.

Both PostScript and modern versions of PCL are *object-oriented*, meaning that they describe a page in terms of geometrical objects such as lines, arcs, and circles.

⇒ See also LASER PRINTER; OBJECT ORIENTED; PCL; POSTSCRIPT.

Page Down key Often abbreviated *PgDn*, the Page Down key is standard on PC and Macintosh keyboards. Its meaning differs from one program to another, but it usually moves the cursor down a set number of lines.

⇒ See also KEYBOARD.

page eject Same as FORM FEED.

page fault An interrupt that occurs when a program requests data that is not currently in virtual memory. The interrupt triggers the operating system to fetch the data from a storage device and load it into RAM.

An *invalid page fault* or *page fault error* occurs when the operating system cannot find the data at all. This usually happens when the virtual memory area, or the table that maps virtual addresses to real addresses, becomes corrupt.

⇒ See also INVALID PAGE FAULT; MMU; PAGING; VIRTUAL MEMORY.

page fault error Same as INVALID PAGE FAULT.

page layout program A program that enables you to format pages of text and graphics. Many word-processing systems support their own page layout functions, but page layout applications designed specifically for this purpose generally give you more control over fine points such as text flow, kerning, and positioning of graphics.

⇒ See also DESKTOP PUBLISHING; KERNING; TEXT WRAP; WORD PROCESSING.

page-mode memory Same as under *FPM RAM*.

page preview See under PREVIEW.

page printer Any printer that processes an entire page at one time. All laser and ink-jet printers are page printers, which means that they must have enough memory to store at least one page.

⇒ See also LASER PRINTER; PAGE DESCRIPTION LANGUAGE (PDL); PRINTER.

pages per minute See PPM.

Page Up key Often abbreviated *PgUp*, the Page Up key is standard on PC and Macintosh keyboards. Its meaning differs from one program to another, but it usually scrolls the document up one screenful.

⇒ See also KEYBOARD.

page-white display A special type of LCD display screen that uses supertwist technology to produce a high contrast between the foreground and background.

⇒ See also FLAT-PANEL DISPLAY; LCD; SUPERTWIST.

pagination 1. Refers to numbering pages in a document. **2.** Refers to dividing a document into pages. Most word processors automatically paginate documents based on a page size that you specify. Some word processors enable you to avoid widows and orphans during pagination.

⇒ See also ORPHAN; WIDOW; WORD PROCESSING.

paging A technique used by virtual memory operating systems to help ensure that the data you need is available as quickly as possible. The operating system copies a certain number of pages from your storage device to main memory. When a program needs a page that is not in main memory, the operating system copies the required page into memory and copies another page back to the disk. One says that the operating system *pages* the data. Each time a page is needed that is not currently in memory, a *page fault* occurs. An *invalid page fault* occurs when the address of the page being requested is invalid. In this case, the application is usually aborted.

This type of virtual memory is called *paged virtual memory*. Another form of virtual memory is *segmented virtual memory*.

⇒ See also DEMAND PAGING; MAIN MEMORY; OPERATING SYSTEM; PAGE; PAGE FAULT; SEGMENT; SWAP; THRASH; VIRTUAL MEMORY.

paint program A graphics program that enables you to draw pictures on the display screen that are represented as bit maps (bit-mapped graphics). In contrast, *draw programs* use vector graphics (object-oriented images), which scale better.

Most paint programs provide the *tools* shown below in the form of icons. By selecting an icon, you can perform functions associated with the tool.

In addition to these tools, paint programs also provide easy ways to draw common shapes such as straight lines, rectangles, circles, and ovals.

Sophisticated paint applications are often called *image editing programs*. These applications support many of the features of draw programs, such as the ability to work with objects. Each object, however, is represented as a bit map rather than as a vector image.

⇒ See also ADOBE PHOTOSHOP; BIT-MAPPED GRAPHICS; DRAW PROGRAM; GRAPHICS; MARQUEE; VECTOR GRAPHICS.

Table 24
Paint Tools

Icon	Tool	Function
	Brush	For freehand painting using the currently selected pattern and color. Most paint programs provide differently shaped brushes for different styles of painting.
	Eraser	For erasing selected areas of the display screen.
	Lasso	For selecting parts of an illustration.
	Pen	For drawing freehand lines.
	Scissors	For cutting a section of a painting.
	Spraycan	For spray painting in the current pattern and color.

PAL 1. Short for *Phase Alternating Line,* the dominant television standard in Europe. The United States uses a different standard, NTSC. Whereas NTSC delivers 525 lines of resolution at 60 half-frames per second, PAL delivers 625 lines at 50 half-frames per second. Many video adapters that enable computer monitors to be used as television screens support both NTSC and PAL signals. **2.** Short for *Programmable Array Logic,* a type of Programmable Logic Device (PLD).

⇒ See also COMMON INTERMEDIATE FORMAT; NTSC; QCIF; VIDEO ADAPTER.

palette 1. In computer graphics, a palette is the set of available colors. For a given application, the palette may be only a subset of all the colors that can be physically displayed. For example, a SVGA system can display 16 million unique colors, but a given program would use only 256 of them at a time if the display were in 256-color mode. The computer system's palette, therefore, would consist of the 16 million colors, but the program's palette would contain only the 256-color subset.

A palette is also called a *CLUT [c(olor) l(ook)-u(p) t(able)].*

On monochrome systems, the term *palette* is sometimes used to refer to the available fill patterns. **2.** In paint and illustration programs, a palette is a collection of symbols that represent drawing tools. For example, a simple palette might contain a paintbrush, a pencil, and an eraser.

⇒ See also DRAW PROGRAM; EGA; GRAPHICS; PAINT PROGRAM; VIDEO ADAPTER.

palmtop A small computer that literally fits in your palm. Compared with full-size computers, palmtops are severely limited, but they are practical for certain functions such as phone books and calendars. Palmtops that use a pen rather than a keyboard for input are often called *hand-held computers* or *PDAs*.

Because of their small size, most palmtop computers do not include disk drives. However, many contain PCMCIA slots in which you can insert disk drives, modems, memory, and other devices.

Palmtops are also called PDAs, hand-held computers, and *pocket computers*.

⇒ See also HANDHELD COMPUTER; NOTEBOOK COMPUTER; PDA; PORTABLE; WINDOWS CE.

Pantone Matching System (PMS) A popular color matching system used by the printing industry to print spot colors. Most applications that support color printing allow you to specify colors by indicating the Pantone name or number. This assures that you get the right color when the file is printed, even though the color may not look right when displayed on your monitor.

PMS works well for spot colors but not for process colors, which are generally specified using the CMYK color model.

⇒ See also CMYK; COLOR MANAGEMENT SYSTEM (CMS); PROCESS COLORS; SPOT COLOR.

PAP Short for *P(assword) A(uthentication) P(rotocol)*, the most basic form of authentication, in which a user's name and password are transmitted over a network and compared with a table of name-password pairs. Typically, the passwords stored in the table are encrypted. The Basic Authentication feature built into the HTTP protocol uses PAP. The main weakness of PAP is that both the username and password are transmitted "in the clear"—that is, in an unencrypted form. Contrast with *CHAP*.

⇒ See also AUTHENTICATION; CHAP.

paper feed The mechanism or method that moves paper through a printer. For example, a *tractor-feed* mechanism is one that pulls the paper with a rotating wheel whose nubs catch in holes on either side of the paper.

⇒ See also PRINTER; TRACTOR FEED.

paperless office The idealized office in which paper is absent because all information is stored and transferred electronically. With the ever-expanding application of computers into business areas as diverse as accounting, desktop publishing, billing, mail, and scheduling, it seemed in the early 1980s that the real paperless office was just around the corner.

Ironically, just the opposite has transpired. The ease with which computers enable people to print all sorts of documents has created a flood of new paper. Indeed, perhaps the most widespread computer application is the fax machine, which uses paper by the ream.

Some analysts believe that the paperless office is still an achievable and desirable goal, but that certain key technologies such as optical character recognition (OCR) must be improved. Others, however, argue that the *tangibleness* of paper documents yields certain benefits that will never disappear.

⇒ See also DOCUMENT MANAGEMENT; FAX MACHINE; OPTICAL CHARACTER RECOGNITION; WORKGROUP COMPUTING.

paper-white display A high-quality monochrome monitor that displays characters in black against a white background. Such monitors are popular for desktop publishing because they most closely mimic real paper with black type. Some manufacturers make a distinction between normal white-background monitors and paper-white monitors, where the background is slightly tinted to look more like bonded paper.

⇒ See also DISPLAY SCREEN; MONITOR.

parallel Refers to processes that occur simultaneously. Printers and other devices are said to be either *parallel* or *serial*. *Parallel* means that the device is capable of receiving more than one bit at a time (that is, it receives several bits *in parallel*). Most modern printers are parallel.

⇒ See also PARALLEL PORT; PORT; PRINTER; SERIAL.

parallel computing Same as PARALLEL PROCESSING.

parallel interface A channel capable of transferring more than one bit simultaneously. Almost all personal computers come with at least one parallel interface. The other type of interface is a *serial interface*.

⇒ See also CENTRONICS INTERFACE; CHANNEL; PARALLEL; PARALLEL PORT; SERIAL PORT.

parallel port A parallel interface for connecting an external device such as a printer. Most personal computers have both a parallel port and at least one serial port.

On PCs, the parallel port uses a 25-pin connector (type DB-25) and is used to connect printers, computers, and other devices that need relatively high bandwidth. It is often called a Centronics interface, after the company that designed the original standard for parallel communication between a computer and printer. (The modern parallel interface is based on a design by Epson.)

A newer type of parallel port, which supports the same connectors as the Centronics interface, is the *EPP (Enhanced Parallel Port)* or *ECP (Extended Capabilities Port)*. Both of these parallel ports support bi-directional communication and transfer rates ten times as fast as those provided by the Centronics port.

Macintoshes have a SCSI port, which is parallel but more flexible.

⇒ See also CENTRONICS INTERFACE; ECP; EPP; IRDA; LOCALTALK; PARALLEL; PORT; SCSI; SERIAL PORT; USB.

parallel processing The simultaneous use of more than one CPU to execute a program. Ideally, parallel processing makes a program run faster because there are more engines (CPUs) running it. In practice, it is often difficult to divide a program in such a way that separate CPUs can execute different portions without interfering with one another.

Most computers have just one CPU, but some models have several. There are even computers with thousands of CPUs. With single-CPU computers, it is possible to perform parallel processing by connecting the computers in a network. However, this type of parallel processing requires very sophisticated software called distributed processing software.

Note that parallel processing differs from multitasking, in which a single CPU executes several programs at once.

Parallel processing is also called *parallel computing.*

⇒ See also CLUSTERING; CPU; DISTRIBUTED PROCESSING; HIGH PERFORMANCE COMPUTING; MPP; MULTITASKING; NUMA; SUPERSCALAR.

parameter 1. Characteristic. For example, *specifying parameters* means defining the characteristics of something. In general, parameters are used to customize a program. For example, filenames, page lengths, and font specifications could all be considered parameters. **2.** In programming, the term *parameter* is synonymous with *argument,* a value that is passed to a routine.

⇒ See also ARGUMENT; ROUTINE.

parameter RAM (PRAM) See PRAM.

parent directory Refers to the directory (or folder) above another directory (or folder). Every directory, except the root directory, lies beneath another directory. The higher directory is called the *parent directory,* and the lower directory is called a subdirectory. In DOS and UNIX systems, the parent directory is identified by two dots (..).

⇒ See also DIRECTORY; ROOT DIRECTORY.

parity The quality of being either odd or even. The fact that all numbers have a parity is commonly used in data communications to ensure the validity of data. This is called *parity checking.*

⇒ See also PARITY CHECKING.

parity bit See under PARITY CHECKING.

parity checking In communications, *parity checking* refers to the use of *parity bits* to check that data has been transmitted accurately. The parity bit is added to every data unit (typically seven or eight bits) that is transmitted. The parity bit for each unit is set so that all bytes have either an odd number or an even number of set bits.

Assume, for example, that two devices are communicating with even parity (the most common form of parity checking). As the transmitting device sends data, it counts the number of set bits in each group of seven bits. If the number of set bits is even, it sets the parity bit to 0; if the number of set bits is odd, it sets the parity bit to 1. In this way, every byte has an even number of set bits. On the receiving side, the device checks each byte to make sure that it has an even number of set bits. If it finds an odd number of set bits, the receiver knows that there was an error during transmission.

The sender and receiver must both agree to use parity checking and to agree on whether parity is to be odd or even. If the two sides are not configured with the same *parity sense,* communication will be impossible.

Parity checking is the most basic form of error detection in communications. Although it detects many errors, it is not foolproof, because it cannot detect situations in which an even number of bits in the same data unit are changed due to electrical noise. There are many other, more sophisticated protocols for ensuring transmission accuracy, such as MNP and CCITT V.42.

Parity checking is used not only in communications but also to test memory storage devices. Many PCs, for example, perform a parity check on memory every time a byte of data is read.

⇒ See also CCITT; COMMUNICATIONS; COMMUNICATIONS PROTOCOL; MNP; MODEM.

park To lock the *read/write head* of a hard disk drive in a safe position so that the disk will not be damaged while the drive is being moved. Parking the disk is particularly important for portable computers, which are moved frequently. The disk will automatically *unpark* itself once you turn the power on.

All modern disk drives support *automatic head parking,* in which the drive automatically parks the head whenever the power is turned off.

⇒ See also DISK DRIVE; HEAD; HEAD CRASH.

parse In linguistics, to divide language into small components that can be analyzed. For example, parsing this sentence would involve dividing it into words and phrases and identifying the type of each component (*e.g.,* verb, adjective, or noun).

Parsing is a very important part of many computer science disciplines. For example, compilers must parse source code to be able to translate it into object code. Likewise, any application that processes complex commands must be able to parse the commands. This includes virtually all end-user applications. For example, each time a Web site displays a Web page, it must first parse the HTML code representing the page.

Parsing is often divided into *lexical analysis* and *semantic parsing.* Lexical analysis concentrates on dividing strings into components, called tokens, based on punctuation and other keys. Semantic parsing then attempts to determine the meaning of the string.

⇒ See also COMPILE; COMPILER; SEMANTICS.

partition *v* **1.** To divide memory or mass storage into isolated sections. In DOS systems, you can partition a disk, and each partition will behave like a separate disk drive. Partitioning is particularly useful if you run more than one operating system. For example, you might reserve one partition for Windows and another for UNIX.

In addition, partitioning on DOS and Windows machines can improve disk efficiency. This is because the FAT system used by these operating systems automatically assigns cluster size based on the disk size: the larger the disk, the larger the cluster. Unfortunately, large clusters can result in a wasted disk space, called slack space. An entire sector of the software industry is devoted to building utilities that let you partition your hard disk.

On Apple Macintosh computers, there are two types of partitioning: *hard* and *soft*. Hard partitioning is the same as DOS partitioning—the disk is physically divided into different sections. Soft partitioning, on the other hand, does not physically affect the disk at all, but it fools the Finder into believing that the disk is partitioned. The advantage of this is that you can partition the disk without affecting the data on it. With hard partitioning, it is usually necessary to reformat the entire disk. —*n* **2.** A section of main memory or mass storage that has been reserved for a particular application.

⇒ See also CLUSTER; DISK DRIVE; FDISK; FILE ALLOCATION TABLE; FINDER; MBR; SLACK SPACE.

Pascal Pronounced *pass-kal,* a high-level programming language developed by Niklaus Wirth in the late 1960s. The language is named after Blaise Pascal, a seventeenth-century French mathematician who constructed one of the first mechanical adding machines.

Pascal is best known for its affinity to structured programming techniques. The nature of the language forces programmers to design programs methodically and carefully. For this reason, it is a popular teaching language.

Despite its success in academia, Pascal has had only modest success in the business world. Part of the resistance to Pascal by professional programmers stems from its inflexibility and lack of tools for developing large applications.

To address some of these criticisms, Wirth designed a new language called Modula-2. Modula-2 is similar to Pascal in many respects, but it contains additional features.

⇒ See also BORLAND INTERNATIONAL; DELPHI; HIGH-LEVEL LANGUAGE; MODULA-2; PROGRAMMING LANGUAGE.

passive backplane See under BACKPLANE.

passive-matrix display A common type of flat-panel display consisting of a grid of horizontal and vertical wires. At the intersection of each grid is an LCD element that constitutes a single pixel, either letting light through or blocking it. A higher-quality and more expensive type of display, called an *active-matrix display*, uses a transistor to control each pixel.

In the mid-1990s, it appeared that passive-matrix displays would eventually become extinct because of the higher quality of active-matrix displays. However, the high cost of producing active-matrix displays, and new technologies such as DSTN, CSTN and HPA that improve passive-matrix displays, have caused passive-matrix displays to make a surprising comeback.

⇒ See also ACTIVE-MATRIX DISPLAY; CSTN; DSTN; FLAT-PANEL DISPLAY; LCD; PIXEL; TFT.

password A secret series of characters that enables a user to access a file, computer, or program. On multiuser systems, each user must enter his or her password before the computer will respond to commands. The password helps ensure that unauthorized users do not access the computer. In addition, data files and programs may require a password.

Ideally, the password should be something that nobody could guess. In practice, most people choose a password that is easy to remember, such as their name or their initials. This is one reason it is relatively easy to break into most computer systems.

⇒ See also ACCESS CODE; AUTHENTICATION; KEY; LOG ON; SECURITY.

Password Authentication Protocol See PAP.

paste To copy an object from a buffer (or clipboard) to a file. In word processing, blocks of text are often moved from one place to another by cutting and pasting. When you cut a block of text, the word processor removes the block from your file and places it in a temporary holding area (a buffer). You can then paste the material in the buffer somewhere else.

Modern operating systems, such as Microsoft Windows, allow you to cut an object from one application and paste it into another. Depending on how the object is pasted, it can be either *linked* or *embedded*.

⇒ See also BUFFER; CLIPBOARD; COPY; CUT; EMBEDDED OBJECT; LINK; OLE.

patch A temporary fix to a program bug. A patch is an actual piece of object code that is inserted into (*patched* into) an executable program.

⇒ See also BUG; EXECUTABLE FILE; OBJECT CODE.

path 1. In DOS and Windows systems, a path is a list of directories where the operating system looks for executable files if it is unable to find the file in the working directory. You can specify the list of directories with the PATH command. **2.** Another name for *pathname*.

⇒ See also DIRECTORY; DOS; EXECUTABLE FILE; PATHNAME; WORKING DIRECTORY.

pathname A sequence of symbols and names that identifies a file. Every file has a name, called a *filename*, so the simplest type of pathname is just a filename. If you specify a filename as the pathname, the operating system looks for that file in your current working directory. However, if the file resides in a different directory, you must tell the operating system how to find that directory. You do this by specifying a path that the operating system must follow.

The pathname always starts from your working directory or from the root directory. Each operating system has its own rules for specifying paths. In DOS systems, for example, the root directory is named \, and each subdirectory is separated by an additional backslash. In UNIX, the root directory is named /, and each subdirectory is followed by a slash. In Macintosh environments, directories are separated by a colon.

⇒ See also DIRECTORY; FILENAME; ROOT DIRECTORY; UNC; WORKING DIRECTORY.

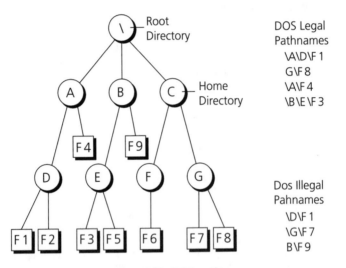

Figure 59: **DOS paths**

pattern recognition An important field of computer science concerned with recognizing patterns, particularly visual and sound patterns. It is central to optical character recognition (OCR), voice recognition, and handwriting recognition.

⇒ See also HANDWRITING RECOGNITION; OPTICAL CHARACTER RECOGNITION; VOICE RECOGNITION.

Pause key A key that you can use to temporarily halt the display of data. Generally, you use the Pause key to freeze data that is being scrolled on the display screen. To continue scrolling, you can press any key.

In DOS, an alternative to using the Pause key is to use the MORE command, which displays one screenful of data at a time.

⇒ See also SCROLL.

PBX Short for *p(rivate) b(ranch) ex(change)*, a private telephone network used within an enterprise. Users of the PBX share a certain number of *outside lines* for making telephone calls external to the PBX.

Most medium-sized and larger companies use a PBX because it's much less expensive than connecting an external telephone line to every telephone in the organization. In addition, it's easier to call someone within a PBX because the number you need to dial typically consists of just three or four digits.

A new variation on the PBX theme is the centrex, which is a PBX with all switching occurring at a local telephone office instead of at the company's premises.

⇒ See also CENTREX; POTS; TELEMATICS.

PC 1. Short for *personal computer* or *IBM PC*. The first personal computer produced by IBM was called the *PC*, and increasingly the term *PC* came to mean IBM or IBM-compatible personal computers, to the exclusion of other types of personal computers, such as Macintoshes.

In recent years, the term *PC* has become more and more difficult to pin down. In general, though, it applies to any personal computer based on an Intel microprocessor, or on an Intel-compatible microprocessor. For nearly every other component, including the operating system, there are several options, all of which fall under the rubric of PC. **2.** *PC* can stand for *printed circuit*, so a *PC board* is a printed circuit board.

⇒ See also CLONE; COMPAQ; COMPATIBLE; DELL COMPUTER; EXPANSION BUS; IBM; IBM PC; LOCAL BUS; MACINTOSH COMPUTER; OPERATING SYSTEM; PERSONAL COMPUTER; PRINTED CIRCUIT BOARD; VIDEO STANDARDS.

PC/AT See under AT.

PCB Short for *printed circuit board*.

PC card A computer device packaged in a small card about the size of a credit card and conforming to the PCMCIA standard.

⇒ See also CARDBUS; PCMCIA; ZV PORT.

PC-DOS The name IBM uses to market its version of the DOS operating system.

⇒ See also DOS.

PC fax Same as FAX MODEM.

PCI Acronym for *P(eripheral) C(omponent) I(nterconnect)*, a local bus standard developed by Intel Corporation. Most modern PCs include a PCI bus in addition to a more general ISA expansion bus. Many analysts, however, believe that PCI will eventually supplant ISA entirely. PCI is also used on newer versions of the Macintosh computer.

PCI is a 64-bit bus, though it is usually implemented as a 32-bit bus. It can run at clock speeds of 33 or 66 MHz. At 32 bits and 33 MHz, it yields a throughput rate of 133 MBps.

Although it was developed by Intel, PCI is not tied to any particular family of microprocessors.

⇒ See also AGP; BUS; BUS MASTERING; CONTROLLER; EXPANSION BUS; I2O; IN-DUSTRY STANDARD ARCHITECTURE (ISA) BUS; INTEL; LOCAL BUS; NuBus.

PCL Abbreviation of *P(rinter) C(ontrol) L(anguage)*, the *page description language (PDL)* developed by Hewlett-Packard and used in many of its laser and ink-jet printers. PCL 5 and later versions support a *scalable font* technology called *Intellifont*.

⇒ See also HP; HP-COMPATIBLE PRINTER; HPGL; INTELLIFONT; LASER PRINTER; PAGE DESCRIPTION LANGUAGE (PDL); POSTSCRIPT; SCALABLE FONT.

PCM Short for *Pulse Code Modulation*, a sampling technique for digitizing analog signals, especially audio signals. PCM samples the signal 8000 times a second; each sample is represented by 8 bits for a total of 64 Kbps. There are two standards for coding the sample level. The Mu-Law standard is used in North America and Japan while the A-Law standard is use in most other countries.

PCM is used with T-1 and T-3 carrier systems. These carrier systems combine the PCM signals from many lines and transmit them over a single cable or other medium.

⇒ See also ADPCM; DIGITIZE; MODULATE; SAMPLING; TDM.

PCMCIA Short for *P(ersonal) C(omputer) M(emory) C(ard) I(nternational) A(ssociation)*, and pronounced as separate letters, PCMCIA is an organization consisting of some 500 companies that has developed a standard for small, credit card–sized devices, called *PC Cards*. Originally designed for adding memory to portable computers, the PCMCIA standard has been expanded several times and is now suitable for many types of devices. There are in fact three types of PCMCIA cards. All three have the same rectangular size (85.6 by 54 millimeters), but different widths.

Type I cards can be up to 3.3 mm thick and are used primarily for adding additional ROM or RAM to a computer.

Type II cards can be up to 5.5 mm thick. These cards are often used for modem and fax modem cards.

Type III cards can be up to 10.5 mm thick, which is sufficiently large for portable disk drives.

As with the cards, PCMCIA slots also come in three sizes:

A Type I slot can hold one Type I card.

A Type II slot can hold one Type II card or two Type I cards.

A Type III slot can hold one Type III card or a Type I and Type II card.

In general, you can exchange PC Cards on the fly, without rebooting your computer. For example, you can slip in a fax modem card when you want to send a fax and then, when you're done, replace the fax modem card with a memory card.

⇒ See also CardBus; Device Bay; hot plugging; IEEE 1394; plug-and-play; USB; ZV Port.

PCS Short for *P(ersonal) C(ommunications) S(ervice)*, the U.S. Federal Communications Commission (FCC) term used to describe a set of digital cellular technologies being deployed in the U.S. PCS includes CDMA (also called *IS-95*), GSM, and North American TDMA (also called IS-136). Two of the most important distinguishing features of PCS systems are:

- They are completely digital
- They operate at the 1900 MHz frequency range

⇒ See also CDMA; cellular; GSM; TDMA.

PC/TV A combination of a personal computer and television. PC/TVs are computers with built-in television boards.

⇒ See also television board; WebTV.

PCX Originally developed by ZSOFT for its PC Paintbrush program, PCX is a graphics file format for graphics programs running on PCs. It is supported by most optical scanners, fax programs, and desktop publishing systems. Files in the PCX format end with a .PCX (pronounced *dot-p-c-x*) extension. Two other common bit map formats are *BMP* and *TIFF*.

⇒ See also bit-mapped graphics; BMP; graphics file formats; TIFF.

PDA Short for *personal digital assistant*, a handheld device that combines computing, telephone/fax, and networking features. A typical PDA can function like a cellular phone, fax sender, and personal organizer. Unlike portable computers, most PDAs are pen-based, using a stylus rather than a keyboard for input. This means that they also incorporate handwriting recognition features. Some PDAs can also react to voice input by using voice recognition technologies.

The field of PDA was pioneered by Apple Computer, which introduced the Newton MessagePad in 1993. Shortly thereafter, several other manufacturers offered similar products. To date, PDAs have had only modest success in the marketplace, due to their high price tags and limited applications. However, many experts believe that PDAs will eventually become common gadgets.

⇒ See also Apple Computer; EPOC; hand-held computer; handwriting recognition; HPC; palmtop; voice recognition; Windows CE.

PDF Short for *Portable Document Format*, a file format developed by Adobe Systems. PDF captures formatting information from a variety of desktop publishing applications, making it possible to send formatted documents and have them appear on the recipient's monitor or printer as they were intended. To create a PDF file, you need special publishing tools from Adobe Systems. To view a file in PDF format, you need Adobe Acrobat Reader, a free application distributed by Adobe Systems.

⇒ See also ACROBAT; FILE FORMAT.

PDL See PAGE DESCRIPTION LANGUAGE.

peer-to-peer architecture A type of network in which each workstation has equivalent capabilities and responsibilities. This differs from client/server architectures, in which some computers are dedicated to serving the others. Peer-to-peer networks are generally simpler and less expensive, but they usually do not offer the same performance under heavy loads.

⇒ See also CLIENT/SERVER ARCHITECTURE; LOCAL-AREA NETWORK.

pel Short for *pixel*.

pen computer A computer that utilizes an electronic pen (called a *stylus*) rather than a keyboard for input. Pen computers generally require special operating systems that support handwriting recognition so that users can write on the screen or on a tablet instead of typing on a keyboard. Most pen computers are handheld devices, which are too small for a full-size keyboard.

⇒ See also HANDHELD COMPUTER; HANDWRITING RECOGNITION; PALMTOP; PDA.

Pentium 2 Same as PENTIUM II.

Pentium II Intel's newest member of the Pentium chip family. The Pentium II builds on the design of the Pentium Pro but adds an additional 2 million transistors to bring the total up to 7.5 million. Current versions of the chip run at speeds of 233, 266, 300, and 333 MHz. In addition, the Pentium II features the following:

- A *Singled Edge Contact (SEC)* cartridge that fits into Slot 1
- Dual Independent Bus (DIB) architecture
- 512K L2 cache
- 32K L1 cache
- MMX support

⇒ See also DESCHUTES; INTEL MICROPROCESSORS; PENTIUM MICROPROCESSOR; PENTIUM PRO; SLOT 1.

Pentium microprocessor A 32-bit microprocessor introduced by Intel in 1993. It contains 3.3 million transistors, nearly triple the number contained in its predecessor, the 80486 chip. Though still in production, the Pentium processor has been superseded by the Pentium Pro and Pentium II microprocessors.

⇒ See also AMD; Cyrix; Deschutes; Intel microprocessors; K6; Merced; microprocessor; Pentium II; Pentium Pro; Socket 7; Tillamook; Triton.

Pentium MMX See MMX.

Pentium Pro The Pentium Pro is Intel's sixth-generation microprocessor (P6). Although it shares the same name as the fifth-generation Pentium microprocessor, the Pentium Pro is architecturally quite different. Thanks to modern design techniques, including superpipelining, dynamic execution, and on-chip L2 cache, the Pentium Pro can perform at nearly twice the speed of previous Pentium microprocessors.

⇒ See also DIB; Intel microprocessors; microprocessor; Pentium II; Pentium microprocessor; Socket 8.

peripheral Short for *peripheral device.*

Peripheral Component Interconnect See PCI.

peripheral device Any external device attached to a computer. Examples of peripherals include printers, disk drives, display monitors, keyboards, and mice.

⇒ See also controller; device; external bus.

Perl Short for *Practical Extraction and Report Language,* Perl is a programming language developed by Larry Wall, especially designed for processing text. Because of its strong text processing abilities, Perl has become one of the most popular languages for writing CGI scripts. Perl is an interpretive language, which makes it easy to build and test simple programs.

⇒ See also awk; CGI; interpreter; Tcl.

Permanent Virtual Circuit See PVC.

persistent cookie See under cookie.

persistent URL See PURL.

Personal Communications Service See PCS.

personal computer A small, relatively inexpensive computer designed for an individual user. In price, personal computers range anywhere from a few hundred dollars to more than $5,000. All are based on the microprocessor technology that enables manufacturers to put an entire CPU on one chip. Businesses use personal computers for word processing, accounting, desktop publishing, and for running spreadsheet and database management applications. At home, the most popular use for personal computers is for playing games.

Personal computers first appeared in the late 1970s. One of the first and most popular personal computers was the Apple II, introduced in 1977 by Apple Computer. During the late 1970s and early 1980s, new models and competing operating systems seemed to appear daily. Then, in 1981, IBM entered the fray with its first personal computer, known as the *IBM PC*. The IBM PC quickly became the personal computer of choice, and most other personal-computer manufacturers fell by the wayside. One of the few companies to survive IBM's onslaught was Apple Computer, which remains a major player in the personal computer marketplace.

Other companies adjusted to IBM's dominance by building IBM clones, computers that were internally almost the same as the IBM PC but that cost less. Because IBM clones used the same microprocessors as IBM PCs, they were capable of running the same software. Over the years, IBM has lost much of its influence in directing the evolution of PCs. Many of its innovations, such as the MCA expansion bus and the OS/2 operating system, have not been accepted by the industry or the marketplace.

Today, the world of personal computers is basically divided between Apple Macintoshes and PCs. The principal characteristics of personal computers are that they are single-user systems and are based on microprocessors. However, although personal computers are designed as single-user systems, it is common to link them together to form a network. In terms of power, there is great variety. At the high end, the distinction between personal computers and workstations has faded. High-end models of the Macintosh and PC offer the same computing power and graphics capability as low-end workstations by Sun Microsystems, Hewlett-Packard, and DEC.

⇒ See also Amiga; clone; computer; home computer; Macintosh computer; microprocessor; PC; workstation.

Personal Computer Memory Card International Association See under PCMCIA.

Personal Digital Assistant See PDA.

personal finance manager A simple *accounting program* that helps individuals manage their finances. Personal finance managers help you balance your checkbook and keep track of investments. Some can even help you pay your bills by printing checks or transferring money electronically from your bank account.

⇒ See also accounting software.

personal information manager See PIM.

petabyte 2^{50} (1,125,899,906,842,624) bytes. A petabyte is equal to 1,024 terabytes.

⇒ See also EXABYTE; GIGABYTE; TERABYTE.

PFE See under INVALID PAGE FAULT.

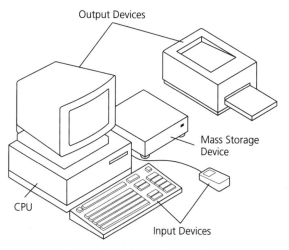

Output Devices

Mass Storage
Device

CPU

Input Devices

Figure 60: **personal computer**

PGA 1. Short for *p(in) g(rid) a(rray)*, a type of chip package in which the connecting pins are located on the bottom in concentric squares. PGA chips are particularly good for chips that have many pins, such as modern microprocessors. Compare with *DIP* and *SIP*. **2.** Short for *P(rofessional) G(raphics) A(dapter)*, a video standard developed by IBM that supports 640 by 480 resolution.

⇒ See also CHIP; DIP; SIP.

PgDn key See PAGE DOWN KEY.

PGP See PRETTY GOOD PRIVACY.

PgUp key See PAGE UP KEY.

phase change disk A type of rewritable optical disk that employs the phase change recording method. Using this technique, the disk drive writes data with a laser that changes spots on the disk between amorphous and crystalline states. An optical head reads data by detecting the difference in reflected light from amorphous and crystalline spots. A medium-intensity pulse can then restore the original crystalline structure.
    Magneto-optical and dye-polymer technologies offer similar capabilities

for developing rewritable optical disks.

⇒ See also MAGNETO-OPTICAL (MO) DRIVE; OPTICAL DISK; SOLID INK-JET PRINTER; WORM.

phase-change printer Same as SOLID INK-JET PRINTER.

Phoenix BIOS A common version of the PC BIOS developed by Phoenix Corporation, one of the largest producers of BIOS firmware for IBM PC clones.

⇒ See also BIOS; CLONE.

phosphor pitch Same as DOT PITCH.

PhotoCD A file format for storing digital photographs developed by Eastman Kodak Co.

⇒ See also PHOTO ILLUSTRATION.

photo illustration A type of computer art that begins with a digitized photograph. Using special image-enhancement software, an artist can then apply a variety of special effects to transform the photo into a work of art.

⇒ See also IMAGE ENHANCEMENT; PHOTOCD.

photo scanner A type of optical scanner designed especially for scanning photographs. Photo scanners are smaller than general-purpose scanners but offer high resolution. A typical photo scanner is a sheet-fed scanner that can scan 3 by 5–inch or 4 by 6–inch photographs at 300 dpi or higher resolution. Some high-end photo scanners can also scan negatives and slides.

⇒ See also IMAGE ENHANCEMENT; IMAGE PROCESSING; OPTICAL SCANNER; SNAP-SHOT PRINTER.

Photoshop See ADOBE PHOTOSHOP.

phreaking Closely related to hacking, using a computer or other device to trick a phone system. Typically, phreaking is used to make free calls or to have calls charged to a different account.

⇒ See also CRACK; HACKER.

physical Refers to anything pertaining to hardware. The opposite of physical is *logical* or *virtual*, which describe software objects. For example, *physical memory* refers to the actual RAM chips installed in a computer. *Virtual memory*, on the other hand, is an imaginary storage area used by programs.

A *physical data structure* refers to the actual organization of data on a storage device. The *logical data structure* refers to how the information appears to a program or user. For example, a data file is a collection of information stored together. This is its logical structure. Physically, however, a file could be stored on a disk in several scattered pieces.

⇒ See also FRAGMENTATION; HARDWARE; LOGICAL; SOFTWARE; VIRTUAL MEMORY.

PIC Short for *Lotus Pic(ture) File*, the graphics file format used to represent graphics generated by Lotus 1-2-3.

⇒ See also GRAPHICS; GRAPHICS FILE FORMATS; LOTUS 1-2-3.

pica In typesetting, a pica is a unit of measurement equal to 1/6 of an inch, or 12 points.

⇒ See also POINT.

PICT file format A file format developed by Apple Computer in 1984. PICT files are encoded in QuickDraw commands and can hold both object-oriented images and bit-mapped images. It is supported by all graphics programs that run on Macintosh computers.

The original PICT format supported 8 colors. Modern versions of PICT, including *PICT2*, support 32-bit color (more than 16 million colors).

⇒ See also GRAPHICS; GRAPHICS FILE FORMATS; MACINTOSH COMPUTER; OBJECT ORIENTED; QUICKDRAW.

pie chart A type of presentation graphic in which percentage values are re-

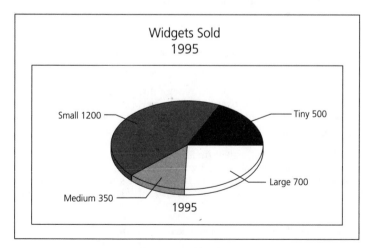

Figure 61: **pie chart**

presented as proportionally sized slices of a pie.

⇒ See also PRESENTATION GRAPHICS.

PIF file Short for *Program InFormation file*, a type of file that holds information about how Windows should run a non-Windows application. For example, a PIF file can contain instructions for executing a DOS application in the Windows environment. These instructions can include the amount of memory to use, the path to the executable file, and what type of window to use. PIF files have a .PIF extension.

⇒ See also DOS; EXECUTABLE FILE; WINDOWS.

PII Short for *Pentium II*.

PIM Acronym for *personal information manager*, a type of software application designed to help users organize random bits of information. Although the category is fuzzy, most PIMs enable you to enter various kinds of textual notes—reminders, lists, dates—and to link these bits of information together in useful ways. Many PIMs also include calendar, scheduling, and calculator programs.

⇒ See also CALCULATOR; CALENDAR; CONTACT MANAGER; SCHEDULER.

pin 1. In dot-matrix printers, the device that presses on the ink ribbon to make dots on the paper. Printers are classified by how many pins they have on the printer head. The more pins a printer has, the higher-quality type it is capable of producing. Dot-matrix printers can have anywhere from 9 to 24 pins. A 24-pin printer can produce letter-quality print. **2.** A male lead on a connector. **3.** Silicon chips have an array of thin metal feet (pins) on their underside that enables them to be attached to a circuit board. The pins are very delicate and easily bent. If they are damaged, the chip will not sit correctly and will malfunction.

⇒ See also CHIP; CONNECTOR; DOT-MATRIX PRINTER; LETTER QUALITY (LQ); NEAR LETTER QUALITY; PINOUT; PRINTER.

pincushion distortion A common type of distortion in CRT monitors in which horizontal and vertical lines bend inward toward the center of the display. The distortion is most noticeable at the edges of the display.

The opposite of pincushion distortion is *barrel distortion*, in which horizontal and vertical lines bend outward toward the edge of the display. A third type of distortion, called *trapezoid distortion*, occurs when vertical lines are straight but not parallel with one another.

Most monitors have pincushion/barrel controls that let you correct these distortions, and many monitors also include a trapezoid distortion control.

⇒ See also CRT; DEGAUSS; DISPLAY SCREEN; MONITOR.

pincushioning See under PINCUSHION DISTORTION.

PINE Acronym for *pine is not elm* or *Program for Internet News and E-Mail,* a character-based e-mail client for UNIX systems. Developed at the University of Washington, PINE replaces an older e-mail program called *elm*.

⇒ See also E-MAIL CLIENT.

pin feed Same as TRACTOR FEED.

PING Short for *P(acket) In(ternet) G(roper),* a utility to determine whether a specific IP address is accessible. It works by sending a packet to the specified address and waiting for a reply. PING is used primarily to troubleshoot Internet connections. There are many freeware and shareware PING utilities available for personal computers.

⇒ See also HOP; ICMP; IP ADDRESS; SMURF; TRACEROUTE.

pin grid array See PGA.

pinout A diagram or table that describes the purpose of each pin in a chip or connector, or each wire in a cable.

⇒ See also CHIP; CONNECTOR; PIN.

PIO Short for *P(rogrammed) I(nput)/O(utput),* a method of transferring data between two devices that uses the computer's main processor as part of the data path. ATA uses PIO and defines the speed of the data transfer in terms of the PIO mode implemented, as shown below:

PIO Mode: Data Transfer Rate (MBps): Standard

0: 3.3: ATA
1: 5.2: ATA
2: 8.3: ATA
3: 11.1: ATA-2
4: 16.6: ATA-2

⇒ See also ATA; DATA TRANSFER RATE.

pipe A temporary software connection between two programs or commands. Normally, the operating system accepts input from the keyboard and sends output to the display screen. Sometimes, however, it is useful to use the output from one command as the input for a second command, without passing the data through the keyboard or display screen. Pipes were invented for these situations.

One of the best examples of pipe usage is linking the command that lists files in a directory to a command that sorts data. By piping the two commands together, you can display the files in sorted order. In UNIX and DOS, the pipe symbol is a vertical bar (|). The DOS command to list files in alphabetical order, therefore, would be:

DIR | SORT

⇒ See also INPUT; OUTPUT.

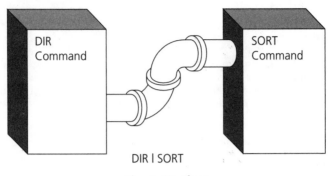

DIR
Command

SORT
Command

DIR I SORT

Figure 62: **pipes**

pipeline See under PIPELINING.

pipeline burst See under PIPELINE BURST CACHE.

pipeline burst cache A type of memory cache built into many modern
DRAM controller and chipset designs. Pipeline burst caches use two techniques—a burst mode that pre-fetches memory contents before they are
requested, and pipelining so that one memory value can be accessed in
the cache at the same time that another memory value is accessed in
DRAM. The purpose of pipeline burst caches is to minimize wait states
so that memory can be accessed as fast a possible by the microprocessor.
The term is often abbreviated as *PBC*.

⇒ See also BEDO DRAM; BURST MODE; CACHE; DRAM; PIPELINING; SDRAM;
WAIT STATE.

pipeline processing See under PIPELINING.

pipelining 1. A technique used in advanced microprocessors where the microprocessor begins executing a second instruction before the first has
been completed. That is, several instructions are in the *pipeline* simultaneously, each at a different processing stage.
The pipeline is divided into segments, and each segment can execute
its operation concurrently with the other segments. When a segment
completes an operation, it passes the result to the next segment in the
pipeline and fetches the next operation from the preceding segment. The
final results of each instruction emerge at the end of the pipeline in rapid
succession.
Although formerly a feature only of high-performance and RISC-based
microprocessors, pipelining is now common in microprocessors used in
personal computers. Intel's Pentium chip, for example, uses pipelining to

execute as many as six instructions simultaneously.

Pipelining is also called *pipeline processing.* **2.** A similar technique used in DRAM, in which the memory loads the requested memory contents into a small cache composed of SRAM and then immediately begins fetching the next memory contents. This creates a two-stage pipeline, where data is read from or written to SRAM in one stage, and data is read from or written to memory in the other stage.

DRAM pipelining is usually combined with another performance technique called burst mode. The two techniques together are called a *pipeline burst cache.*

⇒ See also INTEL MICROPROCESSORS; MICROPROCESSOR; PIPELINE BURST CACHE; RISC; SUPERSCALAR.

piracy See SOFTWARE PIRACY.

pitch 1. For *fixed-pitch* (or *monospaced*) fonts, *pitch* refers to the number of characters printed per inch. Pitch is one characteristic of a monospaced font. Common pitch values are 10 and 12.

In *proportional-pitch* fonts, different characters have different widths, depending on their size. For example, the letter *d* is wider than the letter *I.* Proportional fonts, therefore, have no pitch value. **2.** In graphics, *dot pitch* refers to the spacing between pixels on a monitor. The smaller the dot pitch, the sharper the image.

⇒ See also CPI; DOT PITCH; FIXED PITCH; FONT; MONITOR; PROPORTIONAL SPACING.

pixel Short for *Pic(ture) El(ement),* a pixel is a single point in a graphic image. Graphics monitors display pictures by dividing the display screen into thousands (or millions) of pixels, arranged in rows and columns. The pixels are so close together that they appear connected.

The number of bits used to represent each pixel determines how many colors or shades of gray can be displayed. For example, in 8-bit color mode, the color monitor uses 8 bits for each pixel, making it possible to display 2^8 (256) different colors or shades of gray.

On color monitors, each pixel is actually composed of three dots—a red, a blue, and a green one. Ideally, the three dots should all converge at the same point, but all monitors have some convergence error that can make color pixels appear fuzzy.

The quality of a display system largely depends on its resolution, how many pixels it can display, and how many bits are used to represent each pixel. VGA systems display 640 by 480, or about 300,000 pixels. In contrast, SVGA systems display 1,024 by 768, or nearly 800,000 pixels. True Color systems use 24 bits per pixel, allowing them to display more than 16 million different colors.

⇒ See also ALPHA CHANNEL; CONVERGENCE; GRAPHICS; GRAY SCALING; MONITOR; RESOLUTION; TRUE COLOR.

PKI Short for *public-key infrastructure,* a system of digital certificates, Certificate Authorities, and other registration authorities that verify and authenticate the validity of each party involved in an Internet transaction. PKIs are currently evolving, and there is no single PKI nor even a single agreed-upon standard for setting up a PKI. However, nearly everyone agrees that reliable PKIs are necessary before electronic commerce can become widespread.

A PKI is also called a *trust hierarchy.*

⇒ See also Certificate Authority; electronic commerce.

PKZIP One of the most widely used file compression methods. PKZIP was developed by PKWARE, Inc., in 1989 and distributed as shareware. Files that have been compressed using PKWARE are said to be *zipped.* Decompressing them is called *unzipping.*

The *PK* stands for Phillip Katz, the author of the set of compression and decompression programs.

⇒ See also data compression; shareware; tar; ZIP.

plain text Refers to textual data in ASCII format. Plain text is the most portable format because it is supported by nearly every application on every machine, regardless of operating system. It is quite limited, however, because it cannot contain any formatting commands.

In cryptography, *plain text* refers to any message that is not encrypted. Contrast with *cipher text.*

Plain text is also called *clear text.*

⇒ See also ASCII file; cipher text; encryption.

plasma display A type of flat-panel display that works by sandwiching an ionized gas between two wired panels. In one panel the wires are placed in vertical rows, and in the other they are placed in horizontal rows. Together, the two panels form a grid. An individual point (pixel) can then be charged by passing a current through the appropriate x-coordinate and y-coordinate wires. When the gas is charged, it glows a bright orange.

Plasma displays require much more power than LCD displays and are not used frequently today.

⇒ See also flat-panel display; pixel.

platform The underlying hardware or software for a system. For example, the platform might be an Intel 80486 processor running DOS Version 6.0. The platform could also be UNIX machines on an Ethernet network.

The platform defines a standard around which a system can be developed. Once the platform has been defined, software developers can produce appropriate software and managers can purchase appropriate hardware and applications. The term is often used as a synonym of *operating system.*

The term *cross-platform* refers to applications, formats, or devices that work on different platforms. For example, a *cross-platform programming environment* enables a programmer to develop programs for many platforms at once.

⇒ See also ENVIRONMENT; PPCP; SDK.

platter A round magnetic plate that constitutes part of a hard disk. Hard disks typically contain up to a dozen platters. Most platters require two read/write heads, one for each side.

⇒ See also HARD DISK.

PLD Short for *P(rogrammable) L(ogic) D(evice)*, an integrated circuit that can be programmed in a laboratory to perform complex functions. A PLD consists of arrays of AND and OR gates. A system designer implements a logic design with a device programmer that blows fuses on the PLD to control gate operation.

System designers can use development software that converts basic code into instructions a device programmer needs to implement a design.

PLD types can be classified into the following groups:

PROMs (Programmable Read Only Memory): offer high speed and low cost for relatively small designs

PLAs (Programmable Logic Array): offer flexible features for more complex designs

PAL/GALs (Programmable Array Logic/Generic Array Logic): offer good flexibility and are faster and less expensive than PLAs

⇒ See also CHIP; INTEGRATED CIRCUIT; PROM.

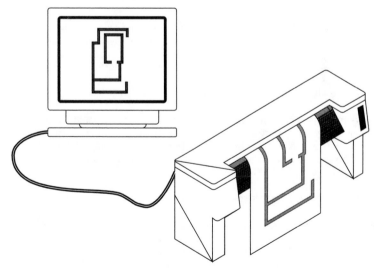

Figure 63: **plotter**

plot To produce an image by drawing lines. You can program a computer to plot images on a display screen or on paper.

⇒ See also PLOTTER.

plotter A device that draws pictures on paper based on commands from a computer. Plotters differ from printers in that they draw lines using a pen. As a result, they can produce continuous lines, whereas printers can only simulate lines by printing a closely spaced series of dots. Multicolor plotters use different-colored pens to draw different colors.

In general, plotters are considerably more expensive than printers. They are used in engineering applications where precision is mandatory.

⇒ See also CAD; PRINTER.

plug A connector used to link together devices.

⇒ See also CONNECTOR.

plug-and-play Refers to the ability of a computer system to configure expansion boards and other devices automatically. You should be able to plug in a device and play with it, without worrying about setting DIP switches, jumpers, and other configuration elements. Since the introduction of the NuBus, the Apple Macintosh has been a plug-and-play computer. The Plug and Play (PnP) specification has made PCs more plug-and-play, although it doesn't always work as advertised.

⇒ See also HOT PLUGGING; IEEE 1394; PnP; SCAM.

plug compatible Able to replace another product without any alterations. Two devices are said to be plug-compatible if either one can be plugged into the same interface. The term is also sometimes used to describe software modules that interface with an application in the same way.

⇒ See also COMPATIBLE; EXPANSION BOARD.

plug-in A hardware or software module that adds a specific feature or service to a larger system. For example, there are number of plug-ins for the Netscape Navigator browser that enable it to display different types of audio or video messages. Navigator plug-ins are based on MIME file types.

⇒ See also COMPONENT SOFTWARE; MODULAR ARCHITECTURE; SHOCKWAVE.

PMS See PANTONE MATCHING SYSTEM (PMS).

PNG Short for *P(ortable) N(etwork) G(raphics),* and pronounced *ping,* a new bit-mapped graphics format similar to GIF. In fact, PNG was approved as a standard by the World Wide Web consortium to replace GIF because GIF uses a patented data compression algorithm called LZW. In contrast, PNG is completely patent- and license-free. The most recent versions of Netscape Navigator and Microsoft Internet Explorer now support PNG.

⇒ See also BIT-MAPPED GRAPHICS; GIF; LZW.

PnP Short for *Plug and Play*, a technology developed by Microsoft and Intel that supports plug-and-play installation. PnP is built into the Windows 95 operating system, but to use it, the computer's BIOS and expansion boards must also support PnP.

⇒ See also BIOS; ESCD; EXPANSION BOARD; PLUG-AND-PLAY; SCAM.

point *v* **1.** To move the pointer on a display screen to select an item. Graphical user interfaces, such as the Macintosh interface, are often called *point-and-click* interfaces because a user typically points to an object on the screen and then clicks a button on the mouse. —*n* **2.** In typography, a point is about 1/72 of an inch and is used to measure the height of characters. (Historically, a point was .0138 inches, a little less than 1/72 of an inch, but this has changed.)

The height of the characters is one characteristic of fonts. Some fonts are referred to as *fixed-point fonts* because their representation allows for only one size. In contrast, a *scalable font* is one that is represented in such a way that the size can easily be changed.

⇒ See also FONT; GRAPHICAL USER INTERFACE; LEADING; MOUSE; POINTER; SCALABLE FONT.

PointCast A company founded in 1992 to deliver news and other information over Internet connections. PointCast's flagship product is PointCast Network, which sends customized news to users' desktops. PointCast Network is free. To use it, you need to download the PointCast client program, which is available from PointCast's Web site and many other places.

PointCast was the first company to successfully combine the Internet with *push* technologies.

⇒ See also CDF; PUSH; WEBCASTING.

pointer 1. In graphical user interfaces, a pointer is a small arrow or other symbol on the display screen that moves as you move the mouse. You can select commands and options by positioning the tip of the arrow over the desired choice and clicking a mouse button. Many text processing programs use an *I-beam pointer*. Pointers are often referred to as *mouse pointers*. **2.** In programming, a pointer is a special type of variable that holds a memory address (that is, it *points* to a memory location).

⇒ See also ADDRESS; GRAPHICAL USER INTERFACE; I-BEAM POINTER; VARIABLE.

pointing device A device with which you can control the movement of the pointer to select items on a display screen. Examples of pointing devices include mice, trackballs, joysticks, touchpads, and light pens.

⇒ See also INPUT DEVICE; JOYSTICK; LIGHT PEN; MOUSE; POINTER; POINTING STICK; PUCK; TOUCHPAD; TRACKBALL.

Grabber pointer   I-beam pointer   Selection pointer

Figure 64: **different types of pointers**

pointing stick A pointing device first developed by IBM for its notebook computers that consists of a miniature joystick, usually with a rubber eraser-head tip, positioned somewhere between the keys on the keyboard. Most pointing sticks are pressure-sensitive, so the pointer moves faster when more pressure is applied.

⇒ See also JOYSTICK; POINTING DEVICE; TRACKBALL.

Point of Presence See POP.

Point-to-Point Protocol See PPP.

Point-to-Point Tunneling Protocol See PPTP.

polling Making continual requests for data from another device. For example, modems that support polling can call another system and request data.

⇒ See also MODEM.

polyline In computer graphics, a continuous line composed of one or more line segments. You can create a polyline by specifying the endpoints of each segment. In draw programs, you can treat a polyline as a single object or divide it into its component segments.

⇒ See also DRAW PROGRAM.

polymorphism Generally, the ability to appear in many forms. In object-oriented programming, *polymorphism* refers to a programming language's ability to process objects differently depending on their data type or class. More specifically, it is the ability to redefine *methods* for *derived classes*. For example, given a base class *shape*, polymorphism enables the programmer to define different *circumference* methods for any number of derived classes, such as circles, rectangles, and triangles. No matter what shape an object is, applying the *circumference* method to it will return the correct results. Polymorphism is considered to be a requirement of any true object-oriented programming language (OOPL).

The type of *polymorphism* described here is sometimes called *parametric polymorphism* to distinguish it from another type of polymorphism called *overloading*.

⇒ See also CLASS; DATA TYPE; OBJECT-ORIENTED PROGRAMMING; OVERLOADING.

POP **1.** Short for *P(ost) O(ffice) P(rotocol)*, a protocol used to retrieve e-mail from a mail server. Most e-mail applications (sometimes called an *e-mail client*) use the POP protocol, although some can use the newer IMAP (Internet Message Access Protocol).

There are two versions of POP. The first, called *POP2,* became a standard in the mid-1980s and requires SMTP to send messages. The newer version, POP3, can be used with or without SMTP. **2.** Short for *P(oint) o(f) P(resence),* a telephone number that gives you dial-up access. Internet service providers (ISPs) generally provide many POPs so that users can make a local call to gain Internet access.

⇒ See also DIAL-UP ACCESS; DIAL-UP NETWORKING; E-MAIL; IMAP; SMTP; SNMP.

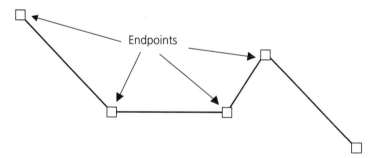

Figure 65: **polyline**

pop **1.** Given a stack of items, *popping* one of the items means to pull it off the stack. Although originally coined to describe manipulation of data stacks, the term is often used in connection with display windows. When two or more windows overlap, you can pop one of them so that it is the topmost window.

The opposite of pop is *push,* which means to move an object onto a stack. **2.** Short for *Point of Presence.* **3.** Short for *Post Office Protocol.*

⇒ See also POP-UP WINDOW; PUSH; WINDOW.

POP3 See under POP.

pop-up menu See under MENU.

pop-up utility A program installed to be *memory resident* so that you can always execute it by pressing a special key, called a *hot key*. When you press the hot key, the pop-up utility appears, regardless of which application you are currently running. When you exit the pop-up utility, the system returns you to your previous program.

In DOS systems, pop-up utilities are also called *TSRs*.

⇒ See also HOT KEY; MEMORY RESIDENT; TSR.

pop-up window A window that suddenly appears (pops up) when you select an option with a mouse or press a special function key. Usually, the pop-up window contains a menu of commands and stays on the screen only until you select one of the commands. It then disappears.

A special kind of pop-up window is a *pull-down menu*, which appears just below the item you selected, as if you had pulled it down.

⇒ See also GRAPHICAL USER INTERFACE; PULL-DOWN MENU; WINDOW.

port *n* **1.** An interface on a computer to which you can connect a device. Personal computers have various types of ports. Internally, there are several ports for connecting disk drives, display screens, and keyboards. Externally, personal computers have ports for connecting modems, printers, mice, and other peripheral devices.

Almost all personal computers come with a serial RS-232C port or RS-422 port for connecting a modem or mouse and a parallel port for connecting a printer. On PCs, the parallel port is a Centronics interface that uses a 25-pin connector. SCSI (Small Computer System Interface) ports support higher transmission speeds than do conventional ports and enable you to attach up to seven devices to the same port. All Apple Macintosh computers since the Macintosh Plus have a SCSI port. **2.** In TCP/IP and UDP networks, an endpoint to a logical connection. The port number identifies what type of port it is. For example, port 80 is used for HTTP traffic. —*v* **3.** To move a program from one type of computer to another. To port an application, you need to rewrite sections that are machine dependent, and then recompile the program on the new computer. Programs that can be ported easily are said to be *portable*.

⇒ See also CENTRONICS INTERFACE; COM; COMPILE; CONNECTOR; INTERFACE; MACHINE DEPENDENT; PARALLEL PORT; PORT REPLICATOR; PORTABLE; PS/2 PORT; SERIAL PORT.

portable 1. When used to describe hardware, *portable* means small and lightweight. A portable computer is a computer small enough to carry. Portable computers include notebook and subnotebook computers, handheld computers, palmtops, and PDAs. **2.** When used to describe software, *portable* means that the software has the ability to run on a variety of computers. *Portable* and *machine independent* mean the same thing—that the software does not depend on a particular type of hardware.

⇒ See also DOCKING STATION; HAND-HELD COMPUTER; MACHINE INDEPENDENT; NOTEBOOK COMPUTER; PALMTOP; PDA; POSIX; SUBNOTEBOOK COMPUTER.

Portable Document Format See PDF.

Portable Network Graphics See PNG.

portrait The terms *portrait* and *landscape* refer to different orientations of the paper—whether it is oriented vertically or horizontally. A page with portrait orientation, typical for letters, memos, and other text documents, is taller than it is wide.

Not all printers are capable of generating text in landscape mode.

Orientation is also a characteristic of monitors. Portrait monitors are often called *full-page monitors*.

⇒ See also LANDSCAPE; MONITOR; PRINTER.

port replicator A device containing common PC ports, such as serial and parallel ports, that plugs into a notebook computer. The purpose of the device is to allow you to easily attach a portable computer to standard, nonportable devices such as a printer and monitor. For example, if you use a computer both at home and at work, you could set up both work areas with a port replicator. Then, you just plug in your notebook computer to the port replicator at either location and you're ready to work.

Most notebook computer manufacturers offer a port replicator as an additional option. A port replicator is similar to a docking station, but docking stations provide additional slots for adding expansion boards and storage devices.

⇒ See also DOCKING STATION; NOTEBOOK COMPUTER; PORT.

port-switching hub See SWITCHING HUB.

POSIX Acronym for *P(ortable) O(perating) S(ystem) I(nterface) for UNIX*, a set of IEEE and ISO standards that define an interface between programs and operating systems. By designing their programs to conform to POSIX, developers have some assurance that their software can be easily ported to POSIX-compliant operating systems. This includes most varieties of UNIX as well as Windows NT.

The POSIX standards are now maintained by an arm of the IEEE called the *Portable Applications Standards Committee (PASC)*.

⇒ See also PORTABLE; UNIX; WINDOWS NT.

POST Short for *p(ower)-o(n) s(elf) t(est)*, a series of diagnostic tests that run automatically when you turn your computer on. The actual tests can differ depending on how the BIOS is configured, but usually the POST tests the RAM, the keyboard, and the disk drives. If the tests are successful, the computer boots itself. If the tests are unsuccessful, the computer reports the error by emitting a series of beeps and possibly displaying an error message and code on the display screen. The number of beeps indicates the error but differs from one BIOS to another.

⇒ See also BIOS; BOOT; POWER UP.

post *v* **1.** To publish a message in an on-line forum or newsgroup. —*n* **2.** A message published in an on-line forum or newsgroup. **3.** Short for *power-on self test.*

⇒ See also FORUM; USENET.

Post Office Protocol See POP.

PostScript A *page description language (PDL)* developed by Adobe Systems. PostScript is primarily a language for printing documents on laser printers, but it can be adapted to produce images on other types of devices. PostScript is the standard for desktop publishing because it is supported by *imagesetters,* the very high-resolution printers used by service bureaus to produce camera-ready copy.

PostScript is an *object-oriented language,* meaning that it treats images, including fonts, as collections of geometrical objects rather than as bit maps. PostScript fonts are called *outline fonts* because the outline of each character is defined. They are also called *scalable fonts* because their size can be changed with PostScript commands. Given a single typeface definition, a PostScript printer can thus produce a multitude of fonts. In contrast, many non-PostScript printers represent fonts with bit maps. To print a bit-mapped typeface with different sizes, these printers require a complete set of bit maps for each size.

The principal advantage of object-oriented (*vector*) graphics over bit-mapped graphics is that object-oriented images take advantage of high-resolution output devices whereas bit-mapped images do not. A PostScript drawing looks much better when printed on a 600-dpi printer than on a 300-dpi printer. A bit-mapped image looks the same on both printers.

Every PostScript printer contains a built-in interpreter that executes PostScript instructions. If your laser printer does not come with PostScript support, you may be able to purchase a cartridge that contains PostScript.

There are three basic versions of PostScript: Level 1, Level 2, and PostScript 3. Level 2 PostScript, which was released in 1992, has better support for color printing. PostScript 3, released in 1997, supports more fonts and better graphics handling and includes several features to speed up PostScript printing.

⇒ See also DESKTOP PUBLISHING; EPS; ISP; LASER PRINTER; OBJECT-ORIENTED GRAPHICS; PAGE DESCRIPTION LANGUAGE (PDL).

PostScript 3 See under POSTSCRIPT.

POTS Short for *p(lain) o(ld) telephone s(ervice),* which refers to the standard telephone service that most homes use. In contrast, telephone services based on high-speed digital communications lines, such as ISDN and FDDI, are not POTS. The main distinctions between POTS and non-POTS services are speed and bandwidth. POTS is generally restricted to about 52 Kbps (52,000 bits per second).

The POTS network is also called the *public switched telephone network (PSTN)*.

⇒ See also ADSL; COMMUNICATIONS; DSVD; IAC; ISDN; K56FLEX; PBX; PSTN; X2; xDSL.

PowerBuilder One of the leading client/server development environments. PowerBuilder supports all the leading platforms—including Windows 95 and 98, Windows NT, UNIX, and Mac OS. Its integrated development environment (IDE) makes it relatively easy to develop and deploy sophisticated client/server applications.

⇒ See also CLIENT/SERVER ARCHITECTURE; INTEGRATED DEVELOPMENT ENVIRONMENT; SYBASE.

power down To turn a machine off.

⇒ See also POWER UP; SHUT DOWN.

power management Efficiently directing power to different components of a system. Power management is especially important for portable devices that rely on battery power. By reducing power to components that aren't being used, a good power management system can double or triple the lifetime of a battery.

⇒ See also ACPI; APM; BATTERY PACK.

power-on self test See POST.

PowerPC A RISC-based computer architecture developed jointly by IBM, Apple Computer, and Motorola Corporation. The name is derived from IBM's name for the architecture, *Performance Optimization With Enhanced RISC.*

The first computers based on the PowerPC architecture were the Power Macs, which appeared in 1994. Since then, other manufacturers, including IBM, have built PCs based on the PowerPC. Although the initial reviews have been good, it remains to be seen whether this new architecture can eventually supplant, or even coexist with, the huge number of Intel-based computers in use and on the market.

There are already a number of different operating systems that run on PowerPC-based computers, including the Macintosh operating system (System 7.5 and higher), Windows NT, and OS/2.

⇒ See also BeOS; CHRP; INTEL MICROPROCESSORS; MACINTOSH COMPUTER; MICROPROCESSOR; MOTOROLA MICROPROCESSORS; PPCP; RISC.

PowerPC Platform See PPCP.

power supply The component that supplies power to a computer. Most personal computers can be plugged into standard electrical outlets. The power supply then pulls the required amount of electricity and converts the AC current to DC current. It also regulates the voltage to eliminate spikes and surges common in most electrical systems. Not all power supplies, however, do an adequate voltage-regulation job, so a computer is always susceptible to large voltage fluctuations.

Power supplies are rated in terms of the number of watts they generate. The more powerful the computer, the more watts it can provide to components. In general, 200 watts should be sufficient.

⇒ See also UPS; VOLTAGE REGULATOR; VRM.

power up To turn a machine on.

⇒ See also POST; POWER DOWN.

power user A sophisticated user of personal computers. A power user is typically someone who has considerable experience with computers and utilizes the most advanced features of applications.

⇒ See also USER.

PPCP Short for *PowerPC Platform*, a computer hardware specification that allows a computer to run multiple operating systems. PPCP was developed jointly by Apple, IBM, and Motorola and was first called the *Common Hardware Reference Platform (CHRP)*. The specification is based on the RISC architecture used for the RS/6000 mini-computer.

A computer that meets the PPCP standard allows you to select an application without regard to the underlying operating system. A PPCP computer can run any Mac, PC, or UNIX-based operating system without the usual modifications required to fit an operating system to a platform.

⇒ See also CHRP; PLATFORM; PowerPC; RISC.

ppm Stands for *p(ages) p(er) m(inute)* and is used to measure the speed of certain types of printers, particularly laser and ink-jet printers. An average speed for laser printers printing text is 8 ppm.

Note that the ppm advertised for printers applies only to text. Complex graphics can slow a printer down considerably. Increasingly, the abbreviation *gppm* is being used for graphics pages per minute.

⇒ See also GPPM; LASER PRINTER; PRINTER.

PPP Short for *P(oint)-to-P(oint) P(rotocol)*, a method of connecting a computer to the Internet. PPP is more stable than the older SLIP protocol and provides error-checking features.

⇒ See also INTERNET; PPTP; PROTOCOL; SLIP.

PPTP Short for *P(oint)-to-P(oint) T(unneling) P(rotocol)*, a new technology for creating *Virtual Private Networks (VPNs)*, developed jointly by Microsoft Corporation, U.S. Robotics, and several remote access vendor companies, known collectively as the *PPTP Forum*. A VPN is a private network of computers that uses the public Internet to connect some nodes. Because the Internet is essentially an open network, the Point-to-Point Tunneling Protocol (PPTP) is used to ensure that messages transmitted from one VPN node to another are secure. With PPTP, users can dial in to their corporate network via the Internet.

Although PPTP has been submitted to the IETF for standardization, it is currently available only on networks served by a Windows NT 4.0 server and Linux.

⇒ See also L2TP; Layer Two Forwarding; PPP; tunneling; VPN; Windows NT.

PRAM Pronounced *pee-ram*, short for *parameter RAM*. On Macintosh computers, PRAM is a small portion of RAM used to store information about the way the system is configured. For example, parameter RAM holds the date and time, desktop pattern, mouse settings, volume settings, and other control data set with control panels. Parameter RAM is powered by a battery, so it does not lose its contents when the power is turned off.

⇒ See also configure; control panel; Macintosh computer; memory; RAM.

precedence A characteristic of operators that indicates when they will be evaluated when they appear in complex expressions. Operators with high precedence are evaluated before operators with low precedence. For example, the multiplication operator (*) has higher preference than the addition operator (+), so the expression

2 + 3*4

equals 14, not 20.

You can override precedence rules by surrounding parts of an expression with parentheses. For example,

(2 + 3)*4

evaluates to 20.

⇒ See also expression; operand; operator.

precision When used to describe floating-point numbers, *precision* refers to the number of bits used to hold the fractional part. The more precision a system uses, the more exactly it can represent fractional quantities.

Floating-point numbers are often classified as *single precision* or *double precision*. A double-precision number uses twice as many bits as a single-precision value, so it can represent fractional quantities much more exactly.

⇒ See also double precision; floating-point number.

preemptive multitasking See under MULTITASKING.

prepress service bureau See under SERVICE BUREAU.

presentation graphics A type of business software that enables users to create highly stylized images for slide shows and reports. The software includes functions for creating various types of charts and graphs and for inserting text in a variety of fonts. Most systems enable you to import data from a spreadsheet application to create the charts and graphs.

Presentation graphics is often called *business graphics*.

⇒ See also BAR CHART; GRAPHICS; LINE GRAPH; PIE CHART; SCATTER DIAGRAM; SPREADSHEET.

Pretty Good Privacy Abbreviated PGP, a technique for encrypting messages developed by Philip Zimmerman. PGP is one of the most common ways to protect messages on the Internet because it is effective, easy to use, and free. PGP is based on the public-key method, which uses two keys—one is a public key that you disseminate to anyone from whom you want to receive a message. The other is a private key that you use to decrypt messages that you receive.

To encrypt a message using PGP, you need the PGP encryption package, which is available for free from a number of sources. The official repository is at the Massachusetts Institute of Technology.

PGP is such an effective encryption tool that the U.S. government actually brought a lawsuit against Zimmerman for putting it in the public domain and hence making it available to enemies of the U.S. After a public outcry, the U.S. lawsuit was dropped, but it is still illegal to use PGP in many other countries.

⇒ See also CRYPTOGRAPHY; PUBLIC-KEY ENCRYPTION; RSA.

preview In word processing, *previewing* refers to formatting a document for the printer, but then displaying it on the display screen instead of printing it. Previewing allows you to see exactly how the document will appear when printed. If you have a WYSIWYG interface, previewing is unnecessary because the display screen always resembles the printed version. For word processors under non-WYSIWYG interfaces, however, previewing is the next best thing. If your word processor does not support previewing, you may be able to buy a separate program that allows you to preview documents.

⇒ See also GREEKING; THUMBNAIL; WORD PROCESSING; WYSIWYG.

primary cache Same as L1 CACHE.

primary key See under KEY.

primary storage A somewhat dated term for *main memory*. Mass storage devices, such as disk drives and tapes, are sometimes called *secondary storage*.

⇒ See also MAIN MEMORY; MASS STORAGE.

printed circuit board Sometimes abbreviated *PCB*, a thin plate on which chips and other electronic components are placed. Computers consist of one or more boards, often called cards or *adapters*. Circuit boards fall into the following categories:

motherboard: The principal board that has connectors for attaching devices to the bus. Typically, the motherboard contains the CPU, memory, and basic controllers for the system. On PCs, the motherboard is often called the *system board* or *mainboard.*

expansion board: Any board that plugs into one of the computer's expansion slots. Expansion boards include controller boards, LAN cards, and video adapters.

daughtercard: Any board that attaches directly to another board.

controller board: A special type of expansion board that contains a controller for a peripheral device. When you attach new devices, such as a disk drive or graphics monitor, to a computer, you often need to add a controller board.

Network Interface Card (NIC): An expansion board that enables a PC to be connected to a local area network (LAN).

video adapter: An expansion board that contains a controller for a graphics monitor.

Printed circuit boards are also called *cards.*

⇒ See also BACKPLANE; CHIP; CONTROLLER; DAUGHTERCARD; EXPANSION BOARD;

Chips

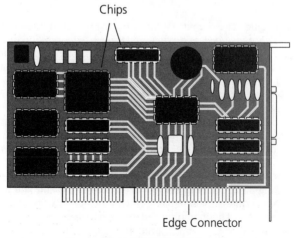

Edge Connector

Figure 66: **printed circuit board**

EXPANSION SLOT; FORM FACTOR; LOCAL-AREA NETWORK; MOTHERBOARD; VIDEO ADAPTER.

printer A device that prints text or illustrations on paper. There are many different types of printers. In terms of the technology utilized, printers fall into the following categories:

daisy-wheel: Similar to a ball-head typewriter, this type of printer has a plastic or metal wheel on which the shape of each character stands out in relief. A hammer presses the wheel against a ribbon, which in turn makes an ink stain in the shape of the character on the paper. Daisy-wheel printers produce letter-quality print but cannot print graphics.

dot-matrix: Creates characters by striking pins against an ink ribbon. Each pin makes a dot, and combinations of dots form characters and illustrations.

ink-jet: Sprays ink at a sheet of paper. Ink-jet printers produce high-quality text and graphics.

laser: Uses the same technology as copy machines. Laser printers produce very high-quality text and graphics.

LCD & LED: Similar to a laser printer, but uses liquid crystals or light-emitting diodes rather than a laser to produce an image on the drum.

line printer: Contains a chain of characters or pins that print an entire line at one time. Line printers are very fast but produce low-quality print.

thermal printer: An inexpensive printer that works by pushing heated pins against heat-sensitive paper. Thermal printers are widely used in calculators and fax machines.

Printers are also classified by the following characteristics:

quality of type: The output produced by printers is said to be either *letter quality* (as good as a typewriter), *near letter quality*, or *draft quality*. Only daisy-wheel, ink-jet, and laser printers produce letter-quality type. Some dot-matrix printers claim letter-quality print, but if you look closely, you can see the difference.

speed: Measured in characters per second (cps) or pages per minute (ppm), the speed of printers varies widely. Daisy-wheel printers tend to be the slowest, printing about 30 cps. Line printers are fastest (up to 3,000 lines per minute). Dot-matrix printers can print up to 500 cps, and laser printers range from about 4 to 20 text pages per minute.

impact or non-impact: Impact printers include all printers that work by striking an ink ribbon. Daisy-wheel, dot-matrix, and line printers are impact printers. Non-impact printers include laser printers and ink-jet printers. The important difference between impact and non-impact printers is that impact printers are much noisier.

graphics: Some printers (daisy-wheel and line printers) can print only text. Other printers can print both text and graphics.

fonts: Some printers, notably dot-matrix printers, are limited to one or a few fonts. In contrast, laser and ink-jet printers are capable of printing an almost unlimited variety of fonts. Daisy-wheel printers can also print different fonts, but you need to change the daisy wheel, making it difficult to mix fonts in the same document.

⇒ See also BILEVEL PRINTER; DAISY-WHEEL PRINTER; DOT-MATRIX PRINTER; DRAFT QUALITY; FONT; GRAPHICS; HOST-BASED PRINTER; HP; IMPACT PRINTER; INK-JET PRINTER; LASER PRINTER; LCD; LCD PRINTER; LED; LETTER QUALITY (LQ); LINE PRINTER; MFP; NEAR LETTER QUALITY; PAGE PRINTER.

Printer Control Language See PCL.

printer driver A program that controls a printer. Whenever you print a document, the printer driver takes over, feeding data to the printer with the correct control commands. Most modern operating systems come with printer drivers for the most common types of printers, but you must install them before you can use the printer. You can also download updated drivers from the printer manufacturer's Web site.

⇒ See also DRIVER.

printer engine The main component of a printer that actually performs the printing. The printer engine determines how fast and at what resolution the printer can print. Although there are many manufacturers of printers, many use the same printer engines. The difference between printers using the same printer engine revolves around other features, such as paper-handling abilities and the console.

⇒ See also PRINTER.

print merge Same as MAIL MERGE.

printout A printed version of text or data. Another term for printout is *hard copy*.

⇒ See also PRINTER.

Print Screen key Often abbreviated *Prt Scr*, the Print Screen key is a useful key supported on most PCs. In DOS, pressing the Print Screen key causes the computer to send whatever images and text are currently on the display screen to the printer. Some graphical user interfaces, including Windows, use the Print Screen key to obtain screen captures.

⇒ See also CAPTURE; HARD COPY.

print server See under SERVER.

⇒ See also SERVER.

print spooling See under SPOOLING.

procedure 1. Same as ROUTINE, *subroutine,* and *function.* A procedure is a section of a program that performs a specific task. **2.** An ordered set of tasks for performing some action.

⇒ See also FUNCTION; ROUTINE.

process *n* **1.** An executing program. The term is used loosely as a synonym of *task.* —*v* **2.** To perform some useful operations on data.

⇒ See also DAEMON; TASK.

process colors Refers to the CMYK color model used in offset printing.

⇒ See also CMYK; COLOR SEPARATION; OFFSET PRINTING.

processor Short for *microprocessor* or CPU.

⇒ See also CPU; MICROPROCESSOR.

processor unit Short for *central processing unit.*

Prodigy An online service developed jointly by IBM and Sears.

⇒ See also ONLINE SERVICE.

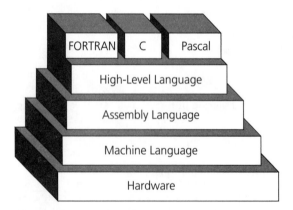

Figure 67: hierarchy of programming language

program *n* **1.** An organized list of instructions that, when executed, causes the computer to behave in a predetermined manner. Without programs, computers are useless.
   A program is like a recipe. It contains a list of ingredients (called *variables*) and a list of directions (called *statements*) that tell the com-

puter what to do with the variables. The variables can represent numeric data, text, or graphical images.

There are many programming languages—C, C + + , Pascal, BASIC, FORTRAN, COBOL, and LISP are just a few. These are all high-level languages. One can also write programs in *low-level languages* called assembly languages, although this is more difficult. Low-level languages are closer to the language used by a computer, while high-level languages are closer to human languages.

Eventually, every program must be translated into a *machine language* that the computer can understand. This translation is performed by *compilers, interpreters*, and *assemblers*.

When you buy software, you normally buy an executable version of a program. This means that the program is already in machine language—it has already been compiled and assembled and is ready to execute. —*v* **2.** To write programs.

⇒ See also ALGORITHM; ASSEMBLER; ASSEMBLY LANGUAGE; CASE; CODE; COMPILER; EXECUTABLE FILE; FLOW CONTROL; HIGH-LEVEL LANGUAGE; INSTRUCTION; INTERPRETER; LANGUAGE; LOW-LEVEL LANGUAGE; MACHINE LANGUAGE; MODULE; PROGRAMMING LANGUAGE; PSEUDOCODE; SOFTWARE.

Programmable Logic Device See PLD.

programmable read-only memory See PROM.

programmer 1. An individual who writes programs. **2.** A device that writes a program onto a PROM chip.

⇒ See also HACKER; PROGRAM; PROM; SOFTWARE ENGINEER.

programming language A vocabulary and set of grammatical rules for instructing a computer to perform specific tasks. The term *programming language* usually refers to high-level languages, such as BASIC, C, C + + , COBOL, FORTRAN, Ada, and Pascal. Each language has a unique set of keywords (words that it understands) and a special syntax for organizing program instructions.

High-level programming languages, while simple compared to human languages, are more complex than the languages the computer actually understands, called *machine languages*. Each different type of CPU has its own unique machine language.

Lying between machine languages and high-level languages are languages called assembly languages. Assembly languages are similar to machine languages, but they are much easier to program in because they allow a programmer to substitute names for numbers. Machine languages consist of numbers only.

Lying above high-level languages are languages called *fourth-generation languages* (usually abbreviated *4GL*). 4GLs are far removed from machine languages and represent the class of computer languages closest to human languages.

Regardless of what programming language you use, eventually you need to convert your program into machine language so that the computer can understand it. There are two ways to do this:

- *compile* the program
- *interpret* the program

See *compile* and *interpreter* for more information about these two methods.

The question of which language is best is one that consumes a lot of time and energy among computer professionals. Every language has its strengths and weaknesses. For example, FORTRAN is a particularly good language for processing numerical data, but it does not lend itself very well to organizing large programs. Pascal is very good for writing well-structured and readable programs, but it is not as flexible as the C programming language. C++ embodies powerful object-oriented features, but it is complex and difficult to learn.

The choice of which language to use depends on the type of computer the program is to run on, what sort of program it is, and the expertise of the programmer.

⇒ See also ADA; ASSEMBLY LANGUAGE; AWK; BASIC; C; C++; COBOL; COMPILER; FLOW CONTROL; FORTRAN; FOURTH-GENERATION LANGUAGE; HIGH-LEVEL LANGUAGE; INTERPRETER; JAVA; LANGUAGE; LISP; LOW-LEVEL LANGUAGE; MACHINE LANGUAGE; MODULA-2; OBJECT-ORIENTED PROGRAMMING; PASCAL; PROLOG; TCL; VBSCRIPT; VISUAL BASIC.

Progress Software A leading software company in the DBMS field. Although Progress Software has its own DBMS system, its real strength is in providing tools to develop applications that can interact with any DBMS.

⇒ See also DATABASE MANAGEMENT SYSTEM.

Prolog Short for *Programming Logic,* Prolog is a high-level programming language based on formal logic. Unlike traditional programming languages that are based on performing sequences of commands, Prolog is based on defining and then solving logical formulas. Prolog is sometimes called a *declarative language* or a *rule-based language* because its programs consist of a list of facts and rules. Prolog is used widely for artificial intelligence applications, particularly expert systems.

⇒ See also ARTIFICIAL INTELLIGENCE; EXPERT SYSTEM; LISP; PROGRAMMING LANGUAGE.

PROM Pronounced *prom,* an acronym for *p(rogrammable) r(ead)-o(nly) m(emory).* A PROM is a memory chip on which data can be written only once. Once a program has been written onto a PROM, it remains there forever. Unlike RAM, PROMs retain their contents when the computer is turned off.

The difference between a PROM and a ROM [r(ead)-o(nly) m(emory)] is that a PROM is manufactured as blank memory, whereas a ROM is programmed during the manufacturing process. To write data onto a PROM chip, you need a special device called a *PROM programmer* or *PROM burner*. The process of programming a PROM is sometimes called *burning* the PROM.

An *EPROM* (erasable programmable read-only memory) is a special type of PROM that can be erased by exposing it to ultraviolet light. Once it is erased, it can be reprogrammed. An EEPROM is similar to a PROM but requires only electricity to be erased.

⇒ See also EEPROM; EPROM; MAIN MEMORY; MEMORY; PLD; ROM.

prompt A symbol on a display screen indicating that the computer is waiting for input. Once the computer has displayed a prompt, it waits for you to enter some information. Generally, it will wait forever, but some programs have built-in time-outs that cause the program to continue execution after it has waited a specified amount of time.

⇒ See also TIME-OUT.

property Characteristic of an object. In many programming languages, including Visual Basic, the term *property* is used to describe attributes associated with a data structure.

⇒ See also ATTRIBUTE.

proportional font A font in which different characters have different *pitches* (widths). Proportional fonts are also called *proportional-pitch fonts*. The opposite of a proportional font is a *fixed-pitch* font.

⇒ See also FONT; PITCH; PROPORTIONAL SPACING.

proportional pitch Same as PROPORTIONALLY SPACED. See under PROPORTIONAL SPACING.

windows

Proportional Pitch

w i n d o w s

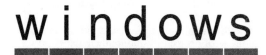

Fixed Pitch (Monospacing)

Figure 68: proportional pitch vs. fixed pitch

proportional spacing Using different widths for different characters. In a proportionally spaced font, the letter *I* is narrower than the letter *q* and the letter *m* wider. This book uses a proportionally spaced font, as do most books, magazines, and newspapers.

The opposite of proportional spacing is *monospacing*. In a monospaced font, each character has the same width. Nongraphics display screens display text in a monospaced font. Almost all printers, with the exception of line printers, are able to print with either proportionally spaced or monospaced fonts.

⇒ See also CPI; FIXED PITCH; FONT; MONOSPACING; PITCH.

proprietary Privately owned and controlled. In the computer industry, *proprietary* is the opposite of *open*. A proprietary design or technique is one that is owned by a company. It also implies that the company has not divulged specifications that would allow other companies to duplicate the product.

Increasingly, proprietary architectures are seen as a disadvantage. Consumers prefer open and standardized architectures, which allow them to mix and match products from different manufacturers.

⇒ See also ARCHITECTURE; OPEN ARCHITECTURE; STANDARD.

protected mode A type of memory utilization available on Intel 80286 and later-model microprocessors. In protected mode, these processors provide the following features:

protection: Each program can be allocated a certain section of memory. Other programs cannot use this memory, so each program is protected from interference from other programs.
extended memory: Enables a single program to access more than 640 K of memory.
virtual memory: Expands the *address space* to more than 1 GB.
multitasking: Enables the microprocessor to switch from one program to another so the computer can execute several programs at once.

Although the DOS operating system is not designed to take advantage of these features, some DOS programs can run in protected mode using special drivers. More sophisticated operating system, such as OS/2, Windows, or UNIX, have built-in support for protected mode.

⇒ See also DOS; EXTENDED MEMORY; INTEL MICROPROCESSORS; MICROSOFT WINDOWS; MULTITASKING; OS/2; UNIX; VIRTUAL MEMORY.

protocol An agreed-upon format for transmitting data between two devices. The protocol determines the following:

• the type of error checking to be used
• data compression method, if any
• how the sending device indicates the end of a message

- how the receiving device will indicate that it has received a message

There are a variety of standard protocols from which programmers can choose. Each has particular advantages and disadvantages; for example, some are simpler than others, some are more reliable, and some are faster.

From a user's point of view, the only interesting aspect about protocols is that your computer or device must support the right ones if you want to communicate with other computers. The protocol can be implemented either in hardware or in software.

⇒ See also CCITT; COMMUNICATIONS; COMMUNICATIONS PROTOCOL; CONNECTIONLESS; HANDSHAKING; MODEM; PROTOCOL STACK.

protocol stack A set of network protocol layers that work together. The OSI Reference Model that defines seven protocol layers is often called a stack, as is the set of TCP/IP protocols that define communication over the internet.

The term *stack* also refers to the actual software that processes the protocols. So, for example, programmers sometimes talk about *loading a stack,* which means to load the software required to use a specific set of protocols. Another common phrase is *binding a stack,* which refers to linking a set of network protocols to a network interface card (NIC). Every NIC must have at least one stack bound to it.

In Windows, the TCP/IP stack is implemented by the Winsock DLL.

⇒ See also NETWORK INTERFACE CARD; OSI; PROTOCOL; TCP/IP; WINSOCK.

proxy See under PROXY SERVER.

proxy server A server that sits between a client application, such as a Web browser, and a real server. It intercepts all requests to the real server to see if it can fulfill the requests itself. If not, it forwards the request to the real server.

Proxy servers have two main purposes:

Improve Performance: Proxy servers can dramatically improve performance for groups of users. This is because it saves the results of all requests for a certain amount of time. Consider the case where both user X and user Y access the World Wide Web through a proxy server. First user X requests a certain Web page, which we'll call Page 1. Sometime later, user Y requests the same page. Instead of forwarding the request to the Web server where Page 1 resides, which can be a time-consuming operation, the proxy server simply returns the Page 1 that it already fetched for user X. Because the proxy server is often on the same network as the user, this is a much faster operation. Real proxy servers support hundreds or thousands of users. The major online services such as CompuServe and America Online, for example, employ an array of proxy servers.

Filter Requests: Proxy servers can also be used to filter requests. For example, a company might use a proxy server to prevent its employees from accessing a specific set of Web sites.

⇒ See also FIREWALL; SERVER; SOCKS; WEB SERVER.

Prt Scr key See PRINT SCREEN KEY.

PS/2 port A type of port developed by IBM for connecting a mouse or keyboard to a PC. The PS/2 port supports a miniature DIN plug containing just 6 pins. Most PCs have a PS/2 port so that the serial port can be used by another device, such as a modem. The PS/2 port is often called the *mouse port*.

⇒ See also PORT; SERIAL MOUSE; SERIAL PORT.

pseudocode An outline of a program, written in a form that can easily be converted into real programming statements. For example, the pseudocode for a bubble sort routine might be written:

while not at end of list
compare adjacent elements
if second is greater than first
switch them
get next two elements
if elements were switched
repeat for entire list

   Pseudocode cannot be compiled or executed, and there are no real formatting or syntax rules. It is simply one step—an important one—in producing the final code. The benefit of pseudocode is that it enables the programmer to concentrate on the algorithms without worrying about all the syntactic details of a particular programming language. In fact, you can write pseudocode without even knowing what programming language you will use for the final implementation.

⇒ See also ALGORITHM; BUBBLE SORT; CODE; PROGRAM.

PSTN Short for *Public Switched Telephone Network,* which refers to the international telephone system based on copper wires carrying analog voice data. This is in contrast to newer telephone networks based on digital technologies, such as ISDN and FDDI.
   Telephone service carried by the PSTN is often called *plain old telephone service (POTS)*.

⇒ See also CIRCUIT SWITCHING; POTS.

public carrier Any of the government-regulated organizations that provide telecommunications services to the public. These include AT&T, MCI, and Western Union. Most public carriers provide *electronic-mail* services that enable you to send messages and documents over a telephone line to other computer users.

⇒ See also E-MAIL.

public-domain software Refers to any program that is not copyrighted. Public-domain software is free and can be used without restrictions. The term *public-domain software* is often used incorrectly to include *freeware*, free software that is nevertheless copyrighted.

⇒ See also FREEWARE; SHAREWARE.

public key See under PUBLIC-KEY ENCRYPTION.

public-key encryption A cryptographic system that uses two keys—a *public key* known to everyone and a *private* or *secret key* known only to the recipient of the message. When John wants to send a secure message to Jane, he uses Jane's public key to encrypt the message. Jane then uses her private key to decrypt it.

An important element to the public key system is that the public and private keys are related in such a way that only the public key can be used to encrypt messages and only the corresponding private key can be used to decrypt them. Moreover, it is virtually impossible to deduce the private key if you know the public key.

Public-key systems, such as Pretty Good Privacy (PGP), are becoming popular for transmitting information via the Internet. They are extremely secure and relatively simple to use. The only difficulty with public-key systems is that you need to know the recipient's public key to encrypt a message for him or her. What's needed, therefore, is a global registry of public keys, which is one of the promises of the new LDAP technology.

Public key cryptography was invented in 1976 by Whitfield Diffie and Martin Hellman. For this reason, it is sometime called *Diffie-Hellman encryption*. It is also called *asymmetric encryption* because it uses two keys instead of one key (*symmetric encryption*).

⇒ See also CERTIFICATE AUTHORITY; CRYPTOGRAPHY; DIGITAL CERTIFICATE; DIGITAL ENVELOPE; ENCRYPTION; LDAP; PRETTY GOOD PRIVACY; RSA; S/MIME; SYMMETRIC-KEY CRYPTOGRAPHY.

public-key infrastructure See PKI.

puck A pointing device used with digitizing tablets. See under DIGITIZING TABLET.

⇒ See also DIGITIZING TABLET; POINTING DEVICE.

pull To request data from another program or computer. The opposite of pull is *push*, where data is sent without a request being made. The terms *push* and *pull* are used frequently to describe data sent over the Internet. The World Wide Web is based on pull technologies, where a page isn't delivered until a browser requests it. Increasingly, however, information services are harnessing the Internet to broadcast information using push technologies. A prime example is the PointCast Network.

⇒ See also PUSH.

pull-down menu A menu of commands or options that appears when you select an item with a mouse. The item you select is generally at the top of the display screen, and the menu appears just below it, as if you had pulled it down.

⇒ See also COMMAND; MENU; OPTION; POP-UP WINDOW.

pulse code modulation See PCM.

punctuation Like punctuation in human languages, punctuation in programming languages serves to separate words and phrases. But unlike human punctuation, which is often optional, computer punctuation is strictly required.

⇒ See also SPECIAL CHARACTER.

purge To remove old and unneeded data systematically and permanently. The term *purge* is stronger than *delete*. It is often possible to regain deleted objects by *undeleting* them, but purged objects are gone forever.

⇒ See also DELETE; RECYCLE BIN.

PURL Short for *Persistent URL*, a type of URL that acts as an intermediary for a real URL of Web resource. When you enter a PURL in a browser, the browser sends the page request to a PURL server, which then returns the real URL of the page. PURLs are *persistent* because once a PURL is established, it never needs to change. The real address of the Web page may change, but the PURL remains the same.
PURLs are managed by the *Online Computer Library Center (OCLC)*.

⇒ See also URL.

push 1. In client/server applications, to send data to a client without the client's requesting it. The World Wide Web is based on a *pull* technology where the client browser must request a Web page before it is sent. Broadcast media, on the other hand, are push technologies because they send information out regardless of whether anyone is tuned in.
Increasingly, companies are using the Internet to deliver information push-style. One of the most successful examples of this is PointCast, which delivers customized news to users' desktops.
Probably the oldest and most widely used push technology is e-mail. This is a push technology because you receive mail whether you ask for it or not—that is, the sender *pushes* the message to the receiver. **2.** In programming, to place a data item onto a stack. The opposite of push is *pop*, which means to remove an object from a stack.

⇒ See also CDF; POINTCAST; POP; PULL; WEBCASTING.

push-button A button in a dialog box. See under button.

⇒ See also DIALOG BOX.

PVC Short for *p(ermanent) v(irtual) c(ircuit)*, a virtual circuit that is permanently available. The only difference between a PVC and a switched virtual circuit (SVC) is that an SVC must be reestablished each time data is to be sent. Once the data has been sent, the SVC disappears. PVCs are more efficient for connections between hosts that communicate frequently.

PVCs play a central role in Frame Relay networks. They're also supported in some other types of networks, such as X.25.

⇒ See also FRAME RELAY; SVC; VIRTUAL CIRCUIT.

QBASIC An interpreter for the BASIC programming language provided by Microsoft with the DOS operating system. The QBASIC interpreter supports many of the more sophisticated features of the BASIC language and replaces GW-BASIC.

⇒ See also BASIC; GW-BASIC.

QBE See QUERY BY EXAMPLE.

QCIF Short for *Q(uarter) C(ommon) I(ntermediate) F(ormat)*, a videoconferencing format that specifies data rates of 30 frames per second (fps), with each frame containing 144 lines and 176 pixels per line. This is one fourth the resolution of Full CIF. QCIF support is required by the ITU H. 261 videoconferencing standard.

⇒ See also COMMON INTERMEDIATE FORMAT; NTSC; PAL; VIDEOCONFERENCING.

Table 25
Common QIC Standards

QIC Type	Capacity	Cartridge Size
QIC-24-DC	60 MB	Full
QIC-40-MC	40 MB	Mini
QIC-80-MC	80 MB 120 MB	Mini
QIC-525-DC	525 MB	Full
QIC-1000-DC	1.01GB	Full
QIC-1350-DC	1.35 GB	Full
QIC-2100-MC	2.1 GB	Mini
QIC-3010-MC	340 MB	Mini
QIC-3020-MC	680 MB	Mini
QIC-3040-MC	1 GB	Mini
QIC-3080-MC	1.6 GB	Mini
QIC-3095-MC	4 GB	Mini
QIC-3210-MC	2.3 GB	Mini
QIC-3220-MC	10 GB	Mini

QIC Abbreviation for *q(uarter)-i(nch) c(artridge)*, pronounced *quick,* a standard for magnetic tape drives. QIC tapes are among the most popular tapes used for backing up personal computers. QIC tapes are divided into two general classes: full-size (also called *data-cartridge*) and mini-cartridge.

The QIC-40 and QIC-80 standards are sometimes referred to as *floppy tape* standards because they are designed to use a personal computer's existing floppy disk drive controller instead of requiring a customized controller.

The newest set of QIC standards is based on the Travan technology developed by 3M.

The various QIC standards are controlled by a consortium of manufacturers called the *Quarter-Inch Cartridge Drive Standards, Inc.* The term *QIC,* therefore, is used to refer both to the type of tape and to the standards-producing organization.

⇒ See also MASS STORAGE; TAPE; TRAVAN.

QoS Short for *Quality of Service,* a networking term that specifies a guaranteed throughput level. One of the biggest advantages of ATM over competing technologies such as Frame Relay and Fast Ethernet is that it supports QoS levels. This allows ATM providers to guarantee to their customers that end-to-end latency will not exceed a specified level.

⇒ See also ATM; CIR; LATENCY; RSVP.

QTVR See QUICKTIME VR.

quad-speed CD-ROM drive A CD-ROM drive designed to run four times as fast as original models. Often denoted as *4X CD players,* they provide data transfer rates of 600K per second and data access times as low as 125 milliseconds (ms).

⇒ See also CD-ROM PLAYER.

Quality of Service See QoS.

quarter-inch cartridge See QIC.

query *n* **1.** A request for information from a database. There are three general methods for posing queries:

   choosing parameters from a menu: In this method, the database system presents a list of parameters from which you can choose. This is perhaps the easiest way to pose a query because the menus guide you, but it is also the least flexible.
   query by example (QBE): In this method, the system presents a blank record and lets you specify the fields and values that define the query.

query language: Many database systems require you to make requests for information in the form of a stylized query that must be written in a special *query language*. This is the most complex method because it forces you to learn a specialized language, but it is also the most powerful.

—*v* **2.** To make a request for information from a database.

⇒ See also DATABASE MANAGEMENT SYSTEM; FIELD; JOIN; MENU; QUERY BY EXAMPLE; QUERY LANGUAGE; RECORD.

query by example In database management systems, *query by example* (QBE) refers to a method of forming queries in which the database program displays a blank record with a space for each field. You can then enter conditions for each field that you want to be included in the query. For example, if you wanted to find all records where the AGE field is greater than 65, you would enter >*65* in the AGE field blank.

QBE systems are considered easier to learn than formal query languages.

⇒ See also DATABASE MANAGEMENT SYSTEM; FIELD; QUERY; QUERY LANGUAGE; RECORD.

query language A specialized language for requesting information from a database. For example, the query

SELECT ALL WHERE age > 30 AND name = "Smith"

requests all records in which the NAME-field is "Smith" and the AGE field has a value greater than 30. The de facto standard for query languages is *SQL*.

⇒ See also DATABASE MANAGEMENT SYSTEM; QUERY; SQL.

queue *v* **1.** To line up. In computer science, *queuing* refers to lining up jobs for a computer or device. For example, if you want to print a number of documents, the operating system (or a special print spooler) queues the documents by placing them in a special area called a *print buffer* or *print queue*. The printer then pulls the documents off the queue one at a time. Another term for this is *print spooling*.

The order in which a system executes jobs on a queue depends on the priority system being used. Most commonly, jobs are executed in the same order that they were placed on the queue, but in some schemes certain jobs are given higher priority. —*n* **2.** A group of jobs waiting to be executed. **3.** In programming, a queue is a data structure in which elements are removed in the same order they were entered. This is often referred to as FIFO (first in, first out). In contrast, a *stack* is a data structure in which elements are removed in the reverse order from which they were entered. This is referred to as LIFO (last in, first out).

⇒ See also BUFFER; DATA STRUCTURE; JOB; OPERATING SYSTEM; SPOOLING.

QuickDraw The underlying graphics display system for Apple Macintosh computers. The QuickDraw system enables programs to create and manipulate graphical objects. Because all Macintosh programs use QuickDraw, they all share a common look.

There are several versions of QuickDraw that offer different color capabilities and other features. The newest, called QuickDraw GX, supports 16.7 million colors.

QuickDraw is currently used primarily for displaying images on monitors, but some printers use it as well.

⇒ See also GRAPHICS; LASERWRITER; MACINTOSH COMPUTER; PIXEL; POSTSCRIPT; SCALABLE FONT.

QuickTime A video and animation system developed by Apple Computer. QuickTime is built into the Macintosh operating system and is used by most Mac applications that include video or animation. PCs can also run files in QuickTime format, but they require a special QuickTime driver. QuickTime supports most encoding formats, including Cinepak, JPEG, and MPEG. QuickTime is competing with a number of other standards, including AVI and ActiveMovie.

In February 1998, the ISO standards body gave QuickTime a boost by deciding to use it as the basis for the new MPEG-4 standard it is defining.

⇒ See also ACTIVEMOVIE; ANIMATION; AVI; CINEPAK; CODEC; INDEO; MPEG; MULTIMEDIA; QUICKTIME VR.

QuickTime Virtual Reality See QUICKTIME VR.

QuickTime VR An enhanced version of the QuickTime standard developed by Apple for displaying multimedia content (animation, audio, and video) on computers. This enhanced version adds the ability to display and rotate objects in three dimensions. A QuickTime VR plug-in is available for most Web browsers.

You prepare visual material for QuickTime VR from computer-generated 3-D artwork or from a series of photographs. To use photographs, an object must be photographed from various angles. The QuickTime viewer is able to stitch the photos together in a realistic way as you move about outside an object or inside a space.

⇒ See also QUICKTIME; VIRTUAL REALITY; VRML.

quit To exit a program in an orderly way. Compare with *abort*, which exits a program in an unorderly fashion.

⇒ See also ABORT.

QWERTY keyboard Pronounced *kwer-tee,* it refers to the arrangement of keys on a standard English computer keyboard or typewriter. The name derives from the first six characters on the top alphabetic line of the keyboard.

The arrangement of characters on a QWERTY keyboard was designed in 1868 by Christopher Sholes, the inventor of the typewriter. According to popular myth, Sholes arranged the keys in their odd fashion to prevent jamming on mechanical typewriters by separating commonly used letter combinations. However, there is no evidence to support this assertion, except that the arrangement does, in fact, inhibit fast typing.

With the emergence of ball-head electric typewriters and computer keyboards, on which jamming is not an issue, new keyboards designed for speed typing have been invented. The best-known is called a *Dvorak keyboard*. Despite their more rational designs, these new keyboards have not received wide acceptance.

⇒ See also Dvorak keyboard; keyboard.

RAD See RAPID APPLICATION DEVELOPMENT.

radio buttons In graphical user interfaces, groups of buttons, of which only one can be on at a time. When you select one button, all the others are automatically deselected. Compare with *check box*, which allows you to select any combination of options.

⇒ See also BUTTON; CHECK BOX; GRAPHICAL USER INTERFACE; SELECT.

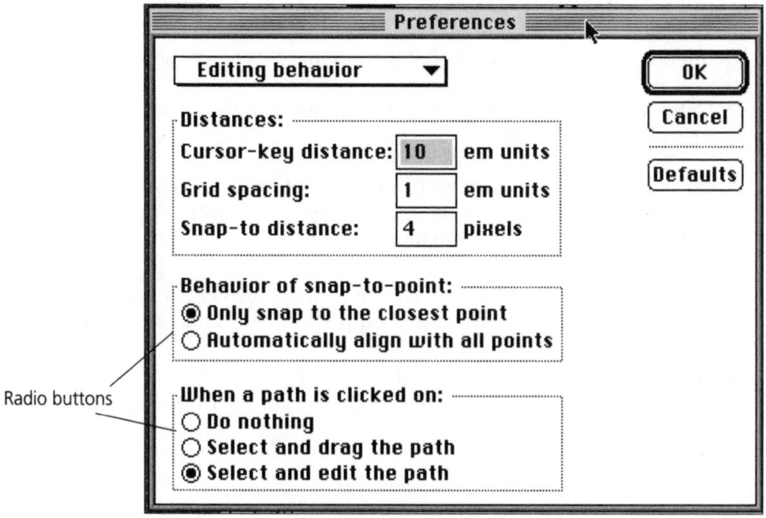

Figure 69: **radio buttons**

RADIUS Short for *R(emote) A(uthentication) D(ial)-I(n) U(ser) S(ervice)*, an authentication and accounting system used by many internet service providers (ISPs). When you dial in to the ISP you must enter your username and password. This information is passed to a RADIUS server, which checks that the information is correct and then authorizes access to the ISP system.

Though not an official standard, the RADIUS specification is maintained by a working group of the IETF.

⇒ See also AUTHENTICATION; DIAL-UP ACCESS; ISP.

ragged In text processing, *ragged* means not aligned along a margin. The opposite of ragged is *flush* or *justified*. The text at the end of this entry has a *ragged right* margin.

Most word processors allow you to choose between ragged and justified margins.

⇒ See also FLUSH; JUSTIFY.

This text has a ragged right
margin because each
line ends at a different
spot.

RAID Short for *R(edundant) A(rray) of I(ndependent) [or I(nexpensive)] D(isks)*, a category of disk drives that employ two or more drives in combination for fault tolerance and performance. RAID disk drives are used frequently on servers but aren't generally necessary for personal computers.

There are number of different RAID levels. The three most common are 0, 3, and 5:

Level 0: Provides *data striping* (spreading out blocks of each file across multiple disks) but no redundancy. This improves performance but does not deliver fault tolerance.
Level 1: Provides disk mirroring.
Level 3: Same as Level 0, but also reserves one dedicated disk for error-correction data. It provides good performance and some level of fault tolerance.
Level 5: Provides data striping at the byte level and also stripe error-correction information. This results in excellent performance and good fault tolerance.

⇒ See also DISK DRIVE; DISK MIRRORING; DISK STRIPING; FAULT TOLERANCE.

RAM Pronounced *ramm,* acronym for *r(andom)-a(ccess) m(emory)*, a type of computer memory that can be accessed randomly; that is, any byte of memory can be accessed without touching the preceding bytes. RAM is the most common type of memory found in computers and other devices, such as printers.

There are two basic types of RAM:

• dynamic RAM (DRAM)
• static RAM (SRAM)

The two types differ in the technology they use to hold data, dynamic

RAM being the more common type. Dynamic RAM needs to be refreshed thousands of times per second. Static RAM does not need to be refreshed, which makes it faster; but it is also more expensive than dynamic RAM. Both types of RAM are *volatile,* meaning that they lose their contents when the power is turned off.

In common usage, the term *RAM* is synonymous with *main memory,* the memory available to programs. For example, a computer with 8MB RAM has approximately 8 million bytes of memory that programs can use. In contrast, *ROM (read-only memory)* refers to special memory used to store programs that boot the computer and perform diagnostics. Most personal computers have a small amount of ROM (a few thousand bytes). In fact, both types of memory (ROM and RAM) allow random access. To be precise, therefore, RAM should be referred to as *read/write RAM* and ROM as *read-only RAM.*

⇒ See also DYNAMIC RAM; MAIN MEMORY; MEMORY; NVRAM; ROM; SRAM; TAG RAM; VRAM; WRAM.

Rambus memory See RDRAM.

RAM cache **1.** Same as L2 CACHE. **2.** On Apple Macintosh computers, the term *RAM cache* refers to a disk cache.

⇒ See also CACHE; DISK CACHE; L2 CACHE.

RAMDAC Short for *Random Access Memory Digital-to-Analog Converter,* a single chip on video adapter cards. The RAMDAC's role is to convert digitally encoded images into analog signals that can be displayed by a monitor. A RAMDAC actually consists of four different components—SRAM to store the color map and three digital-to-analog converters (DACs), one for each of the monitor's red, green, and blue electron guns.

⇒ See also DAC; MONITOR; VIDEO ADAPTER; VIDEO MEMORY.

RAM disk Refers to RAM that has been configured to simulate a disk drive. You can access files on a RAM disk as you would access files on a real disk. RAM disks, however, are approximately a thousand times faster than hard disk drives. They are particularly useful, therefore, for applications that require frequent disk accesses.

Because they are made of normal RAM, RAM disks lose their contents once the computer is turned off. To use a RAM disk, therefore, you need to copy files from a real hard disk at the beginning of the session and then copy the files back to the hard disk before you turn the computer off. Note that if there is a power failure, you will lose whatever data is on the RAM disk. (Some RAM disks come with a battery backup to make them more stable.)

A RAM disk is also called a *RAM drive.*

⇒ See also DISK; EXTENDED MEMORY; RAM.

RAM resident Same as MEMORY RESIDENT.

random access Refers to the ability to access data at random. The opposite of *random access* is *sequential access*. To go from point A to point Z in a sequential-access system, you must pass through all intervening points. In a random-access system, you can jump directly to point Z. Disks are random-access media, whereas tapes are sequential-access media.

The terms *random access* and *sequential access* are often used to describe data files. A random-access data file enables you to read or write information anywhere in the file. In a sequential-access file, you can read and write information only sequentially, starting from the beginning of the file.

Both types of files have advantages and disadvantages. If you are always accessing information in the same order, a sequential-access file is faster. If you tend to access information randomly, random access is better.

Random access is sometimes called *direct access*.

⇒ See also ACCESS; ISAM; RAM; SEQUENTIAL ACCESS.

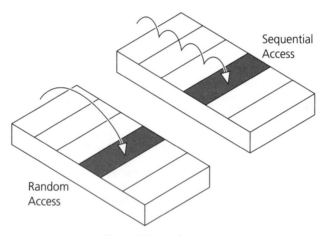

Figure 70: **random access**

random-access memory See RAM.

range In spreadsheet applications, one or more contiguous cells. For example, a range could be an entire row or column, or multiple rows or columns. The only restrictions on ranges is that all the cells of the range must be contiguous and the entire range must be rectangular in shape; that is, you cannot have a range consisting of three cells in one column and four cells in the next.

Once you have defined a range, you can perform operations on it. This is a powerful feature because it allows you to manipulate a set of cells with one expression.

⇒ See also CELL; EXPRESSION; FUNCTION; SPREADSHEET.

rapid application development A programming system that enables programmers to build working programs quickly. In general, RAD systems provide a number of tools to help build graphical user interfaces that would normally take a large development effort. Two of the most popular RAD systems for Windows are Visual Basic and Delphi.

Historically, RAD systems have tended to emphasize reducing development time, sometimes at the expense of generating efficient executable code. Nowadays, though, many RAD systems produce extremely fast code. Conversely, many traditional programming environments now come with a number of visual tools to aid development. Therefore, the line between RAD systems and other development environments has become blurred.

⇒ See also DELPHI; PROGRAMMING LANGUAGE; VISUAL BASIC.

RAS Short for *Remote Access Services,* a feature built into Windows NT that enables users to log into an NT-based LAN using a modem, X.25 connection, or WAN link. RAS works with several major network protocols, including TCP/IP, IPX, and Netbeui.

To use RAS from a remote node, you need a RAS client program, which is built into most versions of Windows, or any PPP client software. For example, most remote control programs work with RAS.

⇒ See also DIAL-UP NETWORKING; REMOTE ACCESS; REMOTE CONTROL; WINDOWS NT.

raster The rectangular area of a display screen actually being used to display images. The raster is slightly smaller than the physical dimensions of the display screen. Also, the raster varies for different resolutions. For example, VGA resolution of 640 by 480 on a 15-inch monitor produces one raster, whereas SVGA resolution of 1,024 by 768 produces a slightly different raster. Most monitors are autosizing, meaning that they automatically use the optimal raster depending on the monitor's size and the video adapter's resolution. In addition, most monitors have controls that allow you move the raster, resize it, and even to rotate it.

⇒ See also AUTOSIZING; BIT-MAPPED GRAPHICS; DISPLAY SCREEN; MONITOR; RASTER IMAGE PROCESSOR; RESOLUTION.

raster graphics See under BIT-MAPPED GRAPHICS.

raster image processor A hardware-software combination that converts a vector image into a bit-mapped image. All PostScript printers contain a RIP that converts the PostScript commands into bit-mapped pages that the printer can output.

⇒ See also BIT MAP; POSTSCRIPT; RASTER; VECTOR GRAPHICS.

raw data Information that has not been organized, formatted, or analyzed.

⇒ See also DATA.

ray tracing In computer graphics, an advanced technique for adding realism to an image by including variations in shade, color intensity, and shadows that would be produced by having one or more light sources. Ray tracing software works by simulating the path of a single light ray as it would be absorbed or reflected by various objects in the image. To work properly, the artist must specify parameters of the light source (intensity, color, etc.) as well as all the objects (how reflective or absorbent the materials are).

Ray tracing requires enormous computational resources and is supported by only the most advanced graphics systems.

⇒ See also 3-D GRAPHICS; GRAPHICS; TEXTURE.

RDBMS Short for *r(elational) d(atabase) m(anagement) s(ystem)* and pronounced as separate letters, a type of database management system (DBMS) that stores data in the form of related tables. Relational databases are powerful because they require few assumptions about how data is related or how it will be extracted from the database. As a result, the same database can be viewed in many different ways.

An important feature of relational systems is that a single database can be spread across several tables. This differs from flat-file databases, in which each database is self-contained in a single table.

Almost all full-scale database systems are RDBMSs. Small database systems, however, use other designs that provide less flexibility in posing queries.

⇒ See also BORLAND INTERNATIONAL; DATABASE; DATABASE MANAGEMENT SYSTEM; DB2; FLAT-FILE DATABASE; MULTIDIMENSIONAL DBMS; NORMALIZATION; QUERY; RDBMS; REFERENTIAL INTEGRITY; SQL SERVER.

RDRAM Short for *Rambus DRAM,* a type of memory (DRAM) developed by Rambus, Inc. Whereas the fastest current memory technologies used by PCs (SDRAM) can deliver data at a maximum speed of about 100 MHz, RDRAM transfers data at up to 600 MHz.

In 1997, Intel announced that it would license the Rambus technology for use on its future motherboards, thus making it the likely de facto standard for memory architectures. However, a consortium of computer vendors is working on an alternative memory architecture called *SyncLink DRAM (SLDRAM).*

RDRAM was first used in place of VRAM in some graphics accelerator boards. Intel and Rambus are also working a new version of RDRAM, called *nDRAM,* that will support data transfer speeds at up to 1,600 MHz.

⇒ See also BEDO DRAM; DRAM; EDO DRAM; FPM RAM; MEMORY; SDRAM; SLDRAM; VIDEO MEMORY.

read *v* **1.** To copy data to a place where it can be used by a program. The term is commonly used to describe copying data from a storage medium, such as a disk, to main memory. —*n* **2.** The act of reading. For example, *a fast disk drive performs 100 reads per second.*

⇒ See also ACCESS.

readme file A small text file that comes with many software packages and contains information not included in the official documentation. Typically, readme files contain late-breaking information that could not be included in the printed or on-line documentation.

⇒ See also DOCUMENTATION.

read-only Capable of being displayed, but not modified or deleted. All operating systems allow you to protect objects (disks, files, directories) with a *read-only attribute* that prevents other users from modifying the object.

⇒ See also ATTRIBUTE; CD-ROM; READ/WRITE; ROM.

read-only memory See ROM.

read/write Capable of being displayed (read) and modified (written to). Most objects (disks, files, directories) are read/write, but operating systems also allow you to protect objects with a *read-only attribute* that prevents other users from modifying the object.

⇒ See also READ-ONLY.

read/write head See HEAD.

real address Same as ABSOLUTE ADDRESS.

RealAudio The de facto standard for streaming audio data over the World Wide Web. RealAudio was developed by RealNetworks and supports FM-stereo-quality sound. To hear a Web page that includes a RealAudio sound file, you need a RealAudio player or plug-in, a program that is freely available from a number of places. It's included in the current versions of both Netscape Navigator and Microsoft Internet Explorer.

⇒ See also REALVIDEO; STREAMING.

real mode An execution mode supported by the Intel 80286 and later processors. In real mode, these processors imitate the Intel 8088 and 8086 microprocessors, although they run much faster. The other mode available is called *protected mode*. In protected mode, programs can access extended memory and virtual memory. Protected mode also supports multitasking. The 80386 and later microprocessors support a third mode called *virtual 8086 mode*. In virtual mode, these microprocessors can run several real-mode programs at once.

The DOS operating system was not designed to take advantage of protected mode, so it always executes programs in real mode unless a protected mode extender is run first.

⇒ See also DOS; EXTENDED MEMORY; INTEL MICROPROCESSORS; MICROSOFT WINDOWS; MULTITASKING; OS/2; PROTECTED MODE; VIRTUAL MEMORY.

real time Immediate response by a computer system. The term is used to describe a number of different computer features. For example, real-time operating systems are systems that respond to input immediately. They are used for such tasks as navigation, in which the computer must react to a steady flow of new information without interruption. Most general-purpose operating systems are not real-time because they can take a few seconds, or even minutes, to react.

Real time can also refer to events simulated by a computer at the same speed that they would occur in real life. In graphics animation, for example, a real-time program would display objects moving across the screen at the same speed that they would actually move.

⇒ See also ISOCHRONOUS; OPERATING SYSTEM; OS/9.

real-time clock A clock that keeps track of the time even when the computer is turned off. Real-time clocks run on a special battery that is not connected to the normal power supply. In contrast, clocks that are not real-time do not function when the computer is off.

Do not confuse a computer's real-time clock with its CPU clock. The CPU clock regulates the execution of instructions.

⇒ See also CLOCK SPEED; CPU.

Real Time Streaming Protocol See RTSP.

Real-Time Transport Protocol See RTP.

RealVideo A streaming technology developed by RealNetworks for transmitting live video over the Internet. RealVideo uses a variety of data compression techniques and works with both normal IP connections as well as IP Multicast connections.

⇒ See also IP MULTICAST; REALAUDIO; STREAMING.

reboot To restart a computer. In DOS, you can reboot by pressing the Alt, Control, and Delete keys simultaneously. This is called a warm boot. You can also perform a cold boot by turning the computer off and then on again.

On Macs, you reboot by selecting the "Restart" option from the Special menu.

⇒ See also BOOT.

recalculate In spreadsheet programs, *recalculation* refers to computing the values of cells in a spreadsheet. Recalculation is necessary whenever you change a formula or enter new data into one or more cells. Depending on the size and complexity of your spreadsheet, recalculation can be a time-consuming process. One criterion for evaluating spreadsheet programs, therefore, is how fast they recalculate.

To make recalculation faster, many spreadsheet programs support *minimal recalculation* (also called *optimal recalculation*), in which the program calculates only the values of cells that will change. In addition, some spreadsheets support background *recalculation*, which allows you to perform other operations while a recalculation is in progress.

⇒ See also AUTOMATIC RECALCULATION; BACKGROUND; CELL; FORMULA; SPREAD-SHEET.

record 1. In database management systems, a complete set of information. Records are composed of *fields*, each of which contains one item of information. A set of records constitutes a *file*. For example, a personnel file might contain records that have three fields: a name field, an address field, and a phone number field. **2.** Some programming languages allow you to define a special data structure called a record. Generally, a record is a combination of other data objects. For example, a record might contain three integers, a floating-point number, and a character string.

⇒ See also DATA STRUCTURE; DATA TYPE; DATABASE; DATABASE MANAGEMENT SYSTEM; FIELD; FILE.

record locking See under LOCK.

recursion A programming method in which a routine calls itself. Recursion is an extremely powerful concept, but it can strain a computer's memory resources. Some programming languages, such as LISP and Prolog, are specifically designed to use recursive methods.

⇒ See also PROGRAM; PROGRAMMING LANGUAGE.

Recycle Bin An icon on the Windows 95 and Windows 98 desktops that represents a directory where deleted files are temporarily stored. This enables you to retrieve files that you may have accidentally deleted. From time to time, you'll want to *purge* the Recycle Bin to free up space on your hard disk. You can also configure Windows so that it doesn't use the Recycle Bin at all, but then you won't be able to retrieve accidentally deleted files.

The Recycle Bin is modeled after the Macintosh trash can, which has been part of the Mac GUI since its inception.

⇒ See also DELETE; PURGE.

Red Book The standard for audio CDs, developed by Phillips and Sony. The specification is formally known as *Compact Disc–Digital Audio (CD-DA)*. It specifies up to 74 minutes of digital audio transferred at 150 Kbps. The first CD-ROM players also transmitted data at this rate, so they came to be called *single-speed* drives.

⇒ See also CD-ROM; COMPACT DISC; GREEN BOOK; ORANGE BOOK; WHITE BOOK.

red-green-blue monitor See RGB MONITOR.

redirection In operating system shells, *redirection* refers to directing input and output to files and devices other than the default I/O devices. By default, input generally comes from the keyboard or mouse, and output goes to the display monitor. With a redirection operator, you can override these defaults so that a command or program takes input from some other device and sends output to a different device.

In DOS and UNIX systems, the redirection operators are < for input and > for output. For example, the DOS command

    sort < c:\list > c:\sorted

takes input from a file called *list*, sorts it, and sends output to a file called *sorted*.

⇒ See also DEFAULT; DEVICE; DOS; FILE; I/O; OPERATING SYSTEM; OPERATOR; SHELL; UNIX.

redlining In word processing, *redlining* refers to marking text that has been edited. Typically, redlining is used when two or more people are working on a document together; each individual can *redline* the text he or she has added or edited. The redlined text will then appear in a special color (or as bold) so that others can see the changes that have been made.

⇒ See also WORD PROCESSING.

reduced instruction set computer See RISC.

Redundant Array of Independent Disks See RAID.

referential integrity A feature provided by relational database management systems (RDBMSs) that prevents users or applications from entering inconsistent data. Most RDBMSs have various referential integrity rules that you can apply when you create a relationship between two tables.

For example, suppose Table B has a *foreign key* that points to a field in Table A. Referential integrity would prevent you from adding a record to Table B that cannot be linked to Table A. In addition, the referential integrity rules might also specify that whenever you delete a record from Table A, any records in Table B that are linked to the deleted record will also be deleted. This is called *cascading delete*. Finally, the referential integrity rules could specify that whenever you modify the value of a linked field in Table A, all records in Table B that are linked to it will also be modified accordingly. This is called *cascading update*.

⇒ See also KEY; NORMALIZATION; RDBMS.

refresh 1. Generally, to update something with new data. For example, some Web browsers include a refresh button that updates the currently displayed Web pages. This feature is also called *reload*. **2.** To recharge a device with power or information. For example, *dynamic RAM* needs to be refreshed thousands of times per second or it will lose the data stored in it.

Similarly, display monitors must be refreshed many times per second. The *refresh rate* for a monitor is measured in hertz (Hz) and is also called the *vertical frequency, vertical scan rate, frame rate,* or *vertical refresh rate.* The old standard for monitor refresh rates was 60Hz, but a new standard developed by VESA sets the refresh rate at 75Hz for monitors displaying resolutions of 640 by 480 or greater. This means that the monitor redraws the display 75 times per second. The faster the refresh rate, the less the monitor flickers.

⇒ See also DYNAMIC RAM; INTERLACING; MONITOR; SCREEN FLICKER.

refresh rate See under REFRESH.

register *n* **1.** A special high-speed storage area within the CPU. All data must be represented in a register before it can be processed. For example, if two numbers are to be multiplied, both numbers must be in registers, and the result is also placed in a register. (The register can contain the address of a memory location where data is stored rather than the actual data itself.)

The number of registers that a CPU has and the size of each (number of bits) help determine the power and speed of a CPU. For example, a 32-bit CPU is one in which each register is 32 bits wide. Therefore, each CPU instruction can manipulate 32 bits of data.

Usually, the movement of data in and out of registers is completely transparent to users, and even to programmers. Only assembly language programs can manipulate registers. In high-level languages, the compiler is responsible for translating high-level operations into low-level operations that access registers. —*v* **2.** To notify a manufacturer that you have purchased its product. Registering a product is often a prerequisite to receiving customer support, and it is one of the ways that software producers control software piracy.

⇒ See also 32-BIT; COMPILER; CPU; LOAD; MICROPROCESSOR; SOFTWARE PIRACY.

Registry A database used by the Windows operating system (Windows 95, 98, and NT) to store configuration information. The Registry consists of the following major sections:

HKEY_Classes_Root: file associations and OLE information
HKEY_Current_User: all preferences set for current user
HKEY_User: all the current user information for each user of the system
HKEY_Local_Machine: settings for hardware, operating system, and installed applications
HKEY_Current_Configuration: settings for the display and printers

HKEY_Dyn_Data: performance data

Most Windows applications write data to the Registry, at least during installation. You can edit the Registry directly by using the Registry Editor (*regedit.exe*) provided with the operating system. However, you must take great care because errors in the Registry could disable your computer.

⇒ See also CONFIGURATION; WINDOWS 95.

relational database See under RDBMS.

relational expression See under RELATIONAL OPERATOR.

relational operator An operator that compares two values. For example, the expression

x < 5

means *x is less than 5*. This expression will have a value of TRUE if the variable x is less than 5; otherwise the value of the expression will be FALSE.
Relational operators are sometimes called *comparison operators*. Expressions that contain relational operators are called *relational expressions*.

⇒ See also BOOLEAN LOGIC; EXPRESSION; OPERATOR.

Table 26		
Relational Operators		
Symbol	**Mnemonic**	**Meaning**
=	EQ	Equal to
<> (or !=)	NE	Not equal to
>	GT	Greater than
>=	GE	Greater than or equal to
<	LT	Less than
<=	LE	Less than or equal to

relative address An address specified by indicating its distance from another address, called the *base address*. For example, a relative address might be B + 15, B being the base address and 15 the distance (called the *offset*).
There are two types of addressing: *relative addressing* and *absolute* addressing. In absolute addressing, you specify the actual address (called the *absolute address*) of a memory location.
Relative and absolute addressing are used in a variety of circum-

stances. In programming, you can use either mode to identify locations in main memory or on mass storage devices. In spreadsheet applications, you can use either mode to designate a particular cell.

⇒ See also ABSOLUTE ADDRESS; ADDRESS; BASE ADDRESS; CELL; MEMORY; OFFSET.

relative cell reference In spreadsheet applications, a reference to a cell or group of cells by indicating how far away it is from some other cell. For example, in Lotus 1-2-3 and many other spreadsheet programs, the cell reference "C2" is relative. Initially it points to the cell in the third column and second row, but it does this by specifying how far away this cell is from some other cell. For example, if you insert this reference in cell A1, the program will translate it to "2 columns right and 1 row down." If you then copy the reference to cell B4, it will now point to cell D5.

In contrast, an absolute cell reference always points to the same cell, no matter where the reference appears.

⇒ See also ABSOLUTE CELL REFERENCE; CELL; SPREADSHEET.

remote In networks, *remote* refers to files, devices, and other resources that are not connected directly to your workstation. Resources at your workstation are considered local.

⇒ See also LOCAL; LOCAL-AREA NETWORK; NETWORK; REMOTE ACCESS; REMOTE CONTROL SOFTWARE; RPC; WORKSTATION.

remote access The ability to log onto a network from a distant location. Generally, this implies a computer, a modem, and some remote access software to connect to the network. Whereas *remote control* refers to taking control of another computer, *remote access* means that the remote computer actually becomes a full-fledged host on the network. The remote access software dials in directly to the network server. The only difference between a remote host and workstations connected directly to the network is slower data transfer speeds.

⇒ See also RAS; REMOTE; REMOTE CONTROL.

remote control Refers to a program's ability to control a computer system from a remote location. Remote-control programs for PCs enable you to access data stored on your home system even when you are traveling.

Remote control is different from *remote access*. In remote control, only keystrokes and screen updates are transmitted between the two machines as all processing takes place in the local computer. In a remote access setup, the user is logged onto the network, using the phone line as an extension to the network. Thus, all traffic has to flow over a low-speed telephone line.

⇒ See also HOST; LOCAL; RAS; REMOTE; REMOTE ACCESS; REMOTE CONTROL SOFTWARE.

remote control software Software, installed in both machines, that allows a user at a local computer to have control of a remote computer via modem or other connection. Remote control operation is used to take control of an unattended desktop personal computer from a remote location as well as to provide instruction and technical support to remote users.

⇒ See also HOST; REMOTE CONTROL.

remote procedure call See RPC.

removable cartridge Same as REMOVABLE HARD DISK.

removable drive Same as REMOVABLE HARD DISK.

removable hard disk A type of disk drive system in which hard disks are enclosed in plastic or metal cartridges so that they can be removed like floppy disks. Removable disk drives combine the best aspects of hard and floppy disks. They are nearly as capacious and fast as hard disks and have the portability of floppy disks. Their biggest drawback is that they're relatively expensive.

⇒ See also CARTRIDGE; DISK; DISK PACK; HARD DISK; JAZ DRIVE; MASS STORAGE.

render Refers to the process of adding realism to a computer graphics by adding three-dimensional qualities such as shadows and variations in color and shade. One technique for rendering graphics is called *ray tracing*. Another type of rendering is scanline rendering, which renders images one vertical line at a time instead of object by object as in ray tracing. In general, scanline rendering doesn't produce as good results as ray tracing, but it is used frequently in animation packages where the image quality of each individual frame isn't so important.

⇒ See also 3-D GRAPHICS; 3-D SOFTWARE; CAD/CAM; MODELING; RAY TRACING; TEXTURE.

repaginate To recalculate page breaks. Word processing and desktop publishing systems decide where to end one page and begin the next based on a set of parameters including the page size, margin size, and widow and orphan settings. Most systems automatically repaginate whenever you modify a document. However, repagination can be time consuming, so some systems allow you to turn off automatic repagination temporarily until you're ready.

⇒ See also ORPHAN; PAGE BREAK; WIDOW.

repeater A network device used to regenerate or replicate a signal. Repeaters are used in transmission systems to regenerate analog or digital signals distorted by transmission loss. Analog repeaters frequently can only amplify the signal while digital repeaters can reconstruct a signal to near its original quality.

In a data network, a repeater can relay messages between subnetworks that use different protocols or cable types. Hubs can operate as repeaters by relaying messages to all connected computers. A repeater cannot do the intelligent routing performed by bridges and routers.

⇒ See also 10BaseT; bridge; hub; router.

replace To insert a new object in place of an existing object. The term is used most often in connection with search-and-replace operations, in which you search for one word or phrase and replace all occurrences with a new word or phrase.

⇒ See also search and replace.

replication The process of creating and managing duplicate versions of a database. Replication not only copies a database but also synchronizes a set of *replicas* so that changes made to one replica are reflected in all the others. The beauty of replication is that it enables many users to work with their own local copy of a database but have the database updated as if they were working on a single, centralized database. For database applications where users are geographically widely distributed, replication is often the most efficient method of database access.

The Lotus Notes system was one of the first to make replication a central component of its design, which has been one of the main reasons for its success.

⇒ See also database; Lotus Notes.

report A formatted and organized presentation of data. Most database management systems include a report writer that enables you to design and generate reports.

⇒ See also report writer; RPG.

report generator Same as report writer.

report writer Also called a *report generator,* a program, usually part of a database management system, that extracts information from one or more files and presents the information in a specified format. Most report writers allow you to select records that meet certain conditions and to display selected fields in rows and columns. You can also format data into pie charts, bar charts, and other diagrams. Once you have created a format for a report, you can save the format specifications in a file and continue reusing it for new data.

The report writer is one of the most important components of a database management system because it determines how much flexibility you have in outputting data.

⇒ See also database management system; field; record; report; RPG.

Request for Comments See RFC.

reserved word A special word reserved by a programming language or by a program. You are not allowed to use reserved words as variable names. For example, in BASIC and COBOL, the word *IF* is reserved because it has a special meaning.

Reserved words are sometimes called *keywords*.

⇒ See also KEYWORD; VARIABLE.

reset button A button or switch on many computers that allows you to reset the computer. When you press the reset button, the computer will enter its start-up procedure as if you had turned the power off and then on again. Generally, you use the reset button only when a program error has caused your computer to *hang*.

Note that on PCs, pressing the reset button is somewhat different from performing a warm reboot by pressing the Ctrl + Alt + Del reboot keys. Pressing the reset button performs a *cold* reboot. When you perform a warm reboot, the system does not repeat the initial start-up stages during which memory is checked.

⇒ See also BOOT; HANG; REBOOT.

resident 1. See MEMORY RESIDENT. 2. See RESIDENT FONT.

resident font Also called an *internal font* or *built-in font,* a resident font is a font built into the hardware of a printer. All dot-matrix and laser printers come with one or more resident fonts. You can add additional fonts by inserting font cartridges or downloading soft fonts.

⇒ See also DOWNLOAD; FONT; FONT CARTRIDGE; PRINTER; SOFT FONT.

resize See under SIZE.

resolution Refers to the sharpness and clarity of an image. The term is most often used to describe monitors, printers, and bit-mapped graphic images. In the case of dot-matrix and laser printers, the resolution indicates the number of dots per inch. For example, a 300-dpi (dots per inch) printer is one that is capable of printing 300 distinct dots in a line 1 inch

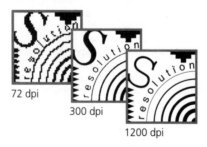

72 dpi

300 dpi

1200 dpi

Figure 71: **resolution**

long. This means it can print 90,000 dots per square inch.

For graphics monitors, the *screen resolution* signifies the number of dots (pixels) on the entire screen. For example, a 640 by 480 pixel screen is capable of displaying 640 distinct dots on each of 480 lines, or about 300,000 pixels. This translates into different dpi measurements depending on the size of the screen. For example, a 15-inch VGA monitor (640 by 480) displays about 50 dots per inch.

Printers, monitors, scanners, and other I/O devices are often classified as *high resolution, medium resolution,* or *low resolution.* The actual resolution ranges for each of these grades is constantly shifting as the technology improves.

⇒ See also BIT MAP; DPI; MONITOR; OPTICAL RESOLUTION; PIXEL; PRINTER; RASTER; VIDEO ADAPTER.

resolution enhancement A collection of techniques used in many laser printers to enable the printer to print at a higher resolution than normal. Most laser printers have printer engines that print at either 300 dpi (dots per inch) or 600 dpi. Using clever algorithms that recognize curved lines, a printer with resolution enhancement can produce output whose resolution appears to be much higher than the print engine's rated resolution. This is why many printer manufacturers characterize their printers with two resolution ratings: the *engine resolution* and the *effective resolution.*

A common resolution-enhancement technique is to vary the size of the dots.

⇒ See also LASER PRINTER; PRINTER ENGINE; RESOLUTION.

resource 1. Generally, any item that can be used. Devices such as printers and disk drives are resources, as is memory. **2.** In many operating systems, including Microsoft Windows and the Macintosh operating system, the term *resource* refers specifically to data or routines that are available to programs. These are also called *system resources.*

⇒ See also UNC.

Resource Reservation Setup Protocol See RSVP.

restore In graphical user interfaces, to *restore* means to return a window to its original size.

⇒ See also GRAPHICAL USER INTERFACE; SIZE; WINDOW; ZOOM.

return A *return* is a special code that causes a word processor or other application to advance to the beginning of the next line. A *soft return* is a return that the application inserts automatically when you reach the end of a line. A *hard return* is a return that you explicitly enter by pressing the Return or Enter key.

⇒ See also CARRIAGE RETURN; HARD RETURN; RETURN KEY; SOFT RETURN.

Return key Almost all computer keyboards have a key marked *Return* or *Enter*; the two names are synonymous. The Return key moves the cursor (or insertion point) to the beginning of the next line. But more important, it returns control to whatever program is currently running. After a program requests information from you (by displaying a prompt), it will usually not respond to your input until you have pressed the Return key. This allows you to correct typing mistakes or to reconsider your entry before it is too late. In many applications, pressing the Return key moves the cursor to the next field.

In word-processing programs, pressing the Return key inserts a hard return into a document.

In technical documentation, the Return key is sometimes signified by an arrow that looks something like < -'.

⇒ See also CURSOR; ENTER KEY; HARD RETURN; INSERTION POINT; KEYBOARD; PROMPT.

Figure 72: **return key**

reverse engineering The process of recreating a design by analyzing a final product. Reverse engineering is common in both hardware and software. Several companies have succeeded in producing Intel-compatible microprocessors through reverse engineering. Whether reverse engineering is legal or not depends on whom you ask. The courts have not yet made a definitive ruling.

⇒ See also SOFTWARE ENGINEER.

reverse video A display method that causes a portion of the display to appear like a negative of the regular display. If the display screen normally displays light images against a dark background, putting it in *reverse video mode* will cause it to display dark images against a light background.

Many programs use reverse video to highlight items, such as selected text or menu options. Also, some systems allow you to change the mode for all displays, so you can choose the display that is most comfortable for you. Some people prefer dark images on a light background, while others prefer light images on a dark background.

⇒ See also BACKGROUND; DISPLAY SCREEN; FOREGROUND.

RFC Short for *Request for Comments*, a series of notes about the Internet, started in 1969 (when the Internet was the ARPANET). An RFC can be submitted by anyone. Eventually, if it gains enough interest, it may evolve into an Internet standard.

Each RFC is designated by an RFC number. Once published, an RFC never changes. Modifications to an original RFC are assigned a new RFC number.

⇒ See also IETF; INTERNET ARCHITECTURE BOARD.

RGB monitor Short for *red, green, blue monitor,* a monitor that requires separate signals for each of the three colors. This differs from color televisions, for example, which use composite video signals, in which all the colors are mixed together. All color computer monitors are RGB monitors.

An RGB monitor consists of a vacuum tube with three electron guns—one each for red, green, and blue—at one end and the screen at the other end. The three electron guns fire electrons at the screen, which contains a phosphorous coating. When the phosphors are excited by the electron beams, they glow. Depending on which beam excites them, they glow either red, green, or blue. Ideally, the three beams should converge for each point on the screen so that each pixel is a combination of the three colors.

⇒ See also COLOR MONITOR; COMPOSITE VIDEO; CONVERGENCE; MASK PITCH; MONITOR; S-VIDEO.

rich text format A standard developed by Microsoft Corporation for specifying formatting of documents. RTF files are actually ASCII files with special commands to indicate formatting information, such as fonts and margins. Other document-formatting languages include the Hypertext Markup Language (HTML), which is used to define documents on the World Wide Web, and the Standard Generalized Markup Language (SGML), of which HTML is a subset.

⇒ See also HTML; SGML; TNEF; WORLD WIDE WEB.

right justify See under JUSTIFY.

ring network A local-area network (LAN) whose topology is a ring. That is, all of the nodes are connected in a closed loop. Messages travel around the ring, with each node reading those messages addressed to it. One of the advantages of ring networks is that they can span larger distances than other types of networks, such as bus networks, because each node regenerates messages as they pass through it.

⇒ See also BUS NETWORK; LOCAL-AREA NETWORK; TOKEN-RING NETWORK; TOPOLOGY.

RIP 1. Pronounced *rip,* acronym for *raster image processor.* See RASTER IMAGE PROCESSOR (RIP). **2.** Short for *Routing Information Protocol.*

RISC Pronounced *risk,* acronym for *r(educed) i(nstruction) s(et) c(omputer),* a type of microprocessor that recognizes a relatively limited number of instructions. Until the mid-1980s, the tendency among computer manufacturers was to build increasingly complex CPUs that had ever-larger sets of instructions. At that time, however, a number of computer manufacturers decided to reverse this trend by building CPUs capable of executing only a very limited set of instructions. One advantage of reduced instruction set computers is that they can execute their instructions very fast because the instructions are so simple. Another, perhaps more important advantage is that RISC chips require fewer transistors, which makes them cheaper to design and produce. Since the emergence of RISC computers, conventional computers have been referred to as CISCs [c(omplex) i(nstruction) s(et) c(omputers)].

There is still considerable controversy among experts about the ultimate value of RISC architectures. Their proponents argue that RISC machines are both cheaper and faster and are therefore the machines of the future. Skeptics note that by making the hardware simpler, RISC architectures put a greater burden on the software. They argue that this is not worth the trouble because conventional microprocessors are becoming increasingly fast and cheap anyway.

To some extent, the argument is becoming moot because CISC and RISC implementations are becoming more and more alike. Many of today's RISC chips support as many instructions as yesterday's CISC chips. And today's CISC chips use many techniques formerly associated with RISC chips.

⇒ See also ALPHA PROCESSOR; CISC; CPU; INSTRUCTION; MICROPROCESSOR; SPARC.

RJ-11 Short for *Registered Jack-11,* a four- or six-wire connector used primarily to connect telephone equipment in the United States. RJ-11 connectors are also used to connect some types of local-area networks (LANs), although RJ-45 connectors are more common.

⇒ See also MODEM; RJ-45.

RJ-45 Short for *Registered Jack-45,* an eight-wire connector used commonly to connect computers onto a local-area networks (LAN), especially Ethernets. RJ-45 connectors look similar to the ubiquitous RJ-11 connectors used for connecting telephone equipment, but they are somewhat wider.

⇒ See also 10BaseT; CONNECTOR; RJ-11.

RJ45 See RJ-45.

RLL Abbreviation of *r(un) l(ength) l(imited),* an encoding scheme used to store data on newer PC hard disks. RLL produces fast data access times and increases a disk's storage capacity over the older encoding scheme called *MFM (modified frequency modulation).*

Technically, any disk drive can use MFM, RLL, or some other encoding scheme. The one used depends on the integrate disk controller within the disk drive.

⇒ See also CONTROLLER; DISK DRIVE; MFM.

RMI A set of protocols being developed by Sun's JavaSoft division that enables Java objects to communicate remotely with other Java objects. RMI is a relatively simple protocol, but unlike more complex protocols such as

CORBA and DCOM, it works only with Java objects. CORBA and DCOM are designed to support objects created in any language.

⇒ See also CORBA; DCOM; Java.

RMON Short for *remote monitoring,* a network management protocol that allows network information to be gathered at a single workstation. Whereas SNMP gathers network data from a single type of Management Information Base (MIB), RMON 1 defines nine additional MIBs that provide a much richer set of data about network usage. For RMON to work, network devices, such as hubs and switches, must be designed to support it.

The newest version of RMON, *RMON 2,* provides data about traffic at the network layer in addition to the physical layer. This allows administrators to analyze traffic by protocol.

⇒ See also DIB; NETWORK MANAGEMENT; SNMP.

robot 1. A device that responds to sensory input. See under ROBOTICS. **2.** A program that runs automatically without human intervention. Typically, a robot is endowed with some artificial intelligence so that it can react to different situations it may encounter. Two common types of robots are *agents* and *spiders.*

⇒ See also ROBOTICS; SPIDER.

robotics The field of computer science and engineering concerned with creating robots, devices that can move and react to sensory input. Robotics is one branch of artificial intelligence.

Robots are now widely used in factories to perform high-precision jobs such as welding and riveting. They are also used in special situations that would be dangerous for humans—for example, in cleaning toxic wastes or defusing bombs.

Although great advances have been made in the field of robotics during the last decade, robots are still not very useful in everyday life, as they are too clumsy to perform ordinary household chores.

The term robotics was coined by the writer Isaac Asimov. In his science fiction book *I, Robot,* published in 1950, he presented three laws of robotics:

1. A robot may not injure a human being, or, through inaction, allow a human being to come to harm.
2. A robot must obey the orders given it by human beings except where such orders would conflict with the First Law.
3. A robot must protect its own existence as long as such protection does not conflict with the First or Second Law.

⇒ See also ARTIFICIAL INTELLIGENCE; CAM; CYBERNETICS.

ROM Pronounced *rahm,* acronym for *r(ead)-o(nly) m(emory).* Computer memory on which data have been prerecorded. Once data have been written onto a ROM chip, they cannot be removed and can be read only.

Unlike main memory (RAM), ROM retains its contents even when the computer is turned off. ROM is referred to as being *nonvolatile*, whereas RAM is *volatile*.

Most personal computers contain a small amount of ROM that stores critical programs such as the program that boots the computer. In addition, ROM is used extensively in calculators and peripheral devices such as laser printers, whose fonts are often stored in ROM.

A variation of a ROM is a *PROM (programmable read-only memory)*. PROMs are manufactured as blank chips on which data can be written with a special device called a *PROM programmer*.

⇒ See also BIOS; BOOT; EEPROM; FIRMWARE; MEMORY; PROM; RAM.

roman In typography, *roman* refers to fonts with characters that are straight up and down rather than slanted. A font designed with characters slanted to the right is *italic*.

⇒ See also FONT; ITALIC.

ROM-BIOS See BIOS.

root directory The top directory in a file system. The root directory is provided by the operating system and has a special name; for example, in DOS systems the root directory is called \. The root directory is sometimes referred to simply as the *root*.

⇒ See also DIRECTORY; FILE MANAGEMENT SYSTEM; HIERARCHICAL.

router A device that connects two LANs. Routers are similar to bridges but provide additional functionality, such as the ability to filter messages and forward them to different places based on various criteria.

The Internet uses routers extensively to forward packets from one host to another.

⇒ See also 3COM; BGP; BRIDGE; BROUTER; GATEWAY; HOP; INTERNETWORKING; IP SPOOFING; IP SWITCHING; OSPF; PACKET; REPEATER; ROUTING; ROUTING INFORMATION PROTOCOL; ROUTING SWITCH.

routine A section of a program that performs a particular task. Programs consist of *modules*, each of which contains one or more routines. The term *routine* is synonymous with *procedure*, *function*, and *subroutine*.

⇒ See also FUNCTION; MODULE; PROGRAM.

routing In internetworking, the process of moving a packet of data from source to destination. Routing is usually performed by a dedicated device called a router. Routing is a key feature of the Internet because it enables messages to pass from one computer to another and eventually reach the target machine. Each intermediary computer performs routing by passing along the message to the next computer. Part of this process involves analyzing a *routing table* to determine the best path.

Routing is often confused with *bridging,* which performs a similar function. The principal difference between the two is that bridging occurs at a lower level and is therefore more of a hardware function, whereas routing occurs at a higher level where the software component is more important. And because routing occurs at a higher level, it can perform more complex analysis to determine the optimal path for the packet.

⇒ See also BGP; CIDR; IP ADDRESS; IP SWITCHING; OSPF; PACKET; ROUTER; ROUTING INFORMATION PROTOCOL; ROUTING SWITCH.

Routing Information Protocol A protocol defined by RFC 1058 that specifies how routers exchange routing table information. With RIP, routers periodically exchange entire tables. Because this is inefficient, RIP is gradually being replaced by a newer protocol called Open Shortest Path First (OSPF).

⇒ See also OSPF; ROUTER; ROUTING.

routing switch A switch that also performs routing operations. Usually a switch operates at layer 2 (the *Data Link layer*) of the OSI Reference Model while routers operate at layer 3 (the *Network layer*). Routing switches, however, perform many of the layer 3 functions usually reserved for routers. And because the routing is implemented in hardware rather than software, it is faster. The downside of routing switches is that they are not as powerful or as flexible as full-fledged routers.

Because they perform some layer 3 functions, routing switches are sometimes called *layer-3 switches.*

⇒ See also IP SWITCHING; ROUTER; ROUTING; SWITCH.

RPC Abbreviation of *remote procedure call,* a type of protocol that allows a program on one computer to execute a program on a server computer. Using RPC, a system developer need not develop specific procedures for the server. The client program sends a message to the server with appropriate arguments and the server returns a message containing the results of the program executed.

Sun Microsystems developed the first widely used RPC protocol as part of its Open Network Computing (ONC) architecture in the early 1980s. The specification has been handed off to the Internet Engineering Task Force (IETF) as a step toward making ONC RPC an Internet standard.

Two newer object-oriented methods for programs to communicate with each other, CORBA and DCOM, provide the same types of capabilities as traditional RPCs.

⇒ See also API; CORBA; MIDDLEWARE; PROTOCOL; REMOTE.

RPG 1. Short for *R(eport) P(rogram) G(enerator),* a programming language developed by IBM in the mid-1960s for developing business applications, especially generating reports from data. The newest version, RPG 400, is still widely used on AS/400 systems. **2.** Short for *r(ole)-p(laying)* g*(ames)*, computer games where one or more players adopt a role and act it out in a virtual reality.

⇒ See also REPORT; REPORT WRITER.

RS-232 See under RS-232C.

RS-232C Short for *r(ecommended) s(tandard)-232C*, a standard interface approved by the Electronic Industries Association (EIA) for connecting serial devices. In 1987, the EIA released a new version of the standard and changed the name to *EIA-232-D*. And in 1991, the EIA teamed up with Telecommunications Industry Association (TIA) and issued a new version of the standard called *EIA/TIA-232-E*. Many people, however, still refer to the standard as *RS-232C*, or just *RS-232*.

Almost all modems conform to the EIA-232 standard, and most personal computers have an EIA-232 *port* for connecting a modem or other device. In addition to modems, many display screens, mice, and serial printers are designed to connect to a EIA-232 *port*. In EIA-232 parlance, the device that connects to the interface is called a *Data Communications Equipment (DCE)*, and the device to which it connects (e.g., the computer) is called a *Data Terminal Equipment (DTE)*.

The EIA-232 standard supports two types of connectors—a 25-pin D-type connector (DB-25) and a 9-pin D-type connector (DB-9). The type of serial communications used by PCs requires only 9 pins so either type of connector will work equally well.

Although EIA-232 is still the most common standard for serial communication, the EIA has recently defined successors to EIA-232 called *RS-422 and RS-423*. The new standards are backward compatible so that RS-232 devices can connect to an RS-422 port.

⇒ See also CONNECTOR; DTE; ELECTRONIC INDUSTRIES ASSOCIATION (EIA); INTERFACE; MODEM; RS-422 AND RS-423; SERIAL PORT.

RS-422 See under RS-422 and RS-423.

RS-422 and RS-423 Standard interfaces approved by the Electronic Industries Association (EIA) for connecting serial devices. The RS-422 and RS-423 standards are designed to replace the older RS-232 standard because they support higher data rates and greater immunity to electrical interference. All Apple Macintosh computers contain an RS-422 port that can also be used for RS-232C communication.

RS-422 supports multipoint connections whereas RS-423 supports only point-to-point connections.

⇒ See also COMMUNICATIONS; CONNECTOR; ELECTRONIC INDUSTRIES ASSOCIATION (EIA); INTERFACE; MODEM; PORT; RS-232C; RS-485.

RS-485 An Electronics Industry Association (EIA) standard for multipoint communications. It supports several types of connectors, including DB-9 and DB-37. RS-485 is similar to RS-422 but can support more nodes per line because it uses lower-impedance drivers and receivers.

⇒ See also ELECTRONIC INDUSTRIES ASSOCIATION (EIA); RS-422 AND RS-423.

RSA A public-key encryption technology developed by RSA Data Security, Inc. The abbreviation stands for Rivest, Shamir, and Adelman, the inventors of the technique. The RSA algorithm is based on the fact that there is no efficient way to factor very large numbers. Deducing an RSA key, therefore, requires an extraordinary amount of computer processing power and time.

The RSA algorithm has become the de facto standard for industrial-strength encryption, especially for data sent over the Internet. It is built into many software products, including Netscape Navigator and Microsoft Internet Explorer. The technology is so powerful that the U.S. government has restricted exporting it to foreign countries.

A similar technology that is also used widely is offered by a company called Cylink.

⇒ See also ENCRYPTION; PRETTY GOOD PRIVACY; PUBLIC-KEY ENCRYPTION; S/MIME; SECURITY.

RSVP Short for *R(esource Re)s(er)v(ation Setup) P(rotocol)*, a new Internet protocol being developed to enable the Internet to support specified Qualities-of-Service (QoSs). Using RSVP, an application will be able to reserve resources along a route from source to destination. RSVP-enabled routers will then schedule and prioritize packets to fulfill the QoS.

RSVP is a chief component of a new type of Internet being developed, known broadly as an *integrated services Internet*. The general idea is to enhance the Internet to support transmission of real-time data.

⇒ See also QoS.

RTF See RICH TEXT FORMAT (RTF).

RTP Short for *R(eal-Time) T(ransport) P(rotocol)*, an Internet protocol for transmitting real-time data such as audio and video. RTP itself does not guarantee real-time delivery of data, but it does provide mechanisms for the sending and receiving applications to support streaming data. Typically, RTP runs on top of the UDP protocol, although the specification is general enough to support other transport protocols.

RTP has received wide industry support. Netscape intends to base its *LiveMedia* technology on RTP, and Microsoft claims that its NetMeeting product supports RTP.

⇒ See also RTSP; STREAMING; UDP; VIDEOCONFERENCING.

RTSP Short for *R(eal) T(ime) S(treaming) P(rotocol)*, a proposed standard for controlling streaming data over the World Wide Web. RTSP grew out of work done by Columbia University, Netscape, and RealNetworks and has been submitted to the IETF for standardization.

Like H.323, RTSP uses *RTP (Real-Time Transport Protocol)* to format packets of multimedia content. But whereas H.323 is designed for videoconferencing of moderately sized groups, RTSP is designed to efficiently broadcast audio-visual data to large groups.

⇒ See also BROADCAST; H.323; MULTICAST; NETSHOW; RTP; SMIL; STREAMING.

rule 1. In word processing and desktop publishing, a straight line that separates columns of text or illustrations. **2.** In expert systems, a conditional statement that tells the system how to react to a particular situation.

⇒ See also EXPERT SYSTEM.

ruler In word processing, a line running across the display screen. It measures the printed-page layout, as measured on paper, in points, picas, inches, or centimeters. It is sometimes called the *ruler line* and is particularly useful for setting margins and tabs. Sophisticated desktop publishing systems and page layout programs sometimes support *movable rulers* that you can move around the display screen to measure particular items of text or graphics.

⇒ See also DESKTOP PUBLISHING; MARGINS; PAGE LAYOUT PROGRAM.

Ruler

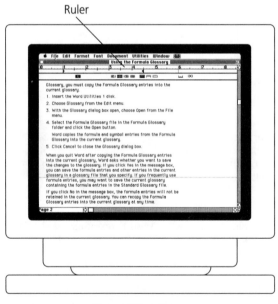

Figure 73: **ruler**

run 1. To execute a program. **2.** To operate. For example, a device that is *running* is one that is turned on and operating properly.

⇒ See also LAUNCH; RUNTIME.

run length limited See RLL.

running head See under HEADER.

runtime Occurring while a program is executing. For example, a runtime error is an error that occurs during program execution, and a runtime library is a library of routines that are bound to the program during execution. In contrast, *compile-time* refers to events that occur while a program is being compiled.

⇒ See also COMPILE; LIBRARY; RUN; RUNTIME ERROR; RUNTIME VERSION.

runtime error An error that occurs during the execution of a program. In contrast, *compile-time* errors occur while a program is being compiled. Runtime errors indicate bugs in the program or problems that the designers had anticipated but could do nothing about. For example, running out of memory will often cause a runtime error.

Note that runtime errors differ from bombs or crashes in that you can often recover gracefully from a runtime error.

⇒ See also BOMB; BUG; COMPILER; CRASH; FATAL ERROR; GPF; RUNTIME.

runtime version A limited version of one program that enables you to run another program. To run a program written in Visual Basic, for example, you need the runtime version of Visual Basic. This allows you to run Visual Basic programs but not to develop them yourself. Many other development applications, particularly database applications, require a runtime version to execute.

Software companies have different approaches to runtime versions. Some allow you to distribute the runtime version freely, while others require that you pay a license fee.

⇒ See also RUNTIME; SOFTWARE LICENSING.

SAA Abbreviation of *System Application Architecture,* a set of architecture standards developed by IBM for program, user, and communications interfaces on various IBM platforms. The main components are:

- Common Programming Interface (CPI)
- Common User Access (CUA)
- Common Communication Support (CCS)

SAA standards were first introduced in the late 1980s. Implementing these standards allows programmers to develop software that is consistent across differing platforms and operating systems.

⇒ See also CUA; STANDARD; USER INTERFACE.

sampling A technique used to capture continuous phenomena, whereby periodic snapshots are taken. If the sampling rate is fast enough, the human sensory organs cannot discern the gaps between snapshots when they are played back. This is the principle behind motion pictures.

Sampling is the key technique used to digitize analog information. For example, music CDs are produced by sampling live sound at frequent intervals and then digitizing each sample. The term *sampling* is also used to describe a similar process in digital photography.

⇒ See also ADPCM; ANALOG; DIGITAL; DIGITAL CAMERA; DIGITIZE; PCM.

sans serif Pronounced *san-serr-if,* refers to a category of typefaces that do not use *serifs,* small lines at the ends of characters. Popular sans serif fonts include Helvetica, Avant Garde, Arial, and Geneva. Serif fonts include Times Roman, Courier, New Century Schoolbook, and Palatino.

According to most studies, sans serif fonts are more difficult to read. For this reason, they are used most often for short text components such as headlines or captions.

⇒ See also FONT.

SAP 1. Short for *S(ervice) A(dvertising) P(rotocol),* a NetWare protocol used to identify the services and addresses of servers attached to the network. The responses are used to update a table in the router known as the *Server Information Table.* **2.** Short for *S(econdary) A(udio) P(rogram),* an NTSC audio channel used for auxiliary transmission, such as foreign language broadcasting or teletext. **3.** (*SAP America, Inc., Lester, PA*) The U.S. branch of the German software company SAP AG. SAP's R/3 integrated suite of applications and its ABAP/4 Development Workbench became popular starting around 1993.

⇒ See also NETWARE; NTSC.

save To copy data from a temporary area to a more permanent storage medium. When you edit a file with a word processor, for example, the word processor copies the entire file, or portions of the file, into an area of main memory called a buffer. Any changes you make to the file are made to the copy in the buffer, not to the real file on the disk. The buffer is temporary—as soon as you exit the program or turn off the computer, the buffer disappears. To record your modifications to the file on the disk, you must save the file. When you do this, the word processor copies the contents of the buffer back to the file on the disk, replacing the previous version of the file.

Because computer crashes due to software bugs and hardware failures are not that uncommon, it is a good idea to save your files periodically. Otherwise, you will lose all the work you have done during an editing session. Many applications automatically save files at regular intervals, which you can specify. These intermediate saves are sometimes called *snapshots*.

⇒ See also AUTOSAVE; CLOSE.

scalability See SCALABLE.

scalable 1. A popular buzzword that refers to how well a hardware or software system can adapt to increased demands. For example, a scalable network system is one that can start with just a few nodes but can easily expand to thousands of nodes. Scalability can be a very important feature because it means that you can invest in a system with confidence that you won't outgrow it. **2.** Refers to anything whose size can be changed. For example, a font is said to be scalable if it can be represented in different sizes.

⇒ See also ARCHITECTURE.

scalable font A font represented in an object-oriented graphics language such as PostScript or TrueType. Such fonts are called *scalable* because the representation of the font defines the shape of each character (the typeface) but not the size. Given a typeface definition, a scalable font system can produce characters at any size (or *scale*).

Aside from offering innumerable sizes of each font, scalable fonts have an added advantage in that they make the most of an output device's resolution. The more resolution a printer or monitor has, the better a scalable font will look.

Scalable fonts are often called *outline fonts* because the most common method of representing scalable fonts is to define the outline of each character. Scalable fonts are also called *object-oriented fonts* or *vector fonts*.

⇒ See also FONT; INTELLIFONT; OUTLINE FONT; POSTSCRIPT; TRUETYPE; TYPE-FACE; VECTOR GRAPHICS.

scale To change the size of an object while maintaining its shape. Most graphics software, particularly vector-based packages, allow you to scale objects freely.

⇒ See also GRAPHICS; SCALABLE FONT; VECTOR GRAPHICS.

SCAM Short for *S(CSI) C(onfiguration) A(uto)m(atically)*, a subset of the PnP specification that provides plug-and-play support for SCSI devices.

⇒ See also PLUG-AND-PLAY; PNP; SCSI.

scan To digitize an image by passing it through an optical scanner. See under OPTICAL SCANNER.

⇒ See also OPTICAL SCANNER.

ScanDisk A DOS and Windows utility that finds different types of errors on hard disks and is able to correct some of them. In DOS, you run ScanDisk by entering **scandisk** at the prompt and pressing the Enter key. In Windows 95, you can run ScanDisk by selecting **Start→Programs→Accessories→System Tools→ScanDisk**.
   Among other things, ScanDisk checks the disk platters for defects and also looks for lost clusters that are sometimes created when a program aborts.

⇒ See also CLUSTER; DEFRAG; HARD DISK.

scanner See OPTICAL SCANNER.

scatter diagram A type of diagram used to show the relationship between data items that have two numeric properties. One property is represented along the x-axis and the other along the y-axis. Each item is then represented by a single point.
   Scatter diagrams are used frequently by computer publications to compare categories of hardware and software products. One axis represents price, while the other represents performance. Typically, all compared products fall near an imaginary diagonal line—that is, performance and price rise together. However, the scatter diagram makes it easy to see items that do not fall near this line, items that are expensive but offer poor performance or items that are inexpensive but provide good performance.

⇒ See also PRESENTATION GRAPHICS.

scheduler 1. A software product designed to help a group of colleagues schedule meetings and other appointments. The scheduler program allows members of a group to view one anothers' calendars so that they can choose a convenient time. Once a time has been selected, the scheduler can automatically send out reminders through e-mail and can even reserve resources such as conference rooms and overhead projectors. **2.** In operating systems, a scheduler is a program that coordinates the use of shared resources, such as a printer.

⇒ See also CALENDAR; GROUPWARE; OPERATING SYSTEM; WORKGROUP COMPUTING.

scientific notation A format for representing real (floating-point) numbers. Instead of writing the full number, scientific notation represents values as a number between 1 and 10 multiplied by 10 to some power. The 10 is often replaced by an uppercase or lowercase *e*.

Scientific notation is much simpler for very large and very small numbers, such as the second and fourth examples in the accompanying table. Most programming languages, and many numeric applications, allow you to enter and display numbers using scientific notation.

⇒ See also FLOATING-POINT NUMBER.

Table 27
Scientific Notation

Number in Normal Notation	In Scientific Notation
0.0004	4.0E-4
1,000,000,000.0	1.0E9
-374.56	-3.7456E2
-0.000000349	-3.49E-7

---

scissoring Same as CLIPPING. See under CLIP.

Scrapbook In Macintosh environments, a desk accessory (DA) that enables you to store objects for future use. The Scrapbook is similar to the clipboard, but it allows more than one item to be stored in it at once. Also, it retains its contents when the computer is turned off.

⇒ See also CLIPBOARD; DESK ACCESSORY (DA).

screen 1. Short for *display screen*. **2.** In offset printing, a mesh used to create halftones. See under HALFTONE.

⇒ See also DISPLAY SCREEN; HALFTONE.

screen capture Refers to the act of copying what is currently displayed on a screen to a file or printer. If the system is in graphics mode, the screen capture will result in a graphics file containing a bit map of the image. If the system is in text mode, the screen capture will normally load a file with ASCII codes.

⇒ See also CAPTURE; PRINT SCREEN KEY.

screen dump Same as SCREEN CAPTURE.

screen flicker The phenomenon whereby a display screen appears to flicker. Screen flicker results from a variety of factors, the most important of which is the monitor's *refresh rate*, the speed with which the screen is redrawn. If the refresh rate is too slow, the screen will appear to glimmer. Another factor that affects screen flicker is the persistence of the screen phosphors. Low-persistence phosphors fade more quickly than high-persistence monitors, making screen flicker more likely. Screen flicker can also be affected by lighting. Finally, screen flicker is a subjective perception that affects people differently. Some people perceive screen flicker where others do not. Most people perceive no screen flicker if the refresh rate is 72 MHz or higher.

⇒ See also INTERLACING; MONITOR; REFRESH.

screen font A font designed especially for a display screen. Typically, display fonts are bit-mapped and must be specially designed to compensate for the relatively low resolution of display screens.

⇒ See also FONT; RESOLUTION.

screen resolution See under RESOLUTION.

screen saver A small program that takes over the display screen if there are no keystrokes or mouse movements for a specified duration. Screen savers were originally developed to prevent *ghosting*, the permanent etching of a pattern on a display screen. For older monochrome monitors, ghosting often occurred if the same pattern was displayed on a display screen for a long period of time. Screen savers would prevent this by either blanking out the screen entirely or by displaying a constantly moving image.

Modern display screens do not suffer so much from this problem. Today, therefore, screen savers are mostly an adornment, a way to liven up the computer. Many screen savers provide another benefit, hiding a user's work from would-be snoopers. These screen savers fill the display with an image or animation until the user either enters a password or activates the mouse or keyboard.

⇒ See also DISPLAY SCREEN; MONITOR.

screen shot Same as SCREEN CAPTURE.

script Another term for *macro* or batch file, a script is a list of commands that can be executed without user interaction. A *script language* is a simple programming language with which you can write scripts.

Apple Computer uses the term *script* to refer to programs written in its HyperCard or AppleScript language.

⇒ See also APPLESCRIPT; BATCH FILE; HYPERCARD; JAVASCRIPT; MACRO.

scroll To view consecutive lines of data on the display screen. The term *scroll* means that once the screen is full, each new line appears at the edge of the screen and all other lines move over one position. For example, when you scroll down, each new line appears at the bottom of the screen and all the other lines move up one row, so that the top line disappears.

The term *vertical scrolling* refers to the ability to scroll up or down. *Horizontal scrolling* means that the image moves sideways.

In theory, the display should move smoothly, as if it were a piece of paper being moved up, down, or sideways. In practice, however, scrolling is not always so smooth.

The scrolling method of viewing documents does not recognize page boundaries. One advantage to scrolling, therefore, is that you can look at the end of one page and the beginning of the next page at the same time.

Another method of viewing data is called *paging*, whereby an entire page is displayed at once. Each subsequent page replaces the previous page on the screen.

⇒ See also PAGE; SCROLL BAR.

scroll bar A bar that appears on the side or bottom of a window to control

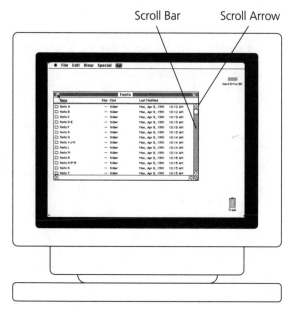

Figure 74: **scroll bar**

which part of a list or document is currently in the window 's frame. The scroll bar makes it easy to move to any part of a file.

Typically, a scroll bar has arrows at either end, a gray or colored area in the middle, and a *scroll box* (or *elevator*) that moves from one end to the other to reflect your position in the document. Clicking on the arrows causes the document to scroll in the indicated direction. You can also quickly move to any part of a document by dragging the scroll box to the corresponding part of the scroll bar.

Many windowing systems support both horizontal and vertical scroll bars.

⇒ See also CLICK; DRAG; GRAPHICAL USER INTERFACE; WINDOW.

scroll box See under SCROLL BAR.

Scroll Lock key A key on PC and enhanced Macintosh keyboards that controls the way the cursor control keys work for some programs. Many applications ignore the Scroll Lock setting.

⇒ See also CURSOR CONTROL KEYS; SCROLL.

SCSI Abbreviation of *S(mall) C(omputer) S(ystem) I(nterface)*, and pronounced *scuzzy*, SCSI is a parallel interface standard used by Apple Macintosh computers, PCs, and many UNIX systems for attaching peripheral devices to computers. Until recently, all Apple Macintosh computers starting with the Macintosh Plus came with a SCSI port for attaching devices such as disk drives and printers. The Apple iMac uses IDE for the hard drive and USB for everything else.

SCSI interfaces provide for faster data transmission rates (up to 80 megabytes per second) than standard serial and parallel ports. In addition, you can attach many devices to a single SCSI port, so that SCSI is really an I/O bus rather than simply an interface.

Although SCSI is an ANSI standard, there are many variations of it, so two SCSI interfaces may be incompatible. For example, SCSI supports several types of connectors.

While SCSI is the only standard interface for Macintoshes, PCs support a variety of interfaces in addition to SCSI. These include *IDE, enhanced IDE,* and *ESDI* for mass storage devices, and *Centronics* for printers. You can, however, attach SCSI devices to a PC by inserting a SCSI board in one of the expansion slots. Many high-end new PCs come with SCSI built in. Note, however, that the lack of a single SCSI standard means that some devices may not work with some SCSI boards.

The following varieties of SCSI are currently implemented:

SCSI-1: Uses an 8-bit bus, and supports data rates of 4 MBps.
SCSI-2: Same as SCSI-1, but uses a 50-pin connector instead of a 25-pin connector, and supports multiple devices. This is what most people mean when they refer to plain *SCSI*.
Wide SCSI: Uses a wider cable (168 pins) to support 16-bit transfers.
Fast SCSI: Uses an 8-bit bus, but doubles the clock rate to support data rates of 10 MBps.

Fast Wide SCSI: Uses a 16-bit bus and supports data rates of 20 MBps.

Ultra SCSI: Uses an 8-bit bus, and supports data rates of 20 MBps.

SCSI-3: Uses a 16-bit bus and supports data rates of 40 MBps. Also called *Ultra Wide SCSI.*

Ultra2 SCSI: Uses an 8-bit bus and supports data rates of 40 MBps.

Wide Ultra2 SCSI: Uses a 16-bit bus and supports data rates of 80 MBps.

⇒ See also ASPI; bus; daisy chain; Fibre Channel; interface; port; SCAM.

SCSI-3 See under SCSI.

SDH Short for *S(ynchronous) D(igital) H(ierarchy).* An international standard for synchronous data transmission over fiber optic cables. The North American equivalent of SDH is SONET.

SDH defines a standard rate of transmission at 51.84 Mbps, which is also called *STS-1.* Higher rates of transmission are a multiple of this basic rate. So, for example, STS-3 is three times the basic rate, or 155.62 Mbps. These are the same as the SONET Optical Carrier (OC) levels.

⇒ See also fiber optics; OC; SONET.

SDK Short for *s(oftware) d(evelopment) k(it),* a programming package that enables a programmer to develop applications for a specific platform. Typically an SDK includes one or more APIs, programming tools, and documentation.

⇒ See also API; JDK; platform.

SDLC Short for *S(ynchronous) D(ata) L(ink) C(ontrol),* a protocol used in IBM's SNA networks. SDLC is similar to *HDLC,* an ISO standard.

⇒ See also HDLC; SNA.

SDRAM Short for *S(ynchronous)* **DRAM,** a new type of DRAM that can run at much higher clock speeds than conventional memory. SDRAM actually synchronizes itself with the CPU's bus and is capable of running at 100 MHz, about three times faster than conventional FPM RAM, and about twice as fast EDO DRAM and BEDO DRAM. SDRAM is replacing EDO DRAM in many newer computers.

Today's fastest Pentium systems use CPU buses running at 100 MHz, so SDRAM can keep up with them, though barely. Future PCs, however, are expected to have CPU buses running at 200 MHz or faster. SDRAM is not expected to support these high speeds, which is why new memory technologies, such as RDRAM and SLDRAM, are being developed.

⇒ See also BEDO DRAM; DDR-SDRAM; DRAM; EDO DRAM; MDRAM; pipeline burst cache; RDRAM; SGRAM; SLDRAM; wait state.

SDRAM II Same as DDR-SDRAM.

SDSL Short for *s(ymmetric) d(igital) s(ubscriber) l(ine)*, a new technology that allows more data to be sent over existing copper telephone lines (POTS). SDSL supports data rates up to 3 Mbps.
    SDSL works by sending digital pulses in the high-frequency area of telephone wires. Because these high frequencies are not used by normal voice communications, SDSL can operate simultaneously with voice connections over the same wires.
    SDSL requires a special SDSL modem. SDSL is called *symmetric* because it supports the same data rates for upstream and downstream traffic. A similar technology that supports different data rates for upstream and downstream data is called *asymmetric digital subscriber line (ADSL)*. ADSL is popular in North America, whereas SDSL is being developed primarily in Europe.

⇒ See also ADSL; ISDN; xDSL.

search and replace A feature supported by most word processors that lets you replace a character string (a series of characters) with another string wherever the first string appears in the document. Most word processors have two search-and-replace modes. In the first mode, the word processor automatically makes all the replacements in the file. In the second mode, the word processor requires you to approve each replacement. This is safer because you may not want to make the change everywhere.
    Search and replace is sometimes called *find and replace.*

⇒ See also CHARACTER STRING; WORD PROCESSING.

search engine A program that searches one or more documents for specified keywords and returns a list of locations where those keywords were found. Although *search engine* is really a general class of programs, the term is often used to specifically describe systems like Alta Vista and Excite that enable users to search for documents on the World Wide Web and in USENET newsgroups.
    Typically, a search engine works by sending out a *spider* to fetch as many documents as possible. Another program, called an *indexer,* then reads these documents and creates an index based on the words contained in each document. Each search engine uses a proprietary algorithm to create its indices such that, ideally, only meaningful results are returned for each *query.*

⇒ See also ALTA VISTA; EXCITE; HOTBOT; INFOSEEK; JUGHEAD; LYCOS; META TAG; OPEN TEXT; SPIDER; VERONICA; WEBCRAWLER; YAHOO!.

secondary cache Same as L2 CACHE.

secondary storage Same as MASS STORAGE.

second normal form See under NORMALIZATION.

sector The smallest unit that can be accessed on a disk. When a disk undergoes a low-level format, it is divided into tracks and sectors. The tracks are concentric circles around the disk, and the sectors are segments within each circle. For example, a formatted disk might have 40 tracks, with each track divided into 10 sectors. The operating system and disk drive keep tabs on where information is stored on the disk by noting its track and sector number.

Modern hard disk drives use a technique called *zoned-bit recording* in which tracks on the outside of the disk contain more sectors than those on the inside.

A sector that cannot be used due to a physical flaw on the disk is called a bad sector.

⇒ See also BAD SECTOR; DISK; FORMAT; INTERLEAVE; TRACK.

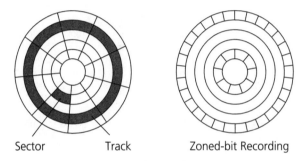

Sector   Track   Zoned-bit Recording

Figure 75: **disk sectors**

Secure Electronic Transactions See SET.

Secure HTTP See S-HTTP.

Secure Socket Layer (SSL) See SSL.

security Refers to techniques for ensuring that data stored in a computer cannot be read or compromised. Most security measures involve data encryption and passwords. Data encryption is the translation of data into a form that is unintelligible without a deciphering mechanism. A password is a secret word or phrase that gives a user access to a particular program or system.

⇒ See also ACCESS CONTROL; AUDIT TRAIL; AUTHENTICATION; AUTHORIZATION; BIOMETRICS; CLIPPER CHIP; CRYPTOGRAPHY; ENCRYPTION; FIREWALL; KERBEROS; NETWORK MANAGEMENT; PASSWORD; RSA; SNIFFER; SSL.

seek time Refers to the time a program or device takes to locate a particular piece of data. For disk drives, the terms *seek time* and *access time* are often used interchangeably. Technically speaking, however, the access time is often longer than the seek time because it includes a brief latency period.

⇒ See also ACCESS TIME; DISK DRIVE.

segment 1. In networks, a section of a network that is bounded by bridges, routers, hubs, or switches. Dividing an Ethernet into multiple segments is one of the most common ways of increasing bandwidth on the LAN. If segmented correctly, most network traffic will remain within a single segment, enjoying the full 10 Mbps bandwidth. Hubs and switches are used to connect each segment to the rest of the LAN. **2.** In virtual memory systems, a variable-sized portion of data that is swapped in and out of main memory. Contrast with *page*, which is a fixed-sized portion of data. **3.** In graphics, a piece of a polyline. See under POLYLINE.

⇒ See also MAIN MEMORY; PAGE; SWAP; SWITCHING HUB; VIRTUAL MEMORY.

select To choose an object so that you can manipulate it in some way. In graphical user interfaces, you usually need to select an object—an icon, file, folder, and so on—before you can do anything with it. To select an object, you move the pointer to the object and click a mouse button. In many applications, you can select blocks of text by positioning the pointer at an end-point of the block and then dragging the pointer over the block.

⇒ See also BLOCK; CHOOSE; DRAG; GRAPHICAL USER INTERFACE; HIGHLIGHT; ICON; MARQUEE; POINTER.

semantics In linguistics, the study of meanings. In computer science, the term is frequently used to differentiate the meaning of an instruction from its format. The format, which covers the spelling of language components and the rules controlling how components are combined, is called the language's *syntax*. For example, if you misspell a command, a syntax error results. If, on the other hand, you enter a legal command that does not make any sense in the current context, a semantic error results.

⇒ See also PARSE; PROGRAMMING LANGUAGE; SYNTAX.

semaphore A hardware or software flag. In multitasking systems, a semaphore is a variable with a value that indicates the status of a common resource. It is used to lock the resource that is being used. A process needing the resource checks the semaphore to determine the resource's status and then decides how to proceed.

⇒ See also FLAG; INTERPROCESS COMMUNICATION (IPC); MULTITASKING.

semiconductor A material that is neither a good conductor of electricity (like copper) nor a good insulator (like rubber). The most common semiconductor materials are silicon and germanium. These materials are then *doped* to create an excess or lack of electrons.

Computer chips, both for CPU and memory, are composed of semiconductor materials. Semiconductors make it possible to miniaturize electronic components, such as transistors. Not only does miniaturization mean that the components take up less space, it also means that they are faster and require less energy.

⇒ See also CHIP; CMOS; INTEGRATED CIRCUIT; NEC; TEXAS INSTRUMENTS; TRANSISTOR.

sequential access Refers to reading or writing data records in sequential order—that is, one record after the other. To read record 10, for example, you first need to read records 1 through 9. This differs from *random access*, in which you can read and write records in any order.

Some programming languages and operating systems distinguish between sequential-access data files and random-access data files, allowing you to choose between the two types. Sequential-access files are faster if you always access records in the same order. Random-access files are faster if you need to read or write records in a random order.

Devices can also be classified as sequential access or random access. For example, a tape drive is a sequential-access device because to get to point q on the tape, the drive needs to pass through points a through p. A disk drive, on the other hand, is a random-access device because the drive can access any point on the disk without passing through all intervening points.

⇒ See also ISAM; RANDOM ACCESS.

serial One by one. *Serial data transfer* refers to transmitting data one bit at a time. The opposite of serial is *parallel*, in which several bits are transmitted concurrently.

⇒ See also COMMUNICATIONS; PARALLEL; SERIAL PORT.

serial interface Same as SERIAL PORT.

Serial Line Internet Protocol See SLIP.

serial mouse A mouse that connects to a computer via a serial port. The other common type of mouse is a *PS/2 mouse*, which plugs into a PS/2 mouse port.

⇒ See also MOUSE; PORT; PS/2 PORT; SERIAL; SERIAL PORT.

serial port A port, or *interface*, that can be used for serial communication, in which only 1 bit is transmitted at a time.

Most serial ports on personal computers conform to the RS-232C or RS-422 standards. A serial port is a general-purpose interface that can be used for almost any type of device, including modems, mice, and printers (although most printers are connected to a parallel port).

⇒ See also ACCESS.BUS; COMMUNICATIONS; GEOPORT; IEEE 1394; INTERFACE; PARALLEL PORT; PORT; PS/2 PORT; RS-232C; RS-422 AND RS-423; UART; USB.

serif A small decorative line added as embellishment to the basic form of a character. Typefaces are often described as being *serif* or *sans serif* (without serifs). The most common serif typeface is Times Roman. A common sans serif typeface is Helvetica.

⇒ See also FONT; SANS SERIF; TYPEFACE.

server A computer or device on a network that manages network resources. For example, a *file server* is a computer and storage device dedicated to storing files. Any user on the network can store files on the server. A *print server* is a computer that manages one or more printers, and a *network server* is a computer that manages network traffic. A database *server* is a computer system that processes database queries.

Servers are often dedicated, meaning that they perform no other tasks besides their server tasks. On multiprocessing operating systems, however, a single computer can execute several programs at once. A *server* in this case could refer to the program that is managing resources rather than the entire computer.

⇒ See also CLIENT; CLIENT/SERVER ARCHITECTURE; DEC; LOAD BALANCING; LOCAL-AREA NETWORK; NETWORK; PROXY SERVER; SERVER MIRRORING; SERVER-SIDE; SGI; SUN MICROSYSTEMS; VIRTUAL SERVER.

server mirroring Utilizing a backup server that duplicates all the processes and transactions of the primary server. If, for any reason, the primary server fails, the backup server can immediately take its place without any down-time.

Server mirroring is an expensive but effective strategy for achieving fault tolerance. It's expensive because each server must be mirrored by an identical server whose only purpose is to be there in the event of a failure. A less expensive technique that is becoming more and more popular is clustering.

⇒ See also DISK MIRRORING; FAULT TOLERANCE; SERVER.

server-side Occurring on the server side of a client/server system. For example, on the World Wide Web, CGI scripts are server-side applications because they run on the Web server. In contrast, JavaScript scripts are client-side because they are executed by your browser (the client). Java applets can be either server-side or client-side depending on which computer (the server or the client) executes them.

⇒ See also CLIENT-SIDE; CLIENT/SERVER ARCHITECTURE; SERVER; SSI.

Server-Side Include See SSI.

service 1. See CUSTOMER SUPPORT. **2.** See ONLINE SERVICE.

Service Advertising Protocol See SAP.

service bureau Short for *prepress service bureau*, a company that provides a variety of desktop publishing services. In particular, service bureaus have imagesetters that can produce high-resolution output on paper or film. This is a necessary step before printing a document with offset printing.

In addition to providing high-resolution output, many service bureaus also offer scanning services, as well as general consultancy. Some service bureaus have computers equipped with desktop publishing software that you can rent by the hour.

⇒ See also DESKTOP PUBLISHING; IMAGESETTER; LINOTRONIC; OFFSET PRINTING; POSTSCRIPT.

Service Profile Identifier See SPID.

service provider Same as INTERNET SERVICE PROVIDER.

servlet An applet that runs on a server. The term usually refers to a Java applet that runs within a Web server environment. This is analogous to a Java applet that runs within a Web browser environment.

Java servlets are becoming increasingly popular as an alternative to CGI programs. The biggest difference between the two is that a Java applet is *persistent*. This means that once it is started, it stays in memory and can fulfill multiple requests. In contrast, a CGI program disappears once it has fulfilled a request. The persistence of Java applets makes them faster because there's no wasted time in setting up and tearing down the process.

⇒ See also APPLET; CGI.

SET Short for *S(ecure) E(lectronic) T(ransaction)*, a new standard that will enable secure credit card transactions on the Internet. SET has been endorsed by virtually all the major players in the electronic commerce arena, including Microsoft, Netscape, Visa, and MasterCard.

By employing digital signatures, SET will enable merchants to verify that buyers are who they claim to be. And it will protect buyers by providing a mechanism for their credit card number to be transferred directly to the credit card issuer for verification and billing without the merchant's being able to see the number.

The first applications based on SET appeared in 1998.

⇒ See also ELECTRONIC COMMERCE.

setup *v* **1.** To install and configure hardware or software. Most Windows applications come with a program called SETUP.EXE or INSTALL.EXE, which installs the software on the computer's hard disk. —*n* **2.** The configuration of hardware or software.

⇒ See also CONFIGURATION.

SGI Short for *S(ilicon) G(raphics) I(ncorporated)*, a company based in Mountain View, California, that provides computer hardware and software. SGI was founded by Dr. James Clark in 1982 and had its initial public offering in 1986. It is best known for products used to develop computer graphics such as those used to create special effects and animation in motion pictures.

SGI formed Silicon Studio in 1994 to serve the interactive digital media market. The company merged with MIPS Computer Systems in 1992, Alias Research and Wavefront Technologies in 1995, and Cray Research in 1996.

SGI provides a wide range of hardware and software products that include high-performance workstations and servers to meet the needs of those developing complex computer graphics or manipulating video images. New products include World Wide Web authoring tools and servers.

⇒ See also ANIMATION; DEC; IBM; OpenGL; SERVER; SUN MICROSYSTEMS; VIDEO EDITING; WORKSTATION.

SGML Abbreviation of *S(tandard) G(eneralized) M(arkup) L(anguage)*, a system for organizing and tagging elements of a document. SGML was developed and standardized by the International Organization for Standards (ISO) in 1986. SGML itself does not specify any particular formatting; rather, it specifies the rules for tagging elements. These tags can then be interpreted to format elements in different ways.

SGML is used widely to manage large documents that are subject to frequent revisions and need to be printed in different formats. Because it is a large and complex system, it is not yet widely used on personal computers. However, the growth of the Internet, and especially the World Wide Web, is creating renewed interest in SGML because the World Wide Web uses HTML, which is one way of defining and interpreting tags according to SGML rules.

⇒ See also HTML; HYPERTEXT; ISO; RICH TEXT FORMAT; TAG; WORLD WIDE WEB; XML.

SGRAM Abbreviation of *S(ynchronous) G(raphic) R(andom) A(ccess) M(emory)*, a type of DRAM used increasingly on video adapters and graphics accelerators. Like SDRAM, SGRAM can synchronize itself with the CPU bus clock up to speeds of 100 MHz. In addition, SGRAM uses several other techniques, such as *masked writes* and *block writes,* to increase bandwidth for graphics-intensive functions.

Unlike VRAM and WRAM, SGRAM is single-ported. However, it can open two memory pages at once, which simulates the dual-port nature of other video RAM technologies.

⇒ See also DRAM; GRAPHICS ACCELERATOR; SDRAM; VIDEO ADAPTER; VIDEO MEMORY; VRAM; WRAM.

shadowing A technique used to increase a computer's speed by using high-speed RAM memory in place of slower ROM memory. On PCs, for example, all code to control hardware devices, such as keyboards, is normally executed in a special ROM chip called the *BIOS ROM.* However, this chip is slower than the general-purpose RAM that makes up main memory. Many PC manufacturers, therefore, configure their PCs to copy the BIOS code into RAM when the computer boots. The RAM used to hold the BIOS code is called *shadow RAM.*

⇒ See also BIOS; BOOT; MAIN MEMORY; RAM; ROM.

shared Ethernet The traditional type of Ethernet, in which all hosts are connected to the same bus and compete with one another for bandwidth. In contrast, a *switched Ethernet* has one or more direct, point-to-point connections between hosts or segments. Devices connected to the Ethernet with a switch do not compete with one another and therefore have dedicated bandwidth.

⇒ See also ETHERNET; SWITCHED ETHERNET.

shareware Software distributed on the basis of an honor system. Most shareware is delivered free of charge, but the author usually requests that you pay a small fee if you like the program and use it regularly. By sending the small fee, you become registered with the producer so that you can receive service assistance and updates. You can copy shareware and pass it along to friends and colleagues, but they too are expected to pay a fee if they use the product.

Shareware is inexpensive because it is usually produced by a single programmer and is offered directly to customers. Thus, there are practically no packaging or advertising expenses.

Note that shareware differs from public-domain software in that shareware is copyrighted. This means that you cannot sell a shareware product as your own.

⇒ See also BULLETIN BOARD SYSTEM; FREEWARE; ONLINE SERVICE; PUBLIC-DOMAIN SOFTWARE; SOFTWARE LICENSING; SOFTWARE PIRACY; WAREZ.

sheet feeder Also called *cut-sheet feeder,* a mechanism that holds a stack of paper and feeds each sheet into a printer one at a time. Sheet feeders are built into laser printers and are optional components for dot-matrix printers. Nearly all modern fax machines also come with sheet feeders, as do some optical scanners.

⇒ See also DOT-MATRIX PRINTER; FAX MACHINE; LASER PRINTER; OPTICAL SCANNER; PRINTER.

shell 1. The outermost layer of a program. *Shell* is another term for *user interface.* Operating systems and applications sometimes provide an alternative shell to make interaction with the program easier. For example, if the application is usually command driven, the shell might be a menu-driven system that translates the user's selections into the appropriate commands. **2.** Sometimes called *command shell,* a shell is the command processor interface. The command processor is the program that executes operating system commands. The shell, therefore, is the part of the command processor that accepts commands. After verifying that the commands are valid, the shell sends them to another part of the command processor to be executed.

UNIX systems offer a choice between several different shells, the most popular being the *Cshell,* the *Bourne shell,* and the *Korn shell.* Each offers a somewhat different command language.

⇒ See also COMMAND DRIVEN; COMMAND LANGUAGE; COMMAND PROCESSOR; INTERFACE; MENU DRIVEN; OPERATING ENVIRONMENT; OPERATING SYSTEM; UNIX; USER INTERFACE.

shift clicking Clicking a mouse button while holding the Shift key down. In Microsoft Windows and Macintosh systems, shift clicking enables you to select multiple items. Normally, when you select an item, the system deselects the previously selected item. However, if you shift click an item, the previously selected item(s) remain selected.

⇒ See also CLICK; GRAPHICAL USER INTERFACE; MACINTOSH COMPUTER; MICROSOFT WINDOWS; MOUSE; SELECT.

Shift key A key on computer keyboards that gives the other keys an alternate meaning. When combined with alphabetic keys, the Shift key causes the system to output a capital letter. The Shift key can also be combined with other keys to produce program-dependent results.

⇒ See also ALT KEY; CONTROL KEY; KEYBOARD.

Shockwave A technology developed by Macromedia, Inc., that enables Web pages to include multimedia objects. To create a Shockwave object, you use Macromedia's multimedia authoring tool called *Director* and then compress the object with a program called *Afterburner.* You then insert a reference to the "shocked" file in your Web page. To see a Shockwave object, you need the Shockwave plug-in, a program that integrates seamlessly with your Web browser. The plug-in is freely available from Macromedia's Web site as either a Netscape Navigator plug-in or an ActiveX control.

Shockwave supports audio, animation, and video and even processes user actions such as mouse clicks. It runs on all Windows platforms as well as the Macintosh.

⇒ See also ACTIVEX CONTROL; MULTIMEDIA; PLUG-IN.

shortcut In Windows 95 and Windows 98, a special type of file that points to another file or device. You can place shortcuts on the desktop to conveniently access files that may be stored deep in the directory structure. Double-clicking the shortcut icon is the same as double-clicking the actual file. However, if you delete the shortcut, you do not affect the original file.

You can control how a shortcut appears by naming it anything you want and associating a particular icon with it.

⇒ See also DESKTOP; SHORTCUT KEY.

shortcut key A special key combination that causes a specific command to be executed. Typically, shortcut keys combine the Ctrl or Alt keys with some other keys. In Windows environments, for example, Ctrl + C is used as the shortcut key to copy. On PCs, the function keys are also often used as shortcut keys.

Most applications come with some shortcut keys already defined. Many, however, allow you to define your own shortcut keys for frequently used commands.

⇒ See also ALT KEY; COMMAND; CONTROL KEY; SHORTCUT.

shtml See under SSI.

S-HTTP An extension to the HTTP protocol to support sending data securely over the World Wide Web. Not all Web browsers and servers support S-HTTP. Another technology for transmitting secure communications over the World Wide Web—*Secure Sockets Layer (SSL)*—is more prevalent. However, SSL and S-HTTP have very different designs and goals so it is possible to use the two protocols together. Whereas SSL is designed to establish a secure connection between two computers, S-HTTP is designed to send individual messages securely. Both protocols have been submitted to the Internet Engineering Task Force (IETF) for approval as a standard.

S-HTTP was developed by Enterprise Integration Technologies (EIT), which was acquired by Verifone, Inc. in 1995.

⇒ See also HTTP; SSL.

SHTTP See S-HTTP.

shut down 1. To turn the power off. **2.** In Windows 95 and Windows 98, the normal way to turn a computer off is to select **Start→Shut Down...**

⇒ See also POWER DOWN.

SIG Acronym for *s(pecial) i(nterest) g(roup)*, a group of users interested in a particular subject who discuss the subject at meetings or via an online service. SIGs exist for almost every conceivable subject. On-line SIGs are sometimes called *forums* or conferences.

⇒ See also BULLETIN BOARD SYSTEM; FORUM; ONLINE SERVICE.

sign A symbol that identifies a number as being either positive or negative. A positive sign is +; a negative sign is -. These two signs are also used to indicate addition and subtraction, respectively.

⇒ See also OPERATOR.

Silicon Graphics See SGI.

Silicon Valley A nickname for the region south of San Francisco that contains an unusually high concentration of computer companies. Silicon is the most common semiconductor material used to produce chips.

⇒ See also CHIP; SEMICONDUCTOR.

SIMM Acronym for *s(ingle) i(n)-line m(emory) m(odule)*, a small circuit board that can hold a group of memory chips. Typically, SIMMs hold up to 8 (on Macintoshes) or 9 (on PCs) RAM chips. On PCs, the ninth chip is often used for parity error checking. Unlike memory chips, SIMMs are measured in bytes rather than bits. SIMMs are easier to install than individual memory chips.

The bus from a SIMM to the actual memory chips is 32 bits wide. A newer technology, called *dual in-line memory module (DIMM)*, provides a 64-bit bus. For modern Pentium microprocessors that have a 64-bit bus, you must use either DIMMs or *pairs* of SIMMs.

⇒ See also CHIP; DIMM; RAM.

Simple Mail Transfer Protocol See SMTP.

Simple Network Management Protocol See SNMP.

simplex Refers to transmission in only one direction. Note the difference between simplex and *half-duplex*. *Half-duplex* refers to *two-way* communications where only one party can transmit at a time. Simplex refers to *one-way* communications where one party is the transmitter and the other is the receiver. An example of simplex communications is a simple radio—you can receive data from stations but can't transmit data.

⇒ See also FULL DUPLEX; HALF DUPLEX.

simulation The process of imitating a real phenomenon with a set of mathematical formulas. Advanced computer programs can simulate weather conditions, chemical reactions, atomic reactions, even biological processes. In theory, any phenomena that can be reduced to mathematical data and equations can be simulated on a computer. In practice, however, simulation is extremely difficult because most natural phenomena are subject to an almost infinite number of influences. One of the tricks to developing useful simulations, therefore, is to determine which are the most important factors.

In addition to imitating processes to see how they behave under different conditions, simulations are also used to test new theories. After creating a theory of causal relationships, the theorist can codify the relationships in the form of a computer program. If the program then behaves in the same way as the real process, there is a good chance that the proposed relationships are correct.

single-density disk A low-density floppy disk. All modern floppies are double-density or high-density.

⇒ See also FLOPPY DISK.

single in-line memory module See SIMM.

single in-line package See SIP.

single-sided disk A floppy disk with only one side prepared for storing data. Single-sided disks have half as much storage capacity as double-sided disks. All modern floppies are double-sided.

⇒ See also FLOPPY DISK.

SIP Abbreviation of *s(ingle) i(n)-line p(ackage)*, a type of housing for electronic components in which the connecting pins protrude from one side. Compare with *DIP* and *PGA*.
A SIP is also called a *Single In-line Pin Package (SIPP)*.

⇒ See also DIP; PGA.

site Short for *Web site*.

680x0 See under MOTOROLA MICROPROCESSORS.

⇒ See also MOTOROLA MICROPROCESSORS.

16-bit Refers to the number of bits that can be processed or transmitted in parallel, or the number of bits used for single element in a data format. The term is often applied to the following:

Microprocessor: indicates the width of the registers. A 16-bit microprocessor can process data and memory addresses that are represented by 16 bits.

Bus: indicates the number of wires in the bus. A 16-bit bus transmits 16 bits in parallel.

Graphics device, such as a scanner or digital camera: Specifies the number of bits used to represent each pixel.

Operating system: Refers primarily to the number of bits used to represent memory addresses. Windows 3.*x* is a 16-bit operating system, whereas Windows 95, Windows 98, and Windows NT are 32-bit operating systems.

Applications: Indicates how a program has been compiled. Programs written for Windows can be compiled to run either as 16-bit applications (for Windows 3.x) or as 32-bit applications (Windows 9x and NT).

Expansion board: Refers to how much data can be sent to and from the card in parallel. 8-bit cards are sometimes called *half-size cards* whereas 16-bit cards are referred to as *full-size cards*.

⇒ See also 32-BIT; BIT; BUS.

size To make an object larger or smaller. In graphical user interfaces, you can size windows to make them larger or smaller.

Other terms for *size* are *resize* and *scale*.

⇒ See also GRAPHICAL USER INTERFACE; SCALE; WINDOW.

slack space The unused space in a disk cluster. The DOS and Windows file systems use fixed-size clusters. Even if the actual data being stored require less storage than the cluster size, an entire cluster is reserved for the file. The unused space is called the *slack space.*

DOS and older Windows systems use a 16-bit file allocation table (FAT), which results in very large cluster sizes for large partitions. For example, if the partition size is 2 GB, each cluster will be 32 K. Even if a file requires only 4 K, the entire 32 K will be allocated, resulting in 28 K of slack space. Windows 95, OSR 2, and Windows 98 resolve this problem by using a 32-bit FAT (FAT32) that supports cluster sizes as small as 4 K for very large partitions.

⇒ See also CLUSTER; FAT32; FILE ALLOCATION TABLE; PARTITION.

slate PC A class of notebook computer that accepts input from an electronic pen rather than from a keyboard. Slate PCs are particularly useful in situations where keyboards are awkward or unnecessary. Typically, slate PCs can decipher clearly written block letters and translate them into their ASCII equivalents. To date, however, they cannot handle script, although the technology of handwriting recognition is progressing rapidly.

⇒ See also HAND-HELD COMPUTER; HANDWRITING RECOGNITION; NOTEBOOK COMPUTER; PDA.

slave Any device that is controlled by another device, called the *master.*

⇒ See also MASTER/SLAVE.

SLDRAM Short for *S(ync)L(ink)* **DRAM**, a new type of memory being developed by a consortium of computer manufacturers called the SyncLink Consortium. SLDRAM is competing with Rambus memory (RDRAM) as the future PC memory architecture. But whereas actual RDRAM chips are already in use on video boards and other devices, SLDRAM is still on paper only. Moreover, Intel is backing RDRAM, which reduces the odds of SLDRAM's becoming an important technology.

⇒ See also BEDO DRAM; DRAM; EDO DRAM; FPM RAM; RDRAM; SDRAM.

sleep mode An energy-saving mode of operation in which all unnecessary components are shut down. Many battery-operated devices, such as notebook computers, support a sleep mode. When a notebook computer goes into sleep mode, it shuts down the display screen and disk drive. Once awakened, the computer returns to its former operating status.

⇒ See also ACPI; green PC.

slimline model A small desktop model computer. See under desktop model computer.

⇒ See also desktop model computer.

SLIP Short for *S(erial) L(ine) I(nternet) P(rotocol)*, a method of connecting to the Internet. Another, more common method is PPP (Point-to-Point Protocol). SLIP is an older and simpler protocol, but from a practical perspective, there's not much difference between connecting to the Internet via SLIP or PPP. In general, service providers offer only one protocol, although some support both protocols.

⇒ See also Internet; ISP; PPP; protocol.

slot An opening in a computer where you can insert a printed circuit board. Slots are often called *expansion slots* because they allow you to expand the capabilities of a computer. The boards you insert in expansion slots are called *expansion boards* or *add-on boards*.

Do not confuse slots with bays. Bays are sites within the computer where you can install disk drives. Typically, slots are in the back of the computer and bays are in the front.

⇒ See also bay; cartridge; chassis; expansion board; expansion slot; printed circuit board.

Slot 1 The form factor for Intel's Pentium II processors. The Slot 1 package replaces the Socket 7 and Socket 8 form factors used by previous Pentium processors. Slot 1 is a 242-contact daughtercard slot that accepts a microprocessor packaged as a Single Edge Contact (SEC) cartridge. A motherboard can have one or two Slot 1s.

⇒ See also form factor; Pentium II; Socket 7.

small computer system interface See SCSI.

Smalltalk An object-oriented operating system and programming language developed at Xerox Corporation's Palo Alto Research Center. Smalltalk was the first object-oriented programming language (Simula was the very first). Although it never achieved the commercial success of other languages such as C++ and Java, Smalltalk is considered by many to be the only true object-oriented programming environment, and the one against which all others must be compared.

⇒ See also C++; Java; object oriented; object-oriented programming.

SMART Acronym for *S(elf)-M(onitoring), A(nalysis) and R(eporting) T(echnology)*, an open standard for developing disk drives and software systems that automatically monitor a disk drive's health and report potential problems. Ideally, this should allow you to take proactive actions to prevent impending disk crashes.

⇒ See also CRASH; DISK DRIVE; HARD DISK; MTBF.

smart battery See under BATTERY PACK.

smart card A small electronic device about the size of a credit card that contains electronic memory, and possibly an embedded integrated circuit (IC). Smart cards containing an IC are sometimes called *Integrated Circuit Cards (ICCs)*.

Smart cards are used for a variety of purposes, including:

- Storing a patient's medical records
- Storing digital cash
- Generating network IDs (similar to a token)

To use a smart card, either to pull information from it or add data to it, you need a *smart card reader,* a small device into which you insert the smart card.

⇒ See also CHALLENGE-RESPONSE; DIGITAL CASH; TOKEN.

Smartdrive A disk-caching system provided by Microsoft with later versions of DOS and used with Windows 3.1. Disk caching provides faster access to data on a hard disk. Smartdrive allows you to monitor how the cache is used and change the cache size to optimize performance.

Starting with Windows 95, Smartdrive was replaced by a disk-caching system called *VCACHE*.

⇒ See also DISK CACHE; VCACHE.

smart terminal A terminal that has some processing capabilities, but not as many as an *intelligent terminal*. Smart terminals have built-in logic for performing simple display operations, such as blinking and boldface. In contrast, a *dumb terminal* has no processing capabilities at all.

⇒ See also DUMB TERMINAL; INTELLIGENT TERMINAL; TERMINAL.

SMB Short for *S(erver) M(essage) B(lock)*, a message format used by DOS and Windows to share files, directories and devices. NetBIOS is based on the SMB format, and many network products use SMB. These SMB-based networks include Lan Manager, Windows for Workgroups, Windows NT, and LAN Server. A number of products also use SMB to enable file sharing among different operating system platforms. A product called *Samba*, for example, enables UNIX and Windows machines to share directories and files.

⇒ See also NETBIOS.

SMDS Short for *S(witched) M(ultimegabit) D(ata) S(ervices)*, a high-speed switched data communications service offered by telephone companies that enables organizations to connect geographically separate local-area networks (LANs) into a single wide-area network (WAN). Prior to SMDS's arrival in 1995, the only way to connect LANs was through a dedicated private line. This is still the way most WANs are connected, but SMDS is becoming an increasingly attractive alternative because it is more flexible and in many cases more economical.

⇒ See also CSU/DSU; WIDE-AREA NETWORK.

SMIL Short for *S(ynchronized) M(ultimedia) I(ntegration) L(anguage)*, a new markup language being developed by the World Wide Web Consortium (W3C) that would enable Web developers to divide multimedia content into separate files and streams (audio, video, text, and images), send them to a user's computer individually, and then have them displayed together as if they were a single multimedia stream. The ability to separate out the static text and images should make the multimedia content much smaller so that it doesn't take as long to travel over the Internet.

SMIL is based on the eXtensible Markup Language (XML). Rather than defining the actual formats used to represent multimedia data, it defines the commands that specify whether the various multimedia components should be played together or in sequence.

⇒ See also MULTIMEDIA; RTSP; STREAMING; XML.

smiley Same as EMOTICON.

S/MIME Short for *S(ecure)/MIME*, a new version of the MIME protocol that supports encryption of messages. S/MIME is based on RSA's public-key encryption technology.

It is expected that S/MIME will be widely implemented, which will make it possible for people to send secure e-mail messages to one another, even if they are using different e-mail clients.

⇒ See also MIME; PUBLIC-KEY ENCRYPTION; RSA.

smoothing A technique used by some printers to make curves look smoother. Most printers that support smoothing implement it by reducing the size of the dots that make up a curved line. In addition, some printers can alter the horizontal alignment of dots to minimize jaggies.

⇒ See also ANTIALIASING; JAGGIES; LASER PRINTER.

SMP 1. Short for *S(ymmetric) M(ulti)p(rocessing)*, a computer architecture that provides fast performance by making multiple CPUs available to complete individual processes simultaneously (multiprocessing). Unlike asymmetrical processing, any idle processor can be assigned any task, and additional CPUs can be added to improve performance and handle increased loads. A variety of specialized operating systems and hardware arrangements are available to support SMP. Specific applications can benefit from SMP if the code allows multithreading.

SMP uses a single operating system and shares common memory and disk input/output resources. Both UNIX and Windows NT support SMP.
2. Short for *S(imple) M(anagement) P(rotocol)*, another name for SNMP2. SNMP2 is an enhanced version of the Simple Network Management Protocol (SNMP) with features required to support larger networks operating at high data transmission rates. SNMP2 also supports multiple network management workstations organized in a hierarchical fashion.

⇒ See also BeOS; MPP; MULTIPROCESSING; MULTITHREADING; NUMA; SNMP; SOLARIS.

SMS Short for *S(ystems) M(anagement) S(erver)*, a set of tools from Microsoft that assists in managing PCs connected to a local-area network (LAN). SMS enables a network administrator to create an inventory of all the hardware and software on the network and to store it in an SMS database. Using this database, SMS can then perform software distribution and installation over the LAN. SMS also enables a network administrator to perform diagnostic tests on PCs attached to the LAN.

SMS runs under Windows NT but can manage PCs running DOS, all varieties of Windows, and OS/2, as well as Macintosh clients.

⇒ See also NET PC; NETWORK COMPUTER; SYSTEM MANAGEMENT; SYSTEMS ADMINISTRATOR.

SMTP Short for *S(imple) M(ail) T(ransfer) P(rotocol)*. A protocol for sending e-mail messages between servers. Most e-mail systems that send mail over the Internet use SMTP to send messages from one server to another; the messages can then be retrieved with an e-mail client using either POP or IMAP. In addition, SMTP is generally used to send messages from a mail client to a mail server. This is why you need to specify both the POP or IMAP server and the SMTP server when you configure your e-mail application.

⇒ See also POP.

smurf A type of network security breach in which a network connected to the Internet is swamped with replies to ICMP echo (PING) requests. A smurf attacker sends PING requests to an Internet broadcast address. These are special addresses that broadcast all received messages to the hosts connected to the subnet. Each broadcast address can support up to 255 hosts, so a single PING request can be multiplied 255 times. The return address of the request itself is spoofed to be the address of the attacker's victim. All the hosts receiving the PING request reply to this victim's address instead of the real sender's address. A single attacker sending hundreds or thousands of these PING messages per second can fill the victim's T-1 (or even T-3) line with PING replies and bring the entire Internet service to its knees.

Smurfing falls under the general category of *Denial of Service attacks*—security attacks that don't try to steal information, but instead attempt to disable a computer or network.

⇒ See also CRACK; IP SPOOFING; PING.

SNA Short for *S(ystems) N(etwork) A(rchitecture)*, a set of network protocols developed by IBM. Originally designed in 1974 for IBM's mainframe computers, SNA has evolved over the years so that it now also supports peer-to-peer networks of workstations.

⇒ See also MAINFRAME; NETWORK; SDLC; VTAM.

snailmail Normal postal mail, where an actual physical letter or package is delivered. The term didn't exist until electronic mail (e-mail) became so prevalent that there was a requirement to differentiate the two. Obviously, the term was invented by e-mail aficionados as a small barb directed at the relative slowness of physical transportation.
   Snailmail is sometimes spelled as two separate words, *snail mail.*

⇒ See also E-MAIL.

snapshot printer A color printer designed to print photographic-quality snapshots. Most snapshot printers require special paper and use dye sublimation, thermal transfer technologies to produce vivid 24-bit color. The devices, however, are limited to prints no larger than about 4 by 6 inches.

⇒ See also COLOR PRINTER; DIGITAL PHOTOGRAPHY; PHOTO SCANNER.

sniff See under SNIFFER.

sniffer A program and/or device that monitors data traveling over a network. Sniffers can be used both for legitimate network management functions and for stealing information off a network. Unauthorized sniffers can be extremely dangerous to a network's security because they are virtually impossible to detect and can be inserted almost anywhere. This makes them a favorite weapon in the hacker's arsenal.
   On TCP/IP networks, where they sniff packets, they're often called *packet sniffers.*

⇒ See also HACKER; NETWORK MANAGEMENT; SECURITY.

SNMP Short for *S(imple) N(etwork) M(anagement) P(rotocol)*, a set of protocols for managing complex networks. The first versions of SNMP were developed in the early 1980s. SNMP works by sending messages, called *protocol data units (PDUs)*, to different parts of a network. SNMP-compliant devices, called *agents,* store data about themselves in *Management Information Bases (MIBs)* and return this data to the SNMP requesters.
   SNMP 1 reports only whether a device is functioning properly. The industry has attempted to define a new set of protocols called *SNMP 2* that would provide additional information, but the standardization efforts have not been successful. Instead, network managers have turned to a re-

lated technology called *RMON* that provides more detailed information about network usage.

⇒ See also IMAP; LOCAL-AREA NETWORK; MIB; NETWORK; NETWORK MANAGEMENT; POP; RMON.

socket 1. In UNIX and some other operating systems, a software object that connects an application to a network protocol. In UNIX, for example, a program can send and receive TCP/IP messages by opening a socket and reading and writing data to and from the socket. This simplifies program development because the programmer need only worry about manipulating the socket and can rely on the operating system to actually transport messages across the network correctly. Note that a socket in this sense is completely *soft*—it's a software object, not a physical component. **2.** A receptacle into which a plug can be inserted. **3.** A receptacle for a microprocessor or other hardware component.

⇒ See also SOCKET 8; TCP/IP; WINSOCK.

Socket 7 The form factor for fifth-generation CPU chips from Intel, Cyrix, and AMD. All Pentium chips, except Intel's Pentium Pro (Socket 8) and Pentium II (Slot 1), conform to the Socket 7 specifications. Intel has decided to phase out Socket 7 and replace it with Slot 1. But Intel's competitors, such as AMD and Cyrix, are sticking with Socket 7 and are developing an enhanced version.

⇒ See also FORM FACTOR; K6; PENTIUM MICROPROCESSOR; SLOT 1; SOCKET 8; ZERO INSERTION FORCE (ZIF) SOCKET.

Socket 8 The form factor for Intel's Pentium Pro microprocessors. The Pentium Pro was the first microprocessor not to use the venerable Socket 7 form factor. The Pentium II microprocessors use an even newer form factor called Slot 1.

Socket 8 is a 387-pin ZIF socket with connections for the CPU and one or two SRAM dies for the Level 2 (L2) cache.

⇒ See also PENTIUM PRO; SOCKET; SOCKET 7; ZERO INSERTION FORCE (ZIF) SOCKET.

SOCKS A protocol for handling TCP traffic through a proxy server. It can be used with virtually any TCP application, including Web browsers and FTP clients. It provides a simple firewall because it checks incoming and outgoing packets and hides the IP addresses of client applications.

There are two main versions of SOCKS—V4 and V5. V5 adds an authentication mechanism for additional security. There are many freeware implementations of both versions. One of the most common V5 implementations is *SOCKS5*, developed by NEC.

SOCKS was recently accepted as an IETF standard and is documented in RFC 1928, 1929 and 1961.

⇒ See also PROXY SERVER; TCP.

soft In computer science, *soft* is used to describe things that are intangible. For example, you cannot touch *software*. It's like music—you can see musical scores and touch CDs and tapes, but the music itself is intangible. Similarly, you can see software instructions (programs), and touch floppy disks on which the programs are stored, but the software itself is intangible.

Soft is also used to describe things that are easily changed or impermanent. In contrast, *hard* is used to describe things that are immutable.

⇒ See also HARD; HARDWARE; SOFTWARE.

soft font A font that is copied from a computer's disk to a printer's memory. Soft fonts can be erased, unlike *resident fonts* (fonts that are built into the printer) or fonts in font cartridges.

Soft fonts are generated by a font program in the computer. You can control the program to specify the font size and other characteristics. The disadvantages of soft fonts are that they require a lot of disk space and printer memory (from 10K to more than 200K for a single font), and it takes time to download the fonts to the printer.

Soft fonts are also called *downloadable fonts*.

⇒ See also DOWNLOAD; FONT; FONT CARTRIDGE; LASER PRINTER; RESIDENT FONT.

soft hyphen See under HYPHENATION.

soft return The term *return* refers to moving to the beginning of the next line in a text document. Word processors utilize two types of returns: *hard* and *soft*. In both cases, the return consists of special codes inserted into the document to cause the display screen, printer, or other output device to advance to the next line.

The difference between the two types of returns is that soft returns are inserted automatically by the word processor as part of its word wrap capability. Whenever too little room remains on the current line for the next word, the word processor inserts a soft return. The position of soft returns automatically changes, however, if you change the length of a line by adding or deleting words, or if you change the margins.

A hard return, on the other hand, always stays in the same place unless you explicitly delete it. Whenever you press the Return or Enter key, the word processor inserts a hard return. Hard returns are used to create new paragraphs or to align items in a table.

⇒ See also HARD RETURN; MARGINS; WORD WRAP.

software Computer instructions or data. Anything that can be stored electronically is software. The storage devices and display devices are hardware.

The terms *software* and *hardware* are used as both nouns and adjectives. For example, you can say, "The problem lies in the software," meaning that there is a problem with the program or data, not with the computer itself. You can also say, "It's a software problem."

The distinction between software and hardware is sometimes confusing

because they are so integrally linked. Clearly, when you purchase a program, you are buying software. But to buy the software, you sometimes need to buy the disk (hardware) on which the software is recorded.
Software is often divided into two categories:

systems software: Includes the operating system and all the utilities that enable the computer to function.
applications software: Includes programs that do real work for users. For example, word processors, spreadsheets, and database management-systems fall under the category of applications software.

⇒ See also APPLICATION; BLOATWARE; DATA; FIRMWARE; HARDWARE; PROGRAM; SYSTEMS SOFTWARE; VAPORWARE.

software development kit See SDK.

software engineer A programmer. The term implies that the individual is more involved with design and management than with actual coding. But in reality, every good programmer is a software engineer because software engineering is required in all aspects of program development. Large applications, however, generally require more emphasis on software engineering aspects than small programs.

⇒ See also PROGRAMMER; SOFTWARE ENGINEERING.

software engineering The computer science discipline concerned with developing large applications. Software engineering covers not only the technical aspects of building software systems but also management issues, such as directing programming teams, scheduling, and budgeting.

⇒ See also COMPUTER SCIENCE; FUNCTIONAL SPECIFICATION; SOFTWARE ENGINEER; UML.

software licensing Allowing an individual or group to use a piece of software. Nearly all applications are licensed rather than sold. There are a variety of different types of software licenses. Some are based on the number of machines on which the licensed program can run, whereas others are based on the number of users that can use the program. Most personal-computer software licenses allow you to run the program on only one machine and to make copies of the software only for backup purposes. Some licenses allow you to run the program on different computers as long as you don't use the copies simultaneously.

⇒ See also APPLICATION; COPY PROTECTION; EULA; SHAREWARE.

software modem A modem implemented entirely in software. Software modems rely on the computer's processor to modulate and demodulate signals.

⇒ See also HOST-BASED MODEM; MODEM.

software piracy The unauthorized copying of software. Most retail programs are licensed for use at just one computer site or for use by only
one user at any time. By buying the software, you become a *licensed user*
rather than an owner. You are allowed to make copies of the program for
backup purposes, but it is against the law to give copies to friends and
colleagues.

Software piracy is all but impossible to stop, although software companies are launching more and more lawsuits against major infractors. Originally, software companies tried to stop software piracy by copy-
protecting their software. This strategy failed, however, because it was
inconvenient for users and was not 100 percent foolproof. Most software
now requires some sort of registration, which may discourage would-be
pirates but doesn't really stop software piracy.

An entirely different approach to software piracy, called *shareware*, ac-
knowledges the futility of trying to stop people from copying software
and instead relies on people's honesty. Shareware publishers encourage
users to give copies of programs to friends and colleagues but ask everyone who uses a program regularly to pay a registration fee to the program's author directly.

Commercial programs that are made available to the public illegally are
often called *warez*.

⇒ See also COPY PROTECTION; DIGITAL WATERMARK; REGISTER; SHAREWARE; SOFT-
WARE; WAREZ.

SOHO Acronym for *S(mall) O(ffice)/H(ome) O(ffice)*. The fastest-growing
market for computer hardware and software. So-called SOHO products
are specifically designed to meet the needs of professionals who work at
home or in small offices.

⇒ See also MFP.

Solaris A Unix-based operating environment developed by Sun
Microsystems. Originally developed to run on Sun's SPARC workstations,
Solaris now runs on many workstations from other vendors.

Solaris includes the SunOS operating system and a windowing system
(either OpenWindows or CDE). Solaris currently supports multithreading,
symmetric multiprocessing (SMP), integrated TCP/IP networking, and
centralized network administration. An emulator, called Wabi, is available to run Windows applications.

⇒ See also SMP; SUN MICROSYSTEMS; UNIX; X-WINDOW.

solid ink-jet printer A type of color printer that works by melting wax-
based inks and then spraying them on paper. Solid ink-jet printers produce very vivid colors and can print on nearly any surface, but they are
relatively slow and expensive.

Solid ink-jet printers are also called *phase-change printers*.

⇒ See also COLOR PRINTER; INK-JET PRINTER; PHASE CHANGE DISK.

SOM Short for *S(ystem)O(bject) M(odel)*, an architecture developed by IBM that allows binary code to be shared by different applications. It serves the same purpose as Microsoft's competing COM standard. SOM is a full implementation of CORBA. A distributed version of SOM that allows binary objects to be shared across networks is known as DSOM.

⇒ See also COMPONENT OBJECT MODEL; CORBA; DSOM.

SONET Short for *S(ynchronous) O(ptical) Net(work)*, a standard for connecting fiber-optic transmission systems. SONET was proposed by Bellcore in the middle 1980s and is now an ANSI standard.

SONET defines interface standards at the physical layer of the OSI seven-layer model. The standard defines a hierarchy of interface rates that allow data streams at different rates to be multiplexed. SONET establishes Optical Carrier (OC) levels from 51.8 Mbps (about the same as a T-3 line) to 2.48 Gbps. Prior rate standards used by different countries specified rates that were not compatible for multiplexing. With the implementation of SONET, communication carriers throughout the world can interconnect their existing digital carrier and fiber optic systems.

The international equivalent of SONET, standardized by the ITU, is called *SDH*.

⇒ See also BROADBAND ISDN (B-ISDN); FIBER OPTICS; OC; SDH; T-1 CARRIER; T-3 CARRIER.

sound card An expansion board that enables a computer to manipulate and output sounds. Sound cards are necessary for nearly all CD-ROMs and have become commonplace on modern personal computers. Sound cards enable the computer to output sound through speakers connected to the board, to record sound input from a microphone connected to the computer, and manipulate sound stored on a disk.

Nearly all sound cards support MIDI, a standard for representing music electronically. In addition, most sound cards are Sound Blaster–compatible, which means that they can process commands written for a Sound Blaster card, the de facto standard for PC sound.

Sound cards use two basic methods to translate digital data into analog sounds:

FM Synthesis mimics different musical instruments according to built-in formulas.
Wavetable Synthesis relies on recordings of actual instruments to produce sound. Wavetable synthesis produces more accurate sound but is also more expensive.

⇒ See also 3-D AUDIO; CD-ROM; MIDI; MULTIMEDIA; WAVE TABLE SYNTHESIS.

source A place from which data is taken. Many computer commands involve moving data. The place from which the data is moved is called the *source*, whereas the place it is moved to is called the *destination* or *target*. If you copy a file from one directory to another, for example, you copy it from the *source directory* to the *destination directory*. The source and destination can be files, directories, or devices (that is, printers or storage devices).

⇒ See also COPY; DESTINATION.

source code Program instructions in their original form. The word *source* differentiates code from various other forms that it can have (for example, *object code* and *executable code*).

Initially, a programmer writes a program in a particular programming language. This form of the program is called the *source program* or, more generically, *source code*. To execute the program, however, the programmer must translate it into machine language, the language that the computer understands. The first step of this translation process is usually performed by a utility called a compiler. The compiler translates the source code into a form called object code. Sometimes the object code is the same as machine code; sometimes it needs to be translated into machine language by a utility called an assembler.

Source code is the only format that is readable by humans. When you purchase programs, you usually receive them in their machine language format. This means that you can execute them directly, but you cannot read or modify them. Some software manufacturers provide source code, but this is useful only if you are an experienced programmer.

⇒ See also ASSEMBLER; CODE; COMPILER; EDITOR; MACHINE LANGUAGE; OBJECT CODE; PROGRAM; PROGRAMMING LANGUAGE.

spam Electronic junk mail or junk newsgroup postings. Some people define *spam* even more generally as any unsolicited e-mail. However, if a long-lost brother finds your e-mail address and sends you a message, this could hardly be called spam, even though it's unsolicited. Real spam is generally e-mail advertising for some product sent to a mailing list or newsgroup.

In addition to wasting people's time with unwanted e-mail, spam also eats up a lot of network bandwidth. Consequently, there are many organizations, as well as individuals, who have taken it upon themselves to fight spam with a variety of techniques. But because the Internet is public, there is really little that can be done to prevent spam, just as it is impossible to prevent junk mail. However, some private online service, such America Online, have instituted policies to prevent spammers from spamming their subscribers.

There is some debate about the source of the term, but the generally accepted version is that it comes from the Monty Python song "Spam spam spam spam, spam spam spam spam, lovely spam, wonderful spam." Like the song, spam is an endless repetition of worthless text. Another school of thought maintains that it comes from the computer group lab at the University of Southern California who gave it the name because it has many of the same characteristics as the lunchmeat Spam:

• Nobody wants it or ever asks for it.
• No one ever eats it; it is the first item to be pushed to the side when eating the entrée.

- Sometimes it is actually tasty, like 1 percent of junk mail that is really useful to some people.

⇒ See also E-MAIL; MODERATED NEWSGROUP.

SPARC Short for *S(calable) P(rocessor) Arc(hitecture)*, a RISC technology developed by Sun Microsystems. The term *SPARC®* itself is a trademark of SPARC International, an independent organization that licenses the term to Sun for its use. Sun's workstations based on the SPARC include the *SPARCstation, SPARCserver, Ultra1, Ultra2,* and *SPARCcluster.*

⇒ See also RISC; SUN MICROSYSTEMS; WORKSTATION.

SPEC 1. Acronym for *S(tandard) P(erformance) E(valuation) C(orporation)*, a nonprofit corporation set up by many computer and microprocessor vendors to create a standard set of benchmark tests. The most widely used set of tests, known as *SPEC95*, results in two sets of measurements, one for integer operations (*SPECint95*) and one for floating point operations (*SPECfp95*). The SPEC95 benchmark tests are also called *CPU95* tests. **2.** Short for *spec(ification)*, as in a *functional specification.*

⇒ See also BENCHMARK; FLOPS; MIPS.

SPEC95 See under SPEC.

special character A character that is not a letter, number, symbol, or punctuation mark. Control characters, for example, are special characters, as are special formatting characters such as paragraph marks.

⇒ See also CONTROL CHARACTER; PUNCTUATION.

special interest group See SIG.

speech recognition Same as VOICE RECOGNITION.

speech synthesis Refers to a computer's ability to produce sound that resembles human speech. Although they can't imitate the full spectrum of human cadences and intonations, speech synthesis systems can read text files and output them in a very intelligible, if somewhat dull, voice. Many systems even allow the user to choose the type of voice—for example, male or female. Speech synthesis systems are particularly valuable for seeing-impaired individuals.

⇒ See also VOICE RECOGNITION.

spell checker A program that checks the spelling of words in a text document. Spell checkers are particularly valuable for catching typos, but they do not help much when your misspelling creates another valid word; for example, if you type *to* instead of *too.*
Many word processors come with a built-in spell checker, but you can also purchase stand-alone utilities.

⇒ See also WORD PROCESSING.

spelling checker See SPELL CHECKER.

SPID Acronym for *S(ervice) P(rofile) Id(entifier)*, a number that identifies a specific ISDN line. When you obtain ISDN service, your telephone company assigns a SPID to your line. Part of the initialization procedure is to configure your ISDN terminal adapter to use this SPID.

Most telephone companies in the U.S. use the *Generic SPID Format*, which is a 14-digit number. The first 10 digits identify the telephone number, called the *Directory Number (DN)*. The remaining four digits identify a particular ISDN device, in the case where multiple devices share the same Directory Number.

⇒ See also ISDN; TERMINAL ADAPTER.

spider A program that automatically fetches Web pages. Spiders are used to feed pages to search engines. It's called a spider because it *crawls* over the Web. Another term for these programs is *webcrawler*.

Because most Web pages contain links to other pages, a spider can start almost anywhere. As soon as it sees a link to another page, it goes off and fetches it. Large search engines, like Alta Vista, have many spiders working in parallel.

⇒ See also ALTA VISTA; ROBOT; SEARCH ENGINE.

spline In computer graphics, a smooth curve that passes through two or more points. Splines are generated with mathematical formulas. Two of the most common types of splines are *Bézier curves* and *b-spline curves*.

⇒ See also BÉZIER CURVE; NURBS.

split screen Division of the display screen into separate parts, each of which displays a different document, or different parts of the same document.

⇒ See also WINDOW.

spoof To fool. In networking, the term is used to describe a variety of ways in which hardware and software can be fooled. *IP spoofing*, for example, involves trickery that makes a message appear as if it came from an authorized IP address.

Spoofing is also used as a network management technique to reduce traffic. For example, most LAN protocols send out packets periodically to monitor the status of the network. LANs generally have enough bandwidth to absorb these network management packets easily. When computers are connected to the LAN over wide-area network (WAN) connections, however, this added traffic can become a problem. Not only can it strain the bandwidth limits of the WAN connection, but it can also be expensive because many WAN connections incur fees only when they are transmitting data. To reduce this problem, routers and other network devices can be programmed to *spoof* replies from the remote nodes. Rather than sending the packets to the remote nodes and waiting for a reply, the devices generate their own *spoofed* replies.

⇒ See also IP SPOOFING; NETWORK MANAGEMENT.

spool See under SPOOLING.

Figure 76: **spreadsheet application**

spooler A program that controls spooling—putting jobs on a queue and taking them off one at a time. Most operating systems come with one or more spoolers, such as a print spooler for spooling documents. In addition, some applications include spoolers. Many word processors, for example, include their own print spooler.

A good print spooler should allow you to change the order of documents in the queue and to cancel specific print jobs.

⇒ See also QUEUE; SPOOLING.

spooling Acronym for *s(imultaneous) p(eripheral) o(perations)* **on-line**, *spooling* refers to putting jobs in a buffer, a special area in memory or on a disk where a device can access them when it is ready. Spooling is useful because devices access data at different rates. The buffer provides a waiting station where data can rest while the slower device catches up.

The most common spooling application is *print spooling*. In print spooling, documents are loaded into a buffer (usually an area on a disk), and then the printer pulls them off the buffer at its own rate. Because the documents are in a buffer where they can be accessed by the printer, you can perform other operations on the computer while the printing takes place in the background. Spooling also lets you place a number of print jobs on a queue instead of waiting for each one to finish before specifying the next one.

⇒ See also BACKGROUND; BUFFER; QUEUE.

spot color Refers to a method of specifying and printing colors in which each color is printed with its own ink. In contrast, *process color* printing uses four inks (cyan, magenta, yellow, and black) to produce all other colors. Spot color printing is effective when the printed matter contains only one to three different colors, but it becomes prohibitively expensive for more colors.

Most desktop publishing and graphics applications allow you to specify spot colors for text and other elements. There are a number of color specification systems for specifying spot colors, but Pantone is the most widely used.

⇒ See also COLOR SEPARATION; PANTONE MATCHING SYSTEM (PMS); PROCESS COLORS.

spreadsheet A table of values arranged in rows and columns. Each value can have a predefined relationship to the other values. If you change one value, therefore, you may need to change other values as well.

Spreadsheet applications (sometimes referred to simply as *spreadsheets*) are computer programs that let you create and manipulate spreadsheets electronically. In a spreadsheet application, each value sits in a cell. You can define what type of data is in each cell and how different cells depend on one another. The relationships between cells are called *formulas*, and the names of the cells are called *labels*.

Once you have defined the cells and the formulas for linking them together, you can enter your data. You can then modify selected values to see how all the other values change accordingly. This enables you to study various what-if scenarios.

A simple example of a useful spreadsheet application is one that calculates mortgage payments for a house. You define five cells:

1. total cost of the house
2. down payment
3. mortgage rate
4. mortgage term
5. monthly payment

Once you defined how these cells depend on one another, you could enter numbers and play with various possibilities. For example, keeping all the other values the same, you could see how different mortgage rates would affect your monthly payments.

There are a number of spreadsheet applications on the market, Lotus 1-2-3 and Excel being among the most well known. The more powerful spreadsheet applications support graphics features that enable you to produce charts and graphs from the data.

Most spreadsheet applications are *multidimensional,* meaning that you can link one spreadsheet to another. A three-dimensional spreadsheet, for example, is like a stack of spreadsheets all connected by formulas. A change made in one spreadsheet automatically affects other spreadsheets.

⇒ See also BORLAND INTERNATIONAL; CELL; FORMULA; LABEL; LOTUS 1-2-3; THREE-DIMENSIONAL SPREADSHEET; VISICALC.

sprite A graphic image that can move within a larger graphic. Animation software that supports sprites enables the designer to develop independent animated images that can then be combined in a larger animation. Typically, each sprite has a set of rules that define how it moves and how it behaves if it bumps into another sprite or a static object.

⇒ See also ANIMATION.

SPX Short for *S(equenced) P(acket) Ex(change),* a transport layer protocol (layer 4 of the OSI Model) used in Novell Netware networks. The SPX layer sits on top of the IPX layer (layer 3) and provides connection-oriented services between two nodes on the network. SPX is used primarily by client/server applications.

Whereas the IPX protocol is similar to IP, SPX is similar to TCP. Together, therefore, IPX/SPX provides connection services similar to those provided by TCP/IP.

⇒ See also IPX; NETWARE; TCP.

SQL Abbreviation of *s(tructured) q(uery) l(anguage),* and pronounced either *see-kwell* or as separate letters. SQL is a standardized query language for requesting information from a database. The original version called *SEQUEL [s(tructured) E(nglish) que(ry) l(anguage)]* was designed by an IBM research center in 1974 and 1975. SQL was first introduced as a commercial database system in 1979 by Oracle Corporation.

Historically, SQL has been the favorite query language for database management systems running on minicomputers and mainframes. Increasingly, however, SQL is being supported by PC database systems because it supports distributed databases (databases that are spread out over several computer systems). This enables several users on a local-area network to access the same database simultaneously.

Although there are different dialects of SQL, it is nevertheless the closest thing to a standard query language that currently exists. In 1986, ANSI approved a rudimentary version of SQL as the official standard, but most versions of SQL since then have included many extensions to the ANSI standard. In 1991, ANSI updated the standard. The new standard is known as SAG SQL.

⇒ See also DATABASE MANAGEMENT SYSTEM; DISTRIBUTED DATABASE; JDBC; ORACLE; QUERY; QUERY LANGUAGE; SQL SERVER; STORED PROCEDURE.

SQL server Generically, any database management system (DBMS) that can respond to queries from client machines formatted in the SQL language. When capitalized, the term generally refers to either of two database management products from Sybase and Microsoft. Both companies offer client/server DBMS products called *SQL Server*.

⇒ See also RDBMS; SQL; SYBASE.

SRAM Short for *s(tatic) r(andom) a(ccess) m(emory)*, and pronounced **ess-ram**. SRAM is a type of memory that is faster and more reliable than the more common DRAM (dynamic RAM). The term *static* is derived from the fact that it doesn't need to be refreshed like dynamic RAM.

While DRAM supports access times of about 60 nanoseconds, SRAM can give access times as low as 10 nanoseconds. In addition, its cycle time is much shorter than that of DRAM because it does not need to pause between accesses. Unfortunately, it is also much more expensive to produce than DRAM. Due to its high cost, SRAM is often used only as a memory cache.

⇒ See also ACCESS TIME; CACHE; CYCLE TIME; DYNAMIC RAM; NVRAM; RAM.

SSI Short for *server-side include,* a type of HTML comment that directs the Web server to dynamically generate data for the Web page whenever it is requested. The basic format for SSIs is:
  < !—#command tag = 'value'... >
Where #command can be any of various commands supported by the Web server. The simplest command is #include, which inserts the contents of another file. This is especially useful for ensuring that boilerplate components, such as headers and footers, are the same on all pages throughout a Web site. To change a boilerplate element, you need only modify the include file, instead of updating every individual Web page.

SSIs can also be used to execute programs and insert the results. They therefore represent a powerful tool for Web developers.

There is no official standard for SSIs, so every Web server is free to support different SSIs in different manners. However, many SSI commands, such as #include and #exec, have become de facto standards.

Web pages that contain SSIs often end with a *.shtml* extension, though this is not a requirement. The filename extension enables the Web server to differentiate those pages that need to be processed before they are sent to the browser.

⇒ See also DYNAMIC HTML; HTML; SERVER-SIDE.

SSL Short for *S(ecure) S(ockets) L(ayer)*, a protocol developed by Netscape for transmitting private documents via the Internet. SSL works by using a private key to encrypt data that's transferred over the SSL connection. Both Netscape Navigator and Internet Explorer support SSL, and many Web sites use the protocol to obtain confidential user information, such as credit card numbers. By convention, Web pages that require an SSL connection start with *https:* instead of *http:*.

Another protocol for transmitting data securely over the World Wide

Web is *Secure HTTP (S-HTTP)*. Whereas SSL creates a secure connection between a client and a server, over which any amount of data can be sent securely, S-HTTP is designed to transmit individual messages securely. SSL and S-HTTP, therefore, can be seen as complementary rather than competing technologies. Both protocols have been submitted to the Internet Engineering Task Force (IETF) for approval as a standard.

⇒ See also DIGITAL CERTIFICATE; DIGITAL SIGNATURE; IETF; IPSEC; S-HTTP; SECURITY; X.509.

ST-412 interface Same as ST-506 INTERFACE.

ST-506 interface An old standard interface for connecting hard disk drives to PCs. Newer standards, such as enhanced IDE and SCSI, support faster data transfer rates.

ST-506 is sometimes referred to as *MFM*, which is the most prevalent encoding scheme used on ST-506 disk drives. ST-506 also supports the RLL encoding format.

⇒ See also HARD DISK; IDE INTERFACE; INTERFACE; MFM; RLL; SCSI.

stack 1. In programming, a special type of data structure in which items are removed in the reverse order from that in which they are added, so the most recently added item is the first one removed. This is also called *last-in, first-out (LIFO)*.

Adding an item to a stack is called *pushing.* Removing an item from a stack is called *popping.* **2.** In networking, short for *protocol stack.* **3.** In Apple Computer 's HyperCard software system, a stack is a collection of cards.

⇒ See also DATA STRUCTURE; HEAP.

stand-alone Refers to a device that is self-contained, one that does not require any other devices to function. For example, a fax machine is a stand-alone device because it does not require a computer, printer, modem, or other device. A printer, on the other hand, is not a stand-alone device because it requires a computer to feed it data.

⇒ See also FAX MACHINE.

standard A definition or format that has been approved by a recognized standards organization or is accepted as a de facto standard by the industry. Standards exist for programming languages, operating systems, data formats, communications protocols, and electrical interfaces.

From a user's standpoint, standards are extremely important in the computer industry because they allow the combination of products from different manufacturers to create a customized system. Without standards, only hardware and software from the same company could be used together. In addition, standard user interfaces can make it much easier to learn how to use new applications.

Most official computer standards are set by one of the following organizations:

- ANSI (American National Standards Institute)
- CCITT (Comité Consultatif Internationale Télégraphique et Téléphonique)
- IEEE (Institute of Electrical and Electronic Engineers)
- ISO (International Organization for Standardization)
- VESA (Video Electronics Standards Association)

IEEE sets standards for most types of electrical interfaces. Its most famous standard is probably RS-232C, which defines an interface for serial communication. This is the interface used by most modems, and a number of other devices, including display screens and mice. IEEE is also responsible for designing floating-point data formats.

While IEEE is generally concerned with hardware, ANSI is primarily concerned with software. ANSI has defined standards for a number of programming languages, including C, COBOL, and FORTRAN.

CCITT defines international standards, particularly communications protocols. It has defined a number of standards, including V.22, V.32, V.34, and V.42, that specify protocols for transmitting data over telephone lines.

In addition to standards approved by organizations, there are also de facto standards. These are formats that have become standard simply because a large number of companies have agreed to use them. They have not been formally approved as standards, but they are standards nonetheless. PostScript is a good example of a de facto standard.

⇒ See also ACM; ANSI; ARCHITECTURE; CCITT; COMPATIBLE; DE FACTO STANDARD; ELECTRONIC INDUSTRIES ASSOCIATION (EIA); IEEE; IETF; INTERNET SOCIETY; ISO; ITU; OPEN ARCHITECTURE; SAA; VESA.

Standard Generalized Markup Language See SGML.

standard input The place from which input comes unless you specify a different input device. The standard input device is usually the keyboard.

⇒ See also INPUT.

standard output The place where output goes unless you specify a different output device. The standard output device is usually the display screen.

⇒ See also OUTPUT.

star network A local-area network (LAN) that uses a star topology in which all nodes are connected to a central computer. The main advantages of a star network is that one malfunctioning node doesn't affect the rest of the network, and it's easy to add and remove nodes. The main disadvantage of star networks is that they require more cabling than other topologies, such as a bus or ring networks. In addition, if the central computer fails, the entire network becomes unusable. Standard twisted-pair Ethernet uses a star topology.

⇒ See also 10BaseT; bus network; hub; local-area network; topology.

start bit In asynchronous communications, the bit that signals the receiver that data is coming. Every byte of data is preceded by a start bit and followed by a stop bit.

⇒ See also asynchronous; bit; byte.

start-stop transmission See under asynchronous.

startup disk Same as bootable diskette.

stateless Having no information about what occurred previously. Most modern applications *maintain state,* which means that they remember what you were doing last time you ran the application, and they remember all your configuration settings. This is extremely useful because it means you can mold the application to your working habits.

The World Wide Web, on the other hand, is intrinsically stateless because each request for a new Web page is processed without any knowledge of previous pages requested. This is one of the chief drawbacks to the HTTP protocol. Because maintaining state is extremely useful, programmers have developed a number of techniques to add state to the World Wide Web. These include server APIs, such as NSAPI and ISAPI, and the use of cookies.

⇒ See also cookie; HTTP; ISAPI; NSAPI.

statement An instruction written in a high-level language. A statement directs the computer to perform a specified action. A single statement in a high-level language can represent several machine-language instructions. Programs consist of statements and *expressions.* An expression is a group of symbols that represent a value.

⇒ See also expression; programming language.

static RAM See SRAM.

static variable A variable that retains the same data throughout the execution of a program. In contrast, a *dynamic variable* can have different values during the course of a program.

⇒ See also dynamic variable; variable.

station Short for *workstation.*

STN Short for *s(uper)t(wist) n(ematic).* See under supertwist.

stop bit In asynchronous communications, a bit that indicates that a byte has just been transmitted. Every byte of data is preceded by a start bit and followed by a stop bit.

⇒ See also ASYNCHRONOUS; BIT; BYTE.

storage 1. The capacity of a device to hold and retain data. **2.** Short for *mass storage.*

⇒ See also HSM; MASS STORAGE; STORAGE DEVICE.

storage device A device capable of storing data. The term usually refers to mass storage devices, such as disk and tape drives.

⇒ See also DISK DRIVE; HSM; MASS STORAGE; STORAGE; TAPE DRIVE.

store To copy data from a CPU to memory, or from memory to a mass storage device.

⇒ See also SAVE.

stored procedure In database management systems (DBMSs), an operation that is stored with the database server. Typically, stored procedures are written in SQL. They're especially important for client/server database systems because storing the procedure on the server side means that it is available to all clients. And when the procedure is modified, all clients automatically get the new version.

⇒ See also DATABASE MANAGEMENT SYSTEM; SQL.

streamer Same as TAPE.

streaming A technique for transferring data such that it can be processed as a steady and continuous stream. Streaming technologies are becoming increasingly important with the growth of the Internet because most users do not have fast enough access to download large multimedia files quickly. With streaming, the client browser or plug-in can start displaying the data before the entire file has been transmitted.

For streaming to work, the client side receiving the data must be able to collect the data and send it as a steady stream to the application that is processing the data and converting it to sound or pictures. This means that if the streaming client receives the data more quickly than required, it needs to save the excess data in a buffer. If the data doesn't come quickly enough, however, the presentation of the data will not be smooth.

There are a number of competing streaming technologies emerging. For audio data on the Internet, the de facto standard is Progressive Network's *RealAudio.*

⇒ See also ACTIVEMOVIE; H.324; MULTIMEDIA; NETSHOW; REALAUDIO; REAL-VIDEO; RTP; RTSP; SMIL.

strikeout A method of highlighting text by drawing a horizontal line through the characters.

Many word processors support edit modes in which deleted sections are displayed with strikeouts. This is particularly effective in workgroups where two or more people are editing the same document.

Strikeout is also called *strikethrough*.

⇒ See also WORKGROUP COMPUTING.

~~This text, for example, has strikeout formatting.~~

strikethrough Same as STRIKEOUT.

string See CHARACTER STRING.

Structured Query Language See SQL.

stub A routine that doesn't actually do anything other than declare itself and the parameters it accepts. Stubs are used commonly as placeholders for routines that still need to be developed. The stub contains just enough code to allow it to be compiled and linked with the rest of the program.

⇒ See also DECLARE; ROUTINE.

style In word processing, a named set of formatting parameters. By applying the style name to a section of text, you can change many formatting properties at once.

⇒ See also FORMAT; STYLE SHEET.

style sheet In word processing and desktop publishing, a style sheet is a file or form that defines the layout of a document. When you fill in a style sheet, you specify such parameters as the page size, margins, and fonts. Style sheets are useful because you can use the same style sheet for many documents. For example, you could define one style sheet for personal letters, another for official letters, and a third for reports.

Stylesheets are also called *templates*.

⇒ See also CSS; DESKTOP PUBLISHING; FONT; LAYOUT; MARGINS; STYLE; WORD PROCESSING.

stylus A pointing and drawing device shaped like a pen. You use a stylus with a digitizing tablet or touch screen.

⇒ See also DIGITIZING TABLET; TOUCH SCREEN.

subdirectory A directory below another directory. Every directory except the root directory is a subdirectory. In Windows 95, Windows 98, and

Windows NT, subdirectories are called *folders*.

⇒ See also DIRECTORY; FOLDER; ROOT DIRECTORY.

subnet A portion of a network that shares a common address component. On TCP/IP networks, subnets are defined as all devices whose IP addresses have the same prefix. For example, all devices with IP addresses that start with 100.100.100. would be part of the same subnet. Dividing a network into subnets is useful for both security and performance reasons. IP networks are divided using a subnet mask.

⇒ See also IP ADDRESS; SUBNET MASK.

subnet mask A mask used to determine what subnet an IP address belongs to. An IP address has two components, the network address and the host address. For example, consider the IP address 150.215.017.009. Assuming this is part of a Class B network, the first two numbers (150. 215) represent the Class B network address, and the second two numbers (017.009) identify a particular host on this network.

Subnetting enables the network administrator to divide the host part of the address further into two or more subnets. In this case, a part of the host address is reserved to identify the particular subnet. This is easier to see if we show the IP address in binary format. The full address is:

    10010110.11010111.00010001.00001001

The Class B network part is:
    10010110.11010111

and the host address is
    00010001.00001001

If this network is divided into 14 subnets, however, then the first 4 bits of the host address (0001) are reserved for identifying the subnet.

The subnet mask is the network address plus the bits reserved for identifying the subnetwork. (By convention, the bits for the network address are all set to 1, though it would also work if the bits were set exactly as in the network address.) In this case, therefore, the subnet mask would be 11111111.11111111.11110000.00000000. It's called a *mask* because it can be used to identify the subnet to which an IP address belongs by performing a bitwise AND operation on the mask and the IP address. The result is the subnetwork address:

- Subnet Mask: 255.255.240.000: 11111111.11111111.11110000. 00000000
- IP Address: 150.215.017.009: 10010110.11010111.00010001.00001001
- Subnet Address: 150.215.016.000: 10010110.11010111.00010000. 00000000

The subnet address, therefore, is 150.215.016.000.

⇒ See also MASK; SUBNET.

subnotebook computer A portable computer that is slightly lighter and smaller than a full-sized notebook computer. Typically, subnotebook computers have a smaller keyboard and screen but are otherwise equivalent to notebook computers.

⇒ See also HANDHELD COMPUTER; NOTEBOOK COMPUTER; PORTABLE.

subroutine Same as ROUTINE.

subscript 1. In programming, a symbol or number used to identify an element in an array. Usually, the subscript is placed in brackets following the array name. For example, AR[5] identifies element number 5 in an array called AR.

If the array is multidimensional, you must specify a subscript for each dimension. For example, MD[5][3][9] identifies an element in a three-dimensional array called MD.

Different programming languages have different rules for specifying subscripts. For example, the BASIC language uses parentheses in place of brackets. **2.** In word processing, a character that appears slightly below the line, as in this example: H_2O. A *superscript* is a character that appears slightly above the line.

⇒ See also ARRAY; SUPERSCRIPT; WORD PROCESSING.

Sun Microsystems A company based in Mountain View, California, that builds computer hardware and software. Sun Microsystems was founded in 1982 by Andreas Bechtolsheim, Vinod Khosla, and Scott McNeally. The firm is best known for developing workstations and operating environments for the UNIX operation system, and more recently for developing and promoting the Java programming language.

Sun products include SPARC workstations and the Solaris operating environment.

⇒ See also DEC; IBM; JAVA; JAVASOFT; MICROSOFT; NETSCAPE; NETWORK COMPUTER; SERVER; SGI; SOLARIS; SPARC; TOPS; UNIX; WORKSTATION.

supercomputer The fastest type of computer. Supercomputers are very expensive and are employed for specialized applications that require immense amounts of mathematical calculations. For example, weather forecasting requires a supercomputer. Other uses of supercomputers include animated graphics, fluid dynamic calculations, nuclear energy research, and petroleum exploration.

The chief difference between a supercomputer and a mainframe is that a supercomputer channels all its power into executing a few programs as fast as possible, whereas a mainframe uses its power to execute many programs concurrently.

⇒ See also COMPUTER; HIGH PERFORMANCE COMPUTING; HIPPI; MAINFRAME.

supercomputing Same as HIGH PERFORMANCE COMPUTING.

SuperDisk A new disk storage technology developed by Imation Corporation that supports very high-density diskettes. SuperDisk diskettes are
etched with a servo pattern at the factory. This pattern is then read by
the SuperDisk drive to precisely align the read/write head. The result is
that a SuperDisk diskette can have 2,490 tracks, as opposed to the 135
tracks that conventional 3.5-inch 1.44 MB diskettes use. This higher density translates into 120 MB capacity per diskette.

Unlike other removable disk storage solutions, such as the Zip drive,
SuperDisk is backward compatible with older diskettes. This means that
you can use the same SuperDisk drive to read from and write to older
1.44 MB diskettes as well as the new 120 MB SuperDisk diskettes.

Imation's current SuperDisk drive is called the *LS-120*.

⇒ See also FLOPPY DISK; HiFD; ZIP DRIVE.

SuperDrive The common name for the *FDHD [f(loppy) d(isk), h(igh) d(ensity)]* disk drive that comes with all models of the Apple Macintosh computer. The SuperDrive can read and write to all three Macintosh disk
sizes (400K, 800K, and 1.44MB) as well as the two PC 3½-inch disk sizes
(720K and 1.44MB).

⇒ See also FDHD; FLOPPY DISK; MACINTOSH COMPUTER.

superscalar Refers to microprocessor architectures that enable more than
one instruction to be executed per clock cycle. Nearly all modern microprocessors, including the Pentium, PowerPC, Alpha, and SPARC microprocessors, are superscalar.

⇒ See also CLOCK SPEED; INSTRUCTION; MICROPROCESSOR; PARALLEL PROCESSING;
PIPELINING.

superscript A symbol or character that appears slightly above a line, as in
this example and the example below: r^2. Footnote numbers appearing in
text are also superscripts. A symbol or character that appears slightly below a line is called a *subscript*.

⇒ See also SUBSCRIPT; WORD PROCESSING.

$$\text{area} = 2\pi r^2$$

supertwist A technique for improving LCD display screens by twisting
light rays. In addition to normal supertwist displays, there also exist *double supertwist* and *triple supertwist* displays. In general, the more twists,
the higher the contrast.

Supertwist displays are also known as *supertwist nematic (STN)* displays.

⇒ See also BACKGROUND; BACKLIGHTING; CSTN; DSTN; FLAT-PANEL DISPLAY; LCD; NOTEBOOK COMPUTER.

Super VGA See SVGA.

Super-Video See S-VIDEO.

support *v* **1.** To have a specific functionality. For example, a word processor that *supports* graphics is one that has a graphics component. The word *support,* however, is vague. It could mean that the word processor enables you to create graphics illustrations, that you can insert graphics created by another program, or something entirely different.

As another example, an operating system that supports multiple users is one that enables several users to run programs at the same time. —*n* **2.** Short for *customer support,* the assistance that a vendor offers to customers. Support can vary widely, from nothing at all to a phone hotline to house calls.

⇒ See also CUSTOMER SUPPORT.

surf To move from place to place on the Internet searching for topics of interest. Web surfing has become a favorite pastime for many Internet users. The links on each page enable you to start virtually anywhere on the Web and eventually find interesting pages. The term *surfing* is generally used to describe a rather undirected type of Web browsing in which the user jumps from page to page rather whimsically, as opposed to specifically searching for specific information.

⇒ See also BROWSE; LURK; WORLD WIDE WEB.

surge protector A device that protects a power supply and communications lines from electrical surges. All computers come with some surge protection built into the power supply, but it is a good idea to purchase a separate device. Many *uninterruptible power supplies (UPSes)* include surge protection.

Surge protectors are also called *surge suppressors.*

⇒ See also UPS.

surround sound See under DOLBY DIGITAL.

SVC Short for *s(witched) v(irtual) c(ircuit),* a temporary virtual circuit that is set up and used only as long as data is being transmitted. Once the communication between the two hosts is complete, the SVC disappears. In contrast, a permanent virtual circuit (PVC) remains available at all times.

⇒ See also PACKET SWITCHING; PVC; VIRTUAL CIRCUIT.

SVGA Short for *Super VGA,* a set of graphics standards designed to offer greater resolution than VGA. There are several varieties of SVGA, each providing a different resolution:

- 800 by 600 pixels
- 1024 by 768 pixels
- 1280 by 1024 pixels
- 1600 by 1200 pixels

All SVGA standards support a palette of 16 million colors, but the number of colors that can be displayed simultaneously is limited by the amount of video memory installed in a system. One SVGA system might display only 256 simultaneous colors while another displays the entire palette of 16 million colors. The SVGA standards are developed by a consortium of monitor and graphics manufacturers called VESA.

⇒ See also 8514/A; palette; resolution; VESA; VGA; video standards.

S-Video Short for *S(uper)*-**Video**, a technology for transmitting video signals over a cable by dividing the video information into two separate signals: one for color (*chrominance*), and the other for brightness (*luminance*). When sent to a television, this produces sharper images than *composite video,* where the video information is transmitted as a single signal over one wire. This is because televisions are designed to display separate Luminance (Y) and Chrominance (C) signals. (The terms *Y/C video* and *S-Video* are the same.)

Computer monitors, on the other hand, are designed for RGB signals. Most digital video devices, such as digital cameras and game machines, produce video in RGB format. The images look best, therefore, when output on a computer monitor. When output on a television, however, they look better in S-Video format than in composite format.

To use S-Video, the device sending the signals must support S-Video output, and the device receiving the signals must have an S-Video input jack. Then you need a special S-Video cable to connect the two devices.

⇒ See also composite video; NTSC; RGB monitor; video.

swap 1. To replace pages or segments of data in memory. Swapping is a useful technique that enables a computer to execute programs and manipulate data files larger than main memory. The operating system copies as much data as possible into main memory and leaves the rest on the disk. When the operating system needs data from the disk, it exchanges a portion of data (called a *page* or *segment*) in main memory with a portion of data on the disk.

DOS does not perform swapping, but most other operating systems, including OS/2, Windows, and UNIX, do.

Swapping is often called *paging.* **2.** In UNIX systems, *swapping* refers to moving entire processes in and out of main memory.

⇒ See also demand paging; main memory; memory; operating system; page; paging; process; segment; thrash; UNIX; virtual memory.

swap file In Windows environments, a hidden file used by the operating system for swapping.

⇒ See also SWAP.

switch 1. In networks, a device that filters and forwards packets between LAN segments. Switches operate at the data link layer (layer 2) of the OSI Reference Model and therefore support any packet protocol. LANs that use switches to join segments are called *switched LANs* or, in the case of Ethernet networks, *switched Ethernet LANs.* **2.** A small lever or button. The switches on the back of printers and on expansion boards are called DIP switches. A switch that has just two positions is called a *toggle switch.* **3.** Another word for *option* or *parameter*—a symbol that you add to a command to modify the command's behavior.

⇒ See also 3COM; DIP SWITCH; OPTION; PARAMETER; ROUTING SWITCH; SWITCHED ETHERNET; TOGGLE.

switched Ethernet An Ethernet LAN that uses switches to connect individual hosts or segments. In the case of individual hosts, the switch replaces the repeater and effectively gives the device full 10 Mbps bandwidth (or 100 Mbps for Fast Ethernet) to the rest of the network. This type of network is sometimes called a *desktop switched Ethernet.* In the case of segments, the hub is replaced with a switching hub.

   Traditional Ethernets, in which all hosts compete for the same bandwidth, are called *shared Ethernets.* Switched Ethernets are becoming very popular because they are an effective and convenient way to extend the bandwidth of existing Ethernets.

⇒ See also 100BASE-T; ETHERNET; SHARED ETHERNET; SWITCH; SWITCHING HUB.

switched virtual circuit See SVC.

switching hub Short for *port-switching hub,* a special type of hub that forwards packets to the appropriate port based on the packet's address. Conventional hubs simply rebroadcast every packet to every port. Because switching hubs forward each packet only to the required port, they provide much better performance. Most switching hubs also support load balancing, so that ports are dynamically reassigned to different LAN segments based on traffic patterns.

   Some newer switching hubs support both traditional Ethernet (10 Mbps) and Fast Ethernet (100 Mbps) ports. This enables the administrator to establish a dedicated Fast Ethernet channel for high-traffic devices such as servers.

⇒ See also HUB; LOCAL-AREA NETWORK; SEGMENT; SWITCHED ETHERNET.

Sybase Based in Emeryville, California, one of the dominant software companies in the area of database management systems (DBMSs) and client/server programming environments. Its DBMS products are branded with the Sybase name, whereas its client/server products, chiefly Power-

Builder, are branded with the name *PowerSoft*. PowerSoft Corporation started as an independent software company but merged with Sybase in 1995.

⇒ See also Informix; Oracle; PowerBuilder; SQL Server.

symmetric digital subscriber line See SDSL.

symmetric encryption A type of encryption where the same key is used to encrypt and decrypt the message. This differs from asymmetric (or public-key) encryption, which uses one key to encrypt a message and another to decrypt the message.

⇒ See also encryption.

symmetric-key cryptography An encryption system in which the sender and receiver of a message share a single, common key that is used to encrypt and decrypt the message. Contrast this with public-key cryptology, which utilizes two keys—a public key to encrypt messages and a private key to decrypt them.

   Symmetric-key systems are simpler and faster, but their main drawback is that the two parties must somehow exchange the key in a secure way. Public-key encryption avoids this problem because the public key can be distributed in a nonsecure way, and the private key is never transmitted.

   Symmetric-key cryptography is sometimes called *secret-key cryptography*. The most popular symmetric-key system is the *Data Encryption Standard (DES)*.

⇒ See also cryptography; DES; key; public-key encryption.

Symmetric Multiprocessing See SMP.

synchronous Occurring at regular intervals. The opposite of *synchronous* is *asynchronous*. Most communication between computers and devices is asynchronous—it can occur at any time and at irregular intervals. Communication within a computer, however, is usually synchronous and is governed by the microprocessor clock. Signals along the bus, for example, can occur only at specific points in the clock cycle.

⇒ See also asynchronous; bisync; bus; clock speed; isochronous.

Synchronous Digital Hierarchy See SDH.

synchronous DRAM See SDRAM.

Synchronous Optical Network See SONET.

SyncLink memory See SLDRAM.

syntax Refers to the spelling and grammar of a programming language.

Computers are inflexible machines that understand what you type only if you type it in the exact form that the computer expects. The expected form is called the syntax.

Each program defines its own syntactical rules that control which words the computer understands, which combinations of words are meaningful, and what punctuation is necessary.

⇒ See also LANGUAGE; SEMANTICS.

sysadmin Short for *system administrator*.

sysop Pronounced *siss-op*, short for *sys(tem) op(erator)*, an individual who manages a bulletin board system *(BBS), online service*, or *special interest group (SIG)*.

⇒ See also BULLETIN BOARD SYSTEM; NETWORK; SIG.

System On Macintoshes, *System* is short for *System file*, an essential program that runs whenever you start up a Macintosh. The System provides information to all other applications that run on a Macintosh. The System and Finder programs together make up the Mac OS.

⇒ See also FINDER; MAC OS; MACINTOSH COMPUTER; OPERATING SYSTEM.

system 1. Refers to a combination of components working together. For example, a *computer system* includes both hardware and software. A *Windows system* is a personal computer running the Windows operating system. A *desktop publishing system* is a computer running desktop publishing software. **2.** Short for *computer system*. **3.** Short for *operating system*. **4.** An organization or methodology. The binary numbering system, for instance, is a way to count using only two digits.

⇒ See also COMPUTER SYSTEM; EMBEDDED SYSTEM; OPERATING SYSTEM; SYSTEM MANAGEMENT.

system administration See under SYSTEM ADMINISTRATOR.

system administrator An individual responsible for maintaining a multi-user computer system, including a local-area network (LAN). Typical duties include:

- Adding and configuring new workstations
- Setting up user accounts
- Installing system-wide software
- Performing procedures to prevent the spread of viruses
- Allocating mass storage space

The system administrator is sometimes called the *sysadmin* or the *systems administrator*. Small organizations may have just one system administrator, whereas larger enterprises usually have a whole team of system administrators.

⇒ See also MIS; SYSTEM MANAGEMENT.

System Application Architecture See SAA.

system board Same as MOTHERBOARD.

system call The invocation of an operating system routine. Operating systems contain sets of routines for performing various low-level operations. For example, all operating systems have a routine for creating a directory. If you want to execute an operating system routine from a program, you must make a system call.

⇒ See also INVOKE; OPERATING SYSTEM; ROUTINE.

System folder A standard folder on Macintoshes that contains the System and Finder programs, as well as other resources needed by the operating system.

⇒ See also FINDER; FOLDER; MACINTOSH COMPUTER; SYSTEM.

system management The general area of Information Technology (IT) that concerns configuring and managing computer resources, especially network resources.

⇒ See also IS; IT; MIS; SMS; SYSTEM; SYSTEM ADMINISTRATOR.

System Object Model See SOM.

system prompt See under PROMPT.

systems administrator See SYSTEM ADMINISTRATOR.

systems analyst A programmer or consultant who designs and manages the development of business applications. Typically, systems analysts are more involved in design issues than in day-to-day coding. However, *systems analyst* is a somewhat arbitrary title, so different companies define the role differently.

⇒ See also PROGRAMMER; SYSTEMS INTEGRATOR.

systems integrator An individual or company that specializes in building complete computer systems by putting together components from different vendors. Unlike software developers, systems integrators typically do not produce any original code. Instead they enable a company to use off-the-shelf hardware and software packages to meet the company's computing needs.

⇒ See also PROGRAMMER; SYSTEMS ANALYST.

Systems Management Server See SMS.

Systems Network Architecture See SNA.

system software See SYSTEMS SOFTWARE.

systems software Refers to the operating system and all utility programs that manage computer resources at a low level. Software is generally divided into systems software and applications software. Applications software comprises programs designed for an end user, such as word processors, database systems, and spreadsheet programs. Systems software includes compilers, loaders, linkers, and debuggers.

⇒ See also APPLICATION; END USER; SOFTWARE; UTILITY.

system unit The main part of a personal computer. The system unit includes the chassis, microprocessor, main memory, bus, and ports but does not include the keyboard or monitor, or any peripheral devices.
   A system unit is sometimes called a *box* or *main unit.*

⇒ See also CHASSIS; MAIN MEMORY; MICROPROCESSOR; PORT.

T-1 carrier A dedicated phone connection supporting data rates of 1. 544Mbits per second. A T-1 line actually consists of 24 individual channels, each of which supports 64Kbits per second. Each 64Kbit/second channel can be configured to carry voice or data traffic. Most telephone companies allow you to buy just some of these individual channels, known as *fractional T-1* access.

T-1 lines are a popular leased line option for businesses connecting to the Internet and for Internet Service Providers (ISPs) connecting to the Internet backbone. The Internet backbone itself consists of faster T-3 connections.

T-1 lines are sometimes referred to as *DS1* lines.

⇒ See also CARRIER; CSU/DSU; FRACTIONAL T-1; ISP; LEASED LINE; OC; SO-NET; T-3 CARRIER; TDM.

T-3 carrier A dedicated phone connection supporting data rates of about 43 Mbps. A T-3 line actually consists of 672 individual channels, each of which supports 64 Kbps.

T-3 lines are used mainly by internet service providers (ISPs) connecting to the Internet backbone and for the backbone itself.

T-3 lines are sometimes referred to as *DS3* lines.

⇒ See also BACKBONE; CARRIER; CSU/DSU; ISP; LEASED LINE; OC; SONET; T-1 CARRIER; TDM.

TA Short for *terminal adapter*.

tab character A special character that can be inserted into a text document.

Different programs react to tab characters in different ways. Most word processors, for example, move the cursor or insertion point to the next *tab stop*, and most printers move the print head to the next tab stop as well. Some programs, however, simply ignore tabs.

⇒ See also TAB KEY; TAB STOP.

Tab key A key on computer keyboards that inserts a tab character or moves the insertion point to the next tab stop. Some applications respond to the Tab key by inserting spaces up to the next tab stop. This is often called a *soft tab*, whereas a real tab character is called a *hard tab*.

Spreadsheet and database management applications usually respond to the Tab key by moving the cursor to the next field or cell. In dialog

table 544

boxes and menus, pressing the Tab key highlights the next button or option.

⇒ See also CELL; CURSOR; FIELD; INSERTION POINT; TAB CHARACTER; TAB STOP.

table Refers to data arranged in rows and columns. A *spreadsheet*, for example, is a table. In relational database management systems, all information is stored in the form of tables.

⇒ See also DATABASE MANAGEMENT SYSTEM; RDBMS; SPREADSHEET.

tablet Short for *graphics tablet, digitizing tablet,* or *electronic tablet.*

⇒ See also DIGITIZING TABLET.

tab stop A stop point for tabbing. In word processing, each line contains a number of tab stops placed at regular intervals (for example, every half inch). They can be changed, however, as most word processors allow you to set tab stops wherever you want. When you press the Tab key, the cursor or insertion point jumps to the next tab stop, which itself is invisible. Although tab stops do not exist in the text file, the word processor keeps track of them so that it can react correctly to the Tab key. That is, a text file may contain tab characters, but each application is free to interpret these characters differently depending on how the tab stops have been configured.

⇒ See also TAB CHARACTER; TAB KEY.

tag *n* **1.** A command inserted in a document that specifies how the document, or a portion of the document, should be formatted. Tags are used by all format specifications that store documents as text files. This includes SGML and HTML. —*v* **2.** To mark a section of a document with a formatting command.

⇒ See also FORMAT; HTML; META TAG; SGML; XML.

Tagged Image File Format See TIFF.

tag RAM The area in an L2 cache that identifies which data from main memory is currently stored in each *cache line*. The actual data is stored in a different part of the cache, called the *data store*. The values stored in the tag RAM determine whether a cache lookup results in a *hit* or a *miss*.

The size of the data store determines how much data the cache can hold at any one time. The size of the tag RAM determines what range of main memory can be cached. Many modern PCs, for example, are configured with a 256K L2 cache and tag RAM that is 8 bits wide. This is sufficient for caching up to 64 MB of main memory. If you add additional main memory, however, it won't be cached unless you also expand tag RAM. Some motherboards allow you to add additional tag RAM chips for this purpose, but many do not.

For Pentium Pro and Pentium II microprocessors, the tag RAM is integrated in the chipset. Pentium Pros have an integrated L2 cache capable of caching up to 4 GB of main memory. Pentium IIs use an SEC daughtercard for L2 caches and can cache up to 512 MB.

⇒ See also CACHE; L2 CACHE; RAM.

tape A magnetically coated strip of plastic on which data can be encoded.

Table 28
Tapes

Type	Capacity	Notes
Half-inch	60MB to 400MB	Half-inch tapes come both as 9-track reels and as cartridges. The tapes themselves are relatively cheap but they require expensive tape drives.
Quarter-inch	40MB to 5GB	Quarter-inch cartridges (QIC tapes) are relatively inexpensive and support fast data transfer rates. Quarter-inch minicartridges are even less expensive, but their data capacities are smaller and their transfer rates are slower.
8-mm Helical-scan	5GB to 40GB	8-mm helical-scan cartridges use the same technology as VCR tapes and have the greatest capacity (along with DAT cartridges), but they require relatively expensive tape drives. They also have relatively slow data transfer rates.
4-mm DAT	2GB to 24GB DAT	(Digital Audio Tape) cartridges have the greatest capacity (along with 8-mm helical-scan cartridges) but they require relatively expensive tape drives. They also have relatively slow data transfer rates.

Tapes for computers are similar to tapes used to store music.

Storing data on tapes is considerably cheaper than storing data on disks. Tapes also have large storage capacities, ranging from a few hundred kilobytes to several gigabytes. Accessing data on tapes, however, is much slower than accessing data on disks. Tapes are *sequential-access* media, which means that to get to a particular point on the tape, the tape must go through all the preceding points. In contrast, disks are *random-access* media because a disk drive can access any point at random without passing through intervening points.

Because tapes are so slow, they are generally used only for long-term storage and backup. Data to be used regularly is almost always kept on a disk. Tapes are also used for transporting large amounts of data.

Tapes come in a variety of sizes and formats.

Tapes are sometimes called *streamers* or *streaming tapes*.

⇒ See also 3480, 3490; BACKUP; DAT; DISK DRIVE; DLT; HELICAL-SCAN CARTRIDGE; MASS STORAGE; QIC; SEQUENTIAL ACCESS; TRAVAN.

tape drive A device, like a tape recorder, that reads data from and writes it onto a tape. Tape drives have data capacities of anywhere from a few hundred kilobytes to several gigabytes. Their transfer speeds also vary considerably. Fast tape drives can transfer as much as 20MB (megabytes) per minute.

The disadvantage of tape drives is that they are *sequential-access* devices, which means that to read any particular block of data, you need to read all the preceding blocks. This makes them much too slow for general-purpose storage operations. However, they are the least expensive media for making backups.

⇒ See also BACKUP; DLT; TAPE; TRAVAN.

TAPI Abbreviation of *T(elephony) A(pplication) P(rogramming) I(nterface)*, an API for connecting a PC running Windows to telephone services. TAPI was introduced in 1993 as the result of joint development by Microsoft and Intel. The standard supports connections by individual computers as well as LAN connections serving many computers. Within each connection type, TAPI defines standards for simple call control and for manipulating call content.

The *Telephony Server Application Programming Interface (TSAPI)* defines similar capabilities for NetWare servers.

⇒ See also API; TELEPHONY; TSAPI.

tar 1. Short for *t(ape) ar(chive)*, a UNIX utility that combines a group of files into a single file. The resulting file has a .TAR extension.

The **tar** command does not compress files. Frequently, therefore, a tar file is compressed with the **compress** or **gzip** commands to create a file with a .TAR.GZ or .TAR.Z extension. These are comparable to files that have been compressed with PKZIP on a PC platform. Most PC compression utilities, including PKZIP, can open (**untar**) a tar file. —*v.* **2.** To combine files with the **tar** command.

⇒ See also PKZIP.

target Synonymous with *destination,* a target is a file, device, or any type
of location to which data is moved or copied. Many computer commands
involve copying data from one place to another. One says that the computer copies from the source to the target (or destination).

⇒ See also SOURCE.

task An operating system concept that refers to the combination of a program being executed and bookkeeping information used by the operating
system. Whenever you execute a program, the operating system creates a
new task for it. The task is like an envelope for the program: it identifies
the program with a *task number* and attaches other bookkeeping information to it.

  Many operating systems, including UNIX, OS/2, and Windows, are capable of running many tasks at the same time and are called *multitasking*
operating systems.

  In most operating systems, there is a one-to-one relationship between
the task and the program, but some operating systems allow a program
to be divided into multiple tasks. Such systems are called *multithreading*
operating systems.

  The terms *task* and *process* are often used interchangeably, although
some operating systems make a distinction between the two.

⇒ See also JOB; MULTITASKING; MULTITHREADING; OPERATING SYSTEM.

taskbar In Windows 95 and 98, a graphical list of active applications. If
the application window is minimized, you can restore it by clicking on its
button in the taskbar. By default, the taskbar appears on the bottom of
your screen, but you can move it to the top or to one of the sides.

task switching Refers to the ability of operating systems or operating environments to enable you to switch from one program to another without
losing your spot in the first program. Many utilities are available that add
task switching to DOS systems.

  Note that task switching is not the same as *multitasking.* In multitasking, the CPU switches back and forth quickly between programs, giving
the appearance that all programs are running simultaneously. In task
switching, the CPU does not switch back and forth but executes only one
program at a time. Task switching does allow you to switch smoothly
from one program to another.

  Task switching is sometimes called *context switching.*

⇒ See also DOS; MULTITASKING; OPERATING ENVIRONMENT; OPERATING SYSTEM.

Tcl Short for *tool command language,* and pronounced *T-C-L* or *tickle,* a
powerful interpreted programming language developed by John Ousterh-
out. One of the main strengths of Tcl is that it can be easily extended
through the addition of custom Tcl libraries. It is used for prototyping ap-

plications as well as for developing CGI scripts, though it is not as popular as Perl for the latter.

⇒ See also INTERPRETER; PERL; PROGRAMMING LANGUAGE.

TCO Abbreviation of *T(otal) C(ost of) O(wnership)*, a very popular buzzword representing how much it actually costs to own a PC. The TCO includes:

- Original cost of the computer and software
- Hardware and software upgrades
- Maintenance
- Technical support
- Training

Most estimates place the TCO at about three to four times the actual purchase cost of the PC. The TCO has become a rallying cry for companies supporting network computers. They claim that not only are network computers less expensive to purchase, but the TCO is also much less because network computers can be centrally administered and upgraded. Backers of conventional PCs, especially Microsoft and Intel, have countered with Zero Administration for Windows (ZAW), which they claim will also significantly reduce TCO.

⇒ See also NETWORK COMPUTER; UPGRADE; ZAW.

TCP Abbreviation of *T(ransmission) C(ontrol) P(rotocol)*, and pronounced as separate letters. TCP is one of the main protocols in TCP/IP networks. Whereas the IP protocol deals only with packets, TCP enables two hosts to establish a connection and exchange streams of data. TCP guarantees delivery of data and also guarantees that packets will be delivered in the same order in which they were sent.

⇒ See also IP; SOCKS; SPX; TCP/IP.

TCP/IP Abbreviation for *T(ransmission) C(ontrol) P(rotocol)/I(nternet) P(rotocol)*, the suite of communications protocols used to connect hosts on the Internet. TCP/IP uses several protocols, the two main ones being TCP and IP. TCP/IP is built into the UNIX operating system and is used by the Internet, making it the de facto standard for transmitting data over networks. Even network operating systems that have their own protocols, such as Netware, also support TCP/IP.

⇒ See also ATM; COMMUNICATIONS; INTERNET; IP; IP ADDRESS; NETWARE; PACKET SWITCHING; PROTOCOL; PROTOCOL STACK; SOCKET; TCP; UDP; WINSOCK.

TCPIP See TCP/IP.

TDM Short for *T(ime) D(ivision) M(ultiplexing)*, a type of multiplexing that combines data streams by assigning each stream a different time slot in a set. TDM repeatedly transmits a fixed sequence of time slots over a single transmission channel. Within T-Carrier systems, such as T-1 and T-3, TDM combines Pulse Code Modulated (PCM) streams created for each conversation or data stream.

⇒ See also CDMA; FDM; LEASED LINE; MODULATE; MULTIPLEX; PCM; T-1 CARRIER; T-3 CARRIER; TDMA; WDM.

TDMA Short for *T(ime) D(ivision) M(ultiple) A(ccess)*, a technology for delivering digital wireless service using time-division multiplexing (TDM). TDMA works by dividing a radio frequency into time slots and then allocating slots to multiple calls. In this way, a single frequency can support multiple, simultaneous data channels. TDMA is used by the GSM digital cellular system.

⇒ See also CDMA; CELLULAR; GSM; PCS; TDM.

teamware A category of software that enables colleagues, especially geographically dispersed colleagues, to collaborate on projects. Typically, teamware uses the Internet and the World Wide Web to facilitate communication among the team. The distinction between *teamware* and *groupware* is extremely fuzzy. Indeed, it seems that *teamware* is just a new name for what was previously called *groupware*. The distinction is made even more confusing by the fact that one of the leading vendors of this type of software is called *TeamWARE Group*.

⇒ See also GROUPWARE; WORKGROUP COMPUTING.

tear-off menu A pop-up menu that you can move around the screen like a window. Regular pop-up menus are attached to the menu selection that caused them to pop up.

⇒ See also MENU.

technical support See CUSTOMER SUPPORT.

telecommunications Refers to all types of data transmission, from voice to video.

⇒ See also COMMUNICATIONS; ITU; TELEMATICS; TELEPHONY.

telecommuting A term coined by Jack Nilles in the early 1970s to describe a geographically dispersed office where workers can work at home on a computer and transmit data and documents to a central office via telephone lines. A major argument in favor of telecommuting over vehicular commuting is that it does not produce air pollution. In addition, many people are more productive working at home than in an office. For others, however, the contrary holds true.

⇒ See also E-MAIL; NETWORK; WORKGROUP COMPUTING.

teleconference To hold a conference via a telephone or network connection. Computers have given new meaning to the term because they allow groups to do much more than just talk. Once a teleconference is established, the group can share applications and mark up a common whiteboard. There are many teleconferencing applications that work over private networks. One of the first to operate over the Internet is Microsoft's NetMeeting.

⇒ See also MULTICAST; NETMEETING; VIDEOCONFERENCING; WHITEBOARD; WORK-GROUP COMPUTING.

telecopy To send a document from one place to another via a fax machine.

⇒ See also FAX MACHINE.

telematics Refers to the broad industry related to using computers in concert with telecommunications systems. This includes dial-up service to the Internet as well as all types of networks that rely on a telecommunications system to transport data.

⇒ See also PBX; TELECOMMUNICATIONS; TELEPHONY.

Telenet One of the largest public data networks (PDNs) in the United States. Telenet is owned by U.S. Sprint Communications Corporation. A competing network, called *Tymnet*, is owned by McDonnell Douglas. Telenet serves as the communications backbone for many online services.

⇒ See also ONLINE SERVICE; WIDE-AREA NETWORK.

telephony The science of translating sound into electrical signals, transmitting them, and then converting them back to sound; that is, the science of telephones. The term is used frequently to refer to computer hardware and software that perform functions traditionally performed by telephone equipment. For example, telephony software can combine with your modem to turn your computer into a sophisticated answering service. Voice mail is another popular telephony application.

⇒ See also CTI; DTMF; INTERNET TELEPHONY; MODEM; TAPI; TELECOMMUNICATIONS; TELEMATICS; TSAPI.

Telephony API See TAPI.

Telephony Server API See TSAPI.

television board An expansion board that enables your computer monitor to do double duty as a television screen. The board contains a TV tuner to select channels and circuitry to convert from the TV video standard (NTSC) to your computer's video standard (normally VGA or SVGA). Most television boards support windowed TVs as well as full-screen viewing. With a TV window you can place a mini television in the corner of your screen while you use the computer for other tasks.

Today's television boards produce TV images comparable to those of normal televisions. Many home computers now come with a television board preinstalled.

⇒ See also EXPANSION BOARD; NTSC; PC/TV.

Telnet A terminal emulation program for TCP/IP networks such as the Internet. The Telnet program runs on your computer and connects your PC to a server on the network. You can then enter commands through the Telnet program, and they will be executed as if you were entering them directly on the server console. This enables you to control the server and communicate with other servers on the network. To start a Telnet session, you must log in to a server by entering a valid username and password. Telnet is a common way to control Web servers remotely.

⇒ See also HOST; INTERNET; TERMINAL EMULATION.

template 1. A plastic or paper diagram that you can put on your keyboard to indicate the meanings of different keys for a particular program. **2.** A sheet of plastic with menus and command boxes drawn on it that you place on top of a digitizing tablet. You can select commands by pressing the digitizing tablet's pen against a command box or by positioning the cursor over a box and pressing one of the cursor keys. **3.** In spreadsheet and database applications, a template is a blank form that shows which fields exist, their locations, and their length. In spreadsheet applications, for example, a template is a spreadsheet in which all the cells have been defined but no data has yet been entered. **4.** In some word processing

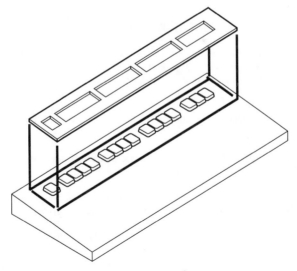

Figure 77: **template**

applications, *template* is used in place of *style sheet*. **5.** DOS uses the term *template* to mean command buffer.

⇒ See also BOILERPLATE; COMMAND BUFFER; CURSOR; DIGITIZING TABLET.

10Base-2 One of several adaptations of the Ethernet (IEEE 802.3) standard for local area networks (LANs). The 10Base-2 standard (also called *Thinnet*) uses 50 ohm coaxial cable (RG-58 A/U) with maximum lengths of 185 meters. This cable is thinner and more flexible than that used for the 10Base-5 standard. The RG-58 A/U cable is both less expensive and easier to place.

Cables in the 10Base-2 system connect with BNC connectors. The Network Interface Card (NIC) in a computer requires a T-connector where you can attach two cables to adjacent computers. Any unused connection must have a 50 ohm terminator.

The 10Base-2 system operates at 10 Mbps and uses baseband transmission methods.

⇒ See also 10BASE5; 10BASET; BASEBAND TRANSMISSION; BNC CONNECTOR; COAXIAL CABLE; ETHERNET.

10Base5 The original cabling standard for Ethernet that uses coaxial cables. The name derives from the fact that the maximum data transfer speed is 10 Mbps, it uses base(band) transmission, and the maximum length of cables is 5(00) meters.

10Base5 is also called thick *Ethernet, ThickWire,* and *ThickNet.*

⇒ See also 10BASE-2; 10BASET; COAXIAL CABLE; ETHERNET.

10BaseT One of several adaptations of the Ethernet (IEEE 802.3) standard for local area networks (LANs). The 10Base-T standard (also called *Twisted Pair Ethernet*) uses a twisted-pair cable with maximum lengths of 100 meters. The cable is thinner and more flexible than the coaxial cable used for the 10Base-2 or 10Base-5 standards.

Cables in the 10Base-T system connect with RJ-45 connectors. A star topology is common with 12 or more computers connected directly to a hub or concentrator.

The 10Base-T system operates at 10 Mbps and uses baseband transmission methods.

⇒ See also 100BASE-T; 10BASE-2; 10BASE5; ETHERNET; HUB; REPEATER; RJ-45; STAR NETWORK; TWISTED-PAIR CABLE.

terabyte 1. 2^{40} (1,099,511,627,776) bytes. This is approximately 1 trillion bytes. **2.** 10^{12} (1,000,000,000,000). This is exactly one trillion.

⇒ See also EXABYTE; GIGABYTE; MEGABYTE; PETABYTE.

terminal 1. A device that enables you to communicate with a computer. Generally, a terminal is a combination of keyboard and display screen.

Terminals are sometimes divided into three classes based on how much processing power they contain:

intelligent terminal: A stand-alone device that contains main memory and a CPU.
smart terminal: Contains some processing power, but not as much as an intelligent terminal.
dumb terminal: Has no processing capabilities. It relies entirely on the computer's processor.

2. In networking, a terminal is a personal computer or workstation connected to a mainframe. The personal computer usually runs terminal emulation software that makes the mainframe think it is like any other mainframe terminal.

⇒ See also CONSOLE; DISPLAY SCREEN; DUMB TERMINAL; EMULATION; HLLAPI; INTELLIGENT TERMINAL; KEYBOARD; MONITOR; NETWORK; SMART TERMINAL.

terminal adapter A device that connects a computer to an external digital communications line, such as an ISDN line. A terminal adapter is a bit like a modem, but whereas a modem needs to convert between analog and digital signals, a terminal adapter needs only to pass along digital signals. As ISDN becomes more common, future computers will probably have terminal adapters built in. Currently, though, you need to purchase a separate terminal adapter if you want ISDN access. You can get an internal adapter or an external adapter that connects to your computer's serial port.

⇒ See also ISDN; MODEM; SPID.

terminal emulation Refers to making a computer respond like a particular type of terminal. Terminal emulation programs allow you to access a mainframe computer or bulletin board service with a personal computer.

⇒ See also BULLETIN BOARD SYSTEM; EMULATION; HLLAPI; MAINFRAME; TELNET; TERMINAL.

terminate and stay resident See TSR.

TeX TeX is a macro processor that provides complete control over typographical formatting. Most people who use TeX, however, utilize one of several macro packages that provide an easier interface. The two most popular are *LaTeX*, originally written by Leslie Lamport, and *plain TeX*, written by Donald Knuth.

⇒ See also LaTeX; MuTeX.

Texas Instruments A large electronics company that has contributed considerably to the computer revolution. In 1958, a TI researcher named Jack Kilby demonstrated the first integrated circuit (IC), and in 1967, TI introduced the first handheld calculator. Today, TI's core business is in producing semiconductors.

⇒ See also DLP; INTEGRATED CIRCUIT; SEMICONDUCTOR; TEXAS INSTRUMENTS GRAPHICS ARCHITECTURE (TIGA); TI 34010.

Texas Instruments Graphics Architecture (TIGA) A high-resolution graphics specification designed by Texas Instruments. Unlike other graphics standards, TIGA does not specify a particular resolution or number of colors. Instead, it defines an interface between software and graphics processors. Programs written for TIGA, therefore, should be able to run on future systems that conform to the TIGA standard, regardless of resolution and color specifics.

Currently, the only graphics standard that conforms to TIGA is TI 34010, which defines a resolution of 1,024 by 768, with 256 simultaneous colors.

⇒ See also 8514/A; GRAPHICS; SVGA; TEXAS INSTRUMENTS; TI 34010; VESA; VIDEO STANDARDS; XGA.

text Words, sentences, paragraphs. This book, for example, consists of text. *Text processing* refers to the ability to manipulate words, lines, and pages. Typically, the term *text* refers to text stored as ASCII codes (that is, without any formatting). Objects that are *not* text include graphics, numbers (if they're not stored as ASCII characters), and program code.

⇒ See also ASCII.

text editor See EDITOR.

text file A file that holds text. The term *text file* is often used as a synonym for *ASCII file,* a file in which characters are represented by their ASCII codes.

⇒ See also ASCII; FILE; TEXT.

text flow Same as TEXT WRAP.

text mode A video mode in which a display screen is divided into rows and columns of boxes. Each box can contain one character. Text mode is also called character mode.

All video standards for the PC, including VGA, support a text mode that divides the screen into 25 rows and 80 columns. In addition to text mode, most video adapters support a *graphics mode,* in which the display screen is divided into an array of *pixels.*

Whereas character-based programs run in text mode, all graphics-based programs run in graphics mode.

⇒ See also CHARACTER BASED; GRAPHICS BASED; GRAPHICS MODE; VIDEO MODE; VIDEO STANDARDS.

texture In 3-D graphics, the digital representation of the surface of an ob-

ject. In addition to two-dimensional qualities, such as color and brightness, a texture is also encoded with three-dimensional properties, such as
how transparent and reflective the object is. Once a texture has been defined, it can be wrapped around any three-dimensional object. This is
called *texture mapping.*

  Well-defined textures are very important for rendering realistic 3-D images. However, they also require a lot of memory, so they're not used as
often as they might be. This is one of the rationales for the development
of a new graphics interface, AGP, which allows texture to be stored in
main memory, which is more expansive than video memory. AGP also
speeds up the transfer of large textures between memory, the CPU and
the video adapter.

⇒ See also 3-D GRAPHICS; 3-D SOFTWARE; AGP; MODELING; RAY TRACING; REN
DER.

texture mapping See under TEXTURE.

text wrap A feature supported by many word processors that enables you
to surround a picture or diagram with text. The text wraps around the
graphic. Text wrap is also called *text flow.*

⇒ See also WORD PROCESSING.

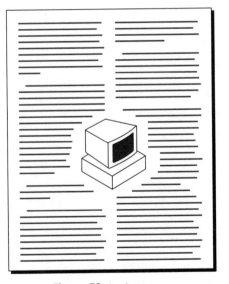

Figure 78: **text wrap**

TFT Abbreviation of *t(hin) f(ilm) t(ransistor)*, a type of LCD flat-panel display screen, in which each pixel is controlled by from one to four transistors. The TFT technology provides the best resolution of all the flat-panel techniques, but it is also the most expensive. TFT screens are sometimes called *active-matrix LCDs*.

⇒ See also ACTIVE-MATRIX DISPLAY; CSTN; FLAT-PANEL DISPLAY; LCD.

TFTP Abbreviation of *T(rivial) F(ile) T(ransfer) P(rotocol)*, a simple form of the file transfer protocol (FTP). TFTP uses the User Datagram Protocol (UDP)and provides no security features. It is often used by servers to boot diskless workstations, X-terminals, and routers.

⇒ See also FTP.

The Open Group An international consortium of computer and software manufacturers and users dedicated to advancing multivendor technologies. The Open Group was formed in February, 1996, by merging two previously independent groups—the *Open Software Foundation (OSF)* and *X/Open Company Ltd.* One of the most important technologies fostered by The Open Group is *DCE*.

⇒ See also DCE; OPEN ARCHITECTURE.

thermal printer A type of printer that produces images by pushing electrically heated pins against special heat-sensitive paper. Thermal printers are inexpensive and are used in most calculators and some low-end fax machines. They produce low-quality print, and the paper tends to curl and fade.

⇒ See also FAX MACHINE; PRINTER.

thin client In client/server applications, a client designed to be especially small so that the bulk of the data processing occurs on the server. The term *thin client* is an especially popular buzzword now because it serves as a symbol dividing the computer industry into two camps. On one side is a group led by Netscape and Sun Microsystems advocating Java-based thin clients running on network computers. The other side, championed by Microsoft and Intel, is pushing ever-larger applications running locally on desktop computers.

   Although the term *thin client* usually refers to software, it is increasingly used for computers, such as network computers and Net PCs, that are designed to serve as the clients for client/server architectures. A thin client is a network computer without a hard disk drive, whereas a fat client includes a disk drive.

⇒ See also CLIENT; CLIENT/SERVER ARCHITECTURE; JAVA; NC; NETWORK COMPUTER; WINFRAME.

thin film transistor See TFT.

ThinNet Same as 10BASE2.

third normal form See under NORMALIZATION.

1394 Short for *IEEE 1394*.

3480, 3490 The IBM designation for families of half-inch magnetic tape drives typically used on mainframes and AS/400s. The 3480 drives use 18-track cartridges at 38000 bpi (bits per inch) to yield 200MB. The 3490 uses built-in compression to obtain 400MB. The 3490e records 36 tracks and uses longer tape to hold 800MB. Tape libraries are available that hold from a handful to thousands of cartridges.

The 3490 drives provide transfer rates of at least 3MB per second. Drives are available that use the ESCON and Fast SCSI-2 interfaces to obtain up to 20MB/sec.

⇒ See also BACKUP; TAPE.

32-bit Refers to the number of bits that can be processed or transmitted in parallel, or the number of bits used for single element in a data format. The term is often applied to the following:

Microprocessor: indicates the width of the registers. A 32-bit microprocessor can process data and memory addresses that are represented by 32 bits.

Bus: indicates the number of wires in the bus. A 32-bit bus transmits 32 bits in parallel.

Graphics device, such as a scanner or digital camera: Specifies the number of bits used to represent each pixel. Typically 24 bits are used for color and the remaining 8 bits are used for control information.

Operating system: Refers primarily to the number of bits used to represent memory addresses.

Applications: indicates how a program has been compiled. Programs written for Windows can be compiled to run either as 16-bit applications (for Windows 3.x) or as 32-bit applications (Windows 9x and NT).

⇒ See also 16-BIT; BIT; BUS; REGISTER.

thrash To make a lot of movements while accomplishing little. In the context of computer systems, *thrashing* usually refers to virtual memory operating systems that are spending most of their time moving data in and out of virtual memory (swapping pages) rather than actually executing programs.

A sure sign that your computer is thrashing is when an application stops responding but the disk drive light keeps blinking on and off. Thrashing is generally caused by too many processes competing for scarce memory resources. To temporarily stop thrashing, you need to terminate one or more applications. To stop it permanently, you need to install more main memory.

⇒ See also PAGING; SWAP; VIRTUAL MEMORY.

thread 1. In on-line discussions, a series of messages that have been posted as replies to one another. A single forum or conference typically contains many threads covering different subjects. By reading each message in a thread, one after the other, you can see how the discussion has evolved. You can start a new thread by posting a message that is not a reply to an earlier message. **2.** In programming, a part of a program that can execute independently of other parts. Operating systems that support multithreading enable programmers to design programs whose threaded parts can execute concurrently.

⇒ See also FORUM; MULTITHREADING; ONLINE SERVICE.

3COM One of the largest networking companies in the world. The name is derived from the prefixes of three terms—com(puter), com(munication), and com(patibility). The company was founded in 1979 by Dr. Robert Metcalfe, one of the co-inventors of Ethernet.

3COM offers a wide array of products, with special emphasis on hubs, switches, routers, modems, and NICs.

⇒ See also CISCO SYSTEMS; HUB; ROUTER; SWITCH.

3-D audio A technique for giving more depth to traditional stereo sound. Typically, *3-D sound*, or *3-D audio*, is produced by placing a device in a room with stereo speakers. The device dynamically analyzes the sound coming from the speakers and sends feedback to the sound system so that it can readjust the sound to give the impression that the speakers are farther apart.

3-D audio devices are particularly popular for improving computer audio where the speakers tend to be small and close together. There are a number of 3-D audio devices that attach to a computer's sound card.

⇒ See also MULTIMEDIA; SOUND CARD.

3D graphics See 3-D GRAPHICS.

3-D graphics The field of computer graphics concerned with generating and displaying three-dimensional objects in a two-dimensional space (e.g., the display screen). Whereas pixels in a two-dimensional graphic have the properties of position, color, and brightness, 3-D pixels include a depth property that indicates where the point lies on an imaginary z-axis. When many 3-D pixels are combined, each with its own depth value, the result is a three-dimensional surface, called a *texture*. In addition to textures, 3-D graphics also supports multiple objects interacting with one another. For example, a solid object may partially hide an object behind it. Finally, sophisticated 3-D graphics use techniques such as ray tracing to apply realistic shadows to an image.

Converting information about 3-D objects into a bit map that can be displayed is known as *rendering* and requires considerable memory and processing power. In the past, 3-D graphics was available only on powerful workstations, but now 3-D graphics accelerators are commonly found in personal computers. The graphics accelerator contains memory and a specialized microprocessor to handle many of the 3-D rendering operations.

⇒ See also 3-D SOFTWARE; AGP; ANIMATION; GRAPHICS; GRAPHICS ACCELERATOR; RAY TRACING; RENDER; TEXTURE; Z-BUFFER; Z-BUFFERING.

three-dimensional spreadsheet A spreadsheet program that allows you to arrange data as a stack of tables, each of which has the same shape and size. You can analyze a single table or an entire group of tables.

⇒ See also SPREADSHEET.

3DO A technology that supports photo-realistic graphics, full-motion video, and CD-quality sound. The first applications of this technology were stand-alone devices used for playing games, but the technology is beginning to find its way into PCs in the form of expansion boards.

⇒ See also EXPANSION BOARD; MULTIMEDIA.

3-D software The category of software that represents three-dimensional objects on a computer. This includes CAD/CAM, computer games, and animation packages.

⇒ See also 3-D GRAPHICS; AGP; ANIMATION; DIRECT3D; MODELING; NURBS; OPENGL; RENDER; TEXTURE.

3-D sound Same as 3-D AUDIO.

3-D spreadsheet See THREE-DIMENSIONAL SPREADSHEET.

386 Short for the *Intel 80386 microprocessor.*

⇒ See also INTEL MICROPROCESSORS.

386DX See under INTEL MICROPROCESORS.

386SX Short for the *Intel 80386SX microprocessor.*

⇒ See also INTEL MICROPROCESSORS.

three-tier A special type of client/server architecture consisting of three well-defined and separate processes, each running on a different platform:

    1. The user interface, which runs on the user's computer (the *client).*

    2. The functional modules that actually process data. This *middle tier* runs on a server and is often called the *application server.*

    3. A database-management system (DBMS) that stores the data re-

quired by the middle tier. This tier runs on a second server called the *database server.*

The three-tier design has many advantages over traditional two-tier or single-tier designs, the chief ones being:

The added modularity makes it easier to modify or replace one tier without affecting the other tiers.

Separating the application functions from the database functions makes it easier to implement load balancing.

⇒ See also CLIENT/SERVER ARCHITECTURE; LOAD BALANCING; MIDDLEWARE; TP MONITOR; TWO-TIER.

throughput The amount of data transferred from one place to another or processed in a specified amount of time. Data transfer rates for disk drives and networks are measured in terms of throughput. Typically, throughputs are measured in Kbps, Mbps, and Gbps.

⇒ See also DISK DRIVE; ISOCHRONOUS; NETWORK.

thumbnail A miniature display of a page to be printed. Thumbnails enable you to see the layout of many pages on the screen at once. Generally, thumbnails are too small to show the actual text, so *greeking* is used to indicate how the text will look.

⇒ See also DESKTOP PUBLISHING; GREEKING; LAYOUT.

thunk *v* **1.** In PCs, to convert a 16-bit memory address to a 32-bit address, and vice versa. Thunking is necessary because Intel's older 16-bit microprocessors used an addressing scheme called *segmented memory,* whereas their new 32-bit microprocessors use a *flat address space.* Windows 95 supports a thunk mechanism to enable 32-bit programs to call 16-bit DLLs. This is called a *flat thunk.*

On the other hand, 16-bit applications running under Windows 3.x and Windows for Workgroups cannot use 32-bit DLLs unless the 32-bit addresses are converted to 16-bit addresses. This is the function of Win32s and is called a *universal thunk.*

According to folklore, the term *thunk* was coined by the developers of the Algol-60 programming language, who realized late one night that the data type of parameters could be known with a little forethought by the compiler. That is, by the time the compiler processed the parameters, it had already thought of (*thunk*) the data types. The meaning of the term has changed considerably in recent years. —*n* **2.** The operation of converting between a segmented memory address space and a flat address space.

⇒ See also ADDRESS SPACE; WIN32s.

TI See TEXAS INSTRUMENTS.

TI 34010 A video standard from Texas Instruments that supports a resolution of 1,024 by 768. TI 34010 conforms to TI's Graphics Architecture

(TIGA). Unlike IBM's 8514/A, which supports the same resolution, TI 34010 is noninterlaced.

⇒ See also 8514/A; INTERLACING; TEXAS INSTRUMENTS; TEXAS INSTRUMENTS GRAPHICS ARCHITECTURE (TIGA); VIDEO STANDARDS.

TIF See under TIFF.

TIFF Acronym for *t(agged) i(mage) f(ile) f(ormat)*, one of the most widely supported file formats for storing bit-mapped images on personal computers (both PCs and Macintosh computers). Other popular formats are BMP and PCX.
   TIFF graphics can be any resolution, and they can be black and white, grayscaled, or color. Files in TIFF format often end with a .TIF extension.

⇒ See also BIT MAP; GRAPHICS; GRAPHICS FILE FORMATS; GRAY SCALING; PCX.

TIGA See TEXAS INSTRUMENTS GRAPHICS ARCHITECTURE.

tiled windows Windows arranged so that they do not overlap one another. Overlapping windows are often called *overlaid* or *cascading windows*.

⇒ See also CASCADING WINDOWS; OVERLAID WINDOWS; WINDOW.

Tillamook Codename for a low-power version of the Pentium microprocessor designed especially for portable devices. The Tillamook processor is Intel's first chip to be manufactured with a new 0.25-micron process, as opposed to 0.35 microns for previous chips. This means that transistors can be packed together more closely, which reduces the power requirements. The Tillamook chip runs at over 200 MHz and support MMX instructions.

⇒ See also PENTIUM MICROPROCESSOR.

Time Division Multiple Access See TDMA.

Time Division Multiplexing See TDM.

time-out An interrupt signal generated by a program or device that has waited a certain length of time for some input but has not received it. Many programs perform time-outs so that the program does not sit idle waiting for input that may never come. For example, automatic teller machines perform a time-out if you do not enter your personal information number (PIN) quickly enough.

⇒ See also INTERRUPT.

time sharing Refers to the concurrent use of a computer by more than one user—users *share* the computer's time. *Time sharing* is synonymous with *multi-user*. Almost all mainframes and minicomputers are time-sharing systems, but most personal computers and workstations are not.

⇒ See also MAINFRAME; MINICOMPUTER; MULTI-USER.

title bar A bar on top of a window. The title bar contains the name of the file or application. In many graphical user interfaces, including the Macintosh and Microsoft Windows interfaces, you move (*drag*) a window by grabbing the title bar.

⇒ See also DRAG; WINDOW.

TLD Short for *t(op)-l(evel) d(omain)*, and refers to the suffix attached to Internet domain names. There are a limited number of predefined suffixes, and each one represents a top-level domain. Current top-level domains include:

com: commercial businesses; this is the most common TLD
gov: U.S. government agencies
edu: Educational institutions such as universities
org: Organizations (mostly nonprofit)
mil: Military
net: Network organizations
ca: Canada
th: Thailand

With the explosion of the Internet over the last few years, competition for domain names has become fierce. Of all the companies named Acme Inc., for example, only one can have the domain name *Acme.com*. The *Internet Ad Hoc Committee (IAHC)* has addressed this problem by creating six new TLDs:

store: merchants
web: parties emphasizing Web activities
arts: arts and culturally oriented entities
rec: recreation/entertainment sources
info: information services
nom: individuals

⇒ See also DOMAIN NAME; IP ADDRESS.

TNEF Pronounced *tee-neff*, and short for *T(ransport) N(eutral) E(ncapsulation) F(ormat)*, a proprietary format used by the Microsoft Exchange and Outlook e-mail clients when sending messages formatted as rich text format (RTF). When Microsoft Exchange thinks that it is sending a message to another Microsoft e-mail client, it extracts all the formatting information and encodes it in a special TNEF block. It then sends the message in two parts—the text message with the formatting removed and the formatting instructions in the TNEF block. On the receiving side, a Microsoft e-mail client processes the TNEF block and reformats the message.

Unfortunately, most non-Microsoft e-mail clients cannot decipher TNEF blocks. Consequently, when you receive a TNEF-encoded message with a non-Microsoft e-mail client, the TNEF part appears as a long sequence of hexadecimal digits, either in the message itself or as an attached file (usually named *WINMAIL.DAT*). These WINMAIL.DAT files serve no useful purpose, so you can delete them.

⇒ See also E-MAIL CLIENT; RICH TEXT FORMAT.

toggle To switch from one setting to another. The term *toggle* implies that there are only two possible settings and that you are switching from the current setting to the other setting.

A *toggle switch* is a switch that has just two positions. For example, light switches that turn a light on or off are toggle switches. On computer keyboards, the Caps Lock key is a toggle switch because pressing it can have two meanings depending on what the current setting is. If Caps Lock is already on, then pressing the Caps Lock key turns it off. If Caps Lock is off, pressing the Caps Lock key turns it on.

Toggle switches exist in software too. For, example a check box in a dialog box is a toggle switch.

⇒ See also DIP SWITCH; KEYBOARD; SWITCH.

token **1.** In programming languages, a single element of a programming language. For example, a token could be a keyword, an operator, or a punctuation mark. **2.** In networking, a token is a special series of bits that travels around a token-ring network. As the token circulates, computers attached to the network can capture it. The token acts like a ticket, enabling its owner to send a message across the network. There is only one token for each network, so there is no possibility that two computers will attempt to transmit messages at the same time. **3.** In security systems, a small device the size of a credit card that displays a constantly changing ID code. A user first enters a password and then the card displays an ID that can be used to log into a network. Typically, the IDs change every five minutes or so.

A similar mechanism for generating IDs is a smart card.

⇒ See also KEYWORD; OPERATOR; PROGRAMMING LANGUAGE; SMART CARD; TOKEN BUS NETWORK; TOKEN-RING NETWORK.

token bus network A type of local-area network (LAN) that has a bus topology and uses a token-passing mechanism to regulate traffic on the bus. A token bus network is very similar to a token-ring network, the main difference being that the endpoints of the bus do not meet to form a physical ring. Token bus networks are defined by the IEEE 802.4 standard.

⇒ See also BUS NETWORK; IEEE 802 STANDARDS; LOCAL-AREA NETWORK; TOKEN; TOKEN-RING NETWORK; TOPOLOGY.

Token Ring See under TOKEN-RING NETWORK.

token-ring network 1. A type of computer network in which all the computers are arranged (schematically) in a circle. A *token*, which is a special bit pattern, travels around the circle. To send a message, a computer catches the token, attaches a message to it, and then lets it continue to travel around the network. **2.** When capitalized, *Token Ring* refers to the PC network protocol developed by IBM. The IBM Token-Ring specification has been standardized by the IEEE as the IEEE 802.5 standard.

⇒ See also ARCNET; IEEE; IEEE 802 STANDARDS; LOCAL-AREA NETWORK; MAU; NETWORK; TOKEN; TOKEN BUS NETWORK; VTAM.

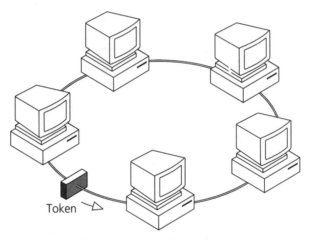

Figure 79: **token-ring network**

toner A special type of ink used by copy machines and laser printers. Toner consists of a dry, powdery substance that is electrically charged so that it adheres to a drum, plate, or piece of paper charged with the opposite polarity.

For most laser printers, the toner comes in a cartridge that you insert into the printer. When the cartridge is empty, you can replace it or have it refilled. Typically, you can print thousands of pages with a single cartridge.

⇒ See also LASER PRINTER.

Top-Level Domain See TLD.

topology The shape of a local-area network (LAN) or other communications system. There are three principal topologies used in LANs.

   bus topology: All devices are connected to a central cable, called the bus or backbone. Bus networks are relatively inexpensive and easy to install for small networks. Ethernet systems use a bus topology.

ring topology: All devices are connected to one another in the shape of a closed loop, so that each device is connected directly to two other devices, one on either side of it. Ring topologies are relatively expensive and difficult to install, but they offer high bandwidth and can span large distances.

star topology: All devices are connected to a central *hub*. Star networks are relatively easy to install and manage, but bottlenecks can occur because all data must pass through the hub.

These topologies can also be mixed. For example, a bus-star network consists of a high-bandwidth bus, called the *backbone*, which connects a collections of slower-bandwidth star segments.

⇒ See also BUS NETWORK; ETHERNET; LOCAL-AREA NETWORK; TOKEN BUS NETWORK.

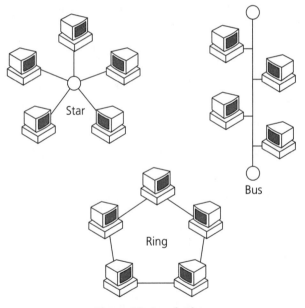

Figure 80: **topologies**

TOPS Acronym for *t(ransparent) o(perating) s(ystem)*, a type of local area network designed by Sun Microsystems that can combine Apple Macintosh computers, PCs, and Sun workstations on the same network. A particular strength of TOPS is that the networking software is *transparent*, meaning that users do not need to adjust to a new operating environment. PC users see their PC interface and Mac users see the Mac interface.

TOPS uses the Macintosh computer's built-in AppleTalk protocol. It is a peer-to-peer network, which means that it does not require any computers to be set aside as file servers. Authorized users can access files from any disk drive connected to the network.

⇒ See also APPLETALK; LOCAL-AREA NETWORK; PEER-TO-PEER ARCHITECTURE; SUN MICROSYSTEMS.

Total Cost of Ownership See TCO.

touchpad A small touch-sensitive pad used as a pointing device on some portable computers. By moving a finger or other object along the pad, you can move the pointer on the display screen. And, on many touchpads, you click by tapping the pad.

⇒ See also DIGITIZING TABLET; POINTING DEVICE.

touch screen A type of display screen that has a touch-sensitive transparent panel covering the screen. Instead of using a pointing device such as a mouse or light pen, you can use your finger to point directly to objects on the screen.

Although touch screens provide a natural interface for computer novices, they are unsatisfactory for most applications because the finger is such a relatively large object. It is impossible to point accurately to small areas of the screen. In addition, most users find touch screens tiring to the arms after long use.

⇒ See also DISPLAY SCREEN; KIOSK; LIGHT PEN; MOUSE; POINT.

touch tablet Same as DIGITIZING TABLET.

tower model Refers to a computer in which the power supply, motherboard, and mass storage devices are stacked on top of one another in a cabinet. This is in contrast to desktop models, in which these components are housed in a more compact box.

The main advantage of tower models is that there are fewer space constraints, which makes installation of additional storage devices easier.

⇒ See also CHASSIS; DESKTOP MODEL COMPUTER.

TPI Short for *t(racks) p(er) i(nch)*, the density of tracks on a disk. For example, double-density 5.25-inch floppies have a TPI of 48, while high-density floppies record 96 TPI. High-density 3.5-inch diskettes are formatted with 135 TPI. Hard disks have TPIs in the thousands.

⇒ See also DISK; TRACK.

TP monitor Short for *t(ransaction) p(rocessing) monitor*, a program that monitors a transaction as it passes from one stage in a process to another. The TP monitor's purpose is to ensure that the transaction processes completely or, if an error occurs, to take appropriate actions.

TP monitors are especially important in three-tier architectures that employ load balancing because a transaction may be forwarded to any of several servers. In fact, many TP monitors handle all the load-balancing operations, forwarding transactions to different servers based on their availability.

⇒ See also CICS; LOAD BALANCING; MIDDLEWARE; THREE-TIER; TRANSACTION PROCESSING.

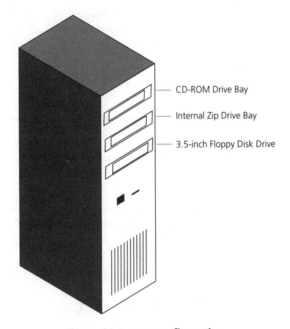

Figure 81: **tower configuration**

traceroute A utility that traces a packet from your computer to an Internet host, showing how many hops the packet requires to reach the host and how long each hop takes. If you're visiting a Web site and pages are appearing slowly, you can use traceroute to figure out where the longest delays are occurring.

The original traceroute is a UNIX utility, but nearly all platforms have something similar. Windows includes a traceroute utility called **tracert**. In Windows 95, you can run **tracert** by selecting **Start→Run...,** and then entering **tracert** followed by the domain name of the host. For example:

tracert www.pcwebopedia.com

Traceroute utilities work by sending packets with low time-to-live (TTL) fields. The TTL value specifies how many hops the packet is allowed before it is returned. When a packet can't reach its destination because the TTL value is too low, the last host returns the packet and identifies itself. By sending a series of packets and incrementing the TTL value with each successive packet, traceroute finds out who all the intermediary hosts are.

⇒ See also HOP; PACKET; PING.

tracert See under TRACEROUTE.

track A ring on a disk where data can be written. A typical floppy disk has 80 (double-density) or 160 (high-density) tracks. For hard disks, each *platter* is divided into tracks, and a single track location that cuts through all platters (and both sides of each platter) is called a cylinder. Hard disks have many thousands of cylinders.

Each track is further divided into a number of *sectors*. The operating system and disk drive remember where information is stored by noting its track and sector numbers.

The density of tracks (how close together they are) is measured in terms of tracks per inch (TPI).

⇒ See also CYLINDER; FORMAT; HARD DISK; INTERLEAVE; SECTOR.

trackball A pointing device. Essentially, a trackball is a mouse lying on its back. To move the pointer, you rotate the ball with your thumb, your fingers, or the palm of your hand. There are usually one to three buttons next to the ball, which you use just like mouse buttons.

The advantage of trackballs over mice is that the trackball is stationary, so it does not require much space to use it. In addition, you can place a trackball on any type of surface, including your lap. For both these reasons, trackballs are popular pointing devices for portable computers.

⇒ See also MOUSE; POINTING DEVICE.

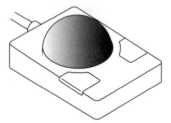

Figure 82: **trackball**

tracks per inch See TPI.

tractor feed A method of feeding paper through an *impact printer*. Tractor-feed printers have two sprocketed wheels on either side of the printer that fit into holes in the paper. As the wheels revolve, the paper is pulled through the printer. Tractor feed is also called *pin feed*.

The other principal form of feeding paper into a printer is *friction feed*, which utilizes plastic or rubber rollers to squeeze a sheet of paper and pull it through the printer.

Tractor-feed printers require special paper (with holes), whereas friction-feed printers can handle most types of cut-sheet paper, including envelopes. Some printers support both types of feeding mechanisms.

⇒ See also FRICTION FEED; PRINTER.

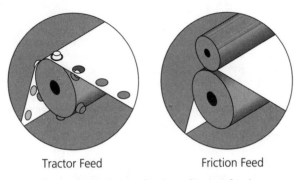

Tractor Feed   Friction Feed

Figure 83: **tractor feed vs. friction feed**

traffic The load on a communications device or system. One of the principal jobs of a system administrator is to monitor traffic levels and take appropriate actions when traffic becomes heavy.

⇒ See also LOAD.

transaction processing A type of computer processing in which the computer responds immediately to user requests. Each request is considered to be a *transaction*. Automatic teller machines for banks are an example of transaction processing.

The opposite of transaction processing is batch processing, in which a batch of requests is stored and then executed all at one time. Transaction processing requires interaction with a user, whereas batch processing can take place without a user's being present.

⇒ See also BATCH PROCESSING; CICS; TP MONITOR; TWO-PHASE COMMIT.

transceiver Short for *trans(mitter)-(re)ceiver*, a device that both transmits and receives analog or digital signals. The term is used most frequently to describe the component in local-area networks (LANs) that actually applies signals onto the network wire and detects signals passing through the wire. For many LANs, the transceiver is built into the network interface card (NIC). Some types of networks, however, require an external transceiver.

In Ethernet networks, a transceiver is also called a *Medium Access Unit (MAU)*.

⇒ See also LOCAL-AREA NETWORK; NETWORK; NETWORK INTERFACE CARD.

transfer rate See DATA TRANSFER RATE.

transistor A device composed of semiconductor material that amplifies a signal or opens or closes a circuit. Invented in 1947 at Bell Labs, transistors have become the key ingredient of all digital circuits, including computers. Today's microprocessors contains tens of millions of microscopic transistors.

Prior to the invention of transistors, digital circuits were composed of vacuum tubes, which had many disadvantages. They were much larger, required more energy, dissipated more heat, and were more prone to failures. It's safe to say that without the invention of transistors, computing as we know it today would not be possible.

⇒ See also CHIP; INTEGRATED CIRCUIT; MOORE'S LAW; SEMICONDUCTOR.

Transmission Control Protocol/Internet Protocol See TCP/IP.

transparent Invisible. In computer software, an action is transparent if it takes place without any visible effect. Transparency is usually considered to be a good characteristic of a system because it shields the user from the system's complexity.

transportable A large portable computer (over 15 pounds). Another term for *transportable* is *luggable*.

⇒ See also LAPTOP COMPUTER; NOTEBOOK COMPUTER; PORTABLE.

trap See under INTERRUPT.

trapezoid distortion See under PINCUSHION DISTORTION.

Travan A magnetic tape technology developed by 3M Corporation that allows for higher data densities. Travan has been standardized by the QIC consortium and is backward compatible with older QIC standards. This means that Travan tape drives can read and write older QIC tapes as well as the newer high-capacity Travan tapes. The following table shows tape capacities (uncompressed) and QIC compatibilities for the different Travan levels, 1 to 4.

Travan Level: Uncompressed Storage: QIC compatibility

TR-1: 400 MB: QIC-80-MC
TR-2: 800 MB: QIC-3010-MC
TR-3: 1.6 GB: QIC-3020-MC

TR-4: 4 GB: QIC-3095-MC

⇒ See also QIC; TAPE; TAPE DRIVE.

tree structure A type of data structure in which each element is attached to one or more elements directly *beneath* it. The connections between elements are called branches. Trees are often called *inverted trees* because they are normally drawn with the *root* at the top.

The elements at the very bottom of an inverted tree (that is, those that have no elements below them) are called *leaves*. Inverted trees are the data structures used to represent hierarchical file structures. In this case, the leaves are files and the other elements above the leaves are directories.

A binary *tree* is a special type of inverted tree in which each element has only two branches below it.

⇒ See also BINARY TREE; BRANCH; DATA STRUCTURE; DIRECTORY; HIERARCHICAL; LEAF.

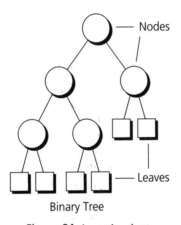

Binary Tree

Figure 84: **tree structure**

Triton Refers to the Intel 430 family of Pentium chipsets. The first in the family, the 430FX, is called the *Triton;* the enhanced 430 HX is called *Triton 2.* The Triton chipset supports the PCI bus and was the first x86 chip to use EDO DRAM. The Triton 2 is one of the fastest Pentium chipsets, with support for multiple CPUs, pipelined burst SRAM cache, memory error checking and correction (ECC), 512 MB of memory, and caching of RAM over 64 MB. The 430VX, a third member of the family, supports USB and uses SDRAM. The VX model is sometimes called *Triton-2* or *Triton-3.*

⇒ See also CHIPSET; INTEL MICROPROCESSORS; PENTIUM MICROPROCESSOR.

Trivial File Transfer Protocol See TFTP.

Trojan horse A destructive program that masquerades as a benign application. Unlike viruses, Trojan horses do not replicate themselves, but they can be just as destructive. One of the most insidious types of Trojan horse is a program that claims to rid your computer of viruses but instead introduces viruses onto your computer.

The term come from a story in Homer's *Iliad*, in which the Greeks give a giant wooden horse to their foes, the Trojans, ostensibly as a peace offering. But after the Trojans drag the horse inside their city walls, Greek soldiers sneak out of the horse's hollow belly and open the city gates, allowing their compatriots to pour in and capture Troy.

⇒ See also VIRUS.

true color Refers to any graphics device or software that uses at least 24 bits to represent each dot or pixel. Using 24 bits means that more than 16 million unique colors can be represented. Because humans can distinguish only a few million colors, this is more than enough to accurately represent any color image.

⇒ See also COLOR DEPTH.

TrueType An outline font technology developed jointly by Microsoft and Apple. Because TrueType support is built into all Windows and Macintosh operating systems, anyone using these operating systems can create documents using TrueType fonts.

Since being introduced in 1991, TrueType has quickly become the dominant font technology for everyday use and is even displacing PostScript in many publishing environments.

⇒ See also FONT; OUTLINE FONT; PostScript.

truncate To cut off the end of something. Usually, the term is used to describe a type of rounding of floating-point numbers. For example, if there are too few spaces for a long floating-point number, a program may truncate the number by lopping off the decimal digits that do not fit: 3.14126 might be truncated to 3.14. Note that truncation always rounds the number down. If the number 1.19999 is truncated to one decimal digit, it becomes 1.1, not 1.2.

⇒ See also FLOATING-POINT NUMBER.

trust hierarchy Same as PUBLIC-KEY INFRASTRUCTURE (PKI).

TSAPI Short for *T(elephony) S(erver) API*, an API developed by Novell and AT&T that enables programmers to build telephony and CTI applications. TSAPI is similar to TAPI, which was developed by Microsoft and Intel. But whereas TAPI has been implemented for the Windows operating system, TSAPI runs on Netware platforms. Another key difference is that TAPI can be used for both client- and server-based applications whereas

TSAPI is strictly a server API.

⇒ See also API; TAPI; TELEPHONY.

TSR Abbreviation of *t(erminate) and s(tay) r(esident)*. Refers to DOS programs that can be *memory resident* (remaining in memory at all times once they are loaded). Calendars, calculators, spell checkers, thesauruses, and notepads are often set up as TSRs so that you can instantly access them from within another program. TSRs are sometimes called *pop-up programs* because they can pop up in applications.

When you install a TSR, you define a special key sequence (usually a control character) that will invoke the TSR program. You can then press this *hot key* from within any application to run the TSR program. Many programs can be installed as a TSR, but TSRs reduce the amount of memory available to other programs. In addition, not all TSRs interact well with one another. You may have difficulties, therefore, if you try to keep too many TSRs in main memory at once.

TSRs are unnecessary with multitasking operating systems such as Windows, OS/2, and the Mac OS.

⇒ See also HOT KEY; LOW MEMORY; MEMORY RESIDENT; MULTITASKING; OPERATING SYSTEM.

TTL 1. Short for *t(ransistor)-t(ransistor) l(ogic)*, a common type of digital circuit in which the output is derived from two transistors. The first semiconductors using TTL were developed by Texas Instruments in 1965. The term is commonly used to describe any system based on digital circuitry, as in *TTL monitor*. **2.** Short for *Time to Live*, a field in the Internet Protocol (IP) that specifies how many more hops a packet can travel before being discarded or returned.

⇒ See also HOP; IP; SEMICONDUCTOR; TTL MONITOR.

TTL monitor TTL stands for *t(ransistor)-t(ransistor) l(ogic)* and refers to a special type of digital circuit. More commonly, however, *TTL* is used to designate any type of digital input or device. A TTL monitor, therefore, is a monitor that accepts digital input. TTL monitors are consistent with older graphics standards such as MDA, but all newer graphics standards, including VGA, require analog signals.

⇒ See also ANALOG MONITOR; DIGITAL MONITOR; MDA; TTL.

tunneling A technology that enables one network to send its data via another network's connections. Tunneling works by encapsulating a network protocol within packets carried by the second network. For example, Microsoft's PPTP technology enables organizations to use the Internet to transmit data across a virtual private network (VPN). It does this by embedding its own network protocol within the TCP/IP packets carried by the Internet.

Tunneling is also called *encapsulation*.

⇒ See also L2TP; LAYER TWO FORWARDING; PPTP; VPN.

turnkey system A computer system that has been customized for a particular application. The term derives from the idea that the end user can just turn a key and the system is ready to go. Turnkey systems include all the hardware and software necessary for the particular application. They are usually developed by *OEMs [o(riginal) e(quipment) m(anufacturers)]* who buy a computer from another company and then add software and devices themselves.

⇒ See also OEM.

TWAIN Acronym for *T(echnology) [or T(oolkit)] W(ithout) A(n) I(nteresting) N(ame)*, the de facto interface standard for scanners. Nearly all scanners come with a TWAIN driver, which makes them compatible with any TWAIN-supporting software. Unfortunately, not all scanner software is TWAIN-compatible.

⇒ See also DRIVER; OPTICAL SCANNER.

tweak To make small changes that fine-tune a piece of software or hardware. *Tweaking* sometimes refers to changing the values of underlying variables slightly to make the results of a program coincide with desired results. In this case, tweaking is not always a good thing since it undermines the integrity of the program.

⇒ See also DEBUG.

tweening Short for *in-betweening*, the process of generating intermediate frames between two images to give the appearance that the first image evolves smoothly into the second image. Tweening is a key process in all types of animation, including computer animation. Sophisticated animation software enables you to identify specific objects in an image and define how they should move and change during the tweening process.

⇒ See also ANIMATION.

TWIP Short for *twentieth of a point*, a typographical measurement.

⇒ See also POINT.

twisted-pair See TWISTED-PAIR CABLE.

twisted-pair cable A type of cable that consists of two independently insulated wires twisted around each other. One wire carries the signal while the other wire is grounded and absorbs signal interference. Twisted-pair cable is used by older telephone networks and is the least expensive type of local-area network (LAN) cable. Other types of cables used for LANs include coaxial cables and fiber optic cables.

⇒ See also 10BaseT; CDDI; COAXIAL CABLE; FIBER OPTICS; LOCAL-AREA NETWORK.

286 Short for the Intel 80286 microprocessor.

⇒ See also INTEL MICROPROCESSORS.

two-phase commit A feature of transaction processing systems that enables databases to be returned to the pre-transaction state if some error condition occurs. A single transaction can update many different databases. The two-phase commit strategy is designed to ensure that either all the databases are updated or none of them, so that the databases remain synchronized.

Database changes required by a transaction are initially stored temporarily by each database. The transaction monitor then issues a "pre-commit" command to each database that requires an acknowledgment. If the monitor receives the appropriate response from each database, the monitor issues the "commit" command, which causes all databases to simultaneously make the transaction changes permanent.

⇒ See also DISTRIBUTED DATABASE; TRANSACTION PROCESSING.

two-tier Refers to client/server architectures in which the user interface runs on the client and the database is stored on the server. The actual application logic can run on either the client or the server. A newer client/server architecture, called a three-tier architecture, introduces a *middle tier* for the application logic.

⇒ See also CLIENT/SERVER ARCHITECTURE; THREE-TIER.

Tymnet One of the largest public data networks (PDNs) in the United States. Tymnet is owned by MCI. A competing network, called *Telenet,* is owned by U.S. Sprint Communications Corporation.

⇒ See also NETWORK.

type *v* **1.** To enter characters by pressing keys on the keyboard. **2.** In DOS, OS/2, and many other operating systems, the TYPE command causes a file to appear on the display screen. —*n* **3.** Short for *data type.*

⇒ See also DATA TYPE.

typeface A design for a set of characters. Popular typefaces include Times Roman, Helvetica, and Courier. The typeface represents one aspect of a *font.* The font also includes such characteristics as size, weight, italics, and so on.

There are two general categories of typefaces: *serif* and *sans serif.* Sans serif typefaces are composed of simple lines, whereas serif typefaces use small decorative marks to embellish characters and make text, in theory, easier to read. Helvetica is a sans serif type and Times Roman is a serif type.

⇒ See also FONT; FONT FAMILY.

Serif   Sans Serif

Figure 85: **typefaces**

typesetter Same as IMAGESETTER.

UART Pronounced *u-art,* and short for *universal asynchronous receiver-transmitter,* the UART is a computer component that handles asynchronous serial communication. Every computer contains a UART to manage the serial ports, and all internal modems have their own UART.

As modems have become increasingly fast, the UART has come under greater scrutiny as the cause of transmission bottlenecks. If you are purchasing a fast external modem, make sure that the computer's UART can handle the modem's maximum transmission rate. The newer 16550 UART contains a 16-byte buffer, enabling it to support higher transmission rates than the older 8250 UART.

⇒ See also ASYNCHRONOUS; DTE; SERIAL PORT.

UDMA Short for *U(ltra)* **DMA**.

UDP Short for *U(ser) D(atagram) P(rotocol),* a connectionless protocol that, like TCP, runs on top of IP networks. Unlike TCP/IP, UDP/IP provides very few error recovery services, offering instead a direct way to send and receive datagrams over an IP network. It's used primarily for broadcasting messages over a network.

⇒ See also CONNECTIONLESS; IP; IPX; RTP; TCP/IP.

UDP/IP See under UDP.

UIDE Short for *U(ltra)* **IDE**. Same as ATA-3.

ULSI Abbreviation of *u(ltra) l(arge) s(cale) i(ntegration),* which refers loosely to placing more than about one million circuit elements on a single chip. The Intel 486 and Pentium microprocessors, for example, use ULSI technology. The line between VLSI and ULSI is vague.

⇒ See also CHIP; PENTIUM MICROPROCESSOR.

Ultra2 SCSI See under SCSI.

Ultra ATA The newest version of the AT Attachment (ATA) standard, which supports burst mode data transfer rates of 33.3 MBps. To take advantage of these high speeds, your computer must also be equipped with Ultra DMA, a protocol that supports faster data transfer rates to and from hard disk drives.

⇒ See also ATA; Uʟᴛʀᴀ DMA.

Ultra DMA A protocol developed by Quantum Corporation and Intel that supports burst mode data transfer rates of 33.3 MBps. This is twice as fast as the previous disk drive standard for PCs and is necessary to take advantage of new, faster Ultra ATA disk drives.

The official name for the protocol is *Ultra DMA/33*. It's also called *UDMA, UDMA/33,* and *DMA mode 33*.

⇒ See also Uʟᴛʀᴀ ATA.

ultra large scale integration See ULSI.

Ultra SCSI See under SCSI.

UML Short for *U(nified) M(odeling) L(anguage)*, a general-purpose notational language for specifying and visualizing complex software, especially large, object-oriented projects. UML builds on previous notational methods such as Booch, OMT, and OOSE. It is being developed under the auspices of the Open Management Group (OMG).

⇒ See also ᴏʙᴊᴇᴄᴛ-ᴏʀɪᴇɴᴛᴇᴅ ᴘʀᴏɢʀᴀᴍᴍɪɴɢ; sᴏғᴛᴡᴀʀᴇ ᴇɴɢɪɴᴇᴇʀɪɴɢ.

UNC Short for *U(niversal) N(aming) C(onvention)* or *U(niform) N(aming) C(onvention)*, a PC format for specifying the location of resources on a local area network (LAN). UNC uses the following format:

\\server-name\shared-resource-pathname

So, for example, to access the file *test.txt* in the directory *examples* on the shared server *silo,* you would write:

\\silo\examples\test.txt

You can also use UNC to identify shared peripheral devices, such as printers. The idea behind UNC is to provide a format so that each shared resource can be identified with a unique address.

UNC is supported by Windows and many network operating systems (NOSs).

⇒ See also ᴅɪʀᴇᴄᴛᴏʀʏ sᴇʀᴠɪᴄᴇ; ᴘᴀᴛʜɴᴀᴍᴇ; ʀᴇsᴏᴜʀᴄᴇ.

underflow Refers to the condition that occurs when a computer attempts to represent a number that is too small for it (that is, a number too close to zero). Programs respond to underflow conditions in different ways. Some report an error, while others approximate as best they can and continue processing. For example, if your computer supports 8 decimal places of precision and a calculation produces the number 0.000000005, an underflow condition occurs.

⇒ See also ғʟᴏᴀᴛɪɴɢ-ᴘᴏɪɴᴛ ɴᴜᴍʙᴇʀ; ᴏᴠᴇʀғʟᴏᴡ ᴇʀʀᴏʀ.

undo To return to a previous state by *undoing* the effects of one or more commands. The undo command is a valuable feature supported by many software products. It lets you try unknown commands with less risk, because you can always return to the previous state. Also, if you accidentally press the wrong function key, you can undo your mistake.

Many programs allow you to undo an unlimited number of commands. Each time you press the undo key, the previous command is undone. You can roll back an entire editing session this way. Other programs impose a limit on the number of commands you can undo.

⇒ See also COMMAND.

undocumented Refers to features that are not described in the official documentation of a product. This lack of documentation can occur for a variety of reasons, including oversight. More often, though, undocumented features are features that were included because they were useful to the programmers developing the product but were deemed either unnecessary or potentially dangerous to end users. Undocumented features can also include untested features that will be officially supported in a future release of the product.

⇒ See also DOCUMENTATION.

Unicode A standard for representing characters as integers. Unlike ASCII, which uses 8 bits for each character, Unicode uses 16 bits, which means that it can represent more than 65,000 unique characters. This is a bit of overkill for English and European languages, but it is necessary for some other languages, such as Chinese and Japanese. Many analysts believe that as the software industry becomes increasingly global, Unicode will eventually supplant ASCII as the standard character coding format.

⇒ See also ASCII; CHARACTER; CHARACTER SET; NTFS.

Unified Modeling Language See UML.

Uniform Naming Convention See UNC.

Uniform Resource Identifier See URI.

Uniform Resource Locator See URL.

uninterruptible power supply See UPS.

universal asynchronous receiver-transmitter See UART.

Universal Naming Convention See UNC.

Universal Serial Bus See USB.

UNIX Pronounced *yoo-niks*, a popular *multi-user, multitasking* operating system developed at Bell Labs in the early 1970s. Created by just a handful of programmers, UNIX was designed to be a small, flexible system used exclusively by programmers. Although it has matured considerably over the years, UNIX still betrays its origins by its cryptic command names and its general lack of user-friendliness. This is changing, however, with graphical user interfaces such as MOTIF.

UNIX was one of the first operating systems to be written in a high-level programming language, namely C. This meant that it could be installed on virtually any computer for which a C compiler existed. This natural portability combined with its low price made it a popular choice among universities. (It was inexpensive because antitrust regulations prohibited Bell Labs from marketing it as a full-scale product.)

Bell Labs distributed the operating system in its source language form, so anyone who obtained a copy could modify and customize it for his own purposes. By the end of the 1970s, dozens of different versions of UNIX were running at various sites.

After its breakup in 1982, AT&T began to market UNIX in earnest. It also began the long and difficult process of defining a standard version of UNIX. To date, there are two main dialects of UNIX: one produced by AT&T known as *System V* and one developed at Berkeley University and known as *BSD4.x,* x being a number from 1 to 3.

Due to its portability, flexibility, and power, UNIX has become the leading operating system for workstations. Historically, it has been less popular in the personal computer market, but the emergence of a new version called *Linux* is revitalizing UNIX across all platforms.

⇒ See also A/UX; AIX; BSDI; C; DAEMON; FreeBSD; GNU; LINUX; MULTI-TASKING; NFS; OPERATING SYSTEM; OS/2; POSIX; SOLARIS; SUN MICROSYSTEMS; VMS.

Unix-to-Unix Copy See UUCP.

unpack To convert a packed file into its original form. A packed file is a file that has been compressed to take up less storage area.

⇒ See also DATA COMPRESSION.

Unshielded Twisted Pair See UTP.

upgrade A new version of a software or hardware product designed to replace an older version of the same product. Typically, software companies sell upgrades at a discount to prevent users from switching to other products. In most cases, you must prove you own an older version of the product to qualify for the upgrade price. In addition, the installation routines for upgrades often check to make sure that an older version is already installed on your computer; if not, you cannot install the upgrade.

In the 1990s, software companies began offering *competitive upgrades,* which means that you can buy a program at a discount if you can prove that you own a competing program.

⇒ See also ESD; TCO.

upload To transmit data from a computer to a bulletin board service, mainframe, or network. For example, if you use a personal computer to log on to a network and you want to send files across the network, you must upload the files from your PC to the network.

⇒ See also BULLETIN BOARD SYSTEM; DOWNLOAD; NETWORK; ONLINE SERVICE.

uppercase Uppercase characters are capital letters; *lowercase characters* are small letters. For example, *box* is in lowercase while *BOX* is in uppercase. The term is a vestige of the days when typesetters kept capital letters in a box above the lowercase letters.

A program that distinguishes between uppercase and lowercase is said to be case sensitive.

⇒ See also CAPS LOCK KEY; CASE SENSITIVE; LOWERCASE.

upper memory Same as HIGH MEMORY.

UPS Abbreviation of *u(ninterruptible) p(ower) s(upply)*, a power supply that includes a battery to maintain power in the event of a power outage. Typically, a UPS keeps a computer running for several minutes after a power outage, enabling you to save data that is in RAM and shut down the computer gracefully. Many UPSs now offer a software component that enables you to automate backup and shutdown procedures in case there's a power failure while you're away from the computer.

There are two basic types of UPS systems: *s(tandby) p(ower) s(ystems) (SPSs)* and *on-line* UPS systems. An SPS monitors the power line and switches to battery power as soon as it detects a problem. The switch to battery, however, can require several milliseconds, during which time the computer is not receiving any power. Standby power systems are sometimes called *Line-interactive UPSes.*

An on-line UPS avoids these momentary power lapses by constantly providing power from its own inverter, even when the power line is functioning properly. In general, on-line UPSs are much more expensive than SPSs.

⇒ See also POWER SUPPLY.

upward compatible Refers to software that runs not only on the computer for which it was designed but also on newer and more powerful models. For example, a program designed to run on an Intel 386 microprocessor, that also runs on a Pentium is upward compatible. Upward compatibility is important because it means you can move to a newer, larger, and more sophisticated computer without converting your data or replacing your software.

In contrast to upward compatibility, *downward (backward) compatible* means that a program runs not only on the computer for which it was designed but also on smaller and older models. For example, a program designed to run under MS-DOS 6.0, that also works under MS-DOS 5.0 is downward compatible.

Upward compatibility is sometimes called *forward compatibility.*

⇒ See also BACKWARD COMPATIBLE; COMPATIBLE; DOS.

URI Short for *U(niform) R(esource) I(dentifier)*, the generic term for all types of names and addresses that refer to objects on the World Wide Web. A URL is one kind of URI.

⇒ See also URL.

URL Abbreviation of *U(niform) R(esource) L(ocator)*, the global address of documents and other resources on the World Wide Web.

The first part of the address indicates what protocol to use, and the second part specifies the IP address or the domain name where the resource is located.

For example, the two URLs below point to two different files at the domain *sandybay.com.* The first specifies an executable file that should be fetched using the FTP protocol; the second specifies a Web page that should be fetched using the HTTP protocol:

ftp://www.microsoft.com/stuff.exe
http://www.pcwebopedia.com/index.html

⇒ See also ADDRESS; INTERNET; PURL; URI; WORLD WIDE WEB.

USB Short for *U(niversal) S(erial) B(us)*, a new external bus standard that supports data transfer rates of 12 Mbps (12 million bits per second). A single USB port can be used to connect up to 127 peripheral devices, such as mice, modems, and keyboards. USB also supports *Plug-and-Play* installation and *hot plugging*.

Starting in 1996, a few computer manufacturers started including USB support in their new machines. Since the release of Intel's 440LX chipset in 1997, USB has become more widespread. It is expected eventually to completely replace serial and parallel ports.

⇒ See also ACCESS.BUS; BUS; DEVICE BAY; HOT PLUGGING; IEEE 1394; PARALLEL PORT; PCMCIA; SERIAL PORT.

USENET A worldwide bulletin board system that can be accessed through the Internet or through many online services. The USENET contains more than 14,000 forums, called *newsgroups*, that cover every imaginable interest group. It is used daily by millions of people around the world.

⇒ See also BULLETIN BOARD SYSTEM; FORUM; INTERNET; NNTP.

user An individual who uses a computer. This includes expert programmers as well as novices. An *end user* is any individual who runs an application program.

⇒ See also APPLICATION; END USER.

User Datagram Protocol See UDP.

user-friendly Refers to anything that makes it easier for novices to use a computer. Menu-driven programs, for example, are considered more user-friendly than command-driven systems. Graphical user interfaces (GUIs) are also considered user-friendly. On-line help systems are another feature of user-friendly programs.

Although the term *user-friendly* represents an important concept, it has been so overused that it has become something of a cliché.

⇒ See also GRAPHICAL USER INTERFACE.

user group A group of individuals with common interests in some aspect of computers. Some user groups cover nearly everything with subgroups (called *SIGs*) for more specialized interests, while others concentrate on a particular area, such as computer graphics, or a particular application.

Nearly every major city in the U.S. has many user groups that meet to share ideas. Joining a local user group is a particularly good way for computer novices to get free expert advice.

⇒ See also SIG.

user interface The junction between a user and a computer program. An interface is a set of commands or menus through which a user communicates with a program. A command-driven interface is one in which you enter commands. A *menu-driven* interface is one in which you select command choices from various menus displayed on the screen.

The user interface is one of the most important parts of any program because it determines how easily you can make the program do what you want. A powerful program with a poorly designed user interface has little value. Graphical user interfaces (GUIs) that use windows, icons, and pop-up menus have become standard on personal computers.

⇒ See also COMMAND DRIVEN; CUA; FUNCTIONAL SPECIFICATION; GRAPHICAL USER INTERFACE; LOOK-AND-FEEL; SAA; XEROX.

username A name used to gain access to a computer system. Usernames, and often passwords, are required in multi-user systems. In most such systems, users can choose their own usernames and passwords.

Usernames are also required to access some bulletin board and online services.

⇒ See also AUTHENTICATION; BULLETIN BOARD SYSTEM; MULTI-USER; ONLINE SERVICE; PASSWORD.

utility A program that performs a very specific task, usually related to managing system resources. Operating systems contain a number of utilities for managing disk drives, printers, and other devices.

Utilities differ from applications mostly in terms of size, complexity, and function. For example, word processors, spreadsheet programs, and database applications are considered applications because they are large programs that perform a variety of functions not directly related to managing computer resources.

Utilities are sometimes installed as *memory-resident* programs. On DOS systems, such utilities are called *TSRs*.

⇒ See also APPLICATION; TSR.

UTP Short for *U(nshielded) T(wisted) P(air)*, a popular type of cable that consists of two unshielded wires twisted around each other. Due to its low cost, UTP cabling is used extensively for local-area networks (LANs) and telephone connections. UTP cabling does not offer as high bandwidth or as good protection from interference as coaxial or fiber optic cables, but it is less expensive and easier to work with.

⇒ See also CDDI; COAXIAL CABLE; ETHERNET; FIBER OPTICS; LOCAL-AREA NETWORK.

UUCP Short for *U(nix)-to-U(nix) C(o)p(y)*, a Unix utility and protocol that enables one computer to send files to another computer over a direct serial connection or via modems and the telephone system. For most file transfer applications, UUCP has been superseded by other protocols, such as FTP, SMTP, and NNTP.

⇒ See also FTP; UNIX.

Uudecode See under UUENCODE.

Uuencode A set of algorithms for converting files into a series of 7-bit ASCII characters that can be transmitted over the Internet. Originally, *uuencode* stood for *U(nix)-to-U(nix)* **encode**, but it has since become a universal protocol used to transfer files between different platforms such as Unix, Windows, and Macintosh. Uuencoding is especially popular for sending e-mail attachments. Nearly all e-mail applications support uuencoding for sending attachments and *uudecoding* for receiving attachments.

Another popular encoding algorithm is *BinHex*, which is often used for transferring Macintosh files, such as PICT graphics files.

⇒ See also BINHEX; E-MAIL; MIME.

V.22 Pronounced *V-dot-twenty-two,* V.22 is short for the CCITT *V.22* communications standard. See under *CCITT.*

⇒ See also CCITT.

V.22bis Pronounced *V-dot-twenty-two-biss*, V.22bis is short for the CCITT *V.22bis* communications standard. See under *CCITT.*

⇒ See also CCITT.

V.32 Pronounced *V-dot-thirty-two*, V.32 is short for the CCITT *V.32* communications standard. See under *CCITT.*

⇒ See also CCITT.

V.34 Pronounced *V-dot-thirty-four,* V.34 is short for the CCITT V.34 communications standard. See under *CCITT.*

⇒ See also CCITT.

V.35 An ITU standard for high-speed synchronous data exchange. In the U.S., V.35 is the interface standard used by most routers and DSUs that connect to T-1 carriers.

⇒ See also CSU/DSU; ITU.

V.42 Pronounced *V-dot-forty-two*, V.42 is short for the CCITT *V.42* communications standard. See under *CCITT.*

⇒ See also CCITT.

V.90 A standard for 56 Kbps modems approved by the International Telecommunication Union (ITU) in February 1998. The V.90 standard resolves the battle between the two competing 56 Kbps technologies—X2 from 3COM and K56flex from Rockwell Semiconductor. Both manufacturers have announced that their future modems will conform to V.90. In addition, most users who already purchased 56 Kbps modems will be able to apply a software upgrade to make their modems support V.90.

⇒ See also K56FLEX; MODEM; X2.

value-added reseller See VAR.

vanilla Without added features. A "vanilla PC," for example, would be a PC with only standard components.

⇒ See also FEATURE.

vaporware A sarcastic term used to designate software and hardware products that have been announced and advertised but are not yet available.

⇒ See also BLOATWARE; SOFTWARE.

VAR Acronym for *value-added reseller*. Same as OEM (ORIGINAL EQUIPMENT MANUFACTURER).

⇒ See also OEM.

variable A symbol or name that stands for a value. For example, in the expression

$x + y$

x and y are variables. Variables can represent numeric values, characters, character strings, or memory addresses.

Variables play an important role in computer programming because they enable programmers to write flexible programs. Rather than entering data directly into a program, a programmer can use variables to represent the data. Then, when the program is executed, the variables are replaced with real data. This makes it possible for the same program to process different sets of data.

Every variable has a name, called the *variable name*, and a data type. A variable's data type indicates what sort of value the variable represents, such as whether it is an integer, a floating point number, or a character.

The opposite of a *variable* is a constant. Constants are values that never change. Because of their inflexibility, constants are used less often than variables in programming.

⇒ See also CHARACTER STRING; CONSTANT; DATA; DATA TYPE; EXPRESSION; LITERAL.

variable length Refers to anything whose length can vary. For example, in databases, a *variable-length field* is a field that does not have a fixed length. Instead, the field length varies depending on what data are stored in it.

Variable-length fields are useful because they save space. Suppose, for example, that you want to define a NAME field. The length of each NAME field will vary according to the data placed in it. For example, *John Smith* is 10 characters long, but *Thomas Horatio Jefferson* is 24 characters long. With fixed-length fields, you would need to define each field to be long enough to hold the longest name. This would be a waste of space for records that had short names. With variable-length fields, the

NAME field in each record would be just long enough to hold its data. The opposite of *variable length* is *fixed length*.

⇒ See also DATABASE-MANAGEMENT SYSTEM; FIELD; FIXED LENGTH; RECORD.

variable-length record A record that has at least one variable-length field. The length of the entire record, therefore, varies according to what data are placed in the variable-length field.

⇒ See also FIELD; FIXED LENGTH; RECORD; VARIABLE LENGTH.

VAX Short for *V(irtual) A(ddress) (e)X(tension)*, Digital Equipment Corporation's successor to its PDP-11 line of minicomputers. As its name implies, VAX systems feature an operating system, VMS, that supports virtual memory.

The VAX was introduced in 1977 and reached its pinnacle of success in the mid-1980s. In the past decade, it has been eclipsed by RISC-based workstations, including DEC's own line of Alpha stations. However, DEC still sells VAXes, though it now calls them servers rather than minicomputers.

⇒ See also DEC; MINICOMPUTER; VMS.

VB Short for *Visual Basic*.

vBNS Short for *v(ery) high-speed B(ackbone) N(etwork) S(ervice)*, an experimental wide-area network backbone sponsored by the National Science Foundation (NSF) and implemented by MCI. vNBS has replaced NSFnet and is designed to serve as a platform for testing new, high-speed Internet technologies and protocols. It currently links several Supercomputer Centers (SCCs) and Network Access Points (NAPs) at OC-12 speeds (622 Mbps). Future versions will support data, voice and video traffic at 2.5 Gbps.

⇒ See also BACKBONE; I2; INTERNET; NGI INITIATIVE.

VBScript Short for *Visual Basic Scripting Edition*, a scripting language developed by Microsoft and supported by Microsoft's Internet Explorer Web browser. VBScript is based on the Visual Basic programming language but is much simpler. In many ways, it is similar to JavaScript. It enables Web authors to include interactive controls, such as buttons and scrollbars, on their Web pages.

⇒ See also INTERNET EXPLORER; JAVASCRIPT; JSCRIPT; VISUAL BASIC.

VBX Short for *V(isual) B(asic) custom control*, a reusable software component designed for use in many different applications. While VBXs can be used in other environments, they were initially created for developing Windows applications with Visual Basic. An application developer can use a number of selected VBXs to develop an application quickly. While similar to objects, VBXs do not have two of the properties (inheritance and polymorphism) required by true object-oriented systems.

Many different companies offer specialized VBXs for tasks such as controlling instruments or image handling. However, VBXs are being superseded by ActiveX controls, which are more flexible.

⇒ See also COMPONENT; CONTROL; DLL; OCX; VISUAL BASIC.

VCACHE The disk cache system in Windows 95/98. VCACHE replaces the Smartdrive system used in older versions of Windows. Whereas Smart-Drive is a 16-bit driver, VCACHE is a 32-bit driver. VCACHE can dynamically change the size of the disk cache depending on available disk space and application requirements.

⇒ See also CDFS; DISK CACHE; SMARTDRIVE.

VCPI Short for *V(irtual) C(ontrol) P(rogram) I(nterface)*, a specification for managing memory beyond the first megabyte on PCs with 80386 or later processors. VCPI can allocate memory to an application as either expanded or extended memory, as required by the application design. The VCPI standard is supported by some memory managers and DOS extenders.

⇒ See also EXTENDED MEMORY; XMS.

VDT Short for *v(ideo) d(isplay) t(erminal)*. See under MONITOR.

VDT radiation The radiation emitted by video display terminals. Like televisions, computer monitors emit various types of radiation. Since the late 1980s, there has been a public debate about whether this radiation poses a health problem. To date, however, there is no conclusive evidence to settle the question once and for all.

⇒ See also ELF EMISSION; MONITOR.

VDU Short for *v(isual) d(isplay) u(nit)*, the old term for display monitors. The older VDUs included a CRT, a serial port to connect to a main computer, and a keyboard.

⇒ See also CRT; MONITOR.

vector 1. In computer programming, a one-dimensional array. A vector can also mean a pointer. 2. In computer graphics, a line that is defined by its start and end point.

⇒ See also ARRAY; VECTOR GRAPHICS.

vector font Same as SCALABLE FONT.

vector graphics Same as *object-oriented graphics*, refers to software and hardware that use geometrical formulas to represent images. The other method for representing graphical images is through bit maps, in which the image is composed of a pattern of dots. This is sometimes called *raster graphics*. Programs that enable you to create and manipulate vector graphics are called *draw programs*, whereas programs that manipulate bit-mapped images are called *paint programs.*

Vector-oriented images are more flexible than bit maps because they can be resized and stretched. In addition, images stored as vectors look better on devices (monitors and printers) with higher resolution, whereas bit-mapped images always appear the same regardless of a device's resolution. Another advantage of vector graphics is that representations of images often require less memory than bit-mapped images do.

Almost all sophisticated graphics systems, including CADD systems and animation software, use vector graphics. In addition, many printers (Post-Script printers, for example) use vector graphics. Fonts represented as vectors are called *vector fonts, scalable fonts, object-oriented fonts,* and *outline fonts.*

Note that most output devices, including dot-matrix printers, laser printers, and display monitors, are raster devices (plotters are the notable exception). This means that all objects, even vector objects, must be translated into bit maps before being output. The difference between vector graphics and raster graphics, therefore, is that vector graphics are not translated into bit maps until the last possible moment, after all sizes and resolutions have been specified. PostScript printers, for example, have a raster image processor (RIP) that performs the translation within the printer. In their vector form, therefore, graphics representations can potentially be output on any device, with any resolution, and at any size.

⇒ See also AUTOTRACING; BÉZIER CURVE; BIT MAP; BIT-MAPPED GRAPHICS; CGM; DRAW PROGRAM; GRAPHICS; GRAPHICS FILE FORMATS; OBJECT ORIENTED; POST-SCRIPT; RASTER IMAGE PROCESSOR; SCALABLE FONT.

Veronica A search engine for Gopher sites. What Archie is to FTP sites, Veronica is to Gopher sites. Veronica uses a spider to create an index of the files on all Gopher servers. You can then enter search keywords into the Veronica system to search all Gopher sites at once.

⇒ See also GOPHER; JUGHEAD; SEARCH ENGINE.

VersaModule Eurocard bus See VME BUS.

vertical frequency See under REFRESH.

vertical justification A feature supported by some word processors and desktop publishing systems in which the system automatically adjusts the vertical space between lines (the *leading*) so that columns and pages have an even top and bottom margin. This is also called *feathering.*

⇒ See also FEATHERING; JUSTIFICATION; LEADING; WORD PROCESSING.

vertical refresh rate See under REFRESH.

vertical scrolling See SCROLL.

very large-scale integration See VLSI.

VESA Short for *V(ideo) E(lectronics) S(tandards) A(ssociation)*, a consortium of video adapter and monitor manufacturers whose goal is to standardize video protocols. VESA has developed a family of video standards that offer greater resolution and more colors than VGA. These standards are known collectively as Super VGA (SVGA).

⇒ See also DDC; SVGA; VL-Bus.

VESA Local Bus See VL-Bus.

VFAT Short for *V(irtual) F(ile) A(llocation) T(able)*, the file system used in Windows for Workgroups and Windows 95. VFAT is the 32-bit version of the older file allocation table (FAT). Unlike the 16-bit FAT, VFAT supports long filenames.

As of OSR 2 and Windows 98, VFAT has been extended with FAT32.

⇒ See also FILE ALLOCATION TABLE; FILE MANAGEMENT SYSTEM; WINDOWS 95.

VGA Abbreviation of *v(ideo) g(raphics) a(rray)*, a graphics display system for PCs developed by IBM. VGA has become one of the de facto standards for PCs. In text mode, VGA systems provide a resolution of 720 by 400 pixels. In graphics mode, the resolution is either 640 by 480 (with 16 colors) or 320 by 200 (with 256 colors). The total palette of colors is 262,144.

Unlike earlier graphics standards for PCs—MDA, CGA, and EGA—VGA uses analog signals rather than digital signals. Consequently, a monitor designed for one of the older standards will not be able to use VGA.

Since its introduction in 1987, several other standards have been developed that offer greater resolution and more colors (see *SVGA, 8514/A graphics standard,* and *XGA*), but VGA remains the lowest common denominator. All PCs made today support VGA, and possibly some other more advanced standard.

⇒ See also SVGA; VIDEO ADAPTER; ZV PORT.

VGA Plus See under SVGA.

video *adj.* **1.** Refers to recording, manipulating, and displaying moving images, especially in a format that can be presented on a television. **2.** Refers to displaying images and text on a computer monitor. The video adapter, for example, is responsible for sending signals to the display device. —*n* **3.** A recording produced with a video recorder (camcorder) or some other device that captures full motion.

⇒ See also DVI; HYPERMEDIA; INDEO; QUICKTIME; REALVIDEO; S-VIDEO; SHOCKWAVE; VIDEO ADAPTER; VIDEO CAPTURE; VIDEO EDITING; VIDEO FOR WINDOWS; VIDEO OVERLAY; VIDEO STANDARDS; VIDEOCONFERENCING; VoD.

video accelerator Same as GRAPHICS ACCELERATOR.

video adapter A board that plugs into a personal computer to give it display capabilities. The display capabilities of a computer, however, depend on both the logical circuitry (provided in the video adapter) and the display monitor. A monochrome monitor, for example, cannot display colors no matter how powerful the video adapter.

Many different types of video adapters are available for PCs. Most conform to one of the video standards defined by IBM or VESA.

Each adapter offers several different video modes. The two basic categories of video modes are *text* and *graphics*. In text mode, a monitor can display only ASCII characters. In graphics mode, a monitor can display any bit-mapped image. Within the text and graphics modes, some monitors also offer a choice of resolutions. At lower resolutions a monitor can display more colors.

Modern video adapters contain memory, so that the computer's RAM is not used for storing displays. In addition, most adapters have their own graphics coprocessor for performing graphics calculations. These adapters are often called *graphics accelerators*.

Video adapters are also called *video cards, video boards, video display boards, graphics cards,* and *graphics adapters.*

⇒ See also 8514/A; ADAPTER; COLOR DEPTH; DDC; DIRECTDRAW; GRAPHICS ACCELERATOR; MDRAM; MONITOR; PAL; RAMDAC; SGRAM; VIDEO MEMORY; VIDEO MODE; VIDEO STANDARDS; VRAM; WRAM.

video capture Converting analog video signals, such as those generated by a video camera, into a digital format and then storing the digital video on a computer's mass storage device. Video capture from analog devices requires a special video capture card that converts the analog signals into digital form and compresses the data. There are also digital video devices that can capture images and transfer them to a computer via a standard serial or parallel interface.

⇒ See also DIGITAL VIDEO; VIDEO EDITING.

video card Same as VIDEO ADAPTER.

videoconferencing Conducting a conference between two or more participants at different sites by using computer networks to transmit audio and video data. For example, a *point-to-point* (two-person) video conferencing system works much like a video telephone. Each participant has a video camera, microphone, and speakers mounted on his or her computer. As the two participants speak to each other, their voices are carried over the network and delivered to the other's speakers, and whatever images appear in front of the video camera appear in a window on the other participant's monitor.

Multipoint videoconferencing allows three or more participants to sit in a virtual conference room and communicate as if they were sitting right next to one another. Until the mid-1990s, the hardware costs made videoconferencing prohibitively expensive for most organizations, but that situation is changing rapidly. Many analysts believe that videoconferencing is one of the fastest-growing segments of the computer industry.

⇒ See also APPLICATION SHARING; COMMON INTERMEDIATE FORMAT; CU-SEEME; DISTANCE LEARNING; GEOPORT; H.323; H.324; QCIF; RTP; TELECONFERENCE; WORKGROUP COMPUTING.

video display board Same as VIDEO ADAPTER.

video editing The process of manipulating video images. Once the province of expensive machines called *video editors,* video editing software is now available for personal computers and workstations. Video editing includes cutting segments (*trimming*), re-sequencing clips, and adding transitions and other special effects.

⇒ See also DIGITAL VIDEO; MPEG; SGI; VIDEO CAPTURE.

Video Electronics Standards Association See VESA.

Video for Windows A format developed by Microsoft Corporation for storing video and audio information. Files in this format have an AVI extension. AVI files are limited to 320 by 240 resolution, and 30 frames per second, neither of which is adequate for full-screen, full-motion video. However, Video for Windows does not require any special hardware, making it the lowest common denominator for multimedia applications. Many multimedia producers use this format because it allows them to sell their products to the largest base of users.

Video for Windows supports several data compression techniques, including RLE, Indeo, and Cinepak. A competing software-only video format is QuickTime.

⇒ See also CODEC; MPEG; QUICKTIME.

Video Graphics Array See VGA.

video memory RAM installed on a video adapter. Before an image can be sent to a display monitor, it is first represented as a bit map in an area of video memory called the *frame buffer.* The amount of video memory, therefore, dictates the maximum resolution and color depth available (see table below).

With a conventional video adapter, the bit map to be displayed is first generated by the computer's microprocessor and then sent to the frame buffer. Most modern video adapters, however, are actually graphics accelerators. This means that they have their own microprocessors that are capable of manipulating bit maps and graphics objects. A small amount of memory is reserved for these operations as well.

Because of the demands of video systems, video memory needs to be faster than main memory. For this reason, most video memory is *dual-ported*, which means that one set of data can be transferred between video memory and the video processor at the same time that another set of data is being transferred to the monitor. There are many different types of video memory, including VRAM, WRAM, RDRAM, and SGRAM.

⇒ See also BIT MAP; GRAPHICS ACCELERATOR; MAIN MEMORY; RAMDAC; RDRAM; SGRAM; VIDEO ADAPTER; VRAM; WRAM.

video mode The setting of a video adapter. Most video adapters can run in either *text mode* or *graphics mode*. In text mode, a monitor can display only ASCII characters. In graphics mode, a monitor can display any bit-mapped image. In addition to the text and graphics modes, video adapters offer different modes of resolution and color depth.

⇒ See also GRAPHICS MODE; TEXT MODE; VIDEO ADAPTER.

Table 29
Popular Video Standards for PCs

Video Standard	Resolution	Simultaneous Colors
VGA (Video	640 by 480	16
Graphics Array)	320 by 200	256
SVGA	800 by 600	16
	1,024 by 768	256
	1,280 by 1,024	256
	1,600 by 1,200	256
8514/A	1,024 by 768	256
XGA (Extended	640 by 480	65,536
Graphics Array)	1,024 by 768	256
TI 34010	1,024 by 768	256

Video-on-Demand See VoD.

video overlay The placement of a full-motion video window on the display screen. There are various techniques used to display video on a computer's screen, depending on whether the video source has been digitized or is still in analog NTSC format.

Since computer monitors are generally analog, NTSC video can be merged with signals coming from the video adapter. Increasingly, faster computer buses (PCI, VL-bus, etc.) and faster video buses (Advanced Feature Connector, VM Channel, etc.) allow analog video to be digitized and stored with other binary data for output. Then the video adapter turns it into analog scan lines for the monitor.

⇒ See also NTSC; VIDEO ADAPTER.

video RAM See VRAM.

video standards There are a variety of video standards that define the resolution and colors for displays. Support for a graphics standard is determined both by the monitor and by the video adapter. The monitor must be able to show the resolution and colors defined by the standard, and the video adapter must be capable of transmitting the appropriate signals to the monitor.

Listed here, in approximate order of increasing power and sophistication, are the more popular video standards for PCs. Note that many of these numbers represent only the minimums specified in the standards. Many suppliers of video adapters provide greater resolution and more colors. For more information, refer to the entries for the specific graphics systems.

⇒ See also 8514/A; MCGA; MDA; SVGA; TI 34010; VGA; VIDEO ADAPTER; XGA.

view In database management systems, a view is a particular way of looking at a database. A single database can support numerous different views. Typically, a view arranges the records in some order and makes only certain fields visible. Note that different views do not affect the physical organization of the database.

⇒ See also DATABASE; DATABASE MANAGEMENT SYSTEM; FIELD.

viewer A utility program that enables you to read a file in its *native format.*. A Lotus 1-2-3 viewer, for example, enables you to read Lotus 1-2-3 files. Many shell utilities and file managers include viewers so that you can display different types of files.

⇒ See also FILE MANAGEMENT SYSTEM; FORMAT; SHELL.

virtual Not real. The term *virtual* is popular among computer scientists and is used in a wide variety of situations. In general, it distinguishes something that is merely conceptual from something that has physical reality. For example, *virtual memory* refers to an imaginary set of locations, or addresses, where you can store data. It is imaginary in the sense that the memory area is not the same as the real physical memory composed of transistors. The difference is a bit like the difference between an architect's plans for a house and the actual house. A computer scientist might call the plans a *virtual house.* Another analogy is the difference between the brain and the mind. The mind is a *virtual brain.* It exists conceptually, but the actual physical matter is the brain.

The opposite of virtual is *real, absolute,* or *physical.*

⇒ See also VIRTUAL MACHINE; VIRTUAL MEMORY; VIRTUAL SERVER; VLAN.

virtual circuit A connection between two devices that acts as though it's a direct connection even though it may physically be circuitous. The term is used most frequently to describe connections between two hosts in a packet-switching network. In this case, the two hosts can communicate as though they have a dedicated connection even though the packets might actually travel very different routes before arriving at their destination. A Telnet session is an example of a virtual circuit.

Virtual circuits can be either permanent (called PVCs) or temporary (called SVCs).

⇒ See also PACKET SWITCHING; PVC; SVC.

Virtual Control Program Interface See VCPI.

virtual desktop A feature supported by some notebook computers that enables them to display images on an external monitor at a higher resolution than is supported by the built-in flat-panel display. For example, most flat-panel displays are limited to a maximum resolution of 800 by 600. With the virtual desktop feature, you could connect the computer to an external monitor and enjoy full SVGA (1,024 by 768) resolution.

The term also refers to a feature supported by some video adapters that enables them to provide a desktop larger than what's actually displayed. Only part of the virtual desktop is displayed at any one time, but you can see hidden areas by scrolling the display. It's as if the display screen is a small window overlaid upon a larger desktop.

⇒ See also FLAT-PANEL DISPLAY; NOTEBOOK COMPUTER.

virtual device driver In Windows systems, a special type of device driver that has direct access to the operating system kernel. This allows them to interact with system and hardware resources at a very low level.

In Windows 95, virtual device drivers are often called VxDs because the filenames end with the *.vxd extension.*

⇒ See also DRIVER.

virtual disk Same as RAM DISK.

Virtual File Allocation Table See VFAT.

virtual LAN See VLAN.

virtual machine A self-contained operating environment that behaves as if it is a separate computer. For example, Java applets run in a Java virtual machine (VM) that has no access to the host operating system. This design has two advantages:

System Independence: A Java application will run the same in any Java VM, regardless of the hardware and software underlying the system.

Security: Because the VM has no contact with the operating system, there is little possibility of a Java program's damaging other files or applications.

The second advantage, however, has a downside. Because programs running in a VM are separate from the operating system, they cannot take advantage of special operating system features.

⇒ See also JAVA; JIT; OPERATING ENVIRONMENT; VIRTUAL.

virtual memory An imaginary memory area supported by some operating systems (for example, Windows but not DOS) in conjunction with the hardware. You can think of virtual memory as an alternate set of memory addresses. Programs use these *virtual addresses* rather than real addresses to store instructions and data. When the program is actually executed, the virtual addresses are converted into real memory addresses.

The purpose of virtual memory is to enlarge the *address space*, the set of addresses a program can utilize. For example, virtual memory might contain twice as many addresses as main memory. A program using all of virtual memory, therefore, would not be able to fit in main memory all at once. Nevertheless, the computer could execute such a program by copying into main memory those portions of the program needed at any given point during execution.

To facilitate copying virtual memory into real memory, the operating system divides virtual memory into *pages*, each of which contains a fixed number of addresses. Each page is stored on a disk until it is needed. When the page is needed, the operating system copies it from disk to main memory, translating the virtual addresses into real addresses.

The process of translating virtual addresses into real addresses is called *mapping*. The copying of virtual pages from disk to main memory is known as *paging* or *swapping*.

⇒ See also ADDRESS SPACE; MAIN MEMORY; MEMORY; MMU; OPERATING SYSTEM; PAGE; PAGE FAULT; PAGING; SWAP; THRASH; VIRTUAL.

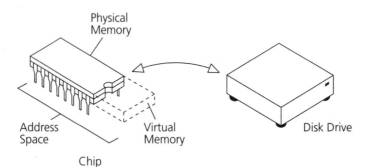

Figure 86: **virtual memory**

Virtual Memory System See VMS.

virtual private network See VPN.

virtual reality An artificial environment created with computer hardware and software and presented to the user in such a way that it appears and feels like a real environment. To "enter" a virtual reality, a user dons special gloves, earphones, and goggles, all of which receive their input from the computer system. In this way, at least three of the five senses are controlled by the computer. In addition to feeding sensory input to the user, the devices also monitor the user's actions. The goggles, for example, track how the eyes move and respond accordingly by sending new video input.

To date, virtual reality systems require extremely expensive hardware and software and are confined mostly to research laboratories.

The term *virtual reality* is sometimes used more generally to refer to any virtual world represented in a computer, even if it's just a text-based or graphical representation.

⇒ See also AVATAR; CYBERSPACE; HMD; MUD; QUICKTIME VR; VIRTUAL; VRML.

Virtual Reality Modeling Language See VRML.

virtual server A server, usually a Web server, that shares computer resources with other virtual servers. In this context, the *virtual* part simply means that it is not a *dedicated* server—that is, the entire computer is not dedicated to running the server software.

Virtual web servers are a very popular way of providing low-cost web hosting services. Instead of requiring a separate computer for each server, dozens of virtual servers can co-reside on the same computer. In most cases, performance is not affected and each web site behaves as if it is being served by a dedicated server. However, if too many virtual servers reside on the same computer, or if one virtual server starts hogging resources, Web pages will be delivered more slowly.

⇒ See also SERVER; VIRTUAL; WEB SERVER.

virus A program or piece of code that is loaded onto your computer without your knowledge and runs against your wishes. Most viruses can also replicate themselves. All computer viruses are made by human beings. A simple virus that can make a copy of itself over and over again is relatively easy to produce. Even such a simple virus is dangerous because it will quickly use all available memory and bring the system to a halt. An even more dangerous type of virus is one capable of transmitting itself across networks and bypassing security systems.

Since 1987, when a virus infected ARPANET, a large network used by the Defense Department and many universities, many antivirus programs have become available. These programs periodically check your computer system for the best-known types of viruses.

Some people distinguish between general viruses and *worms*. A worm is a special type of virus that can replicate itself and use memory but cannot attach itself to other programs.

⇒ See also ANTIVIRUS PROGRAM; ARPANET; BOOTABLE DISKETTE; DATA RECOV-
ERY; HACKER; MACRO VIRUS; MBR; NETWORK; TROJAN HORSE.

VisiCalc The first spreadsheet application, introduced in the late 1970s. The
idea behind VisiCalc was developed by Dan Bricklin, and the actual programming was performed by a friend named Bob Frankston. Bricklin
needed a computer tool to complete repetitive calculations associated
with case studies at the Harvard Business School. After gaining popularity as an Apple application, the product was sold to Lotus Development
Corporation and led to the development of the Lotus 1-2-3 spreadsheet
for the PC in 1983.

⇒ See also LOTUS 1-2-3; SPREADSHEET.

Visual Basic A programming language and environment developed by
Microsoft. Based on the BASIC language, Visual Basic was one of the first
products to provide a graphical programming environment and a paint
metaphor for developing user interfaces. Instead of worrying about syntax
details, the Visual Basic programmer can add a substantial amount of
code simply by dragging and dropping *controls*, such as buttons and
dialog boxes, and then defining their appearance and behavior.

Although not a true object-oriented programming language in the strict-
est sense, Visual Basic nevertheless has an object-oriented philosophy. It
is sometimes called an *event-driven* language because each object can react to different events such as a mouse click.

Since its launch in 1990, the Visual Basic approach has become the
norm for programming languages. Now there are visual environments for
many programming languages, including C, C + +, Pascal, and Java. Visual Basic is sometimes called a Rapid Application Development (RAD)
system because it enables programmers to build prototype applications
quickly.

⇒ See also ACTIVE SERVER PAGES; BASIC; DAO; DELPHI; JET; MICROSOFT; PRO-
GRAMMING LANGUAGE; RAPID APPLICATION DEVELOPMENT; VBSCRIPT; VBX.

Visual Basic custom control See VBX.

Visual Basic Scripting Edition See VBSCRIPT.

Visual C++ An application development tool developed by Microsoft for
C + + programmers. Visual C + + supports object-oriented programming
of 32-bit Windows applications with an integrated development environment (IDE), a C/C + + compiler, and a class library called the Microsoft
Foundation Classes (MFC). The IDE includes an AppWizard, ClassWiz-
ard, and testing features to make programming easier. Visual C + + was
introduced in 1993, and Release 4.0 became available in 1996.

⇒ See also C; C++; IDE; MFC; OBJECT-ORIENTED PROGRAMMING.

visual display unit See VDU.

VLAN Short for *v(irtual) LAN,* a network of computers that behave as if they were connected to the same wire even though they may actually be physically located on different segments of a LAN. VLANs are configured through software rather than hardware, which makes them extremely flexible. One of the biggest advantages of VLANs is that when a computer is physically moved to another location, it can stay on the same VLAN without any hardware reconfiguration.

⇒ See also LOCAL-AREA NETWORK; VIRTUAL.

VLB Short for *V(esa) L(ocal) B(us).*

VL-Bus Short for *V(ESA) L(ocal)-***Bus,** a local bus architecture created by the Video Electronics Standards Association (VESA). Although it was quite popular in PCs made in 1993 and 1994, it has been overshadowed by a competing local bus architecture called PCI.

⇒ See also EXPANSION BUS; LOCAL BUS; PCI.

VLSI Abbreviation of *v(ery) l(arge)-s(cale) i(ntegration),* the process of placing thousands (or hundreds of thousands) of electronic components on a single chip. Nearly all modern chips employ VLSI architectures, or ULSI (ultra large-scale integration). The line between VLSI and ULSI is vague.

⇒ See also CHIP; INTEGRATED CIRCUIT; ULSI.

VM Short for *virtual machine.*

VME See under VME BUS.

VME bus Short for *V(ersa)M(odule) E(urocard) bus.* A 32-bit bus developed by Motorola, Signetics, Mostek, and Thompson CSF. It is widely used in industrial, commercial, and military applications with more than 300 manufacturers of VMEbus products worldwide. VME64 is an expanded version that provides 64-bit data transfer and addressing.

⇒ See also BACKPLANE; BUS.

VMS Short for *V(irtual) M(emory) S(ystem),* a multi-user, multitasking, virtual memory operating system that runs on DEC's VAX and Alpha lines of minicomputers and workstations. VMS was introduced in 1979 along with the first VAX minicomputer. Like the VAX itself, VMS has undergone many changes over the years. DEC now refers to it as *OpenVMS.*

⇒ See also MULTI-USER; MULTITASKING; OPERATING SYSTEM; UNIX; VAX; VIRTUAL MEMORY.

VoD Short for *V(ideo)-o(n)-D(emand),* an umbrella term for a wide set of technologies and companies whose common goal is to enable individuals to select videos from a central server for viewing on a television or computer screen. VoD can be used for entertainment (ordering movies transmitted digitally), education (viewing training videos), and videoconferencing (enhancing presentations with video clips). Although VoD is being used somewhat in all these areas, it is not yet widely implemented. VoD's biggest obstacle is the lack of a network infrastructure that can handle the large amounts of data required by video.

⇒ See also VIDEO.

VOI Short for *V(oice) o(ver the) I(nternet)*; same as *Internet telephony*.

voice mail Refers to e-mail systems that support audio. Users can leave spoken messages for one another and listen to the messages by executing the appropriate command in the e-mail system.

⇒ See also E-MAIL.

Voice over the Internet Same as INTERNET TELEPHONY.

voice recognition The field of computer science that deals with designing computer systems that can recognize spoken words. Note that voice recognition implies only that the computer can take dictation, not that it *understands* what is being said. Comprehending human languages falls under a different field of computer science called *natural language processing*.

A number of voice recognition systems are available on the market. The most powerful can recognize thousands of words. However, they generally require an extended training session during which the computer system becomes accustomed to a particular voice and accent. Such systems are said to be *speaker dependent*.

Many systems also require that the speaker speak slowly and distinctly and separate each word with a short pause. These systems are called *discrete speech* systems. Recently, great strides have been made in *continuous speech* systems—voice recognition systems that allow you to speak naturally. There are now several continuous-speech systems available for personal computers.

Because of their limitations and high cost, voice recognition systems have traditionally been used only in a few specialized situations. For example, such systems are useful in instances when the user is unable to use a keyboard to enter data because his or her hands are occupied or disabled. Instead of typing commands, the user can simply speak into a headset. Increasingly, however, as the cost decreases and performance improves, speech recognition systems are entering the mainstream and are being used as an alternative to keyboards.

⇒ See also ARTIFICIAL INTELLIGENCE; NATURAL LANGUAGE.

VOIP Short for *V(oice) O(ver) IP*. Same as INTERNET TELEPHONY.

volatile memory Memory that loses its contents when the power is turned off. All RAM except the CMOS RAM used for the BIOS is volatile. ROM, on the other hand, is *nonvolatile.*

⇒ See also MEMORY; RAM; ROM.

voltage regulator A small device or circuit that regulates the voltage fed to the microprocessor. The power supply of most PCs generates power at 5 volts, but most microprocessors require a voltage below 3.5 volts. The voltage regulator's job is to reduce the 5-volt signal to the lower voltage required by the microprocessor. Typically, voltage regulators are surrounded by heat sinks because they generate significant heat.

Pentium microprocessors with MMX actually require two voltage regulators—one for the internal (core) voltage, and one for the I/O drivers at 3.3 volts.

Some voltage regulators, particularly those packaged as a voltage regulator module (VRM), are *voltage ID (VID) programmable,* which means that the microprocessor can program the voltage regulator to provide the correct voltage during power-up.

⇒ See also HEAT SINK; MICROPROCESSOR; MOTHERBOARD; POWER SUPPLY; VRM.

voltage regulator module See VRM.

volume A fixed amount of storage on a disk or tape. The term *volume* is often used as a synonym for the storage medium itself, but it is possible for a single disk to contain more than one volume or for a volume to span more than one disk.

⇒ See also DISK; MASS STORAGE.

volume label In DOS systems, the name of a volume (that is, the name of a disk or tape). Specifying a volume label makes it easier to keep track of what kind of data is stored on each medium.

⇒ See also DISK; LABEL; VOLUME.

VON Short for *V(oice) o(n the) N(et).* A coalition of Internet telephony software producers. VON's main goal is to ensure that the telephone companies do not succeed in their bid to outlaw Internet telephony.

VPN Short for *v(irtual) p(rivate) n(etwork),* a *network* that is constructed by using public wires to connect nodes. For example, there are a number of systems that enable you to create networks using the Internet as the medium for transporting data. These systems use encryption and other security mechanisms to ensure that only authorized users can access the network and that the data cannot be intercepted.

⇒ See also L2TP; LAYER TWO FORWARDING; PPTP; TUNNELING.

VRAM Short for *v(ideo)* **RAM**, and pronounced *vee-ram.* VRAM is special-purpose memory used by video adapters. Unlike conventional RAM, VRAM can be accessed by two different devices simultaneously. This enables the RAMDAC to access the VRAM for screen updates at the same time that the video processor provides new data. VRAM yields better graphics performance but is more expensive than normal RAM.

A special type of VRAM, called Windows *RAM (WRAM)*, yields even better performance than conventional VRAM.

⇒ See also GRAPHICS; GRAPHICS ACCELERATOR; MDRAM; MEMORY; MONITOR; PROCESSOR; RAM; SGRAM; VIDEO MEMORY; WRAM.

Table 30
Video RAM Required for Different Resolutions

Resolution	256 colors (8-bit)	65,000 colors (16-bit)	16.7 million colors (24-bit, true color)
640 x 480	512K	1 MB	1 MB
800 x 600	512K	1 MB	2 MB
1,024 x 768	1 MB	2 MB	4 MB
1,152 x 1,024	2 MB	2 MB	4 MB
1,280 x 1,024	2 MB	4 MB	4 MB
1,600 x 1,200	2 MB	4 MB	6 MB

VRM Short for *v(oltage) r(egulator) m(odule)*, a small module that installs on a motherboard to regulate the voltage fed to the microprocessor. Nearly all motherboards have either a built-in voltage regulator or a VRM, the only difference being that the VRM is replaceable.

⇒ See also POWER SUPPLY; VOLTAGE REGULATOR.

VRML Pronounced *ver-mal*, and short for *Virtual Reality Modeling Language*, VRML is a specification for displaying three-dimensional objects on the World Wide Web. You can think of it as the 3-D equivalent of HTML. Files written in VRML have a *.wrl* extension (short for *world*). To view these files, you need a VRML browser or a VRML plug-in to a Web browser.

VRML produces a *hyperspace* (or a *world*), a three-dimensional space that appears on your display screen. And you can figuratively move within this space. That is, as you press keys to turn left, right, up, or down, or go forward or backward, the images on your screen will change to give the impression that you are moving through a real space.

The new VRML 2.0 specification was finalized in August, 1996. It is known officially as ISO/IEC 14772.

⇒ See also BROWSER; CYBERSPACE; HTML; MODELING; QUICKTIME VR; VIRTUAL REALITY; WORLD WIDE WEB.

VSAM Short for *V(irtual) S(equential) A(ccess) M(ethod)*, a file management system used on IBM mainframes. VSAM speeds up access to data in files by using an inverted index (called a *B + tree*) of all records added to each file. Many legacy software systems use VSAM to implement database systems (called *data sets*), though modern relational DBMSs are more efficient and flexible.

⇒ See also FILE MANAGEMENT SYSTEM; LEGACY APPLICATION; MAINFRAME; MVS.

VTAM Abbreviation of *V(irtual) T(elecommunications) A(ccess) M(ethod)*, the software component that controls communications in Systems Network Architecture (SNA) networks. VTAM supports several network protocols, including SDLC and Token Ring.

⇒ See also SNA; TOKEN-RING NETWORK.

VxD See under VIRTUAL DEVICE DRIVER.

W3C Short for *World Wide Web Consortium,* an international consortium of companies involved with the Internet and the Web. The W3C was founded in 1994 by Tim Berners-Lee, the original architect of the World Wide Web. The organization's purpose is to develop open standards so that the Web evolves in a single direction rather than being splintered among competing factions. The W3C is the chief standards body for HTTP and HTML.

⇒ See also HTML; HTTP; WORLD WIDE WEB.

WAIS Short for *Wide Area Information Server,* and pronounced *ways,* a program for finding documents on the Internet. WAIS is rather primitive in its search capabilities.

⇒ See also GOPHER; INTERNET.

wait state A time-out period during which a CPU or bus lies idle. Wait states are sometimes required because different components function at different clock speeds. For example, if the CPU is much faster than the memory chips, it may need to sit idle during some clock cycles so that the memory chips can catch up. Likewise, buses sometimes require wait states if expansion boards run slower than the bus.

A *zero wait state* system is one in which the microprocessor runs at the maximum speed without any time-outs to compensate for slow memory. Wait states can be avoided by using a variety of techniques, including page-mode memory, interleaved memory, a burst mode, and memory caches.

⇒ See also BURST MODE; CACHE; CLOCK SPEED; FPM RAM; INTERLEAVE; LATENCY; PIPELINE BURST CACHE; SDRAM.

WAN See WIDE-AREA NETWORK.

warez Pronounced *wayrz* or *wayrss,* refers to commercial software that has been pirated and made available to the public via a BBS or the Internet. Typically, the pirate (also called a *cracker*) has figured out a way to deactivate the copy-protection or registration scheme used by the software. Note that the use and distribution of warez software is illegal. In contrast, shareware and freeware may be freely copied and distributed.

⇒ See also COPY PROTECTION; FREEWARE; SHAREWARE; SOFTWARE PIRACY.

warm boot Refers to resetting a computer that is already turned on. Resetting it returns the computer to its initial state, and any data or programs in main memory are erased. A warm boot is sometimes necessary when a program encounters an error from which it cannot recover. On PCs, you can perform a warm boot by pressing the Control, Alt, and Delete keys simultaneously. On Macs, you can perform a warm boot by pressing the Restart button.

A cold boot refers to turning a computer on from an off position.

⇒ See also BOOT; COLD BOOT.

WAV The format for storing sound in files developed jointly by Microsoft and IBM. Support for WAV files was built into Windows 95, making it the de facto standard for sound on PCs. WAV sound files end with a . **wav** extension and can be played by nearly all Windows applications that support sound.

⇒ See also AU; MULTIMEDIA.

Wavelength Division Multiplexing See WDM.

wavetable See WAVE TABLE SYNTHESIS.

wave table synthesis A technique for generating sounds from digital signals. Wave table synthesis stores digital samples of sound from various instruments, which can then be combined, edited, and enhanced to reproduce sound defined by a digital input signal. Wave table synthesis reproduces the sound of musical instruments better than Frequency Modulation (FM) synthesis.

The MIDI standard supports a wave table format. Not all sound cards, however, support wave table synthesis.

⇒ See also MIDI; SOUND CARD.

WDM Abbreviation of *W(avelength) D(ivision) M(ultiplexing)*, a type of multiplexing developed for use on optical fiber. WDM modulates each of several data streams onto a different part of the light spectrum. WDM is the optical equivalent of FDM.

⇒ See also FDM; FIBER OPTICS; MULTIPLEX; TDM.

Web Short for *World Wide Web*.

Web Browser See under BROWSER.

webcasting Using the Internet, and the World Wide Web in particular, to broadcast information. Unlike typical surfing, which relies on a pull method of transferring Web pages, webcasting uses push technologies.

⇒ See also BROADCAST; PointCast; PUSH.

WebCrawler A popular Web search engine run by America Online.

⇒ See also ALTA VISTA; EXCITE; INFOSEEK; LYCOS; OPEN TEXT; SEARCH ENGINE.

webcrawler Same as SPIDER.

Webmaster An individual who manages a Web site. Depending on the size of the site, the Webmaster might be responsible for any of the following:

- Making sure that the Web server hardware and software are running properly
- Designing the Web site
- Creating and updating Web pages
- Replying to user feedback
- Creating CGI scripts
- Monitoring traffic through the site

The exponential growth of the World Wide Web has created an unprecedented demand for Webmasters.

⇒ See also CGI; WEB PAGE; WEB SITE.

Web page A document on the World Wide Web. Every Web page is identified by a unique URL (Uniform Resource Locator).

⇒ See also DOM; HOME PAGE; URL; WEB SERVER; WEBMASTER; WORLD WIDE WEB.

Web server A computer that delivers (*serves up*) Web pages. Every Web server has an IP address and possibly a domain name. For example, if you enter the URL *http://www.pcwebopedia.com/index.html* in your browser, this sends a request to the server whose domain name is *pcwebopedia.com*. The server then fetches the page named *index.html* and sends it to your browser.
   Any computer can be turned into a Web server by installing server software and connecting the machine to the Internet. There are many Web server software applications, including public-domain software from NCSA and Apache, and commercial packages from Microsoft, Netscape, and others.

⇒ See also APACHE WEB SERVER; BSDI; CERN; IIS; PROXY SERVER; SERVER; VIRTUAL SERVER; WEB PAGE; WEB SITE; WORLD WIDE WEB.

Web site A site (location) on the World Wide Web. Each Web site contains a home page, which is the first document users see when they enter the site. The site might also contain additional documents and files. Each site is owned and managed by an individual, company, or organization.

⇒ See also E-ZINE; HOME PAGE; WEB SERVER; WEBMASTER; WORLD WIDE WEB.

WebTV A general term for a whole category of products and technologies that enable you to surf the Web on your TV. Most WebTV products today consist of a small box that connects to your telephone line and television. It makes a connection to the Internet via your telephone service and then converts the downloaded Web pages to a format that can be displayed on your TV. These products also come with a remote control device so that you can navigate through the Web.

A future class of WebTV products will not require telephone connections at all but instead will access the Internet directly through the cable TV lines.

⇒ See also CABLE MODEM; OS/9; PC/TV; WORLD WIDE WEB.

what-you-see-is-what-you-get See WYSIWYG.

whiteboard An area on a display screen that multiple users can write or draw on. Whiteboards are a principal component of teleconferencing applications because they enable visual as well as audio communication.

⇒ See also APPLICATION SHARING; TELECONFERENCE.

White Book The specification covering the video CD format.

⇒ See also YELLOW_BOOK.

whitespace Refers to all characters that appear as blanks on a display screen or printer. This includes the space character, the tab character, and sometimes other special characters that do not have a visual form (for example, the bell character and null character).

⇒ See also NULL CHARACTER.

whois An Internet utility that returns information about a domain name or IP address. For example, if you enter a domain name such as *microsoft. com,* whois will return the name and address of the domain's owner (in this case, Microsoft Corporation).

⇒ See also DOMAIN NAME; FINGER; IP ADDRESS.

Wide Area Information Server See WAIS.

wide-area network A computer network that spans a relatively large geographical area. Typically, a WAN consists of two or more local-area networks (LANs).

Computers connected to a wide-area network are often connected through public networks, such as the telephone system. They can also be connected through leased lines or satellites. The largest WAN in existence is the Internet.

⇒ See also BRIDGE; INTERNET; INTERNETWORKING; LOCAL-AREA NETWORK; MAN; NETWORK; PACKET SWITCHING; SMDS.

wide SCSI See under SCSI.

widow 1. In word processing, the last line of a paragraph that appears as the first line of a page. Widows are considered bad form in page layout, so many word processors allow you to avoid them. When the word processor detects a widow, it can end the page one or more lines early so that at least the last two lines from the paragraph start the next page. Some word processors avoid widows by moving all the lines on the page closer together so that the last line can fit on the same page.

The converse of a widow is an *orphan*, the first line of a paragraph appearing as the last line of a page. **2.** The last line of a paragraph that is much shorter than all the other lines in the paragraph.

⇒ See also ORPHAN; PAGINATION; WORD PROCESSING.

wildcard character A special symbol that stands for one or more characters. Many operating systems and applications support wildcards for identifying files and directories. This enables you to select multiple files with a single specification. For example, in DOS and Windows, the asterisk (*) is a wildcard that stands for any combination of letters. The file specification

m*

therefore, refers to all files that begin with *m*. Similarly, the specification

m*.doc

refers to all files that start with *m* and end with *.doc*.

Many word processors also support wildcards for performing text searches.

⇒ See also FILENAME.

Win32 The Windows API for developing 32-bit applications. Win32 is built into Windows 95, Windows 98, and Windows NT, so applications that rely on the API (*Win32 applications*) should run equally well in those environments. It is also possible to run some Win32 applications under older 16-bit versions of windows by installing the Win32s runtime system.

⇒ See also API; WIN32s; WINDOWS; WINDOWS 95; WINDOWS NT.

Win32s Short for *WIN32 s(ubset)*, a software package that can be added to Windows 3.1 and Windows for Workgroups systems to give them the ability to run some 32-bit applications. As the name implies, Win32s is only a subset of the Win32 API used by Windows 95, Windows 98, and Windows NT. The main function performed by Win32s is to convert between 32-bit and 16-bit memory addresses, an operation called *thunking*.

Many applications are designed to run on Win32s-enhanced versions of Windows for performance reasons. When you install such an application on a 16-bit Windows system, the installation procedure automatically installs the Win32s system if necessary.

⇒ See also THUNK; WIN32; WINDOWS.

Win95 Short for *Windows 95*.

Winchester disk drive Another term for hard disk drive. The term *Winchester* comes from an early type of *disk drive* developed by IBM that stored 30MB (megabytes) and had a 30-millisecond access time, so its inventors called it a Winchester in honor of the .30-caliber rifle of the same name. Although modern disk drives are faster and hold more data, the basic technology is the same, so *Winchester* has become synonymous with *hard*.

⇒ See also DISK DRIVE; HARD DISK.

window 1. An enclosed, rectangular area on a display screen. Most modern operating systems and applications have graphical user interfaces that let you divide your display into several windows. Within each window, you can run a different program or display different data.

Windows are particularly valuable in *multitasking environments*, which allow you to execute several programs at once. By dividing your display into windows, you can see the output from all the programs at the same time. To enter input into a program, you simply click on the desired window to make it the foreground window.

Graphical user interfaces, such as the ones supported by the Apple Macintosh or Windows, enable you to set the dimensions and position of each window by moving the mouse and clicking appropriate buttons. Windows can be arranged so that they do not overlap (*tiled windows*) or so they do overlap (*overlaid windows*). Overlaid windows (also called cascading windows) resemble a stack of pieces of paper lying on top of one another; only the topmost window is displayed in full. You can move a window to the top of the stack by positioning the pointer in the portion of the window that is visible and clicking the mouse buttons. This is known as *popping*. You can expand a window to fill the entire screen by selecting the window's *zoom box*.

In addition to moving windows, changing their size, popping, and zooming them, you can also replace an entire window with an icon (this is sometimes called *minimizing*). An icon is a small picture that represents the program running in the window. By converting a window into an icon, you can free up space on the display screen without erasing the window entirely. It is always possible to reconvert the icon into a window whenever you want. **2.** A window can also be a logical view of a file. By moving the window, you can view different portions of the file.

⇒ See also DIALOG BOX; GRAPHICAL USER INTERFACE; ICON; MDI; MICROSOFT WINDOWS; TASKBAR.

Windows When spelled with a capital W, *Windows* is short for *Microsoft Windows*.

⇒ See also MICROSOFT; WIN32S; WINDOWS 98; WINDOWS CE; WINFRAME; WINTEL.

Windows 95 A major release of the Microsoft Windows operating system released in 1995. Windows 95 represents a significant advance over its precursor, Windows 3.1. In addition to sporting a new user interface, Windows 95 also includes a number of important internal improvements. Perhaps most important, it supports 32-bit applications, which means that applications written specifically for this operating system should run much faster. And although Windows 95 can run older Windows and DOS applications, it has essentially removed DOS as the underlying platform. This has meant removal of many of the old DOS limitations, such as 640K of main memory and 8-character filenames.

⇒ See also DIAL-UP NETWORKING; MICROSOFT WINDOWS; OSR 2; REGISTRY; VFAT; WIN32; WINDOWS 98; WINDOWS CE; WINDOWS NT.

Windows 98 The heir apparent to Windows 95, released in mid-1998. Originally it was called *Memphis*, and then *Windows 97*, but Microsoft changed the name when it realized that it was going to miss its target 1997 release date.

Windows 98 offers support for a number of new technologies, including FAT32, AGP, MMX, USB, DVD, and ACPI. Its most visible feature, though, is the *Active Desktop*, which integrates the Web browser (Internet Explorer) with the operating system. From the user's point of view, there is no difference between accessing a document residing locally on the user's hard disk or on a Web server halfway around the world.

⇒ See also INTERNET EXPLORER; WINDOWS; WINDOWS 95; WINDOWS NT.

Windows CE A version of the Windows operating system designed for small devices such as personal digital assistants (PDAs) (or *hand-held PCs* in the Microsoft vernacular). The Windows CE graphical user interface (GUI) is very similar to that of Windows 95, so devices running Windows CE should be easy to operate for anyone familiar with Windows 95.

⇒ See also EPOC; HANDHELD COMPUTER; HPC; OPERATING SYSTEM; PALMTOP; PDA; WINDOWS; WINDOWS 95.

Windows DNA Short for **Windows** *D(istributed) (inter)N(et) (Applications) A(rchitecture)*, a marketing name for a collection of Microsoft technologies that enable the Windows platform and the Internet to work together. Some of the principle technologies that make up DNA include ActiveX, Dynamic HTML (DHTML), and COM.

⇒ See also ACTIVEX; COM; DYNAMIC HTML.

Windows Internet Naming Service See WINS.

Windows Metafile Format See WMF.

Windows NT The most advanced version of the Windows operating system. Windows NT is a 32-bit operating system that supports preemptive multitasking.

There are actually two versions of Windows NT: Windows NT Server, designed to act as a server in networks, and Windows NT Workstation, for stand-alone or client workstations.

⇒ See also ACTIVE DIRECTORY; ALPHA PROCESSOR; MICROSOFT; MICROSOFT WINDOWS; MSCS; MULTITASKING; NTFS; OPERATING SYSTEM; POSIX; PPTP; RAS; WIN32; WINDOWS; WINDOWS 95; WINDOWS 98; WINDOWS TERMINAL; WINFRAME; WOLFPACK.

Windows terminal A dumb terminal especially designed to run Windows applications. Windows terminals are connected to a Windows NT server through a network. All processing and data storage are handled by the server; the terminal does nothing more than send the user's input (keystrokes and mouse movements) to the server and display the results on the display screen. Because Windows NT is not a true multi-user operating system like UNIX, it requires additional software to support Windows terminals. The most popular software for this is called *WinFrame*.

⇒ See also DUMB TERMINAL; NC; NET PC; NETWORK COMPUTER; WINDOWS NT; WINFRAME.

WinFrame A technology developed by Citrix Systems that turns Windows NT into a multi-user operating system. Together with another Citrix technology called *ICA*, WinFrame enables a Windows NT server to function like a minicomputer. The result is that network users on non-Windows machines (e.g., Macintoshes, DOS systems, and UNIX machines) can run Windows applications. The actual applications are executed on the *WinFrame Application Server;* the client machines are just terminals, used only for entering user input and displaying application output.

The ICA protocol is responsible for sending input and output between the client machines and the WinFrame server. Conceptually, the protocol is similar to that of X-Window, which serves the same purpose for UNIX systems.

⇒ See also THIN CLIENT; WINDOWS; WINDOWS NT; WINDOWS TERMINAL; X-WINDOW.

WINMAIL.DAT See under TNEF.

WINS Short for *Windows Internet Naming Service,* a system that determines the IP address associated with a particular network computer. This is called *name resolution.* WINS supports network client and server computers running Windows and can provide name resolution for other computers with special arrangements. Determining the IP address for a computer is a complex process when DHCP servers assign IP addresses dynamically. For example, it is possible for DHCP to assign a different IP address to a client each time the machine logs on to the network.

WINS uses a distributed database that is automatically updated with the names of computers currently available and the IP address assigned to each one.

DNS is an alternative system for name resolution suitable for network computers with fixed IP addresses.

⇒ See also DHCP; DNS; IP ADDRESS.

Winsock Short for *Win(dows) Sock(et)*, Winsock is an Application Programming Interface (API) for developing Windows programs that can communicate with other machines via the TCP/IP protocol. Windows 95 and 98 and Windows NT come with a Dynamic Link Library (DLL) called *winsock.dll* that implements the API and acts as the glue between Windows programs and TCP/IP connections.

In addition to the Microsoft version of winsock.dll, there are other freeware and shareware versions of winsock.dll. However, there is no official standard for the Winsock API, so each implementation differs in minor ways.

⇒ See also API; MTU; PROTOCOL STACK; SOCKET; TCP/IP.

Wintel Refers to the combination of the Windows operating system running on Intel microprocessors. The term is often used sarcastically to indicate the close alliance between Intel and Microsoft. Because Windows 3.x and Windows 95 run only on x86 microprocessor architectures, Intel and Microsoft support each other in ways that many feel is unhealthy for the computer industry as a whole. However, it should be pointed out that Windows NT runs on several non-x86 microprocessors, and there are other operating systems, such as Linux, that run on Intel microprocessors.

⇒ See also INTEL; INTEL MICROPROCESSORS; MICROSOFT; WINDOWS.

wireless modem A modem that accesses a private wireless data network or a wireless telephone system, such as the CDPD system.

⇒ See also CDPD; MODEM.

wizard 1. A utility within an application that helps you use the application to perform a particular task. For example, a "letter wizard" within a word processing application would lead you through the steps of producing different types of correspondence. **2.** An outstanding programmer. Also called a *super-programmer*. Common wisdom holds that one wizard is worth ten average programmers. **3.** The system administrator for a chat room or MUD.

⇒ See also UTILITY.

WMF Short for *W(indows) M(etafile) F(ormat)*, graphics file format used to exchange graphics information between Microsoft Windows applications.

WMF files can hold both vector and bit-mapped images.

⇒ See also GRAPHICS; GRAPHICS FILE FORMATS.

Wolfpack The codename for Microsoft's clustering solution. Wolfpack was released in September, 1997, as part of Windows NT 4.0, enterprise Edition. Its official name is *Microsoft Cluster Server (MSCS)*.

⇒ See also CLUSTERING; MSCS; WINDOWS NT.

word 1. In word processing, any group of characters separated by spaces or punctuation on both sides. Whether it is a real word or not is unimportant to the word processor. **2.** In programming, the natural data size of a computer. The size of a word varies from one computer to another, depending on the CPU. For computers with a 16-bit CPU, a word is 16 bits (2 bytes). On large mainframes, a word can be as long as 64 bits (8 bytes).

Some computers and programming languages distinguish between *shortwords* and *longwords*. A shortword is usually 2 bytes long, while a longword is 4 bytes. **3.** When capitalized, short for *Microsoft Word*.

⇒ See also BIT; BYTE; CPU.

WordPerfect One of the most popular word processors for PCs and Apple Macintoshes.

⇒ See also WORD PROCESSING.

word processing Using a computer to create, edit, and print documents. Of all computer applications, word processing is the most common. To perform word processing, you need a computer, a special program called a *word processor*, and a printer. A word processor enables you to create a document, store it electronically on a disk, display it on a screen, modify it by entering commands and characters from the keyboard, and print it on a printer.

The great advantage of word processing over using a typewriter is that you can make changes without retyping the entire document. If you make a typing mistake, you simply back up the cursor and correct your mistake. If you want to delete a paragraph, you simply remove it, without leaving a trace. It is equally easy to insert a word, sentence, or paragraph in the middle of a document. Word processors also make it easy to move sections of text from one place to another within a document, or between documents. When you have made all the changes you want, you can send the file to a printer to get a hard copy.

Word processors vary considerably, but all word processors support the following basic features:

insert text: Allows you to insert text anywhere in the document.
delete text: Allows you to erase characters, words, lines, or pages as easily as you can cross them out on paper.
cut and **paste:** Allows you to remove (*cut*) a section of text from one

place in a document and insert (*paste*) it somewhere else.

copy: Allows you to duplicate a section of text.

page size and margins: Allows you to define various page sizes and margins, and the word processor will automatically readjust the text so that it fits.

search and replace: Allows you to direct the word processor to search for a particular word or phrase. You can also direct the word processor to replace one group of characters with another everywhere that the first group appears.

word wrap: The word processor automatically moves to the next line when you have filled one line with text, and it will readjust text if you change the margins.

print: Allows you to send a document to a printer to get a hard copy.

Word processors that support only these features (and maybe a few others) are called *text editors*. Most word processors, however, support additional features that enable you to manipulate and format documents in more sophisticated ways. These more advanced word processors are sometimes called *full-featured word processors*. Full-featured word processors usually support the following features:

file management: Many word processors contain file management capabilities that allow you to create, delete, move, and search for files.

font specifications: Allows you to change fonts within a document. For example, you can specify bold, italics, and underlining. Most word processors also let you change the font size and the typeface.

footnotes and cross-references: Automates the numbering and placement of footnotes and enables you to cross-reference other sections of the document easily.

graphics: Allows you to embed illustrations and graphs into a document. Some word processors let you create the illustrations within the word processor; others let you insert an illustration produced by a different program.

headers, footers, and page numbering: Allows you to specify customized headers and footers that the word processor will put at the top and bottom of every page. The word processor automatically keeps track of page numbers so that the correct number appears on each page.

layout: Allows you to specify different margins within a single document and to specify various methods for indenting paragraphs.

macros: A *macro* is a character or word that represents a series of keystrokes. The keystrokes can represent text or commands. The ability to define macros allows you to save yourself a lot of time by replacing common combinations of keystrokes.

merges: Allows you to merge text from one file into another file. This is particularly useful for generating many files that have the same format but different data. Generating mailing labels is the classic example of using merges.

spell checker: A utility that allows you to check the spelling of words.

It will highlight any words that it does not recognize.

tables of contents and indexes: Allows you to create a table of contents and index automatically based on special codes that you insert in the document.

thesaurus: A built-in thesaurus that allows you to search for synonyms without leaving the word processor.

windows: Allows you to edit two or more documents at the same time. Each document appears in a separate *window.* This is particularly valuable when working on a large project that consists of several different files.

WYSIWYG (what-you-see-is-what-you-get): With WYSIWYG, a document appears on the display screen exactly as it will look when printed.

The line dividing word processors from desktop publishing systems is constantly shifting. In general, though, desktop publishing applications support finer control over layout, and more support for full-color documents.

⇒ See also COPY; CUT; DELETE; DESKTOP PUBLISHING; EDITOR; FONT; FOOTER; GRAPHICS; HEADER; HYPHENATION; INSERT; JUSTIFY; LAYOUT; MACRO.

word processor A program or computer that enables you to perform word processing functions.

⇒ See also WORD PROCESSING.

word wrap In word processing, a feature that causes the word processor to force all text to fit within the defined margins. When you fill one line with text, the word processor automatically jumps to the next line so that you are not required to keep track of line lengths and to press the Return key after each line. The word processor divides lines in such a way that a word is never split between two lines (unless the word processor supports *hyphenation*).

Word wrap also occurs if you change the margins. In this case, the word processor readjusts all the text so that it fits within the new margins.

Note that word wrap inserts a *soft return* at the end of each line, not a *hard return.* Soft returns are invisible codes that the word processor utilizes. Hard returns are real characters inserted into the document.

Some word processors allow you to turn off the word-wrap feature. This is useful for writing programs and other types of formatted text where you want complete control over new lines.

⇒ See also HARD RETURN; HYPHENATION; MARGINS; SOFT RETURN; WORD PROCESSING.

workflow The defined series of tasks within an organization to produce a final outcome. Sophisticated workgroup computing applications allow you to define different workflows for different types of jobs. So, for example, in a publishing setting, a document might be automatically routed from writer to editor to proofreader to production. At each stage in the workflow, one individual or group is responsible for a specific task. Once the task is complete, the workflow software ensures that the individuals responsible for the next task are notified and receive the data they need to execute their stage of the process.

⇒ See also WORKGROUP COMPUTING.

workgroup See under WORKGROUP COMPUTING.

workgroup computing A *workgroup* is a collection of individuals working together on a task. Workgroup computing occurs when all the individuals have computers connected to a network that allows them to send e-mail to one another, share data files, and schedule meetings. Sophisticated workgroup systems allow users to define *workflows* so that data is automatically forwarded to appropriate people at each stage of a process.

⇒ See also E-MAIL; GROUPWARE; TEAMWARE; TELECONFERENCE; WORKFLOW.

workgroup productivity package A software package that includes e-mail, calendar programs, scheduling programs, and other utilities that promote communication between users on a local-area network.

⇒ See also CALENDAR; E-MAIL; LOCAL-AREA NETWORK; SCHEDULER; WORKGROUP COMPUTING.

working directory The directory in which you are currently working. Pathnames that do not start with the root directory are assumed by the operating system to start from the working directory.

⇒ See also DIRECTORY; PATHNAME; ROOT DIRECTORY.

worksheet Same as SPREADSHEET.

workstation 1. A type of computer used for engineering applications (CAD/CAM), desktop publishing, software development, and other types of applications that require a moderate amount of computing power and relatively high-quality graphics capabilities.
Workstations generally come with a large, high-resolution graphics screen, at least 64 MB (megabytes) of RAM, built-in network support, and a graphical user interface. Most workstations also have a mass storage device such as a disk drive, but a special type of workstation, called a diskless workstation, comes without a disk drive. The most common operating systems for workstations are UNIX and Windows NT.
In terms of computing power, workstations lie between personal computers and minicomputers, although the line is fuzzy on both ends. High-end personal computers are equivalent to low-end workstations. And high-end workstations are equivalent to minicomputers.
Like personal computers, most workstations are single-user computers. However, workstations are typically linked together to form a local-area

network, although they can also be used as stand-alone systems.

The leading manufacturers of workstations are Sun Microsystems, Hewlett-Packard Company, Silicon Graphics Incorporated, and Compaq. **2.** In networking, *workstation* refers to any computer connected to a local-area network. It could be a workstation or a personal computer.

⇒ See also CAD/CAM; COMPUTER; DEC; DESKTOP PUBLISHING; DISKLESS WORKSTATION; GRAPHICS; LOCAL-AREA NETWORK; MINICOMPUTER; NETWORK; NETWORK COMPUTER; PERSONAL COMPUTER; SGI; SPARC; SUN MICROSYSTEMS; UNIX.

World Wide Web A system of Internet servers that support specially formatted documents. The documents are formatted in a language called HTML (*HyperText Markup Language*) that supports links to other documents, as well as graphics, audio, and video files. This means you can jump from one document to another simply by clicking on hot spots. Not all Internet servers are part of the World Wide Web.

There are several applications called Web browsers that make it easy to access the World Wide Web, two of the most popular being Netscape Navigator and Microsoft's Internet Explorer.

⇒ See also BROWSER; CERN; CGI; HTML; HTTP; HYPERMEDIA; HYPERTEXT; INTERNET; MOSAIC; SURF; W3C; WEB SITE; WEBTV.

WORM Short for *w(rite) o(nce), r(ead) m(any)*. An optical disk technology that allows you to write data onto a disk just once. After that, the data are permanent and can be read any number of times.

Unlike CD-ROMs, there is no single standard for WORM disks, which means that they can be read only by the same type of drive that wrote them. This has hampered their acceptance, although they have found a niche market as an archival medium.

WORM is also called CD-R.

⇒ See also CD-ROM; ERASABLE OPTICAL DISK; MASS STORAGE; OPTICAL DISK; PHASE CHANGE DISK.

WRAM Short for *W(indows)* **RAM**, a type of RAM developed by Samsung Electronics that supports two ports. This enables a video adapter to fetch the contents of memory for display at the same time that new bytes are being pumped into memory. This results in much faster display than is possible with conventional single-port RAM.

WRAM is similar to VRAM but achieves even faster performance at less cost because it supports addressing of large blocks (*windows*) of video memory.

⇒ See also RAM; SGRAM; VIDEO ADAPTER; VIDEO MEMORY; VRAM.

write To copy data from main memory to a storage device, such as a disk.

⇒ See also ACCESS; READ; WRITE-BACK CACHE.

write-back cache A caching method in which modifications to data in the cache aren't copied to the cache source until absolutely necessary. Write-back caching is available on many microprocessors, including all Intel processors since the 80486. With these microprocessors, data modifications (e.g., write operations) to data stored in the L1 cache aren't copied to main memory until absolutely necessary. In contrast, a *write-through cache* performs all write operations in parallel—data is written to main memory and the L1 cache simultaneously.

Write-back caching yields somewhat better performance than write-through caching because it reduces the number of write operations to main memory. With this performance improvement comes a slight risk that data may be lost if the system crashes.

A write-back cache is also called a *copy-back cache.*

⇒ See also CACHE; WRITE.

write once/read many See WORM.

write-protect To mark a file or disk so that its contents cannot be modified or deleted. When you want to make sure that neither you nor another user can destroy data, you can write-protect it. Many operating systems include a command to write-protect files. You can also write-protect 5¼-inch floppy disks by covering the *write-protect notch* with tape. 3½-inch floppy diskettes have a small switch that you can set to turn on write-protection.

Write-protected files and media can be read only; you cannot write to them, edit them, append data to them, or delete them.

⇒ See also FLOPPY DISK; LOCK.

write-through cache See under WRITE-BACK CACHE.

WWW See WORLD WIDE WEB.

WYSIWYG Pronounced *wiz(zy)-wig,* stands for *w(hat) y(ou) s(ee) i(s) w(hat) y(ou) g(et).* A WYSIWYG application is one that enables you to see on the display screen exactly what will appear when the document is printed. This differs, for example, from word processors that are incapable of displaying different fonts and graphics on the display screen even though the formatting codes have been inserted into the file. WYSIWYG is especially popular for desktop publishing.

Note that the WYSIWYGness of an application is relative. Originally, WYSIWYG referred to any word processor that could accurately show line breaks on the display screen. Later WYSIWYGs had to be able to show different font sizes, even when the screen display was limited to one typeface. Now, a word processor must be able to display graphics and many different typefaces to be considered WYSIWYG.

Still, some WYSIWYG applications are more WYSIWYG than others. For example, many desktop publishing systems print text using outline fonts (PostScript fonts, for example). Many of these systems, however, use corresponding bit-mapped fonts to display documents on a monitor. What you see on the display screen, therefore, is not exactly what you see when you print out the document. In addition, standard laser printers have a resolution of at least 300 dpi, whereas even the best graphics monitors have resolutions of only 100 dpi. Graphics and text, therefore, always look sharper when printed than they do on the display screen. And colors often appear differently on a monitor from the way they do when printed.

⇒ See also COLOR MATCHING; DESKTOP PUBLISHING; FONT; POSTSCRIPT; RESOLUTION; WORD PROCESSING; WYSIWYP.

WYSIWYP Short for *What You See Is What You Print,* and pronounced *wizzy-whip,* refers to the ability of a computer system to print colors exactly as they appear on a monitor. WYSIWYP printing requires a special program, called a color management system (CMS), to calibrate the monitor and printer.

⇒ See also COLOR MANAGEMENT SYSTEM (CMS); COLOR MATCHING; WYSIWYG.

X2 A technology developed by U.S. Robotics (now 3COM) for delivering data rates up to 56 Kbps over plain old telephone service (POTS). It was long believed that the maximum data transmission rate over copper telephone wires was 33.6 Kbps, but X2 achieves higher rates by taking advantage of the fact that most phone switching stations are connected by high-speed digital lines. X2 bypasses the normal digital-to-analog conversion and sends the digital data over the telephone wires directly to your modem, where it is decoded.

3COM has announced that future X2 modems will conform to the new V.90 standard approved by the ITU. And users with older X2 modems may upgrade their modems to support V.90.

While X2 offers faster Internet access than normal modems, there are several caveats to using an X2 modem:

1. The high speeds are available only with downstream traffic (e.g., data sent to your computer). Upstream traffic is delivered using normal techniques, with a maximum speed of 33.6 Kbps.
2. To connect to the Internet at X2 speeds, your internet service provider (ISP) must have a modem at the other end that supports V.90.
3. Even if your ISP supports V.90, you might not achieve maximum transmission rates because of noisy lines.

⇒ See also CHANNEL BONDING; K56FLEX; MODEM; V.90.

X.25 A popular standard for packet-switching networks. The X.25 standard was approved by the CCITT (now the ITU) in 1976. It defines layers 1, 2, and 3 in the OSI Reference Model.

⇒ See also CCITT; PACKET SWITCHING.

X.400 An ISO and ITU standard for addressing and transporting e-mail messages. It conforms to layer 7 of the OSI model and supports several types of transport mechanisms, including Ethernet, X.25, TCP/IP, and dial-up lines.

⇒ See also CCITT; E-MAIL ADDRESS; X.500.

X.500 An ISO and ITU standard that defines how global directories should be structured. X.500 directories are hierarchical with different levels for each category of information, such as country, state, and city. X.500 supports X.400 systems.

⇒ See also ACTIVE DIRECTORY; CCITT; DIRECTORY SERVICE; ITU; NDS; X.400.

X.509 The most widely used standard for defining digital certificates. X.509 is actually an ITU Recommendation, which means that it has not yet been officially defined or approved. As a result, companies have implemented the standard in different ways. For example, both Netscape and Microsoft use X.509 certificates to implement SSL in their Web servers and browsers. But an X.509 Certificate generated by Netscape may not be readable by Microsoft products, and vice versa.

⇒ See also DIGITAL CERTIFICATE; SSL.

x86 See under INTEL MICROPROCESSORS.

xDSL Refers collectively to all types of *d(igital) s(ubscriber) l(ines)*, the two main categories being ADSL and SDSL. Two other types of xDSL technologies are *High-data-rate DSL (HDSL)* and *Single-line DSL (SDSL)*.

DSL technologies use sophisticated modulation schemes to pack data onto copper wires. They are sometimes referred to as last-mile technologies because they are used only for connections from a telephone switching station to a home or office, not between switching stations.

xDSL is similar to ISDN inasmuch as both operate over existing copper telephone lines (POTS) and both require the short runs to a central telephone office (usually less than 20,000 feet). However, xDSL offers much higher speeds—up to 32 Mbps for downstream traffic, and from 32 Kbps to over 1 Mbps for upstream traffic.

⇒ See also ADSL; ISDN; POTS; SDSL.

Xenix A version of UNIX that runs on PCs. Xenix was developed by Microsoft Corporation and is compatible with AT&T's System V definition.

⇒ See also OPERATING SYSTEM; UNIX.

Xerox Best known for its copier machines, Xerox Corporation has also had a profound influence on the computer industry. During the 1970s and 1980s, its Palo Alto Research Center conducted pioneering work on user interfaces. Many of their inventions, such as the mouse and the graphical user interface (GUI), have since become commonplace. Xerox continues to do groundbreaking research, especially in the area of document management.

⇒ See also GRAPHICAL USER INTERFACE; USER INTERFACE.

XGA Short for *(e)x(tended) g(raphics) a(rray)*, a high-resolution graphics standard introduced by IBM in 1990. XGA was designed to replace the older 8514/A video standard. It provides the same resolutions (640 by 480 or 1024 by 768 pixels) but supports more simultaneous colors (65,000 compared with 8514/A's 256 colors). In addition, XGA allows monitors to be noninterlaced.

⇒ See also 8514/A; INTERLACING; RESOLUTION; SVGA; VGA; VIDEO STANDARDS.

x-height In typography, the height of a lowercase *x* in a specific font. This is also called the *body height,* as it represents the height of the lowercase character's body, excluding ascenders and descenders.

⇒ See also ASCENDER; BASELINE; DESCENDER; TYPEFACE.

XML Short for *(e)X(tensible) M(arkup) L(anguage),* a new specification being developed by the W3C. XML is a pared-down, simplified version of SGML, designed especially for Web documents. It enables designers to create their own customized tags to provide functionality not available with HTML. For example, XML supports links that point to multiple documents, as opposed to HTML links, which can reference just one destination each. A document tagged according to XML can also be formatted for publication on CD-ROM, in printed book form, etc.

Whether XML eventually supplants HTML as the standard Web formatting specification depends a lot on whether it is supported by future Web browsers. So far, the only major browser vendor to endorse XML is Microsoft, which has stated that XML will be supported in a future version of Internet Explorer.

⇒ See also DOM; HTML; SGML; TAG.

Xmodem Originally developed in 1977 by Ward Christiansen, Xmodem is one of the most popular file transfer protocols. Although Xmodem is a relatively simple protocol, it is fairly effective at detecting errors. It works by sending blocks of data together with a checksum and then waiting for acknowledgment of the block's receipt. The waiting slows down the rate of data transmission considerably, but it ensures accurate transmission.

Xmodem can be implemented either in software or in hardware. Many modems, and almost all communications software packages, support Xmodem. However, it is useful only at relatively slow data transmission speeds (less than 4,800 bps).

Enhanced versions of Xmodem that work at higher transmission speeds are known as *Ymodem* and *Zmodem.*

⇒ See also CHECKSUM; COMMUNICATIONS PROTOCOL; COMMUNICATIONS SOFTWARE; KERMIT; MODEM; PROTOCOL; YMODEM; ZMODEM.

XMS Stands for *(E)x(tended) M(emory) S(pecification),* a procedure developed jointly by AST Research, Intel Corporation, Lotus Development, and Microsoft Corporation for using extended memory and DOS's *high memory area,* a 64 K block just above 1 MB.

⇒ See also EXPANDED MEMORY; EXTENDED MEMORY; HIGH MEMORY AREA; HIMEM. SYS; VCPI.

XOR operator Known as the *exclusive OR* operator, a Boolean operator that returns a value of TRUE only if just one of its operands is TRUE. In contrast, an inclusive OP operator returns a value of TRUE if either or both of its operands are TRUE.

⇒ See also BOOLEAN OPERATOR.

XT form factor Same as BABY AT.

X-Window A windowing and graphics system developed at the Massachusetts Institute of Technology (MIT). MIT has placed the X-Window source code in the public domain, making it a particularly attractive system for UNIX vendors. Almost all UNIX graphical interfaces, including Motif and OpenLook, are based on X-Window.

⇒ See also GRAPHICAL USER INTERFACE; PUBLIC-DOMAIN SOFTWARE; SOLARIS; UNIX; WINFRAME.

Y2K Short for *Year 2000 Problem.*

Yahoo! Short for *Y(et) A(nother) H(ierarchical) O(fficious) O(racle).* Yahoo! is a World Wide Web directory started by David Filo and Jerry Yang at Stanford University. The two began compiling and categorizing Web pages in 1994. By 1996, they had one of the most popular Web sites and a very valuable commodity. Yahoo! Is now the leading *Web portal* —the starting point for Web activities.

⇒ See also ALTA VISTA; EXCITE; HOTBOT; INFOSEEK; LYCOS; MAGELLAN.

Y/C video See under S-VIDEO.

Year 2000 problem The pervasive problem caused by the fact that many applications are designed to handle only twentieth-century dates—dates that begin with '19'. For example, most programs represent dates in the form MM-DD-YY, so the date 10-5-96 is October 5, 1996. But what about the date 10-5-05. Is that 1905 or 2005? There is no way to distinguish between these two dates.

This problem affects a vast amount of software, particularly accounting and database systems. The U.S. Social Security Administration, for example, has estimated that it will need to review about 50 million lines of code to correct this problem in its own system.

The Year 2000 problem is sometimes referred to as the *Millennium bug* or the *Y2K problem.*

⇒ See also ACCOUNTING SOFTWARE.

Yellow_Book The specification for CD-ROMs and CD-ROM/XA.

⇒ See also CD-ROM; CD-ROM/XA; GREEN BOOK; ORANGE BOOK; RED BOOK; WHITE BOOK.

Ymodem An asynchronous communications protocol designed by Chuck Forsberg that extends Xmodem by increasing the transfer block size and by supporting batch file transfers. This enables you to specify a list of files and send them all at one time. With Xmodem, you can send only one file at a time.

⇒ See also BATCH PROCESSING; COMMUNICATIONS PROTOCOL; XMODEM; ZMODEM.

yottabyte 2^{80} bytes, which is approximately 10^{24} (1,000,000,000,000,000,000,000,000) bytes. A yottabyte is equal to 1,024 zettabytes.

The name *yotta* was chosen because it's the second-to-last letter of the Latin alphabet and also sounds like the Greek letter *iota.*

⇒ See also EXABYTE; ZETTABYTE.

ZAW Short for *Z(ero) A(dministration for) W(indows),* a collection of utilities developed by Microsoft that should enable administrators to centrally manage and update software on PCs connected to a LAN. ZAW was developed partly as a response to the emergence of Net PCs. One of the main selling points of Net PCs is that they enable software to be centralized, which greatly simplifies administration of applications. ZAW attempts to offer the same sort of administration ease while letting the applications remain on traditional desktop PCs.

Some pieces of ZAW are included in Windows 98. The remaining pieces of the ZAW puzzle will be part of future versions of Windows.

⇒ See also NET PC; NETWORK COMPUTER; TCO.

Z-buffer An area in graphics memory reserved for storing the Z-axis value of each pixel.

⇒ See also 3-D GRAPHICS; Z-BUFFERING.

Z-buffering An algorithm used in 3-D graphics to determine which objects, or parts of objects, are visible and which are hidden behind other objects. With Z-buffering, the graphics processor stores the Z-axis value of each pixel in a special area of memory called the *Z-buffer.* Different objects can have the same x- and y-coordinate values, but with different z-coordinate values. The object with the lowest z-coordinate value is in front of the other objects, and therefore that's the one that's displayed.

An alternate algorithm for hiding objects behind other objects is called *Z-sorting.* The Z-sorting algorithm simply displays all objects serially, starting with those objects farthest back (with the largest Z-axis values). The Z-sorting algorithm does not require a Z-buffer, but it is slow and does not render intersecting objects correctly.

⇒ See also 3-D GRAPHICS; Z-BUFFER.

Zero Administration for Windows See ZAW.

Zero Insertion Force (ZIF) socket A chip socket that allows you to insert and remove a chip without special tools.

⇒ See also CHIP; SOCKET 7; SOCKET 8.

zero wait state Refers to systems that have no *wait states*—that is, they allow the microprocessor to run at its maximum speed without waiting for slower memory chips.

⇒ See also WAIT STATE.

zettabyte 2^{70} bytes, which is approximately 10^{21} (1,000,000,000,000,000,000,000) bytes. A zettabyte is equal to 1,024 exabytes.

The name *zetta* was chosen because it's the last letter of the Latin alphabet and also sounds like the Greek letter *zeta*.

⇒ See also EXABYTE; YOTTABYTE.

ZIF socket See ZERO INSERTION FORCE (ZIF) SOCKET.

zine Short for *e-zine*.

ZIP A popular data compression format. Files that have been compressed with the ZIP format are called *ZIP files* and usually end with a *.ZIP* extension.

A special kind of zipped file is a *self-extracting file*, which ends with a .EXE extension. You can *unzip* a self-extracting file by simply executing it.

⇒ See also ARC; DATA COMPRESSION; LZW.

Zip drive A high-capacity floppy disk drive developed by Iomega Corporation. Zip disks are slightly larger than conventional floppy disks, and about twice as thick. They can hold 100 MB of data. Because it is relatively inexpensive and durable, the Zip disk has become a popular medium for backing up hard disks and for transporting large files.

⇒ See also FLOPPY DISK; FLOPPY DRIVE; HiFD; SuperDisk.

Zmodem An asynchronous communications protocol that provides faster data transfer rates and better error detection than Xmodem. In particular, Zmodem supports larger block sizes and enables the transfer to resume where it left off following a communications failure.

⇒ See also COMMUNICATIONS PROTOCOL; KERMIT; XMODEM; YMODEM.

zoom In graphical user interfaces, to make a window larger. Typically, there is a *zoom box* in one corner of the window. When you select the zoom box the first time, the system expands the window to fill the entire screen. (This is sometimes called *maximizing*.) When you select it again, the window shrinks to its original size. (This is sometimes called *restoring*.)

Many applications also provide a zoom feature, which enlarges the view of an object, enabling you to see more detail.

⇒ See also BOX; GRAPHICAL USER INTERFACE; MAXIMIZE.

zoomed video See under ZV PORT.

ZV Port Short for *zoomed video port,* a port that enables data to be transferred directly from a PC Card to a VGA controller. The port is actually a connection to a *zoomed video bus.* This new bus was designed by the PCMCIA to enable notebook computers to connect to real-time multimedia devices such as video cameras. The first notebook computers with the ZD port arrived in late 1996.

⇒ See also BUS; LAPTOP COMPUTER; NOTEBOOK COMPUTER; PC CARD; PCMCIA; VGA.